ADVANCES IN
ARTIFICIAL INTELLIGENCE – II

Seventh European Conference on
Artificial Intelligence, ECAI-86
Brighton, U.K., July 20-25, 1986

NORTH-HOLLAND
AMSTERDAM • NEW YORK • OXFORD • TOKYO

ADVANCES IN ARTIFICIAL INTELLIGENCE – II

Seventh European Conference on
Artificial Intelligence, ECAI-86
Brighton, U.K., July 20-25, 1986

Edited by:

Ben du BOULAY
General Chairman
and
David HOGG
Local Arrangements Chairman

The University of Sussex
School of Social Sciences
Arts Building
Falmer, Brighton, BN1 9QN
U.K.

Luc STEELS
Programme Chairman
Vrije Universiteit Brussels
Artificial Intelligence Laboratory
Pleinlaan 2
1050 Brussels
Belgium

1987

NORTH-HOLLAND
AMSTERDAM • NEW YORK • OXFORD • TOKYO

ISBN: 0 444 70279 2

Published by:
ELSEVIER SCIENCE PUBLISHERS B.V.
P.O.Box 1991
1000 BZ Amsterdam
The Netherlands

Sole distributors for the U.S.A and Canada:
ELSEVIER SCIENCE PUBLISHING COMPANY, INC.
52 Vanderbilt Avenue
New York, N.Y. 10017
U.S.A.

Library of Congress Cataloging-in-Publication Data

European Conference on Artificial Intelligence (7th :
    1986 : Brighton, East Sussex)
    Advances in artificial intelligence, II.

    Includes index.
    1. Artificial intelligence--Congresses. 2. Expert
systems (Computer science)--Congresses. 3. Robotics--
Congresses. 4. Learning--Congresses. 5. Knowledge,
Theory of--Congresses. I. Du Boulay, Ben. II. Hogg,
David. III. Steels, Luc. IV. Title. V. Title:
Advances in artificial intelligence, 2. VI. Title:
Advances in artificial intelligence, two.
Q334.E97 1986   006.3   87-13735
ISBN 0-444-70279-2 (U.S.)

PRINTED IN THE NETHERLANDS

OVERVIEW

INTRODUCTION

Although there has been a rapid growth in conferences for subfields of AI (such as expert systems, robotics, logic programming, and natural language) ECAI remains the most important gathering of AI scientists in Europe where the whole field is put in perspective. The papers accepted to the conference focus on basic research directly related to the core problems of artificial intelligence, such as knowledge representation, reasoning and learning. There are also invited presentations and panels to highlight the industrial aspects of AI and there are some sections where innovative basic research results are related to applications.

The invited speakers at the conference were Shapiro, Siekmann, Prini and Hillis. Shapiro and Hillis are at the forefront of research in new architectures for artificial intelligence. They presented two radical alternatives for exploiting the power of parallel computing. One based on the paradigm of logic programming. The other based on data level parallelism and exemplified by the connection machine. Siekmann is representative of the long standing European interest in the exploration of the foundations of logic and their utilisation in automated reasoning. Prini plays an outstanding role in the creation of a new European AI industry.

In addition there were two "visionary speakers": the artist Howard Cohen and the industrialist Sir Clive Sinclair. Both presented fascinating lectures which lead to lively debates.

This book contains a selection of the papers presented at the conference. It is both a record of the conference and also a way to make the most important results available for a large audience. We briefly discuss in this introduction the various topics and also the main themes running in each topic.

1. LEARNING

Learning is one of the subfields of AI that attracted a considerable amount of attention at the conference due to many new recent results. Some of the papers included here address fundamental problems in learning: how the target of learning can be constrained, how heuristic rules can be learned from deep reasoning, how subsumption can be used, and how experiences can be organised. A second set of papers focuses on analogy which is one of the key components of a learning process. A final group involves the study of discovery processes and of human problem solving as a source of inspiration for AI models.

2. KNOWLEDGE REPRESENTATION

Knowledge representation research covers a wide area, from fundamental research to tools for building concrete systems. A first group of papers discusses issues in the foundations of knowledge representation. It covers topics such as default reasoning, and reasoning about time. A second group of papers covers current technical issues in the construction of knowledge representation systems: the use of parallelism, computational reflection, and dependency systems. The final section focuses on logic and deduction. It contains an overview article on unification contributed by Siekmann as invited speaker. Then there are papers developing new algorithms and logical deduction systems. Automatic programming forms the main area of application.

3. NATURAL LANGUAGE

Papers in the natural language subfield range from issues in the representation of the meaning of natural language expressions, to the use of semantic or pragmatic information in parsing. There are also papers on applications of natural language.

4. EXPERT SYSTEMS

The field of expert systems is enjoying an incredible success as application domain of AI. A first group of papers focused on deepening our understanding of expertise as a way to make better expert systems. Part of this is the use of deep models. A second group of papers discussed tools for expert systems, ranging from new techniques for handling uncertainty, shells based on the blackboard model, and technological foundations for expert systems.

5. PLANNING, VISION AND ROBOTICS.

The final section contains papers in robotics. A key problem remains planning. Papers focus on hierarchical planning, temporal planning, and the interaction between planning and sensors. Vision papers continue to search for fundamental constraints on images and for combining different sources of knowledge for retrieving models.

The volume concludes with the visionary speech of industrialist Sir Clive Sinclair.

FINAL REMARK

The conference also contained a lot of position papers which put forward new ideas or small technical results. These papers are not retained for publication in the present volume although some of them contained new exciting ideas. Another important aspect of the conference was a very successful exhibition and events associated with it.

ACKNOWLEDGEMENTS

The processing and selection of ECAI papers was a substantial job which would not have been possible without the help of many people, specifically Karina Bergen and Gina Fierlafijn who did the adminstration, the subfieldchairmen who often responded quickly when the need was high, and of course the many reviewers. The general chairmanship and the local arrangements were handled brilliantly by Ben du Boulay and David Hogg respectively. We are also very much indebted to Sheila Fenton and her team of conference organisers for running such a smooth conference.

Luc Steels
Programme Chairman
ECAI 86

TABLE OF CONTENTS

PART I: LEARNING

1. FUNDAMENTAL PROBLEMS

2. ANALOGY

3. DISCOVERY and HUMAN PROBLEM SOLVING

PART II: KNOWLEDGE REPRESENTATION

1. FOUNDATIONS OF KNOWLEDGE REPRESENTATION

2. KNOWLEDGE REPRESENTATION SYSTEMS

3. LOGIC AND DEDUCTION

PART III: NATURAL LANGUAGE

PART IV: EXPERT SYSTEMS

1. EXPERTISE and USE OF DEEP MODELS

2. TOOLS FOR EXPERT SYSTEMS

PART V: VISION AND ROBOTICS

CONCLUDING VISIONARY PAPER

PART I

LEARNING

1. Fundamental Problems

2. Analogy

3. Discovery and Human Problem Solving

Advances in Artificial Intelligence - II
B. Du Boulay, D. Hogg and L. Steels (Editors)
© Elsevier Science Publishers B.V. (North-Holland), 1987

ANALYTIC GOAL REGRESSION: PROBLEMS, SOLUTIONS AND ENHANCEMENTS

Robin Boswell
Department of Artificial Intelligence
Edinburgh University

80 South Bridge
Edinburgh EH1 1HN
Scotland

Abstract

Analytic goal regression is theoretically a powerful technique for concept learning, but in practice there are very few instances of its successful application in interesting domains. In the following paper I show how the technique can be improved and some of the problems overcome.

In the first section I give a very brief account of learning and problem-solving, in order to provide a framework for discussing goal regression.

In the second, I summarise some points from [Porter and Kibler 85]. In this paper, the authors demonstrate the limitations of goal regression, claim that 'experimental goal regression' (defined in their paper) is in many ways superior, and suggest that the two may be combined. I re-examine the evidence and come to slightly different conclusions: in particular, that further work on goal regression is worthwhile, and that the problems are not insuperable.

In the third section, I suggest some solutions to the problems of goal regression, together with some further generalisations and enhancements.

Keywords

Concept learning, analytic learning, explanation-based learning, goal-regression, back-propagation, algebraic manipulation.

Acknowledgement

I am grateful to Steve Owen for suggesting the possibility of 'forward propagation', and for his ideas on the use of analogous operators.

   This work is supported by a Science and Engineering Research Council Research Studentship for the author.

Concerning the examples

The following programs are referred to later in this paper:

LEX and LEX2 — Mitchell and Utgoff

LEX is divided into modules including a problem-solver and a learning module. The problem-solver solves integrals, and passes the solutions to the learning module, which uses an inductive method to learn heuristics for the application of operators.

   LEX2 is an extension of LEX. It applies goal regression to solution trees in order to generate new concepts and so extend the description language. It uses the same inductive learning technique as LEX (modified in order to handle a changing description language).

   LEX is described in [Mitchell *et al* 80]. LEX2 is described in [Mitchell 82] and [Utgoff 84].

PET — Porter and Kibler

PET [Porter & Kibler 84] is similar to a subset of LEX2. It uses goal regression directly to learn heuristics for the application of operators, and doesn't employ any inductive methods.

LP — Silver

LP [Silver 84] is given worked examples of solutions to equations, analyses them, and hence learns heuristics for the application of operators.

These and other learning programs are examined and compared in [Boswell 85].

1   Learning and Problem-Solving

The purpose of this section is to outline the context in which goal-regression is used.
   The topics covered are:

1. What concept learning is.

2. How concept learning can be applied to problem-solving.

3. *Bias*, and how it affects the performance of a concept learning program.

4. The distinction between two approaches to concept learning: inductive and analytic.

5. Algorithms for inductive concept learning, and the constraints they impose on the description language.

6. A definition of goal regression (normally used as an analytic learning technique).

7. A different use for goal regression

1.1   Concept-learning

The simplest form of concept learning is exemplified by Winston's arch-learning program [Winston 75]. The problem to be solved is

   Given:

   • A representation language $\mathcal{L}$ for concepts.

   • A set of positive (and usually negative) training instances.

Find:

- The unique concept in the description space which best covers all of the positive (and none of the negative) instances.

[Cohen & Feigenbaum 82]

Here a *concept* is simply a partition of the universe of discourse (assumed given). For example, "Prime Number" is a concept which partitions the set of integers. Hence the set of all concepts over $\mathcal{U}$ is $2^{\mathcal{U}}$.

Thus the purpose of a concept-learning program is to search a space of concepts for one that includes all the given positive instances and excludes all the negative ones. Usually the language $\mathcal{L}$ is capable of describing only some small subset of $2^{\mathcal{U}}$, thus reducing the search. (This is a particular example of *bias*, defined below.)

1.2 How concept learning can be applied to problem solving

If operator $\mathcal{A}$, say, proves useful in solving a number of problems, then each of these problems may be regarded as an example of the concept:

Set of problem-states which may be simplified using operator $\mathcal{A}$

The problem-solving module of a learning program may pass such examples to a learning module, which attempts to generalise the concept and hence suggest possible new examples.

1.3 Bias

Given some set of examples, there is likely to be a large choice of concepts all of which correctly classify them. Therefore a learning program must have some way of choosing, out of the range of possible concepts, the ones most likely to be appropriate to the domain. Moreover, to be of any assistance to a problem-solver, the learning program has to generalise from the examples in some way.

For example, the functions $\cos^3 x, \cos^5 x, \cos^7 x$ and $\cos^9 x$ may all be integrated by the same sequence of operators (see fig. 1 in section 3 below, though the details don't matter here), and $\cos^2 x$ may not.

These example are correctly classified by each of the three concepts below.

1. $\{\cos^3 x, \cos^5 x, \cos^7 x \cos^9 x\}$

2. $\{\cos^n x \mid n > 2\}$

3. $\{\cos^n x \mid n \text{ odd}\}$

1. is of no assistance in providing new heuristics for the problem solver, because it doesn't go beyond the examples already given to suggest any new ones. Both 2. and 3. do suggest some generalisation, but the generalisation of 2. happens to be incorrect.

The features of a learning program which lead it to prefer one possible generalization to another are what Utgoff calls *Bias*. He analyses in his thesis [Utgoff 84] different ways in which bias may be introduced, and how the bias of a language may be adjusted.

1.4 Inductive and Analytic Learning Contrasted

Inductive learning (also known as *empirical* or *experimental* learning) seeks by examining examples and non-examples of a concept to determine by syntactic means alone which features in the examples led them to be so classified. Analytic learning (also known as *explanation-based* learning), on the other hand, takes into account whatever process caused the classification to be carried out.

For example, an inductive learner might watch decorators on a number of occasions paint ceilings and then their ladders, and guess that the ceiling should be painted before the ladder, because that's the way it usually happened. An analytic learner, on the other hand, would note that having a non-sticky ladder was a pre-condition to painting the ceiling, and deduce from a single demonstration that the ceiling should be painted before the ladder.

1.5   Algorithms for Inductive Learning

Two similar algorithms are Version Spaces [Mitchell 78] and Focussing [Winston 75].

In both of these, bounds are maintained which indicate the most specific and the most general concepts compatible with the instances so far encountered. As more precise information is acquired, these bounds move closer together, and when they coincide, the concept has been learnt.

The only important feature of these algorithms, for the purposes of this paper, is that both require a hierarchically structured description language (Focussing requires an upper semi-lattice; Version Spaces, any partial ordering). This complicates the problem of extending the language automatically; and extending the language is one application of goal regression.

The authors of LEX2 also require that the description language be context-free. This is not a requirement of Version Spaces, but when new terms in the language are generated by goal regression elsewhere in the program, it simplifies the problem of assimilating these terms into the right place in the hierarchy.

1.6   Analytic Goal Regression

The technique discussed below is usually described in AI literature simply as goal regression, or alternatively as back propagation. It is described in [Porter & Kibler 85] as *analytic* goal regression to distinguish it from *experimental* goal regression, which the authors define in the course of the paper.

In its simplest form, analytic goal regression is used to generalise from a single example as follows:
  Given a sequence of operators

$$S_1 \xrightarrow{op_1} S_2 \xrightarrow{op_2} S_3 \dots S_n$$

back propagation consists of

1. Generalising S_n to S'_n, where S'_n is a term in the description language $\mathcal{L}$ which describes some set of states (including S_n).

2. Reversing the effects of $op_{n-1} \dots op_1$ to give S'_1: a generalisation of S_1

If S_n was an example of a goal state, then a useful generalisation S'_n is a description of the set of all goal states. This is the one LEX2 uses. PET's behaviour may appear different (its heuristic is to generalise state S_i by matching it against the preconditions of op_i), but this difference is only superficial.)

After the application of each reverse operator, the result is unified with the right-hand side of the previous operator, which is then reversed in turn.

Hence a program which carries out goal regression must either be supplied with reverse operators, or else construct them from the forward operators. This problem is discussed in more detail in section 2.2.1.

1.7   An alternative use for Goal-Regression

Mitchell and Utgoff's LEX2 is unique in that it does not use goal regression directly for learning, but rather for extending the description language. The concepts generated can then be used by an inductive learning method (in LEX2's case, Version Spaces).

For example, suppose goal regression through the solution of the integral $\int \cos^7 x\, dx$ by operators $op_i, op_j \dots$ yields a generalisation to $\int \cos^{odd} x\, dx$. The usual way to use this result would be in constructing a heuristic

IF integral is of the form $\int \cos^{odd} x\, dx$
THEN apply operators $op_i, op_j \dots$

However, LEX2 uses the same result to add the term "odd number" to their description language. The above rule can then be learnt by inductive methods.

The use of goal regression to extend the language (adjust the bias, in Utgoff's terminology), makes the inductive method more efficient, and less dependent on the programmer to provide the right description language.

This use of goal regression in this way, to improve the behaviour of an inductive method, is an approach recommended in [Porter & Kibler 85].

2   Problems with Goal Regression

In this section, I first of all summarise [Porter & Kibler 85], then examine their arguments rather more closely, and suggest some alternative conclusions. In order not to obscure the arguments with technical details, I postpone these, as far as possible, until the final section of this paper.

2.1   A summary of [Porter & Kibler 85]

The authors start by pointing out some shortcomings of analytic goal regression, viz. :

1. The operators need to be invertible, or else inverse operators must be supplied by the programmer.

2. The description language must be able to represent the result of goal regression.

3. The heuristic learnt as a result of goal regression may not always lead to the shortest solution.

They then give define a technique which they call *experimental* goal regression. It follows immediately from this definition that experimental goal regression doesn't suffer from either of the first two problems above; and the authors show by means of an example (misleadingly, I claim) how it is superior to analytic goal regression with respect to the third.

They conclude that

1. Experimental goal regression is superior to analytic goal regression.

2. Analytic and experimental goal regression could profitably be combined in one program.

Experimental goal regression is identical to the application of inductive concept-learning to problem-solving described above (section 1.2), with one minor difference. This lies in the method used to determine whether a given operator application is a positive instance. Instead of testing whether the application lies on the shortest solution path (as LEX does), [Porter & Kibler] suggest applying an evaluation function to the problem states before and after operator application. This requires less computation, but depends on the programmer to provide an appropriate function, and in general such a function may not exist.

Since this difference lies in the mechanism for the classification of instances, rather than in the mechanism for learning, I shall ignore it from now on.

2.2   Some answers to Porter & Kiblers' arguments

2.2.1   Inverting Operators

It is true that for goal regression to be applied, inverse operators have to be obtained somehow. In the case of LEX2, they are supplied explicitly. However, PET shows how they can be inferred from the forward operators, even when these are seen as 'black boxes' by the program. Given a single instance of the application of a forward operator, a *relational model* (also known as a set of *inference links* [Geiser 75]) is generated heuristically connecting corresponding subterms of expressions before and after the application of an operator. This relational model is used to construct a reverse operator.

For the purposes of the present discussion, relational models are significant only because they provide a means whereby reverse operators can be deduced heuristically, so the details are unimportant. Moreover, in the section of [Porter & Kibler 85] which deals with the inversion of operators, attention is concentrated not on the problem just discussed, but on the difficulties of reasoning with some operator definitions.

In the case of LEX2, two such problems (of dealing with operator definitions) are experienced, both of which may be illustrated by the same operator, viz. Op 43[1]:

$$\int poly(f(x))f'(x)\,dx \Rightarrow \int poly(u)\,du \,, \ u = f(x)$$

LEX2 is unable to apply goal regression through this operator, firstly because the constraint that whatever matches f' must be the derivative of whatever matches f is not explicit in this representation of the operator, and secondly because in any case, such a relationship is not expressible in LEX2's description language.

The former problem is merely an implementation detail, and can be solved by an appropriate representation of the reverse operator. The second is more serious, because of the constraints imposed on the description language by the inductive learning algorithm (see section 1.5) but is still at least partially solvable — see section 3.1 below.

---

[1]My numbering of operators is taken from LEX and LEX2. In diagrams, I give numbers only to those operators which I discuss in the text.

2.2.2 Relative closure of Description Language

One example of this problem has just been mentioned — viz. the inability of LEX2's description language to represent the fact that one subterm of an expression must be the derivative of another.

Not even simpler STRIPS-like representations [Fikes & Nilsson 71] are immune from this problem. The result of goal regression through operators having **ADD** and **DELETE** lists may contain negations and disjunctions. These can be handled by any language that supports Version Spaces or Focussing, but the number of disjuncts may lead to an exponential explosion [Mitchell *et al* 85]. However, my experience with a reconstruction of LEX2 suggests that this may be less of a problem in the domain of integration: and I give an example in section 3.3 below of how a slight generalisation of goal regression may yield a useful disjunction.

2.2.3 When goal regression leads to an incorrect heuristic

I claim that this problem is easily overcome without any alteration to the algorithm for analytic goal regression as already described. However, I leave the details until paragraph 3.5 in the last section (which mainly deals with enhancements to goal regression) so as to avoid cluttering the present argument with technical details.

2.3 Conclusions

The major weakness in the authors' argument is that nowhere do they acknowledge the drawbacks of the experimental technique as compared to the analytic: viz. the need for several examples, and the dependence on an appropriate bias in the description language. It is significant that when Mitchell had written and tested LEX, which learns by purely experimental methods, its weaknesses led his group to create LEX2, which combines analytic with empirical learning.

My conclusions, therefore, are that the authors' first recommendation (abandoning the analytic method in favour of the experimental) would be a retrograde step. Their second recommendation (combining the two) is potentially valuable; but both the experience of LEX2 and the many valid points in [Porter & Kibler 85] show that the analytic technique must be improved if it is to be of much use in such a partnership.

In the last section of this paper, I show some ways in which the analytic technique *can* be improved.

3 Enhancements and Solutions

In this section, I present a number of enhancements to the goal regression algorithm. Some of these are intended to overcome problems mentioned in the previous section; others are unrelated to these problems, but are valuable because they increase the generality of the result obtained.

All the examples deal with symbolic integration, and are taken from [Utgoff 84]. My justification for choosing symbolic integration as a domain, and LEX2 as a foundation on which to build, is that the difficulties in this domain are greater than in most others, and that LEX2 goes further than other programs towards tackling them [Boswell 85].

My approach is to start with LEX2's treatment of each example, and then to show how this can be improved.

3.1 Constraints imposed by $\mathcal{L}$

The fact that in LEX2 $\mathcal{L}$ is defined to be context-free (section 1.5) means that the program is unable to complete the goal regression shown in figure 1. This is because the l.h.s. of operator 43

$$\int \text{poly}(f(x))f'(x)\,dx \Rightarrow \int \text{poly}(u)\,du\,,\ u = f(x)$$

is not representable within $\mathcal{L}$, so goal regression through this operator is never permitted. However, it is only the result of the goal regression which has to be assimilated into $\mathcal{L}$ and so has to be context-free: there is no reason why one should not allow non context-free expressions to appear somewhere in the course of the goal regression, provided that, as in fig. 1, they disappear before the end. Here the expression $[\text{poly}_2(u(x))]^n u'(x)$ is not context-free, but after back-propagation through Op 52, u is instantiated to $\sin x$ and u' to $\cos x$, and the expression is back in $\mathcal{L}$.

Note, the expressions 'poly$_1$' and 'poly$_2$' in fig. 1 simply denote two different polynomial functions.

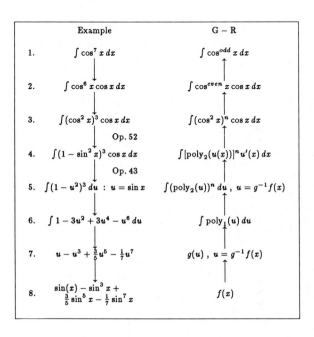

	Example	G − R
1.	$\int \cos^7 x \, dx$	$\int \cos^{odd} x \, dx$
2.	$\int \cos^6 x \cos x \, dx$	$\int \cos^{even} x \cos x \, dx$
3.	$\int (\cos^2 x)^3 \cos x \, dx$	$\int (\cos^2 x)^n \cos x \, dx$
	Op. 52	
4.	$\int (1 - \sin^2 x)^3 \cos x \, dx$	$\int [\text{poly}_2(u(x))]^n u'(x) \, dx$
	Op. 43	
5.	$\int (1 - u^2)^3 \, du \ : \ u = \sin x$	$\int (\text{poly}_2(u))^n \, du \, , \ u = g^{-1}f(x)$
6.	$\int 1 - 3u^2 + 3u^4 - u^6 \, du$	$\int \text{poly}_1(u) \, du$
7.	$u - u^3 + \frac{3}{5}u^5 - \frac{1}{7}u^7$	$g(u) \, , \ u = g^{-1}f(x)$
8.	$\sin(x) - \sin^3 x + \frac{3}{5}\sin^5 x - \frac{1}{7}\sin^7 x$	$f(x)$

Figure 1: Generating the concept "odd"

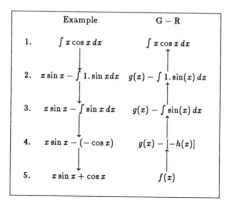

Figure 2: Where Goal-Regression fails to generalise

3.2 The use of families of analogous operators

The process of goal regression may be generalised by grouping the operators into families of analogous operators, and permitting the substitution of analogous operators in the course of goal regression. Thus between lines 3. and 4. of fig. 1, instead of $\cos^2 \Rightarrow 1 - \sin^2$ we may try reversing the analogous operator $\sin^2 \Rightarrow 1 - \cos^2$, and obtain eventually the alternative generalisation $\int \sin^{odd} x\, dx$, instead of $\int \cos^{odd} x\, dx$.

Then, if many more examples of the disjunction $\sin \vee \cos$ arise in this way, there exists a technique for assimilating it into the description language: viz, the method of least disjunction [Utgoff 84].

Secondly, the process may be further generalised by the substituting during goal regression, not of analogous operators, but of more general operators, each of which subsumes a family of more specialised operators. This is illustrated in fig. 2. As it stands, goal regression doesn't lead to any generalisation. This is because the operator linking lines 3 and 4, $\int \sin x\, dx \Rightarrow \cos(x)$, is so specific. If we maximally generalise this operator to $\int f'(x)\, dx \Rightarrow f(x)$, the remainder of the goal regression proceeds as before, but leads to the answer $\int x\, f''(x)\, dx$. It is encouraging that this is the generalisation most mathematicians would choose.

Of course, if a problem-solver is to make use of this result in order to evaluate some new integral $\int x\, g(x)\, dx$, it will have to test whether $g(x)$ is of the form $f''(x)$, i.e. is doubly-integrable. However, this is simpler than the original problem. Moreover, permitting such a precondition does not require an extension of the formalism of existing operator preconditions: for example, when attempting to apply the "integration by parts" operator, we have to test whether the integrand is of the form $f(x)g'(x)$.

3.3 Flexible application of reverse operators

Problems sometimes arise when, in the course of an example, an operator is applied to a subterm within an integrand. When the time comes to reverse this operator, the more general term to which it has to be applied may be found not yet to contain an appropriate subterm. See fig. 3.

If goal regression is carried out in full generality, the value obtained at the end (represented by ? in fig. 3) will be:

$$p[(Op\,1)^{-1}q, (Op\,2)^{-1}r] \tag{1}$$

where p, q, and r are arbitrary functions, with the constraint that $h = p(q, r)$. Thus, the function '+' has been generalised along with all the others (to p).

However, under the more conservative approach used in LEX2, the '+' is not so generalised, and the result obtained is

$$(Op\,1)^{-1}q + (Op\,2)^{-1}r$$

In none of the papers on LEX2 do the authors acknowledge this lack of generality in their implementation of goal regression. However, in practice it makes little difference: the function p in expression (1)

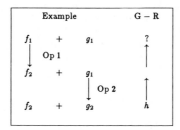

Figure 3: Operators applied to subterms

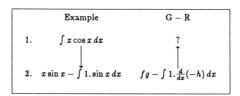

Figure 4: The last step

above would soon be constrained to be '+' in the course of goal regression through an earlier operator. Also, the authors of [Mitchell *et al* 85] do acknowledge this lack of generality in their program LEAP, and explain that it is a deliberate choice, made in order to avoid large disjunctions.

However, if we do adopt the more general goal regression algorithm just described, there are examples in which the greater generality obtained at one particular step is retained throughout the rest of the process and yields a more general solution at the end. Consider line 4 in figure 1. An alternative choice of the subterm to which the reverse of the operator $\cos^2 \Rightarrow 1 - \sin^2$ is applied makes $\text{poly}_2(u) \equiv 1 - u$ rather than $\text{poly}_2(u) \equiv 1 - u^2$. Consequently $u = \sin^2 x$, $u' = 2 \sin x \cos x$, and the generalised integral produced by the goal regression is

$$\int \cos^{odd} x \sin x \, dx$$

This example shows how an alternative generalisation can be obtained by altering the choice of a function (here 'poly'). Alternative generalisations may also be obtained by applying reverse operators to subterms of an expression different from the subterms to which the (forward) operators were applied in the given example. (In fact, this is another way of describing the effect of the change in the choice of polynomial illustrated above.)

Such an alternative generalisation is possible when reversing the step from the line 1 to 2 in fig. 2. This step is illustrated in more detail in fig. 4. (Note: the example in fig. 2 has been modified as described in the section 3.2 above.)

The operator applied here may be represented in the form

$$\int AB' \, dx \Rightarrow AB - \int PQ \, dx \; : \; P = A', Q = B$$

All that is required for the goal regression to give a correct answer (i.e. an integral that may be integrated by the given sequence of operators) is that we should choose A, B, P, and Q such that $P = A'$, $Q = B$, and

$$AB - \int PQ \, dx = fg - \int 1 . \frac{d}{dx}(-h) \, dx$$

In other words, all the is strictly necessary is this algebraic equality: there is no condition on how any of the subterms should match.

Having said this, we note that any match which doesn't match the two integrals is not going to produce a usable result, so we will insist that $AB = fg$ and $\int PQ\,dx = \int 1.\frac{d}{dx} - h\,dx$

The most general values for A and B are then given by

$$p = A \text{ and } \frac{fg}{p} = B$$

Under these conditions, back-propagation generalises the given integral to

$$\int fg' + gf' - \frac{p'fg}{p}\,dx$$

with the condition that $\frac{p'fg}{p}$ be integrable.

3.4 Forward propagation and least commitment

It is interesting to note that goal regression does not have to be carried out 'backwards' i.e. starting at the goal state and finishing with a generalisation of the initial problem state.

The sequence of states in the given example may be generalised by any 'least-commitment' strategy: i.e. keeping each state as general as possible, and imposing specialisations only as required by the intervening operators. This need not be done in any particular order. However, even given the enhancements suggested above, the generality of the result obtained still appears to depend on the order in which the constraints are applied. For example, if the example shown in fig. 1 is processed forwards, then the generalisation of the initial state to $\int \cos^{odd} x \sin x\,dx$ can not be obtained by any method so far discussed.

3.5 When goal regression leads to an incorrect heuristic

Although the set of problem states produced by goal regression are guaranteed solvable by the given sequence of operators, some of these states may be better solved in other ways.

The following example is taken from [Porter and Kibler 85].

The following pair of equations is a positive training instance for operator $subtract(a, b)$:

$$\begin{cases} a: & 2x + 3y = 5 \\ b: & 2x + 4y = 6 \end{cases}$$

Goal regression produces the rule:

$$\begin{cases} a: & Ax + B_1 y = C_1 \\ b: & Ax + B_2 y = C_2 \end{cases} \quad \rightarrow \text{apply } subtract(a, b)$$

This rule is faulty, since it will recommend subtracting equation b from equation a even when one of the coefficients of y is 0, e.g. in

$$\begin{cases} a: & 2x + 3y = 5 \\ b: & 2x + 0y = 6 \end{cases} \tag{2}$$

Porter and Kibler suggest as a solution the use of 'experimental goal regression': i.e. using inductive learning over a set of examples of the application of $subtract$ to obtain the rule

$$\begin{cases} a: & nonzero_1 x + integer_1 y = integer_2 \\ b: & nonzero_1 x + nonzero_2 y = nonzero_3 \end{cases} \quad \rightarrow \text{apply } subtract(a, b) \tag{3}$$

However, analytic goal regression can be applied here, too. From the solution to a single example such as (2), it is possible to learn the rule

$$\begin{cases} a: & Ax + B_1 y = C_1 \\ b: & Ax + 0y = C_2 \end{cases} \quad \rightarrow \text{apply } solve(b)$$

We now have two rules of the form:

IF P_1 THEN apply operator α
IF P_2 THEN apply operator β

From the two examples so far encountered, the program knows that P_1 and P_2 are not disjoint, and that where both are satisfied, operator β leads to a shorter solution. Hence it may rewrite the above rules so that the preconditions are disjoint, thus:

IF $P_1 \wedge \neg P_2$ **THEN** apply operator α
IF P_2 **THEN** apply operator β

The first of these is Porter & Kibler's rule (3) above.

One problem may remain: if $P_1 \wedge \neg P_2$ is not in $\mathcal{L}$ the program must then rewrite the precondition so that it is. However, if $\mathcal{L}$ permits techniques such as Version Spaces or Focussing, then such rewriting must be possible, since it is needed by part of the learning algorithm.

Hence it is possible to discover by analytic goal regression the same rule as Porter and Kibler recommend discovering by experimental goal-regression, but with all the usual advantages of the analytic technique, viz. less examples needed (two, in this case), and assurance that the operator suggested by the rule learnt will lead to a solution.

4 Conclusions

Although analytic goal regression has its difficulties, it should not be entirely rejected in favour of experimental goal regression. The most promising approach appears to be to combine both techniques in a single program, as Mitchell and Utgoff have done in LEX2.

The implementation of analytic goal regression is not as straightforward as is sometimes supposed, since there is scope for many generalisations and enhancements, which have been outlined in this paper.

Further work is needed to place these enhancements on a sounder theoretical footing, and to extend them to other domains.

REFERENCES

[Boswell 85]   Boswell R.A.
                 An Analytic Survey of Analytic Concept-Learning Programs,
                 Working Paper 181, Dept. of Artificial Intelligence, Edinburgh 1985.

[Cohen & Feigenbaum 82]
                 Cohen & Feigenbaum (editors),
                 Handbook of Artificial Intelligence, Vol. 3.,
                 Pitman, 1982.
                 Page 383.

[Fikes *et al* 72]
                 Fikes, R.E., Hart, P.E. and Nilsson, N.J.
                 Some new directions in robot problem solving,
                 in Meltzer B., and Michie D. (editors) *Machine Intelligence 7*,
                     pages 405–430.
                 Edinburgh University Press, 1972

[Geiser 75]   Geiser J.
                 Commenting Proofs,
                 In Winston P. (editor), *Proceedings of the fourth IJCAI*.
                 International Joint Conference on Artificial Intelligence. 1975.

[Mitchell 78]   Mitchell T.M.
                 Version Spaces: An Approach to concept learning,
                 PhD thesis. Stanford University. 1978.

[Mitchell 82]   Mitchell T.M.
                     Towards Combining Empirical and Analytic Methods for
                         inferring Heuristics,
                     Technical Report LCSR-TR-27, Laboratory for Computer Science
                         Research, Rutgers University, 1982.

[Mitchell *et al* 80]
                     Mitchell T.M., Utgoff P.E., and Banerji R.B.
                     Learning Problem-Solving Heuristics by Experimentation,
                     Technical Report CBM-TR-114, Rutgers University, Sept. 1980.

[Mitchell *et al* 85]
                     Mitchell T.M., Mahadevan S., and Steinberg L.I.
                     LEAP: A Learning Apprentice for VLSI Design,
                     in Joshi A. (editor), *Proceedings of the Eighth IJCAI*, vol 1,
                         pages 573–580

[Porter & Kibler 84]
                     Porter B.W. and Kibler D.F.
                     Learning Operator Transformations,
                     In Brachman R. (editor), *Procs. of AAAI-84*, pages 278–282.
                     American Association for Artificial Intelligence, 1983.

[Porter & Kibler 85]
                     Porter B.W. and Kibler D.F.
                     A Comparison of Analytic and Experimental Goal Regression
                         for Machine Learning,
                     in Joshi A. (editor), *Proceedings of the Eighth IJCAI*, vol. 1,
                         pages 555–559

[Silver 83]   Silver B.
                     Learning Equation-Solving Methods from Worked Examples,
                     In Michalski R.S., (editor), *Proceedings of the International*
                         Machine Learning Workshop, pages 99–104.
                     University of Illinois.
                     Also available from Edinburgh as Research Paper 188.

[Utgoff 84]   Utgoff P.E.
                     Shift of Bias for Inductive Concept-learning,
                     PhD thesis, Rutgers University, Oct. 1984.

[Winston 75]   Winston P.
                     Learning Structural Descriptions from Examples,
                     In Winston P.H. (editor), *The psychology of computer*
                         vision. McGraw Hill, 1975.

Advances in Artificial Intelligence - II
B. Du Boulay, D. Hogg and L. Steels (Editors)
© Elsevier Science Publishers B.V. (North-Holland), 1987

GENERALISED SUBSUMPTION
AND ITS APPLICATIONS TO INDUCTION AND REDUNDANCY

Wray Buntine
(N.S.W. Institute of Technology/Macquarie University)

N.S.W. Institute of Technology,
School of Computing Science,
P.O. Box 123,
Broadway, 2007, N.S.W., Australia.

Abstract. A theoretical framework and algorithms are presented that provide a new basis for the induction of definite (Horn) clauses. This hinges on a natural extension of subsumption that forms a strong model of generalisation. Such a model appears crucial to the development of practical induction systems. A useful by–product of the model is a simple but powerful model of redundancy. Both induction and redundancy control are central tasks in a knowledge acquisition system.

1. Introduction

Inductive inference has long been a research topic of Artificial Intelligence (see survey by Dietterich et al. 1982) and Computer Science (see survey by Angluin & Smith 1983). A common application cited is the (semi–)automated acquisition of knowledge for expert systems (Hart 1985, Michie 1983) and knowledge bases (Kitakami et al. 1984). The first commercial products of AI induction research, often based on Quinlan's ID3 algorithm to induce decision trees (Quinlan 1984), are starting to see use in industry (Michie 1985) and pay their way! However, such practical achievements are yet to be demonstrated of definite clause induction systems.

A theoretical foundation for induction of definite clauses has been developed (Shapiro 1981) and some progress has been made towards achieving practicality. For example, by representing an inductive hypothesis as a logic program, that is, as a set of rules, Shapiro's Model Inference System (1981, 1983) demonstrates that the process of induction can be split neatly into two tasks: (1) searching for suitable rules to include; and (2) debugging demonstrably false applications of the rules to pinpoint which rule(s) to subsequently exclude.

Further refinements of definite clause induction methods, specifically, improvements in the search for rules, could be made possible by adapting and unifying known practical methods in use in the field of Machine Learning (for example, see Mitchell 1982, Dietterich et al. 1982). However, the theory of definite clauses currently lacks one important component – a suitable model of generalisation, a key part of many of these induction methods. In the next section, subsumption, a weak model of generalisation, and its associated set of induction tools developed by Plotkin (1970, 1971) and Shapiro (1981), is shown to be sometimes deficient for this purpose.

Intended to fill the gap, the main contribution of this paper is the introduction and development of a stronger *model of generalisation of definite clauses* called *generalised subsumption*, and *key results and algorithms* for its application in a variety of induction styles. The model and algorithms provide a new foundation for more practical definite clause induction systems. A useful by–product of the theory is a model of redundancy. Redundancy control is another central task for a knowledge acquisition system (Kitakami et al. 1984).

Subsumption is shown (in the fourth section) to be a special case of *generalised subsumption*. Consequently, algorithms presented here degenerate to the corresponding subsumption algorithms. As one would expect, the advantages of using generalised subsumption instead of subsumption come with a computational price, for example in some settings termination may not be guaranteed.

1.1. Outline

The paper is organised as follows. The second section discusses the uses of a generalisation model and highlights some deficiencies of subsumption in this respect. The third section provides necessary concepts, notation, and some preliminary results for the theory to follow. Starting from the definition of *generalised subsumption*, a basic theory of generalisation is developed in the fourth section including an examination of some properties pertinent to induction. Applications of the theory are discussed in the remaining sections: a model of redundant clauses and atoms (fifth section) and, the finding of a most specific generalisation (sixth section).

2. Using a Generalisation Model for Induction

A key part of the induction process as it is envisaged by many researchers in the AI discipline regardless of the representation language used, is a *search through a space of rules* (both Dietterich et al. 1982 and Angluin and Smith 1983 discuss this, see also Shapiro 1981). A model of generalisation provides a basis for organising this search space. Briefly, rule $R1$ is *more general* than rule $R2$ (or $R2$ is *more specific* than $R1$) if it can be success-fully applied to prove at least the same facts are true (adapted from Mitchell 1982). Rules are organised into a structure called a hierarchy. All clauses below a node in a *specialisation (generalisation) hierarchy* are specialisa-tions (generalisations) of the node, and furthermore the hierarchy contains all rules more specific (general) than the root. The use of a specialisation or generalisation hierarchy as a search space has several advantages.

Complete branches can be pruned during search on the knowledge that all specialisations of a rule, or generalisa-tions, are guaranteed to inherit some prohibited property. Some such properties are: failure to comply with a con-straint; failure to prove a fact known to be true (Shapiro 1983); and, proving a fact known to be false (Sammut and Banerji 1985).

Furthermore, knowledge of specialisations and generalisations of the desired rule can also be used to delimit the space of potential rules, and, as a by–product, simplify the process of testing whether a potential rule is consistent with the data currently available (Mitchell 1982).

Finally, suppose $R1$ and $R2$ are known specialisations of an unknown rule. A most specific generalisation of $R1$ and $R2$ (that is, a generalisation of both $R1$ and $R2$ more specific than any other generalisation) is a more general rule that is (under conditions pertaining to the nature of the generalisation model) also a specialisation of the unk-nown rule. Applications of an algorithm to compute a most specific generalisation, based on subsumption as a model of generalisation, have been discussed by Plotkin (1970, 1971) and Vere (1977). The LEX system (Mitchell et al. 1981), and the learning system of Fu and Buchanan (1985) employ a similar style of process.

2.1. Problems with Subsumption

Unfortunately, subsumption, an existing weak model of generalisation, in its present form performs poorly at several of the above mentioned tasks. Two simple examples suffice to demonstrate this. Recall that clause C sub-sumes clause D if there exists a substitution θ such that $C\theta \subseteq D$ (Plotkin 1970).

Firstly, suppose we have been advised that any small fluffy dog and any fluffy cat are cuddly pets. In definite clause form (introduced in more detail in 3.1) this can be expressed as follows:

$$(1) \; cuddly\text{–}pet\,(X) \leftarrow small\,(X), fluffy\,(X), dog\,(X).$$
$$(2) \; cuddly\text{–}pet\,(X) \leftarrow fluffy\,(X), cat\,(X).$$

Suppose we also know the following clauses hold:

$$pet\,(X) \leftarrow cat\,(X).$$
$$pet\,(X) \leftarrow dog\,(X).$$
$$small\,(X) \leftarrow cat\,(X).$$
$$tame\,(X) \leftarrow pet\,(X).$$

The most specific generalisation under subsumption of (1) and (2), a possible clause for determining cuddly pets, is:

$$cuddly\text{–}pet\,(X) \leftarrow fluffy\,(X).$$

Given our current knowledge, a more likely clause is:

$$(3) \; cuddly\text{–}pet\,(X) \leftarrow small\,(X), fluffy\,(X), pet\,(X).$$

This should be considered a generalisation of (1) and (2) as it must succeed for any value of X for which either of clauses (1) or (2) does. However, (3) is not more general under subsumption than either (1) or (2), demonstrating a first inadequacy with subsumption.

In similar circumstances, suppose we are trying to find a clause to determine examples of the concept pig. We might consider the clause:

$$(4)\ pig(X) \leftarrow pet(X).$$

If we know of no one with a pet pig this clause can be rejected on the grounds that it does not help explain the available data. From our current knowledge the following three clauses can also be rejected as (5) is essentially the same clause as (4), since all pets are tame, and (6) and (7) are special cases of (4).

$$(5)\ pig(X) \leftarrow pet(X), tame(X).$$
$$(6)\ pig(X) \leftarrow dog(X).$$
$$(7)\ pig(X) \leftarrow cat(X).$$

However, subsumption fails to justify that (5) is as general as (4) and that (6) and (7) are more specific, demonstrating further inadequacies with subsumption. This can result, for instance, in the Model Inference System (Shapiro 1981) doing much unnecessary work during search of a specialisation hierarchy.

The cause of these kinds of inadequacies is that when forming a generalisation or specialisation of a clause, or finding the most specific generalisation of two clauses, subsumption does not allow current knowledge to be utilised. This can be partly alleviated by implementing subsumption relative to some set of background facts (for example in Plotkin 1971, see also Vere 1977). However, in the above example the problem still remains as relevant background facts are not immediatetly available, they need to be inferred.

Fortunately, this problem has already been tackled in the context of constructing generalisations. A more powerful method of generalising a clause than that suggested by subsumption is used in Sammut's Marvin system (Sammut 1985). Marvin induces definite clauses by working in an interactive situation with a knowledgeable trainer. Marvin's technique would for instance generalise either of clauses (1) or (2) to clause (3) and suggests an improved model of generalisation.

3. Preliminaries

Before introducing the model of generalisation, we briefly revise necessary concepts and illustrate the conventions on notation to follow. Appropriate background for logic programming is set out by Lloyd (1984), for subsumption in the context of induction is given by Plotkin (1970), and for a theory of induction in definite clause logic is provided by Shapiro (1981).

The model–theoretic definition of an interpretation from first order predicate logic (for example see Chang and Lee 1973) is assumed here. Herbrand interpretations, the usual class considered in the theory of logic programming, are not sufficient to define whether a clause is more general than another. Essentially, this is because the current Herbrand base continues to expand as an induction system is presented more facts, which it invariably will be. The usual definitions for a formula to be *true in* an interpretation I, and for a formula to be *valid* (that is, true in any interpretation) apply.

3.1. Logic Programming Concepts

Some basic concepts of logic programming follow. The notation is close to that of Lloyd (1984).

A *term* is a constant or the application of a function symbol to the appropriate number of terms. An *atom* is the application of a predicate symbol to the appropriate number of terms. Atoms are usually represented by the letters A or B, sometimes with primes and/or subscripts.

A *goal* has the form $\leftarrow B_1, \cdots B_n$ where $n \geq 0$ and B_i are atoms. Alternatively, this goal may be represented as the set of literals formed by negating each of the atoms B_i, that is, $\{ \neg B_1, \cdots \neg B_n \}$. Goals are usually represented by the letters G or H. If $n=0$ the goal is the empty goal, written $\varnothing$.

A *definite clause*, abbreviated to *clause*, has the form $A \leftarrow B_1, \cdots B_n$ where $n \geq 0$ and A and each B_i are atoms. For $n=0$, the clause is often called a *fact*. If the above clause is represented by the letter C, then $Chead$, the *head* of the clause is the atom A and $Ctail$, the *tail* is written as the goal $\leftarrow B_1, \cdots B_n$. Clauses are usually represented by letters such as C or D.

A *logic program*, for example P or Q, is a finite set of clauses implicitly universally quantified. If the set is empty the program is the null program, represented as $\varnothing$.

A *substitution*, usually represented by lower case greek letters such as θ, σ or τ, consists of a finite number of distinct variables paired with terms. The *instance* of a finite string of symbols F by substitution θ, represented by $F\theta$, is obtained by simultaneously replacing each occurrence of a component variable of θ in F by its corresponding term. Any formula is *ground* if it contains no variables. A substitution for all and only the variables in formula F by ground terms will be referred to as a *ground substitution of F*.

G' is the *resolvent* of G and C on atom A (occurring in G), if there exists a substitution θ, the most general unifier of A and the head of C (that is, the most general or least instantiating substitution θ s.t. $A\theta=Chead\,\theta$), such that $G'=(G\setminus\{A\}\cup Ctail)\theta$.

The existential quantifier ($\exists$) and the universal quantifier ($\forall$) are sometimes used to close a formula. That is, $\forall F$ represents the closed formula obtained by universally quantifying every unbound variable in F. So $\forall\exists_x f(x,y)$ actually represents $\forall_y\exists_x f(x,y)$.

Given a logic program P and a goal $G\equiv\leftarrow A_1,\cdots A_n$, the goal *succeeds* on P if and only if the formula $P\Rightarrow\exists(A_1\wedge\cdots A_n)$ is true. A sound and complete logic programming system can demonstrate this by constructing a *refutation* for G, that is, linear sequence of goals with initial goal G and final goal $\varnothing$ where each is the resolvent of the previous goal and a clause from P.

3.2. A Context for Induction

Next, a theoretical context for induction is considered.

In an induction problem, the *intended interpretation* is that ideal but unknown interpretation giving truth values for formulae consistent with the problem specification and any future observations that could possibly be made in the domain being considered.

An induction system's *current knowledge* consists of *data*, atoms given as true or false, plus *background knowledge* expressed as a logic program. These are assumed true in the intended interpretation. A formula is *known* true if it is a logical consequence of the current knowledge.

An induction system is to find an *inductive hypothesis*, expressed as a set of clauses, consistent with the current knowledge and capable of axiomatising the data. The hypothesis is not considered part of the current knowledge, though at some point a clause may become plausible enough to be included. (This formulation ignores the important problem of truth maintenance (Doyle 1979) to be performed when the truth of part of the system's current knowledge in the intended interpretation becomes falsifiable and so recent induction steps unjustified).

The following key definition (Shapiro 1983) formalises the notion of a clause being *directly responsible* for proving an atom and is an essential building block of the theory to follow. We say a clause $A\leftarrow B_1,\cdots B_n$ *covers* atom A' in interpretation I if there is a substitution θ that unifies A with A', such that each $B_i\theta$ is true in I. Such a clause is called a *covering clause*. The search of the space of rules mentioned in the previous two sections corresponds, more precisely, to a search for covering clauses. Furthermore, a clause is *known to cover* an atom if it does so in every interpretation consistent with the current knowledge.

4. Generalised Subsumption

To avoid confusion, *subsumption*, as considered by Plotkin, will hereafter be referred to as *weak subsumption* and *generalised subsumption* as, more briefly, *subsumption*.

Informally, subsumption corresponds to the *more general* relation for rules considered in the second section. In the following definition, the logic program P represents a system's current knowledge.

Definition (of *generalised subsumption*) We say clause C *subsumes* (or is *more general than*) clause D w.r.t. logic program P, or $C\geq_P D$, if for any atom A and for any interpretation I such that P is true in I, C covers A in I whenever D does. C is referred to as a *generalisation* of D, and D a *specialisation* of C.

To assist in the formulation of hierarchies and redundancy, further definitions are required. We say clause C is *equivalent* to clause D w.r.t. logic program P (represented as $C =_P D$) if $C \geq_P D$ and $D \geq_P C$. $=_P$ is an equivalence relation since $\geq_P$ is transitive and reflexive. The *equivalence class* under $=_P$ of C (denoted $[C]_P$) is the set of all clauses D such that $C =_P D$.

The theorem below (Buntine 1986), a direct consequence of the definition, lays the foundations for an algorithm to test for subsumption.

Theorem 4.1 (Testing for $\geq_P$) Let $C \equiv A_0 \leftarrow A_1, \cdots A_n$ and $D \equiv B_0 \leftarrow B_1, \cdots B_m$ be two clauses containing distinct variables and P be any logic program. Let θ be a ground substitution of D using distinct constants not occurring in C, D or P. $C \geq_P D$ if and only if $A_0 \sigma = B_0$ for some substitution σ and $P \wedge B_1 \theta \wedge \cdots B_m \theta \Rightarrow \exists (A_1 \sigma \theta \wedge \cdots A_n \sigma \theta)$ is true.

The implication in the theorem is of a form suited for testing by a logic programming system. As a consequence, such a test is only semi-decidable. That is, termination of the test is only guaranteed when in fact $C \geq_P D$. Although, if the program contains no recursion, termination is guaranteed.

At this point, the reader may wish to convince themselves that clause (3) given in section 2.1 indeed subsumes both clauses (1) and (2) w.r.t. the logic program given.

The theorem below (Buntine 1986) highlights the close connection between the *subsumption* relation and logical implication.

Theorem 4.2 (Semantics of $\geq_P$) Let D be any clause that is not valid and P a logic program. $P \Rightarrow \forall D$ is true if and only if $C \geq_P D$ for some clause C occurring in P.

Corollary If $C \geq_P D$ then $P \wedge \forall C \Rightarrow P \wedge \forall D$ is true.

The theorem holds because, very briefly, letting D and θ be as given in theorem 4.1, C can be seen to be the first clause used in a refutation to show that $P \wedge (B_1 \theta \wedge \cdots B_m \theta) \Rightarrow B_0 \theta$ is true. As a consequence of the theorem, when a clause in a logic program is replaced by a more general clause, at least the same goals will succeed on the newly constructed program. Furthermore, if $P \subseteq Q$ and $C =_P D$ then $Q \cup \{C\} \Leftrightarrow Q \cup \{D\}$. So, equivalent clauses can be used interchangeably in the right context.

Finally, weak subsumption is a special case of generalised subsumption. For any two clauses C and D, $C \geq_\varnothing D$ if and only if C weakly subsumes D. This follows from theorem 4.1 when the logic program P is the null program. In effect, subsumption degenerates to weak subsumption when no prerequisite knowledge is known about the context in which the clauses will be used. As the knowledge of the system expands, so does the concept of generalisation.

Having covered basic properties of *generalised subsumption*, we now consider additional properties related to the problem of induction.

4.1. Subsumption Hierarchies

Induction can be achieved by searching the space of clauses more general than a known specialisation of a clause (for instance a ground fact, as used in Marvin, Sammut 1985), or the space of clauses more specific than a known generalisation (for instance the fact $sort(X,Y)$ is more general than any clause with the two place *sort* predicate at its head, as used by the Model Inference System, Shapiro 1981). These search spaces are organised into *hierarchies*. Loosely, a *specialisation (generalisation) hierarchy* w.r.t. P *rooted* at a given clause C is some organisation of clauses $\leq_P C$ ($\geq_P C$) such that at least one member from each equivalence class whose members are $\leq_P C$ ($\geq_P C$) is represented. Clauses may be organised into a tree structure where all clauses below a given clause in the tree are $\leq_P$ ($\geq_P$) that clause. Marvin searches a generalisation hierarchy, the Model Inf. Sys. a specialisation hierarchy, and the Version Space method (Mitchell 1982) the intersection of the two hierarchies.

Surprisingly, specialisation and generalisation hierarchies possess very different characteristics. To investigate these, we consider the advantages gained by using a stronger model of generalisation, that is, by increasing the induction systems current knowledge, before searching the hierarchies.

The use of a stronger model of generalisation does not in fact increase the scope of the search space defined by a specialisation hierarchy. The hierarchies still span equivalent clauses. More specifically, let $P \subseteq Q$ be two logic programs, let S_P denote the set of clauses represented in some specialisation hierarchy w.r.t. P rooted at the clause C, and let S_Q denote the same for Q. Then every clause in S_P has a member of its equivalence class w.r.t. Q in S_Q (as a specialisation w.r.t. P is also a specialisation w.r.t. Q), and every clause in S_Q has a member of its equivalence class w.r.t. Q in S_P (let $D \in S_Q$ and $Chead\,\theta=Dhead$, then $(D \cup C\,\theta)=_Q D$ and $\leq_\emptyset C$, hence $\leq_P C$).

However, a stronger model reduces the size though not the scope of the search space as several equivalence classes may collapse into the one (as demonstrated by the second example in the second section where clause (5) becomes the same as (4)), and the stronger model allows more pruning to occur during search (as with clauses (6) and (7) in the same example).

In contrast, the same equivalence of spanned clauses does not hold of the search spaces defined by generalisation hierarchies w.r.t. different logic programs. The stronger the model of generalisation, the greater the number of clauses spanned. In particular, a generalisation hierarchy w.r.t. the current knowledge rooted at a given fact contains representatives of all and only those equivalence classes whose clauses are *currently known to cover that fact*. For example, if the current knowledge is $P=\emptyset$, then the generalisation hierarchy w.r.t. P rooted at the fact *animal (masport)* contains only the fact *animal (X)*. However, if the fact *cat (masport)* is currently known, then the clause *animal (X)←cat (X)* will also occur in the hierarchy.

Thus, when using a generalisation hierarchy to achieve induction, an assumption is being made about the current knowledge, that is, it must be sufficient to justify some clause true in the intended interpretation indeed subsumes the root clause. We call this the *justifiability assumption*. The justifiability assumption dictates that knowledge should be acquired incrementally, with new concepts being built on existing knowledge, and furthermore, greatly restricts the scope of the search space in comparison with a full specialisation hierarchy.

There is one common situation where the justifiability assumption is satisfied by default. This occurs when an unknown concept does not need a recursive definition and all predicates that could be used in the definition are such that all their true instances are known.

We envisage two other situations where the justifiability assumption is applicable. Induction may be controlled by a knowledgeable trainer, as is expected with Marvin (Sammut and Banerji 1985). Before beginning induction, it is not unreasonable to expect them to supply the system with enough relevant knowledge of a few pertinent examples sufficient to justify that a clause is indeed a cover (Sammut 1985, consider also Hart 1985). Secondly, a system may be supplied with all currently available knowledge, that is, observations and a suitably rich description language, and be required to perform induction solely with that knowledge. Any inductive hypothesis can only be accepted if it is currently plausible. We claim that to a first approximation, plausibility of a clause is equivalent to being able to justify that the clause covers at least some facts known true, but none known false.

Having presented some basic features of generalised subsumption and the hierarchies so formed, the remainder of the paper outlines a number of applications of the model.

5. A Model of Redundancy

At least two kinds of redundancy exist in a logic program. A clause can be redundant, and so can an atom within a clause.

We say a clause D is *redundant* in a logic program P if $P \setminus \{D\} \Rightarrow \forall D$. Such a clause can be removed from the logic program and exactly the same goals will still succeed. For example, the third and fourth clauses in the program

$$member (X ,X.Y).$$
$$member (X ,Z.Y) \leftarrow member (X ,Y).$$
$$member (X ,Z.X.\,[]).$$
$$member (1,3.2.1.\,[]).$$

are redundant because they are both logical consequences of the first two.

From theorem 4.2, if a clause D is redundant, their always exists another clause in the logic program that can be considered primarily responsible for rendering D redundant. Several such clauses may exist. In view of this, the subsumption relation can be considered to order clauses in terms of their relative redundancy. More importantly, the subsumption test gives a semi–decidable algorithm to detect redundancy, ideally suited to computation by a logic programming system. This allows, for instance, the redundancy of clauses and not just facts to be detected (compare with Bowen and Kowalski 1982). For example, from theorem 4.1 the third and fourth clauses in the above program are both more redundant than the second clause and the first has no relation to any of the others in the program.

Within clauses themselves, a second type of redundancy is possible. If clauses are being constructed by an algorithm with no proper regard for the underlying semantics, for example if clauses are being enumerated for the purposes of induction, they may contain atoms making no effective contribution to the successful working of the clause. The clause

$$cuddly-cat(X) \leftarrow fluffy(X), cat(X), animal(X)$$

is such a case if it is known that a cat is always an animal as the atom *animal*(X) will be proven true whenever *cat*(X) is. The last atom can be said to be *redundant* as its only effect is to cause additional but unnecessary computation. Formally, this occurs because

$$cuddly-cat(X) \leftarrow fluffy(X), cat(X), animal(X) =_P cuddly-cat(X) \leftarrow fluffy(X), cat(X)$$

if the logic program P contains the clause *animal*$(X) \leftarrow cat(X)$ and as a consequence (by the corollary to theorem 4.2) the shorter clause can replace the longer in any such logic program and exactly the same goals will still succeed. Plotkin (1970) denotes the process of ensuring that a clause contains no further redundant atoms, in the context of weak subsumption, *reducing* a clause. A corresponding concept is appropriate for *generalised subsumption*.

Definition (of a *reduced* form for clauses) We say a clause $A_0 \leftarrow A_1, \cdots A_n$ is *reduced* w.r.t. logic program P if for all i such that $1 \le i \le n$, $A_0 \leftarrow A_1, \cdots A_{i-1}, A_{i+1}, \cdots A_n$ is not equivalent, w.r.t. P to $A_0 \leftarrow A_1, \cdots A_n$.

By the corollary to theorem 4.2, a clause D within a logic program P can be replaced by its reduced form w.r.t. $P \backslash \{D\}$ and the new logic program will have exactly the same goals succeed with perhaps less computation. In addition, the reduced form of a clause will always remain equivalent to the original if the logic program is subsequently expanded.

An algorithm for reducing a clause is the same as Plotkin's but is based on the subsumption test given in theorem 4.1. It suffers the same termination problems as that test. The algorithm can be significantly speeded up in practice by an attempt to reduce small groups of atoms before the full subsumption test is employed. An application of it is demonstrated in the next section.

6. Most Specific Generalisations

A clause C is a *most specific generalisation* w.r.t. logic program P of clauses D_1 and D_2 if C is a generalisation of D_1 and D_2 and for any other generalisation of D_1 and D_2, C', $C' \ge_P C$. Such a clause is unique upto equivalence w.r.t. P. Though it may be a simple matter to devise a logical formula that is a most specific generalisation, finding a clause is a different problem. The concept is important for induction because, assuming that known clauses D_1 and D_2 are specialisations w.r.t. P of some unknown clause true in the intended interpretation, the most specific generalisation w.r.t. P of D_1 and D_2 must also be true. The assumption is similar to the justifiability assumption. Vere (1977) gives a number of illustrative examples where the background information is represented by a set of facts.

The following theorem (Buntine 1986), in conjunction with Plotkin's least generalisation algorithm (1970), suggests a method to find a most specific generalisation if one exists.

Theorem 6.1 (Finding a most specific generalisation of two clauses) Let $C \equiv A_0 \leftarrow A_1, \cdots A_n$ and $D \equiv B_0 \leftarrow B_1, \cdots B_m$ be two clauses containing distinct variables and P a logic program. Let θ be a ground substitution of the variables in C using distinct constants, and ϕ likewise for D. If a most specific generalisation of C and D w.r.t. P exists then it is equivalent to a least generalisation (most specific generalisation w.r.t. $\varnothing$) of $C\theta \cup G$ and $D\phi \cup H$ for some goal G satisfying the following conditions, and H likewise. G has a correct answer substitution on $P \cup \{A_1\theta, \cdots A_n\theta\}$; G contains no constants that occur in both θ and $(C\theta)tail$ but not in $(C\theta)head$; and, no instance of G has the same properties.

A direct implementation of the theorem as it stands is impractical for all but the simplest cases as it essentially involves a computation of all ground facts logically implied by the logic program. The theorem is however of important theoretical significance as it provides a precise characterisation of the technique suggested by Plotkin to use his least generalisation algorithm, extended to allow the least generalisation of clauses, not just facts, and to allow the use of background knowledge expressed as general rules. Furthermore, the resultant clause is to be reduced w.r.t. the logic program and this typically produces a far shorter but equivalent clause.

For example, suppose we are given the logic program P :

$$list([]).$$
$$list(X.Y) \leftarrow list(Y).$$
$$member(X,X.Y) \leftarrow list(Y).$$
$$member(4,3.4.[]).$$
$$member(2,5.1.2.[]).$$
$$member(2,1.2.[]).$$

and that a most specific generalisation w.r.t. P of the facts $C \equiv member(4,3.4.[])$ and $D \equiv member(2,5.1.2.[])$ is to be found under certain assumptions given below. In this case G and H (using the terminology of 6.1) are ground goals with correct answer substitutions on P. To restrict potential goals G and H we assume that any list occurring in the tail of $C \cup G$ must be smaller in length than the list occurring in the head, likewise for H. Furthermore, assume atoms in G or H occur in the Herbrand base of P and that only lists of integers are being considered (not for instance lists of lists of integers). Assumptions of this kind, effectively stating which atoms may be relevant, are generally required to reduce the size of the problem and obtain a more useful answer.

Exhaustive calculation shows that the largest possible G is 11 atoms long and H 58 atoms long. The resultant least generalisation has a tail 335 atoms long! and subsequently reduces w.r.t. P (using an algorithm coded in Prolog and run on an interpreter) to the useful result

$$member(X,U.V.W) \leftarrow member(X,V.W),list(W).$$

It is interesting to note that an attempt to reduce the 335 atom long clause under weak subsumption, rather than subsumption w.r.t. P, using the same algorithm failed due to lack of memory even though the interpreter was using 2 megabytes of memory. To compare the method with Vere's technique of induction in the context of factual background information (1977) and Plotkin's later method (1971), subsumption w.r.t. the set of (possibly non-ground) facts logically implied by P was used. A similar problem arose. These results where typical of a number of experiments. Using the framework of theorem 6.1, useful inductive results could only be obtained by employing the strong model of reduction to reduce the final clause sufficiently.

7. Conclusion and Future Work

An integral part of the induction process is search through a space of clauses. This paper introduces a powerful model of generalisation, incorporating theory and algorithms, on which suitable search spaces can be built. This supersedes weak subsumption as such a model of generalisation.

A number of results presented are: methods to detect redundant clauses in logic programs, and redundant atoms within clauses where the removal of redundant atoms is guaranteed to reduce the size of refutations using the clause; a theoretical characterisation of Plotkin's induction technique of finding a most specific generalisation; a demonstration of the power of the reduction method for producing practical results with this induction technique; and, a significant improvement over an existing tool, weak subsumption.

For the reasons outlined in section 4.1, the model also suggests an improvement over Shapiro's most general refinement operator (1981) for enumerating a specialisation hierarchy.

Further work on the generalisation model would be to account for predicate completion, negation or alternate theories of equality (Jaffer, Lassez and Maher 1984). In addition, improvements in the calculation of a most specific generalisation are obtainable by taking account of the reduction process while the least generalisation is actually calculated (as demonstrated in Buntine 1986) so a more practical implementation of an algorithm to find a most specific generalisation seems feasible.

Of course, to achieve effective induction, a means of heuristically searching the hierarchies needs to be developed. This is currently being investigated.

8. Acknowledgements

I would like to thank Ross Quinlan, Tom Osborn and Jenny Edwards for their encouragement and support, Tom and Jenny for their timely proof–reading of the paper, Paul Brebner for his advice on the Marvin system, and Claude Sammut.

9. References

Angluin D. and Smith, C.H., "Inductive Inference: Theories and Methods". *Computing Surveys*, 15, (1983) 237–269.

Bowen, K.A. and Kowalski, R.A., "Amalgamating Langauge and Meta-language in Logic Programming". In: Clark, K.L., and Tarnlund, S.-A. (Ed.s), *Logic Programming* (1982).

Buntine W.L., "Towards a Practical Theory of Horn Clause Induction". *Proc. of 9th Annual Australian Computer Science Conf.* (Canberra, 1986).

Chang, C.L. and Lee, R.C.T., *Symbolic Logic and Mechanical Theorem Proving*, (Academic, 1973).

Dietterich, T.G., London, R., Clarkson, K. and Dromey, R., "Learning and Inductive Inference". In: Cohen, P. and Feigenbaum E. (Eds), *The Handbook of Artificial Intelligence*, (Kaufmann, Los Altos, 1982) 323–512.

Doyle, J., "A Truth Maintenance system". *Artificial Intelligence*, 12, (1979) 231–272.

Fu, L.-M. and Buchanan, B.G., "Learning Intermediate Concepts in Constructing a Hierarchical Knowledge Base". *Proc. 9th Int. Joint. Conf. Artificial Intelligence*, (UCLA, 1985) 659–666.

Hart, A., "The Role of Induction in Knowledge Elicitation". *Expert Systems*, 2, (1985) 24–28.

Jaffar, J., Lassez J.-J. and Maher M.J., "A Theory of Complete Logic Programs with Equality". *Proc. Int. Conf. on 5th Gen. Computer Systems*, (Tokyo, 1984) 175–184.

Kitakami, H., Kunifuji, S., Miyachi, T. and Furukawa K., "A Methodology for Implementation of a Knowledge Acquisition System". *Proc. IEEE Int. Symp. on Logic Programming*, (Atlanta City, 1984) 131–142.

Lloyd, J.W., *Foundations of Logic Programming* (Springer–Verlag, 1984).

Michie, D., "Inductive Rule Generation in the context of the Fifth Generation". In: Michalski, R.S., Carbonell, J., and Mitchell, T.M., (Ed.s) *Machine Learning, Vol. II* (Tioga, Palo Alto, 1985).

Michie, D., "Expert Systems Today". Invited talk at *Conference on Commercial Applications of Expert Systems* (Sydney, May 1985).

Mitchell, T.M., "Generalisation as Search". *Artificial Intelligence*, 18, (1982) 203–226.

Mitchell, T.M., Utgoff, P.E., Nudel, B., Banerji, R., "Learning Problem Solving Heuristics through Practice". *Proc. 7th Int. Joint. Conf. Artificial Intelligence*, (Vancouver, 1981) 127–134.

Plotkin, G.D., "A Note on Inductive Generalisation". In: Michie, D., (Ed) *Machine Intelligence 5*, (Elsevbier North–Holland, New York, 1970) 153–163.

Plotkin, G.D., "A Further Note on Inductive Generalisation". In: Michie, D., (Ed) *Machine Intelligence 6*, (Elsevbier North–Holland, New York, 1971) 101–124.

Quinlan, J.R., "Learning Efficient Classification Procedures and their Application to Chess End games". In: Michalski, R.S., Carbonell, J., and Mitchell, T.M., (Ed.s) *Machine Learning – An Artificial Intelligence Approach* (Springer–Verlag, 1984).

Sammut, C.A., "Concept Development for Expert System Knowledge Bases". *Australian Computer Journal*, Vol. 17, No. 1, (1985) 49–55.

Sammut, C.A. and Banerji, R.B. "Learning Concepts by Asking Questions". In: Michalski, R.S., Carbonell, J., and Mitchell, T.M., (Ed.s) *Machine Learning, Vol. II* (Tioga, Palo Alto, 1985).

Shapiro, E.Y. "Inductive Inference of Theories from Facts", TR 192, DCS, Yale University (1981).

Shapiro, E.Y., *Algorithmic Program Debugging*, (MIT Press, 1983).

Vere, S.A., "Induction of Relational Productions in the Presence of Background Information", *Proc. 5th Int. Joint. Conf. Artificial Intelligence*, (Cambridge MA, 1977) 349–355.

Advances in Artificial Intelligence - II
B. Du Boulay, D. Hogg and L. Steels (Editors)
© Elsevier Science Publishers B.V. (North-Holland), 1987

UNIMEM, A General Learning System:
An Overview

Michael Lebowitz[1]

Department of Computer Science -- Columbia University

New York, NY 10027

U.S.A

Abstract

Learning by observation is an important area of machine learning, allowing systems to automatically build up knowledge bases from real-world information. We present in this paper UNIMEM, a program that learns by observation. UNIMEM is intended to be a robust program that can be run on many domains with real-world characteristics such as noise and large numbers of examples. We give an overview of the program and show it operating on several different domains: universities, Congressional voting records, and terrorism stories. We illustrate several of UNIMEM's key elements, including automatically created, but non-exclusive, concept hierarchies and the evaluation of concepts over time.

1 Introduction

Learning by observing examples is important in machine learning domains where we cannot expect a teacher to provide carefully selected examples but still wish to analyze and organize large amounts of information intelligently. In this paper we discuss UNIMEM, a program designed to learn from observation by noticing similarities in examples and organizing the examples in terms of an automatically created generalization hierarchy. It is intended as a prototype intelligent information system that will incorporate large amounts of information into memory and allow users to query it. Our research involves the application of cognitive modelling techniques to potential application domains.

Specifically, the task of UNIMEM is to accept a series of examples from a domain that are expressed as collections of features and build up a generalization hierarchy giving us concept descriptions that can be used for a variety of Artificial Intelligence tasks. This process can be viewed as either *generalizing* the examples or *specializing* original concepts in the domain. (See [Fisher and Langley 85] for a classification of learning from examples techniques.) To take an example from one domain, UNIMEM might use information about a collection of universities to derive the concepts of Ivy League universities, European technical universities, and so forth.

The key characteristics of the UNIMEM task are: 1) it learns *by observation* -- it is not explicitly told what concepts to form nor given designated examples of any specific concept; 2) it is *incremental* -- at any point in time it must have made the best possible generalizations and cannot wait for all the examples; 3) it must potentially be able to handle *large numbers of examples*; 4) its generalizations are *pragmatic* -- they do not have to be correct for every case but simply for most, which is crucial in dealing with noisy data. While some learning systems have had various of these characteristics, little work has been concerned with all of them, and yet all are necessary for realistic intelligent information systems.

Much of the concept learning research that has been done in Artificial Intelligence has consisted of either supplying programs with examples of specified concepts and having the programs determine definitions of those concepts ([Winston 72; Mitchell 82; Dietterich and Michalski 83], among many others) or of using largely analytic techniques to classify input (e.g., [Michalski 80; Langley 81]). In "real-world" settings, the crucial concepts to be learned -- those that best help explain and organize information about a domain -- are not pre-supplied; rather, it is necessary to determine these concepts from a stream of very complex

[1]This research was supported in part by the United States Army Research Institute under contract MDA903-85-0103. Many graduate and undergraduate students at Columbia have been involved with UNIMEM. In particular, Ursula Wolz has contributed greatly to the development of the program.

input data. Our research concentrates not just on how to compare examples, but also on methods for determining what examples to compare, which largely determines the concepts to create.

UNIMEM has served as a testbed for studying a variety of issues in machine learning. The research issues that we have used UNIMEM to study include: categorizing input information so that generalization is possible; the evaluation of generalized concepts from further examples in order to recognize the crucial concepts; using concepts that slightly contradict new input items; the study of domain-dependent knowledge on concept formation; and dealing with concepts that change over time.

The name UNIMEM is derived from the phrase UNIversal MEMory model. While "universal" may overstate the case a bit, a key element of UNIMEM is that is can be easily applied to different domains. UNIMEM has been tried on: information about states of the United States, Congressional voting records, software evaluations, biological data, football plays, universities, terrorism stories, and others. This paper is designed to show the flexibility of UNIMEM. We will provide an overview of its operation and then show it in operation on several different domains, using these domains as a vehicle to illustrate its methods and some of the research issues we are studying with UNIMEM.

2 UNIMEM -- The basic model

UNIMEM is intended to take a series of examples in a domain and store them in a permanent long-term memory. As it does this, it notices examples that are similar and generalizes them, forming specialized versions of concepts that can be used in later understanding and question-answering tasks. The key idea of behind UNIMEM (as well as our other prototype intelligent information system, RESEARCHER, which reads, remembers and generalizes from patent abstracts [Lebowitz 83a; Lebowitz 86a]) is Generalization-Based Memory (GBM). The idea of GBM was developed first for IPP, a program that read and learned from news stories about terrorism [Lebowitz 80; Lebowitz 83b]. A system that uses GBM creates a hierarchy of concepts that describe a concept or situation. It begins to build up this hierarchy by generalizing from a small number of examples, and then records in memory specific items (both the examples from which the concepts are generalized and others) in terms of the generalized concepts. More specific generalizations are also recorded along with specific examples under the more general cases. GBM involves identifying and defining multiple concepts, as opposed to maintaining a single model of a concept.

Memory in UNIMEM is built up from a set of input examples, or *instances*. In UNIMEM these are descriptions of objects in a domain. An instance is described in UNIMEM in terms of a set of *features* (essentially property/value pairs). Similar instances are abstracted to form *generalizations* that form the basis of GBM. The manner in which generalizations are combined to form a concept hierarchy is illustrated in Figure 1.

```
concept -------------------------------------> instance A
    |
    > more specific concept ------------------> instances B, C
    |    |
    |    > still more specific concept --------> instances D, E
    |    |
    |    > still more specific concept --------> instances F, G, H
    |
    > more specific concept ------------------> instances H, I, J
```

Figure 1: An abstract generalization-based memory

To provide a less abstract example from the university domain (which we will look at further in Section 3.1), Figure 2 shows how memory might ideally be structured in that domain. We can see how the basic concept of a university is broken down into a number of more specialized versions. Notice that the more specialized versions of a given concept need not be mutually exclusive. In Figure 2, for example, the concepts of "universities with computer science" and "universities in Europe" are obviously not exclusive as a university could be both. As a result of this, an instance can be stored in several places in memory.

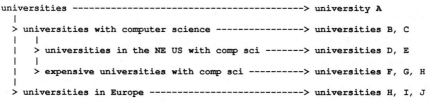

Figure 2: Hypothetical university GBM

Generalization-Based Memory, then, consists basically of one or more hierarchies of generalizations that describe concepts of increasing specificity. Instances and sub-generalizations are stored under each generalization using efficient indexing methods. The exact storage method turns out not to be crucial as there are rarely a large number of instances under a given generalization, since at least one more specific version is likely to be formed.

The use of a hierarchy of generalizations as a method of memory organization allows efficient storage of information, since information in a generalization does not have to be repeated for each instance that it describes, as it can be inherited. In addition, GBM allows relevant generalizations and instances -- and *only* relevant generalizations and instances -- to be found efficiently in memory during processing, allowing further generalizations. This property of GBM is largely independent of the specific knowledge representation being used.

The use of concept hierarchies with inheritance to intelligently and efficiently organize information about concepts is by no means a new one. Semantic networks [Quillian 78], frame systems [Minsky 75], MOPs [Schank 82], among many other formalisms all include this property. A primary feature of the representation language KRL [Bobrow and Winograd 77] is its ability to allow inheritance to be implemented easily. What is important here is the dynamic formation of the concept hierarchy, and its use to guide the development of further concepts. Only a limited amount of work has been done on automatically forming concept hierarchies, including [Michalski and Stepp 83; Sammut and Banerji 83], and this work has not dealt with pragmatic generalizations or particularly large numbers of examples, nor have preliminary commercial products that are beginning to appear.

The basic process of maintaining GBM, which is the learning process we are considering here, is relatively straightforward, once the memory organization method has been defined. As each new instance is processed, the most specific generalization that describes it is found. Since GBM can be thought of as a large discrimination net, UNIMEM starts with its most general node and does a best-first-type search to find the most specific generalization (or generalizations) that best describe the new instance. Then, before the instance is actually indexed under that generalization, a check is made for instances already stored there that have additional features in common with the new instance. For numeric data, various strategies have been used for determining what constitutes similar features [Lebowitz 85]. If there are enough features in common (one of many adjustable parameters of UNIMEM[2]), a new concept is generalized, and the contributing instances indexed there. The assumption is made that the similarities represent some sort of useful generalization about the domain. If no similar existing instances are found, the new instance is simply stored under the existing generalization (or generalizations).

Since concepts are generalized by UNIMEM on the basis of only a few instances, they must be evaluated to eliminate over-generalization (including the elimination of whole concepts). The concept learning process we have described inherently leads to over-generalization due to coincidence, particularly in domains where there is a large amount of information about each instance. Thus, we require that each concept learned be evaluated in light of future input. For each generalization made by UNIMEM, an

---

[2]Future research may look at how the parameters of UNIMEM could be adjusted automatically.

evaluation process continually looks for later instances for which the generalization might be relevant. This occurs as a normal part of the memory search process, since the generalizations to be evaluated are exactly those that might be used to store the new instances. UNIMEM checks whether a relevant generalization is confirmed or contradicted by each new instance.

Rather than simply eliminate bad generalizations when a generalization seems to be disconfirmed, UNIMEM tries to throw away just the "bad" (overly specific) parts and keep the "good" parts. The problem reduces to identifying the components of a generalization that are overly specific, so that they can be deleted, leaving intact a valid generalization. Furthermore, for this to be useful, it must be done at a minimum of cost, hopefully occurring as a natural part of the memory update process, and requiring only a small amount of extra record-keeping.

The solution devised for UNIMEM tracks how often each feature of a generalization is confirmed or contradicted. A confidence level is maintained for each feature of each concept. Confidence modification occurs as UNIMEM determines which generalizations best describe a new instance, as described above. If a confidence level passes a negative threshold (another adjustable parameter), then we can eliminate the feature from the generalization, since it has been wrong much more often than right. UNIMEM sometimes has to eliminate entire generalizations when too many of their features have been eliminated and the generalizations no longer provide useful information.

A final important feature of UNIMEM is the use of an idea known as *predictability*. While space does not permit a discussion of predictability here (see [Lebowitz 83b]), the basic idea is that only the presence of some features of a concept in an instance indicate the relevance of the concept, and that these features can be identified quite easily using GBM.

For the technically curious, UNIMEM runs on both a DECSystem/2060 in UCI LISP and on HP 9861 workstations running PSL. It is quite efficient, being able to incorporate new instances into memory in a matter of seconds. Details of the UNIMEM update process can be found in [Lebowitz 86b].

3 Example UNIMEM domains

3.1 Universities
Although not the first domain on which we used UNIMEM, the "university" domain is perhaps the simplest to illustrate the kinds of generalizations produced by the program. For this domain we collected facts about approximately 230 universities. Data was taken from standard references and from students in an Artificial Intelligence class. As with all of the domains we deal with, we attempted to collect as much information as possible and not pre-judge whether any particular piece of information was likely to be useful in generalization. The data was collected in terms of features for each university such as "percent financial aid = 60", "average math SAT score = 600" and so forth. Some of the features, such as quality of social life, were represented by arbitrary 1-5 scales. Note that while a simple feature representation is clearly inadequate for many tasks, it allows us to very easily get started on a new domain.

Figure 3 shows a typical piece of UNIMEM's memory after about 150 universities had been processed. It shows one "top level" generalization and several more specific versions of it. Each generalization is simply a collection of features, formed by noticing similarities among examples that are assumed to represent regularities in the world.

GND2, the top level generalization in Figure 3, began with 10 features describing a set of universities: average math SAT of 625, 60% of students getting financial aid, academic level 4 out 5, and so on. The generalization could be summarized as "high-quality private universities". At this point in the run, no instances were stored directly under GND2 as they had been used to create sub-generalizations. The numbers in square brackets are predictability information indicating how often that feature appears in other generalizations.

```
GND2
SAT                 MATH            625.0        [1]    (4.87)
%-FINANCIAL-AID     VALUE           60           [2]    (3.54)
ACADEMICS           SCALE:1-5       4            [3]    (15.0)
SOCIAL              SCALE:1-5       3            [3]    (16.4)
NO-APPLICANTS       VALUE           THOUS:4-     [4]    (9.0)
QUALITY-OF-LIFE     SCALE:1-5       3.5          [4]    (15.0)
LOCATION            VALUE           URBAN        [6]    (15.0)
CONTROL             VALUE           PRIVATE      [6]    (15.0)
%-ENROLLED          VALUE           20                  (xxx)
SAT                 VERBAL          625.0               (xxx)
[]

    GND18
    %-ADMITTANCE        VALUE           60               [1]    (-1.98)
    ACAD-EMPHASIS       VALUE           LIBERAL-ARTS     [1]    (-.3)
    MALE:FEMALE         VALUE           RATIO:1:1        [1]    (-.76)
    SAT                 MATH            592.5            [1]    (.09)
    EXPENSES            VALUE           THOUS$:10+       [2]    (4.5)
    QUALITY-OF-LIFE     SCALE:1-5       3.5              [2]    (3.0)
    [BARNARD BOSTON-UNIVERSITY]

    GND21
    SAT                 MATH            620.0            [1]    (1.2)
    EXPENSES            VALUE           THOUS$:7-10      [1]    (-2.7)
    %-ADMITTANCE        VALUE           35.0             [1]    (.9)
    SAT                 VERBAL          612.5            [1]    (3.37)
    QUALITY-OF-LIFE     SCALE:1-5       3.5              [2]    (3.0)
    [CARNEGIE-MELLON COLORADO-COLLEGE COLUMBIA UNIVERSITY-OF-CHICAGO]
```

Figure 3: A university domain example

The values in parentheses in the right hand column of Figure 3 are confidence levels for each feature.[3] As mentioned in Section 2, these values change over time to indicate UNIMEM's belief in that feature. The numbers begin at 0 and move up when confirmed, down when disconfirmed. Above a specified level (15 for this run) a value is "frozen" and the feature assumed to be correct, as happened for academic level and most other features of GND2. If a value reaches a sufficiently low level, the feature is removed, as was done for the last two initial features of GND2 (the ones with "xxx" for confidence levels). By removing these two features, UNIMEM came up with a generalization applicable to a wider range of instances, and yet that still provides useful information.

Under GND2 in Figure 3 are shown two more specific version of it, GND18, which describes expensive, liberal arts schools and GND21, which describes highly selective universities.[4] Notice that these classes are not exclusive, and a university could plausibly fall under both. We can also see that each of these generalizations has actual instances (universities) stored with it. When future instances are found to be described by these generalizations, they will be compared to the examples stored there. Also notice that UNIMEM is still very much in the process of evaluating these generalizations, as many of the confidence levels are quite low. In fact, it may at some point, given enough examples, conclude that GND18 does not really describe a general enough class of instances to be worth keeping, should most of its features be removed.

The generalizations in Figure 3 are not that unlike those that might be formed by statistical clustering techniques (e.g., [Anderberg 73]). The key differences are that UNIMEM's generalizations are done

---

[3]Needless to say, all the decimal places should not be taken seriously. They are the product of the numeric evaluation procedure used for this run.

[4]The fact that the universities in GND18 both start with "B" and those in GND21 with "C" is purely a coincidence. Had we coded up this information as features UNIMEM would have added it to the generalizations. However, unlike other techniques, UNIMEM's confidence evaluation methods would eventually have removed the anomalies from the generalizations.

incrementally (without waiting for all the instances to be available) and that the use of conceptual modelling techniques leads to generalizations that make more intuitive sense than those produced by most clustering techniques. (The work of [Michalski and Stepp 83] has much this same quality, although it uses very different methods than UNIMEM.)

3.2 Congressional voting records

A rather different domain used in UNIMEM was Congressional voting records. Instances were formed by taking information about how each U.S. Congressman voted on a number of major issues combined with information about the district and state represented. (A more complete description of the domain can be found in [Lebowitz 86c]). In the run used here, 100 such instances were added to memory. We were expecting to find generalizations that related the various votes to each other (e.g., "liberal" and "conservative" ideologies) and ones that related the votes to the states represented (e.g., someone representing a highly urban state would support bills that help cities).

Figure 4 shows a generalization that was made and two of its sub-generalizations. Confidence and predictability information is as it was in the university example. The top-level generalization, GND2, describes congressmen from agricultural states with high school expenditures (the third of three categories) who voted for an education bill, parks in Alaska, and so forth. This generalization directly describes the 24th Texas Congressional district. The correspondence between high state school expenditures and a positive vote on the school issue is the kind of generalization we were looking for. We will look at the sub-generalizations of GND2 a bit later.

One thing we immediately noticed in this domain was that the generalizations typically included a large number of features (presumably because there were only two ways to vote on each bill) but that new instances would rarely fit existing generalizations if required to match each feature of a generalization exactly. This problem was partially solved by the evaluation procedure which "trims" the generalizations. However, cognitive modelling ideas suggest another solution. People are perfectly willing to accept a few discrepancies in classifying new instances as examples of old generalizations. So, in this domain, we might accept a congressman as being "conservative but who voted against the MX missile". With this in mind, we modified UNIMEM to allow a generalization to be applied even if it is "a little bit off" (a parameter), though of course reducing confidence in the features that mismatched. This change in the program greatly improved its performance, allowing it to make best use of its generalizations, rather than creating a set of slightly different generalizations for each variation.

The Congressional voting domain also reveals an interesting aspect of the non-exclusive nature of UNIMEM's generalizations. To see it, however, we need to look at another top-level generalization. Figure 5 shows such a generalization along with one of its sub-generalizations.

The top-level node of Figure 5, GND3, would be characterized by someone familiar with U.S. politics as describing a conservative voting record. Similarly, GND2 from Figure 4 would be considered liberal. However, when we compare the two generalizations, we find that they do not, as might be expected, include opposite votes on the same bills. Instead, the generalizations each include votes on different bills and are theoretically not exclusive -- a Congressman could fit into both categories. Presumably this means that the best way to characterize the two groups is not in terms of the same bills. A conservative record can most confidently be identified based on the the votes shown in GND3, against cutting the MX missile, for example, while a liberal record shows up from a positive education vote and other votes in GND2.

The situation becomes particularly interesting when we look at the sub-generalizations of GND2 (GND4 and GND7) and GND3 (GND8). When we examine these generalizations carefully, we see that the features (votes) that we had expected to contrast the top-level generalizations appear in the sub-generalizations. So, for example, the "liberal" generalization, GND2, contains a vote against a cut in social funds. The converse of this vote does not appear in GND3, but it is in GND3's sub-generalization, GND8. Similarly, the opposite of the conservative vote against the MX missile is not included in GND2,

```
GND2
INDUSTRY      TYPE          AGRICULTURE   [1]   (15)
STATE         SCHOOL-EXP    SCH3:3        [2]   (15)
EDUCATION     VOTE          F             [2]    (5)
ALASKA-PARKS  VOTE          F             [3]   (15)
SOC-FUND-CUT  VOTE          A             [4]   (15)
INDUSTRY      TYPE          MANUFACTURING [7]   (15)
STATE         INCOME        INC3:4        [7]   (15)
STATE         MINORITY-PCT  MIN1:2        [9]   (15)
[TEXAS24]


   GND4
   WIND-TAX-LIM    VOTE              A         [1]   (15)
   GAS-CONT-BAN    VOTE              F         [1]    (6)
   HOSP-COST-CONT  VOTE              F         [2]   (15)
   NICARAGUA-BAN   VOTE              A         [2]   (15)
   CANDIDATE       PARTY             D         [3]   (15)
   STATE           FARM-VAL-PER-ACRE FAR5:6    [3]    (8)
   OSHA-CUT        VOTE              A         [4]   (15)
   FOOD-STAMP-CAP  VOTE              A         [4]   (15)
   PAC-LIMIT       VOTE              F         [4]   (15)
   STATE           URBAN-PCT         URB6:6    [4]   (15)
   FAIR-HOUSING    VOTE              F         [5]    (1)
   []
   {CALIFORNIA6 CALIFORNIA7 CALIFORNIA8 FLORIDA15 ILLINOIS8 MASSACHUSETTS7
   MASSACHUSETTS9 MICHIGAN1 MICHIGAN17 MISSOURI1 NEWJERSEY8 WISCONSIN4}


   GND7
   NICARAGUA-BAN   VOTE              A         [2]   (12)
   STATE           DEBT              DEB5:7    [2]    (1)
   INDUSTRY        TYPE              TOURISM   [2]    (3)
   MX-CUT          VOTE              F         [3]    (9)
   DISTRICT        POP-DIR           UP        [3]    (3)
   STATE           FARM-VAL-PER-ACRE FAR5:6    [3]    (7)
   FAIR-HOUSING    VOTE              F         [5]    (1)
   []
   {FLORIDA13 FLORIDA15 MICHIGAN10 MINNESOTA1 MISSOURI1 WISCONSIN1 WISCONSIN6}
```

Figure 4: A voting record example

but is in one of the sub-generalizations, GND7. Many other examples of this phenomenon appear in Figures 4 and 5. It appears that some votes that are not good in distinguishing concepts at the top level are nonetheless useful in refining these concepts.

We view this example as strongly supporting the methodology of UNIMEM. It shows the need for flexibility in building up a concept hierarchy. Rather than simply forcing exclusive generalizations by picking a property and using its values as a discriminant, by allowing non-exclusive generalizations we can capture a wider range of hierarchical information, using the most useful properties to distinguish and subdivide concepts.

The Congressional voting domain provides the opportunity to mention one other aspect of learning. One important way in which UNIMEM's methods differ from what people do is that people always try to *explain* the generalizations that they make. These explanations are useful in a variety of tasks. The use of explanations allows us to learn from a small number of examples, perhaps even just one. This kind of *explanation-based learning* has been explored by [Mitchell 83; DeJong 83; Silver 83] among others. (See [Michalski et al. 86] for other examples.) We believe, however, that such explanation methods must be integrated with similarity-based methods of the sort described here. This is especially true in new domains where even deciding what to explain may be difficult. In this paper we shall only mention the importance of using both methods and refer the reader to [Lebowitz 86c] which describes how we have begun to integrate explanation-based methods into UNIMEM.

```
GND3
HOSP-COST-CONT   VOTE            A                [2]   (15)
WIND-TAX-LIM     VOTE            F                [3]   (15)
DRAFT            VOTE            F                [3]   (15)
NUC-POWER        VOTE            A                [4]   (15)
MX-CUT           VOTE            A                [4]   (15)
STATE            TAXES-PERCAP    TAX2:5           [4]   (15)
DISTRICT         POP-DIR         UP               [5]   (15)
STATE            INCOME          INC3:4           [7]   (15)
INDUSTRY         TYPE            MANUFACTURING    [7]   (15)
STATE            MINORITY-PCT    MIN1:2           [9]   (15)
[]


GND8
STATE            POPULATION      POP6:7           [1]   (3)
EDUCATIQN        VOTE            A                [2]   (5)
CANDIDATE        PARTY           R                [2]   (1)
NICARAGUA-BAN    VOTE            F                [2]   (6)
GAS-CONT-BAN     VOTE            A                [3]   (15)
SOC-FUND-CUT     VOTE            F                [3]   (11)
OSHA-CUT         VOTE            F                [3]   (15)
STATE            URBAN-PCT       URB6:6           [3]   (9)
PAC-LIMIT        VOTE            A                [4]   (15)
[]
{CALIFORNIA34 FLORIDA10 FLORIDA6 ILLINOIS13 ILLINOIS14 MARYLAND4 MICHIGAN9
OHIO17 OHIO8 PENNSYLVANIA15 TEXAS7}
```

Figure 5: Another voting example

3.3 IPP revisited

As alluded to earlier, UNIMEM was developed from the memory and generalization module of IPP, a program that read news stories about international terrorism, added them to a long-term memory, generalizing as it did so [Lebowitz 80; Lebowitz 83b]. Since UNIMEM is now substantially different than its IPP ancestor, and yet still takes input in the same form, we thought it would be interesting to hook the programs together and see if the quality of the resulting generalizations is superior to those of the original IPP.

UNIMEM is different in a number of technical ways from the IPP memory module. Parameters have been added to make it more flexible, different methods of low-level indexing are available, and so forth. The most substantial change, however, is the modification of confidence methods to consider each feature in a generalization separately. IPP only maintained a single confidence level for each generalization. A result of this was that a single anomalous feature could cause an entire generalization to be thrown out. We wanted to see if this would make a dramatic change in the kinds of generalizations made when UNIMEM was connected to IPP.

In order to carry out this experiment we arranged the two systems so that the output of the IPP text understanding module, after being translated into a set of features (as was done for IPP itself) was fed directly into UNIMEM. The experiment was run using about 370 of the stories that IPP "understood" best, all taken from the period of 1979-1980.

The results of the IPP/UNIMEM experiment were quite informative. Overall, the generalizations made seemed intuitively to be "better" or at least more accurate. UNIMEM build up a more complete hierarchy than had IPP. On the other hand, the UNIMEM generalizations seemed rather more "bland" than those of IPP, omitting some of the most interesting generalization that the original system had made. We will illustrate why these results occurred, and why in the long run they are all positive, using the example in Figure 6, which shows a small portion of the UNIMEM memory built up from the extortion stories in the sample set.[5] The features in Figure 6 with "xxx" in their confidence fields have been deleted and should

---

[5]Terrorism stories in IPP are understood as being instances of either extortion, attacks on people, or attacks on facilities.

not be considered part of the generalizations (but were part of the initial ones).

```
S-EXTORT

GND257
RESULTS         AU              HURT-PERSON [1]    (-2.0)
RESULTS         HEALTH          -10         [1]    (0)
METHODS         AU              $TAKE-OVER  [2]    (10.75)
I-MOP           I-MOP           I-TERRORISM [3]    (10.0)
LOCATION        NATION          *ISRAEL*           (xxx)
LOCATION        AREA            THE-MIDEAST        (xxx)
[EV9 EV996 EV1159 EV1162 EV1174 EV1277 EV1319]

    GND262
    SCENES      AU              SS-RELEASE-HOSTAGES [1]   (4.25)
    LOCATION    AREA            LATIN-AMERICA       [1]   (.5)
    HOSTAGES    NUMBER          HUNDREDS                  (xxx)
    LOCATION    NATION          *EL-SALVADOR*             (xxx)
    [EV1028 EV1102]

        GND343
        ACTOR       GROUPNAME       *LEFTIST*     [1]   (0)
        ACTOR       POLITICS        *LEFT-WING*   [1]   (0)
        LOCATION    NATION          *EL-SALVADOR* [1]   (0)
        [EV1025 EV1343]
```

Figure 6: An IPP extortion example

The top-level generalization in this small piece of memory, GND257, describes terrorist takeovers where some of the hostages are killed (HEALTH -10). As can be seen, this generalization was originally formed from stories that took place in Israel. While this made the generalization a bit more interesting than the final version, it was also less widely useful, applying only to Israel. Since other stories were found with the same characteristics, but not occurring in Israel, UNIMEM removed the location from the generalization. This allowed it to apply to a wider range of examples. Specifically, it could then be applied to examples in Latin America that were used to form a simple concept of takeovers in Latin America where hostages were released and a further sub-concept of leftist takeovers in El Salvador. Remember that all the information in higher level concepts is inherited.

It is clear from this example why the UNIMEM generalizations were more "bland" than those of IPP. If a complicated generalization, like "terrorist victims in a given area are always adult policemen", was formed by noticing two coincidental stories, UNIMEM will tend to refine it, and make it less interesting, by removing the coincidental elements so that it covers a wider range of stories. While this is mildly disappointing in the short run, overall it is quite positive. UNIMEM produces the basic generalizations (like terrorist bombings usually hurt people) that we need in an Artificial Intelligence system. Further, the "flashy" generalizations will not be lost, as eventually they will be formed as sub-generalizations. We did not see too much of this in this experiment, as there were not enough examples and, more importantly, the examples did not have a large enough number of features.[6] The next step in the integration of IPP and UNIMEM would be to increase the level of detail in the features produced from IPP representations, which would be easy to do.

Another interesting point about the IPP/UNIMEM integration is the way that multiple concepts are handled. Besides storing an event in several places in the same concept hierarchy, it is possible to store the same event as an example of different concepts. So, a story might be viewed as both an instance of an attack on a person and an instance of how grenades are used. We can get different generalizations from these two perspectives. The integrated IPP/UNIMEM was set up to store each story in terms of both the events and any known objects or groups such as "bomb", "Red Brigades" and so forth. Figure 7

---

[6]Large numbers of features were actually a hindrance to IPP as it had no way to refine over-generalized concepts.

shows two generalizations made from the "object" perspective -- "grenade" being the object. Features are constructed that indicate other roles in events where the object was involved. So, for example, the first feature of GND263 indicates it is about cases where the grenade was part of a "destructive attack" carried out with the method being a "shoot attack".

```
*GRENADE*

GND263
METHODS:S-DESTRUCTIVE-ATTACK  AU                                $SHOOT-ATTACK  [1] (1.0)
VICTIM:S-DESTRUCTIVE-ATTACK   NUMBER                            FEW            [1] (2.75)
RESULTS:S-DESTRUCTIVE-ATTACK  HEALTH                            -5             [1] (.75)
ACTION                        S-DESTRUCTIVE-ATTACK              WEAPON         [2] (10.0)
RESULTS:S-DESTRUCTIVE-ATTACK  HEALTH                            -10            [2] (5.25)
RESULTS:S-DESTRUCTIVE-ATTACK  AU                                HURT-PERSON    [2] (6.5)
LOCATION:S-DESTRUCTIVE-ATTACK AREA                              ASIA           [2] (5.5)
LOCATION:S-DESTRUCTIVE-ATTACK NATION                            *PHILIPPINES*  [2] (5.5)
[PT93 PT146 PT180]

GND276
METHODS:S-DESTRUCTIVE-ATTACK  AU                                $EXPLODE-BOMB  [1] (2.75)
RESULTS:S-DESTRUCTIVE-ATTACK  AU                                HURT-PERSON    [2] (3.75)
LOCATION:S-DESTRUCTIVE-ATTACK AREA                              ASIA           [2] (2.75)
LOCATION:S-DESTRUCTIVE-ATTACK NATION                            *PHILIPPINES*  [2] (2.75)
ACTION                        S-DESTRUCTIVE-ATTACK              WEAPON         [2] (5.0)
RESULTS:S-DESTRUCTIVE-ATTACK  HEALTH                            -10            [2] (3.75)
[PT147 PT156 PT166 PT182]
```

Figure 7: An IPP "object" example

The two generalizations in Figure 7 both describe attacks in the Philippines. GND263 describes attacks that are basically shootings where people are both killed and wounded. GND276 is similar, but the attacks are basically bombings and people were only killed. While these generalizations might have also been made from the event perspective, they might not have if the component events were initially classified differently. Again, the flexible nature of UNIMEM allows it to find useful generalizations.

4 Conclusion

Learning by observation is an important area of machine learning. It allows a system to automatically build up knowledge bases from real-world information. In this paper we have given an overview of UNIMEM, a program that learns by observation. By showing UNIMEM working on several disparate domains we hope to have demonstrated its generality. We have shown several of its key elements, including automatically created, but non-exclusive, generalized concepts and the evaluation of such concepts over time.

While each new domain brings its own problems, the basic methods of UNIMEM have proven quite robust. We feel the system is a promising first step towards the intelligent learning systems that are a crucial next step in Artificial Intelligence.

References

[Anderberg 73] Anderberg, M. R. *Cluster Analysis for Applications.* Academic Press, New York, 1973.

[Bobrow and Winograd 77] Bobrow, D. G. and Winograd, T. "An overview of KRL, a knowledge representation language." *Cognitive Science 1*, 1, 1977, pp. 3 - 46.

[DeJong 83] DeJong, G. F. An approach to learning from observation. Proceedings of the 1983 International Machine Learning Workshop, Champaign-Urbana, Illinois, 1983, pp. 171 - 176.

[Dietterich and Michalski 83] Dietterich, T. G. and Michalski, R. S. Discovering patterns in sequences of objects. Proceedings of the 1983 International Machine Learning Workshop, Champaign-Urbana, Illinois, 1983, pp. 41 - 57. .

[Fisher and Langley 85] Fisher, D. and Langley, P. Approaches to conceptual clustering. Proceedings of the Ninth International Joint Conference on Artificial Intelligence, Los Angeles, 1985, pp. 691 - 697.

[Langley 81] Langley, P. "Data-driven discovery of natural laws." *Cognitive Science 5*, 1, 1981, pp. 31 - 54.

[Lebowitz 80] Lebowitz, M. Generalization and memory in an integrated understanding system. Technical Report 186, Yale University Department of Computer Science, New Haven, CT, 1980. PhD Thesis.

[Lebowitz 83a] Lebowitz, M. RESEARCHER: An overview. Proceedings of the Third National Conference on Artificial Intelligence, Washington, DC, 1983, pp. 232 - 235.

[Lebowitz 83b] Lebowitz, M. "Generalization from natural language text." *Cognitive Science 7*, 1, 1983, pp. 1 - 40.

[Lebowitz 85] Lebowitz, M. "Classifying numeric information for generalization." *Cognitive Science 9*, 3, 1985, pp. 285 - 308.

[Lebowitz 86a] Lebowitz, M. An experiment in intelligent information systems: RESEARCHER. In R. Davies, Ed., *Intelligent Library and Information Systems*, Ellis Horwood, London, 1986.

[Lebowitz 86b] Lebowitz, M. Concept learning in a rich input domain: Generalization-Based Memory. In R. S. Michalski, J. G. Carbonell and T. M. Mitchell, Ed., *Machine Learning: An Artificial Intelligence Approach, Volume II*, Morgan Kaufmann, Los Altos, CA, 1986, pp. 193 - 214.

[Lebowitz 86c] Lebowitz, M. "Integrated learning: Controlling explanation." *Cognitive Science 10*, 1986.

[Michalski 80] Michalski, R. S. "Pattern recognition as rule-guided inductive inference." *IEEE Transactions on Pattern Analysis and Machine Intelligence 2*, 4, 1980, pp. 349 - 361.

[Michalski and Stepp 83] Michalski, R. S. and Stepp, R. E. "Automated construction of classifications: Conceptual clustering versus numerical taxonomy." *IEEE Transactions on Pattern Analysis and Machine Intelligence 5*, 4, 1983, pp. 396 - 409.

[Michalski et al. 86] Michalski, R. S., Carbonell, J. G. and Mitchell, T. M. (Eds.). *Machine Learning, An Artificial Intelligence Approach, Volume II*. Morgan Kaufmann, Los Altos, CA, 1986.

[Minsky 75] Minsky, M. A framework for representing knowledge. In P. H. Winston, Ed., *The Psychology of Computer Vision*, McGraw-Hill, New York, 1975.

[Mitchell 82] Mitchell, T. M. "Generalization as search." *Artificial Intelligence 18*, 1982, pp. 203 - 226.

[Mitchell 83] Mitchell, T. M. Learning and problem solving. Proceedings of the Eighth International Joint Conference on Artificial Intelligence, Karlsruhe, West Germany, 1983, pp. 1139 - 1151.

[Quillian 78] Quillian, M. R. Semantic memory. In M. Minsky, Ed., *Semantic Information Processing*, MIT Press, Cambridge, MA, 1978.

[Sammut and Banerji 83] Sammut, C. and Banerji, R. Hierarchical memories: An aid to concept learning. Proceedings of the 1983 International Machine Learning Workshop, Champaign-Urbana, Illinois, 1983, pp. 74 - 80.

[Schank 82] Schank, R. C. *Dynamic Memory: A Theory of Reminding and Learning in Computers and People*. Cambridge University Press, New York, 1982.

[Silver 83] Silver B. Learning equation solving methods from worked examples. Proceedings of the 1983 International Machine Learning Workshop, Champaign-Urbana, Illinois, 1983, pp. 99 - 104.

[Winston 72] Winston, P. H. Learning structural descriptions from examples. In P. H. Winston, Ed., *The Psychology of Computer Vision*, McGraw-Hill, New York, 1972, pp. 157 - 209.

Advances in Artificial Intelligence - II
B. Du Boulay, D. Hogg and L. Steels (Editors)
© Elsevier Science Publishers B.V. (North-Holland), 1987

EXPLAINABLE KNOWLEDGE PRODUCTION

Walter Van de Velde

Laboratory for Artificial Intelligence
Vrije Universiteit Brussel
Pleinlaan 2, B-1050 Brussels
!mcvax!prlb2!vubarti!walter

ABSTRACT

Recent progress in machine learning seems to provide a promising approach to knowledge engineering for expert systems. Inductive methods have been succesfully used to derive problem solving rules from examples of problems and solutions. However the application of these techniques on less carefully chosen domains may face insurmountable problems. These problems have to do with the applicability of these techniques and the quality of the rules they produce. It is shown how an alternative approach, *learning through progressive refinement*, circumvents these problems. This technique favors an integrated learning system, i.e. a system operating in a real environment which combines a problem solving component and a learning component. In such a *second generation expert system*, the learning component analyses the system's failure to solve some problem and refines the problem solving knowledge to cope with it. This results in a system which gradually solves more problems in a more efficient way. Moreover, for a lot of domains the knowledge it uses (*deep* knowledge) is easier to get at then the expert knowledge itself (*shallow* knowledge).

KEYWORDS: Machine Learning, Incremental Knowledge, Knowledge Acquisition

> What we want is a machine that can learn from experience.
> *Alan Turing, 1947*

1. INTRODUCTION

The possibility of learning machines has received a great deal of attention within the Artificial Intelligence community. Though the high expectations of the early days have been tempered by considerable technical difficulties, recent research justifies some optimism. At several research laboratories programs have been built which are capable of

This research is supported by IWONL contract No. 4465.

generating rules which simulate expert decision making.

For example Michalski (1980) produced a very successful system for identifying soya bean diseases in this way. Ivan Bratko (1985, 1986) reports on systems for medical diagnosis in fields such as heart diseases, breast cancer and primary tumors, the rules of which are also machine generated. Though the size of these applications is relatively small they tackle real problems and some of them are used as a practical tool. Surprisingly, those systems almost invariably show better reliability than the human expert.

Most of these experiments center around the *learning by example* paradigm (see e.g. [Hunt et al., 1966], [Mitchell 1978], [Quinlan 1983]). In this paradigm, also called the inductive approach, the user specifies examples by attribute–value pairs and for each example a class it belongs to. The classes are exclusive and their number is fixed. The output of the learning program is a set of rules which classify some new instance in the class it belongs to.

For example, if the application is diagnosis then an example is a description of a case and the corresponding diagnosis. The learned rules would then assign a diagnosis to each case presented to them. So, an inductive program has to generate, for each possible diagnosis, a rule which associates a pattern of attribute values with that diagnosis.

Rule induction may help to alleviate the painful proces of knowledge acquisition. The classical approach to circumvent this 'Feigenbaum Bottleneck' is to create tools and effective methods to extract heuristic knowledge from the expert. Inductive methods take a rather different stand. There, experts are asked to provide examples of problems and solutions from their domain of competence. No justification for the examples is required. With mechanical aids rules are then induced which show sufficient competence to do those and similar examples.

Knowledge engineering is fairly easy in the inductive approach. The main task is to find the right descriptive attributes for the examples and the appropriate classes. This is nothing compared to the effort required for hand-crafting knowledge bases where one constantly has to worry about incomplete rule-sets, contradictions and exceptions. Since induction has the capability of generating complete and consistent rule sets the systems based on them are systematically more reliable than the experts themselves.

The most optimistic optimists see a new industry arising from these results in machine learning research. According to them the necessary techniques and experience are available to establish an industry with low running costs and great social impact. They envisage *knowledge factories* [Michie 1985] which transform raw data into reliable rule sets. Through those, knowledge from diverse fields can be incorporated into expert systems to yield tools possibly orders of magnitudes more powerful than the human equivalent.

Critiques to this perspective on the future do not deny the possible impact of such technology. They rather object to the term 'knowledge' for the product of this new industry. This is more than just a terminological objection: if, as they claim, knowledge is to be intelligible by humans then their objections may be justified. But there are other problems with induction. They have to do with the applicability of the techniques, the quality of the rules they produce and the requirement to cope with incremental knowledge.

The structure of the rest of the paper is as follows. First we review some of the problems with inductively generated rules as knowledge sources for expert systems. Section 3 discusses an alternative way of rule learning: learning through progressive refinement. The last section shows how this alternative approach remedies some of the problems mentioned before. Also, related research on these problems is described along with suggestions for further work.

2. PROBLEMS WITH INDUCTIVE LEARNING

Techniques to induce general rules from examples have been successfully used to generate knowledge bases for expert systems. Fundamental problems underlying this kind of learning may show up if these techniques are exercised in less carefully chosen situations.

2.1. Intelligible Heuristics

Inductively generated rules constitute an adequate operational model of the expert's knowledge. They are capable of producing the same solutions as the human expert. However, the rules contain no reference to the underlying line of reasoning which justifies them; they are not even derived from it. More specifically, although all conditions play the same logical role, an expert may give different reasons for their presence. The rule structure gives no indication of these differences in status.

As an example consider the two rules in figure 1. Both have to do with diagnosing a start problem with a car. Though they are logically equivalent, the second one has a much richer interpretation because it makes explicit the role of the conditions. It states that if you are trying to get the engine started, explaining why it does not, you have checked that the lights can burn and the problem is not that the car is not in parking mode, then the problem is in the contact-points.

```
Rule R-243                    Rule for start-problem
If Getting-Started            A solution-rule
   and Not Engine=Starts        Preconditions: Getting-Started
   and Lights=Can-Burn          Primary-Symptoms: Not Engine=Starts
   and Not Mode=Parking         Secondary-Symptoms: Lights=Can-Burn
Then fix Contact-Points         Excluded-Solutions: Not Mode=Parking
                                Corrected-Properties: Contact-Points=OK
```

Figure 1: Twice the same rule.

Though the importance of a richer rule structure has been convincingly argued for by several researchers (e.g. [Clancey 1983], [Pople 1982], [Swartout 1983], [Breuker and Wielinga 1985]) no induction method pays attention to it. Of course this does not mean that inductively generated rules are not valid. But the success of the learning by example paradigm depends heavily on the proper choice of attributes to describe examples. The attributes must have causal relevance for the classes and it is this relevance which justifies the resulting rules. However this justification is completely in the head of the designer who initially chose the attributes and the classes. Therefore the rules can be said to be expert intelligible because the expert has the appropriate background knowledge to read the justifications from the rules.

For a non-expert user the system cannot generate a convincing explanation for its answers. It behaves as a black box which is inconvenient, if not dangerous, for applications like air traffic control, military early warning, or nuclear power plant monitoring. Such systems should have intelligible knowledge to allow humans to understand their behaviour and to judge the knowledge using their human common sense.

Even a superficial examination of the techniques which are used to learn from examples shows the difficulty. Learning is similarity based: new instances are classified according to their resemblance to the examples of a certain class. This seems to work – and therefore has its value – but in an ad hoc way. The similarity criterium is a purely syntactic one. It is not based on an understanding of the similarity.

W. Van De Velde

2.2. Natural Heuristics

A good rule base should have intelligible heuristics. Apart from that, it should exhibit a natural and efficient problem solving behaviour. On each problem it should ask questions which are relevant, few and easy to answer by the user. All this is aimed at a reasoning style which is scrutable to the human user, i.e. easy to follow and progressing naturally to a solution. This may be realised using different kinds of rules (see [Pople 82] for motivation).

First of all there should be *solution rules*. Such rules associate a data–pattern (the if–part) immediately with a solution (the then–part). For example, if the application is diagnosis the if–part is a list of symptoms which have to be present for the diagnosis, contained in the then–part, to be valid. The role of the different conditions should be explicitly represented in order to exhibit a natural protocol. The second rule in figure 1 is an example of a good solution rule.

Systems which merely use solution–rules exhibit a *hypothesize and test* behaviour: a list of possible solutions is traversed until a valid one is found. The if–parts of the rules have to be detailed enough to recognise the situations in which the respective solutions are correct. So, if there are many solutions to consider then each if–part may involve a lot of testing.

If *focus rules* are used then the problem solver evolves in a *divide and conquer* style. Focus rules do not yield answers immediately but restrict the set of possible solutions. The rules which have to be invoked to discriminate between remaining solutions can then take aspects of the data for granted and will therefore have more simple if–parts. Figure 2 shows a focus rule zooming in on the start motor in search for a solution of a start problem.

```
Rule for start-problem
A focus rule
   Preconditions: Getting-Started
   Primary-Symptoms: Not Engine=Starts
   Secondary-Symptoms: Starter=Powered
                       Not Starter=Turning
   New Focus: Starter
   New Primary Symptom: Not Starter=Turning
```

Figure 2: A focus rule.

The use of focus–rules allows a structured knowledge base. Rules are grouped in *focusses* (e.g. start–problem, starter). One focus contains the rules relevant for a certain problem–kind, physical part, function. Focus–rules lead from focus to focus until some solution–rule yields an answer. Again, the rule set becomes more amenable to inspection.

One of the problems with the learning from examples paradigm is that it generates only solution rules.[1] If the problem domain is so rich that the set of possible solutions to relevant problems is very large the rules will become complex and their problem solving behaviour unnatural. This problem may be partly remedied by exploiting structural similarity, i.e. grouping common conditions like in the RETE–algorithm of OPS5

---

[1].The inductive package RuleMaster [Michie 1984] provides a limited facility for user guided structuring of the knowledge base.

[Brownston 1985]. This, again, is somewhat ad hoc: the focusses created in this way cannot be guaranteed to correspond to any meaningful concept.

2.3. Relevant Heuristics

The target of any rule learning system should be an efficient set of heuristics to solve a certain class of problems. Such heuristics should of course solve the problems they are supposed to solve. This sounds as a trivial statement but it is not. Especially in rich domains there are far more possible problems than truly relevant ones.

The diagnosis of faults in technical devices like cars is an example. Here there are thousands of things which can go wrong, each causing some characteristic pattern of observations. However, most of these cases will never occur in practice. Though in principal almost anything can go wrong with a car they are usually the same things.

An efficient set of heuristics should not be too clever. Capturing the knowledge relevant for solving all problems in the domain will result in a system which is slow, difficult to follow and asking a lot of questions with trivial answers. A smaller and simpler knowledge base might be equally adequate.

So, it may be difficult to find the good examples if an inductive approach to knowledge engineering is followed. In particular there is a danger that the expert comes up with all the examples he can think of while only few of those will be relevant in practice. Even when he is aware of this he will try to be as complete as possible, if only to save his own credibility.

As a side-effect of having many examples there will be many attributes to describe them. At this point the induction techniques themselves may get into trouble. The required computation increases quickly with the number of attributes and the mere application of the techniques may become infeasible.

2.4. Incremental Knowledge

In order to produce a natural and efficient set of heuristics, its power should be deliberately limited. Thus the heuristics may fail on some problems. Should this happen precautions have to be taken to prevent it in the future. Since those weak spots of the heuristics can only be discovered by experience, systems operating intelligently in a real environment have to cope with unexpected situations.

When the knowledge of a system is inadequate to solve a problem one may follow a *revolutionary* or an *evolutionary* approach [Michalski 1985]. The first option is to throw everything away and develop new knowledge from scratch. In the evolutionary approach the appropriate parts of the existing knowledge are refined to accommodate the previously unanticipated cases. This gives more credit to the incremental nature of heuristic knowledge: they evolve by using them. On the other hand the approach is more difficult to implement because it requires an intricate understanding of the knowledge structures.

Many techniques for learning from examples have difficulty with incremental knowledge. They assume that all examples are present at the time the rules are generated. If later a new example has to be incorporated all the old ones have to be considered again. Thus full memory of examples and a lot of processing on every new experience is required. This contrasts sharply with the ease with which humans adapt their problem solving knowledge to new situations.

2.5. Conclusion

Inductive methods may serve as an alternative solution to the problem of knowledge engineering. Unfortunately they create some new problems and produce unsatisfactory results. The success of the early experiments cannot be denied but may be attributed to the nature of the application. There are few attributes and the problems to be solved (i.e. different classes for classification) are known. However, if one of these conditions is not met induction may face insurmountable problems.

3. LEARNING THROUGH PROGRESSIVE REFINEMENT

Another approach to learning heuristics, and to knowledge engineering in particular, is to reconstruct the process of acquiring expertise. Thus, talking about heuristics as a form of expertise, we want simple processes which incrementally build interesting heuristics from individual experiences. *Learning through progressive refinement* is one way to do this. This method has been introduced in [Steels and Van de Velde 1985]. It is briefly discussed in this section. Section 4 highlights some of its most notable features.

3.1. Deep and shallow knowledge

Human problem solvers learn from experience. We might view an expert as walking through a space of problems to be solved. Each problem is attempted as if not significantly different from those previously seen. The expert tries his *shallow knowledge*, i.e. accumulated know-how in terms of rules which worked for similar problems. Should this fail resort is taken to *deep knowledge*, i.e. the detailed understanding of the structure and underlying principles of the domain. Having solved the problem this way, the expert has traced the causes of his initial failure to solve the problem. At this point the obvious profit is taken: experiencial knowledge is refined to prevent the same failure in the future. (see [Kahn 1984] for discussion on deep and shallow knowledge).

Such a scenario cannot be realised within classical expert systems, which are based purely on shallow knowledge. Though this simple approach allows a uniform representation (i.e. rules) and simple inference (i.e. some form of rule-chaining) it carries a load of problems with it. Among those are the unclear semantics of the rules, the lack of underlying knowledge and common sense, unsatisfactory explanation capabilities, strict applicability region and unpredictable behavior near its boundaries, no learning capabilities.

The introduction of deep knowledge in expert systems solves a number of these problems, at least in principle (see [Steels 1985]). Recent experiments with such *second generation expert systems* (e.g. [Steels and Van de Velde 1985], [Fink 1985]) show the feasibility of this approach. In particular the goal of learning in such a system is to start from a deep model of a problem-domain, and gradually ´compile´ it into an efficient set of heuristics.

It should be stressed that the translation from deep to shallow knowledge is only worthwhile if there are far less relevant problems than possible ones. Otherwise, the shallow level would become as powerful but also as complex as the deep level and little will be gained. Reasoning about technical systems is a typical application. The techniques may be used for vehicles, electronic devices, computer programs or power plants, and for tasks as diverse as discovering design failures, diagnosing faulty components, monitoring, etc.

3.2. Example application

Throughout the rest of this section we continue to use as a source of examples the problem of diagnosing start problems with a car. An experimental second generation expert system has been built for this application. It uses deep reasoning on a *causal model* such as shown in figure 3. A causal model represents enablement relations between properties of a device.

An effective method for diagnostic reasoning on a causal model is discussed in [Van de Velde 1985]. It performs the task of a *causal expert*: given a device described by properties of its components linked in a causal model, given an anomalous property whose value differs from the one expected, find an explanation either in terms of malfunctioning components or in terms of external controls to be changed. The details of the algorithm are irrelevant here, but a glance at the causal model may help to understand the intuitions behind the learning techniques.

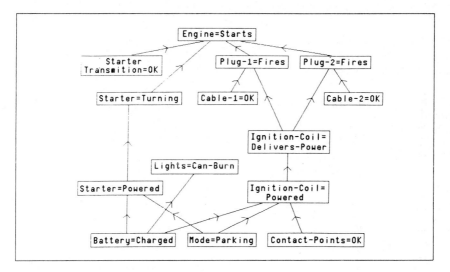

Figure 3: A causal model.

3.3. Abstraction and Integration.

The basic techniques for rule learning are the initial abstraction of a rule from a deep reasoning result, and its integration into the set of previously learned rules (see figure 4).

3.3.1. Rule Abstraction

A deep reasoning process potentially investigates a lot of causal paths and asks for a lot of observations. To be worthwhile heuristic rules must do the opposite: they should be as simple as possible, leaving out details and observations which did not directly contribute to the solution of the problem. Therefore, heuristic rules are learned under the following *circumscriptive assumption*: everything which is not mentioned in a rule is supposed to be normal or irrelevant to the anomaly to be explained. [2]

From a deep reasoning sequence, a heuristic rule is learned which associates the anomaly to be explained (its *primary-symptom*) with the causes which reasoning deemed ultimately responsible (its *corrected-properties*). This rule may be tried whenever its primary-symptom is to be explained (and only then!).

Consider the situation where a car does not start and deep reasoning determines that this was due to it not being in parking mode. The rule in figure 4(a) will be abstracted herefrom. Though some properties (e.g. Battery=Powered) certainly are relevant for starting and probably were used during deep reasoning they are not mentioned. Such a property is treated as being irrelevant (like Lights=Can-Burn) until experience reveals

---

[2] The exact relation to circumscription as discussed in the literature of non-monotonic reasoning (e.g. [McCarthy 1983]) will be discussed elsewhere.

```
Abstracted rules:

Rule for start problem              Rule for start problem
A solution-rule                     A solution rule
  Primary-Symptoms:                   Primary-Symptoms:
    Not Engine=Starts                   Not Engine=Starts
  Corrected-Properties:               Corrected-Properties:
    Mode=Parking                        Battery=Powered

        (a)                                 (b)

After integration:

Rule for start problem              Rule for start problem
A solution rule                     A solution rule
  Primary-Symptoms:                   Primary-Symptoms:
    Not Engine=Starts                   Not Engine=Starts
  Secondary-Symptoms:                 Excluded-Solutions:
    Not Mode=Parking                    Mode=Parking
  Corrected-Properties:               Corrected-Properties:
    Mode=Parking                        Battery=Powered

                        (c)
```

Figure 4: Rule abstraction and integration.

its practical importance.

3.3.2. Rule Integration

The goal of rule integration is to resolve rule conflicts. This is done by adding symptoms to the rules so that they become mutually exclusive. Symptoms which can be added to a rule are the anomalies corresponding to its corrected–properties, or symptoms known to be relevant (because they correspond to a corrected property of another rule with same primary–symptom) but not corresponding to a corrected property of the rule (and thus were certainly normal in the situation the rule was initially learned from).

An example should make this clearer. Suppose the rule in figure 4(a) has been learned. If later a rule is abstracted which explains the malfunctioning of the car by a flat battery (figure 4(b)), then the properties Mode=Parking and Battery=Powered may be used for refinement. The former is chosen because it is easier to observe. Figure 4(c) shows the refined rules.

The process of rule-integration is *monotonic*: a rule never becomes invalid though its applicability may be restricted.[3] Integration may be seen as the partial reconstruction of the situation in which a rule was initially learned. By using circumscription that situation does not have to be explicitly remembered but is implicit in the rule. Its features are made explicit only if this becomes necessary to distinguish between different diagnoses.

---

[3] This does not mean that the theory represented by the rules evolves monotonically. This is impossible since learning is failure driven.

3.4. Other Learning Mechanisms

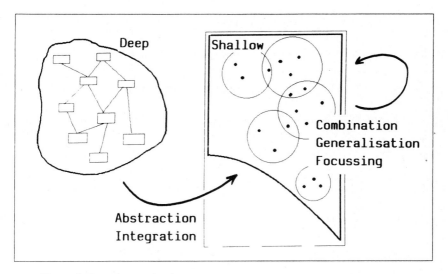

Figure 5: Learning mechanisms.

Rule abstraction and integration account for building a compact memory of past experience. Other learning mechanisms based on similarities between rules or focusses can augment the power of learned rules (figure 5). These processes are triggered by changes in the rule base.[4] Others may be needed to learn a particular kind of heuristics. The next few subsections describe some of these techniques, because of space considerations more in principle than in depth.

3.4.1. Learning Through Generalisation

The goal of learning through generalisation is to decouple learned rules from the particular properties or focus they refer to. Rules may thus be applied to similar regions of the same or another device. Generalisation generates a rule template which is instantiated with the right properties whenever the rule is needed.

For example, if a rule is learned which explains a malfunctioning sparkplug by a bad cable then this may be applied to all sparkplugs and their corresponding cable. (see figure 6). Generalisation requires sophisticated knowledge representation techniques because it is driven by the models (e.g. inheritance relations within a structural model) and influences memory structure in an intricate way.

---

[4] In designing these processes great care was taken to avoid search through the rule base. Therefore the rules are kept in a highly structured memory closely coupled with the various models. At any time appropriate rules become accessible. In fact rules may be scattered over several locations in the memory (e.g. general principles and local constraints). This is somewhat in the spirit of Schank's dynamic memories [Schank 1982].

```
                              Generalised to:
     Rule for start problem            Rule for start problem
     A solution-rule                   A solution-rule
       Primary-Symptoms:                 Primary-Symptoms:
         Not Spark-Plug-1=Fires            Not Spark-Plug=Fires
       Corrected-Properties:             Corrected-Properties:
         Cable-1=OK                        Corresponding-Cable=OK
```

Figure 6: Rule generalisation.

3.4.2. Learning Through Rule Combination

Rules may try to explain different symptoms by the same corrected properties. The simultaneous occurence of these symptoms points strongly to those corrections. So, these rules may be combined to a single one which forces to check the other symptoms as soon as one of them is observed. This mechanism turns out to be capable of generating powerful rules.

```
     Rule for start problem            Rule for start problem
     A solution-rule                   A solution-rule
       Primary-Symptoms:                 Primary-Symptoms:
         Not Spark-Plug-1=Fires            Not Spark-Plug-2=Fires
       Corrected-Properties:             Corrected-Properties:
         Contact-Points=OK                 Cable-2=OK
                                           Contact-Points=OK

     Combined to:

     Rule for start problem            Rule for start problem
     A solution rule                   A solution-rule
       Primary-Symptoms:                 Primary-Symptoms:
         Not Spark-Plug-1=Fires            Not Spark-Plug-2=Fires
         Not Spark-Plug-2=Fires          Excluded-Solutions:
       Corrected-Properties:               Contact-Points=OK
         Contact-Points=OK               Corrected-Properties:
                                           Cable-2=OK
```

Figure 7: Rule combination.

Figure 7 shows an example of rule combination. In this case one rule is discarded, the other one changed and a new one added. Sometimes both the old rules can be discarded. In any case the power of the rules increases. For example before rule combination the situation in which spark-plug-1 does not fire because of a bad cable cannot be explained, while after combination it can. Rule combination accounts for a direction of attention from the anomaly to be explained to other symptoms (e.g. from one spark-plug to another).

3.4.3. Learning of Focus Rules

The goal of learning focus rules is the division of rules in smaller sets according to the problem–type, component or function they relate to, and the learning of rules which lead from one set to another. This division may be based on another kind of model. For instance, focussing along the part–whole relation is learned by identifying in a topological model the part which is investigated by a set of rules.

The various focusses may be predetermined by the deep model. Usually such a model actually is a hierarchy of those. The topmost model represents the general understanding of a device's workings while lower ones describe parts in more detail.

Suppose an engine does not start and deep reasoning on the causal model of figure 3 reveals a problem with the starter (i.e. corrected property Starter=Turning). Deep reasoning will then continue by 'looking inside' the arrow connecting Starter=Powered and Starter=Turning. This arrow will expand into a new network describing the workings of the starter. At this point the focus rule in figure 2 may be learned.

3.5. Conclusion

Learning through progressive refinement is a method for incremental rule learning. The basic techniques of rule abstraction and rule integration account for building a compact memory of past experiences. Additional processes are triggered by changes in the rule set and augment its power in several ways. In this way the initially simple rules evolve to interesting heuristics which closely correspond to our intuitions.

4. DISCUSSION

This paper has introduced a new approach to rule learning. From a practical point of view we wish to simplify the process of knowledge acquisition for expert systems. The following subsection discusses to what extend this has been achieved. Then section 4.2. situates this research within the field of machine learning. Finally achievements are summarised along with suggestions for further work.

4.1. Explainable Knowledge Production?

Learning through progressive refinement clearly circumvents the problems of inductive techniques discussed in section 2. After some time the rules accumulated in a second generation expert system constitute an efficient set of intelligible heuristics. Thus it can be said that the knowledge produced by such a system is of better quality than the inductive product. On the other hand it is not acquired on one pass but is the result of a lengthy series of experiences.

The approach is feasible for those domains where deep models exist, are accessible and an effective method for reasoning about them is available. The first requirement gives preference to scientific and technical problem domains. As to the last requirement, the research on qualitative reasoning [Bobrow and Hayes 1984] provides hopeful results.

The second requirement brings us back to the problem of knowledge acquisition. With second generation expert systems this is transfered from the shallow to the deep level. To be useful as an alternative for knowledge acquisition some additional care is to be taken. Figure 8 shows desirable features for both kinds of knowledge.

The generality of expert system shells stems from the fact that the reasoning mechanism is both domain (e.g. medicine, electrical engineering) and task (e.g. diagnosis, planning, prediction) independent. Unfortunately this implies that the knowledge acquisition effort has to be redone for every new task within the same domain. For example an expert system for repairing a car would contain rather different rules than one for driving a car, though the underlying mechanical principles are the same.

Deep knowledge is ideally task independent, i.e. the same deep model of a car can be used for repairing and for driving it. A different but domain independent reasoning

	Shallow	Deep
Knowledge:		
	Domain dependent	Domain dependent
	Task dependent	Task independent
	Ill structured	Highly structured
Reasoner:		
	Domain independent	Domain independent
	Task independent	Task dependent
	Efficient	Inefficient

Figure 8: Shallow vs. deep knowledge.

mechanism should be used for each different task. Thus one knowledge acquisition effort delivers the basis for a multitude of expert systems.

Deep knowledge is of a much more objective nature and may be acquired from text-books, technical plans or specifications. It has been claimed by P. Sell that "the greater the scientific strength of the field, that much easier is the process of knowledge acquisition". This is but a positive claim in the context of second generation expert systems. Deep reasoning is essentially search and tends to generate unmanageable problem spaces unless extra care is taken (i.e. a suited reasoning mechanism used).

So we see that both inductive and refinement learning have their value for knowledge acquisition. The first approach gives quick results on simple applications like those done so far. The latter approach requires more machinery and is not universally applicable but it generates intelligible knowledge. It may be applied where deep knowledge is available and can be used effectively. Moreover it is only worthwhile if there are far less relevant problems than possible ones (section 3.1).

4.2. Relation to Other Work

Learning by progressive refinement is reminiscent to explanation based learning as dis-cussed by Mitchell (1983) and DeJong (1983). However the latter technique generates overspecified rules when applied to the problem of diagnosis using a deep model. They will mention each property in the causal net which is under the anomaly to be explained (i.e. theoretically relevant). This is absurd if such a property is always nor-mal in practice since testing for it will always return the same value.

The major criticism on explanation based learning is that it is too weak because it can only make explicit what is already implicitly in the theory. Indeed, it takes no risk in generalising from one experience. This does not quite hold for progressive refinement. This technique accounts for the creation of underspecified rules which after some time evolve to interesting heuristics. The circumscriptive assumption as discussed in section 3 is the key to bridging the gap between objective deep knowledge and fallible but useful (i.e. intelligent?) shallow knowledge.

The importance of the circumscriptive assumption cannot be overstated. Learned rules are guaranteed to use a minimal vocabulary and may be interpreted as a compact memory of past experiences. This clearly goes in a different direction than the *full memory* approach to knowledge refinement advocated by Reinke and Michalski (1985) (see also [Michalski 1985]) where both the rules and the facts they were generated from have to be remembered.

Second generation expert systems are among the few *integrated learning systems*. The combination of a problem–solving and learning component in one system is the best way to test the value of what has been learned. It requires to make explicit what constitutes the basic *learning cycle*: how problem solving triggers the learning mechanism, what information it provides and how the learned knowledge is used during problem solving. This is one aspect overlooked by most isolated learning techniques.

The SOAR project (overview in [Rosenbloom 1985]) is related to, and more ambitious then the work on second generation expert systems. Its learning mechanism called *chunking* is similar to ours. Most notably it is also *failure–* (or *impasse*) *driven*. However, the generalisation mechanism it uses is purely explanation based.

The long term goal of this research is to understand expertise. Understanding heuristics is also the goal of *heuretics* [Lenat 1982]. It seems that one essential part of it is missing: the initial birth of a heuristic. As explained above, this research may provide clues for that missing link. Other related research has been done by J.Kolodner (1984). Her work on acquiring expertise is based on the concepts of R.Schank's *dynamic memory* (1982) and uses rather different representations than ours. The most important difference is that it is a full–memory approach.

4.3. Achievements and Future Research

The examples throughout the paper are taken from an actual implementation of a second generation expert system for diagnosis of car failures. A powerful representation system is required in order to deal with different kinds of models and reasoning mechanisms. We have used the knowledge representation system KRS [Steels 1986]. All techniques mentioned in this paper are implemented and research is now going on to use more sophisticated deep reasoning techniques on multiple deep models. Another fruitful line of research is to look at 'the process upside–down', i.e. learning about the deep models.

Learning through progressive refinement shares some fundamental problems of inductive techniques, including the problem of evaluating learning systems and the problems of new terms and noisy data. Among those specific to the techniques described here we mention the problem of exceptions and rare cases (i.e. is the system too eager?) and the influence of the order of experiences on the convergence of the rule base.

5. CONCLUSION

This paper has introduced a method for learning rules from experience: learning through progressive refinement. Its main contribution to the field of machine learning is the use of circumscriptive reasoning to avoid a full–memory approach to incremental learning. Moreover its incorporation in a performance system yields one of the few integrated applications to date of learning. Such a second generation expert system avoids some fundamental problems with classical expert systems. Most practical, it circumvents the problem of knowledge engineering in a better way than inductive methods for rule learning from examples do. Our experiments have shown the feasibility of this second generation expert system technology.

ACKNOWLEDGEMENT

The author wishes to thank all members of the AI–Lab of Brussels Free University for discussions and comments, most notably Luc Steels who proved to be a continuing source of inspiration. I am indebted to him for drawing the general framework of second generation expert systems and sketching a whole landscape of learning techniques within. I also thank Donald Michie for inflicting the germ of this paper. The first outline was produced after an SPL–Insight meeting (october 1985) where he defended his 'knowledge refinery' idea. Vivianne Jonckers, Luc Steels, Pattie Maes and Kris Van Marcke provided useful comments on earlier drafts of the paper.

REFERENCES

Bobrow, D. and Hayes, P. (1984) Special Issue on Qualitative Reasoning. In *Artificial Intelligence Journal*. North Holland Pub. Amsterdam.

Bratko, I., Kononenko, I., Lavrac, N., Mozetic, I., Roskar, E. (1985) Automatic Synthesis of Knowledge. In *Automatika Journal*, Vol. 26, pp. 171-175.

Bratko, I., Mozetic, I., Lavrac, N., (1986) Automatic Synthesis and Compression of Cardiological Knowledge. In *Machine Intelligence 11*. Ellis Horwood. Chichester. (to be published).

Breuker, B.J. and Wielinga, J.A. (1985) KADS: Structured Knowledge Acquisition for Expert Systems. In *Proceedings of the Fifth International Workshop on Expert Systems*. Avignon.

Brownston, L., Farrell, R., Kant, E., Martin, N. (1985) *Programming Expert Systems in OPS5*. Addison Wesley Publishing Company. Reading, Massachusetts.

Clancey, W.J. (1983) The Epistemology of a Rule–Based Expert System– A Framework for Explanation. In *Artificial Intelligence Journal*. North Holland Pub. Amsterdam.

DeJong, G. (1983) An Approach to Learning from Observation. In *Proceedings of the Second International Machine Learning Workshop*. Urbana, Illinois.

Fink, P.K. (1985) Control and Integration of Diverse Knowledge in a Diagnostic Expert System. In A. Joshi (ed.) *Proceedings of Ninth International Joint Conference on Artificial Intelligence*. Morgan Kaufmann, Inc. Los Altos, California.

Hunt, E.B., Marin, J. and Stone, P.J. (1966) *Experiments in Induction*. Academic Press. New York.

Kahn, G. (1984) On when Diagnostic Systems want to do without Causal Knowledge. In *Proceedings of 6th European Conference on Artificial Intelligence*. Pisa, Italy.

Kolodner, J.L. (1984) Towards an Understanding of the Role of Experience in the Evolution from Novice to Expert. In M.J. Coombs (ed.) *Developments in Expert Systems*. Academic Press. London.

Lenat, D.B. (1982) The Nature of Heuristics. In *Artificial Intelligence Journal*. North Holland Pub. Amsterdam.

McCarthy, J. (1983) Circumscription – A form of non–monotonic reasoning. In *Artificial Intelligence Journal*. North Holland Pub. Amsterdam.

Michalski, R.S. and Chilausky, R.L. (1980) Knowledge Acquisition by Encoding Expert Rules versus Computer Induction from Examples: a case study involving soybean pathology. In *International Journal for Man–Machine Studies*.

Michalski, R.S. (1985) Knowledge Repair Mechanisms: evolution vs. revolution. In *Proceedings of the Third International Machine Learning Workshop*. Skytop, Pennsylvania.

Michie, D., Muggleton, S., Riese, C. and Zubrick, S. (1984) RuleMaster: a second generation knowledge engineering facility. In *Proceedings of the First Conference on Artificial Intelligence Applications*.

Michie, D., Johnston, R. (1985) *The Knowledge Machine*. William Morrow and Company, Inc. New York.

Mitchell, T.M. (1978) Version Spaces: An approach to concept learning, Ph.D. dissertation, Rep.No., STAN-CS-78-711, Department of Computer Science, Stanford University.

Mitchell, T.M. (1983) Learning and Problem Solving. Computers and Thoughts Lecture. In A. Bundy (ed.) *Proceedings of Eight International Joint Conference on Artificial Intelligence*. William Kaufmann, Inc.

Pople, H.E. (1982) Heuristic Methods for Imposing Structure on Ill-Structured Problems: The Structuring of Medical Diagnostics. In P. Szolovits (ed.) *Artificial Intelligence in Medicine*. Westview Press. Boulder, Colorado.

Reinke, R. and Michalski, R.S. (1985) Incremental Learning of Concept Descriptions. In J.E. Hayes, D. Michie and J. Richards (eds) *Machine Intelligence 11*. Oxford University Press. Oxford.

Rosenbloom, P.R., Laird, J.E., Newell, A., Golding, A., Unruh, A. (1985) Current Research on Learning in SOAR. In *Proceedings of the Third International Machine Learning Workshop*. Skytop, Pennsylvania.

Schank, R.C. (1982) *Dynamic Memory: a theory of reminding and learning in computers and people*. Cambridge University Press. Cambridge.

Steels, L. (1985) Second Generation Expert Systems. In *Future Generation Computer Systems*. North-Holland Pub. Amsterdam.

Steels, L. and Van de Velde, W. (1985) Learning in Second Generation Expert Systems. In J.S. Kowalik (ed.) *Knowledge Based Problem Solving*. Prentice-Hall Inc. New Jersey.

Steels, L. (1986) The KRS Concept System. Technical Report. A.I. Lab, Brussels Free University.

Swartout, W.R. (1983) XPLAIN: A system for Creating and Explaining Expert Consulting Programs. In *Artificial Intelligence Journal*. North Holland Pub. Amsterdam.

Van de Velde, W. (1985) Naive Causal Reasoning For Diagnosis. In *Proceedings of the Fifth International Workshop on Expert Systems*. Avignon.

Advances in Artificial Intelligence - II
B. Du Boulay, D. Hogg and L. Steels (Editors)
© Elsevier Science Publishers B.V. (North-Holland), 1987

KNOWLEDGE BASED LEARNING:
REDUCING THE DESCRIPTION SPACE FOR RULE LEARNING

Maarten W. van Someren

Department of Social Science Informatics
University of Amsterdam
Herengracht 196
1016 BS Amsterdam

ABSTRACT
Techniques for learning rules from examples may require instances that can not occur in the real world. General facts about the world can be used to reduce the language in which the objects are described, which reduces the complexity of the learning task and may overcome the problem of impossible instances.

1. INTRODUCTION

Techniques for inductive rule learning (see Michalski et.al. (1983) for an overview) generally have the character of "weak methods" (Mitchell (1982), Korf (1985)). They systematically search through the space of possible rules, directed by positive and negative instances. The rules are usually stated in the same terms as the original descriptions of the objects to which they apply. Because of their 'weakness' and the size of the search space, these techniques are insufficient to handle most real life learning tasks. Either the number of instances that is required to learn a rule is too big or the description language must be carefully crafted in advance. Another problem is that fully learning a rule may require instances that never appear during learning, eg. because they cannot exist. It is shown how these problems can be resolved by reducing the description language, using general facts about the data. Search is constrained by reducing the object description language to a simpler rule language in such a way, that the reduced language covers only *possible* instances.

2. PROBLEMS OF AN OVERSIZED DESCRIPTION SPACE

A description space that covers instances which cannot actually exist, can cause several types of problems. It may prevent the method from terminating (ie. knowing that it has found the complete rule) and in any case it will make the search space unnecessarily large.

2.1. Non-termination

Consider the problem of learning the concept "arch" from positive and negative examples, especially "near misses" (*), using the method described by Winston (1975) and refined by Bundy et.al. (1985). Note that Near Miss A is not even a very good example of a near miss, because it differs in two aspects from the first positive instance: the two support relations. If we want to teach the program about the importance of the support relation by showing it a proper near miss, we could use B.

(*) Note that this single positive instance is almost sufficient to explain the concept "near miss", which casts some doubt on the psychological validity of the theory !

However, suppose now that this structure is physically impossible in the blocks world (eg. because the supporting block would collapse). It may be a general fact, that a single block is not strong enough to support any other block.

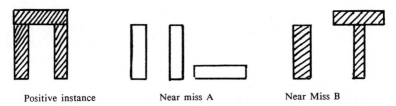

Positive instance   Near miss A   Near Miss B

In that case, it is impossible to construct a proper near miss (with must have only one supporter). Unfortunately, in that case the learning algorithm would never terminate, because it is not possible to present to the program an appropriate sequence of positive examples and "near misses". To teach that **both** "support" relations are necessary, one has to show the program an example that differs from the current concept, because **one** support relation is missing - this is not possible. (*)

The problem is caused by the fact, that the description space contains two properties (the two "supports"), that depend on each other: there cannot be only *one* support relation: it's two or none. Here a better description language would contain the property "support2(X, Y, Z)", meaning that Z is supported by X and Y. If the original description of objects in the blocks world would be in terms of a single support, we could define support2 as a new predicate with values true = *support(X, Z) and support(Y, Z)* and false = *not support(X, Z) and not support(Y, Z)*. Disregarding for the moment the problems with variable bindings that are inherent to this representation, this solves the problem, because we can now apply the original learning technique using "support2", which gives us just what we want.

The non-termination problem would also occur in the version space method. In that case the boundary sets S and G would never converge on a single set.

2.2. Using general knowledge to guide rule learning

Many possible applications of rule learning techniques require very many (positive and negative) examples to learn a rule completely. This contrasts sharply with human learning, which often requires only very few examples. Humans seem to be able to apply knowledge about the domain during learning and thus they can profit much more from a single example than purely inductive techniques. Thus we need techniques that can exploit knowledge about the domain for faster rule learning.

To see how this can be achieved, we should realise that in many rule-based systems we can distinguish several kinds of knowledge (cf. Clancey (1985), Brachman et.al. (1983), Silver (1985), Mitchell (1983)):

* (General) facts about the domain: descriptive knowledge about the world

---

(*) This problem, which inspired the research described here, was noted by Alan Bundy (1982).

* Classification knowledge: knowledge about class membership

* Heuristic or control knowledge: knowledge about when and how to apply facts and classifications

These types of knowledge are not independent and the relation that I shall exploit here, is, that *classification knowledge and heuristic knowledge need only cover possible objects or sitiations, as implied by the facts.* In many rule based systems, these types of knowledge are not separated in the representation. Eg. a system like MYCIN the rules are written in such a way that they don't cover impossible cases, but there is no explicit representation of the fact that they are impossible (thus increasing the efficiency of the rule base).

Thus, we want to augment techniques for learning classification rules (or heuristic rules) with a way to exploit factual knowledge about the domain. Factual knowledge may be available directly from the user, or in the form of a model or theory of the domain (eg. Steels & Van der Velde, 1985) or as the result of a (different) induction about the occurrence of certain events.

3. REDUCING THE DESCRIPTION SPACE: A PARTIAL SOLUTION

The technique that I propose, is to use a general statement about the domain to construct a new (compound) property for the description language, with only the *possible* value combinations of the original properties as values. This effectively reduces the description language, such that it does not cover impossible objects any more. This requires a representation with a variable number of values per unit, eg. features with values (or functions). The details of the method depend on the representation. Here I shall use a feature-value representation.

3.1. Indiscriminative properties - impossible and universal values

A very simple example, is an observable value of a property that, according to the theory given by the expert, cannot occur in any instance. Now learning will not terminate, because neither the generalisation to *any value* nor a specialisation to an inclusion or exclusion of this value can be made. The (obvious) solution is to remove this property from the description language (and perhaps add its negation to all rules, if we want a characteristic rather than a discriminative rule).

The same argument applies to universal properties. If **all** instances have a certain value of a property, it is not possible to show a counterexample to the concept that does not have this value. Again, for this reason learning will not terminate, unless we remove this redundant property from the description language.

We assume that a property can have only a single value "about" an instance, so properties with the same value for all possible instances may also be removed. If a value of a property is impossible, only that value can be removed from the description language.

3.2. Equivalent properties

Another source of problems are interactions between properties. Two forms are equivalences and implications (see next section). Equivalence means that there exists a one to one mapping between the values of two properties. Equivalent properties cause redundancy in the description space and may prevent learning from terminating.

If it is known that two properties are equivalent, they are collapsed into one new property, defined as "P and Q", with as values the possible combinations of values of P and Q. The same applies to negatively equivalent properties. For example, if the user indicates that "bachelor: true" is equivalent to "married: no" and bachelor and married are both binary properties, a new property is defined with values *bachelor and not married* and *not bachelor and married*.

3.3. Implied properties

A slightly more complicated case is that of two properties, one of which entails the other. Suppose that in the blocks world, a ball cannot be used as a supporting block: "if the shape of an object is ball, then it does not support anything". We now remove "supporting balls" from the description by defining a new property **support and shape** that has only the values *support and not ball*, *not support and ball* and *not support and not ball*.

It is possible to construct a more elegant hierarchical representation, in the form of trees, but that leaves us with the choice between two possible trees. Suppose that the expert told us that P implies Q, where P and Q are both two-valued properties, then there are two possible trees:

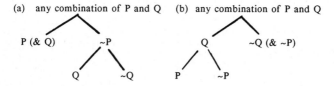

(a) any combination of P and Q   (b) any combination of P and Q

The choice between these two structures can be left to the user or it can be made automatically by the tree hacking method described by Wielemaker and Bundy (1985).

4. APPLICATION AND PRELIMINARY RESULTS

I am currently building a system, that learns from a dialogue that is based on examples, but also allows the user to enter general facts. Experts who are very good at solving cases, are often not able to provide the general rules which they follow. Therefore example cases may be a very useful medium in knowledge elicitation. As in most applications of rule learning techniques that use only examples, the number of examples required is very large. This would make an interactive system impossible. My system relies on the suggestive effect of examples, generated by the program, to elicit (conservative) generalisations from the expert.

Consider the following example taken from the MYCIN-domain. The number of cases that can be constructed by combining all possible parameter values is huge, but consider these parameters:

(1) is the patient an indoor patient ?

(2) is the patient in the intensive care (IC) unit ?

(3) does the patient have a catheter ?

Clearly, these properties do not occur independent of each other. For example, a patient in the IC unit will always have a catheter. A patient with a catheter will usually be an indoor patient, or be in the IC unit. A patient in the IC unit is by definition an indoor patient, unless by "indoor" we mean "indoor but not in IC". If we would present to an expert all cases that can be generated from these features, many of these would be impossible, such as patients in the IC unit, but without catheter, which will make the expert explode, combinatorially or otherwise.

At this moment only a simple prototype is implemented, using only the reduction operators described above. We have not yet done any serious experiments, so we can present only some examples. The reduction operators can be applied at any moment during the learning process. Thus it is possible for the teacher to enter both examples and general facts (about relations between observable data) to an inductive learning system, thereby increasing the practical usefulness of such a system.

To illustrate the effect of the method, consider the context *patient* a mini-version of MYCIN. This context has 17 parameters. If we disregard the name, which plays no role in the inference, the possible allergies and the possible therapies, we have 14 parameters left, one of which can have 4 values and the rest 2 (plus "unknown"). Again, disregarding the "unknowns", this leaves over 16000 possible patients. Obvious interactions between the parameters *has just given birth* and *sex* and between *indoor*, *in intensive care* and *has catheter* reduces this to about 8000 possible patients. More extensive experiments are planned.

Two examples of abstracted properties:

given birth --> female:

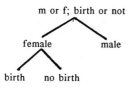

IC --> catheter:

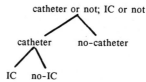

These examples were tree-structured by hand. That these reduction operators are in general not strong enough to realise the interactive knowledge acquisition scenario that I described above, because the search space is still too big. To make a useful system, it will be necessary to combine the reduction rules with other techniques and to enable the expert to enter partial classification rules.

5. RELATED WORK

5.1. Using general facts for rule learning

Bundy (1982) proposes a different solution to the problem of impossible examples. Relations between properties are added to the system as rules, which can reduce the current set of possible classification rules. This has the same effect as our method, but does not affect the description language. Our method has the advantage that facts and examples can be represented in a single representation, but it may produce rather awkward descriptive terms. In the literature several techniques are reported for using knowledge about to domain to improve learning. Buchanan and Mitchell (1978) showed, in META-DENDRAL, how search for a rule can be pruned using a model of the domain. The rules in the candidate sets of the version space method are selected by plausibility according to domain theory. In the case of META-DENDRAL, certain bonds in a molecule are weaker and thus more likely to break than others. Also, attributes of the part of a molecule near to a breaking point are more likely to affect breaking, than attributes of parts that are further away. These attributes are introduced first, thus guiding search for the correct rule. A general version of this heuristic was given by Van Someren (1984).

Mitchell et.al. (1983) point out that the description language needs "bias" to be practically useful and show how *constraint backpropagation* can be used to extend the description space with new terms. Here the description language is refined rather than reduced.

Emde et.al. (1983) infer "properties of (relational) properties" (eg. the transitivity of the relation "south-of") from examples and use these "meta-properties" to generalise much further than would be possible on the basis of the examples. If we look back at the problem of non-termination, the system of Emde et.al could be equipped with a meta-property" *two or none*, that applies to relations. It could then induce from a set of examples, that this property applies to "support" and thus implicitly cut the description space. These "meta-properties" represent a special kind of knowledge about the domain, but it is restricted to a very special kind of knowledge.

5.2. Conceptual clustering

In our case, descriptive terms were constructed from general facts. Another possibility is, to apply empirical clustering techniques, as in BACON (Langley, Bradshaw and Simon, 1983): new properties are constructed by applying an algebraic operator to two existing properties (eg. "area" = "length" * "width"). This is done on the basis of partial correlations. Langley, Zytkow, Bradshaw and Simon (1983) later applied the same approach to categorical data. Michalski (1983, p.111) generalises this method to the "detecting property interdependence" rule (for constructive induction).

6. Conclusions

To be practically useful, a rule learning technique has to meet several requirements:

- The number of instances needed to learn a rule may not be too big

- No irrelevant instances should occur in the learning process

- The learning process should terminate with a completely learned rule

- The resulting rules must be comprehensible to the human user (ie. they should be built from terms that correspond to concepts from natural language or special concepts in the domain; they should not be too complex in terms of nestings; they should contain as few negations and disjunctions as possible)

The technique described here shows how general facts about the domain can be used to reduce the search space for rule learning. New descriptive terms are formed from primitive terms, such that impossible instances are excluded. A knowledge acquisition tool is under development that uses this technique in a dialogue with the expert, that is based on examples.

Acknowledgments

Alan Bundy·pointed out the problem with focussing. Wouter Jansweijer made several useful comments on an earlier draft of this paper.

References:

Brachman, R.J., Fikes, R.E. and Levesque, H.J. (1983) Krypton: a functional approach to knowledge representation, IEEE Computer, vol.16, 67-83.

Buchanan, B. G. and Mitchell, T.M. (1978) Model-directed learning of production rules, in: Waterman, D. and Hayes-Roth, F., **Pattern directed inference systems**, Academic Press.

Bundy, A. (1982) The indispensability of inference in focussing, internal note, Department of Artificial Intelligence, University of Edinburgh.

Bundy, A., Silver, B. and Plummer, D. (1985) An anlytical comparison of some rule-learning programs, **Artificial Intelligence**, **27**, p.137-181.

Clancey, W. (1985) Heuristic classification, **Artificial Intelligence**, **27**, p.289-350.

Emde, W., Habel, C.U. and Rollinger, C.-R. (1983) The discovery of the equator or concept driven learning, Procs. IJCAI-83, Karlsruhe, p.455-458.

Korf, R.E. (1985) Macro-Operators: a weak method for learning, **Artificial Intelligence**, vol.26, p.35-77.

Langley, P., Bradshaw, G.L. and Simon, H.L. (1983) Rediscovering chemistry with the BACON system, in: Michalski ea. (1983).

Langley, P., Zytkow, J.M., Bradshaw, G.L and Simon, H.A. (1983) Three facets of scientific discovery, Procs. IJCAI-83, Karlsruhe, p.465-468.

Michalski, R.S. (1983) A theory and methodology of inductive learning, in: Michalski e.a. (1983).

Michalski, R.S., Carbonell, J. and Mitchell, T.M. (eds) (1983) Machine learning: an AI approach, Tioga Press.

Mitchell, T.M., (1982), Generalization as search, **Artificial Intelligence**, **18**, p.203-226.

Mitchell, T.M., Utgoff, P. and Banerji, R. (1983) Learning by experimentation: acquiring and refining problem solving heuristics, in: Michalski ea., 1983.

Silver, B. (1985) **Meta-level inference**, Amsterdam: North-Holland.

Someren, M.W. van (1984) A heuristic for rule learning, Procs. ECAI-84, Pisa, p.493-496.

Steels, L. and Van der Velde, W. (1985) Learning in second generation expert systems, in: Kowalik, J.S. (ed) **Knowledge-based problem solving**, Prentice-Hall.

Wielemaker, J. and Bundy, A. (1985) Altering the description space for focussing, Expert Systems - 85, Warwick, UK.

Winston, P.H. (1975) Learning structural descriptions from examples, in: Winston, P.H. (ed), **The psychology of computer vision**, McGraw-Hill.

Advances in Artificial Intelligence - II
B. Du Boulay, D. Hogg and L. Steels (Editors)
© Elsevier Science Publishers B.V. (North-Holland), 1987   61

FUZZY REASONING IN A KNOWLEDGE-BASED SYSTEM FOR OBJECT CLASSIFICATION

Catherine Granger

INRIA
Centre de Rocquencourt
78153 Le Chesnay Cedex
FRANCE

An attempt to introduce fuzzy reasoning in an object classification system is presented. The object classification system is caracterized by the presence of objects called prototypes which describe the classes and guide the control strategy, and rules which have the task of inferring abstract knowledge about the unknown object. A possibility theory-based approach was chosen to manipulate fuzzy predicates in the rules and to handle fuzzy matching between the unknown object and the prototypes.

1. INTRODUCTION

The past few years have seen great activity in the field of expert systems. However, this technique is surprisingly not so used in computer vision, although this field is based on an ill understood human capacity of understanding. Ambiguities arise because an image is only a 2D projection of the real world. The appearance of an object may widely change because of a different point of view or a different illumination source, etc...

A way to cope with these problems is to use strong a priori knowledge about the objects we are expecting to find in the image and to provide the system with heuristic rules human beings use, in order to discriminate between different plausible objects.

This approach was chosen for the design of a knowledge-based system for object classification [Granger85]. Because one of the caracteristics of the domain is imprecision and uncertainty, the control structure of the system is based on fuzzy mecanisms issued from the possibility theory and Zadeh's fuzzy sets [Zadeh78]. Among the other features of the system, objects, called prototypes, and production rules represent knowledge. The prototypes are linked in a hierarchical network. They are used to describe the classes and to guide the control strategy; the rules infer abstract knowledge from initial data. During a preliminary phase, in order to improve the efficiency of the system, the rules are automatically attached to the prototypes they correspond to, forming small rule bases which are then compiled into decision trees.

The system has been applied to different domains. A first implementation was an automatic classification of galaxies into their morphological types [Thonnat85]. The examples given in this paper come from this application, which was developed during the design of the system. The good results given by the system in this domain allowed us to validate this approach. Other applications are currently in development: automatic identification of zooplankton [Gandelin85], interpretation of indoor scenes [Thonnat86] and diagnosis of failures for satellite antenna.

2. CARACTERISTICS OF A CLASSIFICATION PROBLEM

The purpose of a classification problem is to identify an unknown object as belonging to a known class of objects. A convenient way to describe one of these classes is to use the notion of stereotypical object which is a perfect representative of its class. These objects (called also prototypes) are naturally hierarchically organized from the most general class to the most specific. Several kinds of sub-hierarchies linked to the object by "part-of" relationships, may also exist

Identifying an object means matching the caracteristics of the object against the different features of the prototypes. A solution to the problem is a prototype which matches the unknown object sufficiently well. If the object does not correspond perfectly to any of the prototypes, the system may provide a ranked list of solutions. There are basically three types of search strategies in the prototype network:

- a data-driven strategy goes forward from data to solutions until all the deductions have been done,
- a hypothesis-driven strategy goes backward from solutions and searches for data to support them,
- a mixed strategy combines data and hypothesis-driven strategies: on the one hand, data trigger rules to infer more knowledge and on the other hand, focusing is performed by the hierarchy of classes to avoid exhaustive search.

The choice of the search strategy greatly depends on the number of data to process and the cost of their acquisition.

Unfortunately, classification problems rarely appear so simple. One problem is that data are rarely at the same level of abstraction than the description of the prototypes (typically, data are numbers and prototypes descriptors have symbolic values). So, the matching process cannot be performed directly and a phase of data abstraction [Clancey84] is necessary. Another problem is that data and knowledge manipulated by the system, issued either from procedures (like the parameters extracted from the image), or from the expert (like the rules), may be imprecise and/or incertain. Standard pattern matching procedures that return only true or false, are in this case, not flexible enough and must be replaced by more "fuzzy" mechanisms.

3. OVERVIEW OF THE SYSTEM

The system is implemented in Le_Lisp/Ceyx [Chailloux84]. Ceyx is an object-oriented extension of Le_Lisp which proved to be very well adapted to the knowledge representation of the system. Besides the possibility of representing objects as records, Ceyx allows to inherit from superclasses, to describe the objects behaviour by methods and to communicate with the objects via messages.

The system is made of different modules : the knowledge base, (see section 4) contains a prototype network, a set of rules and an unknown object; the control structure (see section 5) organizes search in the prototype network and activates the rules; a parser makes knowledge acquisition easier. The user describes prototypes and rules in a simple language defined by a grammar and the parser transforms these descriptions into Lisp objects; the explanation stage is the final stage of the classification. Triggered prototypes and rules are stored in a memory: the history. Explanation of the intermediate and final conclusions are given by consulting the history.

4. THE KNOWLEDGE BASE

4.1. THE PROTOTYPES

A prototype is a special object, considered as a perfect representative of its class. The descriptors of the prototype are stored in the fields (or slots) of the object. The control procedures of the prototype correspond to the behaviour of the object and are stored in its methods. A prototype is always linked to its superclass.

Example : the prototype S (spiral)

```
PROTOTYPE S
     superclass : Galaxy;
     class : S;
     shape : spiral;
     T : [3 7].
```

Different facets are associated with each descriptors of the prototype and depend on the type of the descriptor.

a. The symbolic type : created to store symbolic features, it has a value facet which contains one or more values. Each value is coupled with a number which measures its degree of certainty. A set facet contains a set of plausible values that an object of the same class can take.

Example of a symbolic descriptor :

```
DESCRIPTOR shape
     value : spiral (0.8) , average (0.1);
     set : (elliptical, average, spiral).
```

b. The numerical type : it was created for numerical parameters which are usually input data. It has a value facet which must contain a number, a mesure facet which contains the degree of certainty of the value, and an interval facet which contains the minimun and the maximum value that the descriptor can take for this class.

Example of a numerical descriptor :

```
DESCRIPTOR angle
     value : 15;
     mesure : 1;
     interval : [-90, 90].
```

c. The structured type : It was created to represent a "part of" relationship for aggregated objects. Here, the descriptor is an instance of a class described as a prototype.

Example of a structured descriptor :

```
DESCRIPTOR c1
     class : contour.

PROTOTYPE contour
     superclass : object;
     class : contour;
     angle ... ;
     shape ... ;
```

The unknown object is an instance of the main class (Galaxy for example). At the beginning of the classification, input data are stored in the fields of the unknown object. Then, rules have the task to improve this initial description.

4.2. THE RULES

The rules allow to infer abstract knowledge from input data (parameter level) to reach the level of abstraction used in the prototypes (expert level)

Examples of rules :

RULE 46 :
  if ellipse-err of c1 > 0.25
  then shape of c1 is spiral

RULE 3 :
  if angle of c2 far-from inclination (tol 5)
  and inclination > 0.3
  and ellipticity of c2 >= 0.3
  then bar is present

Several predicates may be used in the rules: <, >, is-between, close-to (with a tolerance), far-from (with a tolerance) etc... They are more or less fuzzy, this depends on the tolerance that follows the predicate but they all require a fuzzy pattern matching mecanism (see 5.1).

Rules are given to the system in an unordered way. This is an important feature for an expert system where knowledge must be described in a modular fashion. On the other hand, problems of efficiency occur when the number of rules increases because the system may spend most of all its time scanning the rule base.

To prevent the combinatorics, the system uses the natural structuration of the knowledge base by the network of prototypes: in a preliminary phase, the system automatically attaches the rules to the prototypes they correspond to so as to create a small rule base at each node of the network.

For example, if a rule concludes to the value of the descriptor "shape" the system will attach this rule to the superclasses of each prototype for which "shape" is a determining descriptor. Therefore, information about the shape of the unknown objet will be provided by the rule at the right moment: just before the selection of the prototypes according to their shape.

5. THE CONTROL STRUCTURE

5.1. FUZZY REASONING

Dealing with imprecise or uncertain data is a crucial problem in most of the fields where expert systems are helpful and especially in vision. In the classification case, the unknown object rarely fits perfectly a unique prototype so we would like that the system could provide a list of solutions with certainty measures attached to them.

For a long time, probability-based models have been the only tools that could manipulate uncertain information. More recently, attempts to build adequate models to subjective knowledge have proposed more empirical approaches (MYCIN [Shortliffe75], PROSPECTOR [Duda76]). On the other hand, the possibility theory [Dubois80] seems to be an attractive and formalized way to handle imprecision and uncertainty in expert systems and other AI works .

5.1.1. Overview

The possibility theory was introduced by Zadeh from his fuzzy sets theory. In this framework, the incertainty of an event is estimated by a possibility measure Π on a universe U. It is a function defined from $\mathfrak{P}(U)$ to $[0, 1]$, where $\mathfrak{P}(U)$ is the set of subsets of U. A possibility measure Π satisfies the following axioms :

$\Pi (\emptyset) = 0$

$\Pi (U) = 1$

$\forall A \in \mathfrak{P}(U), \forall B \in \mathfrak{P}(U), \quad \Pi (A \cup B) = \max (\Pi (A), \Pi (B))$

A consequence of these axioms is the relation between $\Pi(A)$ and $\Pi(\bar{A})$:

$$\forall A \in \mathfrak{P}(U), \quad \max (\Pi (A), \Pi (\bar{A})) = 1$$

Because of the almost complete independence between $\Pi(A)$ and $\Pi(\bar{A})$, a possibility approach seems to be more adapted to knowledge representation than a probabilistic one. In our system, imprecision appears in the rule predicates and their thresholds, incompleteness and uncertainty appears when the object is only partially classified among several plausible classes. However, we presently do not take account of any certainty factor attached to the rules themselves.

5.1.2. Fuzzy pattern matching in the rules

Pattern matching is the process of measuring the similarity between some data and a pattern. Usually this process returns a binary answer: true or false (1 or 0) but this answer lacks flexibility when the data and/or the pattern is imprecise.

For example, the matching of a number x and a pattern $y \geqslant 0.3$ when the pattern is imprecise, is surely true when x is largely greater than 0.3, surely false when x is largely smaller than 0.3 but the answer is incertain when x is close to 0.3.

The possibility based model provides a fuzzy pattern matching procedure [Cayrol82] that measures the possibility of the matching, a number between 0 and 1. For each predicate that appears in the rules, a fuzzy interval is defined (i. e. a fuzzy set of numbers). Then, if I is a fuzzy interval, μ_I (*value*) measures to what extend value belongs or not to I (figure 1).

When a rule has several conditions, the matching of the condition part of the rules returns several possibility measures. These measures are then combined using the conjonctive operator min and this final measure is considered as the possibility measure of the conclusion part of the rule.

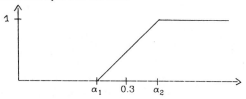

fig 1 : membership function for the pattern $y \geq 0.3$

5.1.3. Fuzzy matching between the prototype and the object

The classification process is mainly achieved by the matching between the unknown object and the prototypes, where each descriptor of both objects are compared in order to evaluate their similaries and their differences. On the prototype side, the descriptor offers a set of plausible values. On the object side, the descriptor may have several values weighed by a possibility measure. The similarities between the object descriptors and the prototype ones provide a measure of compatibility but the differences provide a measure of incompatibility. The final classification of the object depends, of course, on the value of both measures.

- *The measure of compatibility:* there is a compatibility between two descriptors if at least one value of the object descriptor belongs to the set of values of the prototype descriptor. The measurement of this compatibility is given by the following possibility measure: if A_i is the fuzzy set of the possible values taken by the attribute i of the object, if B_i is the set of the possible values allowed for the attribute i of the prototype (in our case B_i is not fuzzy), the possibility that it exists a value for the attribute common to the prototype and the object, is given by :

$$\Pi (B_i \mid A_i) = \max_{v \in B_i} \mu_{A_i} (v)$$

The global compatibility between the object and the prototype is given by the compatibility of *all* the descriptors. This is obtained by minimizing the compatibility measures of all the descriptors : $\min_i \Pi (B_i \mid A_i)$

- *The measure of incompatibility:* a incompatibility is detected between two descriptors as soon as one of the values of the object descriptor does not belong to the set of values of the prototype descriptor. The possibility that it exists a possible value for the descriptor i of the object that is forbidden for the descriptor i of the prototype is given by :

$$\Pi\,(\bar{B}_i\mid A_i)\;=\;\max_{v\,\in\,\bar{B}_i}\mu_{A_i}\,(v)$$

where $\bar{B}_i$ is the complementary set of B_i.

The global measure of incompatibility between the object and the prototype, is given by the incompatibility of *at least* one descriptor. This is obtained by maximizing the incompatibility measures of all the descriptors : $\max_i \Pi\,(\bar{B}_i\mid A_i)$

5.2. THE CONTROL STRATEGIES

The system strategy is mainly hypothesis-driven and follows the prototype network, from the most general classes to the most specific. However, at the rule level, rules are only triggered by data in forward chaining.

5.2.1. The strategy at the prototype level

At the beginning of the classification process, the compatibility of the unknown object with the most general class (the root of the classification tree), is checked and the rules attached to this node are activated. Then the unknown object is taken down the classification tree until no more solution can be found. At each node, two different stages can be distinguished:

- *The selection stage* : the sons of the current prototype are matched to the unknown object. The selection of the sons depends on the compatibility and incompatibility measures that result from the match. If a prototype is selected, its branch will be visited, else the branch is cut

- *The activation stage* : when a prototype is selected, it calls the rule interpreter to activate the rules attached to it. The rules must supply new knowledge about the unknown object and permit to refine the classification.

5.2.2. The strategy at the rule level

It was not necessary to develop complex strategies for the rule interpreter. At a given level of classification, the whole set of rules attached to the current node is useful, as a consequence of the knowledge base structuration. The rules can then be activated in an exaustive way, in forward chaining, to provide a maximum amount of knowledge for the continuation of the classification

A problem may occur when several rules conclude on the same value of the same descriptor and with different possibility measures. A few rules of combination are available, issued from different theoritical framework but these rules may lead to too different results [Dubois85]. In this work, we prefer to adopt a simple and natural approach: $\Pi(conclusion) = \max_i \Pi(cond_i)$ which corresponds to the rule:

if $cond_1$ or $\cdots$ or $cond_n$ then *conclusion*

6. AN EXAMPLE OF FUZZY REASONING

First, input data are given to the system.
Galaxy NGC4474
orientation : 17.60
ellipticity : 0.50
linear-err : 0.031
profile : 0.85
area : 4300.8
contours : center-err ellipse-err compacity angle ellipticity

	center-err	ellipse-err	compacity	angle	ellipticity
c1 :	0	0.15	1.3	6.5	0.46
c2 :	0	0.05	1.9	1.5	0.31
c3 :	4	0.13	4.1	6.2	0.46
c4 :	3	0.07	4.0	5.7	0.58
c5 :	7	0.11	6.1	2.8	0.40

Then, rules are activated at each of the five contour nodes:
at the contour level, activated rules : 95; 47; 10;
at the contour level, activated rules : 96; 48; 30; 13;
at the contour level, activated rules : 97; 53; 16;
at the contour level, activated rules : 98; 54; 19;
at the contour level, activated rules : 99; 44; 42; 22;

Activation of the rules at the root node:
at the Galaxy level, activated rules : 61; 57; 59;
Now, selection stage for the sons of the root node:
Intermediate prototype selected
Activation stage for the Intermediate prototype
at the Intermediate level, activated rules : 27; 9;
Intermediate_B prototype selected
at the Intermediate_B level, activated rules : 90; 89; 87; 84; 91; 92; 93;
LB+ prototype selected
Here the classification arrives at the end of the visited branch
so now, the Intermediate_B brother is selected:
Intermediate_A prototype selected
at the Intermediate_A level, activated rules :
LA+ prototype selected

We arrive now at the explanation phase:
all the rules that were activated are listed.

...

48: as the distance between the second contour and an ellipse
is very small (< 0.1), the shape of this contour is elliptical

...

NGC4474 matches quite well Indermediate
(compatibility: high, incompatibility: null)
NGC4474 matches quite well Intermediate_B
(compatibility: high, incompatibility: medium)
NGC4474 matches quite well LB+
(compatibility: medium, incompatibility: medium)
NGC4474 is not far from SB1a
(compatibility: very low, incompatibility: medium)
NGC4474 matches not badly Intermediate_A
(compatibility: medium, incompatibility: very high)
NGC4474 matches not badly LA+
(compatibility: medium, incompatibility: very high)

Final description of the object:
Object NGC4474

classified :	LB+	(.5, .5)
	LA+	(.5, .9)
isophotes :	unknown	
shape :	average	(.7)
bar :	absent	(.5)
	present	(.9)
inclination :	unknown	
centring :	good	(.5)
	average	(.4)
	bad	(.4)
profile-concavity :	average	(.5)
flatness :	unknown	
bulge :	visible	(1)
arms :	absent	(.7)
validity :	good	(1)

7. CONCLUSION

We proposed a way to handle imprecision and uncertainty in an object classification system. We used fuzzy pattern matching techniques, issued from the possibility theory, to activate the rules and measure the compatibility between an unknown object and the prototypes. The possibility-based framework appeared to be particularly well adequate to our domain. We hope that the applications currently developed will confirm the good results obtained by the system of classification of galaxies. Some points are still under investigation like the delicate problem of combining different incertain sources, especially when rule certainty factors have to be taken into account.

Acknowledgment

I wish to thank Monique Thonnat who contributed to this work by developing the system of galaxy classification and Didier Dubois who introduced me to the principles of the possibility theory.

References

Cayrol82.
    M. Cayrol, H. Farreny, and H. Prade, "Fuzzy Pattern Matching," *Kybernetes* **11**(1982).
Chailloux84.
    J. Chailloux, M. Devin, and J. M. Hullot, "Le_Lisp, a portable and efficient lisp system," *4th ACM Conference on lisp and functional programming*, (August, 1984).
Clancey84.
    W. J. Clancey, "Classification Problem Solving," *Proceeding of the National Conference on AI*, Austin, Texas, (1984).
Dubois80.
    D. Dubois and H. Prade, "Fuzzy Sets and Systems : Theory and Applications," *Mathematics in Sciences and Engineering Series* **144**Academic Press, (1980).
Dubois85.
    D. Dubois and H. Prade, "Combination and Propagation of Uncertainty with Belief Functions -A Reexamination-," *Proceedings of 9th IJCAI*, Los Angeles, (August 1985).
Duda76.
    R. O. Duda, P. E. Hart, and N. J. Nilsson, "Subjective Bayesien methods for rule-based inference systems," *National Computer Conference*, (1976).
Gandelin85.
    M-H. Gandelin, "Etude de faisabilite d'un système expert appliqué a l'identification automatique d'organismes zooplanctoniques," *Diplome d'études superieures spécialisées*, Université de Nice, (1985).
Granger85.
    C. Granger, "Reconnaissance d'objets par mise en correspondance en vision par ordinateur," *Thèse d'Université*, (1985).
Shortliffe75.
    E. H. Shortliffe and B. G. Buchanan, "A model of inexact reasoning in medicine," *Mathematical Biosciences* **23**(1975).
Thonnat85.
    M. Thonnat, "Automatic morphological description of galaxies and classification by an expert system," *Rapport de recherche INRIA*, (1985).
Thonnat86.
    M. Thonnat, "Semantic interpretation of 3D stereo data: finding the main structures," *submitted to 8th ICPR*, (October, 1986).
Zadeh78.
    L. A. Zadeh, "Fuzzy sets as a basis for a theory of possibility," *Fuzzy Sets and Systems* **1**(1978).

Advances in Artificial Intelligence - II
B. Du Boulay, D. Hogg and L. Steels (Editors)
© Elsevier Science Publishers B.V. (North-Holland), 1987

HEURISTICS FOR ANALOGY MATCHING

Stephen Owen

Dept. Artificial Intelligence
University of Edinburgh
80 South Bridge
Edinburgh EH1 1HN
Scotland

Abstract

We analyse the heuristics that underlie analogy matching algorithms, in particular the matchers of Munyer and Kling. These matchers are reconstructed, tested, modified and assessed, and the underlying heuristics are abstracted. We propose a more principled approach to analogy matching, involving flexible application of the heuristic criteria.

Keywords

Analogy, Partial Matching, Problem Solving.

1 Introduction - Motivation for Analogy

The desirability of having computers which can reason by analogy has been argued for many times in the AI literature, usually by reference to the usefulness of the analogical abilities of humans. My area of interest is analogical reasoning within automated or interactive problem solvers working within mathematics. Given a problem to solve which is suitably similar or analogous to one which has previously been solved, such a system would use its experience of solving the previous problem to help it solve the given problem. The time taken to solve the given problem in this way could be much less than that if the analogy had not been used.

If previously solved problems were stored together with their solutions, and could be retrieved efficiently, the problem solver could become more efficient and powerful over the course of its problem solving experience.

Analogy would also give a useful way of providing advice to an interactive proving system such as PRL [Staff 85].

Matching and Application

There are two main stages involved in solving a problem by analogy: firstly finding and then using the analogy. Finding an analogy means retrieving a previously solved problem and constructing an **analogy match** between the two; this stage is known as **analogy matching**. Using the analogy means applying the match obtained in the first stage to the solution of the solved problem (the **base** problem), and using the result to guide the search for a solution to the given problem (the **target** problem); this stage is known as **analogy application**. The process is illustrated in figure 1.

1..1 Matching

The matching stage is performed by an **analogy matching algorithm**. This takes as input logical representations of the two problems and either outputs an **analogy match** between them, or fails. A match is a correspondence between symbols in the logical representations of the two problems. Previous systems have differed in their representation of matches: in Kling's system, ZORBA [Kling 71], the correspondence is between symbols alone, the information about where the symbols occur in the problem statements being discarded. Thus, when given the two statements,

```
P(f(b, c), g(b))        Q(g(s), f(s,d)),
```

the following match might be returned :

```
Predicates : { P <---> Q }
Functions  : { f <---> f, g <---> g }
Constants  : { b <---> s, c <---> d }.
```

(In the Kling-matches displayed below, the distinctions between predicate, variable and constant associations are not shown, in order to show the order in which associations are made.) So analogy matches in ZORBA are *translations*. In Munyer's system [Munyer 81], the information about where the symbols occur in the formulae is retained in the match. The match is a correspondence between *nodes* in the *trees* which represent the statements. Thus, given the same statements, his matcher might return

```
P(f(b, c), g(b))


Q(g(s), f(s, d)).
```

Munyer calls the individual associations in a match **local maps**.

1..2   Application

Analogy systems **apply** analogies by first constructing the analogues of either the steps in the base solution (Munyer), the axioms used in the base solution (Kling), or perhaps both (see [Owen 85a]), according to the match between the problem statements. This is done with an **analogue construction rule**, the purpose of which is to produce a best guess at what the analogue of a given term is under a given analogy match. The result of the analogue construction is then used to guide the search for a solution to the target problem in some way. In Kling's system, this latter stage is very simple - the axiom base used for the target proof attempt is restricted to the set of analogous axioms. Munyer's system is more ambitious in that it uses the analogues of the base steps as *plan* for the solution of the target. The details of application, while important, will not concern us in this paper.

2   Motivation for reconstructions

There seems to be no general, formal rule which tells us what constitutes a good analogy match. It is in the nature of analogy that it is partly empirical - that is, we only know for sure whether a particular match is good or not after the application procedure has used it in trying to solve the target problem. Therefore

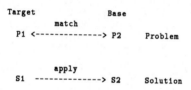

Figure 1: Overview

analogy matching algorithms use *heuristic criteria* to guide them in searching for good analogies. The heuristics that a particular matcher uses determine its *idea* (or rather its designer's) of what is a promising analogy.

But the descriptions given in the literature of existing matchers do not make it at all clear what heuristics they are using - there has been little discussion of the assumptions which matchers make. This makes it very hard to compare the existing matchers as to their performance - how much they achieve relative to the information they are given (see the discussion about semantic types below) - and hard also to extend and improve them.

I have reconstructed the matchers of Kling and Munyer (both in Prolog) in order to analyse their performance and underlying assumptions. The rationale behind such rational reconstructions of previous work is as follows: firstly, the discipline of having to transform the sometimes ambiguous descriptions of the algorithms given by their authors into computer programs forces one to examine the algorithms much more closely than one might do otherwise; secondly, having a working version of an algorithm makes it easy to test it on different examples from those around which it was designed, and thus to assess its generality.

Analogy matching, being in a poor state of explanation as described above, seemed a suitable area for rational reconstruction. More detailed reports of both reconstructions are available from the author.

3 Descriptions of algorithms and reconstructions

The first analogy matcher which I reconstructed was that of Munyer [Munyer 81].

3.1 Munyer

Munyer calls the terms input to his matcher **logical terms**. They are not necessarily first-order, since variables can have arguments (i.e. there can be variable functions and predicates). Munyer's matcher makes no distinction between predicates and functions. If logical *formulae* are to be matched, the logical connectives in them are treated as predicate/function symbols. So the matcher operates with an unrestricted and rather uniform syntax. Furthermore, it uses only the problem statements, and so has no semantics for the symbols in the statements. It is thus **purely syntactic**.

3.1.1 The algorithm

Munyer's matcher works in three stages, constructing intermediate matches from the first two. They are : grounding, deleting and adding.

Grounding

In this stage, an initial map is created in which

- Any pair of identical symbols, one from each term, are associated.
- Any variable in either term is associated with all symbols in the other term.

Deleting

This stage takes as input the output of the previous stage, ie two terms and an initial map between them, and deletes some (or all or none) of the local maps in the initial match. To explain how this stage works we need some definitions.

For symbols a and b in a term, define a > b if b occurs in the (unique) subterm headed by a. For local maps (a1,a2) and (b1,b2), (a1,a2) **dominates** (b1,b2) if a1 > b1 and b1 > b2. (a1,a2) **directly**

dominates (b1,b2) (in a match M) if (a1,a2) dominates (b1,b2) and there is no (c1,c2) in M, dominated by (a1,a2), which dominates (b1,b2).

If (a1,a2) directly dominates both (b1,b2) and (c1,c2), (b1,b2) and (c1,c2) **left-compete** (w.r.t. (a1,a2)) if b1 and c1 are in the same argument position of a1. (b1,b2) **left-supports** (a1,a2) if it has minimal **left penalty** among the maps with which it left-competes. The left penalty of (b1,b2) w.r.t. (a1,a2) is defined as

$$\text{C.P.} + \text{P.P.}$$

where C.P., the containment penalty, is the number of *unmapped* symbols between a1 and b1 in the tree structure of the left term, and P.P., the permutation penalty, is 1 if (b1,b2) permutes arguments of (a1,a2) and 0 if it doesn't. Right-competing and right-supporting are defined analogously.

Lastly, (b1,b2) **reinforces** (a1,a2) if it **either** left-supports **or** right-supports (a1,a2).

The deleting stage works by first calculating the reinforcement relations in the initial match, and then deleting any local maps which (a) share a node with another map **and** (b) do not reinforce any other map in the match. The latter stage is iterated, as a map which is deleted may be the only map which another had reinforced, so the latter should be deleted also.

The motivation behind this complicated procedure seems to be that we should retain a set of local maps which preserve the structure of the terms (this is behind the notion of direct dominance), and remove any alternative sets (this is behind the notion of competition).

Adding

This stage takes as input the result of the deleting stage and adds a local map between any pair of nodes in the two terms which are both unmapped in the existing match but whose parent nodes are mapped to each other.

Also, if the head symbols of the two terms are both unmapped a local map between them is added.

This step is not iterated.

3.1.2 Reconstruction

The reconstruction of Munyer's algorithm in Prolog proved to be fairly straightforward, although the details of the deleting stage are fiddly and make the program larger than might be expected. I have not been particularly concerned with efficiency, which I am sure could be improved, but the algorithm seems to be unavoidably expensive.

The structure of the entire program corresponds closely with the description of the algorithm given above, with predicates corresponding to the concepts of the algorithm (directly_dominates, perm_penalty, containment_penalty etc.). It has therefore been quite easy to modify the program when definitions in the algorithm have been changed (the program is **modular**).

The program has 60 Prolog predicates and 132 clauses.

3.1.3 Performance and modifications

Among the examples of analogy matches which Munyer claims his matcher finds are the following four:

(Note the second order variable, X, in the fourth example). Munyer does not go into *why* these matches are suitable analogies, but lists them as matches which a matcher should be able to construct. The matches produced by my reconstruction on the same examples are as follows:

```
   f(X)        f(a, g(a))        f(a,f(b,c))        f( g(a, h(a)), g(b, h(b)) )
   |            \                 |\ | |             \          /
   f(g(a))       h(a)             f(f(a,b),c)        f( X(a), X(b) )
```

(I subsequently confirmed these matches by going through the algorithm by hand). Analysis of the third example suggested that it is wrong to count only **unmapped** intermediate nodes in computing the containment penalty - this is why the internal (f,f) map is deleted in favour of the (a,a) and (c,c) maps. If this restriction was dropped, (f,f) would have equal left penalty with (c,c) and equal right penalty with (a,a) and would thus be exempted.

I made this change to the program, and tested the new version on Munyer's examples. The only change in result was in the third example above, for which the desired match was found. Since the performance wasn't worse on any of the examples, I will call this an improvement to the algorithm - improvement A.

Note that the first example should produce a first-order unification. But Munyer gives a 'proof' that his algorithm is complete for first-order unifiable terms (i.e. finds the m.g.u.). Analysis of the obviously faulty proof suggested that the proof would be valid if (B) the definition of reinforcement is strengthened so that (b1,b2) reinforces (a1,a1) if it supports (a1,a2) **both** on the left **and** on the right, and (C) any map which is maximal in the match w.r.t. **partial dominance** (a suitably defined refinement of dominance) is exempted from deletion.

With these changes made to the program, I tested it again on Munyer's examples. It got the right answers on all but one, the remaining one being the example with which Munyer illustrates his algorithm! Again, performance is not impaired on previously successful examples. I therefore call these changes improvements as well - improvements B and C. First-order completeness is finally achieved. (Without C, the algorithm is not even complete for *identical* first-order terms, a(a(a(b))) being a counter-example!)

3.1.4 Assessment of the algorithm

Munyer's matcher is extremely expensive computationally: since variables are associated with all symbols in the other term in grounding, the match which is passed to the deleting stage is usually large. In deleting, complex computations are performed on this match: this is where most of the c.p.u. time is spent. For example, in constructing the match

```
   even(X) & even(Y) --> even(X*Y)
   |  | | | /  |   | | ///
   odd(X) & odd(Y) --> odd(X*Y)
```

the program took 30 seconds of c.p.u. time. Considerable computational cost seems inherent to the structure of the algorithm. However, there are ways in which the matcher could be guided more than it is:

- consistency: no attention is paid, during matching, to the consistency of the match, particularly the variable bindings which it entails. Matches with inconsistent variable bindings are rejected at a later stage of the analogy process (see [Munyer 81]). But the complexity would be reduced if only consistent sets of variable bindings were considered in the first place. This would involve the development of several possible matches between a pair of terms which Munyer, for some reason, seems to want to avoid. The (relative) consistency of the predicate and variable mappings could be used to prune unpromising matches.

- syntactic types: Munyer's matcher blurs some syntactic distinctions which analogies tend to respect, for example the special status of the propositional connectives, and the distinction between predicates and functions. One way of exploiting these would be to construct only those local maps which respect the syntactic types during grounding, and put in those which don't, if at all, during adding.

3.1.5   General assessment of syntactic matching on terms

A purely syntactic analogy matcher, such as Munyer's is based on the hope that there will be enough clues about an analogy in the syntax for the solution of the base problem to be of use in the search for a solution to the target. In studying Munyer's matcher, the following problems with this philosophy have become apparent:

- Sometimes the analogy is not apparent in the syntax, for one of the following reasons:
  - **Ambiguous syntax problem**: there are several plausible syntactic matches and no syntactic clue as to the 'correct' one: in the following example, the correct match is given, which pairs cosine terms whose arguments are in corresponding arithmetic progression, but note that a syntactic matcher would have no reason for distinguishing this map from the other possible pairings of terms :

  - **Superficial difference problem**: the syntactic structures of the terms are substantially (but unimportantly for the analogy) different:

    A purely syntactic matcher is not able to 'see through' the irrelevant differences in representation (e.g. X^2 for $X*X$). Yet the analogy is clear to a human.

- **Multiple matches problem**: even if the analogy seems clear in the syntax, and one would expect a syntactic matcher to find it, for example

    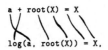

    it may well be that other, non-analogous, formulae would match just as well:

    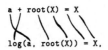

    for example, would be an equally valid match - the two pairs are syntactically indistinguishable - but would not be a fruitful one (the equations cannot be solved in the same way).

Of these three problems, we could live with the first two - we would just miss a proportion of useful matches. The multiple matches problem is more serious: as the knowledge base of solved problems expands, the chances of finding a fruitless match would increase until it was not worth the effort of the application routine.

The problems show that syntactic matching is not strong enough: it can't distinguish different plausible matches with the same term or with different terms.

3.1.6 Possible solutions

Adding extra (semantic) information along with the terms could help to solve the problems of the last section:

Ambiguous syntax

The method of solution for the base problem relies on the cosine arguments being in arithmetic progression. Numerical features of problem statements are often crucial to their solutions. By applying **constraint back-propagation** [Utgoff 83] (or related techniques), these features could be extracted from the base solution and used to *guide* matching - fruitless matches could be rejected quickly in favour of those which (approximately) preserve the features of the base.

Superficial difference

In order to 'see through' irrelevant syntactic differences between formulae, the matcher will need to construct analogies **modulo a theory**. In the example given above, it would need to know that $X^2 = X*X$ and that $A\&A \longleftrightarrow A$. This is very similar to 'built-in' unification [Raulefs 78]. The incorporation of such ability into a matcher would not be easy, involving extra search; it would also permit extra matches to be found, while not, in itself, blocking any; and so it would be best used along with the suggestions for **guiding** the matcher made above and below.

Multiple matches

It might be possible to use knowledge about the symbols in the terms to distinguish the promising matches from the bad ones. One fairly obvious way of doing this would be to use a **type hierarchy** so that, the closer two symbols were in the hierarchy, the more plausible they would be considered as analogues.

Kling uses 'semantic templates' in his matcher, which seem very similar to a type hierarchy. I went on to a reconstruction of Kling's matcher, with particular reference to its use of semantic types, which I describe next.

3.2 Kling

Kling's analogy matcher, INITIAL_MAP, is part of his analogy system ZORBA. INITIAL_MAP accepts as input two theorem descriptions, each of one of the forms

$$H_1 \& H_2 \& \ldots \& H_n \rightarrow C_1 \& C_2 \& \ldots \& C_m \quad \text{or} \quad C_1 \& C_2 \& \ldots \& C_m,$$

where each of the H's and C's is of the form

$$P(x_1, \ldots, x_r),$$

P being a predicate and the x's variables. The variables are implicitly universally quantified. Thus there are no functions or constants. Note that this is a more restricted syntax than that accepted by Munyer's matcher. Kling's claim that this syntax is suitable for mathematics is surely unfounded, but the algebra theorems around which Kling designed his matcher do fit naturally into this form.

INITIAL_MAP also has access to **semantic templates** for each of the predicates in the sentences to be matched. For example, the predicate group/2 has semantic template

$$structure(set, operation).$$

3.2.1 The algorithm

I.M. matches the hypotheses of the theorems with each other and similarly the conclusions; it does one of these first, then the other, using the match obtained from the first to guide the second.

Kling doesn't say in what order the two sub-matches are attempted. In my reconstruction, whichever of the conclusions and the hypotheses contains fewest atoms is attempted first, on the basis that it is usually easier to match smaller structures.

So, if the theorems to be matched are

$$A_1 \& A_2 \& \ldots \& A_n \rightarrow B_1 \& B_2 \& \ldots \& B_m \quad \text{and} \quad C_1 \& C_2 \& \ldots \& C_n \rightarrow D_1 \& D_2 \& \ldots \& D_m$$

and $m+s < n+r$, the module SETMATCH is called first on the conclusions, then the hypotheses.

SETMATCH breaks up into two submodules, SINGLEMATCH and MULTIMATCH. SINGLEMATCH pairs up the atoms in the sets which have unique semantic templates, and then MULTIMATCH pairs up the rest using the partial match from SINGLEMATCH as guidance.

Whenever a pair of atoms is associated, ATOMATCH is called to extract predicate and variable correspondences, which are added to the evolving match. If the atoms have identical semantic templates, the correspondences added are just those which preserve argument order. But Kling also wants to be able to find analogies in which, for example, group(Set, Op) is associated with ring(Set1, Op1, Op2), and these predicates do not have the same semantic templates. Their templates are structure(set,operation) and structure(set,operation,operation) respectively. Kling's solution to this problem is a hack. He allows a variable in one of the atoms to be associated with a consecutive sequence of variables in the other as long as (a) all the types involved are the same and (b) the correspondences preserve argument order. In this case, he would get

group <--> ring,   Set <--> Set1   and   [Op] <--> [Op1,Op2] .

If conditions (a) and (b) cannot be satisfied, ATOMATCH fails. I describe this as a hack because there is no reason, in general, why associations should preserve argument order - this depends on arbitrary choices made in formally representing the theorems.

The job of SINGLEMATCH and MULTIMATCH, then, is to decide on pairs of atoms to pass to ATOM-ATCH. SINGLEMATCH uses the following criteria in its decision:

1. If there is only one unpaired atom left on each side, associate them by default.

2. Associate pairs of atoms having the same semantic template.

3. Associate pairs of atoms whose predicate symbols are associated in the existing match.

4. Associate pairs of atoms whose predicate symbols have the same type.

1 is checked after any association is made. Otherwise 2, 3 and 4 are checked in that order.

If SINGLEMATCH cannot pair up all the atoms with unique semantic templates on each side, it fails. If it can, the partial match produced is passed on to MULTIMATCH, which considers the atoms on each side which have the same semantic templates as others. First, the atoms are grouped into their semantic blocks; then blocks are paired up using the following criteria in the same way that SINGLEMATCH used its criteria:

1. If there is only one unpaired block on each side, associate them by default.

2. Associate pairs of blocks which contain atoms whose predicate symbols are associated by the existing match.

3. Associate pairs of blocks whose atoms have predicates with the same semantic type, where this gives a unique association.

When a pair of blocks is associated by the above criteria, the submodule MULTIMATCH1 is called to pair up the atoms within the blocks. MULTIMATCH1 has a single criterion for doing this, based on the existing variable associations: if there is a pair of variables associated by the existing match, each of which occurs in only one atom in the appropriate block, then pair up the two atoms.

This completes the description of INITIAL_MAP.

3.2.2 Reconstruction

The reconstruction of INITIAL_MAP in Prolog turned out to be straightforward - considerably easier than Munyer's algorithm. The code has 46 predicates and 102 clauses. The modules in Kling's description of the algorithm translated easily into Prolog predicates.

3.2.3 Performance and modifications

I first tried the matcher on the algebra examples that Kling gives in [Kling 71]. There are several different ways of translating these (given in natural language) into logic. If 'corresponding' ways for analogous theorem pairs are not chosen, I.M. will almost certainly fail (there would be a superficial difference problem).

The performance of the reconstruction was satisfactory on most of the algebra examples that Kling gives in [Kling 71]; where there were representation choices, the matcher was successful on at least one of them. The following is one of Kling's theorem pairs and the resulting match obtained by the program:

```
HYPOTHESES                          HYPOTHESES
group(g,*)                          ring(r,**,++)
propernormal(m,g,*)                 properideal(n,r,**,++)
factorstructure(x,g,m)              factorstructure(y,r,n)
simplegroup(x,*)                    simplering(y,**,++)

CONCLUSION                          CONCLUSION
maximalgroup(m,g,*)                 maximalring(n,r,**,++)
```

```
                          MATCH

        maximalgroup <-------> maximalring
                   m <-------> n
                   g <-------> r
                 [*] <-------> [**,++]
      factorstructure <-------> factorstructure
                   x <-------> y
         propernormal <-------> properideal
               group <-------> ring
          simplegroup <-------> simplering
```

The reader is encouraged to work through this example by hand.

While the program performed as desired on Kling's algebra examples, the heavy use of the semantic templates worried me. All of Kling's theorem pairs come from essentially the same global analogy between group theory and ring theory. It seemed to me that it was Kling's knowledge of this global analogy which led him to choose the particular semantic templates which he did for the examples. Thus it is no surprise and no great achievement that the algorithm finds the correct matches in these cases. There is a strong suspicion of circularity about this.

After going through Kling's algebra examples, I tried the matcher on some new examples. One of these was the following pair:

$$-(x + y) = -x + -y \qquad \text{and} \qquad 1/(x.y) = 1/x \ .1/y$$

When transformed into Kling's syntax, these become:

Example A

```
(times(x,y,z)                    (plus(x,y,z)
& inv(z,z1)                      & minus(z,z1)
& inv(x,x1)                      & minus(x,x1)
& inv(y,y1)                      & minus(y,y1)
& times(x1,y1,r))                & plus(x1,y1,r))


--> equal(z1,r)                  --> equal(z1,r)
```

where new functional predicates are introduced to replace the functions. I chose very general types - 'relfn' for all the functional predicates and 'rel' for equal/2. I.M. fails on this easy example, because MULTIMATCH fails on the hypotheses, not being able to pair up the semantic blocks with condition 3. If MULTIMATCH is given the extra semantic template condition that SINGLEMATCH has, the problem would be solved. With this change made to the program, performance is not impaired on any previous examples.

Another example which I tried the matcher on was:

```
    rational(p)                      rational(p)
& irrational(q)                  & irrational(q)
& plus(p,q,r)                    & unequal(p,0)
                                 & times(p,q,r)
--> irrational(r)                --> irrational(r) .
```

General semantic templates were again used. The matcher fails on this example, since it requires a 1-1 association of atoms in order to succeed. The failure occurs in SINGLEMATCH. Since extra conditions on one side often occur in analogies, allowing SINGLEMATCH to succed if there is one atom left on one side seems sensible. With this change made, the matcher finds the right match, and, again, performance on previous examples is not impaired.

Another example where the performance of the matcher was not as I expected is shown below:

```
HYPOTHESES                       HYPOTHESES
group(g,*)          ⌐             ⌐ring(r,**,++)
abeliangroup(h1,*)  |             | commutativering(s1,**,++)
abeliangroup(h2,*)  ⌐             ⌐ commutativering(s2,**,++)
subgroup(h1,g,*)    ⌐             ⌐ subring(s1,r,**,++)
subgroup(h2,g,*)    ⌐             ⌐ subring(s2,r,**,++)
intersection(h1,h2,h3)           intersection(s1,s2,s3)

CONCLUSION                       CONCLUSION
abeliangroup(h3,*)               commutativering(s3,**,++)
```

```
        abeliangroup <-------> commutativering
                  h3 <-------> s3
                 [*] <-------> [**,++]
        intersection <-------> intersection
                  h1 <-------> s1
                  h2 <-------> s2
            subgroup <-------> subring
                   g <-------> r
```

The match lacks the expected group <—> ring association. This is because MULTIMATCH1 cannot pair up the group and ring atoms within the first pair of semantic blocks shown.

There seem to me to be two possible solutions to this problem:

- MULTIMATCH1 could be given a default condition, like those in SINGLEMATCH and MULTI-MATCH. The group and ring atoms would then be ATOMATCHed by default and the final match would be complete.

- The application of MULTIMATCH1 to the pairs of semantic blocks could be more flexible, allowing it to interleave work on the various pairs, so that if it gets stuck on one, it can move on to another one and return to the first if progress is made on the second.

The second modification is more principled than the first (defaults should be avoided if possible). Again, performance is not impaired on previous examples.

3.2.4 Assessment

SINGLEMATCH, MULTIMATCH and MULTIMATCH1 all try to pair up parts of the sentences by reference, in part, to the existing partial match. But all of the tests are *monotonic* in the existing match - that is, they force an association if some related association has already been made. The existing match is never used to explicitly *inhibit* an association, which might be a good thing to do if the association in question would be inconsistent with the match. The lack of lateral inhibition in INITIAL_MAP may be the result of the fact that it never had to search for analogies in a knowledge base of solved problems (Kling fed it with pairs of problems which he knew were analogous). In the more realistic situation, it is important for the matcher to fail on non-analogous problems as well as to succeed on analogous ones, and this is where consistency checks (and other strength criteria) could be useful.

A more serious problem with the matcher is shown up by the following example:

Equation	In Kling's syntax
root(x) + a = b	root(x,z) & plus(z,a,x) & equal(x,b)
root(x+1) + a = b	plus(x,1,y) & root(y,z) & plus(z,a,x) & equal(x,b)

In the first sentence, all the atoms have unique semantic templates, whereas in the second the two plus atoms are in a semantic block together. Thus, SINGLEMATCH pairs up the two root atoms and the two equal atoms, and leaves the plus atom in the top sentence un-matched. Then MULTIMATCH is called between a single block on one side and nothing on the other, and so fails.

It is the basic SINGLEMATCH/MULTIMATCH distinction which is at fault here: where there is an atom which ought to be unmatched, its semantic template may coincide with that of another which ought to be matched by SINGLEMATCH, which will prevent the latter from ever being considered by SINGLEMATCH. It seems likely that this situation will occur often in non-trivial analogies, and thus that the whole matching strategy of INITIAL_MAP will have to be changed to cope.

3.2.5 Assessment of the use of semantic types in matching

The idea behind the use of semantic types in analogy matching is that symbols of the same/similar type make good analogues. Thus types are used to give *a priori* plausibility judgements for analogies. Semantic types can be thought of as expressing information about global analogies within the domain; i.e. symbols of the same/similar type are likely to have structurally similar axioms/operators associated with them. Thus, given that the symbols occur in structurally similar formulae, and regarding a solution as a sequence of structural rearrangements leading from a start to a finish, each arising from an axiom or operator, it is likely that the two formulae will have similar solutions. Thus semantic types will be effective, when used along with the **partial homomorhism heuristic** (see below).

However, as noted earlier, there is a danger of circularity in the use of types i.e. that the types encode the analogies that the matcher is supposed to find for itself. This will be so if (a) the types are specified by the user *and* (b) the matcher does not go beyond the analogies encoded in the types. These conditions are, unfortunately, met by Kling's matcher, which repeatedly reconstructs the global analogy between group theory and ring theory which is represented by the types.

To avoid (b), the matcher would need to use the types more flexibly than Kling does - it ought not to be based around the enforcement of type preservation, as I.M. is. A more structured type **hierarchy** would be helpful for this, as it would give a notion of *similar* type.

To avoid (a), the analogy system could create/refine its type hierarchy over the course of its analogical problem solving experience: roughly, the new types would be sets of symbols which had often been associated in previous analogies. In [Owen 85b], the learning of types using analogies is gone into in detail.

4   Summary and conclusions

Neither of the algorithms described provides a robust and useful analogy matcher. Munyer's algorithm, even with the improvements, is dogged by the fact that it is purely syntactic, and thus suffers from all the problems of synactic matching discussed above. Kling's algorithm has no solution to the first two problems, and its solution to the third is inflexible and circular. Furthermore, Kling's matcher is incapable of producing matches which involve (a) any argument permutation and (b) matched predicates with one or more unmatched arguments, both of which occur often in analogies.

The purpose of this paper is to describe heuristics for analogy matching. The following five heuristics are the basis of the matchers which have been reconstructed:

- partial homomorphism heuristic: an analogy match is likely to be a partial homomorphism between the terms to be matched i.e. the associations in a match are expected to respect the structure of the matched terms. Kling uses this heuristic in ATOMATCH, where variable associations which preserve argument order are extracted from prior associations of the containing predicates. Munyer uses the heuristic both in the deleting and adding stages, which are based around the idea that associations in a match should reinforce each other if the pairs of symbols they connect are in the same relative positions within their terms.

- syntactic type heuristic: symbols which are associated in a match are likely to be of the same syntactic type. This heuristic is built in to the structure of Kling's algorithm, which never considers associating symbols unless they have the same syntactic type. Surprisingly, Munyer makes no use of this heuristic.

- consistent/efficient translation heuristic: the translation between symbols implied by an analogy match ought to be consistent, in the sense that the mapping should be as near to 1-1 as possible, and efficient, in the sense of matching relatively large structures with a relatively small mapping. (This heuristic is used in the related field of **inductive generalisation** [Diettrich 79].) Kling uses a form of the heuristic in SINGLEMATCH, MULTIMATCH and MULTIMATCH1, when atoms are paired whose predicates or variables are already associated in the match; i.e. the expected consistency of the match is used to enforce correspondences which in turn increase the efficiency of the match. An additional use of the heuristic, not made by Kling, would be to explicitly inhibit associations inconsistent with the developing match. Munyer does not use this heuristic at all during matching.

- identical symbols heuristic: symbols which are associated in a match are (*a priori*) likely to be identical. Munyer uses this heuristic in order to get his algorithm going, and then proceeds with the partial homomorphism heuristic. Kling does not use this heuristic.

- semantic type heuristic: symbols which are associated in a match are (*a priori*) likely to have the same (Kling) or *similar* (more general) semantic type. This heuristic dominates Kling's algorithm, being the main source of possible predicate associations. As discussed above, this heuristic is important but problematic.

These heuristics all have validity. My criticism of the matchers discussed here is that they are used rather inflexibly (particularly the last two). It seems that any heuristic criterion will only be valid some of the time. Therefore it would be better to use the heuristics flexibly within a best partial match framework, such as that proposed by Hayes-Roth [HayesRoth 78]. The matcher would prefer, and be guided towards, matches which respect the heuristics, but would not be precluded from finding those which didn't. This is particularly important for the learning of types, which can only be achieved when existing type information is overridden.

References

[Diettrich 79]   T.G. Diettrich and R.S. Michalski. Learning and generalization of characteristic descriptions: evaluation criteria and comparative review of selected methods. In *Proceedings of the Sixth IJCAI*, International Joint Conference on Artificial Intelligence, 1979.

[HayesRoth 78] F. Hayes-Roth. The role of partial and best matches in knowledge systems. In *Pattern-Directed Inference Systems*, Academic Press, 1978.

[Kling 71]   R.E. Kling. A paradigm for reasoning by analogy. *Artificial Intelligence*, 2, 1971.

[Munyer 81]   J.C. Munyer. *Analogy as a Means of Discovery in Problem-Solving and Learning*. PhD thesis, Univ. Calif. Santa Cruz, 1981.

[Owen 85a]   S.G. Owen. *Analogy in Artificial Intelligence - Thesis Proposal*. Working Paper 176, Edinburgh University, 1985.

[Owen 85b]   S.G. Owen. Getting better at analogy. 1985.

[Raulefs 78]   Siekmann J. Szabo P. Raulefs, P. and E. Unvericht. A short survey on the state of the art in matching and unification problems. *AISB Quarterly*, issue 32:17–21, December 1978.

[Staff 85]   The PRL Staff. *Implementing Mathematics with the NUPRL proof development system*. 1985.

[Utgoff 83]   P.E. Utgoff. Adjusting bias in concept learning. In *Proceedings of the Eighth IJCAI*, International Joint Conference on Artificial Intelligence, 1983.

Advances in Artificial Intelligence - II
B. Du Boulay, D. Hogg and L. Steels (Editors)
© Elsevier Science Publishers B.V. (North-Holland), 1987

GENERALIZATION-BASED RETRIEVAL

Lisa F. Rau

General Electric Company
Corporate Research and Development
Schenectady, NY 12301 USA
and
Computer and Information Sciences Department
University of Massachusetts, Amherst
Amherst, Massachusetts, USA 01003

ABSTRACT

The ability to intelligently store, retrieve and generalize experiential knowledge helps a system understand the present, predict the future, and learn from the past. There are problems with previous approaches to conceptual indexing and retrieval. Some require the ability to anticipate indices that might be useful in the future, or the ability to know the point at which all relevant input has been seen. Other organizations of episodic knowledge for retrieval preclude or make more difficult the incorporation and use of semantic and world knowledge.

A modified form of spreading activation is used to attack the problem of implicit, knowledge-intensive indexing for appropriate retrieval and generalization of experiences. This technique has certain advantages over other approaches to conceptual episodic retrieval. First, indexing and retrieval are *automatic* and *incremental*. Second, it not only makes use of explicit semantic connections, but requires them. Finally, experiences stored or entered at an abstract level index specific experiences and *vice versa*.

The importance of an explicit theory of the structure of memory is stressed, and the distinction between episodic and semantic information maintained, with a middle layer of conceptual abstraction that facilitates learning via generalization. The indexing and retrieval techniques described have been implemented in a set of tools called MEMORE (MEmory Mechanism for Organization and REtrieval).

1. Introduction

Intelligent, appropriate retrieval of experiential knowledge is a difficult and important problem (Schank, 1982). It can be restated as the problem of retrieving long-term memory structures that might be useful or necessary to help in performing intelligent tasks in a knowledge-based system. Some of these intelligent tasks are predicting, inferencing, drawing analogies, generalizing, planning and understanding. The problem is hard because index information obtained from a current situation or experience to be used in retrieval may or may not be present, and if present, may appear at varying levels of conceptual abstraction, or contain irrelevant or unimportant information. Closely associated with the retrieval problem is the problem of storing experiential knowledge

---

Special thanks go to Dr. Paul Jacobs and Professors Wendy Lehnert, Paul Utgoff, and Robert Wilensky for their helpful comments on various versions of this paper.

appropriately so that it may be efficiently retrieved in the future.

A simple technique of semantic priming and intersection search within an appropriately structured episodic memory addresses problems with previous approaches, both in the physical organization of memory for retrieval (Kolodner 1980, Lebowitz, 1983) and with different marker passing schemes (Charniak, 1982). This process produces a structural match between arbitrary graphs, by utilizing semantic constraints on nodes that can be said to match, and relations between nodes for graph-orienting information. Some important questions answered by this technique are:

1) How does one efficiently match arbitrary graph structures present in a network-style representation?

2) How does one decide *a priori* what features of experiences will be used in the future for retrieval?

3) How does one know that there might be a relevant experience in memory, and how does one know when enough indexical information has been given to retrieve it?

It is often most effective to treat the problem of determining where to store new experiences in memory along with the problem of retrieving related experiences and generalizing them. This is because regardless of any particular implementation, the right "place" for a new experience is often "near" where other similar experiences are stored. Thus, finding the "place" for a new experience allows one more easily to find similar experiences for generalization at the same time. It is because of this phenomenon that the approach to retrieval of experiences discussed here is said to be "generalization-based". The focus of this paper, however, is on the retrieval mechanism and associated requirements for conceptual indexing, and not on the generalization process.

In this paper, two parts of a four-part memory mechanism which has been implemented will be described. These are the memory organization, storage and integration component and the spreading activation retrieval components of the MEMORE (MEmory Mechanism for Organization and REtrieval) system. The parts that will not be described are (1) the generalization component that generalizes similar experiences retrieved, and (2) the retrieval filter component, which filters experiences retrieved by performing a simple structural matching operation. Below is a flowchart illustrating the flow of control and system organization of the components of the MEMORE system. Asterisks designate the components which will be presented here.

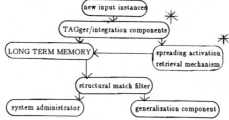

After the description of the system, it will be compared and contrasted to other relevant work. Finally, the limitations of this approach along with future directions will be discussed.

2. Overview

Indexing and retrieval in the MEMORE system have some important features which have advantages over other approaches. These are:

1) Indexing and retrieval are automatic and spontaneous

2) Indexing and retrieval are incremental

3) Cross-indexing is automatic between specific concepts and abstract concepts

Indexing and retrieval are automatic in that the instantiation of new experiences in the system is all that is necessary for them to be appropriately indexed, and for retrieval to occur. That is, there is no function in the system called "integrate-into-memory" or "fetch". In this regard, a demon-driven retrieval mechanism may also be classified as having the property of automatic retrieval (Charniak, Riesbeck and McDermott, 1980). Indexing is automatic because experiences stored are contents-addressable. The components of experiences automatically induce the indices used to retrieve the experiences.

Briefly, this happens as follows. As new experiences unfold to the system, instances of existing semantic categories in the system are created. This instantiation causes parts of previously stored memories to be marked. At the point at which enough components of one or more memories are marked, the memory or memories are automatically considered as potentially relevant to the situation at hand. Indexing and retrieval are incremental in that a series of input concepts continues to contribute activation to episodes in memory until enough components have been activated to overcome the episode's threshold level of activation. Cross-indexing occurs automatically from specific concepts to abstract concepts and *vice versa* by virtue of the spreading activation process to be described.

3. Structure of Knowledge in Memory

The MEMORE system manipulates long-term memory conceptual structures which are represented in the KODIAK (Wilensky, 1984) Knowledge Representation language. This is a hierarchical, network-type language, capable of expressing arbitrary concepts in a uniform manner.

One omission in many AI systems is the lack of a clear theory of the structure of memory. At one extreme, there are theories of memory such as the dynamic memory theory of Schank (Schank, 1982) that do not explictly incorporate semantic knowledge into their primarily episodic memories. At another extreme, there are some story understanding or inferencing systems *(cf.* Charniak, 1982; Quillian, 1958) that treat knowledge about the relationship between suicide and rope, for example, as semantic and have no concern for the presence of experiences in memory of such situations, or how to store *new* inputs and experiences in such a memory. That is, there is another connection between "rope" and "suicide" in an intelligent system besides the hypothesized semantic intersection at the "hanging" node. That connection is that both rope and suicide are elements of specific experiences we have heard about happening, where victims have commited suicide by hanging.

In the MEMORE system, knowledge stored is either specific, abstract or semantic. An example of a specific memory is the memory of John hanging himself with a rope yesterday. A traditional episodic memory (Tulving, 1972) is composed of specific memories. An example of an abstract memory is the abstraction or generalization across all specific experiences we may have heard about where people have hung themselves. Abstract memories are on the border between specific memories and semantic memory. Semantic memory is the memory or knowledge of what "ropes" are and what "hanging" is. Semantic memory is used in understanding and making inferences about the input to the system.

This tri-partite division of memory represents a continuum, where the three divisions represent the most specific level, the most general level, and everything else in between. At the most specific level, there are things that happen in the world, composed of particular unique instantiations of concepts. Specific memories may abstract through generalization, and these abstractions may abstract. The following diagram illustrates the structure of long-term memory with associated examples.

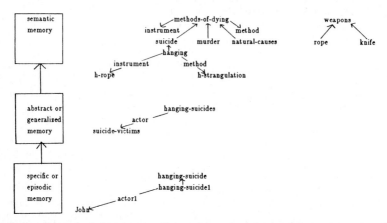

Both specific and abstract memories are quantized into memory packets, not unlike Memory Organization Packets or MOPs (Schank, 1982). Associated with each experience is a simple numerical threshold, representing the number of features in the experience that must be marked before retrieval of that experience will occur.

4. Description of System - Integration of New Experiences

Concepts are instantiated by other components of the system during the understanding and response to the input. These components may be a parsing mechanism, a deep understanding or goal-analyzing mechanism, a planning mechanism, or an inferencing mechanism to name a few. The concepts instantiated represent the understanding of the input and the new concepts created in making inferences or reasoning about the input. These new concepts are instantiations of existing categories in the system. For example, given an input experience "John hung himself", a new instance of hanging-suicide would be created with actor John, as illustrated above.

All the instances instantiated in an experience must be connected together so they are known to be part of the same experience. In some sense, in the MEMORE system, the determination of what will be used as an index to a memory has been changed to the problem of how to assign components to memories. This is because all elements of a given experience are indices to that experience. This is nice because the problem becomes one of knowledge representation instead of processing, and indices are implicitly declaratively defined. What has not been discussed here is how the determination is made of where one memory starts and another starts. In this system and others, this problem is finessed, or perhaps ignored.

In the real world, however, experiences are not cleanly divided into discrete packages. Multiple experiences happen in parallel, overlapping, discontinuously and constantly. In light of this, the issue of determining what is a conceptually coherent, identifiable experience becomes important. This problem is difficult and critical, and has not been adequately addressed here or in other work. However, the need to have a dynamic and incremental retrieval process becomes very important when one cannot tell when all the relevant information has become available, and the process described here does have this property.

The retrieval algorithm in the MEMORE system presupposes that the components of specific or abstract (as opposed to semantic) memories be tagged with a TAG that indicates to which memories they belong. Any given component may be tagged with more than one TAG, signifying that it is a component of more than one identifiable memory. Thus the "Mary" concept is TAGged with (connected to) every experience that involves her. TAGs can be thought of as associative links which link together the components of memories. For example, if a system experienced walking down an icy sidewalk and then slipping, the concepts that make up the experience of walking down an icy sidewalk would be marked with a TAG. Slipping would be marked with a different TAG. Also, the combined episode of walking down the icy sidewalk and slipping would be marked with yet another TAG.

TAGging simply connects components of experience together, and allows the same component (i.e., Mary) to be shared with all experiences that contain that component. The TAGger is the process by which new experiences are integrated with existing experiences and semantic memory.

Each experience has two registers associated with it. One is the experience's threshold value, and the other is the current level of activation of the experience. When the current level of activation exceeds the threshold, the experience is retrieved.

5. Description of System - Retrieval Algorithm

Retrieval is performed by a process of priming or spreading activation. As concepts are instantiated in the system, instances of concepts that are related via category membership links are marked (primed; activated). When a certain subset of the concepts in a memory are marked, the entire memory or memories are either handed to the system administrator for further consideration (this corresponds to spontaneous retrieval). The system administrator is the component of the system which receives experiences that have been spontaneously retrieved, and evaluates them for their potential use in generating expectations of what might happen next in the current situation, or what to do in the current situation, based on the experiences retrieved.

The system operates in the following manner:

1) At the time of instantiation, concepts are marked according to the rules which follow (see "priming rules" below). Each concept marked adds one to all of its TAG's episode level of activation.

2) Concepts which are marked check their TAG threshold to see if enough other concepts in the experience have also been marked.

3) If the TAG threshold has been exceeded, an *intersection* has been detected.

4) Memories satisfying the check made in (3) are passed to the filter. The filter performs a simple check to ensure that the match is valid, and if so, the entire experience is handed to system administrator for consideration.

5) All memories that are passed to the system administrator component are unmarked.

The retrieval algorithm effectively ignores components of the input experiences which do not have corresponding components in other episodes that might be retrieved. That is, components of experiences in the input cause other concepts to be marked, but if those other concepts are not components of relevant experiences, the marking does not contribute to retrieval. In this sense, stored memories "pick out" or activate what is relevant to them and disregard other inputs, in the same way that the process of set intersection yields only the common components of the sets being intersected. This is one factor which makes the retrieval algorithm robust, and memories contents-addressable. The algorithm is incremental in that experiences may mark parts of memories at one time and other parts at some later time.

The rules which guide how activation or marks are passed through the conceptual hierarchy are given below. These rules were formulated to decrease the possibility of retrieving memories that have limited predictive capacity or relevance to the current situation.

5.1. Priming Rules

The rules given below produce the effect that all instances of concepts that are components of memories and are children of the incoming parent of the parent of the incoming instance in the conceptual hierarchy get marked. Also, all instances of concepts that are components of memories and are *direct* instances of concepts that are parents of the incoming instance get marked. This rule prevents everything in the hierarchy from being marked, and limits what is marked to a level of conceptual abstraction supported by the presence of a direct instance at that level.

The following examples show where components of memories would cross-index each other, and when components of memories would not. Double arrows between instances (concepts with numbers following them) signify cross-indexing. Single headed arrows signify where the instantiation of one concept will activate the concept pointed to, but not *vice versa*. Note that each instance is part of a specific memory which is not shown in this diagram. For example, "fish3" may be part of the memory of the fish you ate for dinner last night that was of an indeterminate variety.

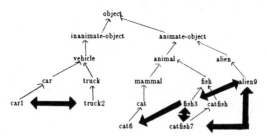

Rules

1) Mark only concepts that are components of specific or abstract memories. These concepts are marked with TAGs.

2) The categories the incoming instance belongs to are determined (Categories-of A).

3) Determine the concepts in the reflexive, transitive closure along category membership links of Categories-of(Categories-of A).

4) Direct instances of concepts in this reflexive, transitive closure are marked. Each marked concept increases the current activation value of each of its TAGs.

5) Episodes which just had components marked are checked if the current activation exceeds the threshold level.

Example

The following diagram illustrates a simple example of how an experience of driving on a wet road and slipping would remind a system of walking on a icy sidewalk and slipping. The curved arrows indicate the flow of activation through the network. Once all the components in the experience of walking on an icy sidewalk and slipping have been marked, the entire episode would be handed to the system administrator, for a spontaneous reminding ("This road is as slippery as the sidewalk I slipped on last night"), a prediction, ("The pedestrians must be having trouble on the sidewalk as well"), a plan formation ("I better drive more slowly to avoid slipping some more"), or a generalization ("I guess wet, icy surfaces are slippery").

The numbers assigned to concepts play the role of TAGs in this example. Note that not all the curved arrows are included in this diagram for simplicity. For example, "slip1" and "slip2" are both instances of the "slip" category, so that the instantiation of "slip1" would mark the remembered slipping of "slip2". Also note that in this particular example, all instances shown are marked, and the match occurs with other instances at the same level of conceptual abstraction.

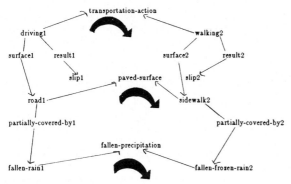

6. Related Research

The approach to retrieval taken in the MEMORE system has a number of intellectual antecedents. Amongs these are work on episodic memory indexing and retrieval (DeJong 1979, Kolodner 1980, Lebowitz 1983, Dyer 1981, Schank 1982), work on spreading activation, marker passing and distributed representations (Quillian 1968, Collins and Loftus 1975, Charniak 1982), and work on learning by analogy (Winston, 1980). In this section, the major similarities and differences between MEMORE and the above work will be briefly outlined.

6.1. Learning by Analogy

Winston (Winston, 1980) describes a similar algorithm for matching plot units of Shakespearean plays to do learning and reasoning with analogy. The most obvious difference between this work and the MEMORE system is the purpose of retrieval. In the MEMORE system, matches where all components of experiences correspond are useful as indicated in the slipping example above, whereas in Winston's system, if all components correspond, nothing would be left to predict by analogy.

Winston's system explicitly examines every episode against the input to determine a numerical degree to which they match. In the MEMORE system, such a computationally complex process is reduced to an automatic mark-and-compare operation. After a new instance is instantiated, a set of existing instances are marked according to the priming rules given. Each TAG count is incremented, and it is compared to the TAG threshold. When a TAG threshold is exceeded, it is a match worth considering.

Finally, Winston's program attaches TAGs (called APPEARS-IN) not only to the instances in the experiences, but to every semantic concept above those instances in the hierarchy as well. For example, given "Juliet loves Romeo", not only would Juliet, loves and Romeo be TAGged with the same APPEARS-IN TAG, but woman (above Juliet), man (above Romeo) etc. Such TAGging would certainly become excessive if the database contained more stories. In MEMORE, these marks are computed and removed as needed.

6.2. Memory indexing and Retrieval

For the purposes of this discussion, I will refer to work related to memory retrieval and organization included in (DeJong 1979, Kolodner 1980, Lebowitz 1983, Dyer 1981, Schank, 1982) as "MOPs systems" after the common data structure used in this work. The goals of appropriate reminding, combined with processes to perform memory storage and generalization are the same goals as in the MEMORE system. In both the MOPs system and the MEMORE system, intelligent reminding of experiences in memory is used to guide the formation of inferences, expectation and generalizations.

The primary difference between the MEMORE and the MOPs system lies in the method of retrieval of memories, and how that retrieval subsequently governs the formation of generalizations. The MEMORE system indexes episodes incrementally and opportunistically. What this means is that as concepts are instantiated in the system, related concepts get primed. Whenever enough concepts have been instantiated to cause a memory to be retrieved, retrieval occurs. Thus there is no need to know beforehand *when* to "fetch", or *what* to use as an indexing key. All information is a potential candidate. This includes high level thematic information like the kind used by Dyer in his BORIS and MORRIS systems (Dyer, 1981, 1983). In CyFr (Schank, Kolodner, and DeJong, 1980) for example, only information that *differentiates* the current episode from episodes known about is used in retrieving that episode.

Finally, the approach to indexing is fundamentally different from the discrimination net-based approach to indexing used in the MOPs systems. Lebowitz (Lebowitz, 1983) identifies the central problem with discrimination nets to perform matching of arbitrary structural descriptions, which the MEMORE system addresses. An example he gives of a limitation with his RESEARCHER system is its inability to recognize that a read/write head that is described as "a direct part of a disc-drive" is the same as a read/write head that is described as part of a "read/write assembly" in another. In MEMORE, spreading activation from input concepts allows for more flexible matching of concepts.

6.3. Spreading Activation

Spreading activation as implemented in the MEMORE system is more accurately described as a form of marker passing (Charniak, 1982), in that digital markers are passed from node to node, not analog values. Analog values will probably be used in the future to weight components, however, this has not been shown to be necessary with the current implementations, and introduces some additional complexity into the system. The spreading activation algorithm differs from traditional spreading activation schemes *(cf.* Quillian, 1968, Collins and Loftus, 1975) in two significant ways.

First, the form of intersection search employed differs from most forms of intersection search in that markers do not intersect except at the episode level. Intersections are not necessarily binary. In marker passing schemes (*cf.* Charniak, 1982), the path between two concepts indicates the information being searched for. For example, given "John wanted to commit suicide and bought a rope", the connection between "rope" and "suicide" leads through the "hanging" node, where this path could be used to represent an inference that John meant to hang himself, or a plan to commit suicide when a rope was present. In the MEMORE system, there need be no semantic connection between the concept of "rope" and the concept of "suicide". Intersections of concepts matter only when some subset of concepts in any given episode have been marked. Thus both rope and suicide concepts are present in an abstract episode of people hanging themselves, and it is this episode that is retrieved.

Second, and related to the above point, input concepts prime only specific or abstract episodic memories. Traditionally, spreading activation is used to prime members of semantic categories, and find connections between concepts in semantic memory. In this formulation, there is no marking of concepts in semantic memory at all. Semantic categories are used to guide the marking of instances in memories, but the semantic categories themselves are not marked.

7. Future Topics for Discussion

There are some important aspects of the marker passing algorithm not discussed here. One is the mechanism by which marks are deleted from memory. Components of episodes retrieved are explictly unmarked, but unless something is done about all the other marks, saturation of the knowledge base would ensue. Briefly, marks decay and are deleted as a function of time between incoming episodes, and their potential relevance in processing. Also, when an episode has components marked from instances widely spread out in time, the integrity of those marks is questioned.

Another system component that plays an important role in the MEMORE system and not discussed here is the system administrator. Ultimately, the applicability and potential for use of experiences retrieved lies with this component. The retrieval algorithm described here is best viewed as a first pass, with many experiences retrieved never actually being of use in processing.

Also not discussed here is how the value of the episode threshold level is determined. Thresholds are chosen somewhat arbitrarily, but conservatively. Having a threshold that errs on the low side prevents potentially useful memories from being ignored. Memories retrieved that are not used are filtered by the system adminstrator, as discussed above.

Spreading activation applied to retrieval and generalization of episodic memories should allow for the easy incorporation of weights on components of memories, to facilitate retrieval weighted by interesting features. The next step is to develop heuristics to guide the assignment of weights to components of memories, based on the frequency of use, and predictive power.

8. Conclusions

Spreading activation is a simple yet powerful tool when applied to the problem of retrieval of arbitrary conceptual clusters, represented in a network language. Using semantic priming as a retrieval mechanism has not previously been applied to the task of retrieving complicated network-style memories. It has a number of clear advantages to other methods. First, it takes the computationally intractable problem of determining all possible matches between arbitrary graphs and makes it into a simple problem through the exploitation of semantic constraints of possible node and link values and orientations.

Second, spreading activation allows for incremental retrieval. That is, multiple components of experiences may combine in memory to cause retrieval of one or more memories. Using spreading activation also facilitates obtaining the goals of automatic or spontaneous retrieval, and eliminates the need for specifying the indices to retrieve memories *a priori.*

Because memories are contents-addressable, the content of a new incoming experience is what causes similar experiences to be retrieved. Memories stored are *automatically* indexed by other instances of the categories that the components of the memories are categories of. They are also indexed by instances of categories both more abstract than and more specific than the categories the components of the memories are instances of in the conceptual hierarchy. It is because of this rich conceptual indexing that specific memories stored at a very detailed level may cause specific memories stored at a general level to be retrieved and *vice versa.*

9. References

Charniak, E. Passing markers: A theory of contextual influence in language comprehension. *Cognitive Science, 7,*(3), pp. 171-190, 1983.

Charniak, E., Riesbeck, C. K., and McDermott, D.V. *Artificial Intelligence programming,* Hillsdale, NJ: Lawrence Erlbaum Associates, 1980.

Collins, A.M. and Loftus, E.F. A spreading-activation theory of semantic processing. *Psychological Review,* 82, pp. 407-425. 1975,

DeJong, G.. *Skimming Stories in Real Time: An Experiment in Integrated Understanding* (Research Report #158). Department of Computer Science, Yale University, New Haven, CT, 1979.

Dyer, M.G. In *Proceedings of the Eight International Joint Conference on Artificial Intelligence*, Understanding stories through morals and remindings, Karlsruhe, West Germany, 1983.

Dyer, M. G. The role of TAUs in narratives. In *Proceedings of the Third Annual Conference of Cognitive Science Society*, Berkeley, CA 1981.

Kolodner, J. *Retrieval and Organizational Strategies in Conceptual Memory: A Computer Model.* Research Report #187. Yale University Press. November, 1980.

Lebowitz, M. Researcher: An overview In *Proceedings of the National Conference on Artificial Intelligence*. pp. 232 - 235, Washington, D.C., August, 1983.

Lebowitz, M. Generalization from natural language text. *Cognitive Science* 7,(1), pp. 1 - 40, 1983.

Quillian, M.R. Semantic memory. In M. Minsky (Ed.) *Semantic Information Processing*, Cambridge, MA: MIT Press, 1968.

Schank, R.C. *Dynamic Memory: A Theory of Reminding and Learning in Computers and People.* Cambridge University Press, MA 1982.

Schank, R.C, Kolodner, J. and DeJong, G. *Conceptual Information Retrieval*, Research Report #190, Department of Computer Science, Yale University, 1980.

Tulving, E. Episodic and semantic memory. In E. Tulving and W. Donaldson (eds.), *Organization and Memory.* New York: Academic Press, 1972.

Wilensky, R. . KODIAK - A knowledge representation language. In *Proceedings of the Sixth Annual Conference of the Cognitive Science Society*, Boulder, Colorado, 1984.

Winston, P. Learning and Reasoning by Analogy. *Communications of the ACM.* Volume 23, (12), pp.689-703, 1980.

Advances in Artificial Intelligence - II
B. Du Boulay, D. Hogg and L. Steels (Editors)
© Elsevier Science Publishers B.V. (North-Holland), 1987

COMPUTATIONAL ANALOGY

Ken Wellsch and Marlene Jones

Logic Programming and Artificial Intelligence Group
University of Waterloo
Waterloo, Ontario
N2L 3G1, CANADA

ABSTRACT

Evidence suggests that analogy is a key component in human reasoning and learning situations. Exploiting past experience via analogies is an important aspect of *intelligent behavior*. We briefly review the research of Burstein, Gentner and Winston, then present a particularly simple (polynomial complexity) but powerful algorithm for detecting and applying analogies. The algorithm, which is based on subtree matching, employs a hierarchical representation; we investigate the power of such a representation. The effectiveness of the algorithm is examined using two-dimensional scenes as the major test domain. The results are discussed herein along with suggestions for future research.

1. Introduction

The study of analogy is a relatively new area, and the development of a computational model for analogical reasoning has remained largely unexplored. One of the problems with the the notion of analogy is understanding exactly what it is. At the most basic level, *analogy is a relation of likeness between two things*. These *things* may be objects, relations or complex concepts, taken from either the same domain or disparate domains. One dominant characteristic of analogy is that there often appears to be no apparent relationship between the two *things*. On a more complex level, analogy manifests itself in the literary world as *metaphors* and *similes*. For example, consider the well-known metaphor:

> *"What light from yonder window breaks?*
> *It is the east, and Juliet is the sun! ..."*

A second example, illustrating the lack of an obvious relationship between the *objects* is (Quine and Ullian 1978):

> *"knowledge in some ways is like a good golf score ..."*

The complete statement removes the mystery:

> *"knowledge in some ways is like a good golf score: each is substantially the fruit of something else, and there are no magic shortcuts to either"*

One of the meanings of the Greek word "analogia", from which analogy originates, is *proportion* (Polya 1954). The notion of proportion appears in a problem-solving environment; a common example are intelligence-tests. A proportion problem often has the form "A:B::C:?", i.e. *A* is to *B* as *C* is to what? The familiar geometric-analogy intelligence-test problem is an example of a proportion problem with grouped two-dimensional objects for *A*, *B*, and *C*.

As far as terminology goes, the structure of an analogy is divided up into two parts: the *base* (or *vehicle*) and the *target* (or *topic*, traditionally called the *tenor*). The base of an analogy is the domain which the reader is assumed to be familiar with (the *base* from which to infer). The target of an analogy is the domain that the reader has little or no knowledge of (the *target* of the inferences). Analogy in teaching and communication is used to impart a better foundation for understanding new domains (of which little or nothing is known by the listener) in relation to a domain familiar to the listener. Good analogies represent extremely efficient (compact yet rich) representations of knowledge.

2. Current Research

The study of analogy is a fairly modern endeavor (within the past 30 to 40 years), although the use of analogy is old. The diversity in existing research on analogy makes it difficult to produce a concise summary of the complete area. Instead, we will concentrate on the most influential work during the last few years, research from Gentner (1982, 1983), Winston (1980), and Burstein (1983). For a comprehensive survey of previous research, see (Wellsch 1985).

Gentner is a researcher in Cognitive Psychology who has published several works in the 80's that defines the current model for analogy. Her *structure-mapping* theory of analogy provides a set of principles for the representation and derivation of analogies. Here is the definition of structure-mapping (Gentner 1982):

> *attributes*   – predicates taking one argument,
> *relations*   – predicates taking two or more arguments.
>
> T *target* containing object nodes $t_1, t_2, \cdots t_m$
> B *base* containing object nodes $b_1, b_2, \cdots b_n$
>
> A, R, and R' *predicates*

Example :

> *"The hydrogen atom is like the solar system"*

Predicates:

> sun (hot), sun (massive)
> revolves-around (planets , sun)
> more-massive-than (sun , planets)
> more-massive-than (nucleus , electron)

Map object nodes of B onto object nodes of T

> M: $b_i \rightarrow t_i$
>
> (i.e. sun $\rightarrow$ nucleus , planet $\rightarrow$ electron)

Using node substitutions found above:

> M: $[R(b_i, b_j)] \rightarrow [R(t_i, t_j)]$
>
> where $R(b_i, b_j)$ is a relation that holds in domain B.
> and so on for higher order predicates...

> (i.e. revolves-around(planets,sun) $\rightarrow$ revolves-around(electron,nucleus))

A distinguishing characteristic of analogy (so claims Gentner) is that attributes from B tend not to be mapped into T :

> M: $[A(b_i)] \nrightarrow [A(t_i)]$
>
> (i.e. sun (hot) $\nrightarrow$ nucleus (hot)).

In addition to the structure mapping theory, Gentner adds the following principle:

> " ... *Systematicity Principle: A predicate that belongs to a mappable system of mutually inter-connecting relationships is more likely to be imported into the target than is an isolated predicate.*" (Gentner 1982)

Winston has done a wide range of work that, to varying degrees, has incorporated analogy. One paper in particular (Winston 1980) is devoted to the study of learning by analogy via a computational model. Winston deals mainly with representing story plots (such as *Romeo and Juliet*, and *Macbeth*) and the determination of some measure of plot similarity. For example, the play *Romeo and Juliet*, and *Cinderella* have a lot in common. These stories are represented via a network of frames (i.e a graph), and using a constrained matcher, a value representing the number of similar components is determined. An exhaustive matcher would be far too computationally expensive, so Winston selected a set of constraints to limit the combinatorial explosion; these constraints include: *cause*, *importance*, and *classification*. One criticism of Winston's approach is his reliance on well-bounded domains. The story plot is clearly a self contained world in terms of the story. A point worth noting is that Winston is looking at generalizing the target and base (i.e. schema induction) rather than transferring specific relations using some (supposed) similarity between the domains. His approach is different from those people studying analogical reasoning; his task is somewhat easier, relying on some external source for accurate representation of the domain knowledge.

Burstein takes a different approach. He is interested in the reasoning aspect; to extend incrementally a small target domain with the aid of an external teacher and some knowledge about the base domain (Burstein 1983). The method he employs is less clear than Winston's but based on the structure-mapping model of Gentner. Burstein criticizes the well-defined knowledge necessary for the work of Evans and Winston as well as the complexity of a partial-pattern matching approach. Burstein suggests a hierarchical knowledge structure to reduce the volume of potential pairings. He also deals with non-identical mappings, something he claims is not embodied in Gentner's model. A *virtual* relation is created when a non-identical mapping occurs to preserve the other relationships in the mapping. Burstein employs an incremental process of mapping so that any potential errors can be recognized and corrected by the external instructor before making any further inferences. Work such as Winston's is exhaustive; the matcher goes through all of the data before returning any result.

3. The Algorithm

The problem of detecting and applying analogies is very hard and although a great deal of work has been directed at analogical reasoning, it remains an open problem (for a fuller discussion of analogy and analogical reasoning, see (Wellsch 1985)). In the context of this paper, the subproblem of detecting analogies is tackled using a simple, but powerful polynomial algorithm.

A method for modelling analogy consists of **matching** two bodies of knowledge (base and target) obtaining pairwise correspondences between the two bodies (in order to determine the analogy). The analogy (these pairwise correspondences) can be used to **map** relationships known to hold in the base domain to the target domain (i.e. analogical reasoning).

If one accepts this matching paradigm for modelling analogical reasoning, then a number of key issues remain to be formalized. An effective matching procedure and mapping procedure are two obvious issues. A third, equally important issue is the form of knowledge representation (KR) to be used by these two procedures. A proportion of existing analogy research has dealt with matching and mapping trying to remain above actually selecting a KR form; unfortunately the computational feasibility of any approach relies on selecting a form of KR and providing concrete procedures. The algorithms which provide matching and mapping rely on the KR chosen.

3.1. Knowledge Representation

The array of potential KR forms (frames, networks, and logic for example), all revolve around one basic (fundamental) representation structure: a **graph**. A **tree** and a **list** are restricted forms of graphs that are also used when the complexity associated with graphs is unnecessary and undesirable. The disadvantage of an unrestricted graph in a matching situation is well-known: the *subgraph isomorphism problem* is *NP complete* (Gary and Johnson 1979) i.e. graph matching is computationally expensive and potentially infeasible. Conversely, restricted forms of graphs are more computationally attractive, for example, *the tree isomorphism problem* has a linear-time solution (Aho, Hopcroft and Ullman 1974).

In addition to computational superiority, a hierarchical representation has a basis in the current Psychological research on knowledge structuring (Bourne, Dominowski and Loftus 1979; Dember and Warm 1979; Reynolds and Flagg 1977). The fact that people have a limited short-term memory capacity has lead to the *chunking* model for short-term memory (Miller 1956). A limit of 7 ± 2 *chunks* of information as the human short-term memory capacity is well accepted and experimentally verified. For people to remember more than such a restricted number of specific things requires some way of encapsulating the surplus within each *chunk*. The theory of *chunking* encorporates an explicit hierarchy by *chunking chunks* to form larger and large units of information. Hierarchical recoding of information is a common component in cognitive models for human memory; a tree structure provides such a hierarchical representation.

A hierarchical representation is also used in Pattern Recognition. Scene and picture analysis are two important applications of pattern recognition (and analogies in these visual domains are common in human reasoning). Syntactic pattern recognition, one of the two general pattern recognition approaches (Fu 1982), represents two and three-dimensional scenes using a hierarchical description.

It would seem that a hierarchical representation (without cycles and a specific rooted node) is an attractive knowledge structure. The question of descriptive power immediately arises; do trees have sufficient descriptive power compared with graphs? The most obvious disadvantage of a hierarchical structuring is the problem of multiple representation. By this we mean that a given scene can be "ordered" in several different ways within a tree. Gestalt psychology does provide what amounts to heuristics that describe how people mentally order scene hierarchies, but these "guides" have not been tested in this research area. This is one of the issues we will address herein.

3.2. Matching

Tree matching is an extension of the tree isomorphism problem. When a tree is used to represent *knowledge*, the nodes of the tree correspond to objects and the relationships between the objects (i.e. the tree has labelled nodes). The tree isomorphism problem requires that the structure and labels be identical between the two trees (with branch permutations) for them to be isomorphic; a strict form of equality. On the other hand, an exact match between the base and target of an analogy (assuming one would call such a comparison an *analogy*) is of little value. To deviate from strict equality (to flexible equality) relies on some additional knowledge about the labels. Clearly, if our model of equality relies on labels being identical for equality and otherwise being not equal, then our model of analogy could not function. The background information regarding labels provides a means of judging the *similarity* of two labels (not just "equal" or "not equal"); strict equality is inadequate in this situation.

The area of judging similarity has received a reasonable amount of attention (Ortony 1979; Tversky 1977); the method used here does not attempt to achieve the same level of sophistication of today's similarity models, but has proved adequate for developmental purposes. The relationships between the various tree labels of the domain trees are represented in a single hierarchy called a *background knowledge tree (BKT)* (see Figure 1). The *similarity function* σ, given two labels, computes a value from the relative positions of the two labels within the BKT, i.e. a measure of distance. Greater "distance" implies lower similarity between the two labels. This form of measure is certainly not ideal, but whatever metric is chosen, as long as it yields values such that a larger value signifies lower similarity, then the exact definition of σ will not effect the matching algorithm.

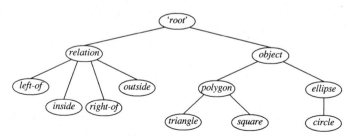

Figure 1
General background knowledge hierarchy (BKT)

Returning once again to the idea of tree matching, given the function σ, one can develop an algorithm of "flexible" matching for trees. There are a variety of ways of combining the values of individual node pairings (obtained from σ) to judge the similarity of two trees. For example, the worst node-pair rating, the best node-pair rating, and the sum of all the node-pair ratings (cost) are three such measures; others certainly exist. In the research discussed here, the worst node-pair rating and the total "cost" are used to judge tree similarity. Matching two trees t_1 and t_2 yields the ordered pair $<cost\,(t_1,t_2),worst\,(t_1,t_2)>$. Notice that the *cost* function pairs the most appropriate (least costly) branches, and the overall cost is penalized for any remaining unmatched branches (the *cost* function presented here assumes, without loss of generality, that $|t_1|\leq|t_2|$).

Consider now the subtree isomorphism problem: given two trees, t_1 and t_2, is one tree isomorphic to a subtree of the other? Note that a subtree s of a tree t can be the tree t itself (i.e. $s=t$) and that we are not considering the problem of matching **all** the subtrees of t_1 with all the subtrees of t_2 (That would be grim indeed!). Here we have a selection problem: which subtree of t_1 *best* matches with t_2 as given by the $<cost\,,worst>$ rating? The selection strategy used is one that picks the matching with the lowest worst node-pair rating (i.e minimize worst node-pair rating), and if there is more than one that has this minimum rating, then break such a tie by minimizing the cost rating among the minimum worst node-

$$cost\,(t_1,t_2) \equiv \textbf{if } root\,(t_1) = root\,(t_2) = \textbf{nil then } 0$$
$$\textbf{else if } \delta\,(root\,(t_1)) \neq \delta\,(root\,(t_2)) \textbf{ then LARGE-CONSTANT} \times (|t_1| + |t_2|)$$
$$\textbf{else } \sigma(root\,(t_1),root\,(t_2)) + \sum_{i=1}^{\delta(root(t_1))} cost\,(child\,(i,t_1),child\,(i,t_2)) \textbf{ endif.}$$

$$worst\,(t_1,t_2) \equiv \textbf{if } root\,(t_1) = root\,(t_2) = \textbf{nil then } 0$$
$$\textbf{else if } \delta\,(root\,(t_1)) \neq \delta\,(root\,(t_2)) \textbf{ then LARGE-CONSTANT}$$
$$\textbf{else } \underset{i=1}{\overset{\delta(root(t_1))}{\text{MAX}}} \left\{ \sigma(root\,(t_1),root\,(t_2))\,,\,worst\,(child\,(i,t_1),child\,(i,t_2)) \right\} \textbf{ endif.}$$

$$pair\text{-}min\;(<cost_1,worst_1>,<cost_2,worst_2>) \equiv \textbf{if } (worst_1<worst_2) \textbf{ or}$$
$$((worst_1=worst_2) \textbf{ and } (cost_1<cost_2)) \textbf{ then } <cost_1,worst_1>$$
$$\textbf{else } <cost_2,worst_2> \textbf{ endif.}$$

$$\sigma\;(l_1,l_2) \equiv \textbf{if } inconsistent\,(l_1,l_2) \textbf{ then LARGE-CONSTANT}$$
$$\textbf{else } (\,|depth\,(l_1)-depth\,(l_2)| \,+\, \text{MAX}(\,|depth\,(l_1)-depth\,(\rho)|\,,$$
$$|depth\,(l_2)-depth\,(\rho)|\,))\times\text{MAX}(priority\,(l_1),priority\,(l_2)) \textbf{ endif.}$$
$$where$$

$depth\,(n)$ is the depth in the background knowledge hierarchy of node n and ρ is the common ancestor of l_1 and l_2.

$$tree\text{-}match\;(t_1,t_2) \equiv <cost\,(t_1,t_2),worst\,(t_1,t_2)>.$$

$$subtree\text{-}match\;(t_1,t_2) \equiv \underset{t \text{ subtree of } t_1}{pair\text{-}min} \left\{ tree\text{-}match\;(t,t_2) \right\}.$$

$$forest\text{-}match\;(f_1,f_2) \equiv \underset{t \in f_1}{pair\text{-}min} \left\{ \underset{\text{eliminate } t_j \text{ from } f_2}{subtree\text{-}match\;(t,t_i)} \mid t_i \in f_2 \right\}.$$

Figure 2
Matching algorithm

pair matchings (i.e. pick the matching with the lowest cost rating). Subtree matching consists of selecting the "best" subtree pairing.

Finally, at the level of the base and target representation, is *forest* matching. Both the base and target domains are represented by forests, i.e. sets of trees. It is at this level of representation that we refer to matching as that associated with analogy. Forest matching uses the same basic approach taken with subtree matching (i.e. the selection technique) but with a few twists. Things become a bit more complicated because the trees in a domain forest are significantly more independent than the nodes in a tree (other than pertaining to the same domain, there isn't necessarily any more of a connection). This structure independence (and common-sense) implies that combining an unequal number of structures (trees) taken from one domain with another has no basis. The natural approach might be to simply eliminate each of the already paired trees (obtained from "best" matching) from consideration and use only the remainder for later pairings (i.e. a process of elimination).

Two obvious problems can occur using such a matching algorithm. The first is *multiplicity*, i.e. a one-to-many mapping of an object or relation to another. In terms of a tree representation, this manifests itself when a single leaf node is paired to a subtree composed of more than one node. The second problem is *inconsistency*, i.e. a mapping that contains an object or relation that seems to map to more than one distinct object or relation (or visa versa). This is much like multiplicity, but simpler to deal with than multiplicity. The algorithm penalizes a matching that results in inconsistent mappings (in function σ). The algorithm (Figure 2) handles both of these problems (although there are undoubtedly other approaches).

3.3. Mapping

The mapping process is quite straight-forward given the node-wise pairings obtained in the matching stage. In most cases, the direction of the mapping is from the base domain to the target domain (a characteristic of analogy). The mapping stage can be carried out by simply **substituting** the label names in the base structures by their paired label names from the target structures. In this way the base structures can be *looked upon in terms of the target domain*. One question that immediately arises is: "What happens when there are labels in the base structures which have no correspondence in the target structures as determined by the matcher?". A second question relates to consistency: "What happens when there is more than one possible substitution for a given label, i.e. a non one-to-one mapping of labels?". Figure 3 illustrates two examples that contain potential mapping conflicts.

(a)   (b)

Figure 3
Pictures with mapping conflicts

Regarding the first question, these unpaired labels may be objects or relations that have some equivalence in the target domain but the reasoner does not have sufficient knowledge of the target domain. It is also possible that such objects and relations do not have any correspondence in the target domain. Here is where analogical reasoning takes on its full characteristics. Analogies are prone to causing reasoning errors (lead to false conclusions); this is an accepted characteristic. Analogy is not a proof technique, but merely a powerful guide. Thus it is necessary that some form of *alias* be established for these unpaired objects and relations so that at some later time their existence in the target domain can be tested and either verified, discounted, or left as still unknown.

As a means of dealing with the unpaired labels, the choice of determining a **mapping union** or a **mapping intersection** is available. *Union* consists of ignoring the lack of a pairing and just directly transferring the label into the target domain. On the other hand, the *intersection* eliminates any labels that are not integral within the portion of the structure that contains paired labels. For example, if a subtree contains paired labels and the root label has no pairing, then the root label must has some correspondence within the target domain. In such a case, an *alias* is established for the label.

Regarding the question of consistency, either the matching algorithm must take it into account in the selection process, or should inconsistency remain in a matching, then some other strategy must be followed by the mapping stage (such as ignoring the inconsistent pairings all together). It is straightforward to extend the node matching function to consult a list being maintained by the tree matching algorithm to see if the node pairing in question is consistent with the preceding node pairings in the match. If it is not, some large value akin to (LARGE-CONSTANT) can be assigned the pairing to indicate the inconsistency.

One interesting extension to the simple substitution algorithm for mapping is a **generalized mapping** (see Figure 4). Such a mapping consists of replacing the *most-specific* labels paired by the matcher with successive generalizations obtained from the background knowledge tree (BKT). Since the background hierarchy is based on abstraction, tracing successive generalizations until the common ancestor of the two original labels is encountered is a simple task. By augmenting the simple substitution with generalized substitutions the wealth of potentially useful reasoning structures increases. The full use and implications of these generalized mappings remains to be studied.

4. Implementation and Testing

The algorithm described in section 3 has been implemented and tested in several domains; the major domain being two-dimensional shapes (as in geometric analogy intelligence test questions). Consider, for example, the two pictures (1) and (2) in Figure 5. Each picture is representable by a tree structure (shown for picture (1)) and can also be described by a nested predicate notation (shown for all three pictures).

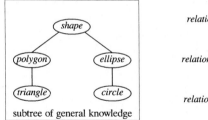

subtree of general knowledge

$$relation(shape,...) \rightarrow relation(shape,...)$$

$$\uparrow$$

$$relation(polygon,...) \rightarrow relation(ellipse,...)$$

$$\uparrow$$

$$relation(triangle,...) \rightarrow relation(circle,...)$$

Figure 4
Range of generalized substitutions

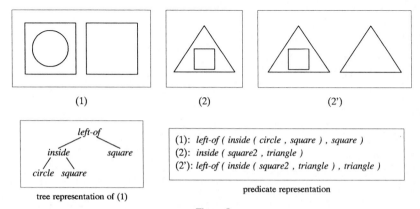

(1)   (2)   (2')

left-of
    inside   square
  /   \
circle square

tree representation of (1)

(1): *left-of (inside (circle , square) , square)*
(2): *inside (square2 , triangle)*
(2'): *left-of (inside (square2 , triangle) , triangle)*

predicate representation

Figure 5
Two simple pictures, (1) & (2),
and resulting analogical inference (2')

Does an analogy exist between pictures (1) and (2)? Applying the algorithm in Figure 2 by pairing the root node (i.e. *inside*) of picture (2) to each node of picture (1) yields:

inside with *left-of*	☞	<(1+4×LARGE-CONSTANT+1),(LARGE-CONSTANT)>
inside with *inside*	☞	<(0+2+1),(2)>
all other pairings	☞	<(4×LARGE-CONSTANT),(LARGE-CONSTANT)>

The pairing between picture (2) and the left half of picture (1) produces a strong matching (<3,2>) over the other possible matchings. The resulting node-pairings are consistent: *inside* → *inside*, *square* → *triangle*, and *circle* → *square2*, and picture (2') is the result of the analogical inference.

Our second example (see Figure 6) is only slightly more complicated than the first; it consists of a matching that results in consistent object pairing but an inconsistent relation pairing. Intuitively, the four identical objects (the squares) are paired with four identical objects of a different form (the circles). The problem is obvious, all of the circles are positioned along the horizontal, while the last square in the left-hand picture lies below the horizontal. The two tree representations below each picture have the offending positional relation circled. The algorithm successfully matches corresponding circles with squares.

This particular example also illustrates the problem of multiple representation of a scene using a tree structure. One will notice in Figure 6 that the tree representations shown group the left pair and right pair together, and then group these as a pair. Another possible ordering would be to group them from left to right, or right to left (i.e. group the left pair, then group that with the next object, and finally group that subtree with the last object on the right). Should different ordering strategies be employed for the base and target scenes, the matching usually fails to produce anything. We will discuss this problem in our concluding remarks.

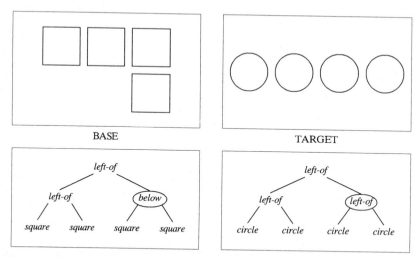

Figure 6
Single relation mismatch

Our third example is taken from a paper by Evans (Evans 1968); it represents the classic geometric analogy intelligence test problem. One interesting application for the algorithm is to group the upper A and C pictures into a forest, and the possible solution choices plus B into a second forest. The matching obtained was that A matched "best" with B and C matched "best" with 3, the solution. This remarkable result must be qualified though; in order to obtain the correct solution to the problem, it was necessary to take into account an important property of visual analogies. It has been suggested that in many analogies, relationships are more *important* than objects, and in turn, objects are more *important* than their attributes (Carbonell 1981). This is where the notion of *priority* comes from in the node similarity function σ. Relations can be given a higher priority than objects; providing this additional constraint allows for the solution of a wider array of visual analogies. The use of a *fudge factor* is not very satisfactory, but the notion of priorities and importance is not simply a *fudge factor* but a real characteristic used in human visual perception (Gestalt Psychology).

Figure 8 is our first real look at object **multiplicity**. Multiplicity is the *multiplication* (or replication) of an object in a pairing (i.e. one-to-many mapping). The simplistic belief that all matchings will be one-to-one is unrealistic. Intuitively, the matching between the figures in the left picture have a mapping to those in the right-hand picture. Object consistency implies that we cannot pair one circle with a triangle, and the other circle with the square; careful study shows that each pair *(triangle-square)* consistently maps to a circle. This requires that a subtree of the left representation be paired with a leaf-node (circle) of the right picture (matching multiplicity). Again, the algorithm found the forementioned solution.

Our last example illustrates more clearly regular multiplicity (irregular multiplicity exists when the multiplication factor is not the same for each object-cluster pairing). Again, the algorithm obtained the accepted matching *(circle → circle×2, triangle → triangle×2, etc.)*.

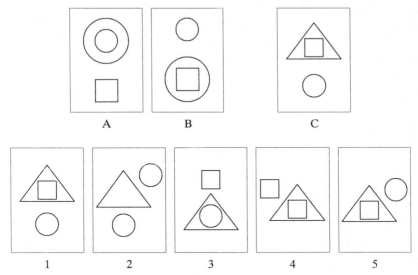

Figure 7
Geometric analogy intelligence test question (Evans, case 5)

Figure 8
An example of Multiplicity

Figure 9
An example of Regular Multiplicity

5. Concluding Remarks

Although the initial testing has been restricted mainly to two-dimensional geometric shapes, the results have been encouraging. As illustrated by the test cases presented in the previous section, the results do correspond with one's intuition i.e. the analogies detected by the algorithm are easily explained. This is also true of the limited testing we made within the domain of ballet (for the automated generation of student models used in instructional systems); the results of which are discussed in (Wellsch 1985). At this point the full power of the algorithm has not been investigated; analogies in other domains remain to be studied using the algorithm.

Regarding the multiple representation problem associated with a hierarchical representation, this does not make such a representation any less effective. The ability to "group" or "cluster" objects and relations is what causes this problem, but "clustering" adds immensely to the descriptive power of a hierarchy over a general graph. The influence of multiple representation and methods of dealing with it remain to be investigated.

With regard to more general issues concerning analogy testing, the handling of *inconsistency* and *multiplicity*, and the usefulness of *generalized mapping* warrant further study. Again our initial results within both the domains of two-dimensional geometric shapes and introductory ballet instruction, are very encouraging; the current approach (although simple) appears to be very effective. Although a more sophisticated method of handling these issues *may* improve applicability, one does not want to increase the computational complexity of the algorithms (which is polynomial in the size of the trees).

6. References

Aho, A. V., Hopcroft, J. E. and Ullman, J. D. (1974), *The Design and Analysis of Computer Algorithms,* Addison-Wesley.

Bourne, L. E., Dominowski, R. L. and Loftus, E. F. (1979), *Cognitive Processes,* Prentice-Hall.

Burstein, M. H. (1983), "A Model of Learning by Incremental Analogical Reasoning and Debugging", *Proceedings of the AAAI,* 45-48.

Carbonell, J. G. (1981), "A Computational Model of Analogical Problem Solving", *Proceedings of the IJCAI,* 147-152.

Dember, W. N. and Warm, J. S. (1979), *Psychology of Perception,* Holt, Rinehart and Winston.

Evans, T. G. (1968), "A Program for the Solution of a Class of Geometric-Analogy Intelligence-Test Questions", in *Semantic Information Processing,* 271-353, MIT Press.

Fu, K. Sun (1982), *Syntactic Pattern Recognition and Applications,* Prentice-Hall.

Garey, M. R. and Johnson, D. S. (1979), *Computers and Intractability,* W. H. Freeman and Company.

Gentner, D. (1982), "A Structure-Mapping Approach to Analogy and Metaphor", *IEEE Proceedings, International Conference on Cybernetics and Society,* 75-79.

Gentner, D. (1983), "Structure-Mapping: A Theoretical Framework for Analogy", *Cognitive Science,* 7, 155-170.

Gentner, D. and Gentner, D. R. (1983), "Flowing Waters or Teeming Crowds: Mental Models of Electricity", in *Mental Models,* 99-129, L. Erlbaum Assoc. Inc.

Gick, M. L. and Holyoak, K. J. (1980), "Analogical Problem Solving", *Cognitive Psychology,* 12, 306-355.

Gick, M. L. and Holyoak, K. J. (1983), "Schema Induction and Analogical Transfer", *Cognitive Psychology,* 15, 1-38.

Miller, G. A. (1956), "The Magical Number Seven, Plus or Minus Two: Some Limits on Our Capability for Processing Information", *American Psychologist,* 17, 748-762.

Ortony, A. (1979), "Beyond Literal Similarity", *Psychological Review,* 86, 161-180.

Polya, G. (1954), *Induction and Analogy in Mathematics,* Princeton University Press.

Quine, W. V. and Ullian, J. S. (1978), *The Web of Belief,* Random House, Inc.

Reynolds, A. G. and Flagg, P. W. (1977), *Cognitive Psychology,* Winthrop.

Tversky, A. (1977), "Features of Similarity", *Psychological Review,* 84, 327-352.

Wellsch, K. C. (1985), *A Computational Model for Reasoning by Analogy,* M. Math Thesis, Department of Computer Science, University of Waterloo; also available as Research Report CS-85-19, 167p.

Winston, P. H. (1980), "Learning and Reasoning by Analogy", *Communications of the ACM,* 23, 689-703.

Advances in Artificial Intelligence - II
B. Du Boulay, D. Hogg and L. Steels (Editors)
© Elsevier Science Publishers B.V. (North-Holland), 1987

BIG FLOOD IN THE BLOCKS WORLD
OR
NON-CUMULATIVE LEARNING *

Werner Emde **
Technische Universität Berlin
Institut für Angewandte Informatik
CIS, Projekt KIT-Lerner, Sekr. FR 5-8
Franklinstr. 28/29
D-1000 Berlin 10

The knowledge acquisition process of many Machine Learning approaches is idealized, e.g., with respect to the exclusion of noisy data. The consequence of abandoning the idealization is: the system may be led to a dead end. In this paper the reasons for this assertion are given and heuristics of the system METAXA.3 are described. METAXA.3 is able to leave such dead ends by replacing old theories by new, differently structured theories with an exchange of parts of the factual knowledge. It is argued that the development of a 'paradigm' is advantageous and possibly necessary in learning processes.

1. Introduction

The knowledge acquisition process of many machine learning approaches is based on the view of knowledge acquisition as a quasi-cumulative process in which single hypotheses are sometimes rejected, but theories as a whole are never replaced by a new, differently structured theory. A method that is built up on this view will only lead to success if the knowledge acquisition process is idealized for example with respect to the exclusion of noisy data, the applicability of backtracking methods, or the presentation of concept examples by a teacher. If the idealization must be abandoned, the system may be led to a dead end.

One way out from such dead ends is to throw away a piece of knowledge and develop another one from scratch, in other words, to use the 'revolutionary approach' as Michalski (85) has called it somewhat misleading (because a revolution should start with an idea). But learning from scratch is (at least) difficult, often inefficient and time consuming. Another approach to knowledge improvement is presented in this paper.

2. Origin and Necessity of "Paradigms"

In many approaches the knowledge acquisition process is idealized with respect to the exclusion of noisy data. An exception is, e.g., the work of Langley et al. (83). The usual way of handling noisy data is to compute a threshold score and to retain only those rules exceeding the threshold value. The problems that have been neglected are those that will arise if the rules are applied in further induction processes as described below.

----

* The term 'non-cumulative' has been used by Stegmüller (79) to describe differences between views of scientific discovery processes (cf. Feyerabend 75). In this paper the terms 'quasi-cumulative' and 'non-cumulative' are used to describe different kinds of incremental learning. An earlier version of this paper has been presented on the 'European Working Session on Learning ~86' (Orsay, France 1986).
** The work of the author has been supported by the BMFT (Bundesministerium für Forschung und Technologie) under grant ITW8501B1. The author would like to thank Ch. Habel and C.-R. Rollinger for comments on earlier versions of this paper.

If it is not possible to guarantee the correctness of the data, each input must be classified by the system according to whether or not it should be 'accepted'. Furthermore, the system must decide if an input should lead to a rectification of its 'theory'. As this classification will be made with the help of the generalized and possibly (partly) faulty 'theory', the system runs the risk of classifying correct data as 'noisy' and incorrect data as 'correct', whereas the latter will cause the contamination of the knowledge base. Therefore, the correctness of the knowledge base can be called in question if a faulty element of a 'theory' (e.g. a single rule) has been detected. One attempt to identify faulty knowledge base entries could be the reclassification of all facts given to the system between the introduction of the faulty 'theory' element (e.g. the single rule) and its refutation, in other words, to initiate an expensive backtracking process. But from the standpoint of cognitive economy it seems - at least in cases where a 'theory' has proven useful for a long time - inappropriate to ensure the applicability of backtracking methods. And another point should be made with regard to cognitive economy.

In some cases counterexamples to a 'theory' can appear as rare exceptions to the factual knowledge; nevertheless it may be impossible to reject them under given circumstances (e.g. because they occur repeatedly). Many learning systems treat counterexamples of this kind like any other counterexamples; that means they can cause the refutation of central hypotheses. A defence of core hypotheses would be more reasonable at least if the 'theory' has been successful over a long period.

This seems especially appropriate with regard to the fact that it is hardly possible to find a 'theory' without counterexamples, and therefore it is hardly possible to find a 'theory' which will improve the system's behavior at all. Since a simple 'theory' is better then no 'theory' and a simple 'theory' can serve as a good starting-point for the development of complicated 'theories', a system should try to exclude uncommon counterexamples with ad hoc hypotheses (cf. Salzberg 85), e.g., through the use of the "Monster-barring" method of Lakatos (cf. Hayes-Roth 83).

Here it is argued that a system will develop a 'paradigm' rather than a theory (in a mathematical sense) when no or incomplete backtracking is used and certain hypotheses are protected against refutation (cf. Emde 83, Kuhn 62). The contaminated knowledge base and the (central) faulty hypotheses will influence the system's 'perception'. Single hypotheses may still be rejected and replaced by other hypotheses; quasi-cumulative knowledge acquisition may take place but the 'paradigm' will be resistant to refutations.

The use of a 'paradigm' is advantageous and possibly necessary in learning processes. A 'paradigm' may help to achieve a fully operational system in the early stages of induction, which is important with regard to the fact that 'a learning component should improve the efficiency and effectiveness of a performance element'. But of course the use of a 'paradigm' is also accompanied by a disadvantage. In the later stages of a learning process a 'paradigm' can cause a crisis like the 'crisis in science' as described by Kuhn and will make 'paradigm changes' necessary. The system has to change to non-cumulative knowledge acquisition. The entire paradigm has to be refuted and replaced.

The substitution of an obsolete 'theory' by an alternative (differently structured) 'theory' takes place in several steps. First, one or more new 'theories' have to be constructed. Second, the most promising 'theory' has to be selected and third, this 'theory' must be introduced ('counterinductively') against the contaminated knowledge base (cf. Feyerabend 75)) and extended.

Finally, a choice has to be made between the old 'theory' and the probably more complicated new 'theory'. This decision may be based on a competition between the two 'theories' (probably with regard to a particular application).

In the following the problems are illustrated by an example. For this purpose the task of METAXA.3 is defined as to search for 'a law of floating bodies' that can be used to classify floating/ non-floating objects. A description of the generalization approach of METAXA is ommitted here as the idea of non-cumulative learning is independent of the generalization approach. The knowledge acquisition process of METAXA is based on higher cognitive concepts like 'transitivity' or 'conversity' and can be characterized as 'incremental learning with heuristically generated rule models'. The generation of hypotheses and the test of these hypotheses is triggered by each input to the inference engine of METAXA. The theoretical concepts of the knowledge acquisition process are described in (Emde/Habel/Rollinger 83). The search of the rule space and the system METAXA.2 is discussed at length in (Emde 84). In the following the term 'theory' is used to denote a number of interrelated inference rules 'explaining' the systems epistemic (factual) knowledge. A hypotheses is called 'central' if the hypothesis has been used to infer other hypotheses.

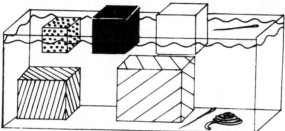

Fig. 1: Floating and non-floating objects

3. An Example

In the first step, a description of objects involved in a scene illustrated in figure 1 has been given to the system. Some of these nearly 100 facts are shown in figure 2 with their natural language 'equivalents'. Each factual input has triggered the induction process. At the end of this first step the system has made the generalizations that are shown in figure 3. Five of the rules are correct but one rule (R3) is incorrect. Rule R3 states that one object is bigger than another object if its weight is greater than the weight of the other object. The result of applying this rule will be correct sometimes. Therefore it may be better to have this rule than no rule. In addition, there is another advantage of this rule: positive evidence for Rule R1 and R2 have been inferred via 'meta-rules' as each operator for a conclusion of a rule like R3 must be asymmetrical and transitive.

At the end of step 1, about 40 new facts have been inferred using the new rules. Two inputs (2) were not compatible with the inferred facts.
(2) ~bigger-than(needle1,needle2)
     bigger-than(needle2,needle1)
(3) heavier-than(needle1,block1)
Therefore this input data (2) was classified as noisy although other facts were given to the system describing the length of needle2 as greater than the length of needle1. The reason for the rejection is that the system had generalized that the relation bigger-than depends on the weight of objects rather than their size (R3). On the other hand, one noisy input (3) stating

```
is-block(block1)                    "Object block1 is a block"
heavier-than(block2,block1)         "Block2 is heavier than block1"
is-heavy(block5)                    "Block5 is heavy"
volume(block1,216)                  "The volume of block1 is 216"
is-ice-object(block3)               "Block3 is an ice-object"
material(needle1,iron)              "The material of needle1 is iron"
```

Fig. 2: Some facts about a block world

```
R1: bigger-than(x,y) & bigger-than(y,z) -> bigger-than(x,z)
R2: bigger-than(x,y) -> ~bigger-than(y,x)
R3: weight(x,x-n) & weight(y,y-n) & gt(x-n,y-n) -> bigger-than(x,y)
R4: smaller-than(x,y) & smaller-than(y,z) -> smaller-than(x,z)
R5: smaller-than(x,y) -> bigger-than(y,x)
R6: bigger-than(x,y) -> smaller-than(y,x)
```

Fig. 3: Generalized inference rules after the first step

that needle1 is heavier than block1 is not detected. The corresponding
inference rule that is necessary to deduce the 'heavier-than' relation from
facts about the weight of objects was rejected by METAXA because only one
'comparative'-relation for each operator is allowed by the meta knowledge of
the system in order to restrict the search space.

A few words are necessary here to finish the description of the handling of
noisy data in METAXA.3. If an input is classified as noisy, it is not
'accepted' (or: not 'perceived') as ('told') true. The noisy input will be
used neither in induction processes nor in deduction processes. But the data
is stored as noisy data. If an input that has been classified as 'noisy'
occurs once more the input will be 'accepted' (or 'perceived'). This will lead
to a contradiction in the knowledge base and the the contradiction handler
will try to eliminate the contradiction by analyzing and restructuring the
support sets of one or more rules with minimum changes in the factual and
inferential knowledge (cf. Emde/Habel/Rollinger 83). Now, back to the
example.

In the next step METAXA.3 is given one more fact about the objects in figure
1. As the fact is not consistent with the system's factual knowledge it is
classified as 'noisy', too. Now, the experimental threshhold of the maximum
number of noisy data that is allowed has been reached and the system tries a
'paradigm shift'.

4. A 'Paradigm Shift'

Several reasons to try a 'paradigm shift' can be found. The set of noisy data
may be to large, the set of contradictory facts that cannot be reduced by
support set restructuring is too large or other 'interesting observations'
(see below) may have occurred. Similarly, many starting points to develop a
new and better theory may be available. Two examples are discussed below.

The first one deals with 'alternative core hypotheses'. An alternative
hypothesis is a hypothesis that has been rejected in the knowledge acquisition
process in favor of another hypothesis which seems more advantageous (cf.
Langley et al. 83). An alternative hypothesis is called 'core hypothesis' if
it implies other hypotheses (probably inconsistent with the old 'theory' of
the system). In the example above the 'comparative'-relation between
'heavier-than' and 'weight' has been noted as alternative core hypothesis by
the system.

This alternative is considered in order to develop a new theory. The inference rules that lead to the recommitment of the alternative are deleted and the alternative hypotheses are added to the rule base. Then, all rules that can be inferred via meta rules from the alternative hypothesis are added to the rule base. The 'truth maintenance'-component of the inference engine is responsible at this point for updating the factual and inferential knowledge, e.g., deleting facts that have been inferred only with recommited rules.

```
R1: bigger-than(x,y) & bigger-than(y,z) -> bigger-than(x,z)
R2: bigger-than(x,y) -> ~bigger-than(y,x)
R4: smaller-than(x,y) & smaller-than(y,z) -> smaller-than(x,z)
R5: smaller-than(x,y) -> bigger-than(y,x)
R6: bigger-than(x,y) -> smaller-than(y,x)
R7: heavier-than(x,y) -> ~heavier-than(y,x)
R8: heavier-than(x,y) & heavier-than(y,z) -> heavier-than(x,z)
R9: weight(x,x-n) & weight(y,y-n) & gt(x-n,y-n) -> heavier-than(x,y)
```

Fig. 4: Rules after the first 'paradigm shift'

In the next step of the 'paradigm shift', a part of the factual knowledge is classified once more in 'noisy' and 'correct' data. The part that will be inspected contains the facts that have been classified with deleted rules and facts that can be classified 'better' with the new set of rules. Furthermore, all facts that have been classified as 'noisy' will be classified once more. The result of the 'paradigm shift' is shown in figure 4. During the new classification of data two facts (2) were re-classified as 'not noisy'. On the other hand a fact (3) that was accepted with the first theory has been rejected as 'noisy' with the second theory.

```
R10: smaller-than(x,y) -> ~smaller-than(y,x)
R11: smaller-than(x,y) -> heavier-than(y,x)
R12: heavier-than(x,y) -> smaller-than(y,x)
R13: smaller-than(x,y) & is-light(y) -> is-light(x)
R14: lighter-than(x,y) & lighter-than(y,z) -> lighter-than(x,z)
R15: lighter-than(x,y) -> bigger-than(y,x)
R16: heavier-than(x,y) -> lighter-than(y,x)
R17: bigger-than(x,y) -> lighter-than(y,x)
R18: lighter-than(x,y) -> heavier-than(y,x)
R19: is-light(x) & ~equal(x,block3) -> is-floating(x)
R20: is-floating(x) & ~equal(x,block3) -> is-light(x)
R21: is-small(x) -> is-floating(x)
R22: is-floating(x) -> is-small(x)
R23: lighter-than(x,y) & is-floating(y) -> is-floating(x)
```

Fig. 5: Further generalized rules after the first 'paradigm shift'

In the next step METAXA.3 is supplied with data about floating and non-floating objects. The rules that were induced in this step are shown in figure 5. Together with the rules of figure 4 the 'theory' of the system can be stated as follows: Light objects are small, heavy objects are big, small objects are able to float and big objects will not float. The 'theory' is simple, but it is useful in some situations.

During the development of this 'theory' several inputs have been rejected as noisy. For example, the statement that needle2 is a non-floating object has been rejected, because needle2 is known to be a small and light object. That needle1 is a floating object has been accepted - not, of course, because the system has developed the concept of 'surface tension', but because needle1 is

known as a small object.   Other inputs have not been   rejected although they
are wrong,   e.g.,   the input that cablel is floating.   Problems occurred with
block3,   the biggest floating object.   Block3 was described as a small but not
light object.   A contradiction lead to the   restriction of the support set of
the synonym-relation   between 'is-light' and 'is-floating' to all objects with
the exception   of block3.   This restriction is   represented as   an additional
premise of the corresponding rule (R19).

In the   next step   METAXA.3 was given   more facts about   the materials   of the
different   objects   in   the   blocks world.   These   facts   lead   to   another
generalization: for all objects made of the same material the ratio of weight
to volume   is constant.   The   corresponding rule that   was added to   the rule
knowledge from this observation is shown in (4).
   (4)   R24: weight(x,x-w) & volume(x,x-v) & material(x,x-m) &
                const is (x-w / x-v) & material(y,x-m) & weight(y,y-w) &
                y-v is (y-w / const)   -> volume(y,y-v)
This is   a nice rule for   inferring the volume   of objects if their   weight is
known.   But this rule is interesting in   another sense as well: METAXA.3 has
heuristics (coded in PROLOG or as rules   of the inference engine)   to look for
useful extreme values. One heuristic says: If constant proportionalities   have
been   found,   look   for   extreme   values of   all   ratios   to refine   the   core
hypotheses.   If some positive examples for a refined rule can be found as well
as some negative examples, try to establish this rule via 'paradigm shift'.

Good   candidates   for   a refinement   are   rules   describing   synonym-relations
between   operators, such as R19,   R20,   R21 and R22 in figure 5.   These rules
are   preferred as   it is   assumed   that a   (representation) language   usually
contains no synonyms   unless the meaning of   the language has not   been worked
out entirely.   Because   negative examples may give a hint   in which direction
the refinement   might be   promising,   rules   with known   exceptions are   tried
first.

```
R10:  smaller-than(x,y) -> ~smaller-than(y,x)
R11:  smaller-than(x,y) -> heavier-than(y,x)
R12:  heavier-than(x,y) -> smaller-than(y,x)
R13:  smaller-than(x,y) & is-light(y) -> is-light(x)
R14:  lighter-than(x,y) & lighter-than(y,z) -> lighter-than(x,z)
R15:  lighter-than(x,y) -> bigger-than(y,x)
R16:  heavier-than(x,y) -> lighter-than(y,x)
R17:  bigger-than(x,y) -> lighter-than(y,x)
R18:  lighter-than(x,y) -> heavier-than(y,x)
R24:  weight(x,x-w) & volume(x,x-v) & material(x,x-m) & const is (x-w/x-v) &
      material(y,x-m) & weight(y,y-w) & y-v is (y-w/const)  -> volume(y,y-v)
R25:  weight(x,x-w) & volume(x,x-v) & is-ice-object(y) & weight(y,y-w) &
      volume(y,y-v) & (x-w / x-v) < (y-w / y-v) -> floating(x)
R26:  weight(x,x-w) & volume(x,x-v) & is-ice-object(y) & weight(y,y-w) &
      volume(y,y-v) & (x-w / x-v) > (y-w / y-v) -> ~floating(x)
```

Fig. 6: Rules after the second 'paradigm shift'
(in addition to the rules of figure 4)

In   the case   described in   this paper   the development   of a   new theory   was
triggered by the rule   R24 (4).   The triggered heuristic tried   to refine the
rule R19 by replacing   the original premises by new premises   with a reference
to an interesting   ratio of weight to volume.   The   interesting proportion was
found with two ice-objects.   The proportion of weight to volume of ice-objects
seemed to mark the borderline between floating and non-floating objects.
Thus, the 'paradigm shift' was tried with the following hypothesis (5) similar
to the   starting point 'alternative   hypothesis' (see above).   The hypothesis

states that objects whose weight-to-volume ratio is smaller than that ratio for ice-objects will be able to float.

(5) weight(x,x-w) & volume(x,x-v) & is-ice-object(y) & weight(y,y-w) &
     volume(y,y-v) & (x-w / x-v) < (y-w / y-v) -> floating(x)

This starting point for the development of the alternative theory is used in the same way as for the first 'paradigm shift'. First, the rule (5) is added to the rule knowledge and all rules which are incompatible with this rule are deleted. Second, rules that can be inferred via metarules from the 'starting-point hypothesis' are added to the knowledge base. Third, a part of factual knowledge is classified once more in correct and incorrect data (see above). Finally, all facts that have been classified as 'noisy' will be classified once more. The result of this second, more radical 'paradigm shift' is shown in figure 6.

5. Discussion and Remarks

In this paper the necessity of using non-cumulative knowledge acquisition has been discussed and some ideas have been presented as to how a system may change its 'paradigm' by replacing its theory by a new one and by updating the factual knowledge with regard to the new theory. It is possible to renounce 'expensive' backtracking methods if a learning system is able to perform jumps in the search space of possible theories ('paradigm changes'). The heuristics involved in 'paradigm changes' will determine if a particular theory is within reach of the learning system. The search space in the induction of single hypotheses is significantly restricted by the use of a 'paradigm'. This may help to avoid increasing search spaces in progressive knowledge acquisition. Many questions remain unanswered, such as how a competition between theories can be modelled or when a re-structuring of an old theory should be tried.

It is beyond the aim of this approach to build a system which is capable of performing a 'paradigm change' from say Newtonian mechanics to an Einsteinian mechanics, but it is argued that 'small paradigm changes' are ubiquitous in learning (cf. Inhelder/Piaget 68).

METAXA.3 is fully operational in Waterloo-PROLOG 1.4 on an IBM 4381 computer comprising about 1600 lines of source code (without the code of the inference engine) and about 85 domain-independent (meta)rules of the inference engine.

6. References

Emde, W. (83): "Kontrainduktives Lernen von Konzepten aus Fakten"; In: B.Neumann (ed.): GWAI-83, 7th German Workshop on Artificial Intelligence; Springer, Berlin, 1983
Emde, W. (84): "Inkrementelles Lernen mit heuristisch generierten Modellen"; Technische Universität Berlin, KIT-Report 22, 1984
Emde, W./ Habel, Ch./ Rollinger, C.-R. (83): "The Discovery of the Equator"; In: Proc. IJCAI-83, Karlsruhe, 1983
Feyerabend, P. (75): "Against Method"; New Left Books, 1975
Hayes-Roth, F. (83): "Using Proofs and Refutations to Learn from Experience"; In: Michalski/Carbonell/Mitchell (eds.): Machine Learning; Tioga Press, Palo Alto, 1983
Inhelder, B./ Piaget, J. (68): "The Law of Floating Bodies and the Elimination of Contradictions"; In: Inhelder/Piaget:The Growth of Logical Thinking; Routledge & Kegan Paul Ltd., London, 1968
Kuhn, T.S. (62): "The Structure of Scientific Revolutions"; University of Chicago Press, Chicago, 1962
Langley, P./Zytkow, J./Simon, H.A./Bradshaw, G.L. (83): "Mechanism for Qualitative and Quantitative Discovery"; In: Proc. 2nd ML Workshop, Monticello, Illinois, 1983
Michalski, R.S. (85): "Knowledge Repair Mechanisms"; In: Proc. 3rd ML Workshop, Skytop, Pennsylvania, 1985
Salzberg, S. (85): "Heuristics for Inductive Learning"; In: Proc. IJCAI-85, Los Angeles, 1983
Stegmüller, W. (79): "Hauptströmungen der Gegenwartsphilosophie"; Band II, Kröner Verlag, Stuttgart, 1979

Advances in Artificial Intelligence - II
B. Du Boulay, D. Hogg and L. Steels (Editors)
© Elsevier Science Publishers B.V. (North-Holland), 1987

111

Discovery Systems

Kenneth W. Haase Jr.
Artificial Intelligence Laboratory
Massachussets Institute of Technology
Cambridge, Massachussets 02139

ABSTRACT

Cyrano is a thoughtful reimplementation of Lenat's controversial Eurisko program, designed to perform automated discovery and concept formation in a variety of technical fields. The "thought" in the reimplementation has come from several directions: an appeal to *basic principles*, which led to identifying constraints of modularity and consistency on the design of discovery sytems; an appeal to *transparency*, which led to collapsing more and more of the control structure into the representation; and an appeal to *accountablity*, which led to the explicit specification of dependencies in the concept formation process.

The process of reimplementing Lenat's work has already revealed several insights into the nature of Eurisko-like systems in general; these insights are incorporated into the design of Cyrano. Foremost among these new insights is the characterization of Eurisko-like systems (which I call *inquisitive* systems) as search processes which dynamically reconfigure their search space by the formation of new concepts and representations. This insight reveals requirements for modularity and "consistency" in the definition of new concepts and representations.

Keywords: Discovery, Learning, Representation, Eurisko, Subsumption.

1 Introduction

Cyrano is a thoughtful reimplementation of Eurisko [Len83a] developed over the last year at the MIT AI lab. Like Lenat's controversial program, Cyrano is designed to discover new concepts and representations in a variety of technical domains. For example, from an initial definition of set theoretic operations, the program synthesizes the concept of numbers and various operations on numbers.

While the development of Cyrano is still in progress, early results have produced insights into the design and performance of discovery systems in general. Discovery is so fundamental a process that any success requires fundamental explanations. Lenat and Brown in [LB83] propose that discovery systems succeed due to a close connection between syntax and semantics in their representation. I believe that this is only part of the story. In this article I describe four additional insights into the nature and design of discovery systems.

- In Section 2, I show how **Eurisko-like systems may be viewed as search processes which reconfigure their own search space.** I call these sorts of processes *inquisitive processes*: processes which extend — during search — the conceptual vocabulary in which their search is cast. Inquisitive processes are contrasted with acquisitive processes which acquire new descriptions by search or instantiation in a representational space whose form is initially — and invariably — fixed. This view is a significant extension of Lenat's analysis in [Len76,Len82].

- In Section 3, I explain why **concept formation in discovery systems must be functionally modular.** Since the progress of an inquisitive process is driven by concepts formed (or provided) at earlier moments of the process, the inputs and outputs of each moment of the process must be explicitly accessible to the preceding and succeeding moments of the process. This requirement for explicitness demands that the formation of new concepts be a module characterized by its explicit inputs and outputs. To illustrate this requirement, several non-modular parts of AM are detailed and criticized.

- In Section 4, I argue that **the formation of new concepts must be "consistent" as well as modular.** Given that a concept formation module has — on the basis of experimentation and empirical analysis — produced an array of extended concepts, these generated concepts must be amenable to further experimentation and extension by the same module. Informally, the inputs and outputs of the module must "talk about" the same sorts of things. Many of AM's most powerful heuristics were crippled by this lack of consistency.

- In Section 5, I describe why **an inquisitive process must ultimately be introspective.** As the conceptual vocabulary of the process grows, the empirical performance of its search and concept formation engine will decline. The process must ultimately reflect on, modify, and extend this engine if it is to proceed effectively past this point. This reflection is a property the design of Cyrano shares with Eurisko.

Finally, in Section 6, I describe the integration of these insights into the design of Cyrano. Among the highlights of this design are: a uniform representation of concepts in a subsumption lattice of types; a general representation of empirical regularities, structured around the confirmation process; and a control structure based on the organization of tasks into experimentally determined classes.

2   Inquisitive Exploration

The operation of a system like AM or Eurisko is often described as a heuristic search through a space of operators and concepts; in this framework, the power of the program arises from the effectiveness of the generating and pruning heuristics for this search space. As with any search process, it is critical that the representation of the search space expose the constraints of the domain. In particular, the representation syntax and the represented semantics must be closely coupled, ensuring that small syntactic variations (steps in the search space) produce meaningful (or even interesting) semantic definitions. I call this coupling of syntax to semantics the "tightness" of the representation.

But the search space of operators and concepts is described in terms of the operators and concepts themselves, a representational vocabulary which is being constantly extended by the ongoing search process. For each generation or cycle of the discovery process, the conceptual vocabulary of its search is determined by concepts formed in the preceding generations. To succeed, the concept formation mechanism must maintain the tightness of its representation over indefinitely many generations of discovery and abstraction. The consistency of this concept formation process is at least as critical as any semantic-syntactic tightness in the starting representation.

Tightness of representation — a property critical to any heuristic search — is the principle to which Lenat and Brown [LB83] attribute the success of AM and Eurisko. AM succeeded, they argue, because the language in which AM represented its mathematical concepts was LISP, which was designed — at its roots — from a mathematical basis. Small changes in the LISP definitions of simple recursive functions produced simple and meaningful changes in the mathematical structures they defined or operated upon. While this analysis is correct, it is incomplete; the credit for the success of AM (and the blame for its eventual malaise) is at least as much due to its mechanisms for extending its conceptual vocabulary and representational search space.

The novelty and power of inquisitive systems lies in this careful incremental evolution of representations and definitions. The significance of AM is not that it discovered multiplication, but that it defined numbers; not that it generated the operation Divisors-Of, but that it defined primes and noticed they were interesting. From AM's initial configuration, the first definition of multiplication was only one syntactic step away, and Divisors-Of only five. An exhaustive search would have eventually found them. What led to these discoveries and marked them as interesting were the concepts which AM defined along its path to them. These generated concepts allowed AM to focus sufficiently to make (and find interesting) its later discoveries and allowed us (or particularly, Lenat) to relate AM's derivations to recognized mathematical concepts. The semantically transparent and tight representation space provided for mathematics by LISP is certainly important, but at least equally important are the mechanisms which extend that space *while preserving its transparence and tightness.*

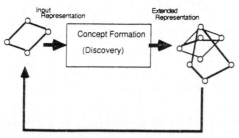

Figure 1. Discovery can be profitably viewed as a cycle of representational extension; concepts formed in one cycle of discovery are used as terms in the vocabulary given to the next.

3   Modularizing Concept Formation

The first step to tightness is transparence and the first step to transparence is explicitness; this yields a constraint on the form of an inquisitive process which we describe here as the **modularity constraint**. The insight of this section is that the formation of new concepts must be a **module** with clearly and explicitly defined inputs and outputs. The inputs are an experimental vocabulary and a way of generating (or referencing) its empirical behavior; the outputs are new concepts and representations (new vocabulary) which capture or exploit certain empirical properties of the inputs (regularities, coincidences, etc). Because each cycle of an inquisitive process builds on the representations (the results) of the cycles before it, the output of each cycle must be accessible as input to the next. This requirement of the discovery cycle is pictured in Figure DiscoveryCycle. In order for the connection between output definitions and input representations to be realized, the output of the formation process must be **explicit**.

An example of modular concept formation is the following heuristic from AM, Eurisko, and Cyrano:

> **If**   Some (but not most) examples of an interesting class C
> are also examples of an interesting class D, and D is not
> already a specialization of C,
> **Then**   Define and study a specialization of C and D which is the
> intersection of C and D.

This heuristic catches one particular sort of empirical regularity: coincidental overlap of classes. The class it produces is accessible, even to the same heuristic, for further analysis and specialization. Further, the concepts it defines actually enhance the explicitness of the representational search space by separating off and declaring possibly interesting cases of predicate/property intersection. Modular extensions like this maintain the transparency of the search space from cycle to cycle in the inquisitive process.

An example of non-modular concept formation is the CANONIZE operation (or heuristic) of AM. The CANONIZE operation takes two related two-place predicates (one is a generalization of the other over the same domain) and produces an automorphism of their domain which preserves the algebraic structure they define over it. Precisely, given $p : A \times A \Longrightarrow \{T, F\}$ and a generalization $r : A \times A \Longrightarrow \{T, F\}; p(x, y) \rightarrow r(x, y)$, CANONIZE finds a function $f : A \Longrightarrow A$ such that $r(x, y) \longleftrightarrow p(f(x), f(y))$. This function f generates a "canonical representation" of A which preserves the equivalence partition defined over A by r. In generating f, CANONIZE recognizes the algebraic structure of A under r and exploits it, but the partition of A is never explicitly and accessibly declared.

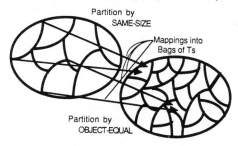

Figure 2 . AM's CANONIZE heuristic found a partition preserving mapping from the domain of SAME-SIZE to the domain of OBJECT-EQUAL. This mapping transformed each element of SAME-SIZE lists into the unique symbol T, producing OBJECT-EQUAL lists.

CANONIZE plays a critical role in AM's progress, defining the canonicalization of bags (multisets) under the SAME-SIZE relation (cardinality) relative to LIST-EQUAL. Given a synthesized notion of SAME-SIZE (a generalization of LIST-EQUAL), AM tried to find a mapping of lists into lists such that lists of the same size would be mapped into lists that were equal. The successful result of this attempt was a mapping (f) which took every element of a list and replaced it with the single symbol T. BAGS-OF-Ts, the range of this mapping (representing the equivalence partitions of SAME-SIZE), was interesting because of where it came from and was later renamed **Numbers** by Lenat. This one discovery, depicted in Figure CanonizeDiagram, was the basis of AM's forays into number theory, where all of its more significant discoveries were made.

CANONIZE is an instance non-modular concept formation because AM never explicitly constructed the partition of the set of bags, but merely exploited its structure to produce the canonicalization f. The recognition of p and r as equivalence relations is never explicitly declared; if it had been, it would be available for confirmation, identification, or exploitation by either later phases of the inquisitive process or a human user interacting with the program. These properties are buried inside the CANONIZE heuristic and never see the light of accessibility by later phases of concept formation and analysis.

In Cyrano, the recognition of structures like equivalence classes is noted explicitly; the class of bags is specialized into the set of bags qua algebraic group (i.e. the subset of bags over which same-size is an equivalence relation), and then this is specialized into its disjoint equivalence classes. These equivalence classes then become the objects of new operations 'raised' from the class the relation was originally defined over.

Equivalence partitions are only one of a broad class of structural properties which Cyrano looks for in its empirical observations; these broad empirical classes are axes of concept formation which support the *consistency* of the concept formation process. This consistency is demanded by the second constraint on concept formation in an inquisitive process: *the consistency constraint.*

4   Consistent Construction

The modularity requirement arises from the structure of inquisitive processes in general: the "discovery cycle" which grinds experiment into representation must close on itself. A "semantic" version of the modularity constraint is the **consistency requirement** placed on the inputs and outputs of a concept formation module.

The experiments performed and the patterns looked for in concept formation are determined by the "sensibility space" and the "interest space" of the input representation. These are specified (of necessity) syntactically and, as pointed out in [LB83], the success of the formation process (to which I will append "at any moment or generation of the inquisitive process") depends critically on the tightness with which these syntactic specifications match the actual space of sensible or interesting constructions.

The consistency constraint arises from this tightness requirement; the concept formation process should preserve — in the new representational vocabulary it generates — the tightness of the original syntactic specification. Since this tightness arises from the representations recognized by the inputs, the forms produced by the outputs of the formation module must be *consistent* with the forms recognized and exploited by its inputs. This requirement is a constraint placed on both the inputs and the outputs of a concept formation module: informally, they must talk about the same sorts of things.

Many of the heuristics in AM and Eurisko satisfy the consistency constraint. The class coincidence heuristic mentioned above, for instance, deals with arbitrary classes and produces a class which refines already established regularities and — at need — may be analyzed and further specialized by the same or other heuristics. AM's operation restriction heuristic also satisfies the consistency constraint:

> **If**   The domain D of an interesting operation O has an interesting specialization C,
>
> **Then**   Define and study O' which is the operation O restricted to Cs.

The new operation this defines can be analyzed by the same heuristics which found the original O to be interesting and further extended on the basis of this analysis. In one instance, AM used this heuristic to study addition restricted to primes, leading to the proposal of Goldbach's conjecture (that any even number may be expressed as the sum of two primes).

On the other hand, AM's CANONIZE heuristic — to criticize it once more — violates the consistency constraint. We will recall that CANONIZE recognizes an relative algebraic property of two relations over their common domain and produces a canonicalization of the domain to itself which preserves this property. But this description invests CANONIZE with more generality than it deserves; CANONIZE actually recognized only a handful of **particular** equivalence partitions defined over the set of list structures by various structural mutations such as element variance, permutation or deletion. In this, CANONIZE violates the consistency constraint because its outputs — the fixed points of simple structural mutations in a space defined by the two predicates — are distinctly separate from the forms recognized by its inputs (arbitrary structures). Put simply, structural canonicalization immediately obsoletes itself.

A more general version of CANONIZE — modularly working off of generally recognized and explicitly declared equivalence partitions — could define a canonicalization by selecting distinguished elements from each partition and defining that as a canonical set. Or more generally, it could define the set of equivalence partions as a class of its own with operations which are defined in terms of operations on the objects partitioned. Such a version of CANONIZE would satisfy both the modularity and consistency constraints we have formulated. We can imagine this more general (and more modular) version of CANONIZE eventually examining (and finding structure in) synthesized notions like vectors (lists of numbers) or dot-products, once it had defined numbers. But AM's clumsy and impoverished CANONIZE was impotent once its objects moved beyond simple structures to numbers, a class it had itself defined.

Lenat recognized that the primary reason for AM's eventual malaise was a particular violation of the consistency constraint: AM's concepts outgrew its heuristics. His solution, proposed in [Len76] and implemented in Eurisko [Len83a], was to make the inquisitive process itself — heuristically defined — a domain for discovery and evolution by meta-heuristics. Instead of making consistency a constraint on the initial design of the concept formation engine, consistency was to be dynamically maintained by a battery of evolutionary meta-heuristics.

In Cyrano, we have instead chosen to implement the consistency constraint directly, having the program always operate with a vocabulary of functions, operators, and classes. The concept formation module extends this vocabulary by recognizing and acting on certain highly exploitable domain independent regularities — called "concept germs" by Minsky [Min86] and "cognitive cliches" by Chapman [Cha83] — to which are attached batteries of reasoning, problem solving, and exploration/experimentation heuristics. The outputs of the concept formation module are concepts and functions reflecting these regularities and therefore exploitable — in virtue of their batteries of attached heuristics — by the next cycle of the inquisitive process. By choosing experiments based on these regularities and forming new concepts around them, the consistency constraint is embedded in the concept formation module of Cyrano.

In the final analysis, this principle also emerged from Eurisko's development, as Lenat's meta-heuristics began to express the same sort of domain independent properties incorporated into Cyrano's design. The meta-heuristics presented in [Len83b] capture the same sort of domain independent properties as concept germs or cognitive cliches. Lenat identifies these concept formation principles or heuristics as methods significantly more specific than weak methods like "Generate and Test" but still far more general than domain specific methods like "Try the choke." It is not surprising that these methods emerged from Eurisko's development; they are the result of designing around the consistency constraint to find principles prevailing over many domains or many generations of an inquisitive process.

From Eurisko's eventual convergence with the consistency constraint, it would appear that Lenat's original reply to the AM's consistency crisis — having meta-heuristics dynamically maintain consistency — failed and was superseded by embedding the consistency constraint in the domain independent formation heuristics of the program. This is true insofar as the only metric of consistency of represenation was the overall performance of the heuristics using it. But such a blanket condemnation of Lenat's solution is unfair. Even when consistency has been built into the structure of the inquisitive process, ensuring that it continues to run, meta-heuristics still play a pivotal role in the inquisitive process, ensuring that it continues to succeed.

5   Inquisitive Introspection

The twin constraints of modularity and consistency maintain and constrain the evolving representational search space of an inquisitive process. But this space is still enormous and ever growing; an inquisitive process must choose one path of representational experimentation from among many possibilities. If we don't want this choice to be arbitrary, the inquisitive process must become a heuristic search.

This characteristic of inquisitive processes has been an implicit bias in previous sections, whose examples were taken from three heuristic discovery programs: AM, Eurisko, and Cyrano. Taken alone, the constraints of modularity and consistency describe a representational space which — in theory — could be enumeratively searched; but most of the nodes reached in such a search would be — while syntactically plausible and apparently suitable for further exploration — dead-ends of little or no utility to the program in the future. Empirically, no examples or patterns will be found and the program's labors in the direction would be wasted.

We would like our heuristic search to avoid such short term dead-ends. But the sorts of paths which are successful in any given domain or generation of discovery (the paths we would like our heuristics to select) are particular to that domain or generation; in order to maintain the effectiveness of its search, the inquisitive process must modify — or appropriately extend — the heuristic engine by which it proceeds along paths constrained by consistency.

This process of modification or extension could be managed by a special separate process (working independently of the inquisitive process itself), but it seems more sensible (and ultimately more powerful) to manage this modification by turning the inquisitive process on itself. Eurisko and Cyrano (AM was not introspective) work in this way, turning its own performance into a domain for empirical experimentation and examination. In Cyrano, the heuristics that drive the inquisitive process become operators in a space of tasks and concepts, and these operations and tasks are analyzed, organized, modified, and specialized based on their empirical performance. The new concepts and operations developed in this domain specify new heuristics, specialized or synthesized for particular domains or new representations.

But in describing this introspection we intrude on the structure of the inquisitive program itself, a matter of design and implementation rather than of theoretical properties. Having so intruded, we shall complete our step and begin a description of Cyrano's particular implementation.

6   Cyrano: The Implementation

The principles above arose from a careful study of reports on AM and Eurisko, scattered conversations with Lenat himself, some hours interacting with Eurisko at Xerox PARC, and — most importantly — a prototypical implementation of Cyrano which duplicated about half of AM's reported performance. This prototypical implementation duplicated most of the control structure and representation of Eurisko and based on its development, the principles above were formed and clarified. A program implementing these principles — the latest version of Cyrano — is still under development, but enough of its design has been specified to sketch its critical components and new innovations.

The implementation of Cyrano revolves around a subsumption lattice of types and classes. All of Cyrano's concepts are defined as nodes in this lattice and Cyrano's experiments and observations are all described by relations embedded in or attached to the lattice. New concepts are well-formed extensions to the lattice which then are amenable to further experimentation and extension. Cyrano's control structure is also organized around the lattice, which places the program's activities and projects in particular classes within the lattice. This organization replaces the priority queues of AM and Eurisko with myriad "focus classes" of related activities.

These components of Cyrano's design remain essentially experimental; they may be abandoned or changed as their actual performance or behaviour is revealed. Most derive from experience with Eurisko and the prototypical Cyrano: the reasoning behind each design decision is presented below.

6.1   The Type Lattice

All of Cyrano's concepts are represented as "types" in a lattice of generalization and specialization. A fragment of this lattice is shown in Figure LatticeFragment. All of Cyrano's discoveries about the properties of its representations are described in this lattice and the program's new definitions consist of additions to the lattice. Many of Cyrano's actions begin with *classifying* some object in this lattice and using the resulting classification to determine some set of actions. Some of the types in the lattice are the natural classes of various domains; others are empirically collected sets of objects or types (which are also objects); but most are *analytic types* which combine other types into new definitions.

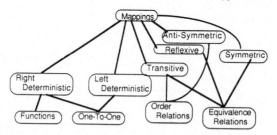

Figure 3. All of Cyrano's concepts and meta-concepts are uniformly represented in a lattice of types.

Some of the types represented in the lattice are *composite*: they specify types of tuples satisfying particular element or inter-element constraints. Functions and relations, for instance, are represented as pairs of other objects and the fact that a function has a particular LISP implementation is merely a heuristic for finding examples of such object pairs. This generality is an attempt to move Cyrano beyond completely specified domains into areas where examples are not always effectively enumerable, such as the real world!

Types in the lattice are of two basic sorts: analytic and synthetic. Analytic types are types whose definition is solely in terms of other types; for instance, the intersection or union of two established types or a constraint on some component of a composite structure. Synthetic types are types whose definition is provided by the "world": for instance, enumerated sets, LISP predicates, or user defined classes. One important sort of synthetic type is the *empirical class* which I describe below; it defines and implements Cyrano's notion of regularities and experimentation.

New types are defined in a combinator language in terms of either existing types or — in the case of some synthetic types — in terms of the behaviour some external interface. The following are examples of type definitions:

```
;;; Defining a type by intersecting two existing types.
(define bachelors (type-intersection men unmarried))
;;; Defining a type by merging two existing types.
(define agents (type-union humans intelligent-programs))
;;; This defines a function call by saying that the image
;;; of the function CAR for function calls is function names.
(define function-calls
   (image-constraint CAR function-names))
;;; This defines points in 3-space as a cross product of
;;; reals.
(define points (cross-product reals reals reals))
;;; This defines the class of LISP functions in a particular
;;; implementation; its uses the LISP predicate functionp.
(define functions (simple-type functionp))
;;; This defines chord triads which the user says are harmonious.
(define harmony
   (type-intersection
   (query-type "harmonious?")
   (cross-product notes notes notes)))
```

Definitions like these describe both Cyrano's initial domain and the constructed domains it develops over time; the program's defining actions construct new types and place these types — as objects — in appropriate classes in the lattice. The central process in Cyrano generates examples for classes in the lattice, in turn triggering the definition of new classes for which examples must be found.

Each of the combinators above possesses a type-inference procedure for computing — on creation — the types neccesarily above and below it in the lattice. One of the properties of the lattice is that for any two given types, no new subsumption relations will ever be established between them. Any newly created type will have new subsumption relations, but those new relations will never posit new relations between types already in the lattice.

It has been shown that type inference in a distributive lattice with complementation is NP-complete[BL84]; my lattice implementation gets around this intractability by weakening representing complementation to representing *disjointness*. Complementation — information that any object not in one class IS in another — allows the inference of certain subsumption relations not otherwise computable from the lattice; this asymmetry makes subsumption in complementary lattices an NP-complete problem. Information about disjointness, on the other hand, only enables further inferences about disjointness, a weaker inference. This weakening is sufficient to make the type inference problem tractable, though still enabling many useful inferences.

Using the lattice to represent all the program's knowledge — both provided and defined — ensures that the modularity constraint is satisfied. Each cycle of concept definition produces extensions to the lattice and places these extensions in meta-classes in the lattice; all of this information is then available to the next phase of discovery.

6.2 Empirical Classes

An inquisitive process proceeds by a cycle of recognition and definition: empirical regularities noticed in one domain vocabulary are used to define terms in the domain vocabulary of the next cycle. The recognition of regularities is one key component of any inquisitive process. In Cyrano, all regularities are represented by subsumption relations in the lattice of concepts.

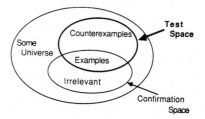

Figure 4 . Empirical classes describe empirical regularities by potential accidental subsumption/subset relations in the lattice.

In particular, Cyrano defines an *empirical class* as a class of classes whose members accidentally (i.e. not by definition) satisfy some empirical property. An empirical class K is determined by two functions: a test function K_{Test} and a confirmation function $K_{Confirm}$. These functions translate an individual class into a *test class* and a *confirmation class*. A regularity K is true of a class c if all instances of $K_{Test}(c)$ are also instances of $K_{Confirm}(c)$ (e.g. for all known examples: $K_{Test}(c) \subseteq K_{Confirm}(c)$). Figure EmpiricalClassesDiagram illustrates a view of confirmation classes as overlapping sets.

The simplest empirical classes have a constant

$$K_{Confirm} = C$$

and

$$K_{Test}(x) = x.$$

These classes encode the simple regularity that some set is contained in a particular constant set. "All X's are red" or "R is a reflexive relation" are instances of such classes. More complicated empirical classes generate test and confirmation classes which combine instances of the class they are testing. For instance, the regularity "F preserves R" has a test class of "pairs of Fs whose inputs are related by R" and a confirmation class of "pairs of Fs whose outputs are related by R."

Membership in an empirical class is determined by defining a class of examples $K_{Test}(c) \wedge K_{Confirm}(c)$ and a class of counterexamples $K_{Test}(c) \wedge \neg K_{Confirm}(c)$. Each of these has classification daemons which — when a counterexample or some quota of positive erexamples is discovered — assert the membership of the class being tested in either the appropriate empirical class or its complement. The representation of all empirical regularities in this manner is an attempt to satisfy the consistency constraint; any defined concept is likely to be amenable to this level of raw empirical analysis. It depends only on definitions of sets and tuples, rather than on arbitrary properties of mutatable list structures.

Of course, setting up a test situation is only part of the confirmation process; it is also neccesary to generate the examples which will fall into the situation. When a test situation is created, a *task* is created for generating examples of $K_{Test}(c)$. The scheduling of these tasks, again using the type lattice, is introduced below.

6.3   Control Structure

Cyrano's control structure has two components: a set of *classification daemons* and a set of active *projects*. A classification daemon is a procedure run on new examples of particular types; a project is an activity divided into quanta of action.

Classification daemons work as follows. Whenever a new potentially interesting object is found or generated, its terminal types (the most specific types it satisfies) are collected. The lattice is then climbed — in the generalization direction — from this set, and at each type along its ascent the classification daemons of that type are applied to the object. This process is called *classification* and is Cyrano's fundamental action.

When a new definition is generated by Cyrano, the definer gives it some set of properties and classifies it. This classification triggers daemons which — based on the properties of the definition — propose hypotheses in terms of empirical classes. These hypotheses set up the confirmation machinery described in the previous section, which then waits for confirming or disconfirming examples. When a hypothesis is confirmed or disconfirmed, it is given the appropriate empricial property (added to the appropriate class) and classified again. This classification may produce either new hypotheses or new definitions, which will once more turn the crank of analysis and definition.

Cyrano's discovery activities divide classification daemons into two interleaved control phases: recognition and extension. In recognition, empirical regularities in an input vocabulary are recognized; in extension, new representations are defined based on these noted regularities. Recognition and extension are further divisible into two control stages each: recognition begins by the *hypothesis* of possible regularities and continues to the *confirmation* of these regularities through analysis by empirical classes; extension begins by definition of primitive concepts and proceeds to their elaboration by pragmatic example-generation information, or the definition of associated operations and functions. These phases, while conceptually distinct, are interleaved into the classification process. Classifying a definition produces hypotheses which set up confirmation machinery; classifying a definition with some noticed empirical property produces new definitions which captialize on that property. Classification of examples and counterexamples drives the confirmation machinery set up by previous classifications of definitions; classification of new definitions produces auxiliary definitions which elaborate simple constructions.

Despite this complexity of actions and triggers, classification daemons are a more or less passive mechanism, reacting to some source of examples streaming in from the world. Cyrano applied to analyzing a mass of scientific data might function precisely in this mode. On the other hand, in many domains (perhaps eventually in all) Cyrano may have to seek or generate examples. For this purpose, AM and Eurisko's notion of *tasks* has been partially appropriated.

Eurisko's tasks were organized into several separate agendas and ordered by a universal priority within each agenda. At any moment, Eurisko worked on a single agenda, selecting and executing the highest priority task on the agenda. Cyrano abandons Eurisko's priority mechanism, choosing instead to enrich the agenda structure. At any point, Cyrano is working on a class of tasks — its *focus class* — which are related in some way. When focussing on a class of tasks, Cyrano executes all the tasks in the class, either in some order or at random. Over time, Cyrano observes the empirical properties of these classes, defining new classes of tasks to which the focus may eventually shift.

Task execution occurs in three stages: triage, execution, and post mortem. In *triage*, the classifier runs on the task description, and daemons construct an "implementation" for the task. This implementation is then used in an *execution* of the task. After the task completes, it is classified again as a *post mortem* perhaps triggering changes in focus or new defintions of task types. Task execution may be thought of as a generator for examples of actions, as well as a mechanism for acting.

Unlike AM and Eurisko's tasks, Cyrano's tasks are never completed in one shot. Instead, they describe ongoing processes divided into quantized actions. The one shot actions of Eurisko are replaced by simple procedure calls, generally from the execution of a classification daemon.

Currently, Cyrano's tasks are only example generation tasks; in the future they will become the backbone of evolving problem solvers for the domains Cyrano is learning in.

7 Conclusion

In conclusion, I will restate the insights into discovery systems put forth in this paper:

* Eurisko-like systems may be viewed as search processes which reconfigure their own search space.
* Concept formation in discovery systems must be functionally modular.
* The formation of new concepts must be "consistent" as well as modular.
* An inquisitive process must ultimately be introspective.

The implementation described here is in active progress, and the results in six months will offer new insights on the mechanisms described in the last section. In the same way that the prototpyical implementation of Cyrano produced the insights above, I look forward to the next phase of implementation as fertile ground for newer insights.

8 Acknowledgements

This work was done at the MIT Artificial Intelligence Laboratory, with support from the Defense Advanced Research Projects Agency under contract number N00014-85-K-0124. Of course, the opinions herein are those of the author and in no way reflect the opinions of the Department of Defense or the US Government. In turn, the opinions of the Department of Defense also in no way reflect the opinions of the author. This research was further supported by a generous equipment grant from Hewlett-Packard.

120   K.W. Haase, Jr.

9 References

[BL84]   Ronald J. Brachman and Hector J. Levesque. The Tractability of Subsumption in Frame-Based Description Languages. In *AAAI-84*, American Association for Artificial Intelligence, 1984.

[Cha83] David Chapman. *Naive Problem Solving and Naive Mathematics*. Working Paper 249, MIT Artificial Intelligence Laboratory, 1983.

[LB83]   Douglas B. Lenat and Jon S. Brown. Why AM and Eurisko Appear to Work. *Artificial Intelligence*, 23, 1983.

[Len76] Douglas B. Lenat. *AM: An Artificial Intelligence Approach to Discovery in Mathematics as Heuristic Search*. PhD thesis, Stanford University, 1976.

[Len82] Douglas B. Lenat. AM: Discovery in Mathematics as Heuristic Search. In Douglas B. Lenat and Randall Davis, editors, *Knowledge Based Systems in Artificial Intelligence*, McGraw-Hill Book Company, 1982. Several appendices of examples were trimmed from the original version of the thesis in this book version.

[Len83a] Douglas B. Lenat. Eurisko: A program which learns new heuristics and domain concepts. *Artificial Intelligence*, 21, 1983.

[Len83b] Douglas B. Lenat. Theory Formation by Heuristic Search. *Artificial Intelligence*, 21, 1983.

[Min86] Marvin Minsky. *The Society of Mind*. Simon and Schuster, 1986. Forthcoming.

Advances in Artificial Intelligence - II
B. Du Boulay, D. Hogg and L. Steels (Editors)
© Elsevier Science Publishers B.V. (North-Holland), 1987

The Expertise of Novice Problem Solvers

W.N.H. Jansweijer, J.J. Elshout, B.J. Wielinga

Institute for Cognitive studies, University of Amsterdam
Weesperplein 8
1018 XA Amsterdam, The Netherlands

ABSTRACT

PDP-O is a computational model of human problem solving behaviour. The model is based on the analyses of protocols from novices solving problems in a semantically rich domain, while thinking aloud. It models part of the general expertise in problem solving that humans have. In the model difficulties in problem solving arise caused by inoperationallity of domain knowledge and lack of domain specific problem solving strategies. These impasses in the object problem solver are repaired by a meta- problem solver. The repairs used are domain independent and independent of the level of domain expertise. We argue that the impasse and repair mechanism plays an integral part in normal problem solving. In addition to this we assume that the impasse can focus learning by doing. We present a trace of the model working on a problem. We show that the behaviour of the implemented model closely matches the behaviour of a subject, when the model is equipped with similar knowledge deficiencies as the subject has.

keywords: problem solving, cognitive modelling, repair theory, learning by doing

1. INTRODUCTION

Computational models of human problem solving usually model *successful* problem solving behaviour only. Examples are the models of human competence in physics problem solving e.g. ABLE (Larkin et.al. 1980), MECHO (Bundy 1979, Luger 1981) and PDP (Konst et. al., 1983). The ACT[*] theory of Anderson (1983a) is a similar theory of human learning and problem-solving behaviour, which is based on succesful performance. Although these models are capable to model *incorrect* behaviour, they can only do this by mutilating the knowledge base or by representing the knowledge in either too restrictive or too general rules. All these models however come to a grinding halt if their knowledge is really defective or inconsistent. They are not able to recover from unexpected problems. The reason is obvious. They miss flexibility in the *process* of problem-solving. They are adequate as long as everything goes well, but they show their insufficiency as a computational model for *human problem solving* whenever an unexpected difficulty comes up. Humans, in contrast to the aforementioned models, use the declarative (factual) knowledge of the domain in a variety of ways, hence controlling problem solving activity. They switch between strategies when an alternative has the better chance and are not apt to just quit when an unexpected difficulty arises. In this way humans usually come to a solution --albeit a suboptimal one--, even when the conditions under which they have to solve a problem(e.g. with inperfect or incomplete knowledge about the domain) are not optimal.

In this paper we will present a computational model of problem solving, that behaves in a flexible way and does not just quit if a difficulty comes up. This model is based on fine grain analyses of think aloud protocols of human problem solvers, solving series of problems in the domain of thermo-dynamics (physics). These analyses were carried out with help of the semi automatic protocol analysis program PDP (Konst et.al., 1983).

We choose to study novices that solve problems because their problem solving behaviour is characterised by many difficulties. They lack full *operationality* of the just acquired domain knowledge and have to resort to general problem solving strategies. Novices (first year psychology students in our study) will give us an extensive sight of the range of problem solving strategies used, because they are naïve in the domain, but have a problem solving ability high enough to be able --at least in principle-- to solve the problems at the presented level of difficulty.

2. NOVICE PROBLEM SOLVING BEHAVIOUR

Novice problem solvers solved series of 35 problems in thermo-dynamics after having followed a short written introductory course on the subject. Their problem solving behaviour was audio and video taped and, later, transcribed verbatim. At first sight their behaviour seems chaotic and unstructured. Further inspection however shows that the problem solving behaviour of beginners is goal directed. Beginners (as all humans) use schemata to decompose a task in several subtasks. The think aloud protocols of these subjects prove that they are strongly aware of their problem solving activity. This can be illustrated with statements in their think aloud protocols that comment the ongoing problem solving activity. Examples of such statements are: *"Now we have to find a principle"* and *"Is it an ideal gas again?"*.   Beginners however lack operational domain knowledge and have to do without domain specific strategies, since this is not the type of knowledge usually presented in course texts. Beginners miss these specific, domain dependent, problem solving strategies used by experts, they have to use more general and therefore *weaker*, problem solving strategies. Therefore they frequently come to dead ends that have to be solved in turn. In this way problem solving is guided alternately by goals and impasses. Impasses set the context for changing the original plan or to switch strategies.

As an example of beginners behaviour we present a fragment taken from the protocol of subject L solving his second problem. First he reads the problem aloud:

A container contains air with a temperature of 290 Kelvin and a pressure is 40 Kpa. The piston is fixed, so the volume does not change. Then heat is added until the pressure has become 80 Kpa. What will be the new temperature in the container?

The subject identifies givens and unknown, and then immediately selects a principle. This brings him in various impasses because he did not analyse the problem in sufficient detail in advance. The example shows that a repair for an impasse can cause a new impasse and that the same impasse can be solved in different ways.[1]

1- 25	⊲these lines contain reading of the problem and identification of givens and unknown⟩
26	Well,
27	Now... ehh... we take Boyle's law *{Subject points to PV= RT}*
28	again they don't...,
29	is it an ideal gas *again* ?
30	that is not mentioned
31	"The temperature in the container is 290
32	volume..., then heat is added until
33	the pressure..."
34	it is *not* mentioned.
35	That is annoying... How about this one? *{Subject points to PV= nRT}*
36	where... ehh.?.. 'n'???
37	then...
38	it *must* be this one *{Subject points to PV= RT}*, I think
39	Let us just try it.

In line 27 subject L selects a principle that relates the unknown to the givens. Checking the precondition for use of this principle fails because information about the ideality of the gas is missing. This deadlock is repaired by reading the problem text again, because the subject knows that this is the kind of information that may be obtained from the problem text. The 'rereading' however does not solve the problem. Then the subject tries to do without this information by trying another principle (line 35), but this immediately leads to a new impasse, namely not knowing what 'n' (molecular mass) stands for. Although itt is not directly clear from *this* part of the protocol that subject L misses knowledge about molecular mass, the following protocols show that subject L actively avoids the use of molecular mass until problem 11 that has this variable as the unknown. There he finally solves this impasse by studying the coursenotes on this subject. After the impasse about 'n'

---

[1] The protocol fragments are translated from Dutch

L decides that his former principle did give the better perspective, but there still is the problem of the missing information about the ideality of gas. This impasse is solved finally, in third instance, by *assuming* it is an ideal gas (line 39).

The preceding protocol fragment of problem 2 continues with an immediate new impasse that is caused by missing knowledge about R (the universal gas constant). It is solved, as it was solved in problem 1, by making an assumption. In problem 1 however (fragment not shown) there was a long impasse about R wich subject first perceived as a variable to compute ("R= 8.314 $Joule/Mol.$ $Kelvin$····· So let me find the Joule.... etc"), before he assumed it to be constant in thats case.

    40   The 'P' is given, it is 40...
    41   The volume .... is constant....
    42   The 'R' .... is it?......
    43   let me see ehm...
    44   does it remain... ehm, stays it constant also?
    45   Yes,... in the last one it remained constant also
    46   So ... why not this time.

Almost all protocols of our novice-subjects contain one or more passages expressing these impasses. As a last illustration we show a fragment of the same subject, this time working on problem 1. It shows an impasse that is solved by doing *nothing* "since the units cancel each other".

    1- 125 <after a lot of muddlement a new principle is selected>
    126   Now I am not sure whether I ehm...
    127   have to write litres or ehm... cubic meters.
    128   How many litres are a cubic metre? 1000?
    129   because a litre is a cubic decimetre...., or not?
    130   no! .... well
    131   it doesn't make any difference,
    132   since the units cancel each other.

From these examples we can see that L actively tries to repair the intervening difficulties. Clearly repairing impasses is not a trial and error procedure. The subject is aware of *profits and losses* of applying a repair and estimates the uncertainty introduced by applying a repair. In the first example for instance subject L does not *start* making an assumption. In the second example the repair is justified because it was successfully applied earlier. In the third example the subject seems to be aware that he does not introduce uncertainty by the repair of doing nothing. He knows that this repair is cheaper than a repair consisting of: 1. finding out what the required units are; 2. finding out the relations between litres, cubic metres and cubic decimetres; 3. doing the transformation.

We conclude that the impasse, and solving it, is an important part of normal problem solving. We assume a problem solver on a meta-level that solves the problems occuring at the object level. The knowledge used by this meta-problem solver is general, domain independent and presented in more detail in § 5.

3. A THEORY OF NOVICE PROBLEM SOLVING

Here we will present a theory of novice problem solving as a computational model. Based on the protocol analyses of novice problem solving we postulate the following properties for such a model:

-   Problem solving is knowledge driven, i.e. the model will have knowledge about 1.) the domain objects and about the 2.) relations between these objects and 3.) knowledge how to exploit this domain knowledge, i.e. knowledge about 3.) problem solving strategies.
-   The object problem solver will be goal driven, since novice problem solving is goal driven. The current goal will determine which strategy from a library will be used.
-   When the problem solver comes to a dead end, a meta- problem solver is needed to solve the problems in the object problem solver.
-   There will be a goal tree that, as a dynamic structure, represents the current plan and determines behaviour at the object level.

- This goal tree will have an *explicit structure* annotated by a trace of the object problem solver actions, since the meta- problem solver has eventually to be able to adjust this control structure.
- There will be a supervising component that checks progress and detects problems in the object level problem solving component. This supervising component can decide to give control to the meta- problem solver for the adjustment of the plan. It can also decide to switch between several plans, that may have been activated during successive problem solving and repair steps.
- There will be a working memory that contains all activated knowledge structures.

The goal tree represents the tasks that must be achieved. It is a dynamic structure created during problem solving. At any time the problem solver focusses on one task, using this as a guide to bring to mind that knowledge that is relevant to the subtask at hand. This knowledge either specifies how this goaltree will be expanded, or what inferences must be made at the object level.

We suppose that the strategies that can be brought to mind with a task are organised in a hiërarchy. The root then represents the general but weak problem solving methods. Towards the leaves of the tree the strategies become more specific and more powerful. The expert will have locally (for his domain of expertise) a "deep" structure, with the leaves representing powerful strategies to solve a small range of problems. These strategies are "compiled expertise": they are a synthesis of strategies and domain knowledge. The beginner will have only the more general strategies with a task. In § 6 we will present an example of the general but weak task decomposition of subject L.

In our model the goal tree fulfills multiple functions. It is the central control structure since each of its nodes is (or becomes) annotated with the problem solving history (side effects, difficulties, repairs). It can have multiple layers, orthogonally organised in a context hiërarchy, representing the different plans that have been activated during repairing impasses. Together these components are configured as shown in Fig 1.

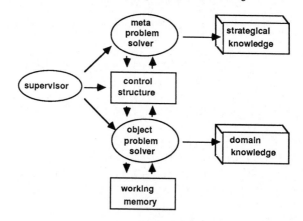

Fig 1.: Architecture of **PDP-0**

The declarative domain knowledge in our model is represented in a ISA- hiërarchy, in a formalism based on KL-One (Brachman, 1978). The Object Problem Solver (called **GOPS** in earlier papers) is driven by a hierarchy of goals (the control structure), dynamically representing the current plan. The strategical knowledge is represented in production rules grouped into small packets (schemata) serving a particular goal. The interplay between the production rules and the KL-One hierarchy of domain concepts enables the formulation of powerful inference rules. Details can be found in Jansweijer and Wielinga (1983). The model is implemented in CProlog.

4. SUPERVISOR

The supervisor inspects continuously the control structure and detects the following problems in the object problem solver:

- there is no known strategy to reach a goal.
- although a strategy to reach a goal is known, it cannot be used because application is currently not allowed.
- a production rule with a true condition side failed unexpectedly on the action side.
- although a strategy to reach a goal is known, it is not effective since none of the production rules did fire.
- An explicit gripe coming from the object level.

Besides the detection of these problems, the supervisor keeps track of progress in problem solving by recording how much time was spent with each (sub)goal. If this exceeds a prespecified amount an impasse will be generated.

If there is an impasse the supervisor will ask the meta- problem solver to propose an adjustment of the plan to continue the stuck problem solving process.

5. META PROBLEM SOLVER

The meta- problem solver tries to solve the difficulties of the object problem solver, that were detected by the supervisor, in a three step process. First the difficulty is categorized into one of a few types of impasses. Then there are general heuristics that propose repairs with each class of impasse. The final step is the specification of the general repair into a concrete new or adjusted plan.

The classification part inspects the control structure and uses rules to classify difficulties in classes of impasses. These classes are:

- wasting resources
    Too much effort (computing time) is spent in a subpart of the problem solving process or --while repairing an impasse-- almost immediately a new difficulty did come up.
- missing information about Concept
    Information is needed that is not available or not in the right form.
- missing declarative knowledge about Concept
    There is no useable domain knowledge available
- missing procedural knowledge about Goal
    There is no known method to reach a goal.
- conflicting information
    During problem solving contradictory information is generated (currently not implemented).

The classification rules are general and independent of the domain. An example (paraphrased in English) is:

> **If** there is an impasse
> *and* this impasse occurs during a repair
> *and* we have spent less effort on this repair than $committing-repair-time-parameter
> **Then** we are wasting resources

The argument for this rule is that there is probably an easier repair for the previous impasse. On the other hand, if we have already invested a lot in solving the problem along this line, it may not be wise to change strategy while there is perhaps an easy repair for the new impasse.

An example of another rule, dealing with the impossibility to foresee (and the undesirability to *have* to foresee!) any possible state of the world, is:

If the impasse was caused by an unexpectedly failing action side of a production rule
   and concept $Concept is mentioned in the rule
   and there is declarative domain knowledge about $Concept
   and $Concept was never referred to before (i.e. it is *not* in working memory).
Then there is missing information about $Concept.

After having classified the difficulty, the second step is to propose a repair to resolve the impasse. There is a collection of general repairs that differ in ease of application and in reliability.

The following repairs can *usually* be done:
   - If you know how to do it, do it now.
   - gather information or knowledge from an external source (a human expert or teacher, a textbook, the written problem), resulting in a changed or improved domain knowledge.
   - switch to an alternate previous plan.
   - if several outcomes are possible with one procedure, try an alternative outcome.
   - if several methods are known to reach a (sub)goal, back-up to that (sub)goal and try an alternative method.
   - make an assumption.
   - check, working backwards, the outcomes of earlier procedures.

A repair that *always* can be done is:
   - ignore the problem.[2]
   - start anew.
   - give up and quit.

In the second phase we use heuristics that link impasses to repairs. As an example we present the heuristic for the impasse *wasting resources* :

   If we are wasting resources
   Then back up to the previous plan and try to proceed with it

for the impasse *missing information* the heuristic is:

   If there is missing information about $Item
   Then consider the following repairs as possible candidates
      - if $Item is something that could be a given then read the problem text again.
      - if a strategy, used earlier, has other possible outcomes then try one of the alternative outcomes.
      - if there is, with an earlier goal, a known alternative strategy, then apply that strategy.
      - if there is a known method to gather $Item, then apply that method.
      - if $item has properties that make it possible to make assumptions about $Item, then assume $Item.
      - if $Item has properties that make it likely that the course text will present that information, then study the course notes (this will result in a changed domain knowledge base).
      - ask $Item.
      - ignore the problem.

The repairs in these rules are ordered with respect to the uncertainty they introduce and to the resources they will demand to execute. The first one found will be proposed as repair for the impasse, with the restriction that never a repair will be proposed that is considered before in the same situation, but was ineffective.

The third and final phase of the three steps process is the particularization of the proposed repair in a specific adaptation of the goal tree. The adaptations are done in a (partial) copy of the control structure. The original plan and repair plans are organized in a context-hiërarchy that is orthogonal to the goal hiërarchy so that it is known within which plan, what repair was executed. This enables switching from one plan to another and the return to a previous plan later. The repairs effectively take the form of:

---
[2] At first sight this a not a usefull "repair", but it is a repair we see with human problem solvers!

- insertion of a specific goal into the goal hiërarchy (control structure) just before the node that caused the difficulty.
- a back- up to the point were there was either a choice made between methods or there was a method with alternative outcomes.
- scream and give up.

6. WORKED EXAMPLE

Here we will present a worked example of our model, simulating part of the problem solving behaviour comparable to that of the presented protocol of subject L working at problem 2. The model is equipped with general, but weak, strategies to solve the problem. This strategy decomposes the task of problem solving in a sequence of three new tasks: *Orientate, Solve* and *Evaluate.* The *Orientation* task strategy is: *Read the problem and Identify the variables.* The solution task strategy consists of a *description of the variables in general terms* followed by the *selection of a principle* . Then the *applicability* and the *preconditions* of this principle are tested. There are two methods in the model for selecting a principle. The first one being *"Select a principle with the asked variable appearing in isolation at the left hand side"* . The second being: *"Select from the list of principles in the coursetext a principle that mentions the asked"*. The declarative domain knowledge about molecular mass is deleted from the knowledge base.

The implemented computer model generates the following problem solving and repair behaviour. The first a problem solving plan generated is retrieved from the task strategy knowledge base of the model. (In the following only the relevant parts of the planning and problem solving process is showed in a condensed form. Also only the solution part is presented, without the orientation part that preceedes it).

Original problem solving plan:

Solve unknown$_1$ [3]

    generalise-variables$_1$ -->   *[pressure, volume, temperature]*

    select-principle-on-pattern$_1$ -->   *[Pressure= Force/ Surface]*

    check-applicability$_1$ -->   **nothing known about 'surface'**

    check-preconditions$_1$

Check-applicability fails (really a subgoal of this goal) and the impasse is diagnosed as missing knowledge about surface. The proposed repair is to read the coursenotes on the subject of surface.

First repair plan:

Solve unknown$_1$

    generalise-variables$_1$ -->   *[pressure, volume, temperature]*

    select-principle-on-pattern$_1$ -->   *[Pressure= Force/ Surface]*

    read-coursenotes$_1$ -->   **nothing In course notes**

    check-applicability$_2$

    check-preconditions$_2$

The plan still fails because the read coursenotes part does not deliver any new information about *surface* . It is diagnosed as a waste of resources (a new difficulty is reached while we just started a repair for the impasse of missing knowledge about 'surface'). The proposed repair is to back up to the former plan, but then the situation is identical to the failing original plan and the impasse is not yet solved. The second repair tried with this impasse is to back- up to a place where a choice was made. The select-principle-on-pattern strategy does not know any other principle of the form *pressure= ......* But there is known an entirely different method to select a principle (select-principle-on-variables).

---

[3] The numbers denote specific instances of the goals

Second repair plan:

Solve unknown$_1$

generalise-variables$_1$	-->	*[pressure, volume, temperature]*
select-principle-on-variables$_1$	-->	*[PV= RT]*
check-applicability$_3$	-->	*ok*
check-preconditions$_3$	-->	**no information about ideality of gas**

This fails because the precondition test fails. The impasse is diagnosed as: "missing information about ideality of gas" and the proposed repair is to reread the problem text.

Third repair plan:

Solve unknown$_1$

generalise-variables$_1$	-->	*[pressure, volume, temperature]*
select-principle-on-variables$_1$	-->	*[PV= RT]*
read-problemtext$_1$	-->	**not in problemtext**
check-applicability$_4$		
check-preconditions$_4$		

Here again a new impasse is reached while just solving the former one. It is diagnosed as wasting resources, therefore it is not attempted to repair this impasse. An alternative repair for the former impasse (no information about ideality of gas) is tried and found as an alternative outcome with the method 'select-principle-on-variables'

Fourth repair plan:

Solve unknown$_1$

generalise-variables$_1$	-->	*[pressure, volume, temperature]*
select-principle-on-variables$_2$	-->	*[PV= nRT]*
check-applicability$_5$	-->	**nothing known about 'n'**
check-preconditions$_5$		

Check-applicability of principle fails again (one of its subgoals) and the impasse is diagnosed as missing knowledge about 'n'. Again however it is also diagnosed as a waste of time to go on along this line (with this new principle) and the proposed repair is to back up to the former plan (repair plan 2) and to repair this plan alternatively with making an assumption about the ideality of gas.

Fifth repair plan:

Solve unknown$_1$

generalise-variables$_1$	-->	*[pressure, volume, temperature]*
select-principle-on-variables$_1$	-->	*[PV= RT]*
check-applicability$_3$	-->	*ok*
make-assumption$_1$	-->	*ok*
check-preconditions$_6$	-->	*ok*

This repair finally solves the problem within the solution part of the problem solving task.

7. CONCLUSIONS AND DISCUSSION

The computational model proves the power that can be obtained with a "two level" problem solver. In such a problem solver the problems as presented are solved at one level, using well known operational knowledge sources. The unexpected difficulties in the object problem solver are solved at another level, using general and domain independent problem solving knowledge. The techniques and the knowledge in the model can be used to build more robust reflective problem solvers.

In **PDP-0** the strategies are explicitly represented and sometimes different strategies are known. This is different from e.g. MECHO that implements a rigid backward search strategy, or the physics model of Larkin that can run in two modes; a backward search mode (modelling novices) and a "knowledge development" mode (modelling experts). The earlier PDP model (Konst et.al.) implemented a mixture of strategies; first a forward working strategy that elaborated the presented problem into a formal description suitable for using physical principles; second a backward search strategy to find principles to solve for the unknown. All these models are however not able to switch strategies if a chosen strategy leads to a dead end.

Our work is related to work in the expert systems field where there is a trend to separate domain knowledge from strategic knowledge, to get explicit control on problem solving. Clancey (1985) for instance represents a task decomposition in a separate goal tree just like we do. This enables him to *explain* the ongoing problem solving activity. We differ from Clancey in our use of such a goaltree, namely to model impasse and repair behaviour as integrated parts of problem solving behaviour of novices. The goaltree in **PDP-0** controls the entire problem solving process.

In building a problem solver that can reason about its problem solving behaviour we can point to related work on *reflective* problem solvers at CMU. SOAR of Laird (Laird, 1984) is an example. He describes a universal subgoaling technique were a difficulty in a problem solving process is solved in subgoals. This technique requires complete knowledge of the problem space. This is however not possible in our domain that is, contrary to the domains suitable for SOAR, semantically rich and ecological valid for *human* problem solving.

The impasse repair mechanism has been described earlier by Brown & vanLehn (1980). Their repair theory however does not explain the *rationality* of the repair mechanism. They describe the repair mechanism as a local problem solver of the generate (a repair) and test (with a critic) type. They present the repair mechanism as necessary to introduce a *manifest bug* . In our opinion the repair mechanism plays an integral part of the normal problem solving activity. Evidence for this can be found in the protocols of our novices. They solved 78% of the problems with a *correct answer.* The solution process of these problems however is paved with repair activities, only 9% of the protocols being without an impasse!

Our think aloud protocols show, besides human problem solving capabilities, also human learning capabilities. This learning however appears to be a complicated process. Humans eventually learn a problem solving strategy that is different from any of the successful problem solving instances. In the above example for instance the successful solution was obtained by making an assumption about the ideality of gas. It would be silly to learn this as a correct problem solving procedure.

It is evident that simple learning mechanism like automatic generalization and discrimination of production rules as proposed by Anderson (Anderson 1983a) are too simple to explain the learning processes in the human. As Anderson himself recently has noted is ".... the discrimination process .... a conscious process operating on declarative memory" (Lewis & Anderson, 1985). We agree with this revision of his ACT[*] theory and think that learning by doing is the *result* of a conscious problem solving process much similar to the repair mechanism presented in this paper. We think that impasses during problem solving can set the right stage for learning by doing.

An apparently important way of learning is the activation of inactive knowledge or the *proceduralization* (c.f. Anderson, 1983b) of knowledge that was previously only declarative. An impasse may focus a learning process based on *proceduralization.* Instructions with problem solving in a new domain usually take the form of advice (e.g. first select the thermo-dynamical system), without specifying *how* that must be done or *why* it is necessary. An impasse gives information about the reason for the action and presents a context to explore how it must be done. Learning techniques similar to the "operationalizing advice" technique of Mostow (Mostow, 1983) can be used to convert initially inoperational advice into an executable strategy. The operationalizing can be guided by information obtained from an impasse and its repair. If a problem solver is capable to *explain* the impasse with use of previously inoperational knowledge or with use of "justification structures" (c.f. Smith e.a., 1985), it can use this explanation to refine the old or learn a new strategy. In the presented example it is essential that, in future, information about ideality of gas is obtained before a principle is selected, since the availability of that information solved the impasse.

We intend to show in future with our model on a few examples the *learning by doing* based on impasses, where a difficulty focusses the learning process.

8. REFERENCES

Anderson, J.R. (1983a): *The Architecture of Cognition.*   Harvard University Press. Cambridge Massachusettes.

Anderson, J.R. (1983b): *Acquisition of Proof skills in geometry.* in: R.S. Michalski, J.G. Carbonell and T.M. Mitchel (Eds.). Machine Learning: An Artificial Intelligence Approach. Tioga Publishing Company. Palo Alto, Californië.

Brachman, R.J. (1978): *A structural paradigm for representing knowledge.* Techn. Report No. 3605. Cambridge, MA: Bolt Beranek and Newman.

Brown, J.S. and K. VanLehn (1980): *Repair theory: A Generative Theory of Bugs in Procedural Skills.* Cognitive Science 4, pp 379-426.

Bundy, A., Byrd, L., Luger, G., Mellish, C., and Palmer, M. (1979): *Solving mechanics problems using meta-level inference.* Proceedings of the 6th IJCAI, pp 1017-1027.

Clancey, W.J. (1985): *Acquiring, Representing and Evaluating a Competence Model of Diagnostic Strategy.* Report No. KSL-84-2, Stanford Knowledge Systems Laboratory. Palo Alto, CA.

Jansweijer, W.N.H & B.J. Wielinga (1984): *Modelling Novice Problem Solving Behaviour.* in: T. O'Shea (Ed.) ECAI-84: Advances in Artificial Intelligence, pp 449-454. Elsevier Science Publishers B.V. (North-Holland).

Konst, L., B.J. Wielinga, J.J. Elshout and W.N.H. Jansweijer (1983): *Semi Automated Analysis of protocols from novices and experts solving physics problems.* Proceedings of the 8th IJCAI, pp 97-100, Karlsruhe W-Germany.

Laird, J.E. (1984): *Universal Subgoaling.*   Doctoral Dissertation. Report CMU-CS-84-129. Carnegie-Mellon University., Pittsburgh, PA.

Larkin, J.H., McDermott, J., Simon, D.P., and Simon, H.A. (1980): *Models of Competence in Solving Physics Problems.* Cognitive Science 4, pp 317-345.

Lewis, M.W. and J.R. Anderson (1985): *Discrimination of Operator Schemata in Problem Solving: Learning from Examples.* Cognitive Psychology 17, pp 26-65.

Luger, G.F. (1981): *Mathematical Model Building in the Solution of Mechanics Problems: Human protocols and the MECHO trace.* Cognitive Science 5, pp 55-77.

Mostow, D.J. (1983): *Learning by being told: Machine transformation of advice into a heuristic search procedure.* in: R.S. Michalski, J.G. Carbonell and T.M. Mitchel (Eds.). Machine Learning: An Artificial Intelligence Approach. Tioga Publishing Company. Palo Alto, Californië.

Smith R.G., H.A. Winston, T.M. Mitchell and B.G. Buchanan (1985): *Representation and Use of Explicit Justification for Knowledge base Refinement.* Proceedings of the 9th IJCAI, pp 673-680, Los Angeles.

Advances in Artificial Intelligence - II
B. Du Boulay, D. Hogg and L. Steels (Editors)
© Elsevier Science Publishers B.V. (North-Holland), 1987   131

EXPLORING ALGORITHMS THROUGH MUTATIONS

Viviane Jonckers

Artificial Intelligence Laboratory
Vrije Universiteit Brussel
.Pleinlaan 2
1050 Brussels
Belgium

ABSTRACT

An experiment is reported to explore variants of an existing algorithm by mutating its components. We aim at investigating algorithm variants that change the underlying principles or improve the algorithm's functionality. The explicit representation of high level programming constructs is argued to be crucial for this experiment. Algorithms are modeled as structured combinations of high level computational concepts. A set of possibly interesting mutations is associated with each high level computational concept. Nodes in the algorithm model can be marked as candidates for exploration depending on their role. Application of the transformations in some cases leads to new useful algorithms. A classic router known as the LEE grid expansion router is used as an example.

1. INTRODUCTION.

An experiment in algorithm exploration by mutation of an initial algorithm is discussed. Exploring algorithms means to investigate variants of it which are more optimal solutions to the same problem or similar solutions to similar problems. We will not address the exploration of alternatives to optimise implementation but aim at exploring variants that change the underlying principles or improve the algorithm's functionality in an aspect meaningful to the application domain.

The following issues must be addressed :

*   How can an algorithm be represented or modeled to support a task like algorithm exploration.
*   How can the mutations or transformations be formalised.
*   How can the exploration process draw upon domain knowledge to choose and evaluate mutations.

Research sponsored by Bell Telephone mfg. Co.

The experiment is conducted as an exercise to investigate and evaluate different aspects of knowledge in the domain of programming. Our overall objective is to develop a framework in which expert programming knowledge can be expressed and used in various tasks related to programming such as: algorithm design or synthesis, design and implementation of abstract data types, automatic selection of data structures and algorithms, and in general program synthesis, verification, debugging, exploration and optimisation.

This framework is based upon formalisations of an expert programmer's vocabulary. This vocabulary reflects the broad knowledge an experienced programmer has about the the domain of programming. Besides concrete programming concepts such as the primitive data types, primitive operations and basic control structures of a specific programming language he masters a range of abstract programming concepts including abstract data concepts, standard programming forms, general problem solving paradigms and associated programming techniques. He knows how to implement the abstract concepts using the more concrete ones, views the same concept differently in different situations, knows about several types of relations between different concepts and exploits all these types of knowledge when confronted with various programming tasks.

Development of this programing environment requires both identification and formalisation of the expert vocabulary and associated expert programming knowledge. Representions for different types of programming knowledge that enhance the exploitation of the captured knowledge must be developed. We are using the knowledge representation system KRS currently under development at the VUB AI-LAB (Steels 86) as a foundation. KRS consists of a concept system and various libraries of formalisms each implementing specific knowledge representation styles including rules, frames and logic. The notations used in this paper are informal reflections of actual code written in the KRS concept language. Their meaning and purpose should be intuitively clear from the surrounding discussions.

The remainder of this paper discusses an experiment in algorithm exploration conducted in this environment. It illustrates the power of the high level programming constructs supported explicitly in the environment. In particular attention is given to the modeling of algorithms as structured combinations of high level computational concepts. It is shown how the exploration task is enhanced by these explicit representations in different aspects. High level computational concepts are associated with a set of possibly interesting mutations that can be performed on them. Nodes in the model of the algorithm can be marked as candidates for exploration depending on their role in the algorithm. Application of the transformations leads in some cases to new useful algorithms.

The paper is structured as follows. The next section introduces the example algorithm used in the experiment: a classic router known as the LEE grid expansion router. Section 3 presents the high level computational concepts and develops the algorithm model for the example. In section 4 mutations on the computational concepts are discussed and applied to the algorithm model of the example algorithm. Relations to other research are discussed to conclude the paper.

2. THE LEE GRID EXPANSION ROUTER.

The example algorithm is a router, commonly used in CAD for VLSI design to draw connections between modules, known as a LEE grid expansion router (Lee 1961). The basic problem is to draw a line or wire from a start point to a target point in a grid. Some places in the grid are occupied by modules, others are occupied by previously routed connections. The start point serves as the initial front wave. The diamond-shape front wave is stepwise expanded to include the neighbouring grids until the target-point is reached. Then a route is found for the connection and marked by tracing the information kept in the work table. Figure 1 captures the basic idea of the technique by showing a simplified form of both the work table and the result for routing just one connection.

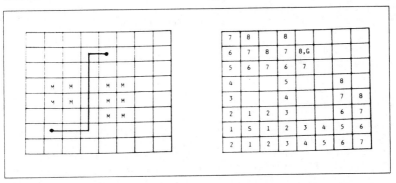

Figure 1: Simplified view of the result and work-table for the Lee grid expansion technique.

3. EXPLICIT ALGORITHM MODELS.

3.1. Introduction.

The algorithm presented in the previous section can be coded in a few hundred lines of code in most programming languages. Why can't we use the source code of the algorithm as a representation in our experiment? There are several problems:

* Syntactic distinctions on source code level do not reflect the semantic distinctions meaningful to the domain of the algorithm. The source code is in this view a too fine grained representation and making mutations on it will produce mostly nonsense.

* Often only many coordinated mutations on source code level will produce a useful transformation on the algorithm. Pieces of code that together

constitute a complete step or action of the implemented technique are shatered through the source code.

* Any implementation of an algorithm contains parts of code that do not really contribute to the implemented technique but only provide some environment and initialisations needed for implementation issues. This distinction is not reflected in the source code.

In an algorithm model that supports algorithm exploration the operations must be abstracted to a level where the abstractions capture combinations that perform complete steps of the implemented technique. The rest of this section introduces high level programming concepts explicitly supported in our programming environment. Special attention is given to the high level computational concepts and it is shown how they can be exploited for our purpose in different aspects including:

* Algorithms are modeled as structured combinations of high level computational concepts.

* The role performed in the global algorithm by each computational concept is marked at the corresponding node in the algorithm model.

* The set of possibly meaningful mutators on a computational concept is explicitly associated with the concept.

3.2. High level programming constructs.

In our environment explicit representations for high level programming concepts are supported that can be used to model a problem solution. They include representations of concrete and abstract data structures and of computational constructs such as functions, predicates, control structures, standard programming forms and general programming techniques. We will focus here on the formalisations of the computational constructs relevant to the experiment.

Besides abstractions of more basic operations which often correspond to functions in the underlying language, abstractions for complex computational constructs, called **cliches** have been introduced. They capture standard programming forms and techniques known by expert programmers. Cliches differ from operations in our terminology because they take other operations such as predicates, functions or other cliches as inputs which makes them higher order functions. This implies that cliches can also be used to model control abstractions.

Informal descriptions of cliches used in the example algorithm are shown in figure 2.

–   When initialising the tables used in the implementation a collection of modules must be marked on the grid. Later the routing of each connection in a collection of connections must be activated. Both tasks need a control structure that applies or calls the same action or function over each member of a collective data structure. The *map* cliche captures this control abstraction.

- Finding a path through the grid from one point to another is basically a search problem. The name of the algorithm 'grid expansion' indicates that the search is implemented here as the repetitive expansion of an initial collection of (reached) points in the grid. The search terminates when the target point is reached or when the expansion cannot proceed (for example when the collection to expand becomes empty). This common technique of enlarging an initial collection until a condition on the collection is satisfied is abstracted as the *expand* cliche. This cliche is in a certain respect a control abstraction but it at the same time the abstraction of a general problem solving technique.

- Typical examples of a class of cliches abstracting powerful operations are various *transform* cliches that define a collection by applying the same transformation function to each object of a given collection and collecting the results. A *transform&unite* cliche is used in the example algorithm to expand the collection of reached grid points to the collection of neighbouring grid points.

```
A CLICHE
  MAP
    MAP-OVER a collection
    MAP-ACTION a mutating-operation

A CLICHE
  EXPAND
    EXPAND-OVER a variable
    INITIALLY a collection
    NEXT an operator over a collection and defining a collection
    TERMINATE-WHEN a predicate

  A CLICHE
    TRANSFORM&UNITE
      TRANSFORM-WHAT a collection
      TRANSFORMER an operation
```

Figure 2 : Specification of computational concepts.

The informal specifications such as those shown in figure 2 intend to capture the creation of corresponding *concepts* in the KRS concept graph. Only the input/output descriptions of functions and cliches are shown here. The specifications are sufficient to use the concepts for modeling solutions to problem tasks. In practice many more types of information are associated with the concepts. For example associating *definitions* with computational concepts (in the implementation encapsulations of lisp forms) yields the functionality of a high level programming language. This aspect is not elaborated in detail in this context, more information can be found in Steels (1985) and Jonckers (1986). In the remainder of this paper different other aspects of the concepts will be made explicit. This is possible because of the object–oriented approach to the formalisation of programming concepts.

3.3. A model for the Lee grid expansion router.

Modeling an algorithm with cliche's resembles at the surface programming in a very high level language. To illustrate the use of concepts to model an algorithm the Lee routing technique is modeled to some level of detail in figure 3. Some parts are not completely worked out because of space limitations. Enough material is provided to illustrate the idea of algorithm transformation later on. Some cliches are used which were not introduced in the previous section but their meaning can be determined from the names used.

```
AN ALGORITHM  LEE-ROUTER
              MODULES a typed collection of modules
              CONNNECTIONS a typed collection of connections
              WORK-TABLE a table
              KEEP-TABLE a table
              TEMPLATE
                A SEQUENCE
                  MARK-ALL-MODULES
                    ROLE initialisation
                    A MAP
                      MAP-OVER  the modules
                      MAP-ACTION mark module in the work table
                  ROUTE-ALL-CONNECTIONS
                    ROLE control
                    A MAP
                      MAP-OVER  the connections
                      MAP-ACTION  the route-connection
                  read out the keep-table

              ROUTE-CONNECTION
                CONNECTION a connection
                  A SEQUENCE
                    clear the work-table
                    SEARCH-FOR-ROUTE
                    ROLE technique
                    AN EXPAND
                      USING [access front-wave]
                      INITIALLY singleton including start-point of the connection
                      NEXT  A TRANSFORM&UNITE
                      TRANSFORM-WHAT the front-wave
                      TRANSFORMER mark and collect all neighbours
                      TERMINATE-WHEN goal-point of connection in the front-wave
                    mark connection in keep table
```

Figure 3 : Model for the Lee grid expansion router.

Again it is important to emphasise that the informal specifications used in figure 3 are abstractions of the actual code written in the KRS concept-language. That code in turn stands for much more than the syntax of a programming language. It serves to create corresponding concepts and establish explicitly all the necessary relations between them. The algorithm model is a structured combination of high level programming concepts.

4. MUTATIONS ON THE ALGORITHM MODEL.

4.1. Associating mutators with cliches.

Different cliches are likely to be meaningfully transformable with different mutations. Some examples are provided in this section but clearly a lot of work
remains to be done to provide a catalog of mutations for each cliche. The possible mutations are explicitly represented as *mutator* concepts and are associated
with the involved cliches. The mutators introduced in this section will be used in
the following section to explore the Lee grid expansion router.

A first example is the map cliche introduced as abstraction for applying the same
action over each element of a collection. The effect of the map is produced by
the side effect(s) of the *map-action*. Mutating this action results in a mutation
on the global construct. The task of detecting useful transformations can be
delegated to the involved action. Delegation is a general but weak mutator that
controls exploration of useful transformations on algorithm components. More
powerful are the mutations that are specifically interesting to a particular construct.

Since in the map cliche side effects are involved, the order of execution of the
action over the members of the collection can be important. Therefore introducing an ordering, depending on some specific property of the collection elements,
before executing the map is a possible mutation. This *introduce–order* mutator
will try out several ordering strategies on the collection elements. The ordering
strategies are either choosen from explicitly modeled domain knowledge or are
orderings on some attribute of the collection elements that has an order relation
defined on it.

```
MUTATORS OF MAP
    A DELEGATION                AN INTRODUCE-ORDER
        TO the map-action           ON the map-over


MUTATORS OF EXPANSION
    A DELEGATION                A DELEGATION
        TO the initially            TO the terminate-when

    A DELEGATION                AN INTRODUCE-SELECTION
        TO the next                 ON the input of the next
```

Figure 4 : Specification of mutators on cliches.

As second example the various mutators associated with the expand cliche are
shown. Changing the initial collection and changing the termination condition
will change the overall construct. Other interesting mutations concern the function or operator that constructs in each step the current collection from the previous one. There are two possibilities. The first is again a delegation to the next
function or operator. But more interesting in the context of expansion is the idea

that it is not necessary to expand the current collection as a whole.

An *introduce-selection* mutator is used to explore this possibility. This mutator will try out several selection criteria on the collection elements. These criteria are either choosen from explicitly modeled domain knowledge or are standard criteria such as orderings on some attribute of the collection elements. This type of mutation imposes additional changes to the control and data structures since not expanding all collection elements in one step will make it necessary to preserve unhandled elements for later use. The specifications in figure 4 associate the discussed mutators with the cliches.

4.2. Transformations on the Lee grid expansion router.

Once an algorithm is modeled as a combination of cliches, every single cliche can be given the opportunity to try out some or all of its mutators. This can be automated by setting up a control process that takes care of resource distribution and bookkeeping operations. Any implementation of an algorithm, and this proves also to be true for an implementation in high level constructs, contains parts of code that do not really contribute to the core of the implemented technique but only initialise some environment or are necessary for some implementation issues. It must be avoided to spend resources on these components. Nodes worth exploring can be explicitly marked as such (as was done in the algorithm model in figure 3) or can receive a higher credit to start with.

A few mutations on the Lee grid expansion router are explored here manually and the improvement or different result as compared to the original algorithm is explained.

4.3. Exploring mutations on the map cliche.

A first candidate for transformation is the route-all-connections node which is just a single map over a colletion of connections. The *introduce-order* mutator associated with the map cliche is used on it. Figure 5 shows the different results produced by the algorithm when the subject length of connection was used as ordering criterium. Routing long wires before short ones results in a solution that is more balanced, meaning that the maximal wire length was improved. The inverse ordering results is a solution where the total wire length is improved but the result is less balanced. Maximal wire length, total wire length, mean wire length, etc. are known evaluation criteria in the context of connection routing.

Figure 6 shows a mutated version of the node in the algorithm model that controls the routing of all connections. Sort-decending is an existing function. The introduce-order mutator associated with the map cliche automatically selected to use this function on the length of a routing connection because the function sort-decending is known to introduce order on numbers and the length of a connection is a number attribute. In the literature on routing techniques a lot of attention is given to ordering criteria for routing connections. When specific ordering techniques on connections are explicitly modeled as domain knowledge in the routing domain, the introduce-order mutator can use them.

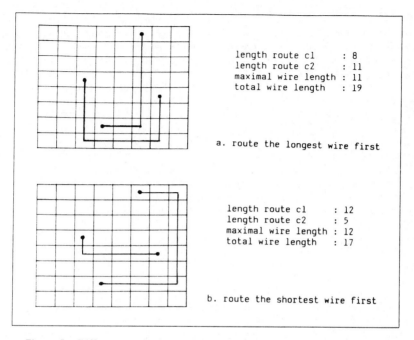

length route c1   : 8
length route c2   : 11
maximal wire length : 11
total wire length   : 19

a. route the longest wire first

length route c1   : 12
length route c2   : 5
maximal wire length : 12
total wire length   : 17

b. route the shortest wire first

Figure 5 : Different results for routing two connections in different order.

```
ROUTE-ALL-CONNECTIONS of LEE-ROUTER
   A MAP
   MAP-OVER  A SORT-DECENDING
                SORT-WHAT the connections
                SORT-ON the length of one-connection
   MAP-ACTION  the route-connection
```

Figure 6 : The transformed version of the node controlling the routing
              of all connections.

Although the node controlling the marking of the modules in the keep-table is
very similar it was not investigated because it was marked as being non contributing to the technique since it performs just some initialisations.

4.4. Exploring mutations on the expand cliche.

A more complicated example is found in the route–connection node implementing the search for a route for one connection. The mutator *introduce-selection*
looks again for attributes of the elements of the collection that can be used to
select elements to be treated by preference. The distance between a wave–point
and the target–point of the connection to be routed is such an interesting attribute.

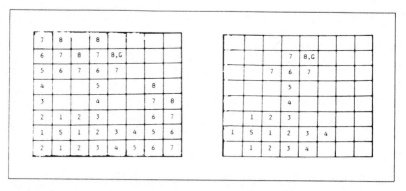

Figure 7 : View on the work table of the initial and transformed algorithm.

Figure 7 shows the result of running a transformed version of the algorithm
where the points in the wave closest to the target–point are expanded first. The
work–table contents for the original and transformed version of the algorithm are
compared for an example where just one connection had to be routed.   The
transformation proves to be meaningful, not because it produces different results
but because the result is in general obtained faster which means by visiting less
grids. The number of grids visited is a standard evaluation criterium in the context of search in a grid.

Writing out this mutation is more complicated since some extra work needs to be
done to keep around the points in the wave that were not selected for immediate
expansion and recombine them to the newly produced points to make them available for later use. A simple (but unefficient) variant is to select the points from
the collection just before the expansion and then unite the set of newly attained
points with the set of points that were not selected. The next operation of the
route–connection node of the mutated algorithm model is shown in figure 8. The
other parts of the algorithm model remain unchanged.

```
NEXT OF ROUTE-ONE-CONNECTION OF LEE-ROUTER
   A BLOCK
      SPLITTED-COLLECTION
         A SPLIT-BY-SELECTION
            SELECT-FROM the input of the next
            SELECT-ON minimal distance to target point
      A UNITE
         UNITE-WHAT
            A TRANSFORM&UNITE
               TRANSFORM-WHAT the selected-elements of the splitted-collection
               TRANSFORMER mark and collect all neighbours
            UNITE-WITH the unselected-elements of the splitted-collection
```

Figure 8 : The mutated route–connection node of the Lee grid expansion router.

5. CONCLUSIONS

The overall goal of our research is to identify and investigate representations for different types of programming knowledge. They are integrated in a programming environment and used for conducting experiments in knowledge based programming. Our approach follows a line of research on the use of AI techniques to support programming. The common theme is the embedding of expert programming knowledge in computer systems to exploit it for automatic or partial automated programming. Work originating from the PSI project started at Stanford illustrates the knowledge based approach to program synthesis (Green&Barstow 1978 ; Barstow 1979). At MIT research on the Programmer's Apprentice Project (Rich&Shrobe 1978 ; Waters 1981) addresses the representation of knowledge and reasoning techniques needed to support intelligent interactive software development.

In this paper the explicit representation of abstract data concepts and abstract computational concepts is argued to be a fundamental contribution to this environment. The abstract data concepts and abstract computational concepts introduced in our environment are in many aspects similar to the *plans* introduced as formal representations in the Programmer's Apprentice (Rich 1981). The high level programming concepts are in our environment fully exploited as hooks for the formalisation of various types of knowledge.

The paper discussed in particular an experiment in algorithm exploration by mutation of an initial algorithm model. Our experiment relates to Lenats experiments with AM and EURISKO (Lenat 1979; Lenat 1983) for getting machines to learn by discovery. Discovery is certainly to big a word for what we want to achieve in this experiment but some of the representation issues are common. In Lenat's experiments the choice of the representations also proved to be of critical importance for getting some useful results (Lenat&Brown 1984).

Program transformation is a long standing approach to automatic programming. Some transformation systems have as objective program improvement. Changing

programs written in a target language by application of transformations is introduced by various researchers: Darlington and Burstall (1976); Baltzer, Goldman
and While (1976). Other transformation systems address the automatic selection
of efficient implementations for abstract data concepts. An example is the
approach to program synthesis by refinement of abstract programs reported by
Barstow (1981) and Kant (1979). Relevant issues are the identification of the
programming knowledge to embody in these transformation systems and the techniques necessary to conduct the transformations.

An earlier paper (Jonckers 1985) describes how AI techniques can be used to
guide the selection and coordination of existing specialised algorithms. It was
argued there that explicit representations of available algorithms are necessary to
conduct this task. Moreover it introduced the notion of modeling the computational part of such an algorithm at a much higher level of abstraction than provided by a classical programming language in order to capture the structure or
core of the implemented technique. This was exploited to introduce additional
structure in the hierarchies of algorithm models. The present experiment showed
that the same algorithm model could be exploited to explore meaningful variants
on an algorithm.

ACKNOWLEDGEMENTS

I would like to thank all members of the VUB AI–LAB for the environment,
discussions and comments. In particulary Luc Steels who provides continuous
support and read previous drafts of this paper.

REFERENCES

Balzer, R., Goldman, N., and While, D. (1976) On the transformational implementation approach to programming. In *Proceedings of the Second International Conference on Software Engineering.* Long Beach, California.

Barstow, D.R. (1979) *Knowledge–based Program Construction.* New–York:
Elsevier North–Holland.

Barstow, D.R. (1981) An Experiment in Knowledge–Based Automatic Programming. In B.L. Webber and N.J. Nilsson (eds.): *Readings in Artificial
Intelligence.* Tioga Publishing Company, Palo Alto California.

Darlington, J., and Burstall, R. (1976) A System which Automatically improves
Programs. *Acta Informatica,* 6, 41–60.

Green, C.C., and Barstow, D.R. (1978) On Program Synthesis Knowledge.
Artificial Intelligence, 10 (no.3), 241–279.

Jonckers, V. (1985) Knowledge Based Selection and Coordination of Specialised
Algorithms. In *Proceedings of the Fifth International Workshop on Expert
Systems and their applications,* Avignon, May.

Jonckers, V. (1986) Generalisation Hierarchies in Knowledge Based Programming. In *Proceedings of the Sixth International Workshop on Expert Systems and their applications,* Avignon, April.

Kant, E. (1979) Efficiency in Program Synthesis. In H.S. Stone (ed.): *Computer Science: Artificial Intelligence, No.8.* Umi Research Press, Ann Harbor Michigan.

Lee, C.Y. (1961) An Algorithm for Path Connections and Its applications. *IRE Transactions on Electronic Computing* 346–365, September.

Lenat, D.B. (1979) On Automated Scientific Theory Formation : A Case Study Using the AM Program. In J.Hayes, D.Mitchie, L.I.Mikulish (eds.): *Machine Intelligence 9,* Halstead Press, New-York.

Lenat, D.B. (1983) EURISKO: A Program That Learns New Heuristics and domain concepts. *Artificial Intelligence, 21* (no. 1,2) 61–98.

Lenat, D.B.; Brown, J.S. (1984) Why AM and EURISKO Appear to Work, *Artificial Intelligence, 23* (no. 3) 269–294.

Rich, C. (1981) A Formal Representation for Plans in the Programmer's Apprentice. In *Proceedings of the Seventh International Joint Conference on Artificial Intelligence.* Vancouver, Canada.

Rich, C., and Shrobe, H. (1978) Initial Report on a LISP Programmers Apprentice. *IEEE Transactions on Software Engineering,* 4 (no. 6), 456–467.

Steels, L. (1985) Algorithmic Concepts in KRS. In *Proceedings van het NGI-SION symposium 3.* Utrecht, Nederland.

Steels, L. (1986) The KRS Concept System. Technical Report 86–1 A.I. Lab. Brussels University.

Waters, R.C. (1979) A Method for Analyzing Loop Programs. *IEEE Trans. on Software Eng.,* SE–5 (no.3), 237–247.

Advances in Artificial Intelligence - II
B. Du Boulay, D. Hogg and L. Steels (Editors)
© Elsevier Science Publishers B.V. (North-Holland), 1987

CO-ADAPTATION AND THE DEVELOPMENT OF COGNITIVE STRUCTURES

Robert W. Lawler
GTE Laboratories
Waltham, MA 02254, USA

Things developed for one purpose often can be used for something else. Systems, individuals, and even their component parts evolved under one set of environmental pressures may function well and with significantly different impact in changed circumstances. The general name for this circumstance is the **coadaptation** of structures[1]. The idea of coadaptation is extremely useful in explaining saltations in performance. I aim to produce a more articulate description of the role of coadaptation in the development of structures for thinking.

Within a function-oriented structuralist view of human learning, a central challenge is explaining the transition from naïveté to mastery. This is likewise a major issue for machine learning. I report here progress on that theme with programming experiments taking guidance from a human case study[2]. The domain is tictactoe. The human case serves as the developmental prototype; it answers the question "why this way?" The machine case serves as an experimental laboratory for asking "how hard or simple might the development be?" For a sketch of program modules and control structure see Figure I. Performance objectives are to develop programs that will achieve primitive forms of abstraction, create internal reflections of external objects and processes, and learn without instruction.

From Anterior Structures to Mature Performance

Piaget's "conservation" experiments are strong evidence that knowledge in the naive mind leads to reasoning surprisingly different from that in expert minds (see, for example, Piaget 1952). Such studies lead us to focus on the issues of what are the precursors of and the processes leading to mature performances. With humans, mature skills can arise from small but significant changes in the organization of pre-existing, fragmentary bodies of common-sense knowledge[3] which represent the things of everyday experience and operations on them. If one could specify the character and function of antecedent structures, he could explain large scale behavior changes as saltations emergent from minimal internal organizational changes.

The Neophyte: particularity and egocentricity

Children's early cognition is usually described as "concrete", a term which has two significant dimensions of meaning. The broader meaning is that the child's knowledge is based upon personal experience. It is in this sense that concrete knowledge is very **particular**, that is, depending on the specific details of the learner's interaction with people and things. Lawler's subject was observed beginning to play tictactoe strategically by imitating a three-move plan for establishing a fork another child performed. The characteristics of her knowledge at that time were particularity and egocentricity. **Particularity:** when her sole plan was blocked, she was unable to develop any alternative[4]. **Egocentricity:**[5] she did not attend to the moves of her opponent unless they directly interfered with her single plan. In the setting of a competitive game, this was bound to change. But how, if a mind constructs itself from such beginnings, is it possible to escape the particularity and egocentricity characteristic of early experiences? The journey from neophyte to master is a long one. One hope of the human study was tracing the path of such development. One objective of the machine study is constructing such a path.

---

[1] This is a technical use of the term, following Satinoff in "Neural Organization and the Evolution of Thermal Regulation in Mammals", 1978: "...most, if not all thermoregulatory reflexes evolved out of systems that were originally used for other purposes.... This illustrates **the principle of evolutionary coadaptation: a mechanism evolved for one purpose has as a side benefit an adaptive value in an entirely different system.**" For a profound and more general discussion of related views, see Jacob's "Evolution and Tinkering", 1977/1982. See also Caple, Balda, and Willis.

[2] The material used here is detailed in Chapter 4 of **Computer Experience and Cognitive Development** (CECD), Lawler, 1985. The subject will be referred to as "Lawler's subject".

[3] Such a viewpoint is detailed in Chapter 2 of CECD.

[4] The detailed background for the subject and this incident are presented at pp. 120-122 in CECD.

[5] Piaget introduced this characterization in **The Language and Thought of the Child.**

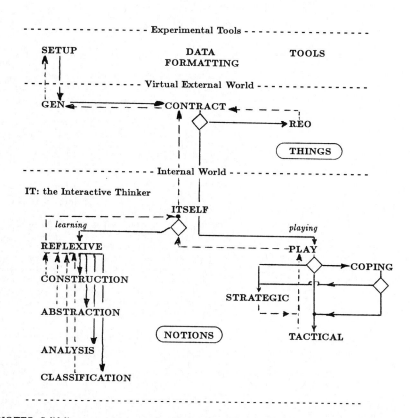

FUNCTIONING MODULES OF A VIRTUAL UNIVERSE

FIGURE I

NOTES: Solid lines represent invocation; dashes show control return. GEN represents the the possibility of various experiences, and is thus part of the world rather than an experimental tool. REO is a "reasonably expert opponent". THINGS are external tokens perceptible by both REO and IT; NOTIONS are things of the internal world available to IT for both playing and learning.

Representation of Knowledge

The representation used to model Lawler's subject's naive knowledge, presented in detail in "Learning Strategies through Interaction" by Lawler and Selfridge, 1985, has the parts necessary for adaptive functioning. Learning what to do is essential: GOALS are explicitly represented. Knowing how to achieve a goal is essential: ACTION PLANS are explicitly represented. Knowing when a planned action will work and when it won't is essential: CONSTRAINTS limiting application of actions are represented explicitly. The structure composed of this triad, a GAC (Goal, Action, Constraints), is my representation of a strategy for achieving a fork in tictactoe. Goals are considered as a three element set of the learner's marks which take part in a fork. This is the first element of a strategy. Plans of three step length, which add the order of achieving goal steps, are represented as lists. Constraints on plans are two element sublists, the first element being the step of the plan to which the constraint attaches and the second being the set of cell numbers of the opponent's can win, block, and apply various rules of cell choice – though ignorant of any strategies of the sort IT is learning. Within the execution of a simulation, the structure of GAC 1 below will lead to the three games shown depending on the opponent's moves (letters are for IT's moves, numbers for REO's):

	GOAL	ACTION	CONSTRAINT
GAC 1:	{1 3 9}	[1 9 3]	< [3{258}] >
win by plan	plan defeat	constrained draw	cell numbers

A	3	C
	1	D
2		B

A		C
2	1	3
		B

A	C	3
4	1	E
D	2	B

1	2	3
4	5	6
7	8	9

The representation and learning mechanisms are committed to cell-specificity; they are also self-centered, focussing on the learner's own plans and knowledge (as they must since, by principle, IT begins not knowing what the opponent will do; IT does not have the ability to model or predict an opponent's moves in any abstract way). The result of learning simulations is a **descent network** which specifies all the goals and plans learned as modifications of the generating precursors of each.

ESCAPING FROM PARTICULARITY

If we ask where symmetry comes from in a world of highly particular descriptions, the answer MUST involve abstraction, but which form of those kinds possible? Abstraction by feature-based classification is the most commonly recognized form, but there are others. Piaget emphasizes a kind of abstraction, focussing more on **what one does** rather than on **what one attributes to external things** as a quality. This **reflexive abstraction** is a functional analysis of the genesis of some knowledge[6], as presented in Bourbaki's description of the generality of axiomatic systems:

> A mathematician who tries to carry out a proof thinks of a well-defined mathematical object, which he is studying just at this moment. If he now believes that he has found a proof, he notices then, as he carefully examines all the sequences of inference, that only very few of the special properties in the object at issue have really played any significant role in the proof. It is consequently possible to carry out the same proof also for other objects possessing only those properties which had to be used. Here lies the simple idea of the axiomatic method: instead of explaining which objects should be examined, one has to specify only the properties of the objects which are to be used. These properties are placed as axioms at the start. It is no longer necessary to explain what the objects that should be studied really are....
>
> N. Bourbaki, in Fang, p. 69.

Robust data argue that well articulated, reflexive forms of thought are less accessible to children than adults. The possibility that mature, reflexive abstraction is unavailable to naive minds raises this theoretical question: **what process of functional abstraction precedes such fully articulated reflexive abstraction**; could such a precursor be the kernel from which such a mature form of functional abstraction may grow?

The Multi-modal Mind

Let us discriminate among the major components of the sensori-motor system and their cognitive descendents, even while assuming the preeminence of that system as the basis of mind. Imagine the entire sensori-motor system of the body as made up of a few large, related, but distinct sub-systems, each characterized by the special states and motions of the major body parts, thus:

BODY PARTS	SENSORI-MOTOR SUB-SYSTEM	MAJOR OPERATIONS
trunk	somatic	being here
legs	locomotive	moving from here to there
head-eyes	visual	looking at that there
arms-hands	manipulative	moving that there
tongue, etc.	linguistic	saying whatever

We will assume the representations of mind remain profoundly affected by the modality of interactions with experience through which they were developed. One implication is that the representations built through

---

[6]   Piaget contrasts reflexive abstraction with classificatory or Aristotelian abstraction, (p. 320 in **Biology and Knowledge**) demeaning the latter somewhat by referring to it as "simple".

experience will involve different objects and relations, among themselves and with externals of the world, which will depend upon the particular mode of experience. Even if the atomic units of description (e.g., condition action rules) are shared between modes, the entities which are the salient objects of concern and action are different; and in relation to each other only through learned correspondences. This general description of mind contrasts with the more uniformitarian visions which dominate psychology today. These major modal groupings of information structures are imagined to be populated with clusters of related cognitive structures, called "microviews", with two distinct characters. Some are "task-based" and developed through prior experiences with the external world; others, with a primary character of controlling elements, develop from the relationships and interactions of these disparate, internal microviews. The issue of cognitive development is cast into a framework of developing control structure within a system of originally competing microviews[7].

Redescriptive Abstraction

I propose that the multi-modal structure of the human mind permits development of a significant precursor to reflexive abstraction. The interaction of different modes of the mind in processes of explaining unanticipated outcomes of behavior can alter the operational interpretation and solution of a problem. Eventually, a change of balance can effectively substitute an alternative representation for the original; this could occur if the alternative representation is the more effective in formulating and coping with the encountered problem. In terms of the domain of our explorations and our representations, there is no escape from the particularity of the GAC representation unless some other description is engaged. A description of the same circumstance, rooted in a different mode of experience, would surely have both enough commonality and difference to provide an alternative, applicable description. I identify the GAC absolute grid as one capturing important characteristics of the visual mode[8]; other descriptions based on the somatic or locomotive subsystems of mind could provide alternative descriptions which would by their very nature permit escape from the particularity of the former.

Why should explanation be involved? Peirce argues that "doubt is the motor of thought" and that mental activity ceases when no unanswered questions remain[9]. Circumstances requiring explanation typically involve surprises; the immediate implication is that the result was neither intuitively obvious nor were there adequate processes of inference available beforehand to predict the outcome (at least none such were invoked).

We propose that a different set of functional descriptions, in another modal system, can provide explanation to a set of structures controlling ongoing activity. The initial purpose served by alternative representations is explanation. Symmetry, however, is a salient characteristic of body centered descriptions; this is the basis of their explanatory power when applied where other descriptions are inadequate. Going beyond explanation, when such an alternative description is applied to circumvent frustrations encountered in play, one will have the alternate structure applied with an emergent purpose. Through such a sequence of events, the interaction of multiple representations permits a concrete form of abstraction to develop, an abstraction emergent from the application of alternative descriptions. In the following scenario, I will trace the interaction of different modes of mind as an example of how this early form of functional abstraction, a possible precursor to any consciously articulated reflexive abstraction because it involves "external interpretation" more than reflexive analysis, permits breaking out of the original description's concreteness with its limitations of particularity. To do so, I need to establish the basic kinds of alternative descriptions to be involved.

---

[7] This view of mind is presented and applied Chapter 5 of CECD.

[8] The GAC description is cast in terms of an external thing seen by the person referring to it, with no hint of an imaginary homunculus in view. Further, the absolute reference assigning numbers to specific cells preserves a top-down, left to right organization. Notice however, that even if a specific person's internal representation were different – based perhaps on a manipulative mode of thought and representation – the essential points of following arguments remain sound.

[9] Peirce's position (presented lucidly in "The Fixation of Belief" but ubiquitous in his writing) was the primary observation leading me to focus on on this theme. He uses the term doubt because his discussion is cast in terms of belief; mine, cast in terms of goals, finds its equivalent expression as surprise. Doubts require evidence for elimination (but see Peirce on this); surprises require explanations. Surprise is accessible to mechanical minds as the divergence between expectation and outcome under a specific framework of interpretation.

Alternative Descriptions in Tictactoe

I begin with the assumptions that the GAC formulation is primarily visual in character and that one should seek familiar schemes for representing things, relations, and actions that are from a different mode of experience. Descriptions based on activity lead to the somatic and locomotive body-part systems as the two obvious, primary candidates. I offer two suggestions for concretizing this search: let's consider first an "imaginary body-projection" onto the tictactoe grid as the somatic candidate description; and second, an "imaginary walk" through the tictactoe grid as the locomotive candidate description[10]. How would this work in practice?

Somatic Symmetries

Let's consider two essentially different types of symmetry for the tictactoe grid. **Flipping symmetry** will name the relation between a pair of forks (or more complex structures) when they are congruent after the grid is rotated around some axis lying in the plane of the grid. Examples of symmetrical forks might be {1 3 9} and {1 7 9}[11]. An example of an explanation for this **fork symmetry** based upon an alternative, somatic description would be the following:

> If I sat in the center of the grid and lay down on my back with my head in cell 1 and my feet in cell 9, then cell 3 would be at my left hand. The forks {1 3 9} and {1 7 9} are the same in the way that my right and left hands are the same, for cell 7 would be at my right hand.

Such an explanation focusses on symmetry with respect to the body axis. A similar argument can be made for **plan symmetry** in the common fork {1 3 7} achieved by the two plans [1 3 7] and [1 7 3].

> If I sit in the center of the grid and lie down on my back with my head in cell 1, the cell 3 is at my left hand and cell 7 at my right. If the plan is to move first at the head, next at the left hand, then at the right [1 3 7] then the other plan is the same to the same extent that it doesn't matter if I lie there with my face up or my face down.

It is harder to argue that such flipping forms of description are as natural for symmetries such as those of forks {1 3 9} and {1 3 7} because the axis of symmetry lies where no ego-owned markers are placed (along the cells {2 5 8}) and because other body parts have to be invoked as placeholders, as in the following:

> If I sat in the center of the grid and lay down on my back with my head going up between cells 1 and 3, my **shoulders** would be there at 1 and 3 and the other parts of the forks would be the same as are my right and left hands.

As this elaboration departs from the explanatory simplicity of the former, one should consider contrasting another model, and thus turn to explanations based on walking around.

Locomotive Symmetry

In contrast with the last explanation which placed a body axis along a line of empty cells, the locomotive symmetries involve moving from one ego-occupied cell to another. Consider now the type of locomotive description that could be used to explain the equivalence of forks {1 3 9} and {1 3 7}[12].

> Suppose I start at cell 1, walk to cell 9, then turn and walk to cell 3. Facing center in place leaves me with occupied cells at my right and left hands. For the fork {1 3 7}, if I stood at cell 1, I would also have other occupied cells at my right and left hand. The forks are the same if nothing is changed by my jumping from one corner to the next and swinging around to the center.

This Jump-and-Swing model of symmetry does more than explain a surprising win; the outcome is creative, as can be seen in the following scenario where it enables breaking out of the particularity of the GAC representation.

---

[10] The following descriptions are rather like imputing thought experiments to subjects but such with a decidely personal and everyday content; the "dramatic style" seems natural enough for people. If it seems unnatural for machines, the reason is that we do not yet provide our machines with so rich and powerfully various a collection of interacting descriptions as humans are fortunate enough to inherit from the long history of life's evolution.

[11] Referring only to the set of markers here, we need not distinguish between the forks achieved by various plans such as [1 9 3] or [3 1 9].

[12] Under IT's learning mechanisms, the plan [1 9 3] will generate the goal {1 3 7} via the game [1974325] or [1932745]. These goals are essentially related. REO's move directly blocking IT's plan leads directly to the other determinate games.

SCENARIO 1: From one corner to another:

After describing different types of symmetries, and justifying their activitation to explain surprising serendip-itous victories in play, we now ask whether they can have more than explanatory value. The conclusion is that the "flipping symmetries" do not generate novelties through interactions in this model even though they are natural explanations of surprises. The rotational or jump-and-swing symmetries can do so, however, through the kind of tortuous but feasible path presented in the following scenario.

Generating a Second Descent Network

Let's suppose the IT plays with minimal look ahead. Remember also that IT knows nothing of opening advantage. IT has played successfully to victories even when the second and third step of its known plans were foiled, but never so when the first step was blocked. Suppose now that REO begins a game with a move to cell one. All of the existing plans in IT's repertoire are useless. But IT knows that the GOAL {1 3 7} is the same as {1 3 9} by rotational symmetry, therefore it can try to generate the alternative plan for that symmetrical goal. The attempt to create and use a plan, based on "jumping from a pivot at cell 3 to a new pivot at cell 1," will fail on a later move, but IT doesn't know that[13].

That game establishes the plan [7 3 1] in IT's repertoire. When IT once again has the first move, should it choose to begin a game in cell 7, it has a decent chance of winning either the game [7 5 3 1 9 ...] or [7 5 3 9 1 ...]. Such a victory will establish a new prototypical game, comparable in status to [1 9 3] from which a second descent network can be derived. This does NOT argue that such a second descent network will actually be developed in all its fullness (though it may). What it DOES show is one plausible scenario for how the incredibly particular descriptions of GACs can break away from one element of their fixity – commitment to opening in cell 1. The alternative description has served as a bridge to permit developing a second set of equally particular goals and plans.

Emerging Abstraction

If alternative representations can serve as explanation for surprises developed through play, and if they can serve as a bridge to break away from the rigid formulation of the GAC representation, it is not impossible to believe they may begin to provide dynamic guidance as well – exactly of the sort found useful by adults in their play. When this occurs, the alternative description, useful initially as an explanation for the more particular system of primary experiences, will become the dominant system for play. Then the symmetry implicit in the body-centric imagery will become a salient characteristic of the player's thinking about tictactoe as the highly specific formulations of early experience recede into the background. Abstraction has taken place – because the descriptions of the body mode are implicitly less absolute in respect of space than are those supposed to operate with the GAC representation. But the abstraction is not by features, nor is it by the articulate analysis of reflexive abstraction, as described by Bourbaki. This is an EMERGENT ABSTRACTION via REDESCRIPTION, a new kind of functional abstraction. Redescriptive abstraction is a primary example of the coadaptive development of cognitive structures. As a kind of functional abstraction which does not yet require reflexive analysis of actions taken within the same mode of representation, but merely the interpretation of actions in one mode in terms of possible, familiar actions in another mode[14], it needs bear less of an inferential burden than would the more analytic reflexive abstraction described by Bourbaki.

Redescriptive Abstraction and Analogy

One might say that emergent abstraction via redescription is "merely analogy". I propose an antithetical view: emergent abstraction explains why analogy is so natural and so important in human cognition. Redescriptive abstraction is a primary operation of the multi-modal mind; it is the way we must think to explain surprises to ourselves. We judge analogy and metaphor important because redescriptive abstraction is subsumed under those names.
Further, I speculate it is THE essential general developmental mechanism. This process can be the bootstrap for ego-centric cognitive development because it is accomplished without any reference to the moves or the actions of the other agent of play.

---

[13] IT does not look ahead, therefore IT doesn't notice that the use of cell 1 is relevant to plan [7 3 1]. Nor does moving second inhibit the attempt to escape the frustration of cell 1 being taken because IT does not understand opening advantage; but then, neither did Lawler's subject at age six years.
[14] The point here is that the process is more like Peirce's abduction than any inductive process of learning. See "Deduction, Induction, and Hypothesis" for Peirce's introduction to this distinction or K.T.Fann's "Peirce's Theory of Abduction" for an analysis of Peirce's developing ideas on abduction.

ESCAPING FROM EGOCENTRICITY

"...The internalization of socially rooted and historically developed activities is the distinguishing feature of human psychology, the basis of the qualitative leap from animal to human psychology. As yet, the barest outline of this process is known...."

L. S. Vygotsky

If the higher psychological processes to which Vygotsky refers are characteristic of productive intelligence in all forms, the issues of the progressive development of self-control and the internalization of exterior agents and context are profound transformations which need to be understood in both natural and artificial intelligence. The general objective of this section is to describe how it is possible for an egocentric system to transcend its limited focus. The central idea is that the system will adapt to an environmental change because of an insistent purpose; it will do so by interpreting the actions of its antagonist in terms of its own possibilities of play. Two essential milestones on the path of intelligent behavior in interactive circumstances are first, simulation of the activity of an opponent, and second, the internalization of some control elements from the context of play.

In the human case, learning sometimes goes forward by homely binding, an instruction by people or things in what this or that means or how it works. Another kind of learning, which I call "lonely discovery," is the consequence of commitment to continuation of an interaction, despite the loss of the external partner. Such a desire, which can definitionally permit only vicarious satisfaction, is the motor of that internalization of "the world and the other" which is the quintessence of higher psychological processes[15]. We use the case study experiences in respect of these issues to guide the development of two examples/scenarios of how a machine can confront such challenges. We will consider how a system can develop through interaction in such a way that when the environment becomes impoverished, the system can begin to function more richly, and therefore become generally more capable. The particular problems through which I will approach these issues are the inception of multi-role play (one player as both protagonist and antagonist) and the inception of guarded (or mental) play. I do not want to impute to IT the motive of understanding the play of an opponent to whom it initially pays little attention. Therefore, we grant the system an initial purpose of continuing play even under such limitations as to amount to a crippling of the environment. From this initial purpose emerges another, that of the proper understanding of an antagonist's game. A major side effect of the solution I propose to this problem is creativity, in the specific sense of enabling the discovery of strategies of play not known beforehand nor learned by another's instruction. The ultimate achievement of such developmental mechanisms as I propose here is to learn new strategies through analysis of games played by others, i.e., learning by observation.

SCENARIO 2: The Beginning of Multi-role play:

The Human Case

After many sessions of her playing tictactoe with me, in one experiment I asked the subject to play against her brother so that I might better observe her play with another person. She surprised her brother by her significant progress at play (she beat him honestly and knew she would do so in specific games). When I was called away to answer a knock at the door, I asked the children not to play any more games together until I returned. Coming back, I found the game below on the chalk board. When I asked if she had let herself win, she explained that she had been 'making smart moves for me and the other guy.'

A	3	C
	1	D
2		B

---

[15] This episode dealt with here is neither singular nor domain specific in character. The original observations on which this view is based were about the behavior of a newly verbal infant. See CECD pp. 113-115 in Chpt. 4. This issue became prominent for me through its advocacy by Minsky and through its manifest importance in empirical observations on the learning of my children. The ideas can be cast in a Freudian framework for relative simplicity of explanation. The essential idea I advance for developing self-control can be read into Freud's description of the tripartite mind – Id, Ego, and Super-ego – which depends for development, first, on the introjection of authority figures by the child. After this introjection of an 'other', which we can take to be an adoption of goals of the Superego not compatible with existing goals of the Id, the Ego, by mediating interior conflicts between the Id and Super-ego, can develop control over both through **virtual experiences**; this permits the system of the self to become somewhat better able to deal with the disparity between the desires of the Id and the constraints of the external world.

My formulation of this episode is as follows. She wanted to continue playing tictactoe. Her ability to do so was hindered by my specific prohibition: the normal environment was crippled. She adapted her earlier developed skills, partitioning them so that strategic play remained her prerogative while tactical play was assigned to her newly effective internal antagonist, 'the other guy'. Could such a process be made effective in a machine?

The Form of the Solution for Machines

If the deprivation of interaction in the social milieu is one motor of human cognitive development, within the world of machine intelligence the corresponding circumstance would be the crippling of some function of other programmed modules of the system. The desired consequence of this crippling should be one where continuing in the well worn path is an easily detectable, losing maneuver, thus necessitating changes in the functions of existing structures. Further, there should exist some alternative which is the marginally different application of an already existing structure capable of providing a functional solution to the problem which the "social" vagary creates. This paper offers two examples of such challenges and possible outcomes in the reorganization of this system of game simulation functions.

The deprivation of interaction leads to the introjection of "the other" within the "self" through the assignment of one of alternative functions (strategic play) to the "ego" (IT) and another (tactical play) to the "alter-ego" (let's call this agent **REO-sim**). What forces this reassignment is crippling the environment so that a decision needs to be taken on an issue which was immanent in but transactionally insignificant in the interactive context[16]. What makes this introjection possible is the successful application of established structures for a new function. Obviously, not every attempt to apply an old structure for a new function would be successful[17]; consequently, the character of structures which permits such successful re-application, their functional lability, needs to be established through some sort of experience, either of actual or imaginative interaction. In a system within which such imaginative experience is not yet possible, actual interchanges are needed.

The question raised by simulations was how extensive would be changes required to permit the system of programs to mimic the kind of behavior Lawler's subject showed in this incident. For IT, the situation equivalent to having no opponent is: whenever IT returns its latest move, IT receives control again with no move made by REO. There are three possible responses to this situation:

1. IT could make its next planned move (without even noticing something novel had happened); the consequence of continuing to play with no responses from the antagonist is a sort of **rehearsal** of IT's plan.

2. IT could respond making moves for the antagonist but do so in an imperfectly discriminated manner (for example, using the moves of its own plan for both its own moves and those of REO-sim); when IT attempts to assign moves without making a strategy/tactic division of moves, the play appears random, but is best characterized as **confused tactical play** by both (that is, IT's first move for REO-sim blocks IT's own plan after which both agents play tactically.).

3. IT could partition its own capabilities so that IT alone made strategic moves and REO-sim made tactical moves; when IT's own internal structure is respected in the allocation of roles, play procedes in the normal fashion. This is the **articulation of complementary roles**.

I have programmed IT to function in each of these three different manners under control of global switches. The question remains of how one should view the transition from the states of rehearsing, to confusion, to articulated multi-role play[18].

---

[16] Chapter 4 of CECD argues that in the human case "whose-turn?" at play was one issue upon which judgments were made at each move to prohibit or permit the effecting of intentions in behavior. Lawler's subject knew what she wanted to do, and when she knew also that the turn was not hers she suppressed her next intended move until it was her turn. Further, one of the ways the child cheated when she feared her plan might be frustrated was to make multiple moves in a single turn.

[17] Because my simulations, in fact, share tactical code, the internalization of REO as REO-sim is perfect. Such need not have been the case. REO could have been any arbitrarily baroque system of decisions; IT's simulation of such an alternative REO would still be the same as described here. Allocating a part of itself to represent the other is all that IT can do. When it is successful, however, this functional re-application of existing structure is very powerful.

[18] The path is straightforward. Here is how the program works. IT can tell when it receives control out of turn. The manifest failure of rehearsal need only require that IT do something different from the next step of its own plan, which could be nothing else but making some move for the non-existent antagonist. The

For the transition from one mode of response to another I offer no general, theoretical justification. There are reasons. Very little change was required to the original code because of the modular separation of strategic and tactical play. This is an important observation if and only if the modularity of the code for tactical and strategic play is justified by psychological data or epistemological argument.

The assumption of the modularity of cognitive structures and IT's pervasive use of modularity is based on the empirical witness of Lawler's case study. If the human mind is organized as that study suggests, then it should be easy for the kinds of developments described here to occur. Further, if the transition is representable by no more than the **insertion of a control element**, choosing between formerly competing or serialized subfunctions; and if the transition is **driven by events in the environment upsetting ongoing processes which "want" to continue**, the only "theory" possible is one about the characteristics of structure which permit this adaptivity. My structural assertion in this context is that the **coadaptation of disparate cognitive structures is the key element of mind enabling the "internalization" of external agents and objects**[19].

SCENARIO 3: The Beginning of Guarded play:

The Human Case

When she was already quite adept at playing Tictactoe against an internalized opponent, Lawler's subject was confronted with a new challenge: given the first two moves of a game, to tell whether she could certainly win, might possibly win, or would certainly lose. When she was refused her request for materials on which to represent possible games graphically, she proceeded to play out mentally sequences of moves which led to determinate games. This is the quintessence of mental play.

In this example, as in the former, constraints upon interaction with the external world – in a framework committed to continuing the activity – led to the application of existing structures to the satisfaction of new ends[20]; the ends are new in the specific sense that knowledge and know-how developed for playing games against an opponent, worked out with graphical tokens, were applied to answer speculative questions about the possible outcomes of games worked out in the mind. This functional lability of structure is the key to adaptive behavior and thus to learning.

The Machine Case

In the inception of multi-role play, the prohibition of the antagonist role was the stimulus for the reorganization of functioning knowledge. In the machine case, this was achieved through a "crippling" of the output function of the opponent, REO. The next extension asks what function should be crippled to impel the development of guarded play.

Tree generation within the module GEN is the primary function which creates all the possibilities of play; thus it is the candidate program from whose internalization mental play might emerge. GEN contains a mixture of interrelated LOOP macros and recursive invocations. Note, however, that these programs were created as experimental tools, as mechanisms to explore the learning of IT through experiencing particular games. Consequently, the mechanisms have no grounded epistemic status; their functions need be replicated but their mechanisms may be replaced freely by some alternative if that seems more natural.

Because IT does not contain any such tree-generation modules, rebuilding the GEN module structures within IT would require creating such structure from nothing. Because subfunction invocation with arguments is the primary mechanism within IT for transferring control, an invocation oriented solution is the preferred one: this is doing something already given within the module.

The essential insight IT needs for an invocation solution is that **if it can be called** with an argument by GEN, **it can call itself** successively with a series of arguments drawn from a list[21].

---

manifest failure of IT's own plan application for both roles requires refined discrimination; again, a single decision to route control to either one or the other of the strategic and tactical functions based on turn taking is all that's required for the more precise articulation of roles.

[19] The animism of the young child is not at all bizarre if his only means of understanding "the other" is through self knowledge. Like Descartes, he knows he has a mind because he thinks; he believes in his own past because of memory; and he imputes will to things because he feels the meaning of wanting.

[20] Here, guarded play began because of my experimental intervention. However, to the extent that children believe keeping their plans secret will help them win (they surely learn that by the age of seven), the development of mental play with the initial purpose of guarding plans is to be expected in general.

[21] This is done in the simplest fashion, by tail recursion of IT with the cdr of the candidate moves-list until it is empty. The branching condition for entry into IT's handler is a data anomaly: a list of atoms

The remaining issue is how the outcomes of these generated executions of games are handled; that is, the record keeping function is affected as well as the tree generation function. Two alternatives appear to be first, the (unjustified) rebuilding within IT of the list-manipulation aspects of record keeping, or second, the acceptance of an imperfect result in the following specific sense. If the aim of the game is to win, the desired outcome of play is a specific string of cell numbers which comprise a valid win for the first player. If such a single game is the result of the recursive internalization of the GEN module's tree-generation function, the result is an impoverished one (as compared to a list of all possible outcomes) but nonetheless one that will serve the everyday function of winning a game[22].

Conclusions

The immediate cause for internalizing some exterior function is a constriction of the surrounding context. Given the objective of continuing activity despite this constriction, a person or a programming module can proceed by simulating the crippled functions of the environment with components of its own function. The functional lability of existing structures in response to a changed external circumstance is the key to internalization of exterior agents and context elements. In the very simple cases presented here, a machine learning system can internalize portions of the outer world as people do. There is no guarantee that any structure will work when applied in some non-intended function. On the other hand, setting up systems of programs to employ this technique in coping with an uncomprehended environment is surely worth considering for any mechanized learning system.

The test of the value of such a capability is creativity. If learning from one's own experience is a criterion of intelligence, is it not smarter to learn from another's experience? Such a capability is an emergent, with a few simple programming changes, of the facilities for multi-role and guarded play.

LEARNING WITHOUT INSTRUCTION

With the developments sketched so far, all the capabilities needed for learning from another by observation are in place. The most dramatic evidence for the accuracy of this claim in the human case comes from Lawler's subject's invention of a new strategy of play based upon her later analysis of a game played against herself at an earlier time[23]. In summary, reviewing a game played only to the point where she believed a draw would follow, Lawler's subject recognized that she had abandoned the game while a single further move would have led to her winning. She then worked through the moves she had made, both as protagonist and antagonist, and convinced herself that she had created a new strategy with which to win on condition that her opponent made any one of four responses to her opening corner selection. The kinds of abilities employed in her analysis were those of multi-role play, guarded play, and specific knowledge of three sorts: of the particular game, about her own habits (starting in cell one), and procedures of play (she knew that SHE would have made forced moves at need)[24].

SCENARIO 4: Analysis through synthesis

The Machine Case

What then need be added for IT to perform a similar feat of creative analysis? When presented with an externally generated game, nothing would be easier for IT to analyze IF the order of moves were preserved.

---

is expected; when the previous game move is determined to be a list of atoms itself, "something different" must be done. If IT's handler for this condition takes the first element of the end-list of the game and invokes itself with the game made of the prior state and the first member of that list it received, calling itself with the residue of that list will either route a path of execution in a second instantiation through normal IT processing or through the same condition handler, thus leading to further recursions and instantiations of IT. The lists created by GEN's tree generator will be replaced by the recursively generated structure of IT's multiple instantiations. (I do **not** claim people do this naturally.)

[22] This is implemented by choosing to return only a won game to the primary instantiation of IT with a throw. If only nil is returned, then no game can be won from the given initial moves. The objective implicit in GEN to fill the space of possible games is the experimenter's objective; the objective of program IT is to return the next move for any game presented to it.

[23] The detail of this story and its analysis are presented in pp. 139-141 of CECD.

[24] Lawler's subject's discovery or invention of a new strategy is obviously a creative application of her knowledge, but is it appropriate to claim that it represents learning from another? The sense in which the answer is "yes" to this question is the following: Lawler's subject used all the relevant knowledge she had. If she encountered a game by some other person, she would have been incapable of interpreting it by any other means than this very analysis. The claim then is that this is what people do when they analyze the thought of another, that this is all they can do.

HERE the challenge is different: the set of moves to be made is prescribed, but the order is to be determined. Lawler's subject's game is below; the tree of possible games following after. When a string is forced into a forbidden move (one not part of the **presented** pattern), the branch is pruned[25]. The * marks the late discovered move to cell 4.

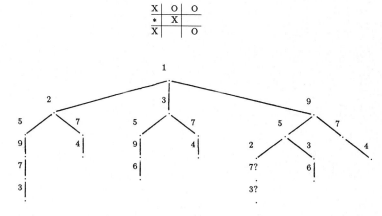

Given as prerequisite a system that is capable of multi-role play and guarded play (the latter implies the former), the following changes need be made to existing code:

FUNCTIONS IMPLEMENTED:

    Limiting Proposed Moves to those used:

        by intersecting possible moves with "visible" markers.

    Pruning Strings requiring forbidden moves:

        this requirement is satisfied when a failure occurs, not by look ahead.

    Exit from model based learning to **example based learning**:

        this is a hook to an additional learning routine.

    Example Based Learning:

        a routine fixing actual ego moves of the reconstructed game as a plan.

    Quitting when done:

        a test for exhaustion of the "visible" set of tokens.

If these seem like extensive changes, note that two of the five are control transfers on a single condition (EXIT and QUITTING), one is a control transfer to toplevel on a set membership condition (PRUNING), one is a set intersection of normally available possible moves with the given set of actual moves (LIMITING). The final change (EXAMPLE BASED LEARNING) extracts the ego-owned moves from the selected game in order (a subfunction common to all playing routines in the programs) and installs them as a list with other known plans. The basic mechanism is no more than is required to learn by instruction when shown an example – but **now the instructor is no longer needed.**

As a player becomes more adventurous with guarded play – willing to start in the center and various corner cells, willing to move to side cells as well – the number of winnable games possible becomes quite large. This explosion of possible won games, the fact that there is too much to remember and all the games are superficially similar, introduces the need to impose a more abstract order on the experience. Answering that need demands feature based abstraction and conceptualization, the focus of work still ongoing.

---

[25] The process depends upon forcing as an operation of tactical play but it does not require a **concept** of forcing. Such a concept could however come as an **explanation** from mental trials such as this. Forcing is important initially less because it leads to a win, than because it is easier to think about a string than a tree.

156   R.W. Lawler

CONCLUSIONS

Coadaptive development of cognitive structures is central to human learning. Human studies can provide valuable guidance for machine learning work to the extent that one both can analyze mature performance and can uncover anterior structures whose reorganization permits the emergence of that mature performance. Specifically, Lawler's case study permitted a characterization of the cognitive state of a young child (one quite congenial with the literature on young children) and more, a trace of the particular child's path of development to relatively more mature performances. This developmental path provided significant guidance for constructing programs that model the learning behavior of the individual child. More generally, the constructed model illuminates in a computational form the elements and processes that enter into coadaptive development. The programs pass from learning by prototype modification to learning from experience by analysis without instruction.

Going beyond earlier conclusions in the human study, the discovery remarked here is the role of the multi-modal mind in creating the potential for abstraction emerging from redescription. This is an example of the functionality of coadaptation in cognitive development. The conjecture is advanced that the multi-modal structure is central to understanding the possibility of human cognitive development. Further, emerging abstraction through redescription can be appreciated as a primitive form of functional abstraction, of which reflexive abstraction is a more mature form. Redescriptive abstraction helps explain the importance of analogy and metaphor in human thinking and learning.

In this research, we have focussed only on the interaction between visual and kinesthetic systems. The other modes of mind, related to the linguistic system and and the touch-salient manipulative system, add significant further dimensions of possible complexity to this non-uniformitarian model of mind. Such models, although basically simple, are complex enough to permit interesting development through plausible, internal interactions; that is, they permit the possibility of learning through thinking – a desirable outcome for any view of human minds, and one that may prove of some value with machines as well.

References

Caple, Balda, and Willis. Work reported in "How Did Vertebrates Take to the Air?" by Roger Lewin, Science, July 1, 1983. See also the American Naturalist, 1983.

Fang, J. Towards a Philosophy of Modern Mathematics. Hauppauge, New York: Paideia Series in Modern Mathematics, Vol.1, 1970.

Fann, K. T. Peirce's Theory of Abduction. The Hague: Martinus Nijhoff.

Jacob, F. "Evolution and Tinkering" in Science, June 10, 1977 and The Possible and the Actual. New York, Pantheon Books, 1982

Lawler, R. Computer Experience and Cognitive Development. Chichester, England and New York: Ellis Horwood, Ltd. and John Wiley Inc., 1985.

Lawler, R. and Selfridge, O. "Learning Concrete Strategies through Interaction". Proceedings of the Cognitive Science Society Annual Conference, 1985.

Piaget, J. The Child's Conception of Number. New York: Norton and Co., 1952.

Piaget, J. Biology and Knowledge. Chicago: University of Chicago Press, 1971.

Piaget, J. The Language and Thought of the Child. New York: New American Library.

Peirce, C.S. "The Fixation of Belief" in Chance, Love and Logic, M. Cohen, (ed.). New York: George Braziller, Inc., 1956

Peirce, C.S. "Deduction, Induction, and Hypothesis" in Chance, Love and Logic.

Satinoff, N. "Neural Organization and the Evolution of Thermal Regulation in Mammals", Science, July 7, 1978.

Selfridge, M.G.R. and Selfridge, O.G. "How Children Learn to Count: A Computer Model", 1985.

Vygotsky, L.S. Mind in Society. Eds. Michael Cole, Vera John-Steiner, Sylvia Scribner, and Ellen Souberman. Cambridge, Mass: Harvard University, 1978.

Acknowledgements

This paper began in a collaboration with Oliver Selfridge to extend work in "How Children Learn to Count" (Selfridge and Selfridge) with ideas of CECD. With Oliver's genial prodding, I have carried forward that effort to confront the issue of abstraction from highly particular descriptions. Special thanks are due to Sheldon White, who first pointed out the similarity of my conclusions to those of Vygotsky. He has repeatedly emphasized the importance of ideas about the internalization of external processes and urged me to develop them.

PART II

KNOWLEDGE REPRESENTATION

Advances in Artificial Intelligence - II
B. Du Boulay, D. Hogg and L. Steels (Editors)
© Elsevier Science Publishers B.V. (North-Holland), 1987

INTERPRETING PROPOSITIONAL ATTITUDE REPORTS:
TOWARDS GREATER FREEDOM AND CONTROL

John Barnden

Computer Science Department
Indiana University
Bloomington, IN 47405-4101
USA

ABSTRACT

Propositional attitudes — beliefs, hopes, desires, etc. — are of central concern in knowledge
representation and natural language semantics. A long-standing problem is to design a representation scheme that can adequately express interpretations of sentences about agents' propositional
attitudes. In common with some other researchers, I argue that the most promising design approach is to allow the scheme to contain items denoting conjectured mental objects. However, the
mental-object approach and several others are prone to "imputation" difficulties. That is, they
tend to impute possibly-implausible ideas to agents. This problem arises particularly in connection
with nested-attitude reports (concerning belief about beliefs, and so on). I show how a particular
form of the mental-object approach can avoid some imputational pitfalls. The proposal also differs
from others in being freer, yet more controlled, in its travel within the space of attitude-report
interpretations.

1. INTRODUCTION

Sentences reporting the propositional attitudes (PAs) of cognitive agents present some difficult
problems in natural language semantics and representation theory. See, for example, Barwise &
Perry (1983, 1985), Creary (1979), Fagin & Halpern (1985), Fodor (1978), Hintikka (1983), Konolige
(1984, 1985), Levesque (1984), Linsky (1983), Maida & Shapiro (1982), Moore (1977), Peters &
Saarinen (1982: introduction), Rapaport & Shapiro (1984), and Barnden (1983, 1985, 1986).

PA reports can be interpreted in a complex variety of ways, but discussions in AI rarely go beyond
what are commonly called "de-dicto" and "de-re" interpretations. I shall argue that when the
whole of the rich space of PA-report interpretation types is kept in mind, and when PA reports are
seen properly in the context of natural language as a whole, the "mental object" or "mental representation" approach to the formal expression of PA report interpretations becomes very attractive.
The mental-object approach dictates that the formal representation scheme should in some sense
directly represent the (conjectured) mental objects — ideas, concepts, representations, expressions
— in the minds of the attitude-holding agents. The mental-object approach can be viewed as a
special case of the "syntactic" or "symbol manipulation" approach to PA representation.

160   J. Barnden

The mental-object approach has been supported by other researchers, e.g. McCarthy (1979), Creary (1979), Fodor (1978), Moore & Hendrix (1982), Konolige (1984). However, even here there has been insufficient attention to an important issue: namely, the propensity of PA-oriented representation schemes to generate undesirable *imputations*, to ordinary agents, of arcane representational features on which the schemes themselves are based. This arises especially in the treatment of nested-attitude reports. The representational proposal presented below is relatively free of imputation difficulties, as we shall see.

2.   THE RICHNESS OF THE PA-REPORT INTERPRETATION SPACE

Consider the phrase "Jim's wife" in the PA report

((1)) Mike believes Jim's wife is clever.

This sentence could be taken to mean that Mike is mentally describing the supposedly clever person as the wife of Jim; more precisely, that Mike's belief employs a mental person-description that is some sense *preserves the structure* of the phrase "the wife of Jim".

This interpretation would commonly be called the "de-dicto" interpretation (with respect to "Jim's wife"). On the other hand, a "de-re" interpretation would take Mike's belief to "refer" to or "denote" some person, who happens to be Jim's wife, but the interpretation would not constrain Mike to use a description based on Jim and the wife-of relation. Notice that the de-re interpretation takes "Jim's wife" to refer to an actual person, whereas the de-dicto interpretation leaves the reference issue open.

An immediate complication is that there are several different theoretical assumptions that one could make about the nature of the person-concept that Mike is using. For instance, in the de-re case:

(a) One might assume that the concept is Mike's "standard concept" of the person.

(b) One might partially specify the intrinsic nature of the concept (whether or not it is constrained to be standard). For instance, one might specify that it is perceptually based, or includes an appeal to the person's name or role with respect to Mike, or is sufficiently "vivid" in some sense [Kaplan (1971)].

(c) One might leave the nature of the concept completely unconstrained. It would then be *possible* for the concept to be, say, Mike's standard concept of the person; or, it might be some non-standard description or other of the person.

Consider now the possibility of different interpretations of

((2)) Mike believes Sally is clever

arising from different construals of "Sally". One type of interpretation of this sentence is analogous to the de-re interpretations of (1). That is, it is assumed that a person called "Sally" exists, and that Mike has some sort of concept of her. We again have a variety of positions that could be taken about the nature of this concept.

It is not clear what a de-dicto interpretation of (2) would be, since "Sally" is not a structured description. However, there is an interesting interpretation that does not assume existence of a Sally — namely, to take Mike to be using an internal description analogous to "the person called 'Sally' ". [cf. Rapaport & Shapiro (1984), and also Yagisawa (1984).] There need be no person called "Sally".

One source of complexity in the case of sentences like (1) has, strangely, received little attention. In that sentence, the word "Jim" is subject to multiple interpretations just as "Sally" is in sentence (2). To say that the Mike concept that underlies "Jim's wife" preserves the structure of this phrase leaves open the question of the Mike concept underlying the word "Jim".

We should also consider the question of multiple interpretations of the possessive phrase " 's wife". The literature on PA reports has concentrated almost exclusively on the variety of interpretations of *proper names and physical-object descriptions* in PA-report complements. (The "complement" of a PA report is the clause governed by the attitude verb.) There has been little discussion, even in the contemporary philosophy literature, of the analogous variety of interpretations of "predicational" or "functional" phrases, such as " 's wife", "is clever" and "is taller than". One exception is Swoyer (1983). It seems to be almost universally assumed that sentences like (1) and (2) are to be understood as meaning that Mike is using some (unspecified and undiscussed) standard mental representations of the wife relationship and the property of cleverness. However, it is equally possible for interpretations of those sentences to exclude any assumption that the representations are Mike's standard ones. It is even possible, for instance, that Mike happens to be asserting cleverness by means of an internal structure analogous to "has the property called 'clever' ", just as it is possible for Mike to refer to Jim by a "the person called ..." description. Therefore, there should be interpretations that allow Mike to use such a means of ascribing cleverness. Similarly, in a de-dicto interpretation of sentence (1) with respect to "Jim's wife", the nature of the mental handle that Mike has on the wife relationship might be allowed to be non-standard. This allows the handle to be, say, analogous to "the woman mentioned on ...'s marriage certificate" (to over-simplify a little) assuming that this description is not Mike's standard way of representing wifeness.

Quantification within PA-report complements, as in

((3)) Mike believes some person is green

has received a lot of attention. Most discussions convey the impression that there would be only two types of construal of the indefinite description "some person". On one construal, we would take the sentence to say merely that Mike's belief is analogous to the sentence "some person is green" — i.e. Mike has no specific person in mind. The other construal (de-re) would have Mike believing of some particular, existing person that he or she is green.

But there is a third important type of interpretation which is seldom discussed (two exceptions being Hellan (1981) and Saarinen (1981)): viz, that Mike's belief involves an (unknown) internal person-description that is of *definite* form but may perhaps fail to identify any actual person. E.g. the description could be "the person who first walked on Mars", even though there is no such person. Notice that we are presenting a *class* of possible interpretations here: one interpretation in the class leaves the nature of Mike's person-description open except in requiring it to be of definite form; another interpretation might require it to have some general characteristic such as vividness; and so on.

In sum, there is an extremely rich variety of constraints that can be placed on the mental objects that an attitude-holder is assumed to be entertaining. We have looked at examples of but a few aspects of this richness. Some of these constraints involve appeal to the notion of reference. Others require a mental object to have some general psychological feature such as vividness, or to have some structural feature such as preserving the predicate-application structure of phrase like "Jim's wife". Considerable richness is provided by the fact that functional and predicational phrases can be subject to multiple interpretations.

Generally, a particular PA researcher will recognize the existence of a few very particular forms of PA-report interpretation. For instance, the researcher might definitely assume that mental objects involved in de-re interpretations are vivid or are standard representors (or he might refrain from placing any such constraint on the mental objects). It is rare to find a researcher allowing the possibility of a rich space of possible interpretation types, each based on a particular set of decisions about constraints. However, there is no particular justification for picking on just a few interpretation types. This is better appreciated in some of the philosophy literature [e.g. Elgin (1985), Grandy (1981), Kraut (1983), Saarinen (1981)] than in the AI literature.

3.   SUPPORT FOR THE MENTAL-OBJECT APPROACH

The previous section has set the stage for some observations in support of the mental-object approach to PA-report interpretation. See Fodor (1978), Konolige (1984) and Moore & Hendrix (1982) for other supporting discussion.

In the following, we suppose that we wish to design a representation scheme "RS_{SYS}" for use by an AI program "SYS", and that SYS translates incoming sentences into expressions in the scheme.

Observation 1

Our informal discussion of interpretations was couched in terms of conjectured mental objects (concepts) in the minds of the attitude-holders in PA reports. Further, this style of discussion seems to be the natural one to use, and does justice to the way people commonly interpret PA reports. This point is similar to the claim in Moore & Hendrix (1982) that PA reports really do seem to be *about* mental representations. It *suggests* that it is reasonable for RS_{SYS} to contain items that stand for mental objects. The motivation here is that matching the scheme's ontology to that of language-using humans will give the scheme a head start in matching human linguistic abilities.

Observation 2

PA-report interpretations can require mental objects to be "vivid", or to have a perceptual aspect, or to have some other general psychological feature. The most straightforward way to ensure that RS_{SYS} has control over the application of such constraints is to let it denote mental objects. Indeed, any other approach has a difficult issue of expressive power to face.

Even the *reference* or denotation of a mental object can (in agent SYS's view) be in part an intensely psychological matter. System may take a mental object's reference relationship to an object to involve, say, causal chains in the psychological history of the attitude-holder. Although in many cases SYS will not need to appeal to any such explication, sometimes it will need to do so. This need may arise, for instance, in situations where the attitude-holder's description of an object is erroneous, and the sources of the error are important to SYS's proper understanding of the situation. SYS may interpret the sentence "Mike believes that the man drinking red wine is a spy" in a way that ascribes to Mike a mental object analogous to "the man drinking red wine", even though SYS knows there is no man drinking red wine. SYS may, however, apply its knowledge of Mike's appreciation of the situation to recognize that he is trying in his belief to refer to the man who is drinking some other red drink. SYS may thereby allow Mike's mental object an "attempted reference" to that man.

Observation 3

We frequently talk explicitly about ideas, concepts and other supposed mental objects, in ordinary sentences other than PA reports. Mundane examples are: "Mike's ideas are always very good" and "Mike has no clear notion of justice". If sentences such as these are to be translated into RS_{SYS}, then a reasonable strategy in designing RS_{SYS} is to include items that can stand for ideas and the like. No doubt there are other ways of proceeding — e.g. we might suggest interpreting the sentences in terms of Mike's dispositions to act or converse in certain observable ways — but the burden of proof is on the proponents of other approaches to show that they can cope as well with the sentences as the mental-object approach does.

If, then, RS_{SYS} is in any case to include items standing for mental objects, it is perverse not to try to use such items in interpreting PA reports.

Observation 4

Further, explicit talk of mental objects can enter into PA reports in a way which strongly suggests that PA reports in general are implicitly *about* mental objects. Consider:

((4)) Mike believes that some person, of whom he has only a hazy idea, is green.

How would a representational approach not based directly on mental objects deal with such a (perfectly mundane) sentence? In particular, isn't it reasonable for an RS_{SYS} interpretation to contain (i) an item that stands for Mike's person-idea, (ii) a statement that this idea is hazy, and (iii) a statement that Mike's belief is a structure involving the idea? If it is reasonable to proceed in this way, then surely, by continuity, a similar approach is called for in treating sentence (3).

Sentences such as (4) have, to my knowledge, not been properly discussed in the philosophy or AI literature.

4. IMPUTATION DIFFICULTIES WITH NESTED-ATTITUDE REPORTS

Consider the sentence

((5)) George believes that Mike believes that Sally is clever.

Such nested-attitude reports are important both practically and theoretically. I show in Barnden (1986) how some PA-orientated representation schemes run foul of "undesirable imputation" problems when nested attitudes are considered. In particular, I explain in detail how such difficulties arise in modal schemes, quotational schemes, and in the schemes of Creary (1979), Barwise & Perry (1983) and Maida & Shapiro (1982).

Here I shall very briefly describe the difficulties that are most relevant to my present purposes. Consider a quotational scheme that provides as one prime interpretation of sentence (2) the formula

((6))   B(m, 'clever(s)')

where B denotes a relation on agents and formulae in the scheme itself. One might then be forgiven for being seduced into supposing that a prime interpretation for sentence (5) is

((7))   B(g, 'B(m, 'clever(s)')').

This is because it seems that one standard way of getting an interpretation of a sentence of form "A believes that C" is to construct an application of B to an expression denoting agent A and the quotation of the scheme's translation of C. However, formula (7) embodies a possibly-undesirable "imputation" to George, because it is as least as naturally to be regarded as an interpretation of

((8)) George believes that Mike bears-the-B-relation-to the formula clever(s)

as of sentence (5). For, surely, symbol B stands for the predicate bears-the-B-relation-to, and the quotation 'clever(s)' stands for the RS_{SYS} formula clever(s). So, (7) expresses a natural interpretation of (8).

The sort of interpretation we have in mind here for (8) is structure-preserving, in the sense that it imputes to George mental objects corresponding to the "bears-the-B-relation-to" phrase and the quotational phrase in (8). This is just the sort of interpretation that occurs when we take the sentence "George believes that Mike loves Sally" to mean that George has mental objects corresponding to the phrases "loves" and "Sally". But the difference is that the mental-object imputations in the case of (8) are quite likely to be wrong. That is not to say that, according to these imputations, George has any information on the detailed nature of the formula clever(s) or of the bears-the-B-relation-to relation. The problem is rather that George's mental representation scheme may not "carve up the world" in such a way as to cast believing agents as being in relationships to formulae.

Tom put it another way, the scheme is effectively guilty of an *opacity-violation* and *unwarranted inference*, in that it is as if the complement "Mike believes Sally is clever" of (5) has been replaced by the complement "Mike bears-the-B-relation-to the formula 'clever(s)'" of (8). These complements are equivalent *from the scheme's standpoint*, but that equivalence should not be assumed to infect George's beliefs.

Undesirable imputations of a similar sort arise in the BR-based scheme described in Barwise & Perry (1983), if it is extended in the natural way to deal with nested belief reports. The extension causes imputations, to ordinary agents, of beliefs about *the Barwise & Perry scheme's* "situation types" and mental-classification (BR) relation.

The mental-object scheme in Creary (1979) also leads to undesirable imputation, but of a slightly different sort. For instance, the formula blv(g, Blv(M, Clever$(Sally$))) would be a prime, natural interpretation of sentence (5). As I show in Barnden (1986), this situation is once again tantamount to a sort of opacity violation, unwarranted inference and implausible mental-object imputation, since that formula is at least as natural as an interpretation of sentence

((9)) George believes that Mike believes the-cleverness-proposition-constructed-from the-standard-Sally-concept.

interpreted in a structure-preserving way to state that George believes something about one of *Creary's* proposition-construction functions.

5. A REPRESENTATIONAL PROPOSAL

Here I show how a suitably designed representation scheme in the mental-object tradition can provide sufficient control over, and freedom in, the conjectured nature of mental objects to cater for the richness of the space of possible interpretations of PA reports. In particular, the proposal supports multiple interpretations of functional and predicational phrases and avoids imputational problems of the sort described in the previous section. The present section sketches a particular scheme that we simply call RS_{sys}.

RS$_{SYS}$ is a descendant of the schemes reported in Barnden (1983), Creary (1979) and McCarthy (1979). RS$_{SYS}$ in the form represented here is a first-order logic scheme. Often, RS$_{SYS}$ relates mental objects in a reported attitude-holder to expressions in RS$_{SYS}$ itself. Thus RS$_{SYS}$ is also strongly related to quotational PA-orientated proposals, such as those of Quine (1981), Burdick (1982) and Perlis (1985). RS$_{SYS}$ will be described in more detail elsewhere.

So far, we have used phrases like "concepts" and "mental objects". Henceforth, we will talk about "mental expressions" instead, using that term in a very broad sense. Mental expressions could be akin to logic expressions, pieces of semantic network, specialized structures underlying visual imagery, or what you will. An expression may be an entity we would be happy to call a "concept", but it need not be.

One possible interpretation of sentence (2) is expressed as the following formula. Constants m and s denote Mike and Sally respectively.

((10))   blv(m, ϕ_m(\$$_m$('clever(x)'),\$$_m$('s'))).

The \$$_m$('s') term denotes Mike's standard correlate for the RS$_{SYS}$ constant s. RS$_{SYS}$ need contain no detailed information on the nature of such a correlate: the main assumption is simply that there *is* one. In particular, it can be an arbitrarily complex expression. We assume the axiom

((11))   denotes$_m$(\$$_m$('s'), s).

We may also have the axiom

((12))   \$$_m$('s') = σ_m(s)

where σ_m delivers Mike's standard expression for an entity.

Formula (10) uses *templates*. The expression clever(x) is an RS$_{SYS}$ template with one hole-name. (In all our examples the RS$_{SYS}$ templates will actually be open formulae, an important special variety of template, and the hole names will be free variables.) Mike's standard correlate of the template is obtained by applying the \$$_m$ function to it, and is itself *a template with respect to Mike's mental representation scheme* (which need not be a logic). A Mike-template has named holes that can be plugged to obtain a well-formed expression in Mike's scheme. The \$$_m$ function when applied to an RS$_{SYS}$ template preserves the number of hole-names. We do *not* assume that a Mike-template is *itself* necessarily a mental object that Mike can entertain or manipulate.

Hole filling for Mike's scheme is done by the ϕ_m function. An important intuitive assumption about hole filling is that the items that are plugged into the holes maintain their integrity as distinguishable entities. Thus the term ϕ_m(\$$_m$('clever(x)'), \$$_m$('s')) denotes a structure that contains, undisturbed, the expression denoted by \$$_m$('s'), no matter what form is taken by the template denoted by \$$_m$('clever(x)').

If, for the sake of example, Mike's representation scheme were a logic, then it *could* be that $\$_m$('clever(x)') and $\$_m$('s') denote the template m-clever(y) and the expression m-sally, say. Therefore $\$_m$('clever(s)') would denote the expression m-clever(m-sally). However, we make no general assumption that matters are always as simple as this.

The mental object that Mike uses to refer to Sally according to formula (10) is constrained in that Mike is taken to use his *standard* correlate for constant s. An interpretation in which the mental object underlying "Sally" is completely unconstrained, except in that it must refer to Sally, is

$$((13)) \quad (\exists E)[\text{denotes}_m(E,s) \wedge \text{blv}(m, \phi_m(\$_m('clever(x)'), E))].$$

Here E is just some Mike-expression that denotes Sally. For a more constrained interpretation we could include further conjuncts placing constraints on E. As a simple illustration, the extra conjunct could be contains-perceptual-description(E).

The following is also a possible interpretation of (2):

$$((14)) \quad \text{blv}(m, \$_m('clever(s)')).$$

We appeal here to Mike's standard correlate of the formula clever(s). In the absence of constraining axioms, RS_{SYS} embodies no assumption whatsoever about the structure of this correlate. One possible and natural constraining axiom that *could* be included is

$$((15)) \quad \$_m('clever(s)') = \phi_m(\$_m('clever(x)'), \$_m('s')).$$

We turn now to sentence (1). One interpretation is

$$((16)) \quad \text{blv}(m, \phi_m(\$_m('clever(x)'), \sigma_m(\text{wife}(j)))).$$

This is constrained in that Mike's expression for the person is deemed to be his standard expression for her. Notice that Mike is *not* being said to be using a structured expression for her based on expressions for wifeness and Jim (unless there is some background statement that Mike's standard expression for the woman is in fact this structured expression).

Another constrained interpretation is

$$((17)) \quad \text{blv}(m, \phi_m(\$_m('clever(x)'), \phi_m(\$_m('wife(x)'), \$_m('j')))).$$

This constrains Mike's mental expression underlying "Jim's wife" to be a wifeness template whose single hole has been plugged with his standard correlate for j. Thus, in some weak sense, the mental expression preserves the structure of the phrase "Jim's wife". Structure-preservation of stronger forms is mentioned below.

Formula (17) also requires Mike to be using his standard correlate for constant j (which may also be his standard expression for Jim), but, just as with Sally in sentence (2), there are other possibilities. Thus, (17) could be modified to use other Mike expressions for Jim. The formula would still be weakly preserving the structure of the phrase "Jim's wife".

Nor is it necessary for an interpretation to require Mike to use his *standard* correlate for the template $\texttt{wife(x)}$. He might merely be constrained to use *some* correlate of it. It would also be possible to place restrictions of various sorts on it. Similarly, the interpretations presented above could be modified by deleting the standardness of the Mike-correlates for the template $\texttt{clever(x)}$.

Now consider sentence (3). One version of the third, somewhat ignored, interpretation we identified earlier is

((18)) $(\exists H)[\texttt{blv}(m,\ \phi_m(\texttt{'is-person(x)'}),H)) \wedge \texttt{blv}(m,\ \phi_m(\$_m(\texttt{'green(x)'}),H))]$.

We could get a more constrained interpretation by placing restrictions on H. In this vein we could get an interpretation of sentence (4) by including in the body of (18) the conjunct $\texttt{hazy(H)}$.

Versions of the second previously identified interpretation of (3), according to which Mike believes greenness of some existing person, can be constructed on similar lines. The first type of interpretation, under which the quantification is inside Mike's belief, requires the use of quantificational templates (unless the interpretation $\texttt{blv}(m,\ \$_m(\texttt{'∃h.is-person(h)∧is-green(h)'}))$ is used).

Templates: Freedom and Control

Consider the term $\$_m(\texttt{is-bachelor(x)})$. This *may* denote a Mike template akin to the simple logical predication $\texttt{is-bachelor(x)}$ in structure. But, equally, there may be nothing in Mike's representation scheme that is like an is-bachelor predicate symbol. Mike may, for instance, explicitly represent bachelors as being unmarried and male. What this point brings out is that to take $\phi_m(\$_m(\texttt{'is-bachelor(x)'}),\ \$_m(\texttt{'j'}))$ to be an application of an is-bachelor predicate is to *impute* to Mike a feature of RS_{SYS}. Such imputations may be undesirably inaccurate, as I argue in detail in Barnden (1986).

Accordingly, RS_{SYS} is able to leave open the nature of the template denoted by the term $\$_m(\texttt{'is-bachelor(x)'})$. It is possible, for instance, that it is structurally similar to the open logic formula $\neg\texttt{married(x)} \wedge \texttt{male(x)}$. If we really do want an interpretation that foists a predicate-application on Mike, then we can have an explicit or implicit constraint that does the work. Thus, we could have as an interpretation of

((19)) Mike believes that Jim is a bachelor

the formula

((20))   blv[m, ϕ_m($\$_m$('is-bachelor(x)'), $\$_m$('j'))]
∧ applicational($\$_m$('is-bachelor(x)')).

The second conjunct here is an explicit constraint stating that Mike's standard template for the is-bachelor property is analogous to an open logic formula of form p(x) where p is a symbol or expression with no free variables.

The constraint does not of itself imply that Mike has an *atomic* predicate-like item referring to the is-bachelor property. It may be, for instance, that the term $\$_m$('is-bachelor(x)') denotes a template analogous to [λy. ¬ married(y) ∧ male(y)](x), so that ϕ_m($\$_m$('is-bachelor(x)'), $\$_m$('j')) denotes Mike's analogue of [λy. ¬ married(y) ∧ male(y)](j). Observe carefully that this is still of predicate-application form: we do not assume that a β-reduction happens here so as to deliver ¬ married(j) ∧ male(j).

Similar points can be made about the application of $\$_m$ to functional templates, such as wife(x). Thus, perhaps the term $\$_m$('wife(x)') denotes a template akin to [ιy. female(y) ∧ married-to(y,x)], where ιy can be read as "the y such that", or akin to [λz. ιy. female(y) ∧ married-to(y,z)](x), or akin to wife(x). If necessary, an interpretation can include constraints that hone down the space of possibilities for the nature of a template.

We thus see that the space of possibilities for the Mike-expression underlying a phrase like "Jim's wife" in a PA report is even more subtle than was previously apparent. All three possible wifeness templates in the preceding paragraph lead to expressions that in some sense preserve some structure in "Jim's wife". The last of the three does so more strongly than the second, and the second more strongly than the first. But even the first preserves structure, in the sense that it leads to a expression that it purports to use a reference to Jim in order to define a unique person.

Moreover, since Mike's conjectured correlates of templates are represented by terms in RS_{SYS}, it is possible to place arbitrary constraints on the nature, structure and relationships of the correlates. And we have already seen that Mike need not be assumed to be using standard correlates. These features of RS_{SYS} provide a degree of freedom in *and* control over the nature of interpretations that goes considerably beyond what previous PA-representation proposals have catered for.

Nested Attitudes: Avoiding Imputations

There is an imputation problem we must be aware of in RS_{SYS}. It is analogous to the one pointed out for quotational schemes in section 4.

We have seen that one prime interpretation for sentence (2) is formula (10). Suppose for simplicity that we do have axiom (15), so that (10) is actually equivalent to (14), which we repeat here:

((14))   blv(m, $\$_m$('clever(s)')).

It appears therefore that we get a prime interpretation of a PA report by taking the RS_{SYS} interpretation I of its complement ("Sally is clever" in this case) and a term A denoting the attitude-holder, and then constructing the formula blv(A, $\$_A$('I')).

But suppose we apply this technique to sentence (5), "George believes that Mike believes that Sally is clever". We get

((21))   blv(g, $\$_g$('blv(m, $\$_m$('clever(s)')')')).

The trouble with this is that it is also the formula we would get from applying our interpretation technique to the sentence

((22)) George believes that Mike believes his-standard-correlate-of clever(s).

The formula is as least as natural as an interpretation of this sentence as of (5), so that the formula embodies an imputation to George of items referring to arcane entities such as the Mike's-standard-correlate-of function.

We can view this imputation problem in another way. Assume that the natural decomposition axiom (analogous to axiom (15)) for terms of form $\$_g$('blv(...)') is present. Then formula (21) is equivalent to

((23))   blv(g, ϕ_g($\$_g$('blv(x,y)'), $\$_g$('m'), $\$_g$('$\$_m$('clever(s)')'))).

Then we are saying that *George's* representation scheme contains an item that denotes Mike's mental contents. This item is the George-expression denoted by $\$_g$('$\$_m$('clever(s)')'). This George-expression denotes the mental object in Mike that RS_{SYS} denotes with $\$_m$('clever(s)'). (We make the natural assumption here that SYS has the axiom denotes$_g$($\$_g$('E'), E) for each denoting expression E in RS_{SYS}. Recall also that the ϕ_g application preserves the integrity of the items it uses to fill holes in templates.) Thus, SYS is *imputing to George* a way of viewing belief that originates in *its* representation scheme.

I am inclined to say that the imputation is heuristically a reasonable one, in that it will tend not to lead agent SYS to make undesirable inferences about the behaviour, plans, etc. of cognitive agents. However, it is instructive to observe that RS_{SYS} is flexible enough for it to be able to avoid making the imputation. Consider the following alternative interpretation of (5):

((24))   blv(g, ϕ_g($\$_g$('blv(x, $\$_x$('y'))'), $\$_g$('m'), $\$_g$('clever(s)'))).

Our case rests on the freedom allowed in what the term

((25)) $\$_g$('blv(x, $\$_x$('y'))')

could denote. By way of simple illustration, suppose that George's expressions are all expressions in a modal logic scheme, containing constants and predicate symbols like those in RS$_{SYS}$. Assume that the terms $\$_g$('m') and $\$_g$('clever(s)') denote m and clever(s) respectively, and that term (25) denotes the template B_x(y), where for any agent-denoting term x, the symbol B_x is a modal belief operator. Then, according to (24) George is mentally asserting the expression B_m(clever(s)). Thus, there is no imputation to George of mental objects that denote Mike's mental objects.

6. DISCUSSION AND CONCLUSIONS

We have suggested by example that a particular type of representation scheme based on terms denoting mental expressions and "mental templates" can cope easily with the rich variety of ways of interpreting PA reports. In particular, the freedom and control provided by the proposal allows varying interpretations of the functional and predicational phrases in PA-report complements. A special case of such a phrase is the inner "believes that" in a nested-belief report, and a consequence of the freedom and control provided is the avoidance of certain "imputation" problems associated with the treatment of nested reports by other representational proposals.

The freedom and control is afforded by the use of "templates" that when filled become expressions either in the proposed scheme itself or in the conjectured schemes of other agents. The use of templates is not itself claimed to be a wide departure from other work (for instance, they are similar to the abstracted expressions used in Quine (1981)). Rather, the proposal's main contribution is its particular way of using templates to avoid imputations and to control multiple interpretations of functional/predicational phrases.

Moreover, my intent in this paper is *not* to put forward a fully worked out representation scheme, but rather to make suggestions about how the development of the mental-object approach should proceed. For one thing, systems that are able to denote their own expressions (and also have truth-predicates and the like) are notorious for introducing paradoxes and inconsistencies. Although I also have suggestions about these, the problem is long-standing and likely to remain so. (I am considering the technique of taking the connections between "formula F is true" and F itself to be merely ones of plausible inference. I am also considering avoiding own-expression denotation in the first place and using instead complex, high-order terms denoting properties and relationships [cf. Barnden (1986)], but this technique has problems of its own.)

Finally, although I have presented a logic-based proposal here, I am not committed to using logic notation as opposed to, say, network notation. Still less am I committed to a classical, Tarskian view of the semantics of representation schemes. Thus, when I say representational items in an agent SYS "denote" things (including mental objects), I am merely using a heuristic form of expression to describe SYS's acting in the world *as if* it contained those things. I am inclined to an operational/ecological view of the "semantics" of representational schemes, be they in human agents or artificial ones.

172

J. Barnden

REFERENCES

+Barnden, J. A. (1983). Intensions as such: an outline. *Procs. 8th Int. Joint Conf. on Artificial Intelligence*, Karlsruhe.

Barnden, J. A. (1985). Representations of intensions, representations as intensions, and propositional attitudes. Tech. Rep. 172, Computer Science Dept., Indiana University, Bloomington, Indiana.

Barnden, J.A. (1986). Imputations and explications: representational problems in treatments of propositional attitudes. Tech. Rep. 187, Computer Science Dept., Indiana University, Bloomington, Indiana. Submitted to *Cognitive Science*.

Barwise, J., & Perry, J. (1983). *Situations and attitudes*. Cambridge, Mass.: MIT Press.

Barwise, J., & Perry, J. (1985). Report of interview with Barwise and Perry in *Linguistics and Philosophy, 8*, 105–161.

Burdick, H. (1982). A logical form for the propositional attitudes. *Synthese, 52*, 185–230.

Creary, L. G. (1979). Propositional attitudes: Fregean representation and simulative reasoning. *Procs. 6th. Int. Joint Conf. on Artificial Intelligence*, Tokyo.

Elgin, C. Z. (1985). Translucent belief. *J. Philosophy, 82*, 74–91.

Fagin, R. & Halpern, Y.J. (1985). Belief, awareness, and limited reasoning: preliminary report. In *Procs. 9th. Int. Joint Conf. on Artificial Intelligence*, Los Angeles, 1985.

Fodor, J. A. (1978). Propositional attitudes. *The Monist, 61*, 501–523.

Grandy, R. E. (1981). Forms of belief. *Synthese, 46*, 271–284.

Hellan, L. (1981). On semantic scope. In Heny (1981).

Heny, F. (ed). (1981). *Ambiguities in intensional contexts*. Dorcrecht: D. Reidel.

Hintikka, J. (1983). Situations, possible worlds, and attitudes. *Synthese, 54*, 153–162.

Kaplan, D. (1971). Quantifying in. In L. Linsky (Ed.), *Reference and modality*. Oxford: Oxford University Press.

Konolige, K. (1984). A deduction model of belief and its logics. Report No. STAN-CS-84-1022, Department. of Computer Science, Stanford Univ., Stanford, Calif.

Konolige, K. (1985). A computational theory of belief introspection. In *Procs. 9th. Int. Joint Conf. on Artificial Intelligence*, Los Angeles, 1985.

Kraut, R. (1983). There are no *de dicto* attitudes. *Synthese, 54*, 275–294.

Levesque, H. J. (1984). A logic of implicit and explicit belief. *Procs. Natl. Conf. on Artificial Intelligence*, Univ. of Texas at Austin.

Linsky, L. (1983). *Oblique contexts*. Chicago: U. Chicago Press.

McCarthy, J. (1979). First order theories of individual concepts and propositions. In J. E. Hayes, D. Michie & L. I. Mikulich (Eds.), *Machine Intelligence 9*. Chichester: Ellis Horwood.

Maida, A. S. & Shapiro, S. C. (1982). Intensional concepts in propositional semantic networks. *Cognitive Science, 6*, 291–330.

Moore, R. C. (1977). Reasoning about knowledge and action. *Procs. 5th. Int. Joint Conf. on Artificial Intelligence*, MIT.

Moore, R. C. & Hendrix, G. G. (1982). Computational models of belief and the semantics of belief sentences. In Peters & Saarinen (1982).

Perlis, D. (1985). Languages with self-reference I: Foundations. *Artificial Intelligence, 25*, 301–322.

Peters, S., & Saarinen, E. (Eds.) (1982). *Processes, beliefs and questions*. Dordrecht: Reidel.

Quine, W.V.O. (1981). Intensions revisited. In W.V. Quine, *Theories and things*. Cambridge, Mass: Harvard U. Press.

Rapaport, W. J., & Shapiro, S. C. (1984). Quasi-indexical reference in propositional semantic networks. *Procs. 10th Int. Conf. on Computational Linguistics*, Stanford Univ.

Saarinen, E. (1981). Quantifier phrases are (at least) five ways ambiguous in intensional contexts. In Heny (1981).

Swoyer, C. (1983). Belief and predication. *Noûs, 17*, 197–220.

Yagisawa, T. (1984). The pseudo-Mates argument. *Phil. Revw., 93*, 407–418.

Advances in Artificial Intelligence - II
B. Du Boulay, D. Hogg and L. Steels (Editors)
© Elsevier Science Publishers B.V. (North-Holland), 1987

MINIMIZATION OF ABNORMALITY:
A SIMPLE SYSTEM FOR DEFAULT REASONING

Witold Łukaszewicz

Institute of Informatics
University of Warsaw
P.O. Box 1210
00-901 Warszawa, POLAND

ABSTRACT

We specify a simple system intended to model default reasoning.
The system employs general ideas of circumscription. In particular, it assumes common sense knowledge representation corresponding closely to McCarthy's abnormality formalism.

In contrast to circumscription, the presented system works within the framework of first-order logic. This leads to several advantages. In particular, a simple interface with first-order
theorem provers can be specified.

INTRODUCTION

A fundamental property of common sense reasoning is its <u>nonmono-
tonicity</u>, i.e., the ability of drawing conclusions which may be
invalidated by new information.

An important form of nonmonotonic reasoning is <u>default reasoning</u>,
that is the drawing of plausible inferences from incomplete information in the absence of evidence to the contrary. A typical
example is the following. If Joe is a child, then in the absence
of evidence to the contrary, we normally assume that he has parents. But if we later learn that Joe is an orphan, we shall reject our previous conclusion.

One of the most interesting approaches to the problem of formalizing nonmonotonic inference patterns, including default reasoning, is <u>circumscription</u> (McCarthy, 1980, 1984). This formalism
captures the idea that the objects that can be shown to have a
certain property are all the objects that satisfy this property.
In other words, to circumscribe a property is to assume that the
property has the minimal possible extension.

To express a default rule admitting exceptions, McCarthy introduces a predicate symbol ab, standing for "abnormal", with intuitive interpretation that the abnormal objects are those violating the rule. Assume, for instance, that our common sense knowledge consists of the default "Typically adults are married" and
the proposition "John is an adult". These facts can be represented by the following first-order theory:

(1) $\forall x (\text{adult}(x) \land \sim ab(x) \supset \text{married}(x))$

(2) $\text{adult}(\text{John})$

Of course, applying deductive structure of classical logic, it
is impossible to use (1) to infer that John is married. The problem is that classical logic offers no way to conclude that John
is not abnormal. But circumscription does. Circumscribing the
property of being abnormal, i.e., minimizing its extension, we
can infer that all the adults that cannot be proved abnormal are

normal and, in the consequence, that they are married.

To express the fact that Bill is an unmarried adult, we extend
our theory by adding the following axiom:

(3)   adult(Bill) $\wedge \sim$married(Bill).

Observe that (1) and (3) imply that Bill is abnormal. This means
that Bill is now the only element of the minimal extension of ab.

Suppose now that we want to introduce a new default stating that
a typical adult is employed. Taking into account that being abnormal with regard to the employment status is something quite
different from being abnormal with respect to the marital one,
we choose a new abnormal predicate, say ab1, and we add

(4) $\forall x(\text{adult}(x) \wedge \sim \text{ab1}(x) \supset \text{employed}(x))$.

It should be stressed that dealing with several kinds of abnormality, extensions of all the abnormality predicates have to be
minimized. In our case, we must assume the joint minimization of
ab and ab1.

There are default rules requiring many-place abnormality predicates. Consider, for instance, the rule "Typically if x has a
birthday and y is a friend of x, then y gives x a gift". The appropriate representation of this default requires using a two-
place abnormality predicate:

$\forall x \forall y(\text{birthday}(x) \wedge \text{friend}(x,y) \wedge \sim \text{ab}(x,y) \supset \text{gives-gift}(x,y))$.

For lack of space we are not able to discuss the abnormality
formalism in full detail. The reader should consult (McCarthy,
1984), (Grosof, 1984), (Lifschitz, 1984).

There are two problems connected with circumscription. First,
involving quantifying over predicate variables, circumscription
cannot be generally handled by first-order theorem provers (but
see (Lifschitz, 1985)). Second, unrestricted application of circumscription can lead to implausible conclusions.

The purpose of this paper is to specify a simple system intended
to model default reasoning. The system employs general ideas of
circumscription. In particular, it assumes common sense knowledge representation corresponding closely to McCarthy's abnormality formalism. The major distinction between circumscription
and the presented system arises from different deductive structures given to this representation. In circumscription this
structure is defined syntactically by means of a second-order
formula. In our system the set of theorems nonmonotonically derivable from a given set of premisses is defined by means of an
algebraic construction. This allows us to work entirely within
the framework of first-order logic, and to avoid problems connected with unrestricted application of circumscription.

For lack of space some proofs will be omitted, and the others
will be only sketched. Complete proofs will be published elsewhere.

ABNORMALITY THEORIES AND THEIR EXTENSIONS

We are dealing with the usual first-order language over an alpha-
bet of variables, function and predicate letters, logical constants and punctuation signs. We assume that the set of predicate letters contains countable many n-place abnormality predi-

<u>cates</u>: ab_1^n, $ab_2^n, \ldots,$ for each $n \geqslant 0$.

The objects under consideration are <u>abnormality theories</u>, i.e., sets of well-formed closed formulae over the above language. If A is an abnormality theory, then by Th(A) we denote the set of formulae monotonically derivable from A.

We shall limit our attention to a specific class of abnormality theories, namely <u>universal abnormality theories</u>. A theory is universal if the prenex normal form of each of its axioms contains no existential quantifier. Since circumscription of non-universal theories can lead to inconsistency (see Etherington, Mercer and Reiter, 1985)), this restriction does not make our system essentially weaker than circumscription (for details concerning the satisfiability of circumscription see (Lifschitz, 1985a)). On the other hand, universal theories include the Horn theories, which have turned out to be sufficient for many applications. In what follows, the term "abnormality theory" refers to "universal abnormality theory".

Nonmonotonic deductive structure given to an abnormality theory must capture the idea of minimizing all the abnormality predicates occurring in the theory. In contrast to circumscription, this minimization will be achieved algebraically. To make it possible, first a set of individuals for a given theory A must be specified. Since A is a universal theory, it is natural to identify this set with the Herbrand universe for A, i.e., with the set of all ground terms constructable from constant and function letters occurring in A. Now, to minimize an n-place abnormality predicate ab, occurring in a theory A, we should add to A a maximal (with respect to consistency) set of formulae of the form $\sim ab(t_1, \ldots, t_n)$, where t_i's are ground terms from the Herbrand universe for A. The formal details follow.

Let A be an abnormal theory. By Terms(A) we denote the set of all ground terms constructable from constant and function letters occurring in A. By ABP(A) we denote the set of all the abnormal predicates occurring in A. By ABF(A) we denote the <u>set of abnormality formulae for</u> A, i.e., the set of all the formulae of the form $ab(t_1, \ldots, t_n)$, where $ab \in ABP(A)$ and $t_1, \ldots, t_n \in Terms(A)$.

<u>Example.</u>   Consider the abnormality theory A given by

(1)   bird(Tweety)
(2) $\forall x \big(bird(x) \supset bird(father(x))\big)$
(3) $\forall x \big(bird(x) \wedge \sim ab(x) \supset flies(x)\big)$

We have:

Terms(A) = $\{$ Tweety, father(Tweety), father(father(Tweety)),..$\}$
ABP(A) = $\{$ ab $\}$
ABF(A) = $\{$ ab(Tweety), ab(father(Tweety)),... $\}$.

A set of theorems nonmonotonically derivable from a given abnormality theory is called an <u>extension of the theory</u>. There are three conditions which such an extension S of a theory A has to satisfy:

(i)   It should be deductively closed; $S = Th(S)$
(ii)   It should contain all the axioms of A; $A \subseteq S$.

(iii)   It should contain a maximal (with respect to consistency)
        set of formulae of the form $\sim ab(t_1,..,t_n)$, where
        $ab \in ABP(A)$; $t_1,\ldots,t_n \in Terms(A)$.

This motivates the following definition. Let A be an abnormality
theory. A set of closed formulae S is an extension of A iff

$$S = Th(A \cup \{\sim\alpha: \ \alpha \in ABF(A) \ \text{and} \ S \not\vdash \alpha\}).$$

The theory given by (1)-(3) above has a single extension

$$S = Th(\{(1)-(3)\} \cup \{\sim ab \ (\text{Tweety}), \ \sim ab \ (\text{father}(\text{Tweety})),\ldots\}).$$

Consider now a theory A given by:

(4) $\forall x(\text{republican}(x) \land \sim ab_1(x) \supset \sim\text{pacifist}(x))$

(5) $\forall x(\text{quaker}(x) \land \sim ab_2(x) \supset \text{pacifist}(x))$

(6) $\text{republican}(\text{John}) \land \text{quaker}(\text{John})$

The set of abnormality formulae for A is $ABF(A) = \{ ab_1(\text{John}),$
$ab_2(\text{John})\}$. Note that we can consistently add to A "$\sim ab_1(\text{John})$"
or "$\sim ab_2(\text{John})$", but not both. This results in two extensions:

$$S_1 = Th(\{(4)-(6)\} \cup \{\sim ab_1(\text{John})\})$$

$$S_2 = Th(\{(4)-(6)\} \cup \{\sim ab_2(\text{John})\}).$$

Observe that $\sim\text{pacifist}(\text{John}) \in S_1$; $\text{pacifist}(\text{John}) \in S_2$.

In the case of many extensions of a theory A, each of them is
regarded as an alternative set of theorems nonmonotonically derivable from A, and is interpreted as a possible set of beliefs
one may hold about a world being modelled by the theory A.

Theorem 1. Each abnormality theory has an extension.

Proof (outline): Let A be an abnormality theory. If A is (monotonically) inconsistent, then the set of all closed formulae is
clearly an extension of A. Thus assume that A is consistent.
Let $\alpha_0, \alpha_1,\ldots$ $[\alpha_0,\ldots,\alpha_n]$ be any sequence of all abnormality formulae for A. We define a sequence of sets of for-
mulae $S_0 \subseteq S_1 \subseteq \ldots$ $[S_0 \subseteq S_1 \subseteq \ldots \subseteq S_n]$ by

$$S_0 = A,$$

$$S_{i+1} = \begin{cases} S_i & \text{if} \quad S_i \vdash \alpha_i \\ S_i \cup \{\sim \alpha_i\} & \text{otherwise} \end{cases}$$

Put $S = Th(\cup S_i)$. It is easily verified that S is an extension
of A.

SEMANTICAL CHARACTERIZATION OF EXTENSIONS

The general idea is to restrict the set of all first-order models for a theory A in such a way that

(1)   Any restricted set of models is the set of all models for
      some extension of A.

(2)   If S is any extension of A, then there is some such re-
      stricted set of models which is the set of all models for A.

Some preliminary terminology. Let A be an abnormality theory,
and suppose that Mod(A) is the set of all first-order models for
A. If $M \in Mod(A)$, then by $ABF(A,M)$ we denote the set of all abnormality formulae for A which are true in M. Formally:

$$ABF(A,M) = \{ab(t_1,..t_n): \ t_i's \in Terms(A) \ \text{and} \ M \models ab(t_1,..,t_n)\}.$$

We say that a model M∈Mod(A) is <u>AB-minimal wrt</u> A iff for each M1∈Mod(A), ABF(A,M1) ⊆ ABF(A,M) implies ABF(A,M1) = ABF(A,M).

Let X ⊆ Mod(A) be the set of all AB-minimal models wrt A. The relation $\rho_A \subseteq X \times X$ such that M1 ρ_A M2 iff ABF(A,M1) = ABF(A,M2) is clearly an equivalence relation. We state without proofs the following theorems showing that equivalence classes of ρ_A characterize extensions of A.

Theorem 2. Let A be an abnormality theory, and suppose that a set of models X is an equivalence class of ρ_A. Then X is the set of all models for some extension of A.

Theorem 3. Let A be an abnormality theory, and suppose that S is an extension of A. Then the set of all models for S is an equivalence class of ρ_A.

PROOF THEORY

By a proof theory we understand the following problem. Given an abnormality theory A and a closed formula α, determine whether A has an extension containing α.
The key result is the following theorem.

Theorem 4. Let A be an abnormality theory, and suppose that α is a closed formula. Then α belongs to some extension of A iff there exists a finite set of formulae X such that:

(1) Each element of X is the negation of an abnormality formula for A, i.e., it is a formula of the form $\sim$ab(t1,...,tn), where ab∈ABF(A), t1,...,tn∈Terms(A).

(2) A ∪ X $\vdash$ α.

(3) If X $\neq$ $\emptyset$ (the empty set), then A ∪ X is consistent.

<u>Proof</u> (outline): Assume first that α belongs to an extension S of A. From the definition of an extension we have

$$S = Th(A \cup \{\sim ab(t1,..,tn): \quad S \nvdash ab(t1,...,tn)\}).$$

If A is inconsistent, then it is sufficient to take X = $\emptyset$. So, assume that A, and thus S, is consistent. Since $\alpha \in S$, there is a classical first-order proof of α. Define:

$$X = \{\sim ab(t1,..,tn): \sim ab(t1,..,tn) \text{ belongs to the proof of } \alpha\}.$$

X is finite. Moreover, it is easily seen that X satisfies (1)-(3).

Assume now that for some X the conditions (1)-(3) hold. If A is inconsistent, then α clearly belongs to the unique extension of A. Assume, therefore, that A is consistent. It is sufficient to show that there is an extension of A containing A ∪ X. Let $\alpha 1$, $\alpha 2$,..., αn be a sequence of all formulae from X. The construction given in the proof of Theorem 1 leads to an extension containing A ∪ X.

This completes the proof of Theorem 3.

The above theorem suggests a method of applying a standard resolution theorem prover for the purpose of our system. This will be illustrated for a theorem prover based on linear resolution (Loveland, 1970).

A linear resolution proof of α from some set of clauses S has the form

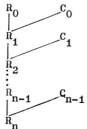

where

(i) R_0 is a clause of $\sim\alpha$.

(ii)   For $1 \leqslant i \leqslant n$, R_i is a resolvent of R_{i-1} and C_{i-1}.

(iii) For $0 \leqslant i \leqslant n-1$, $C_i \in S$ or C_i is a clause of $\sim\alpha$ or C_i is R_j for some $j < i$.

(iv) $R_n = \square$, (the empty clause).

We shall need the following terminology. Let A be a theory. We say that a formula α is a <u>final clause</u> <u>for</u> A, iff α is the empty clause or α is of the form $\alpha 1 \vee \alpha 2 \vee \ldots \vee \alpha n$, where each αi is an abnormality formula for A, i.e., each $\alpha i \in ABF(A)$. We say that a formula α is a <u>good final</u> <u>clause</u> <u>for</u> A, iff α is the empty clause or $\alpha = \alpha 1 \vee \alpha 2 \vee \ldots \vee \alpha n$ is a final clause for A such that $A \cup \{\sim\alpha 1, \sim\alpha 2, \ldots, \sim\alpha n\}$ is consistent.

<u>Example</u>   Consider the theory A given by:

$\forall x (\text{fish}(x) \wedge \sim ab1(x) \supset \text{swims}(x))$;   fish (Tweety);

$\forall x (\text{bird}(x) \wedge \sim ab2(x) \supset \text{flies}(x))$;   bird (Tao) $\wedge \sim$ flies (Tao).

Examples of final clauses for A are the following:

(1) $\square$;   (2) ab1 (Tao) $\vee$ ab2 (Tao);   (3) ab1 (Tweety);
(4) ab2 (Tweety).

All of the above clauses, except (2), are good final clauses for A. Since $A \cup \{\sim ab1(\text{Tao}), \sim ab2(\text{Tao})\}$ is inconsistent, (2) is not a good final clause for A.

Let A be an abnormality theory. Since all the theories under consideration are universal theories, without the loss of generality, we can assume that A is in clausal form.

A <u>nonmonotonic</u> <u>proof</u> of α wrt A is a linear resolution proof of α from the set of clauses A, where the condition (iv) from the definition of standard linear resolution proof is replaced by

(iv') R_n is a good final clause for A.

<u>Example</u>   Consider the theory A given by:

$\forall x (\text{bird}(x) \wedge \sim ab1(x) \supset \text{flies}(x))$
$\forall x (\text{flies}(x) \wedge \sim ab2(x) \supset \text{has-wings}(x))$
bird (Tao)

The clausal form of A is
$\sim$bird(x) $\vee$ ab1(x) $\vee$ flies(x)
$\sim$flies(x)$\vee$ ab2(x) $\vee$ has-wings(x)
bird(Tao)

A nonmonotonic proof of "has-wings Tao " from A is given below:

has-wings(Tao) $\sim$flies(x) $\vee$ ab2(x) $\vee$ has-wings(x)

$\sim$flies(Tao) $\vee$ ab2(Tao) $\sim$bird(x) $\vee$ ab1(x) $\vee$ flies(x)

ab2(Tao) $\vee \sim$bird(Tao) $\vee$ ab1(Tao)   bird(Tao)

ab2(Tao) $\vee$ ab1(Tao)

Note that since A$\cup\{\sim$ab2(Tao), $\sim$ab1(Tao)$\}$ is consistent, the clause ab2(Tao) $\vee$ ab1(Tao) is a good final clause for A.

Combining Theorem 4 and the fact that standard linear resolution is complete, it is routine to prove the following theorem.

Theorem 5. Let A be an abnormality theory, and suppose that α is a closed formula. Then α belongs to some extension of A, iff there exists a nonmonotonic proof of α wrt A.

It should be stressed that the proof theory of our system, as in other nonmonotonic formalisms, is generally non-semi-decidable. This result is due to consistency test while determining whether a final clause is a good one. This means that any computational implementation of the system must necessarily apply an heuristic mechanism and will, sometimes, lead to mistaken results.

CONCLUSIONS

We have presented a simple system modelling default reasoning. The system employs general ideas of circumscription. The major advantage of our system is that it entirely works within the framework of first-order logic.

As has been pointed out by an anonymous referee, a large number of naturally occurring abnormality theories are Horn theories. This poses the interesting question of how to modify standard Prolog interpreters to make them applicable to the presented system. We plan to study this problem in the near future.

An important distinction between circumscription and our system arises from different interpretation of individuals in both the formalisms. While in circumscription individuals under consideration should be thought of as all the elements of universe, in our system they are only those objects which can be referred by ground terms. This makes some plausible conclusions, represented by general formulae, underivable in our system. Consider, for instance, the theory A given by:

$\forall$x(bird(x) $\wedge \sim$ab(x) $\supset$ flies(x))

bird(Tweety)

bird(Clyde)

Given the theory A, circumscription allows us to infer
$\forall x(\text{bird}(x) \supset \text{flies}(x))$.

To infer this formula in our system, the domain closure axiom
$\forall x(x = \text{Tweety} \lor x = \text{Clyde})$
has to be added. Of course, such a solution is impossible for
theories containing function symbols.

ACKNOWLEDGEMENTS

I am indebted to Barbara Dunin-Kęplicz for her comments on earlier drafts of this paper.

REFERENCES

Etherington, D., Mercer, R., Reiter, R. (1985) On The Adequacy
   of Predicate Circumscription for Closed-World Reasoning,
   Computational Intelligence 1.

Grosof, B. (1984) Default Reasoning as Circumscription, AAAI
   Workshop on Non-Monotonic Reasoning, 115-124.

Lifschitz, V. (1984) Some Results on Circumscription, AAAI
   Workshop on Non-Monotonic Reasoning, 151-164.

Lifschitz, V. (1985) Computing Circumscription, Proc. 9th IJCAI,
   121-127.

Lifschitz, V. (1985a) On The Satisfiability of Circumscription,
   Stanford University, draft.

Loveland, D. (1970) A Linear Format for Resolution, Proc. IRIA
   Symp. Automatic Demonstration, Springer-Verlag, New York,
   163-190.

McCarthy, J. (1980) Circumscription - A Form of Non-Monotonic
   Reasoning. Artificial Intelligence 13, 27-39.

McCarthy, J. (1984) Applications of Circumscription to Formalizing Commonsense Knowledge, AAAI Workshop on Non-Monotonic
   Reasoning, 295-323.

Advances in Artificial Intelligence - II
B. Du Boulay, D. Hogg and L. Steels (Editors)
© Elsevier Science Publishers B.V. (North-Holland), 1987

Reified Temporal Logics:
Semantical and Ontological Considerations

Yoav Shoham

Yale University
Computer Science Department

Abstract

One way to represent temporal information in a logical formalism is through what are known as "reified" propositions. What would otherwise be propositions or formulas, actually appear as arguments to some predicate, say *TRUE*, as in *TRUE(t_1, t_2, color(house,red))*. This way time is referred to explicitly, while retaining its special notational and conceptual status. Reified propositions have been widely adopted in AI.

We examine this method by looking closely at two of the more influential formalisms featuring reified propositions, those of Allen and McDermott. We show that these do not have completely clear semantics, and that they make some unfortunate and unnecessary ontological commitments. Finally, we present a new formalism and demonstrate that it does not suffer from these disadvantages.

1 Introduction

Most research areas within AI involve reasoning about time in one way or another: medical diagnosis systems try to determine the time at which the virus infected the blood system; circuit debugging programs must reason about the period over which the charge in the capacitor increased; automatic programmers and program synthesizers must deduce that after procedure P is executed the value of variable X is zero; robot programmers must make sure that the robot meets various deadlines when carrying out a set of tasks. One particular subfield of AI, which has become known as the area of *temporal reasoning* (henceforth TR), acknowledges this central role of time. While most subfields merely employ temporal terminology, the very goal of TR is a general theory of time.

In contrast to much of the work in AI which is rather informal, work in TR consists primarily of "formalisms," which is to say logics with more or less well-worked-out syntax and semantics. Still, the body of work has a somewhat episodic nature; the motivation of each system is slightly different, and it's not always clear how to compare two formalisms. Elsewhere I propose criteria by which to evaluate and compare temporal formalisms [6]. In this paper I have a more specific aim.

How does one represent temporal information? Suppose we want to represent in logic the fact that the color of a particular house is red at time t. We have several options:

- We can simply include time as an argument to the predicate: *color(house,red,t)*, where *t* is a time argument (a point, an interval or otherwise; we will return to this later).

- We can refrain from mentioning time at all! Instead, we complicate the interpretation of our formulas. If in classical logic a formula φ is either true (written $\models \varphi$) or false, now a formula is either true *at a given time t* (written $t \models \varphi$) or false *at that time*. (Here again we have of the choice of choosing t to be a point, an interval or some other temporal entity.)

- We can "reify" (or, as John McCarthy once proposed, "thingify") the proposition: *TRUE(t,color(house,red))*. This option requires that we be careful about the logical status of *color(house,red)*, about what consitute well-formed formulas, and about the meaning of these formulas.

The first option is not acceptable from the standpoint of TR. If time is represented as an argument (or several arguments) to predicates then there is nothing general you can say about the temporal aspect of propositions. For example, you cannot say that "effects cannot precede their causes"; at most you can say that about specific causes and effects. Indeed, this first option accords no special status to time — neither conceptual nor notational — which goes against the grain of the TR spirit.

The second option, which appears in the form of modal temporal logic and which has been favored in formal philosophy and theoretical computer science, has for the most part been ignored in AI until very recently [5,2].

The third option has been, in one guise or another, widely accepted in TR. My aim in this paper is to look closely at what is involved in exercising this third option without sacrificing rigor. I will do so by looking closely what are probably the two most influential temporal formalisms in AI, both of which feature reified propositions: James Allen's interval calculus [1] and Drew McDermott's temporal logic [4]. More specifically, I'd like to do the following:

1. Identify the part common to both formalisms, and in the process point out problems in each one.

2. Show that the part of each formalism that can be given adequate semantics is exactly that common part.

3. Suggest a new formalism whose expressiveness subsumes that of the common part of these two formalisms, which is simpler than either one, and which enjoys clear formal semantics.

2   Allen's and McDermott's formalisms

I begin by discussing the relevant parts of the formalisms developed by Allen and McDermott. I'll first discuss Allens's *properties*, *events* and *processes*, and then McDermott's *facts* and *events*.

2.1   Allen

For Allen, the basic entities that are associated with time are *properties*, *events* and *processes*. The fact that a property holds for an interval is denoted by the formula $HOLD(p,i)$, where p is a property type and i is an interval. A property is true for an interval iff it holds for every subinterval. (In fact, Allen requires a stronger axiom; more on his Axiom H.2 later.) Three examples of properties are that a particular object is green, elongated and tasty. The fact that an event occurred over an interval is denoted by the formula $OCCUR(e,i)$, where e is an event type. In contrast with properties, an event cannot occur over two intervals one of which contains the other. An example Allen gives of an event type is $CHANGE\text{-}POS(ball1, pos1.pos2)$. Finally, processes are a hybrid case, which are intended to be typified by the sentence "I am walking"; it is (according to Allen) true of an interval if it occurred in a "substantial" number of subintervals. In fact Allen has to make do with the following definition: a process occurred over an interval iff it occurred over *some* subinterval. The fact that a process p took place from over interval i is denoted by the formula $OCCURRING(p,i)$.

This describes Allen's basic ontology. He goes on to discuss weighty issues such as actions, causation, intentions and planning, but I'd like to halt here and see to what degree the basic formalism is well defined. What defines the meaning of $HOLD(p,i)$? For that matter, what is the set of all properties? If we have a property of the form *color(house.red)*, which Allen allows, what is the criterion by which we allow the property *color(roof(house).red)* but not the property *roof(house)*? Also, Allen introduces connective-like functions: "To allow properties to name complex logical expressions, there is a set of functions *and, or, not, all* and *exists*, that correspond to the logical operators ..." (p.130). So, apparently, one can apply functions to properties and obtain new properties. Are these all the functions one can apply? Furthermore, the *all* and *exists* functions imply that properties contain variable-like entities; what does *that* imply about the structure of well-formed preperties? In short, the set of properties look suspiciously like the set of first-order formulas. If that is the case, then not only has Allen not given precise syntax and semantics for the new language, but in fact he gave up the off-the-shelf FOPC and the associated model theory.

The reason Allen goes to all this trouble is because he tries to accommodate both his wish to grant time a special status and his desire to retain the expressiveness of FOPC, all that without resorting to a logic which he views as more complex: "Note that if we had introduced *HOLD* as a modal operator we would not need to introduce properties into our ontology. We have not followed this route, however, since it seems more complicated in the later development of occurrences." Actually I see no difficulty in taking the modal route, but at any rate I will show that even if we wish to remain within the "reified" framework there is a better way of doing so, one that does not obscure the first-order (or propositional) nature of our assertions.

There are other points where I think Allen made the wrong choice. The first is his insistence on not mentioning time points. Reasoning about intervals is essential and it would be foolish to disallow it, but discarding the notion of points altogether is also bad, especially in this context of a formal system with notions such as density. Consider, for example, Allen's Axiom H.2. (p.130), $HOLD(p,i) \equiv \forall\, i' \in i\, \exists\, i'' \in i'\, HOLD(p,i'')$. This strange looking formula would be greatly simplified if we allowed points into the ontology; what the formula really means is that a property holds over an interval iff it holds at all points during the interval. This awkwardness is propagated onwards. For example, Theorem H.7. (p.131) reads: $HOLD(OR(p,q),i) \equiv \forall\, i' \in i\, \exists\, i'' \in i'\, (HOLD(p,i'') \lor HOLD(q,i''))$. Again, if we had points at our disposal, the theorem would state simply that $OR(p,q)$ holds over an interval iff at any point in the interval either p holds or q does.

Finally, I think Allen made the wrong choice in the property/event/process trichotomy, at least as the "assembly language" of the logic. Certainly there are propositions that are wholistic in nature ("the robot solved the problem") and those that are not ("the robot's batteries were fully charged"), but for some purposes the distinction between these kinds of propositions is unnecessary and it would be useful to have a term covering both. For example, much of Allen's discussion of event causation (*ECAUSE*) should apply to pairs of properties and mixed pairs of properties and events.[1] Furthermore, this distinction is insufficient to express some other properties of propositions, such as that if a proposition holds over two overlapping intervals then it holds over the union of the two intervals, though not necessarily vice versa ("I ran for more than two miles"). In the new reified logic I will propose a different categorization of temporal propositions.

2.2   McDermott

McDermott's construction is similar to Allen's. McDermott's building blocks are *fact types*, *event types*, and time points (or states.) The formula[2] $T(t,p)$ means that the fact type p holds at time t. The formula $TT(t1,t2,p)$ is merely an abbreviation for the formula $\forall\, t\, (t1 \leq t \leq t2 \supset T(t,p))$. Finally, the formula $OCC(t1,t2,e)$ means that event type e took place between t_1 and t_2.

McDermott starts out by giving precise semantics to the sentences. The construction is set theoretic: the meaning of a fact type is simply a set of time points, and the meaning of an event type is a set of pairs of time points. McDermott treats $T(t,p)$ as merely an abbreviation for $t \in p$, $TT(t1,t2,p)$ as an abbreviation for $[t1..t2] \subset p$, and $OCC(t1,t2,e)$ as an abbreviation for $\langle t1,t2 \rangle \in e$. McDermott's semantics are essentially those

---

[1]This is beside the fact that Allen, like McDermott and a score of philosophers and other AI researchers, does not give semantics to the causation. While he isn't to be discredited for not doing so, it brings out once again the seductive unclarity of the logic: there is nothing that is obviously ill-formed in the formula *ECAUSE(e1,i1,e2,i2)*, whereas the corresponding formula in first-order logic (or for that matter in the reified logic that I will present shortly) is obviously illegal on syntactic grounds.

[2]I'm using standard notation rather than McDermott's LISP-like notation for the sake of uniformity.

of propositional modal logic, although he introduces them differently by using set-theoretic notions in the language itself in a way that makes the semantics explicit.

McDermott too goes on to discuss important issues such as chronicles, causation and persistences, which I will ignore. What concern me here are the T, TT and OCC statements. Although, unlike Allen, McDermott gives precise semantics to his statements, in the rest of his formulations he goes far beyond the sentences to which the semantics apply. McDermott too uses fact types and event types that look suspiciously similar to first order sentences, including not only relation symbols but also function symbols and variables (p.135: $T(t.CLEARTOP(x))$, p.131: $WATER\text{-}VOL(TANK1)$.) In the new reified logic that I'll present such statements can be made, and the formal semantics can be viewed as generalizing McDermott's semantics to the first order case.

There are, however, formulas used by McDermott which will not be given meaning even by the new logic. For example, in discussing causation McDermott uses the formula $ECAUSE(e1.e2)$ (McDermott's $ECAUSE$ is different from Allen's and actually has more that two arguments; the rest are suppressed here.) The only "predicates" which are given meaning either in McDermott's logic or in the new logic are T, TT and OCC, which leaves the predicate $ECAUSE$ undefined. Again, it's not surprising that the meaning of a causal construct doesn't fall out of the truth-functional semantics of some theory, but it's important to recognize that it doesn't.

3 A new reified interval logic

To summarize the previous section, both McDermott's and Allen's logic suffer in two respects. Semantically, neither give their sentences a clear meaning, although McDermott does give the semantics of what may be regarded as the propositional theory. Conceptually, Allen's trichotomy of properties/events/processes and McDermott's dichotomy of facts/events are unnecessary at some times and insufficient at others. Also, Allen's exclusion of time points from the ontology leads to some awkward formulations. In the formulation I offer below I try to retain the appealing characteristics of the two logics without suffering from their drawbacks.

Omitting the propositional case, I directly define the first-order version, with time viewed simply as a total order on time points. I don't consider the cases of metric time or branching time; these will be simple extensions of the given logic. Equality is also a simple addition to the logic. Let me add that the logic I'm defining is by no means earthshakingly novel. For readers familiar with modal logic, I am simply encoding possible-worlds semantics in the logic itself. The reason it's worth doing is that it happens to be a *right* way of constructing reified temporal logics, and that it hasn't been done so far. The literature abounds with distorted and confused versions of it; I discussed Allen's and McDermott's systems because they are among the clearest in AI.

3.1 Syntax

The formulas I define have a uniform structure. Each formula is a pair $\langle i, \varphi \rangle$, where i is an interval symbol and φ is any first-order formula. An interval symbol i is really a pair $\langle t_1, t_2 \rangle$, where the t_is are time point symbols. For notational convenience I'll follow Allen's and McDermott's lead and replace the formula $\langle \langle t_1.t_2 \rangle.\varphi \rangle$ by the more appealing $TRUE(t_1.t_2.\varphi)$. The precise definition of the syntax is given below.

Given:

T: a set of time point symbols,

C: a set of constant symbols that is disjoint from T,

U: a set of temporal variables,

V: a set of variables that is disjoint from *U*,

TF: a set of temporal function symbols (typical ones being the arithmetic operators),

F: a set of function symbols that is disjoint from *TF*, and

R: a set of relation symbols,

The set of *(purely) temporal terms* is defined inductively as follows:

1. All constant symbols (*T*) are temporal terms.

2. All variables (*U*) are temporal terms.

3. if $trm_1, \ldots, trm_n$ are temporal terms, and $f \in TF$ is an n-ary function symbol, then $f(trm_1, \ldots, trm_n)$ is a temporal term.

The set of *nontemporal terms* is defined in exactly the same way, with *T* replaced by *C*, *U* replaced by *V*, and *TF* replaced by *F*.

The set of well-formed formulas (wffs) is defined inductively as follows:

1. If trm_1 *and* trm_2 are temporal terms, then $trm_1 = trm_2$ and $trm_1 \preceq trm_2$ are wffs. These wffs will be called *(purely) temporal* wffs.

2. If trm_i *and* trm_j are temporal terms, $trm_1, \ldots, trm_n$ are nontemporal terms, and $r \in R$ an n-ary relation symbol, then $TRUE(trm_i . trm_j . r(trm_1, \ldots, trm_n))$ is a wff. These wffs will be called *atomic* wffs.

3. If *x* and *y* are wffs then so are $x \wedge y$ and $\neg x$.

4. If *x* is a wff and $z \in U \cup V$ is a variable, then $\forall z\, x$ is a wff.

We assume the usual definitions of $\vee$, $\supset$, $\equiv$, $\exists$ and so on. We can also use the following syntactic sugar: $TRUE(trm_1 . trm_2 . x \wedge y)$ is shorthand for $TRUE(trm_1 . trm_2 . x) \wedge TRUE(trm_1 . trm_2 . y)$, $TRUE(trm_1 . trm_2 . \neg x)$ is shorthand for $\neg TRUE(trm_1 . trm_2 . x)$, and so on (one may prefer a different interpretation of $TRUE(trm_1 . trm_2 . \neg x)$; more on "strong negation" later).

A wff with no free variables is called a *sentence.* Below are some examples of sentences:

$TRUE(t_1 . t_2 . COLOR(HOUSE17, RED))$

$\exists u\ TRUE(t_3 . t_4 . ON(u, B))$

$\forall\, v\ (1776 < v < 1986 \supset TRUE(t_v . t_v . GENDER(PRESIDENT(USA).MALE)))$

$\forall v_1 . u\, \exists v_2\ ((TRUE(v_1 . v_1 . SOLID(u)) \wedge v_2 = v_1 + 30_{min} \wedge TRUE(v_1 . v_2 . HEATING(u))) \supset TRUE(v_2 . v_2 . LIQUID(u)))$

Notice that in the third example the term *PRESIDENT(USA)* is a function that depends implicitly on time. Such functions, which have also been called *fluents*, will therefore be interpreted in a way that takes time into account. The same applies to the interpretation of relation symbols. Constant symbols, on the other hand, will be interpreted in a time-independent fashion.

The respective intended meanings of these sentences are that *HOUSE17* is red from t_1 to t_2, that there's something on *B* from t_3 to t_4, that at any point between 1984 and 1988 the name of the American president is Reagan, and that if you heat a solid object for half an hour it melts.

The next subsection guarantees that these indeed *are* the meanings.

3.2 Semantics

An *interpretation* is a tuple $S = \langle W. \leq .D.TFN.FN.RL.M \rangle$, where

W is a nonempty universe of time points,

$\leq$ is a (relexive) total order on W.

D is a nonempty universe of individuals that is disjoint from W,

TFN is a set of total functions $\{fn: 2^W \to W\}$,

FN is a set of total functions $\{fn: 2^D \to D\}$,

RL is a set of relations over D, and

$M = \langle M1.M2.M3.M4.M5 \rangle$ is a meaning function as follows. $M1: T \to W$, $M2: C \to D$, $M3: TF \to TFN$, and $M4: W \times W \times F \to FN$, and $M5: W \times W \times R \to RL$. We also require that $M4$ and $M5$ be commutative in the first two arguments; that is, $M4(w_1.w_2.f) = M4(w_2.w_3.f)$ etcetera. This convention, suggested by Johan van Benthem, makes explicit the intuition that a pair of time points denotes a single interval.

A *variable assignment* is a function $VA = \langle VAU.VAV \rangle$, such that VAU $U: \to T$ and VAV $V: \to D$. M and VA induce a meaning MVA on arbitrary terms in the following way.

We first define the meaning of arbitrary temporal terms. If $u \in U$, then for all $w_1.w_2$, $MVA(\langle w_1.w_2 \rangle.u) = VAU(u)$. If $t \in T$ then for all $w_1.w_2$ $MVA(\langle w_1.w_2 \rangle.t) = M1(t)$. If $f \in TF$ and $trm = f(trm_1, \ldots .trm_n)$ is a temporal term, then $MVA(\langle w_1.w_2 \rangle.trm) = M3(f)$ $(MVA(\langle w_1.w_2 \rangle.trm_1), \ldots, MVA(\langle w_1.w_2 \rangle.trm_n))$.

If $v \in V$, then for all $w_1.w_2$, $MVA(\langle w_1.w_2 \rangle.u) = VAU(u)$. If $t \in T$ then for all $w_1.w_2$ $MVA(\langle w_1.w_2 \rangle.t) = M1(t)$. Finally, If $f \in F$ and $trm = f(trm_1, \ldots .trm_n)$ is a nontemporal term, then $MVA(\langle w_1.w_2 \rangle.trm) = M4(\langle w_1.w_2 \rangle.f)$ $(MVA(\langle w_1.w_2 \rangle.trm_1), \ldots, MVA(\langle w_1.w_2 \rangle.trm_n))$.

The interpretation S and the variable assignment VA satisfy a wff φ (written $S \models \varphi[VA]$) under the following inductively defined conditions.

- $S \models trm_1 = trm_2 [VA]$ iff $MVA(trm_1) = MVA(trm_2)$,

- $S \models trm_1 \preceq trm_2 [VA]$ iff $MVA(trm_1) \leq MVA(trm_2)$,

- For any atomic wff $\varphi = TRUE(trm_i.trm_j.r(trm_1, \ldots .trm_n))$,
  $S \models \varphi[VA]$ iff $\langle MVA(\langle MVA(trm_i).MVA(trm_j) \rangle.trm_1), \ldots, MVA(\langle MVA(trm_i).MVA(trm_j) \rangle.trm_n) \rangle \in M5(\langle MVA(trm_i).MVA(trm_j) \rangle.r)$.

- $S \models x \wedge y[VA]$ iff $S \models x[VA]$ and $S \models y[VA]$.

- $S \models (\neg x)[VA]$ iff $S \not\models x[VA]$

- $S = \models \forall z\, x[VA]$ iff
  $S \models x[VA']$ for all VA' that agree with VA everywhere except possibly on z.

We will say that an interpretation S satisfies a wff φ (written $S \models \varphi$) just in case $S \models \varphi[VA]$ for some variable assignment VA. Clearly, a sentence (i.e., a closed wff) is satisfiable under some variable assignment iff it is satisfiable under *any* variable assignment.

If an interpretation satisfies a formula then it is called a *model* of the formula. A formula is *satisfiable* if it has a model. A formula is *valid* if its negation is not satisfiable.

3.3 Categorizing propositions

We now have a logic with precise syntax and semantics, but it might leave one feeling disappointed. When all is said and done, all we are left with are *propositions*, rather bland objects that enjoy none of the glamour of events, properties or processes. (Of course, even in Allen's and McDermott's systems these notions had very specific intended meanings, much narrower than in ordinary English usage.) In this subsection I'll try to recapture that lost sparkle. I will provide the means for making the distinctions between event-like propositions, property-like propositions, etcetera. In fact I will give a categorization of propositions that is richer than either Allen's or McDermott's.

Let us call the φ part of a proposition $TRUE(t_1.t_2.\varphi)$ a *proposition type*.

Definition 1: downward-hereditary types
A proposition type φ is *upward-hereditary* iff whenever it holds in some interval it holds in all subintervals, or in other words if the following holds: $\forall\ t_1 \leq t_3 \leq t_4 \leq t_2\ TRUE(t_1.t_2.\varphi) \supset TRUE(t_3.t_4.\varphi)$

Definition 2: upward-hereditary types
A proposition type φ is *upward-hereditary* iff whenever it does not hold for an interval then it does not hold for some proper subinterval.

Definition 3: liquid types
A proposition type φ is *liquid* if it is both upward-hereditary and downward-hereditary.

Definition 4: concatenable types
A proposition type φ is *concatenable* if whenever it holds in two consecutive intervals it holds in the interval that is the union of the two.

Definition 5: clay-like types
A proposition type φ is *clay-like* if it is both downward-hereditary and concatenable.

Definition 6: solid types
A proposition type φ is *solid* if whenever it holds in some interval it does not hold in any overlapping interval.

One can devise further categories of propositions, but I'll stop here. Let me point out that Allen's properties are exactly the liquid propositions, and his events are exactly the solid propositions. In fact, at this point the utility of the finer-grained categorization can be demonstrated. Consider Allen's definition of negation: $NOT(p)$ holds over an interval if p does not hold for any subinterval.[3] For Allen NOT can be applied only to properties, of course, and not (for example) to events. He then asks what is the meaning of the operator $NOT(NOT(\ldots))$, and shows that NOTs cancel out. In the new logic we are in a position to perform a broader analysis, by subjecting arbitrary proposition types to strong negation (using Allen's exact same definition.) Doing that, we can prove the following much stronger theorems.

Theorem 1.
If φ is downward-hereditary then $TRUE(t_1.t_2.\varphi) \supset TRUE(t_1.t_2.NOT(NOT(\varphi)))$.

Theorem 2.
If φ is upward-hereditary then $TRUE(t_1.t_2.NOT(NOT(\varphi))) \supset TRUE(t_1.t_2.\varphi)$.

Corollary 3.
If φ is liquid then $TRUE(t_1.t_2.\varphi) \equiv TRUE(t_1.t_2.NOT(NOT(\varphi)))$.

---

[3]This is what philosophers call *strong negation* [3]. I think this is the wrong notion to adopt, since it can easily be defined in terms of weak negation, but use it here in order to demonstrate how my categorization sheds light on otherwise somewhat mysterious theorems.

4   Conclusions

In the introduction I listed three options that are available for representing temporal information in a logic. This paper explored the one that is most commonly used in AI, which reifies the propositions in order to mention time explicitly without losing its special notational and conceptual status. Examining two of the more influential formalisms, those of Allen and McDermott, I identified problems in assigning meaning to sentences in the logic. I also showed that it is desirable to include time points in the ontology, and that there is no need to make premature distinctions such as the one between events and properties.

I proposed a new reified temporal logic, which borrows heavily from the intuitions and formulations of Allen and McDermott. It is an improvement on those for two main reasons. First, it has precise syntax and semantics. Second, it allows finer distinctions than the simple property/event/process trichotomy or the fact/event dichotomy, and at the same time does not force any.

A word about the computational properties of the logic. Since the logic is really the encoding of Kripke semantics of modal logic, it inherits the properties of the corresponding modal logic. In [2] we show that these depend critically on the underlying model of time; depending on whether time is unbounded, infinite and complete, deciding validity can be recursive, r.e.-hard, co-r.e.-hard or Π_1^1-hard. In the last two cases this means that there is no finite axiomatization of the logic.

In conclusion let me make clear some of the problems that I have *not* addressed. First, I have taken it for granted that we need to represent the temporal information in logical form, and that our logic must have formal semantics. I actually believe that these are correct claims, but realize that neither is unanimously accepted in AI. Since I clearly will not settle the issue of the role of logic in AI in these notes, I'll save my ammunition for the future. Second, I must emphasize the obvious fact that both Allen and McDermott have much broader goals than I had in formulating the new logic. In this paper I really just cleaned up the basis for their formulations, making no contribution to our understanding of causation, counterfactual conditions, intention, planning or acting. In fact I've made it clear that Allen's and McDermott's formulations concerning these notions do not fit in with the logic, and for the most part require much more sophisticated machinery. I believe, however, that having firm foundations in the form of a well-defined temporal ontology is a prerequisite for tackling those hard issues.

Acknowledgements. I have benefitted from discussions with and comments by Drew McDermott, James Allen, Brad Alpert, Joe Halpern and Pat Hayes.

Bibliography

[1] J. F. Allen, *Towards a General Theory of Action and Time*, Artificial Intelligence, 23/2 July (1984), pp. 123–154.

[2] J.Y. Halpern and Y. Shoham, A Propositional Modal Logic of Time Intervals, *Proc. Symp. on Logic in Computer Science*, IEEE, Boston, MA, June 1986.

[3] I. L. Humberstone, *Interval Semantics for Tense Logics: Some Remarks*, Journal of Philosophical Logic, 8 (1979), pp. 171–196.

[4] D. V. McDermott, *A Temporal Logic for Reasoning about Processes and Plans*, Cognitive Science, 6 (1982), pp. 101–155.

[5] B. C. Moszkowski, *Executing Temporal Logic Programs*, Technical Report 71, University of Cambridge, Computer Laboratory, August 1985.

[6] Y. Shoham, *Ten Requirements for a Theory of Change*, New Generation Computing, 3/4 (1985).

Advances in Artificial Intelligence - II
B. Du Boulay, D. Hogg and L. Steels (Editors)
© Elsevier Science Publishers B.V. (North-Holland), 1987

REFERENCE WITHOUT CAUSAL LINKS

Aaron Sloman
Cognitive Studies Programme
University of Sussex
Brighton BN1 9QN England

Abstract

This enlarges on earlier work attempting to show in a general way how it might be possible for a machine to use symbols with 'non-derivative' semantics. It elaborates on the author's earlier suggestion that computers understand symbols referring to their own internal 'virtual' worlds. A machine that grasps predicate calculus notation can use a set of axioms to give a partial, implicitly defined, semantics to non-logical symbols. Links to other symbols defined by direct causal connections within the machine reduce ambiguity. Axiom systems for which the machine's internal states do not form a model give a basis for reference to an external world without using external sensors and motors.

Keywords

Understanding, semantics, symbols, reference, reality, logic, inference rules, models, meaning postulates.

Introduction

Before knowledge there must be understanding. In order to know or wrongly believe that something is or is not the case you must understand some representation of the possibility. How? What conditions would enable a machine to understand symbols that it manipulated? Unlike most philosophers who discuss meaning and understanding (e.g. Putnam 1975) I am not concerned with the use of an *external* language for communication. The question is - how can a machine understand a language used internally for planning, reasoning, remembering, etc. This question has had little attention from AI theorists, probably because most regard it as obvious that machines understand programming languages, or at least machine codes. (But see Woods 1981, Cohen forthcoming.) Clearly computers can already manipulate symbols that *people* understand, but not everyone agrees that computers themselves could ever understand symbols, or have any other mental states or processes. There are three main attitudes. Behaviourists take our question to be: could a machine produce behaviour indicative of understanding (e.g. passing the 'Turing test')? Dualists ask: can apparently non-physical but introspectable mental processes like ours exist in machines? A third option is to ask: what sorts of internal mechanisms could enable a machine, or person, to understand?

The behaviourist often relies on the old argument that we can never know anything about the contents, or existence, of other people's minds except on the basis of their observable behaviour. We assume that our parents, children, friends and enemies all have minds and mental states, though we have nothing but their behaviour to go on, albeit very subtle kinds of behaviour. Tests that are adequate for people should be adequate for machines, never mind what processes produce the behaviour. This answer is implicit in much AI work.

Neither behaviourists nor dualists are concerned about explanatory power. Yet 'understands' is an explanatory concept. Neither behaviour nor a peculiar unanalysable kind of entity like a soul can in itself explain success in thought, action and communication, whereas understanding does. Moreover, the primary use of symbols is NOT to communicate with others but to provide a usable store of information, instructions, plans, to allow inferences to be made, and to formulate questions, problems, and goals: in short *representation is prior to communication*. This understanding of internal symbols cannot be tested directly by external behaviour. (Does behaviour show whether dogs use symbols, or what sort?) Understanding processes may not even be internally accessible. The introspectible and the mental are not co-extensive.

Explanatory insight requires the third approach, adopting what Dennett (1978) calls the 'design stance', exploring mechanisms that might support meaningful uses of symbols. I'll start with a logic-based machine, then generalise.

Recapituation
In Sloman (1985c) I discussed general conditions for using symbols to refer, listing an (incomplete) collection of 'prototypical' conditions satisfied by human uses of symbols, and showing that many of the conditions are satisfied even by computers without AI programs.

Unprogrammed computers can interpret symbols in the machine language because of built-in causal links between on the one hand bit patterns and on the other hand memory locations or their contents, properties and relations or operations on the memory. Some symbols influence the selection of memory location, others influence the action to be performed there. Conversely, when a machine interrogates its memory, states of the memory can cause appropriate new symbols to be constructed and stored. So, the mapping from symbols to locations, properties and relations is significant for and can be used by the machine itself because of two-way causal links. (The word 'use' does not imply purpose or consciousness: plants use oxygen and supports.)

Built-in causal connections explain how machines can interpret symbols as instructions or questions about internal states and processes. Assertion and external reference, usually require additional programming. (See Sloman 1985c. Cohen [forthcoming] makes similar points.) Let's examine internal reference more closely, and then return to external reference.

All reference is to virtual worlds
Causal mechanisms give machine codes for addresses and instructions a semantics that attributes a formal structure to the designated world. This world is usually taken to be a linear configuration of bit-patterns. Yet it is not physically linear, and the bit-patterns are abstractions relevant to the way the machine works, rather than objective physical entities.

Implementations of equality of bit-patterns can vary enormously, and usually do not require physical identity: measurements may be thresholded so that different patterns of voltages are treated as identical bit-patterns. Other differences in the fine structure of physical components may be ignored completely. New technologies can use new physical representations for a string of bits. They may even differ from one part of a computer to another: bits in a fast memory cache may be very different from both bits other parts of the memory. A portion of the memory may be replaced with a component using a new, but functionally equivalent device. The class of potentially usable physical mechanisms is quite open-ended.

So two implementations of logically the same structure may differ radically in how symbolic patterns are represented and how they are translated into physical processes representing the same action, such as comparing the contents of two memory locations. The internal world of a computer is therefore an abstraction. Symbols referring to memory locations, their contents or actions thereon, refer to 'virtual' entities, relations and processes, that may be implemented in the physical world in different ways. The common use of the phrase 'virtual memory' is a partial acknowledgement of this.

The referents of symbols in a machine language therefore do not form 'natural kinds' from the point of view of a physicist, for there is no simple correspondence between the truth of any assertion about the computer's memory, and the state of the world as viewed by a physicist. I am not denying that the machine uses symbols to refer to physical objects. Rather, the reference is indirect and 'wholistic', in the sense that individual symbols make sense because the whole system can be attached to the world. (This is explained further below. See also Quine 1953.)

Related arguments show that people do not refer directly to objectively individuated physical entities or their intrinsic properties, relations, states, etc., but rather to a reality conceived of in terms of a system of concepts we find useful. This must be true of concepts used by any thinker or perceiver, even a physicist during office hours. The environment, as conceived of by a symbol user, is inevitably a 'virtual' world with properties defined by the system of concepts used. Usually these will have been selected because of their relevance to the needs or functions of the user (or a class of users). Other people, other animals, or other machines may conceive of the same reality in a totally or partially different way. We all inhabit, think about, and act in virtual worlds, in this sense. So would a robot.

Virtual worlds are not mere abstractions: they are *implemented* or *embodied* in one physical world, much as a particular design of computer can be implemented in actual hardware, whose failings may show up in bizarre behaviour of the virtual machine. In philosophical jargon, one world can be 'supervenient' on another, as temperature is supervenient on motion. Two supervenient worlds may share a substrate. So the fact that two organisms inhabit different virtual worlds doesn't mean they live in totally unrelated realities, as relativists claim. An event in the common underlying world may affect them both, albeit differently. Living in a different virtual world doesn't help a mouse escape being eaten by an owl or one culture being destroyed by another. However, it would be incoherent to try to describe the common underlying reality in neutral terms.

Theory-based reference
An ordinary computer's ability to refer to its simple internal virtual world is severely restricted. For example, it can check the contents of a location at a certain time, but cannot answer a question about what the contents were at some past time. It can't obey instructions like:
> If you've changed the value of X more than three times then perform action A.

Some information about the past could be stored, but no machine could keep complete and explicit historical records of its internal states and events unless the memory was constantly growing to include the new information -- an explosive requirement. A practical system would keep only partial records. A theory about its constraints could then allow inferences about unrecorded facts.

The need to use a theory is even more obvious if the machine has to answer questions about the future. Like a software designer, it could answer questions about the future contents of its memory if it examined its programs to infer their effects, or non-effects. If no instructions refer to a certain location and that location is not connected to external transducers, the machine could infer that the location will not be changed. Of course, inferences about a virtual machine can founder if the underlying reality misbehaves.

The important point is that the ability to use symbols to refer to past and future states of a world capable of change, even a 'totally accessible' world like that of the machine's own memory, requires the use of an explicit or implicit theory about the constraints governing the world and the sorts of changes that can occur in it. The same applies to reference to the present, in a partly inaccessible world. Put another way: no interesting world can be totally accessible: theory-based inference will always be required for reference to some portions of the world. In this sense knowledge (or at least belief) is prior to some forms of understanding. So the dependence between knowledge and understanding is mutually recursive.

The theory used may be explicit in a representation manipulated by the machine, or implicit — 'compiled' into mechanisms, as in most vision systems. The best understood technique is to use a logical language to express the theory and logical principles for making inferences. Before examining more general capabilities, let's examine what is involved in giving a machine a grasp of logic (extending my 1985c).

Giving a machine a grasp of logic

Computers easily manipulate boolean values and use logical symbols analogous to 'and', 'or', 'not' with semantics defined by truth-tables. Circuits can be built with such operations wired in. This is a primitive inference-making capability. If truth-values for p and for q are checked directly, then the machine can infer the truth-value for p & q. Similarly for 'or' and 'not'. Computers can also be programmed to store and derive consequences from collections of axioms expressed in predicate calculus. But can a machine really understand first-order logic's unrestricted quantification? What does it mean to talk about all the real numbers, all the possible people that might exist, all the legal programs in a certain language.

Quantifiers 'For all x', and 'For some x', (first analysed by Frege) are not definable by truth-tables, though when predicates with finite extensions are used, it is possible to use truth-tables. If the extension of P is a finite set (e.g. a set of locations in the computer's memory), then

(1)   'Ax(Px -> Qx)'   ('For all x, if Px then Qx'),

can be shown to be true or false by treating it as the conjunction of all instantiations of 'Qx' with members of the set. So if a and b are the only elements of P's extension, then (1) is equivalent to 'Qa & Qb', and a truth-table can be used to evaluate it. Similarly, if P has a finite extension, then

(2)   'Ex(Px & Qx)'   ('For some x, x is P and Q)

can be treated as a disjunction of instantiations of Q.

Despite the factual equivalence, there is no definitional equivalence, since quantifiers would be needed to assert that there are no other individuals to consider in addition to those listed in the conjunction or disjunction. The inference rules for universal and existential quantifiers are not restricted to finite sets. Some of the inferences are unproblematic, even for infinite sets, for example:

Universal Instantiation (UI):
    AxFx   =>   Fa

Existential Generalisation (EG):
    Fa   =>   ExFx

More problematic are the reverse inferences: universal generalisation (UG) and existential instantiation (EI), especially if the domain is infinite. In fact, it is not at all clear in what sense people understand unrestricted quantifiers (as shown in part by the existence of non-standard models for any consistent set of axioms for arithmetic).

For dealing with finite sets, we can avoid problematic quantifiers by introducing a form of assertion that certain individuals a1, a2, .. ak comprise the total extension of a predicate P, e.g.

    Extension(P,a1,a2,a3,..ak)

If we allow sets, then this could be expressed as a binary relation:

(3)   Extension(P, {a1,a2,a3,..ak})

Using the Extension predicate it is possible easily to express a fact of the form 'a, b and c are the only M's present', making it unnecessary to use non-monotonic reasoning to infer that there are no other instances of M. Extension facts could be expressed in ordinary first order logic, but the notation would be very clumsy, including a component something like:

    Ax {Mx -> (x = a V x = b V x = c)}

('everything that is M is identical with a or with b or with c'). The search space for proofs involving expressions like this is very awkward. For assertions about relations, the use of ordinary logic is even more clumsy, whereas a slight generalisation of our notation copes with the extensions of n-ary relations, e.g.

(4)   Extension(Loves, {{John,Mary},{Fred,Mary},{Mary,Tom}})

Lambda-notation could be used to represent complex predicates occurring as the first argument, but in some contexts a notation using a new form of quantifier might be more convenient, e.g. expressing (3) and (4) as

(3')   AOx{a1,a2,a3,..ak}P(x)
and
(4')   AOxy{{John,Mary},{Fred,Mary},{Mary,Tom}}Loves(x,y)

Where 'AO' can be read as 'All and only', and the quantified variables range over the specified set.

Mechanisable procedures could directly check the truth of such 'Extension' assertions in the machine's accessible world. Perceptual mechanisms, for example, need the ability to check bounded quantified assertions: X is a square only if the extension of the predicate 'side of X' has exactly four members. Such inferences may be disguised by being compiled into special-purpose modules, such as structure matchers. By making them explicit we may explore their power and limitations. For instance, checking an Extension assertion may require knowledge analogous to 'naive physics' (Hayes 1969, 1985) for interpreting perceptual evidence. When I look into a small box I can easily discern the extension of 'apple in this box', but not necessarily 'flea in this box'; whereas visual data doesn't suffice to determine the extension of 'apple in this room' unless the room contains no objects large enough to hide an apple. Learning such meta facts may be an important form of child development. (These notions need further exploration and elaboration.) Quantifiers ranging beyond known individuals would still be required for a world where extensions of sets are not known, even if they are knowable. For example, this would be needed in questions, like 'Extension(P,{a,b,x..})' ('is there an x other than a and b which is P').

New inference rules like the following would allow Extension facts to play a role in reasoning with quantifiers:

Given:
    Extension(P,{a1,a2}) & Qa1 and Qa2
infer:
    Ax(Px -> Qx)

Given:
    Extension(P,{a1,a2}) & Ex(Px & Qx)
infer:
    Qa1 V Qa2

The use of 'Extension' or the 'AO' quantifier would not add expressive power to ordinary logic, since every occurrence can be replaced by a translation including a very clumsy disjunction of equalities, as indicated above. Similarly, the above rules would not validate any new conclusions. However, they would permit in a single step useful inferences that would otherwise require several awkward steps and additional searching.

The main point is that there appears to be a useful subset of logic involving a concept of bounded quantification that could be clearly understood by a finite mechanism, since quantification over infinite sets would not be allowed. Even if the actual universe is infinite, the portion an intelligent agent will need to think about for most practical purposes will be finite. So, giving a machine the ability to handle formulas of this restricted predicate calculus may enable it to have an adequate understanding of logical operators, though not yet an understanding suitable for advanced mathematics. (A similar restriction may apply to many animals, young children and perhaps even most adults.)

Once quantifiers have been introduced in this way, it may be that the restriction to finite sets can be dropped, using a syntactic manoeuvre to extend semantic power. Unfortunately, the history of mathematical logic shows that there are deep problems of interpretation of logical symbols in infinite domains.

Anyhow, the claim is that by extending existing AI techniques we could enable a machine to employ a store of symbols using a logical notation to formulate instructions, questions or assertions concerning its 'accessible' world, and using inference rules that define the semantics of logical operators.

Implicitly defined non-logical symbols

Non-logical symbols can be interpreted as names or predicates via direct causal links, but this won't do for reference to an inaccessible reality. Machines will need to refer to external objects, events, locations, etc. How can they use symbols to describe objects, properties, and relationships to which they have no direct access? Direct causal links via sensors and motors are often practically impossible, and may even be logically impossible, for instance when referring to hypothetical objects in hypothetical situations that never arise, as when I talk about the children my still-born elder sister might have had, or when a robot contemplates disasters it then manages to avoid. Though we cannot have causal links to events that never occur, or to non-existent individuals we can refer to them. How? The answer is implicit in our preceding discussion: using a logical formalism allows a set of 'axioms' implicitly to define semantics for non-logical symbols referring beyond what is immediately accessible. The ideas are familiar to philosophers studying theoretical concepts in science.

The basic idea is an old one: a collection of axioms for Euclidean geometry can partially and implicitly define predicates like 'line', 'point', or 'intersects', so that their possible interpretations are restricted. Tarski (1951) showed formally, in his recursive definition of what makes an assertion true, how some portion of reality can be or fail to be a model for a set of axioms (sentences in a logical formalism). Carnap (1956) suggested that, in a logical notation new symbols can be defined implicitly by 'meaning postulates'. This was used to account for theoretical concepts of physics and dispositional concepts like 'brittle'. Our machine could do something similar.

A model for an axiom set is not, as sometimes suggested, another symbolic structure denoting the world. Models cam be portions of the real world. (Hayes 1985 explains this very clearly.) More precisely, they are virtual systems *implemented* in the physical world just as a computer's memory was shown above to be a virtual system implemented in the world. Put another way, a model may be seen as a bit of the world 'carved up' in a certain way, just as people using the concepts 'finger', 'thumb', 'knuckle' and 'palm' conceptually carve up human hands in one way, whereas an anatomist, or a dog licking its master's hand, might use a different ontology.

Axioms alone do not pin down meanings unambiguously, since there are always different possible models. Any model for axioms of projective geometry has a dual in which points and lines are interchanged, for example. Axioms merely define the non-logical symbols to refer to aspects of the structure common to all the acceptable models. So meanings defined purely axiomatically have structure without content. They cannot be used to talk about specific properties of our world, or particular individuals, but only about possible types of worlds or world-fragments, though their features might happen to exist in our world. Adding new axioms can narrow the range of possible models, but will never pin the interpretation down to any actual portion of reality.

If, however, some of the symbols already have meanings determined independently of the axioms, then this will restrict the set of possible models, and thereby the possible interpretations of the new symbols. It may even attach the new symbols to a particular bit of the world. (See Nagel 1961, Pap 1963 on theoretical terms in science).

Semantic links between binary codes and objects or events in the machine's memory are based on causation not axioms. This semantic attachment to the actual world can be inherited by axiomatically defined terms, if the axioms link new and old terms. A theory that links unobservables, like 'neutrino', to observables, like 'flash' may limit possible models of the theory to things in this world. A blind person may attach meanings to colour words not too different from those of a sighted person, because much of the meaning resides in rich interconnections with concepts shared by both, such as 'surface', 'edge', 'pattern', 'stripe', etc. Likewise, a machine with logical powers could interpret symbols as formulating assertions or questions about things beyond its immediately accessible world, as follows.

Using logic to think about inaccessible objects
In addition to symbols referring to its memory locations and their contents and relationships, a machine could use a logical formalism to express axioms for predicates analogous to 'before', 'after', 'inside', 'outside', 'further', and and perhaps even 'cause'. (How this comes about does not matter for now: it could arise from random processes, external input or some kind of creative learning. I am trying only to explain how the machine could interpret such symbols.) The predicates could then be combined with names of locations to make assertions about the contents of or events in the machine's memory, which would form a Tarskian model for the database of axioms. The model could be a unique minimal model because some of the symbols had causal links with this portion of the world. Adding assertions using existential quantifiers would allow the formation of a new database for which the accessible world would not be a complete model. For example, an assertion might state that there exists a location 'beyond' the last known memory location. Such assertions would then be about inaccessible entities.

More formally, consider an existentially quantified assertion of the form:
   (5) Ex(Rxa)

('There is an x such that x stands in the relation R to a', where a is a known object). If (5) is consistent with the rest of the database, but the machine can establish that no *known* object stands in the relation R to a, then it must express a hypothesis, or question, about some hitherto unknown entity. There could be a sub-set of the larger world containing the machine, that forms a Tarskian model for the extended database including (5).

Thus the machine uses symbols to formulate a proposition about something beyond its known world, without relying on any external causal links. It requires only some relations (e.g. spatial and temporal relations) linking internal entities to which it can already refer (using causal links) with external objects and events. 'Causes' is merely one of several internal/external relations able to support external reference.

The machine might have symbols for several such relationships defined partly axiomatically and partly by mechanisms for creating or checking internal instances of the relations. These symbols could be used to formulate collections of assertions for which the accessible world was not large enough to provide a model. The relations need not, but might, include a notion something like our concept 'cause', implicitly defined by a set of axioms, including axioms for the practical uses of causal relations. How exactly 'cause' should be defined is an old and unsolved problem. (A sophisticated machine might use the meta-level notion of a type of relationship whose detailed definition is not yet completely known, and build descriptions of relationships — of unknown types — between accessible objects and others — also of unknown types. Cf Woods 1981)

Notice that I am only talking about the machine using symbols with a certain semantics. I am not discussing conditions for *successful* reference. I.e. the machine may use symbols that purport to refer, but don't actually, just as a deluded person can use a phrase like 'the burglar upstairs' even though it actually refers to nothing. The conditions for meaning, or understanding, are weaker than the conditions for knowledge (though more fundamental). Nothing is implied about the machine being *aware* of using symbols with a meaning. It seems that very young children and many animals use internal symbols without being aware of the fact. They lack the required self-monitoring.

The machine might think of its own internal states as embedded in a larger structure with a web of named relationships, and speculate about the properties of that structure, which it could refer to as: 'this world'. (It could do this even though some of its speculations were false, and not all important relationships are already known about.) External objects would then be referred to in terms of their supposed relationships to known internal objects. (This is an old idea in philosophy. cf. Strawson, 1959, ch.3). Such reference need not depend on sensors or motors providing causal links with the remote particulars. However, I am not, like philosophical phenomenalists, proposing that external objects be *defined* in terms of concepts relating to the internal world. This is not a reductionist theory.

It is sometimes argued that the semantics of empirical predicates must always be partly probabilistic, since often only probabilistic assertions are justified by available evidence. For instance, when only part of the extension of a predicate is accessible, statistical rules can be used to order, and perhaps assign probabilities to hypotheses compatible with available evidence. These rules, however, are simply heuristics for dealing with incomplete information and do not affect the semantics of the language used.

The indeterminacy of model-based semantics
The kind of semantics described here will always be indeterminate in that alternative models can exist. Like other relations, causal linkage via sensors, motors, or computer terminals used for purely verbal communication, can reduce, but never totally eliminate, semantic indeterminacy. It can narrow down reference to particulars, such as a particular place, or object or other agent, but such reference is never totally unambiguous in the way philosophers often dream of. There's always the possibility that some hidden complexity in the world prevents uniqueness of reference — as when mischievous identical twins fool a teacher into thinking he knows who he is dealing with when he doesn't. Human and machine uses of symbols must be subject to exactly the same indeterminacy. Anyone designing machines to interact with people will need to take account of this fact.

New axioms can extend the ontology
This indeterminacy is an important aspect of the growth of knowledge, since it is always possible (except in very simple cases) to add new independent axioms that constrain the possible models and add precision to the implicitly defined terms. It is also generally possible to add axioms postulating both additional entities and new relations between those entities and the previous ones, just as science advances partly by postulating new sorts of entities: like atoms, neutrinos, genes, gravitational forces, and new relationships between them and familiar objects. This

often adds coherence to disparate observations.

A similar process might occur in our machine — and perhaps in a child. Some parts of the memory (e.g. a retina connected to external transducers) might be changed by external events. A machine that cannot think about an external world will be forced to treat these events simply as inexplicable occurrences. If the 'axioms' are (somehow) extended to refer to a suitably structured external environment including a process whereby structures are 'projected' into its memory (usually with considerable loss of information) it may be able to make sense of the phenomena, e.g. explaining 2-D retinal changes as resulting from different views of the same external 3-D scene.

The machine may also discover that certain changes that it can produce in parts of its memory (connected perhaps to motors) are followed by changes in its sensory registers. The relationship between the two sorts of changes may at first seem arbitrary and inexplicable, but by adding axioms describing suitable external structures and causal connections, the whole thing may be made to fit into a coherent framework. (A more complicated story is required if the system is to allow that its senses can sometimes malfunction and deceive it. Similarly scientific theories accommodate faulty instruments.)

A machine using an explicit set of axioms describing external (and internal) structures may be contrasted with one that merely uses perceptual and planning mechanisms that happen to be consistent with such a set of axioms (a 'compiled' version of the axioms, or a compiled theory about the world). This may be relevant to understanding differences between animal species. The latter system could not support some explicit learning processes, for example.

Loop-closing semantics for non-propositional symbols
So far the discussion has assumed that the machine uses a logical language to for..ulate axioms and record beliefs. Though little is known about the high level representations used by brains, it seems unlikely that birds, baboons or babies use explicit Carnapian meaning postulates or logic with Tarskian semantics to enable them to perceive and act on things in the world. Yet many animals appear to have rich mental lives including awareness of external objects. Might something other than logical and propositional representations explain this?

Perhaps a generalisation of Tarskian semantics is applicable to a wider range of intelligent systems. Not all internal representations have to be propositional, any more than our external representations are. There are good reasons for using a variety of forms of representations, including analogical representations such as diagrams, maps, ordered lists, networks, etc. Visual systems use some representations related to image structures. Many of these non-logical symbolisms can be implemented in computers. They can be used for a variety of purposes, including representing goals, percepts, beliefs, instructions, plans, and so on. (See Sloman 1985a).

If we think of such representations as having a semantics partly defined by their use in perception, planning, acting, etc., then the notion of a model might be defined as 'an environment which can coherently close the feedback loops'. Roughly, this requires the environment to be rich enough for external objects and events, to project (via perceptual mechanisms and action mechanisms) into internal representations of beliefs, goals and behaviour. The projection need not preserve structure (as neither geometric image-forming projections, nor Tarskian mappings do), but must support some notion of valid inference. That is, certain transformations of correct representations must be useful for making predictions, or drawing inferences about the environment. An environment that allows successful predictions to be made and goals to be achieved, and checked using perception, provides a model in this sense. This notion of semantics requires further investigation. Tarskian semantic theory takes a God-like perspective, contemplating mappings between symbols and things independently of how anything uses those mappings. This may not be possible in general, for instance, if semantic relations are highly context sensitive. We'd then need to adopt a design stance and think about the mechanisms.

The meaning attributed to a symbolic structure will be relative to the system's ability to have precise and detailed goals and beliefs. How specific the semantic mapping is will depend on how rich and varied is the range of percepts, goals and action strategies the system can cope with. An image representing a desired view of a scene may be constantly checked against current percepts as the machine moves. If the matching process requires very detailed correspondence between image and percept, the semantics will allow more different situations to be represented distinctly, than if matching is very tolerant. If different degrees of tolerance are required for different purposes, the semantics will be context sensitive.

Like Tarskian semantics, 'loop-closing' semantics leaves meanings indeterminate. For any level of specification at which a model can be found, there will be many consistent extensions to lower-levels of structure (in the way that modern physics extends the environment known to our ancestors). In both cases, as John McCarthy has pointed out in conversation, if the total system is rich enough, and works in enough practical situations, the chance that we've got it wildly wrong may be small enough to be negligible, except for sceptical philosophers.

Methodological note: do we need the design stance?

Why isn't it enough to describe a Turing test that a machine might pass? Because how behaviour is produced is important. Two systems producing the same behaviour over all the tests that can be dreamed up in a lifetime, might differ in how they would perform in some test not yet thought up. For example, there is a difference between a program with a generative ability to solve problems in arithmetic, and one that uses an enormous table of problems and solutions that happens to include answers to all the arithmetic questions that any human being will ever formulate. (Compare the distinction (Cohen [forthcoming]) between 'simulated understanding' and 'simulated parroting'.) Mere use of a look-up table would not constitute competence at arithmetic. Success in passing tests would be partly a matter of luck: the missing problems were never posed. Correct answers are produced simply because the entries happen to be in the table. Such a program can be described as successful but unreliable. It would not work in all the cases that could possibly arise. A table could not be checked except by examining every entry, whereas meta-level reasoning can be used to check a generative mechanism. So there are good engineering reasons for rejecting the Turing test as adequate.

A follower of Ryle (1949) might attempt to deal with all possible tests by postulating an infinite set of behavioural dispositions. We'd still need an explanation of the infinite capability in terms of a finite mechanism that can reliably generate the required behaviour. So the behaviourist analysis of mental states is unsatisfactory from an engineering point of view. From a naive philosophical point of view it is also unsatisfactory because it seems to leave something important out. Many people are convinced, on the basis of their own experience, that mental states like understanding have a kind of existence which is plain enough to those who have them, but which is quite unlike and independent of the existence of physical bodies or their behaviour. No amount of behaviour by a machine, however similar to human behaviour, could demonstrate the existence of this non-physical sort of state or entity. Dualists often admit that they lack conclusive evidence that other people have the same mental states as they do. But because of similarities of constitution and origin they are willing to give other people, or even other animals, the benefit of the doubt -- but not so computers.

Dualist objections to behaviourism assume that mental objects and events are non-physical entities directly perceivable only by introspection. So, unlike the postulated entities of theoretical physics, each person has direct and infallible access to a different subset. There is an element of mystery, since we have no explanation of how these entities can generate and control behaviour in physical systems. Nevertheless, it is a compelling view and is at least part of the motivation of many who object to the claim that computational mechanisms can explain the existence of mind. No amount or type of symbol manipulation could bring into existence new entities with the required properties.

There are reasons for the persistence of the dualist view. Like the theory that the sun and stars revolve around the earth, it is supported by common observations and also satisfies a powerful need to think of oneself as special. A theory thus motivated cannot be undermined simply by evidence and argument. Something analogous to therapy, or moral persuasion, is required, but there is no guarantee that the same techniques are relevant to everyone. Homo sapiens may not be unique in the space of possible intelligent machine-types, but each individual human being has a uniquely tangled web of reasons spawning motives and beliefs.

Since therapy cannot be conducted in a public essay, I have concentrated only on scientific and engineering considerations relevant to the design stance. A key issue is reliability: unless there is an underlying generative mechanism there is no reason to believe that intelligent behaviour will continue, no matter how many tests have already been passed. This is the key reason for rejecting the Turing test. Even common sense concepts, I believe, work on the assumption that explanatory mechanisms underly observed generalisations of all kinds, even when nobody knows what the mechanisms are, and even when there's a wide-spread confusion over what would be an adequate explanation.

Conclusion

This paper extends earlier suggestions about how it is possible in principle for a machine to use symbols *it* understands. Here I've concentrated on what I had previously called 'structural conditions' (Sloman 1985c). Analysis of 'functional conditions' for meaningful use of symbols would require a description of mechanisms for symbols representing the machine's own goals, desires, plans, preferences, policies, likes, dislikes, etc. (For an initial sketch see Sloman and Croucher 1981.) A surprising conclusion is that external causal connections are not needed to support reference to an external world, provided that there are internal causal links between symbols and the machine's innards. Of course, external links are needed for reducing indeterminacy and checking truth or falsity: a requirement for knowledge. But understanding meanings is a more fundamental ability, with fewer requirements.

Theoretical AI investigates what can (or might) occur, what should occur and what does occur. I have been concerned only to explore some possible designs for cognitive systems. What the best designs for practical purposes might be, and how biological systems actually work, remain open questions.

Acknowledgements
This work is supported by a Fellowship from the GEC Research Laboratories, and a grant from the Rennaisance Trust. I have profited from conversations with many colleagues, especially Bill Woods. Woods (1985) expresses, I believe, very similar views, using very different terminology.

BIBLIOGRAPHY
Carnap, R., *Meaning and Necessity* Phoenix Books 1956.

Cohen, L.J., 'Semantics and the computer metaphor' in R. Barcan Marcus, G.Dorn, P. Weingartner (eds) *Logic Methodology and Philosophy of Science VII*, Amsterdam: North-Holland, forthcoming. (Initially circulated in 1983)

Dennett, D.C., *Brainstorms*, Harvester Press 1978.

Evans, Gareth, *The Varieties of Reference*, Oxford University Press, 1982.

Fodor, J.A., *The Language of Thought* Harvester Press 1976.

Frege, G., *Translations from the philosophical writings*, ed. P. Geach and M. Black. Blackwell, 1960.

Hayes, P.J., 'The naive physics manifesto' in D. Michie (ed) *Expert Systems in the Microelectronic Age*, Edinburgh University Press, 1979.

Hayes, P.J. 'The secnd naive physics manifesto' in R.J.Brachman and H.J.Levesque (eds), *Readings in Knowledge Representation*, Morgan Kaufmann, 1985.

Hempel, C.G, 'The Empiricist Criterion of Meaning' in A.J. Ayer (Ed.) Logical Positivism, The Free Press, 1959. Originally in *Revue Int. de Philosophie,_Vol.4.* 1950.

Nagel, E. *The Structure of Science*, London, Routledge and Kegan Paul, 1961

Pap, A., *An Introduction to the Philosophy of Science* Eyre and Spottiswoode (Chapters 2-3). 1963.

Putnam, A., *Mind Language and Reality: Philosophical Papers Vol 2*, (chapters 11, 12, 13), Cambridge University Press, 1975.

Quine, W.V.O., 'Two Dogmas of Empiricism' in *From a Logical point of view* 1953.

Ryle, G. *The Concept of Mind*, Hutchinson, 1949.

Searle, J.R., 'Minds, Brains, and Programs', with commentaries by other authors and Searle's reply, in *The Behavioural and Brain Sciences* Vol 3 no 3, 417-457, 1980.

Searle, J.R., *Minds Brains and Science*, Reith Lectures, BBC publications, 1984

Sloman, A. and M. Croucher, 'Why robots will have emotions' in *Proc. IJCAI* Vancouver 1981.

Sloman, A., D. McDermott, W.A. Woods 'Panel Discussion: Under What conditions can a machine attribute meaning to symbols' *Proc 8th International Joint Conference on AI*, Karlsruhe, 1983.

Sloman, A., 'Why we need many knowledge representation formalisms', in *Research and Development in Expert Systems*, ed M. Bramer, Cambridge University Press, 1985. [1985a]

Sloman, A., 'Strong strong and weak strong AI', *AISB Quarterly*, 1985. [1985b]

Sloman, A., 'What enables a machine to understand', in *Proc 9th International Joint Conference on AI*, UCLA, 1985. [1985c]

Sloman, A., 'Did Searle attack strong strong or weak strong AI?', in A. Cohn and R. Thomas (eds) *Proceedings 1985 AISB Conference*, Warwick University, Forthcoming.

Strawson, P. F., *Individuals: An Essay in Descriptive Metaphysics*, Methuen. 1959.

Tarski, A., 'The concept of truth in formalized languages' in his *Logic Semantics Metamathematics*, New York, 1951.

Woods, W.A., 'Procedural semantics as a theory of meaning', in *Elements of discourse understanding* Ed. A. Joshi, B. Webber, I. Sag, Cambridge University Press, 1981.

Advances in Artificial Intelligence - II
B. Du Boulay, D. Hogg and L. Steels (Editors)
© Elsevier Science Publishers B.V. (North-Holland), 1987

CONCURRENT STRATEGY EXECUTION IN OMEGA

Giuseppe Attardi

DELPHI SpA
via della Vetraia 11
I-55049 Viareggio, Italy

Abstract. Omega is a description system for knowledge embedding which enables representation of knowledge in conceptual taxonomies. Reasoning on this knowledge can be carried out by a process called taxonomic reasoning, which is based on operations of traversing the lattice of descriptions. This process can be performed with a high degree of parallelism, by spreading the activities among the nodes of the lattice. Reasoning strategies expressed at the metalevel of Omega can be used to tailor deductions to specific applications. A message-passing approach is proposed to implement the deduction in Omega. An extension to Common LISP is suggested to provide the necessary message-passing primitives.

Introduction. Performing reasoning on a significant body of knowledge is a formidable task, which poses stringent requirements on the underlying knowledge representation system, both in terms of size of the knowledge base and in terms of performance. In the work on the Omega description system [Attardi 81] the following ideas are being explored:

- to use a description based knowledge representation system, where information is structured in conceptual taxonomies

- to base all reasoning on the traversal of such networks, using algorithms that can be executed with a high degree of parallelism.

An actor language is the natural choice for implementing a description system like Omega for several reasons. Omega descriptions, which represent collections of objects, are naturally implemented with actors. Concurrency in exploring the network of descriptions is suitably obtained by message passing between such descriptions. Ideally the greatest benefits of this approach could be obtained on an actor machine supporting efficient message passing primitives. In order to experiment with concurrent reasoning algorithms in a practical setting, I have defined an extension to the Common Lisp language to provide a minimum set of message passing primitives.

In the following sections, I introduce the description system Omega, then I sketch CLAVE, an extension to Common Lisp with message passing. I describe the form of taxonomic reasoning perfomed in Omega and how exsistence query are processed. Finally I illustrate how reasoning strategies can be programmed and executed in parallel.

The description language Omega. Omega is a logic system, which consists of a language, an axiom system and a set of inference rules. A brief introduction to Omega appears in these proceedings [Attardi 86]. I just recall here that the basic construct in Omega is the description, which is used to represent a collection of individuals. Descriptions can be related by inheritance with the relation **is**, which is transitive, so that one can conclude:

Socrates **is** (a Mortal)

from

Socrates **is** (a Man)   and   (a Man) **is** (a Mortal)

Descriptions form a boolean lattice, induced by the partial ordering relation **is**. The bottom of the lattice is the description **Nothing**, a special constant which plays the role of the null entity. The top of the lattice is the description **Something**, another special constant which represents the most generic, universal description.

CLAVE.   CLAVE (Common Lisp Actor Virtual Extension) is an extension to Common Lisp which provides facilities for concurrency in object-oriented programming. The design of CLAVE was inspired by COMMONLOOPS [Bobrow 85]. CLAVE provides a way to define polymorphic functions over object types.

According to the actor theory, actors have acquaintances and a behavior. The acquaintances are other actors that are known to the actor. The behavior determines which actions the actor performs when it receives a message. Actors are implemented as standard Lisp objects to which a behavior can be attached using the primitive *defmethod*.

Communication Primitives. In an actor language, basic communication is asynchronous and buffered. The following primitive is provided to perform an asynchronous send:

(**asend** *target message* [:cont *continuation*] [:sponsor *sponsor*])

The message is transmitted to the actor target with an optional keyword argument which represents the continuation. The continuation is the actor to which the reply for the request should be sent. The execution of an **asend** returns immediately after having enqueued the message for delivery by the mail system. *sponsor* is the sponsor assigned to manage the activity, i.e. all the events generated either directly or indirectly by this message, which are not explicitly assigned to a different sponsor.

Replies are themselves asynchronous communications which are issued by means of the following primitive:

(reply *target value*)

Actor Definition.   The *structure* of an actor is defined using the standard *defstruct* primitive of Common LISP. An *:actor* option is used to indicate the definition of an actor.

(defstruct (*name* :actor)
      (*attr-1* ...)
      ...
      (*attr-n* ...))

An actor of the kind defined with *defstruct* can be created with the function *make* applied to the name used in the definition. Such actor will have attributes as those described in the definition.

In order to determine which is the most specific method to apply, in CLAVE one must be able to determine a precedence between types. This precedence is defined by extending the standard subtype hierarchy of Common LISP, in a similar way to Common LOOPS.

Among actors, inheritance relations can be established by means of the *:include* option of *defstruct* like in this example from [Bobrow 85]:

```
(defstruct (3d-point (:include 2d-point)) (z 0))
```

The *behavior* of an actor is specified by means of *defmethod*:

```
(defmethod operation
        ((var-1 type-1 [&LOCK])
        ...
        (var-n type-n [&LOCK])
        [&CONT continuation])
    body
    )
```

The type specifiers *type-i* indicate the type of the corresponding argument of the operation. If no type is indicated, the definition applies as a default when no other definition is applicable. It is possible to associate a method to an individual object, by using as the type specifier the quoted value of such individual.

An actor might want to *delegate* further processing of a message to another actor, using the primitive:

```
(delegate-to actor)
```

A frequent case of delegation is when the actor wants to delegate the handling of a message to a more generic method. Such method is also determined on the basis of the ordering among argument types, and it can be invoked with:

```
(delegate-to-superior)
```

Examples. The following example is taken from [Hewitt 79]. A checking account is implemented as an actor that can accept messages for operations like withdrawal and deposit. The checking account actor protects the data: in this case a single value representing the current balance on the account. The actor enforces orderly access and modification to such data.

```
(defstruct (ACCOUNT :actor)
    (BALANCE 0))                    ; the initial balance is 0

(defmethod CURRENT-BALANCE ((the-account ACCOUNT))
    (BALANCE the-account))          ; access and return current balance

(defmethod WITHDRAW ((the-account ACCOUNT &LOCK) amount)
    (if (> amount (BALANCE the-account))
        "Overdraft"
        (setf (BALANCE the-account)
             (— (BALANCE the-account) amount))))
```

Notice that only the withdraw method locks the account. Thereby it is possible that several requests for balance proceed concurrently with a single withdrawal operation.

If we wish to use continuations explicitly, the code becomes:
```
(defmethod CURRENT-BALANCE ((the-account ACCOUNT) &CONT customer)

  (reply (BALANCE the-account) customer))

(defmethod WITHDRAW ((the-account ACCOUNT &LOCK) amount &CONT customer)

  (if (> amount (BALANCE the-account))
    (reply "Overdraft" customer)
    (reply (setf (BALANCE the-account) (— (BALANCE the-account) amount))
    customer)))
```

Sponsors. The sponsor mechanism is used to control activities that are started concurrently. Sponsors perform those tasks which in standard Lisp implementations are handled by processes.

When using processes, some confusion arises in the model of coordination between activities. Since processes are the only handle available to the programmer, facilities are usually provided for inter-process communication. However, in most cases the programmer has no interest in communicating with a process, but wants just to interact with the activity managed by the process, either by stimulating further activity or inhibiting the current one. In a purely functional language this means asking for a certain function to be called, in an actor system this means that a message is delivered to a certain actor.

As an example, consider a window-based interactive system which needs to get input from mouse. The standard solution is to have two processes: process W which manages the interactive system, and process M which manages the mouse. The mouse process overlooks the mouse, taking care of updating the cursor. When the mouse enters the window, the mouse process needs to inform W. In the process model, this is performed by an inelegant solution of forcing keyboard input to the process W.

The solution derives from the consideration that the activity spurred by the mouse-input should not be done within the mouse process, but is part of the interactive system and should be managed by W. The mouse process, after informing W, wants to resume immediately its job without having to provide resources for the processing of the request by the interactive system.

In the actor/sponsor model, we would have two actors: MA (the mouse actor) and WA (the window actor), and two sponsors: MS (the mouse sponsor) and WS (the window sponsor). MA runs under the control of MS. When the mouse moves over the window, then MA sends a message to WA with sponsor WS. WA will react to this message by performing some work under the control of WS, therefore without drawing any resource out of MS.

Notice that in this model we have separated the activator of an actor from the sponsor of its activity, while in the traditional model, the two parties coincide. An actor can perform one task on behalf of a sponsor and another task on behalf of another sponsor. For instance a printer-spooler actor will act on behalf of the many different sponsors of the clients requiring printer service.

Concurrent Search. As an example of concurrency and the sponsor mechanism, I present a program to search a tree for a node that has a particular label.

```
(defstruct (tree (:class actor))
    (label mark sons))

(defmethod find ((node tree &LOCK) search-label &CONT customer)
    (unless (mark node)                      ; first time we visit this node
       (setf (mark node) t)                  ; mark this node
       (if (eq (label node) search-label)
          (reply node customer)              ; return the node
          (loop for son in sons
             do
             (asend son :find search-label :cont customer)))))
```

By calling:

```
(asend root :find the-label :cont the-customer)
```

we will obtain the first node that is discovered which has the indicated label.

A problem arises when no node exists with the specified label. Under such conditions, with the above solution the-customer would wait indefinitely, without ever receiving a reply. In order to avoid this, a special kind of sponsor is introduced, which monitors the activity in order to discover when the activity is completed. The implementation can accomplish this for instance by examining the internal message delivery queue of the sponsor. When such a queue becomes empty, there is nothing else to be done within the activity managed by the sponsor.

We will activate the search by the following request:

```
(asend root :find the-label :cont the-customer
    :sponsor (create-sponsor :final-reply 'no-more-answers :cont the-customer))
```

Notice that the same mechanism can be used when one wishes to determine all the nodes with a certain label. The continuation needs just to collect all the answers it will receive by the nodes, and stop when it will receive the message 'no-more-answers from the sponsor. Despite unpredictable delivery times in communications, the final message will be sent only after all previous messages to the continuation have been processed.

The primitive:

```
(create-sponsor [:parent sponsor] [:share percent] [:final-reply reply :cont continuation])
```

builds a new sponsor, which can draw up to *percent* (default: 100) of resources from the parent *sponsor* (default: the current sponsor). A reply with value *reply* will be sent to *continuation* when no more messages will remain to be processed within the activity managed by the sponsor. A sponsor created with the :final-reply option is allowed to manage only one communication, therefore any subsequent *asend* referring to that sponsor will result in an error.

Taxonomic Reasoning. Omega explores the idea of *taxonomic reasoning*, that is to base all reasoning on traversal of the lattice of descriptions. All knowledge in Omega is represented in a single lattice: from factual knowledge, to general rules, to dependencies and constraints. When a description needs to be accessed to answer a problem, all relevant and related facts and assertions can be found directly connected to it. The deduction is performed traversing the lattice, but it is controlled by user specified strategies which determine which part of the lattice to consider, and how to move around it. To tailor reasoning strategies to specific applications, strategies can be programmed in the metalanguage of Omega.

Metalevel strategies. The language for expressing strategies has been largely influenced by the ETHER language for parallel problem solving [Kornfeld 1982]. However, while ETHER uses a broadcast communication primitive for interaction among actors, in our language only direct communication between actors is involved.

The *Strategy Interpreter* of Omega builds and manipulates a goal structure according to the applicable strategies for each goal. A goal structure is a tree of alternating and-or nodes. "And" nodes are called attempts, and contain a list of goals, all of which are to be solved for the attempt to be successfull. "Or" nodes represent goals: a goal contains a list of attempts, each one corresponding to an alternative way to solve the goal. Only one attempt needs to succeed for the goal to be established.

For example :

```
        G0
         |
        A1
       /  \
      G1   G4
     /  \
    A2   A3
     |    |
    G2   G3
```

The initial goal G0 can be solved uniquely with attempt A1. A1 in turn, to be solved, requires that goals G1 and G4 be solved. G1 can be solved by attempts A2 and A3 ... and so on.

The strategy interpreter runs a loop like this:

```
for each outstanding attempt A do:
    for each unsolved goal G in A do:
        if G is true
            then execute (succeeds G)
```

else
for each backward strategy S applying to G do apply S
if no such strategy exists execute (fails G)

Each strategy, when applied to a goal, generates an attempt to establish the goal, and associates to the attempt the list of necessary subgoals. In practice, a strategy expands by two levels the and-or goal tree.

This interpreter leaves three hooks where the user can plug in its own code, namely at the places where a goal fails or succeeds, and where the strategy is invoked.

The language for strategies. I will illustrate the language for writing strategies with an example of a strategy that implements the following inference rule of the calculus of descriptions:

δ is $\delta1$, δ is $\delta2$

δ is ($\delta1$ **and** $\delta2$)

With the cap-notation ($\uparrow$) we can denote meta-level descriptions, so that

$\uparrow$(=d **is** (=d1 **and** =d2))

stands for

(a Predication (**with** subject =d) (**with** predicate (**an And** (**with** arg1 =d1) (**with** arg2 =d2))))

This provides Omega with the ability to express a strategy in the following way:

$\uparrow$(=d **is** (=d1 **and** =d2))
is
(a Predication (**with** backward-strategy
'(let ((attempt (new-attempt)))
(let ((goal-1 (goal $\uparrow$(=d **is** =d1) attempt))
(goal-2 (goal $\uparrow$(=d **is** =d2) attempt)))
(on-success goal-1
(on-success goal-2
(succeeds attempt)))
(on-failure goal-1
(fails attempt))
(on-failure goal-2
(fails attempt))))))

The strategy is asserted in Omega as a value for the attribute backward-strategy of the concept Predication. The subject of this statement is a metadescription of a statement.

Any statement of this form will appear lower in the lattice than this description, and therefore will inherit the strategy.

The strategy presented above states that in order to prove a statement of the form (=d **is** (=d1

and =d2)), a subgoal to prove (=d **is** =d1) is set up. When this succeeds, a second subgoal is generated to prove (=d **is** =d2). When also this goal is established, the whole attempt succeeds.

The primitives used in the example are the following:

(goal *statement attempt*)

sets up one subgoal of *attempt* whose objective is to prove *statement*.

(on-success *subgoal body*)

(on-failure *subgoal body*)

correspond to defining methods for the *subgoal* to handle respectively the cases of success or failure in attempting the subgoal. For instance, in the above example the strategy could have been defined as:

```
(let ((attempt (new-attempt)))
 (let ((goal-1 (goal ↑(=d is =d1) attempt)))
  (defmethod succeeds ((goal ',goal-1))
   (let ((goal-2 (goal ↑(=d is =d2) attempt)))
   (defmethod succeeds ((goal ',goal-2))
    (succeds attempt))
   (defmethod fails ((goal ',goal-2))
    (fails attempt))))
   (defmethod fails ((goal ',goal-1))
      (fails attempt)))))
```

Strategies for proving composite statements. The following is a strategy corresponding to the axiom of implication introduction which is interesting since it involves hypotethical reasoning, which is handled by means of the viewpoint mechanism of Omega. Informally the strategy can be formulated as follows: *if you want to prove "σ1 → σ2", assume σ1 and prove σ2.*

The corresponding strategy can be expressed as:

```
↑(=s1 → =s2)
is
(a Statement
  (with backward-strategy
    '(let ((nvp (create-viewpoint))
          (attempt (new-attempt)))
      (vp-goto nvp)
      (assert =s1)
      (on-success (goal =s2 attempt)
       (vp-goto (vp-parent nvp))
       (vp-kill nvp)
        (succeeds attempt)))))
```

I just recall that viewpoints are defined as collections of statements (therefore represented at the metalevel of Omega) [Attardi 84]. They represent the set of assumptions valid in that viewpoint. The function "create-viewpoint" creates a new viewpoint which inherits from the current one, and so that it contains initially the same assumptions as the current one. Asserting =s1 in the new viewpoint means to add =s1 to its set of assumptions.

For example if the user had asked:

(is? ((John **is** (a Man)) → (John **is** (a Mortal))) **true**)

since

$\uparrow$(John **is** (a Man)) → (John **is** (a Mortal)) **is**
   (**an** Implication [antecedent $\uparrow$(John **is** (a Man))]
                   [consequent $\uparrow$(John **is** (a Mortal))])])

by transitivity it is also

  (**a** Statement
    (**with** backward-strategy
      '(let ((nvp (create-viewpoint))
          (attempt (new-attempt)))
       (vp-goto nvp)
       (assert '(John **is** (a Man)))
       (on-success (goal '(John **is** (a Mortal)) attempt)
        (vp-goto (vp-parent nvp))
        (vp-kill nvp)
        (succeeds attempt)))

therefore this strategy is triggered to answer the query.

Conclusions. A few basic constructs for providing message-passing functionality within Common LISP have been suggested as a practical framework to experiment with concurrent reasoning algorithms. Taxonomic reasoning within the Omega description system appears as an interesting candidate for such experiments. Deductive strategies in Omega can be programmed at the metalevel and executed concurrently.

Related work. The design of Omega has its origins in the studies performed at MIT Artificial Intelligence Laboratory on the languages AMORD [deKleer 78], Ether [Kornfeld 82], and Omega itself [Hewitt 80, Attardi 81].

Acknowledgements. Carl Hewitt has been the leading force in the early stages of the design of Omega. Maria Simi has contributed to all significant developments of Omega. Andrea Corradini, Stefano Diomedi and Maurizio De Cecco of the ESPRIT team at DELPHI have contributed to the implementation of the ideas presented in this paper.

References.

[Agha 85]   Agha, G.A. "Actors: A Model of Concurrent Computation in Distributed Systems", MIT, AI-TR 844, 1985.

[Attardi 81]   Attardi, G. and M. Simi "Semantics of Inheritance and Attributions in the Description System Omega", MIT, AI Memo 642, 1981.

[Attardi 84]   Attardi, G. and M. Simi "Metalanguage and Reasoning across Viewpoints" Proc. of Sixth European Conference on Artificial Intelligence, Pisa, 1984.

[Attardi 85]   Attardi, G. et al. "Building Expert Systems with Omega", DELPHI, Tech. Rep. ESP/85/2, 1985.

[Attardi 86]   Attardi, G., Corradini, A., Diomedi, S., Simi, M. "Taxonomic Reasoning", Proc. of ECAI '86, Elsevier, 1986.

[Attardi 86b]   Attardi, G., Simi, M. "A Description Oriented Logic for Building Knowledge Bases", to appear in **The Proceedings of the IEEE**.

[Bobrow 85]   Bobrow, D.G., et al. "COMMONLOOPS - Merging COMMON LISP and Object-Oriented Programming", Xerox PARC, ISL-85-8, 1985.

[De Kleer 78]   deKleer. J., Doyle, J., Rich, C., Steele, G.L., Sussman, G.J., "AMORD: a Deductive Procedure System", MIT AI-Memo 435, 1978.

[Hewitt 79]   Hewitt, C., Attardi, G., Lieberman, H., "Specifying and Proving Properties of Guardians for Distributed Systems", **Semantics of Concurrent Computations**, (Ed. G. Kahn), *Lecture Notes in Computer Science*, No. 70, Springer-Verlag, Berlin, 1979.

[Hewitt 80]   Hewitt, C., Attardi, G., Simi M. "Knowledge Embedding in the Description System Omega", Proc. of First AAAI Conference, Stanford, 1980.

[Kornfeld 82]   Kornfeld, W. "Using parallel processing for problem solving" M.I.T. Ph.D. Thesis, 1982.

[Steele 84]   Steele, G.L. "Common Lisp: the Language", Digital Press, 1984.

Advances in Artificial Intelligence - II
B. Du Boulay, D. Hogg and L. Steels (Editors)
© Elsevier Science Publishers B.V. (North-Holland), 1987

Knowledge Representation and Communication Mechanisms

in LORE

Ch. Benoit, Y. Caseau, Ch. Pherivong

Laboratoires de Marcoussis
Centre de Recherches de la C.G.E
Route de Nozay
91460 Marcoussis

LORE is an object oriented language based on the notion of behaviour associated with an object. Its originality lies in its relational and set-theoretical approach, in its factorization mechanisms for generic descriptions and behaviour definition, and in its asynchronous and synchronous communication primitives. We present the underlying notions of LORE: relations, sets, definition by selection, message passing and mailing system, with examples. LORE is available for UNIX/Franz-Lisp (VAX, SUN) and Common-Lisp (MAIA, SYMBOLICS 3600).

1. Some principles

1.1. LORE in four axioms

In LORE, an object is defined by its behaviour

According to this view, the object is not defined as a pluri-functional entity equipped with a knowledge base, but as a *behaviour*, i.e a set of reactions to different messages. A behaviour is described by a list of *properties*. Each property is composed of a *filter* and an *action-object* (the LORE object associated to the filter). For example, the property *inspect* is defined on the set of all LORE objects. This property possesses the filter *inspect* and the corresponding object-action is the method: *inspect*. This method allows us to have a graphic description of a LORE object. LORE is characterized by three fundamental axioms:

> A1: all entities are objets.
>
> A2: an object is characterized by its behaviour.
>
> A3: Messages are the means by which an object exhibits one of its properties.

Sets and properties

In the relational and set-theoretical model of LORE [Caseau.85], these properties are expressed in terms of n-ary relations on sets of objects. For example, the properties *x-axis* and *y-axis* of a point are described in terms of binary relations on $Point \times Number$, where *Point* is the set of points and *Number* the set of numbers. The movement of a point $P(x,y)$ to another point $P'(x',y')$, *move-to-x'-y'*, is considered as a n-ary relation on $(Point \times Number \times Number) \times Point$. This relation can be considered as a function from *Point* to *Point*, with two arguments belonging to *Number*. The properties *x-axis, y-axis* and *move-to-x'-y'* are defined on the set of points *Point*.

LORE distinguishes several types of binary and n-ary relations. These sets possess many subsets as we shall see in the next section. At this time, we shall retain two sets: *relation*, a subset of the binary-relation set and *method*, a subset of the n-ary-relation set. The set *Point*, being the definition domain of the three properties *x-axis, y-axis* and *move-to-x'-y'*, is described as follows:

```
┌─────────────────────────────────────────────────────────┐
│ Point                                                     │
│    Relations:                    Method:                  │
│       x-axis                        move-to-x'-y'         │
│          target Number              filter (Number, Number)│
│       y-axis                        target Point          │
│          target Number                                    │
└─────────────────────────────────────────────────────────┘
```

The set *Point* is then described by the set of properties of which it is the definition domain.

In **LORE**, *x-axis* and *y-axis* being relations of domain *Point*, for any element *aPoint* of this domain, x-axis(aPoint) and y-axis(aPoint) are defined. This remark allows us to consider the following axiom:

> A4: A property is attached to an object if and only if
> it belongs to the domain of the associated relation.

In **LORE**, attributes and methods are properties defined on a given set. Thus, the basic entities are sets and properties. In **LORE** all is object, so particular behaviours will be associated to these properties.

1.2. The is-a link

The traditional method of factorizing properties in existing object oriented languages is to distinguish between two kinds of entities in the language: *classes* and *instances*. Every object is an instance of a class which possesses a dictionary of properties, to which it is linked by an "is-a" link. Moreover, classes are also linked together by an "is-a-subclass-of" link which allows the user to factorize common properties between classes. In these languages, a class is both a concept and a set. This situation does not contribute to clarifying the notion of a class in the user's mind. That is the reason why we prefer a set-theoretical model where the "is-a" link has no conceptual sense. Such elementary notions as inclusion and membership are more intuitive for the user than class and instance notions. These notions are expressed in the following table:

common object concept	**LORE** object	mathematical concept
class	set	set
instance	element	element
subclass	subset	subset
instanciation link	is-a	membership relation
inheritance link	included-in	inclusion relation
attributes, methods	properties on a set	relations on sets

In **LORE**, all entities are grouped into sets. These sets, ordered by inclusion, constitute an inclusion lattice. Thus, there are two fundamental rules:

■   Sets are put into this lattice at the time of their creation.

■   Among classes containing an object, there exists a minimal set for the inclusion relation named the type of the object.

1.3. Examples

In **LORE**, properties of an object are exhibited by sending messages to it. We will see in section 5 different communication primitives. At this time, we shall use in the following examples an immediate request primitive: *ask-i*, written as:

    (ask-i <object> <message>) or [<object> <message>]

The circle object illustrates the definition of a number of mathematical properties of an object in terms of stored data and in terms of other properties. The property *pi* illustrates the definition of a property as a constant. Many properties of a circle are defined using references to other properties.

```
;; Creation of a class:
['circle is-a class included-in obj]
```

```
;; Definition of relations:
[circle has relation 'center target point]
[circle has relation 'radius target number]
```

```
;; A constant of a class:
[circle has constant 'pi target number value 3.1415926]
```

Mathematical properties of a circle are defined in terms of methods. A method possesses three characteristics: a domain of values (target), a filter which is the list of domains of its arguments and a formula defined by a lambda-expression or a **LISP** function. The first parameter of the lambda-list is the receiver of the message.

```
;; Some methods. ? symbolizes a reading access to a property.
[circle has method 'diameter   target number   filter nil
       for   '(lambda (c) (times [c radius ?] 2))]
```

```
[circle has method 'area   target number   filter nil
       for   '(lambda (c) (times [c pi ?] (expt [c radius ?] 2)))]
```

```
[circle has method 'area+100   target circle   filter nil
       for '(lambda (c)
              [c radius is
                 (sqrt (quotient (plus (times [c pi ?]
                                         (expt [c radius ?] 2))
                              100)
                         [c pi ?]))]
           c)]
```

Some manipulations of circles are given in figure 1.

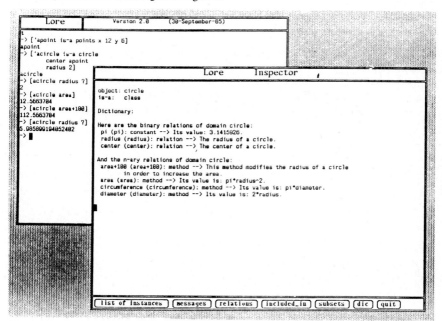

Figure 1 : Circle objects

2. Creating sets

The inheritance and class/instance links are still present in **LORE**, but integrated in a relational and set-theoretical model. A **LORE** object is thus described as a set of relations, and properties are factorized via sets with the inclusion relation. These sets, ordered by inclusion, constitute an inclusion lattice. The inclusion lattice of the basic sets of **LORE** is given in figure 2.

The set of all objects (*god, for General Object Domain*) possesses two subsets: *lisp* is the set of all Lisp-entities which then become **LORE** objects, and *obj*, the set of all pure **LORE** objects. In this manner, *god* allows us to attach different worlds to **LORE** preserving a consistent model. Included in *obj*, there are two trees: a tree of root *abstract-set* which describes sets in **LORE** and a tree of root *property* which describes sets of properties. This last tree is studied in section 3. Hereafter, we examine what are sets in **LORE**: sets describing the **LORE** universe, sets created by inclusion definition and sets created by selection definition.

2.1. Different kinds of sets

A **LORE** set is defined by its place in the **LORE** lattice: it is necessary to know which are its super-sets and subsets, and its behaviour which can be enriched after the creation of the set. The set *set* describes all of this information in terms of properties.

A user deals with two kinds of sets: real sets and virtual sets. The former are defined by inclusion definition, the latter by selection definition. Real sets are elements of *class*, the set of generic objects which ensures the correct management of instances, or of *sys-set*, the set of predefined sets such as the Lisp universe. Virtual sets are elements of *select* and are attached to a real set as we shall see in section 2.3.

2.2. Classes

Sets which have the property of generating objects are called classes. *Class* is the set of such sets. A new class is defined by inclusion into existing classes. For example, the class of red circles is included both into the class *circle* and the class *red-objects*:

['*red-circle* is-a *class* included-in '*(circle red-object)*]

The default properties of *red-circle* are a combination of the properties associated to *circle* and *red-object*. This set of properties can be modified and enriched by the user.

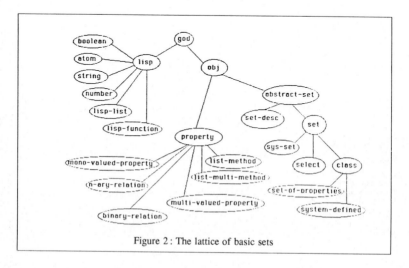

Figure 2: The lattice of basic sets

2.3. The definition by selection

Our inheritance relation is a specialization/generalization relation, but we have introduced the notion of the definition by selection. For instance, we can write in **LORE**:

A = { x belongs to B and P(x) } where P is any predicate.
i.e
['A is-a *select* included-in 'B pred 'P(x)]

This means that each element x of B such that P(x) becomes an element of A, and in addition, that each element of A satisfies P and belongs to B. This gives the user a dynamic inheritance graph which can be modified at any time.

These domains, defined by selection, are maintained in **LORE** in an economical and dynamic way using the lattice of the different relation domains (ordered by inclusion). The following example of geometry shows how the user can describe different kinds of parallelograms. A parallelogram has the following characteristics:

■   a length and a width,

■   the length of the first diagonal and the length of the second diagonal. So,

['parallelo is-a *class* included-in *obj*]
[parallelo has *relation* 'length target *number*]
[parallelo has *relation* 'width target *number*]
[parallelo has *relation* 'diag1 target *number*]
[parallelo has *relation* 'diag2 target *number*]

The set *rectangle* is defined by selection:

Rectangle = { parallelogram / diag1 = diag2 }

So:

['rectangle is-a *select*   included-in   *parallelo*
    pred '(lambda (p) (= [p diag1] [p diag2]))]

In the same way, we can defined the set *lozenge* by selection:

Lozenge = { parallelogram / length = width }

So:

['lozenge is-a *select*   included-in   *parallelo*
    pred '(lambda (p) (= [p length] [p width]))]

The set *square* is then defined as the intersection of the two sets *rectangle* and *lozenge*:

Square = Rectangle ∩ Lozenge,
['square is-a *class* included-in '(rectangle lozenge)]

As both sets *rectangle* and *lozenge* are virtual sets, the set *square* will be also defined by **LORE** as a virtual subset of the class *parallelo*. The **LORE** system assures the user that at any time, the inclusion lattice of **LORE** is a v-graph [Caseau.85]. So, if P1 (resp. P2) is the predicate associated to the set *rectangle* (resp. *lozenge*), then the set *square* is defined by the **LORE** system with the following definition by selection:

Square = { parallelogram / P1 and P2 }

3. Creating properties

Sets of properties are particular classes: they belong to the "meta-class" *set-of-properties*. When an object, which is an element of a set of properties, receives a message such as reading or writing accesses, a special behaviour is activated. This behaviour is described by the class *set-of-properties* and can be viewed as a re-writing as opposed to an evaluation.

3.1. Classes of properties

Property is the set of properties. This set regroups common characteristics of properties: domain, target and the processing of the inheritance relation. In [Caseau.86], the reader will find an explaination of how some conflicts of properties are solved in **LORE**.

Several sets of properties are defined as subsets of *property*. As properties are n-ary relations, two criteria distinguish them:

- a property may be a binary relation or a n-ary relation with n > 2 ;
- a property may be mono- or multi-valued.

The classic notions of attributes and methods of an object are respectively considered as elements of the subsets *binary-relation* and *n-ary-relation*. In the next two sections, we present an overview of these two subsets of *property*.

3.2. Binary relations

In **LORE**, we distinguish two subsets of binary relations: *relation*, the subset of mono-valued binary relations and *multi-relation*, the subset of multi-valued binary relations.

A binary relation is mono-valued if a single value is associated to each element of its definition domain. For example, the age of a person is a mono-valued binary relation: it is defined on the cartesian product *Person* × *Number*. So, it is an element of *relation*.

   [*person* has *relation* '*age* target *number*]
   [*'john is-a person age 9*]]
   [*john age ?*] ==> 9

A binary relation is multi-valued if a set of values is associated to each element of its definition domain. For example, a set of sports played by a person is a multi-valued binary relation: it is defined on the cartesian product *Person* × *Hobbies*. So, it is an element of the set *multi-relation*.

   [*person* has *multi-relation* '*sports* target *hobbies*]
   [*john sports* is *football*]
   [*john sports* add *rugby*]
   [*john sports ?*] ==> (rugby football)

Several methods have been defined on the set *multi-relation* in order to take into account different manipulations on sets of values: add, erase, remove,... The user will be able to imagine others manipulations. Properties such as initialization by default, procedural attachments, which exist in frame languages [Greiner-et-al.80], are also associated to binary relations. Such facets as if-needed daemons are defined in terms of binary relations on the cartesian product *Binary-relation* × *Method*.

3.3. N-ary relations

Let A_i, $i \in [n]$, $n \geq 2$, be sets. An n-ary relation R is a relation on $A_1 \times A_2 \times ... \times A_n \times A_{n+1}$. The domain of the relation R is $A_1 \times A_2 \times ... \times A_n$ and its target is A_{n+1}. This relation can be viewed as a function from $A_1 \times A_2 \times ... \times A_n$ to A_{n+1} if R is mono-valued and to A_{n+1}^* if it is multi-valued. The filter associated to an n-ary relation R on $A_1 \times A_2 \times ... \times A_n \times A_{n+1}$ is $(A_1 \ R \ A_2 ... \ A_n)$. Therefore, the property, corresponding to an n-ary relation R, is associated to an object O if and only if O is an element of the set A_1.

We find here, differently expressed, the notion of a method associated to a class:

- A_1 indicates the domain of the method: *domain*,
- R indicates the name of the method: *name*,
- (A_2 ... A_n) indicates the list of sets of its arguments: *filter*,
- and A_{n+1}, the target of the method: *target*

The formula associated to a method is given by the property *for*.

In **LORE**, n-ary relations belong to the set *n-ary-relation*. *Method* and *multi-method* are respectively the subsets of mono-valued and multi-valued n-ary relations. For example, the method *move-to-x'-y'* defined on the set *Point*, given in section 1, is described by:

> [*point* has *method 'move-to-x'-y'* target *point* filter *'(number number)*
>   for *'(lambda (p x' y') [p x is x'] [p y is y'] p)*]

The method *move-to-x'-y'* is then considered as a relation on (*Point* × *Number* × *Number*) × *Point*.

Another example is the description of daemons or facets existing in frame languages. These properties belong to a subset of *relation*: *relation-with-daemons*. They are defined on *relation-with-daemons* × *method*. So, daemons are methods that are activated at each access to a property they are associated with. A parking lot having three attributes - *total*, the total number of places, *occupied*, the number of occupied places and *free*, the number of free places -, can be described in **LORE** as follows:

> [*'parking-lot* is-a *class* included-in *obj*]
>
> [*parking-lot* has *relation 'total* target *number*
>   com *"The total number of places"*]
>
> [*parking-lot* has *relation-with-daemons 'occupied* target *number*
>   write *'(lambda (occupied p)*
>   *(format *standard-output* "Not more than ˜ A places.˜ %"*
>   *(- [p total ?] [p occupied ?])))*
>   com *"Number of occupied places"*]

After writing access to *occupied*, the method associated to *write* will be activated.

> [*parking-lot* has *relation-with-daemons 'free* target *number*
>   need *'(lambda (free p) (- [p total ?] [p occupied ?]))*
>   com *"Number of free places"*]

At each reading access to *free*, the method associated to *need* will be activated.

4. Control and communication

Messages are the way to make an object exhibit one of its properties. When an object receives a message , its behaviour permits it to activate the corresponding property. But the way a message is sent to an object concerns the communication mechanisms. With this in mind, we propose for **LORE** a communication protocol based on a framework that is not purely sequential or applicative. In this section, we present the communication primitives of **LORE** and an example of the mailing behaviour of objects.

4.1. A double dichotomy

The usual *ask/send* dichotomy discriminates between two kinds of messages: those for which an answer is needed and those just sending an order to other objects. This dichotomy is still present in **LORE**. Moreover, the consideration of both *synchronous* and *asynchronous* communications led us to introduce a new dichotomy "orthogonal" to the previous one. **LORE** distinguishes between two execution modes, namely *immediate* and *buffered* execution.

- In the *immediate* mode: the message is taken into account without further delay. The processing is done in the workspace (memory, execution stack, processor,...) of the sender.

- In the *buffered* mode: the message is appended to the mailbox of the receiver. It waits for its turn to be treated.

The double dichotomy induces twice two primitives for communication in **LORE**. We present below these four communication primitives with their semantic.

ask-buffer:

> O1 executes an *ask-buffer* request to O2: the message is added to the mailbox of O2, and O1 is descheduled. Another object (perhaps O2 itself) becomes the current active one. O1 will become active again when the response to its request arrives.

send-buffer:
O1 executes a *send-buffer* request to O2: the message is added to the mailbox of O2, and O1 carries on execution. O2 will process the message in its turn according to the scheduling strategy but this message requires no answer. This primitive allows asynchronous communication by the propagation of messages through the universe of the objects.

ask-immediate:
O1 executes an *ask-immediat* request to O2: O1 keeps the control, and the message is interpreted by O2 without any further delay. The *ask-immediate* primitive is a function call, so the request and, later, the answer are carried by the mechanism of function calls. Thus, it allows messages to behave like methods. Typically O1 wants to make an access to an O2's attribute and this primitive is the fastest way to do so. Being a bridge to the functionnal world, the *ask-immediate* primitive allows recursive mailing requests inside LORE. Recursive buffered requests lead to a deadlock. This primitive is the classic communication primitive in most object oriented languages.

send-immediate:
O1 executes a *send-immediate* request to O2: control is immediately given to O2, which processes the message. The *send-immediate* primitive takes the request into account without any further delay. It corresponds to a kind of software interrupt.

4.2. A mailing system

For such a protocol, we need to construct a real *mailing system* because the **LISP** interpreter cannot deal on its own with mailing requests. Thus, we have implemented for **LORE** a scheduler devoted to the mailing activity, treating also the concurrency conflicts that arise in a buffered communication mode. The following example shows how this mailing system interacts with the behaviour of the concerned objects.

All mailing requests, using any one of the four primitives of communication, are sent under the control of one particular object called the master. At the top-level of **LORE**, the master is the object *lore-top-level*.

Suppose it is John's birthday. John, as a person, knows perfectly well what to do when it is birthday. The state of the mailing system during the execution time of the method *birthday* is given in figure 3.

This method implies that the object *person* becomes active with the message *(all welcome john)*, and that the object *la-Tour-d-Argent* becomes the second active object with the request *(reserved-dinner)*, both placed in their mailboxes by *john* under the control of *lore-top-level*. This last request descheduled the current master *lore-top-level* (*john* cannot be descheduled because [*john birthday*] was just a function call to the behavior of *john*). The scheduling strategy gives the control to the active object *person* for treating the message *(all welcome john)*. This message contains immediate requests to *john*, such as reading access to its name, considered as a subcontractor of the master *person*. During this time, *lore-top-level* is waiting for the answer to its request to *la-Tour-d-Argent*, which is now the first active object.

5. Conclusion

In **LORE**, objects can be thought of as independent processing units operating concurrently with their own "instruction sets", "memory", and the ability to communicate with other objects by message passing. As memory and processor costs fall, it is possible to seriously envisage machines whose computational power will be derived from interconnected processors where each processor has its own memory. Such an architecture is often called message-passing architecture. So, the work to be done may be defined as follows. Existing architectural proposals (such as the Cosmic cube, the Connection Machine, the Transputer) will be studied to determine whether they can provide reasonable support for Object Oriented Languages such as **LORE**, and more generally for Knowledge Representation Systems.

Acknowledgements

LORE is the result of a collective brain-storming where most of the people working on object oriented languages in Marcoussis were involved. Special thanks are due to Gérard Guiho, Jean-Pascal Aubert, Eric Papon, François Jakob and Stéphane Kaplan who were very influential on the design of the language.

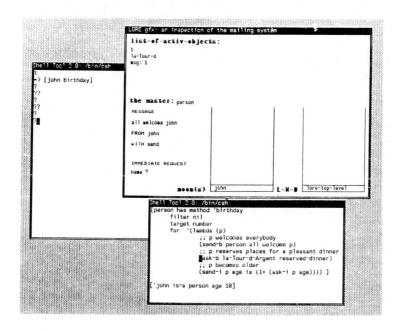

Figure 3 : A mailing system

References

[Agha.85] : G.A Agha,
"Actors, a model of concurrent computation in distributed systems", MIT, AI-TR 844, 1985
[Attardi.86] : G. Attardi,
"Concurrent strategy execution in Omega", DELPHI, Tech. Report, 1986.
[Benoit-Caseau-Pherivong.86] : Ch. Benoit, Y. Caseau, Ch. Pherivong,
"LORE: un Langage Objet Relationnel et Ensembliste" Actes des 3ème Journées d'Etudes sur les Langages Orientés Objets, Paris, Janvier 1986.
[Benoit-Pherivong.85] : Ch. Benoit, Ch. Pherivong,
"The object model : Analysis and Evolution". Actes des Journées AFCET, Groupe Génie Logiciel, Paris, Octobre 1985.
[Bobrow-Kahn et al.85] : D.G Bobrow, K. Kahn, G. Kiczales, L. Masinter, M. Stefik, F. Zdybel,
"Common Loops : merging Common LISP and Object-Oriented Programming". Xerox Palo Alto Research Center, Intelligent System Laboratory, ISL-85-8, August 1985.
[Brachman.83] : R. Brachman,
"What Is-A is and isn't: an analysis of taxonomic links in semantic networks". Proc. of IEEE Computer, pp. 30-36, October 1983.
[Caseau.85] : Y. Caseau,
"Objects and Sets in LORE". Actes du 5ème congrès RFIA, Grenoble, Novembre 1985.
[Caseau.86] : Y. Caseau,
"An overview of LORE", IEEE Software, January 1986.
[Fahlman.79] : S. Fahlman,
"NETL a system for representing and using real world knowledge". MIT Press, Cambridge, MA, 1979.
[Ferber.84] : J. Ferber,
"MERING, an open-ended object-oriented language for knowledge representation". Proc. of ECAI.84, Pisa, September 1984.
[Hillis.85] : W.D. Hillis,
"The connection machine". The MIT Press, Series in Artificial Intelligence, 1985.
[Novak.83] : G. Novak,
"GLISP User's Manual". Tech. Report HPP-82-1, STAN-CS-82-895, Revised September 1983, Stanford University, September 1983.

[Seitz.85]: C.L Seitz,
"The Cosmic Cube". Comm. of ACM, Vol. 28, No. 1, pp 22-33, January 1985.
[Steels.83]: L. Steels,
"Descriptions as constraints in Object-Oriented representation". Proc. IJCAI-83, pp. 395-397, Karlsruhe, August 1983.
[Steels.84]: L.Steels,
"Object-oriented knowledge representation in KRS" Proc. of ECAI-84, pp. 333-336, Pisa, September 1984.
[Stefik-Bobrow.86]: M. Stefik, D.G Bobrow,
"Object-Oriented Programming: Themes and Variations". AI Magazine, Vol. 6, No. 4, Winter 1986.
[Yonesawa-Matsumoto.85]: A. Yonesawa, Y. Matsumoto,
"Object Oriented Concurrent Programming and Industrial Software Production". Formal Methods and Software Development.
Lecture Notes in Computer Science, No. 186, pp 395-409, 1985.
[Van Damme-Van Nerom.85]: P. Van Damme, L. Van Nerom,
"A general framework for message-passing architectures". Proc. of AI Europa Conference, Wiesbaden, September 1985.

Advances in Artificial Intelligence - II
B. Du Boulay, D. Hogg and L. Steels (Editors)
© Elsevier Science Publishers B.V. (North-Holland), 1987

The OBJVLISP Model: Definition of a
Uniform, Reflexive and Extensible Object Oriented Language

Jean-Pierre BRIOT[*]   Pierre COINTE[†]

Abstract

This paper presents the ObjVlisp model designed to experiment and synthesize the expanding activities of the Object Oriented world. The goal is to specify a minimal kernel whose semantic is perfectly uniform, then to modelize other Object semantics by extending this concentrate kernel. We propose a unification of the metaclass, class and object concepts which allows an optimal uniformity. This unification is obtained as a reflexive definition of the language. We rapidly describe some ObjVlisp variations establishing the malleability of the system.

The kernel is built on a portable virtual machine defined as a set of Lisp primitives which preserve the Lisp evaluator and maintain the spirit of dynamic (or lexical) scoping.

Keywords:

object, class, metaclass, uniformity, instance variable, classe variable, message, instantiation, CLASS, inheritance, OBJECT, Lisp, Smalltalk, ObjVlisp, virtual machine, dynamic scoping, lexical scoping, portability, reflexive, extensible.

1   Uniformity

"One way of stating the Smalltalk philosophy is to choose a small number of general principles and apply them uniformly" [Kra83].

---

[*] Tokyo Institute of Technology, Dept. of Information Science, Ookayama, Meguro-ku, Tokyo 152, & LITP, 4 place Jussieu, 75005 Paris.

[†] Centre Mondial Informatique, 22 Avenue Matignon, 75008 Paris, electronic mail: ...!mcvax!inria!cmirh!pc & LITP 4 place Jussieu, 75005 Paris.

1.1   Is a class an object?

In most common Object Oriented Languages, besides Krasner's uniformity "wish", a class is not a REAL object. Some of them however, like Smalltalk-80 [GR83] and Loops [BS83], introduced the new *metaclass* concept to provide a greater abstraction. To definitively suppress the gap between *class* and *object*, we propose a unification of the *metaclass*, *class* and *object* concepts.

We claim [Bri85] that a class must be an object, allowing greater clarity and expressive power. As a consequence, we no longer need to introduce the *class variable* and *class method* concepts of Smalltalk which are not real variables and methods.

1.2   Class and terminal instance

The reverse question is "*is every object a class?*", whose answer is "no". [1] Some objects are "only" instances of a class, and don't define a model. An instance of a POINT class, e.g. an object *a_point*, or an instance of the NUMBER class, e.g. 3, are such objects. We call them *terminal instances*.

1.3   How many object types?

We consider only one kind of objects, without structure or nature distinction between generators (*classes*) and non generators (*terminal instances*).

---

[1] In the *actor* model, an *actor* describes its own structure and exists without a class. Defining generator actors [Yon86] or using a copy mechanism [Lie86] [CBS86] are alternatives to the class model.

In fact, they only differ by their capacity to react to the instantiation message. If the class of an object owns the primitive instantiation method (*new* selector, owned by the primitive class **CLASS**) or inherits it, this object is a generator, otherwise a terminal instance.

1.4   Metaclasses are usual classes

A metaclass (or a metagenerator) is simply a class which generates other classes. Every class declared as a subclass of the metaclass **CLASS** inherits its *new* method, and becomes a metaclass. Therefore the introduction of the metaclass concept is unnecessary and "the distinction between metaclasses, classes and terminal instances [2] is only a inheritance consequence and not a type distinction. There is now only one type of objects in the model."
This unification induces a simplification of the instantiation and inheritance concepts but imposes to use them simultaneously: for example a metaclass is created as the subclass of another one (as an "ultimate" subclass of **CLASS**).

2   The ObjVlisp Model

Historically the ObjVlisp model comes from our work on Smalltalk-76 [Coi83], and our wish to present a synthesis in an operational semantic expressed in Lisp [Coi84b]. We present here the new reflexive version which exactly integrates the previous unification and gives a fine solution to the problem of < *class* , *instance* > dichotomy.

2.1   ObjVlisp in five Postulates

Following the classical presentation of Smalltalk-76 [Ing78], five postulates fully describe the new ObjVlisp model:

P1:   every entity of the language is an *object*. An object represents a piece of knowledge and a set of potentialities:

---

[2] To easily distinguish them, we use upper-case for classes, upper-bold for metaclasses, and lower-case for terminal instances.

$$object = < data , procedures >$$

P2:   the only control structure is *message passing*: the protocol to activate an object. A message specifies which procedure to apply (denoted by its name, the *selector*), and the arguments to pass:

$$(send\ object\ selector\ Args_1\ ...\ Args_n)$$

P3:   every object belongs to a *class* that specifies its data (attributes called *fields* or *instance variables*) and its behavior (procedures called *methods*). Objects will be dynamically generated from this model, they are called *instances* of the class. Following Plato, all instances of a class have same structure and shape, but differ through the values of their common *instance variables*.

P4:   a class is also an object, generated from a class, called a *metaclass* (because describing a class). Consequently (P3), to each class is associated a metaclass. The initial primitive metaclass is the class **CLASS**.

P5:   a class can be defined as a subclass of one (or many) other class(es). This subclassing mechanism allows inheritance of fields and methods, and is called *inheritance*. The class **OBJECT** represents the most common behavior shared by all objects.

2.2   Classes and objects

2.2.1   Structure of an object

The postulates P1 & P3 define an object as a "chunk" of knowledge and actions whose structure is defined by its class. More precisely:

fields: This environment (also called a dictionary) is split in two parts:
a) the set of *instance variables* specified by the object's class,
b) the set of associated values.
The set of instance variables belongs to the

class, and is shared by all its instances. The set of values is owned by each instance. An object cannot exist without its class.

Each object implicitly holds three "pseudo-fields"; **self** and **isit** [3] are bound to the object itself and its class, **metaisit** denotes the metaclass of the object and is characteristic [4] of the ObjVlisp model.

methods: The methods define the procedures shared by all the instances of a class and owned by it.

To realize the unification between class and instance we represent this method environment as a particular field of a class; the methods dictionary of a class is the value associated to a specific instance variable called *methods*. As a common object, a class is defined by its (meta)class and the values of the associated instance variables.

2.2.2 Structure of a class

We present now the three instance variables describing a class. They are owned by **CLASS** as the primitive metaclass:

supers :   the list of super-classes of the class,

i_variables :   the list of instance variables that the class specifies,

methods :   the list of methods held by the class organized in a P-list way, with pairs < *selector* , *lambda-expression* > .

2.2.3 Instantiation of a class

A class is instantiated by sending it a message of selector *new*. The *new* message received by a class provides the generation of a new object built on the class model. For example, we define the class POINT by instantiating the metaclass **CLASS**; we specify the name of the object (value

---

[3] respectively analogs to SELF and ISIT in Smalltalk-72 [GK76]

[4] We use it to simulate the *class variables* even if we have the double equality: **metaisit = (class-of isit) = (send isit 'is)**

---

of self) and the three values associated to the **CLASS**'s instance variables:

```
; (send 'CLASS 'new <name> <supers> <i_variables> <methods>)
(send 'CLASS 'new 'POINT '(OBJECT) '(x y)
   '( draw    (lambda () (tty-print x y " * ")) ) )
```

Then we create an instance of POINT, using the same *new* message: [5]

```
; (send 'POINT 'new <name> <x> <y>)
(send 'POINT 'new 'a_point 40 15)
(send 'POINT 'new 'another_point 24 12)
```

The semantic and syntax of the *new* method are totally uniform. The *new* message always receives as arguments: the name of the instance to generate, and the values related to the instance variables specified by the receiver-class. Unlike the SMALLTALK-80 system, ObjVlisp uses only one method (named *new*) to create an object (by using the **make-object** primitive of the virtual machine). This method is owned by the metaclass **CLASS** as expressed by its reflexive definition.

3 Reflexivity

Because we need a complete transparency in the objects definitions to give more complete control to the users, we adapt the reflexive interpreter technic [dRS84] to the construction of our model. ObjVlisp is supported by two graphs: the *instantiation graph* and the *inheritance graph*. The instantiation graph represents the "*instance of*" relation (P3 & P4), and the inheritance graph the "*subclass of*" one (P5). **CLASS** and OBJECT are the roots of these two graphs: they are defined in ObjVlisp .

---

[5] This table shows the half-dictionary of values owned by each object:

```
? (send 'a_point 'i_values)
= (40 15)
? (send 'POINT 'i_values)
= ((OBJECT) (x y) (draw ..))
? (send 'CLASS 'i_values)
= ((OBJECT) (supers i_variables methods) (new ..))
```

3.1 CLASS: Instantiation

CLASS is the first object of the system, as the root of the instantiation graph, it will recursively generate all other objects. CLASS is also its own instance and we have the equality:

$$\boxed{\text{class [CLASS]} = \text{CLASS}}$$

3.1.1 Self pattern-matching of CLASS

To verify the previous equality we have to guarantee that the instance variables specified by CLASS match the corresponding values also held by CLASS, as its own instance:

```
i_variables :    supers          i_variables                    methods
i_values :       (OBJECT)    (supers i_variables methods)    (new (lambda1 ..) ... menu (lambdan ..))
```

The value associated to the instance variable *i_variables* is exactly the list of instance variables itself, this self pattern-matching illustrates the definition of CLASS as an object.

3.1.2 Boot-strap

"A natural and fundamental question to ask, on learning of these incredibly interlocking pieces of software and hardware is: "How did they ever get started in the first place?". It is truly a baffling thing" [Hof79].

Defining CLASS from itself necessitates to precise the boot-strap mechanism. We create the skeleton of CLASS using the **make-object** primitive. We just need to introduce the *new* method which supports the self-instantiation of CLASS:

```
; (make-object <metamodel> <model> <instance> <i_variables> <i_values>)
(make-object 'CLASS 'CLASS 'CLASS
  '( supers              i_variables                    methods )
  '( (OBJECT)    (supers i_variables methods)    (new (lambda (name . i_values)
                                                    (make-object isit self name i_variables i_values))) ) )
```

This bootstrap prepared, we can define ObjVlisp in ObjVlisp :

3.1.3 Self-instantiation of CLASS

```
; (send 'CLASS 'new <name> <supers> <i_variables> <methods>)
(send 'CLASS 'new 'CLASS '(OBJECT) '(supers i_variables methods)
  '( new            (lambda (name . i_values) (make-object isit self name i_variables i_values))
    supers          (lambda () supers)
    i_variables     (lambda () i_variables)
    methods         (lambda () methods)

    ...             ...

    methodfor       (lambda (selector) (methodfor selector methods))
    change          (lambda (selector method) (changemethod selector method methods))
    understand      (lambda (selector method) (defmethod selector method methods))
    menu            (lambda () (selectors methods)) ) )
```

This definition is given for a dynamically scoped Lisp (Le_Lisp [CDH84]) as other ones and examples. Then all the instance variables are automatically bound to their values in a method body. Consequently the lambda-methods associated to the *supers*, *i_variables* and *methods* selectors are quite easy to express.

Similarly, in the *new* method, *isit* denotes the metagenerator (here **CLASS**), *self* the generator (again **CLASS**), and *i_variables* the variables to instantiate with i_values. They are used as free variables in the **make-object** call.

3.2 OBJECT: Inheritance

(P5) precises the inheritance mechanism which concerns only classes. Inheritance allows to connect together fields and methods of several classes but in two differents ways.

The inheritance of fields is static and done once at creation time.

When defining a class, its instance variables are calculated as the union of a copy of the instance variables owned by the superclasses with the instance variables specified at creation (the value associated to *i_variables* in the *new* message).

On the contrary, the methods inheritance is dynamic and uses the virtual copy mechanism realized by the linkage of classes in the inheritance graph.

If the lookup of a method fails in the receiver class, then the search continues in a depth/breadth way. This graph is supported by the *supers* instance variable.

3.2.1 Classes vs Terminal Instances

The inheritance mechanism of fields is applied only when creating classes. Thus we need to discriminate creation of classes and creation of terminal instances. We have the equivalence:

create a class $<=>$ *creator is a metaclass*

As we pointed out already, a class inheriting from **CLASS** is a metaclass and inherits statically the *supers*, *i_variables* and *methods* instance variables. The predicate-method *metaclass?*, presented below, implements this test. It is used by the **make-object** primitive, thus no inheritance will occur when creating a terminal instance.

3.2.2 OBJECT the most common class

The second primitive class is OBJECT, instance of **CLASS**. OBJECT is usually the default specified superclass (e.g. **CLASS** is a subclass of OBJECT), so it represents the most common class (intersection of all classes), describing the most common behavior (for classes and terminal instances).

```
; (send 'CLASS 'new <name> <supers> <i_variables> <methods>)
(send 'CLASS 'new 'OBJECT () ()
  '( is         (lambda () isit)
     ?          (lambda (i_var) (eval i_var))
     ?<-        (lambda (i_var i_val) (set i_var i_val))
     i_values   (lambda () (i_values self))
     metaclass? (lambda () (memq 'supers i_variables))
     class?     (lambda () (send isit 'metaclass?))
     ...          ...
     print      (lambda () (pretty self))
     error      (lambda msg '(lambda bs ',msg)) ) )
```

From this definition, each ObjVlisp object answers to the *< selector>* by *< action>*:

is	giving the name of its class
?	returning the value of the field i_var
?<-	writing i_var with the new value
i_values	returning the values of the fields
metaclass?	testing if the object is a metaclass
class?	testing if the object is a class
print	printing an external representation
error	precising the standard error treatment

Notice that the ? and ?<- methods which access to the instance variables are conform to the dynamic binding of Le_Lisp .

3.3 Self-Extensions

3.3.1 Class variables by Example

Let us return to the POINT class, previously defined. Now we would like the constant character " ★ " to be a class variable shared by all the points of a same class. We redefine the POINT class as before, but metaclass of which (let's call it **METAPOINT**) specifies this common character:

```
; (send 'CLASS 'new <name> <supers> <i_variables> <methods>)
(send 'CLASS 'new 'METAPOINT '(CLASS) '(char) ())


; (send 'METAPOINT 'new <name> <supers> <i_variables>
  <methods>
  <char>)
(send 'METAPOINT 'new 'POINT '(OBJECT) '(x y)
  '( draw    (lambda () (tty-print x y char)) )
  " ★ " )
```

METAPOINT is declared as a subclass of CLASS (thus it is a metaclass). It inherits the instance variables supers, i_variables and methods from CLASS and adds them the instance variable char. Consequently, POINT specifies the associate value of char, i.e. " ★ ".
Now we could create such a point:

```
? (send 'POINT 'new 'a_point 20 10)
= a_point
? (send 'a_point 'draw)
      ★
= ★
```

Parametrization of a class: The POINT class is now parametrized by the "display" character and the METAPOINT metaclass represents this abstraction. Let's define two new classes, called POINT# and POINT@ with two other different display characters. Obviously, they are defined as a subclass of POINT:

```
? (send 'METAPOINT 'new 'POINT# '(POINT) () () "#" )
= POINT#
? (send 'METAPOINT 'new 'POINT@ '(POINT) () () "@" )
= POINT@
? (send (send 'POINT# 'new 'a_point# 1 2) 'draw)
  #
= #
? (send (send 'POINT@ 'new 'a_point@ 3 4) 'draw)
  @
= @
```

Such a simple and intuitive construction is IMPOSSIBLE in Smalltalk, because class variables are implemented like pool variables [GR83], and are not inheritable.
With the ObjVlisp model we have the identification:

```
class variable [an_object] =
instance variable [an_object's class]
```

3.3.2 Architecture of the ObjVlisp model

We summarize the general structure of the ObjVlisp model by connecting together the instantiation graph and the inheritance graph to explain the "POINT construction":

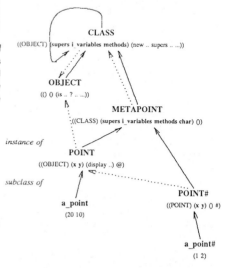

Below an object, appears its half-dictionary of values; they correspond to the instance variables of its class, this list (in bold) being itself a value corresponding to the i_variables instance variable owned by CLASS, and inherited by METAPOINT. There is no longer any depth limitation of the instantiation graph. We can extend it as much as we want to specify different levels of shared knowledge and methods.

3.3.3 Class methods by Example

As for class variables, class methods are specified in the metaclass as usual methods. Suppose we want to define a new class method for POINT to create and initialize a new point. We simply define the newinit method of METAPOINT (assuming we define also an init method in the POINT class, or at least in the OBJECT class):

```
(send 'METAPOINT 'understand 'newinit
  '(lambda (name)
    (send (send self 'new name) 'init)) )
```

3.3.4 Filiation link

To use classes registering all their instances, we define a new metaclass **SET**, as a subclass of **CLASS** with a new instance variable *sons* pointing the list of instances. We just have to redefine the **CLASS'** *new* method to add the newly instance at the end of the *sons* list:

```
(send 'CLASS 'new 'SET '(CLASS) '(sons)
    '( new          (lambda (name . i_values)
                        (nconc sons (cons name ()))
                        (run-super))
      mapsons       (lambda (selector)
                        (mapc
                          (lambda (an_object)
                            (send an_object selector))
                          sons)) ) )
```

The *mapsons* method distributes an unary message (without argument) to all the instances of a particular set. The "(run-super)" form (same as in CommonLoops [BKK*85]) recalls the current message, but the lookup for the method will begin in the superclasses of the current class.

4 Implementation

ObjVlisp means OBJect extension of a Virtual LISP and is implemented along the virtual machine technic allowing a quick installation on any Lisp (dynamically or lexically scoped). The classical difficulty when defining such a machine is to choose general primitives available on major aimed systems without privileging particular constructions, even if they are powerful for a given target. Consequently we have decided to preserve the <eval , apply> engine, and to use classical Lisp data structures such as atom, list, structure or environment. The Le_Lisp instantiation of this virtually machine is totally described in [Coi84a], and we are just finishing its Scheme and CommonLisp mergings.

To synthesize our previous presentation we conclude this paper with Le_Lisp & Scheme definitions of an object:

ObjLe_Lisp : an object is implemented as a Lisp atom whose functional value (**send** is equal to the *funcall* function) is a self-referenced closure:

```
(defun an_object (selector . args)
-1-  (let ( (self 'an_object) (isit 'A_CLASS)
-1-         (metaisit 'A_METACLASS) )
-2-    (letdic (i_variables metaisit) (i_values isit)
-2-      (letdic (i_variables isit) (i_values self)
-3-        (protect (apply (lookup selector isit) args)
-3-          (rewrite self isit metaisit))))))
```

1. The pseudo instance variables are dynamically bound by the "let" function. [6] Notice that those variables allow a factorization of the script of an object, the parts -2- to -3- defining a completely parametrized (and shared) piece of code,

2. in the spirit of a dynamic Lisp, the activation of an object is done in its fields' context. This double environment is dynamically set by the two "letdic" (let dictionary) functions:
"(letdic (i_variables metaisit) (i_values isit)"
sets the class environment,
and "(letdic (i_variables isit) (i_values self)"
the object's one,

3. when the object is disactivated, the updating of the double closure is automatically done with the function "rewrite". Consequently, the usual Lisp affectation functions (set, setq, nextl, incr ...) can be used to assign the instance (and class) variables.

ObjScheme: an object is now anonymous and represented as a *compound-procedure* grouping together the environment of the instance variables (i_dico) and a lambda-expression:

```
; i_dico = < (metaisit . ?) (isit . ?) (i_variable₁ . ?) ... (i_variableₙ . ?) >
(define (self selector . args)
-1-  (apply (lookup selector (access isit i_dico))
-2-         (cons* self i_dico args)))
```

---

[6]We propose (cf. ObjScheme) to replace these "let" pseudo-variables bindings by real instance variables, defining OBJECT with *isit* and *metaisit* (facultative) as instance variables. Objects can also be anonymous by using structures in place of atoms (notice that naming classes is useful for documentation and debugging, therefore **CLASS** will own the new *name* instance variable).

1. the "i_dico" is built as a Scheme environment by the "make-environment" primitive.

2. each method takes "i_dico" as argument allowing the explicit access to each field.

5   Improvements and Possibilities

The ObjVlisp model first advantage is UNIFORMITY. There is now only one kind of objects. This allows a simplification and reduction of concepts, which are thus more powerful and general. The second property is REFLEXIVITY which provides a language totally and uniformly accessible by the user. Finally, EXTENSIBILITY authorizes various applications and semantics modelizations. For example the study of inheritance strategies of such systems like Flavors [MW80], Smalltalk-80 [GR83] or Loops [BS83] are simulated by defining new metaclasses [Coi84a].

The ObjVlisp project is part of the "O.O.P. Methodology, GRECO de Programmation" Research Group.

References

[BKK*85] G. Bobrow, K. Kahn, G. Kiczakes, L. Masinter, M. Stefik and F. Zdybel: COMMONLOOPS: Merging Common Lisp and Object-Oriented Programming (IJCAI85 draft), 16 August 1985.

[Bri85] J.P. Briot: *Les Métaclasses dans les langages Orientés Objets*. Vol. 2, p. 755-764, AFCET/INRIA, Grenoble, 27-29 Novembre 1985.

[BS83] D. Bobrow and M. Stefik: *The LOOPS Manual*. Xerox PARC, December 1983.

[CBS86] P. Cointe, J. P. Briot, and B. Serpette: The FORMES Language: a Musical Application of Object Oriented Concurrent Programming. In *Object Oriented Concurrent Programming*, A. Yonezawa & M. Tokoro ed., MIT Press, Cambridge, Mass., May 1986.

[CDH84] J. Chailloux, M. Devin, and J.M. Hullot: LeLisp a Portable and Efficient Lisp System. In *Conference Record of the 1984 ACM symposium on LISP and Functional Programming*, p. 113-123, ACM, Austin, Texas, 5-8 August 1984.

[Coi83] P. Cointe: A Vlisp implementation of Smalltalk-76. In *Integrated Interactive Computing Systems*, P. Degano & E. Sandewall ed., p. 89-102, North-Holland, Amsterdam, 1983.

[Coi84a] P. Cointe: *Implémentation et interprétation des langages objets, application aux langages Formes, ObjVlisp et Smalltalk (thèse d'Etat)*. Technical Report 85-55, LITP/IRCAM, 17 Décembre 1984.

[Coi84b] P. Cointe: Une extension de Vlisp par les objets. *Science of Computer Programming*, Vol. 4, No 161, p. 291-322, 1984.

[dRS84] J. des Rivières and B. C. Smith: The implementation of proceduraly reflective languages. In *Conference Record of the 1984 ACM symposium on LISP and Functional Programming*, p. 331-347, ACM, Austin, Texas, 5-8 August 1984.

[GK76] A. Goldberg and A. Kay: *SMALLTALK-72 Instruction Manual*. Technical Report, Xerox PARC, Palo Alto, CA, March 1976.

[GR83] A. Goldberg and D. Robson: *SMALLTALK-80 The Language and its Implementation*. Addison-Wesley, Reading, 1983.

[Hof79] D. R. Hofstadter: *GOEDEL, ESCHER, BACH: an Eternal Golden Braid*. The Harvester Press, Stanford Terrace Publisher, 1979.

[Ing78] D. H. Ingalls: *The Smalltalk-76 Programming System Design and Implementation*. Conference Record of the 5th Annual ACM Symposium on Principles of Programming Languages, Tucson, January 1978.

[Kra83] G. Krasner: *Smalltalk-80: Bits of History, Words of Advice*. Addison-Wesley, Reading, 1983.

[Lie86] H. Lieberman: Delegation and Inheritance, two modular mechanisms. In *Conf. Record of the 3rd Workshop on OOP, AFCET/IRCAM*, J. Bezivin & P. Cointe ed., Bigre + Globule No 48, Centre Georges Pompidou, Paris, January 1986.

[MW80] D. A. Moon and D. Weinreb: *Flavors: Message Passing In The Lisp Machine*. Technical Report, MIT, Cambridge, Mass., November 1980.

[Yon86] A. Yonezawa: An approach to Object Oriented Concurrent Programming - A language ABCL. In *Conf. Record of the 3rd Workshop on OOP, AFCET/IRCAM*, J. Bezivin & P. Cointe ed., Bigre + Globule No 48, Centre Georges Pompidou, Paris, January 1986.

Advances in Artificial Intelligence - II
B. Du Boulay, D. Hogg and L. Steels (Editors)
© Elsevier Science Publishers B.V. (North-Holland), 1987

MULTILOG : MULTIple worlds in LOGic programming

Hervé Kauffmann

Alain Grumbach

Laboratoires de Marcoussis
C.G.E. Research Center
Route de Nozay
91460 Marcoussis
France

Ecole Supérieure d'Electricité
Plateau du Moulon
91190 Gif
France

ABSTRACT

MULTILOG is a Logic Programming language intended for **knowledge representation** and manipulation. Its main features are the following :

- knowledge is distributed among different **worlds**

- each world has his own **inference mechanism**

- several **inheritance relations** are provided.

Possible applications of MULTILOG include : hypothetical reasoning, default reasoning, viewpoints representation, distributed reasoning.

1. INTRODUCTION

Our purpose is to use logic programming to represent and manipulate knowledge. Unfortunately, there are features essential in knowledge representation that are difficult to handle if we use a logic programming language such as Prolog <Coimerauer 79>, <Kowalski 79a> :

- Representing and manipulating large amounts of knowledge.
  example : If we want to perform symbolic integration, we need a lot of knowledge ; general knowledge on integration (e.g. the integral of a sum is the sum of the integrals), as well as specific knowledge on rational functions (e.g. how to use the method of partial fractions), on trigonometric expressions (e.g. which are the interesting substitutions such as u = tan(t/2)) , etc.
  This knowledge needs some structure to achieve clarity and efficiency.

- Default reasoning.
  example : We often have to represent facts such as :
  - if you do not know where somebody lives, then it is reasonable to assume that he lives where his work is located.
  - typically, a mammal has four legs.
  Such facts can be expressed in Prolog only through using such extra features as metalevel features (e.g. "clause" built-in predicate) or control facilities (e.g. "!").

- Hypothetical reasoning.
  example : Suppose that we wish to perform troubleshooting on logic circuits. To show that a given component may be responsible for the failure, we hypothesize the faultiness of this component and then check to see whether the circuit outputs observed match the outputs expected.
  It is possible to do this kind of reasoning in Prolog, but side effects built-in predicates such as "assert" and "retract" must be used. Besides, if we want to compare the consequences of two different hypothesis, the problem becomes much more complicated.

- Defining one's own strategy.

example : An expert system in process control has to react to all events that may arise. Therefore it should be data driven and the inference engine should work through forward chaining.

The problem with Prolog is that there is a single strategy : depth first backward chaining. If we want forward chaining, the inference engine of Prolog can not be directly used. Therefore, we will have to build a new level on top of Prolog which provides this forward chaining. Our program will contain both declarative knowledge (the facts and rules) and procedural knowledge telling how to use the declarative knowledge (the inference engine). As argued by Kowalski with his well known formula "Algorithm = Logic + Control" <Kowalski 79b>, it would often be better to separate these two components.

- Simulating an evolution.

example : When trying to generate a plan in the block world, we may wish to represent explicitly the time, i.e. the state of the blocks at each stage of our plan. It would allow us to perform time-based reasoning, for example in order to detect that we are in a loop or that we are farther from the desired state than we were before.

In Prolog, there is a single knowledge base. Therefore, it is difficult to represent the different states of the blocks and hence to perform time-based reasoning.

- Simulating cooperation.

example : When a prime minister has to make a decision, he may ask his different ministers for their opinion and then try to make a synthesis of these opinions.

Prolog is not very well suited for this kind of problems because of the following points :

- again, there is a single knowledge base and therefore it is difficult to represent the viewpoints of different ministers.

- there is no facility to simulate communication between two viewpoints.

Considering such problems led us to the design of MULTILOG, a language which is based on the notion of **world**. A world consists of two components :

- a **knowledge base**, which is a set of clauses.

- an **inference mechanism**, describing *which* inferences can be made from the clauses of the knowledge base and *how* to perform these inferences.

Different worlds can be connected using three **inheritance relations :** a full inheritance relation, an inheritance relation with exceptions and a default inheritance relation.

Several Prolog interpreters already provide the notion of world : Prolog II <Van Caneghem 84>, MProlog <Szeredi 82>, Prolog/KR <Nakashima 84>, ESP <Chikayama 84>, Mandala <Furukawa 84> ... However, their notions of world have not been introduced for the same reason as ours. In Prolog II and MProlog, the goal is the modularity of the language (e.g. ability for two different users to use the same predicate names without ambiguity) and its efficiency (e.g. garbage collection or separate compilations). In Prolog/KR, worlds are used to simulate a Frame based language and in ESP an object oriented language (we will give an example of such uses of worlds in section 2.2). In Mandala, one of the main reasons for introducing worlds is allowing parallelism (several worlds can be active simultaneously). As in ESP, worlds are also used to allow object oriented programming.

Some knowledge representation languages which use another formalism than first order logic also provide notions similar to the one of world : viewpoints in OMEGA <Attardi 84> and in ART <Inference 85>, contexts in SRL <Wright 83>, net spaces in semantic networks <Hendrix 75>, etc.

Compared with all these systems, the main feature of MULTILOG is that reasoning is **local to each world**, with a **specific inference mechanism**. Another interesting feature of MULTILOG is that it provides **several inheritance relations**.

The next section consists in a description of MULTILOG. Then we will describe how MULTILOG could be used in a concrete application : troubleshooting of logic circuits.

2. A DESCRIPTION OF MULTILOG

2.1. Standard clauses and Multiclauses

The knowledge base of a world consists in a set of clauses. There are in fact two kinds of clauses : **standard clauses** and **multiclauses.**

- a standard clause is a classic Horn clause.

- a multiclause has the same form as a standard clause except that each literal of its tail can be either a standard literal or a term of the form "Literal *in* World", where "Literal" and "World" are variables of the metalanguage (English) denoting, respectively, a standard literal and the name of a world, and where "*in*" is a built-in operator of MULTILOG.

Intuitively, when a term of the form "Literal *in* World" lies in the tail of a clause, it means that the literal "Literal" must be proven in the world "World" instead of in the current world.

examples :
- the prime minister.

To represent the fact that a prime minister asks his different ministers for their opinion before making a decision, we could have a world corresponding to each minister. The knowledge base of the prime minister's world could contain a clause such as :

decision(D) :- opinion(O1) in minister1,
opinion(O2) in minister2,
opinion(O3) in minister3,
synthesis(O1,O2,O3,D).

- simulating the "*demo*" predicate introduced by Bowen and Kowalski.

In a well-known paper <Bowen 82>, Bowen and Kowalski argue that logic programming systems should be extended by adding to the original object language the portion of the metalanguage that deals with the derivability relation of the object language. To do this, a predicate "*demo*(X,Y)" is introduced, which means that the goal Y can be proven from the set of clauses X. Such a predicate can be simulated in MULTILOG by creating a world world_X which contains the set of clauses X and by replacing "*demo*(X,Y)" by "Y *in* world_X". This allows us to do for example some non-monotonic reasoning (or default reasoning), as described in <Bowen 82>.

2.2. Three inheritance relations

Three inheritance relations allow us to build an acyclic directed graph of worlds :
- a full inheritance relation
- an inheritance relation with exceptions
- a default inheritance relation.

• **inheritance(World1,World2,full)** is the full inheritance relation. It means that World1 inherits all the clauses of World2.

example : symbolic integration

In this example, we could have a world containing general knowledge and several worlds which inherit from this world and which contain specific knowledge :

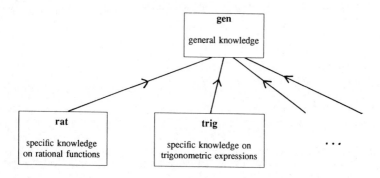

- inheritance(World1,World2,except(List)) is the inheritance relation with exceptions. It means that World1 inherits each clause of World2 whose head can not be unified with a literal of the list List.

example : planning in the block world

The inheritance relation with exceptions makes it very easy to represent an evolution such as :

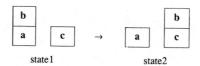

We use a world for each state of the blocks in the following way :

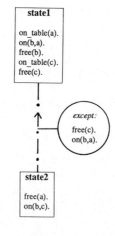

$\uparrow$
: = *inheritance*(state2,state1,except([free(c),on(b,a)]))

remark : Inheritance with exceptions can be seen as providing a solution to the Frame problem

<Mc Carthy 69>. A state change can be simulated by creating a new world containing the new facts and inheriting everything from the previous world except those facts that are no longer true.

• **inheritance(World1,World2,default)** is the default inheritance relation. It means that World1 inherits each clause of World2 except if there is already in World1 - or if World1 inherits through full inheritance or inheritance with exceptions - a clause of the same name. We say that two clauses have the same name if their head literals have the same predicate symbol and the same arity.

example : simulating a Frame-based language.

With MULTILOG, it is very easy to simulate a Frame-based language <Minski 75>. Incidentally, this is the way worlds are used in languages such as Prolog/KR or ESP.

- To each Frame, we assign a world.
- IS-A links are represented by default inheritance relations.
- Each slot of a Frame is represented by a unit clause.
- If-needed demons are represented by non unit clauses (including multiclauses).

The following figure gives an example of this use of MULTILOG. It also illustrates multiple inheritance :

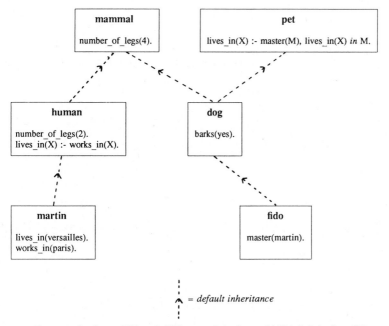

= *default inheritance*

For example, the goal "lives_in(X)" succeeds in the world "fido". It leads to "X = versailles".

2.3. Each world has its own semantics

As said before, a world consists of two components :
- a knowledge base
- an inference mechanism.

The inference mechanism of a world tells both *which* inferences can be made from the knowledge base clauses (declarative semantics) and *how* to perform these inferences (procedural semantics).

The declarative semantics will be mostly the classic semantics given to Horn Clauses (i.e. a goal is true if it is the head of some clause instance and each of the literals in the tail of that clause instance is true). But through the inference mechanism, we can provide some extensions to this classic semantics, for example handling hypothetical implications as in N-Prolog <Gabbay 84>. Further it is possible to give a completely different semantics to the knowledge base clauses : we could imagine a "Mister No" inference mechanism, making nothing and giving the answer "no" to every query.

Concerning the procedural semantics, it is possible to use backward chaining (which can be improved, for example, by adding an intelligent backtracking mechanism <Dincbas 80> or a loop detection mechanism <Brough 84>), or forward chaining (which can include detection of contradictions). It is also possible to combine these two types of control.

MULTILOG provides both some predefined inference mechanisms, for example :
- a pure Prolog inference mechanism
- a local saturation inference mechanism
and the ability to define one´s own inference mechanism.

Defining one´s own inference mechanism for a world World consists in defining three procedures which are :

- **add(World,Head,Tail)** i.e. what to do to add the clause "Head :- Tail" to the world World.

- **remove(World,Head,Tail)** i.e. what to do to remove the clause "Head :- Tail" from the world World.

- **show(World,Goal)** i.e. what to do to show the goal Goal in the world World.

To define these three procedures, we use the language Prolog, considered as a programming language rather than a declarative knowledge representation language. The fact that Prolog is a good tool to write logic programming interpreters has already been mentioned, for example in <Pereira 82>. MULTILOG provides some built-in predicates which can be used to write these three procedures. The five basic ones are :

- **assert_w(World,Head,Tail)** i.e. assert the clause "Head :- Tail" in the knowledge base of the world World.

- **retract_w(World,Head,Tail)** i.e. retract the clause "Head :- Tail" from the knowledge base of the world World.

- **local_clause(World,Head,Tail)** i.e. search for a clause of the world World whose head and tail unify with Head and Tail respectively.

- **global_clause(World,Head,Tail)** i.e. search for a clause of the world World or one inherited by the world World whose head and tail unify with Head and Tail respectively.
Clauses are inherited in the following order : depth first, using first full inheritance relations, then inheritance relations with exceptions, and default inheritance relations last.

-     **add_inheritance_link(World1,World2,Type)**   i.e.   create   the   inheritance   link "inheritance(World1,World2,Type)".

In addition to these five basic built-in predicates, MULTILOG provides many others (e.g. create a new world, remove all the clauses of the knowledge base of a world, delete a world, delete an inheritance link ...)

2.4. Inference mechanism examples

• The "Mister No" inference mechanism can be defined by :
add(World,Head,Tail) :- assert_w(World,Head,Tail)
remove(World,Head,Tail) :- retract_w(World,Head,Tail).
show(World,Head,Tail) :- fail.

• A pure Prolog inference mechanism can be defined by :
add(World,Head,Tail) :- assert_w(World,Head,Tail).

remove(World,Head,Tail) :- retract_w(World,Head,Tail).

show(World,Goal) :- global_clause(World,Goal,Tail),
showlistgoal(World,Tail).

showlistgoal(World,[]).

showlistgoal(World,[Hlist|Tlist]) :-show(World,Hlist),
showlistgoal(World,Tlist).

• A local saturation inference mechanism without removals (e.g. for the process control expert system) could be :
add(World,Head,Tail) :- instanciate([Head|Tail],[Head1|Tail1]),
local_clause(World,Head1,Tail1), !, fail.
/* If "Head :- Tail" is an instance of a clause which already exists in the world World, nothing needs to be done. *instanciate(X,X1)* is a predicate which transforms a term X to a term X1, where each of the variables of X is instanciated. */

add(World,Head,Tail) :- assert_w(World,Head,Tail), fail.
/* The clause is asserted */

add(World,Head,[]) :- !, local_clause(World,H,T), member(Head,T),
verify(World,T), add(World,H,[]).
/* When adding a fact (unit clause), we look for all the clauses which have this fact among their hypotheses and try to apply them. */

add(World,Head,Tail) :- verify(World,Tail), add(World,Head,[]).
/* When adding a rule (non unit clause), we try to apply it. */

remove(World,Head,Tail) :- write('no removals').

show(World,Goal) :- local_clause(World,Goal,[]).
/* we do not take inheritance into account */

verify(World,[]).
verify(World,[Hlist|Tlist]) :- show(World,Hlist), verify(World,Tlist).

• Hypothetical reasoning :
An inference mechanism can be extended to handle clauses with hypothetical implications <Gabbay 84>. A clause with hypothetical implications is a clause where each literal of the tail can be

either a standard literal or a term of the form "P => Q", where P and Q denote standard literals. "P => Q" succeeds from a set of clauses S, if Q succeeds from the set of clauses (S+{P}).

Such hypothetical implications can be handled very easily in MULTILOG : when we have to show an implication "P => Q" in a world W, we first create a world hyp_W which inherits from W and contains only the clause P, then try to show Q in hyp_W and finally delete the world hyp_W. This can be done by adding to the inference mechanism of W the two clauses :

show(W,P=>Q) :- create_world(hyp_W,Inference_mechanism,[]),
                add_inheritance_link(hyp_W,W,full)),
            . *add(hyp_W,P,[]),*
                show(hyp_W,Q),
                !,
                delete_world(hyp_W).

show(W,P=>Q) :- delete_world(hyp_W), fail.

"create_world(Name,Inf_Mech,List)" is a built-in predicate of MULTILOG which :
- creates a world with name Name and with inference mechanism Inf_Mech (either a predefined one or the name of a file which contains a user-defined inference mechanism).
- adds to the knowledge base of Name all the clauses of the files of the list List.

The inference mechanism of Hyp_W can be the same as that of W. It can be also a different one, as will be seen in section 3.

remark : Of course it is possible to handle clauses with hypothetical implications in Prolog. To show an implication "P => Q", we assert P, try to show Q, and then retract P. But two conditions must be satisfied : there must be no free variables in P nor in Q (otherwise, there are some quantification problems), and the call of the goal Q must not create any side effects. The solution presented with MULTILOG leaves unaddressed the problem of free variables in P or Q, but allows what was called side effects in the call of Q. This can be very interesting, because for example it makes it possible to work in forward chaining.

• Combining various inference mechanisms

MULTILOG makes it possible to combine various inference mechanisms within different worlds. For example, it seems interesting to combine backward chaining and local saturation in the following way :

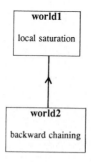

We could imagine such an organization with world1 containing knowledge that is often used and world2 other knowledge.

2.5. Sketch of syntax and semantics

2.5.1. Syntax

A MULTILOG program can be viewed as a set of triplets (where each triplet describes a world) plus a set of inheritance relations :

<program>	=	{<w-name>,<knowledge-base>,<inf-mech>}* <inheritance-rel>*
<w-name>	=	<atom>
<knowledge-base>	=	<kb-clause>*
<inheritance-rel>	=	inheritance(<w-name>,<w-name>,<inh-type>)
<inf-mech>	=	<add-clause>* <remove-clause>* <show-clause>* <clause>*
<kb-clause>	=	<unit-clause> | <non-unit-clause>
<unit-clause>	=	<literal>
<non-unit-clause>	=	<literal> :- <kb-tail>
<kb-tail>	=	<goal> | <goal> , <kb-tail>
<goal>	=	<literal> | <literal> in <w-name>
<inh-type>	=	full | default | except(<list-of-literals>)
<list-of-literals>	=	[ ] | [<literal> ¦ <list-of-literals>]
<add-clause>	=	add(<w-name>,<var>,<var>) :- <tail>
<remove-clause>	=	remove(<w-name>,<var>,<var>) :- <tail>
<show-clause>	=	show(<w-name>,<var>) :- <tail>
<tail>	=	<literal> | <literal> , <tail>

where :
<atom> denotes a Prolog atom
<var> denotes a Prolog variable
<literal> denotes a standard literal, i.e. a term which is not a variable or a number.
<clause> denotes a standard Prolog clause.

2.5.2. Semantics

• Prolog pure built-in predicates and Multiclauses

As has been said, the semantics of knowledge base clauses is provided by the inference mechanism of the considered world, i.e. by definition of the three primitives "add", "retract" and "show". However, MULTILOG automatically provides an extension to the "show" primitive of each world, in order to handle Prolog pure built-in predicates and multiclauses :

- Prolog pure built-in predicates

All the "pure" built-in predicates of Prolog can be used in the clauses of the knowledge base of a world. By pure built-in predicates we mean most of them, except those that modify the knowledge base, the "cut" and the "not". In fact, everything happens as if there were in the inference mechanism of each world World a set of clauses of the form :
show(World,Predef) :- call(Predef). /* where Predef is any pure built-in predicate */

- Multiclauses

Multiclauses can be understood by viewing "*in*" as a built-in predicate, whose definition would be :
"*(Goal* in *World) :- show(World,Goal)*"

Again, everything happens as if there were in the inference mechanism of each world World the following clause :
show(World,Goal in *World1) :- show(World1,Goal).*

• MULTILOG built-in predicates

Inference mechanisms are written in Prolog, using the new built-in predicates provided by MULTILOG. Therefore, their semantics is based on the standard Prolog semantics extended by the new built-in predicates semantics. We will give the semantics of the five basic ones. But before doing this, we first have to state a few definitions of sets used by these predicates.

Let IL be the *ordered* set of all the inheritance links.

Let KB(W), FIKB(W), EIKB(W), DIKB(W) and GIKB(W) be *ordered* clause sets and let $\oplus$ and Σ be, respectively, binary infix and n-ary prefix ordered sets concatenation operators :

KB(W) = {(H,T) | "H :- T" $\in$ knowledge base of world W}.

$$FIKB(W) = \sum_{W' \mid inheritance(W,W',full) \in IL} GKB(W')$$

$$EIKB(W) = \sum_{W' \mid inheritance(W,W',except(L)) \in IL} \{(H,T) \mid (H,T) \in GKB(W') \& (\not\exists X \in L \mid unifiable(X,H))\}$$

$$DIKB(W) = \sum_{W' \mid inheritance(W,W',default) \in IL} \{(H,T) \mid (H,T) \in GKB(W') \&$$
$$(\not\exists (H1,T1) \in KB(W) \cup FIKB(W) \cup EIKB(W) \mid$$
$$predname(H) = predname(H1) \& args\_nbr(H) = args\_nbr(H1))\}$$

GKB(W) = KB(W) $\oplus$ FIKB(W) $\oplus$ EIKB(W) $\oplus$ DIKB(W)

Now, we can give the semantics of the five basic built-in predicates of MULTILOG. In the following description, concepts as environment, backtracking point list, and functions such as car, cdr, append, remove, first_clause and backtrack denote usual Prolog interpreter entities.

Let K be the knowledge base set :   K = {KB(W)} for all W.

E   environment (variable links).
R   remaining goals.
B   backtracking point list.

MULTILOG manages states which are 5-upple :   S := (K,IL,E,R,B).

Initial state is : $S_0 := (K_0,IL_0,\varnothing,g,\varnothing)$ where g is the goal.

Final state is : $S_f := (K_f,IL_f,E_f,\varnothing,B_f)$ where E_f contains g goal variable links and B_f remaining backtracking points.

Let us describe how MULTILOG basic built-in predicates modify the state S : $S_{i+1} := step(S_i)$. Only changing state variables are described.

step(S$_i$)

  case car(R$_i$)

    = *assert_w(W,H,T)*

        $KB_{i+1}(W) := append(KB_i(W),\{(H,T)\})$

        $R_{i+1} := cdr(R_i)$

    = *retract_w(W,H,T)*

        $(TF,E,B,(H1,T1)) := first\_clause(KB_i(W),(H,T))$

/* TF : true or false; E : new variable links; B : new backtracking points; (H1,T1) : the founded clause. */

        if TF = true then

            $KB_{i+1}(W) := remove((H1,T1),KB_i(W))$

            $E_{i+1} := append(E,E_i)$

            $R_{i+1} := cdr(R_i)$

            $B_{i+1} := append(B,B_i)$

        if TF = false then $(E_{i+1},R_{i+1},B_{i+1}) := backtrack(E_i,R_i,B_i)$

    = *add_inheritance_link(W1,W2,IT)*

        $IL_{i+1} := append(IL_i,inheritance(W1,W2,IT))$

        $R_{i+1} := cdr(R_i)$

    = *local_clause(W,H,T)*

        $(TF,E,B,\_) := first\_clause(KB_i(W),(H,T))$

        if TF = true then

            $E_{i+1} := append(E,E_i)$

            $R_{i+1} := cdr(R_i)$

            $B_{i+1} := append(B,B_i)$

        if TF = false then $(E_{i+1},R_{i+1},B_{i+1}) := backtrack(E_i,R_i,B_i)$

    = *global_clause(W,H,T)*

        $(TF,E,B,\_) := first\_clause(GKB_i(W),(H,T))$

        if TF = true then

            $E_{i+1} := append(E,E_i)$

            $R_{i+1} := cdr(R_i)$

            $B_{i+1} := append(B,B_i)$

        if TF = false then $(E_{i+1},R_{i+1},B_{i+1}) := backtrack(E_i,R_i,B_i)$

3. A LOGIC CIRCUIT TROUBLESHOOTING SYSTEM

3.1. The problem

In this section, we will describe how MULTILOG (and hypothetical reasoning) could be used to make some troubleshooting on logic circuits. Here is the kind of circuits we would like to consider :

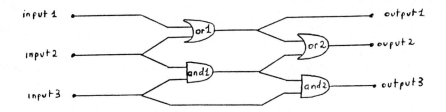

To restrict the problem, we will make the hypothesis that there is a single failure and assume that this failure can only be a faulty component (whose output is stuck at 0) or a short circuit.

3.2. Our solution

Therefore it seems to be a good solution to use three worlds :

- a world world1 contains the description of the circuit and some general knowledge. For example :

or_gate(or1).
/* or1 is an or gate */

link(input1,input1(or1)).
/* there is a link between input1 and the first input of or1 */

link(output(and1),input2(or2)).
/* there is a link between the output of and1 and the second input of or2 */

transforms(Component,Value1,Value2,Value) :- or_gate(Component),
or_function(Value1,Value2,Value).

or_function(0,0,0).
or_function(1,_,1).
or_function(_,1,1).

- a world world2, which fully inherits from world1, describes the behaviour of the circuit when there may be a faulty component but when there is no other failure. This world contains the following clauses :

value(output(C),0) :- faulty(C).
/* when a component is faulty, we assume that its output is stuck at 0 */

value(output(C),V) :- not faulty(C),
value(input1(C),V1),
value(input2(C),V2),
transforms(C,V1,V2,V).

value(X,V) :- link(Y,X), value(Y,V).
/* there is no short circuit */

- a world world3, which also fully inherits from world1, describes the behaviour of the circuit when there may be a short circuit but when there is no other failure :

value(X,Value) :- link(Y,X),
                        shortcircuit(link(Y,X),link(Y1,X1)),
                        value(Y,V),
                        value(Y1,V1),
                        or_function(V,V1,Value).

/* shortcircuit(link(Y,X),link(Y1,X1)) means that there is a short circuit between the links Y → X and Y1 → X1 */

value(X,V) :- link(Y,X),
                   not shortcircuit(link(Y,X),_),
                   value(Y,V).

value(output(C),V) :- value(input1(C),V1),
                            value(input2(C),V2),
                            transforms(C,V1,V2,V).

/* all components are good */

By now, we can simulate the behaviour of the circuit either when a component is faulty or when there is a short circuit. But how can we troubleshoot ? To show that a given component (or a given short circuit) may be responsible for the failure, we hypothesize the faultiness of this component (or the existence of this short circuit) and check to see whether the circuit outputs observed match the outputs expected. This can be done using clauses with hypothetical implications.

in world2 :

suspect_component(C) :- observed_output(O1,O2,O3),
                                    (faulty(C) => output(O1,O2,O3)).

in world3 :

suspect_shortcircuit(L1,L2) :- observed_output(O1,O2,O3),
                                             (shortcircuit(L1,L2) => output(O1,O2,O3)).

We then need in the knowledge base of world1 the following two multiclauses :

suspect(component(C)) :- suspect_component(C) in world2.

suspect(shortcircuit(L1,L2)) :- suspect_shortcircuit(L1,L2) in world3.

Concerning the inference mechanisms, we can use a prolog-like inference mechanism in world1, world2 and world3. We could also use such an inference mechanism in hyp_world2 and hyp_world3 but it would lead to serious efficiency problems because the same facts (i.e. the values of the different terminals) would have to be proven many times. Therefore, we prefer to use in these two worlds a forward chaining inference mechanism.

3.3. Summary

Let us describe what happens if we want to know whether and1 is a suspect component. We first have to add to world1 the values of the inputs and observed outputs. Then we call the goal "suspect(component(and1))" in the world world1. It leads to the creation of a world hyp_world2 (see next figure), which will be later deleted.

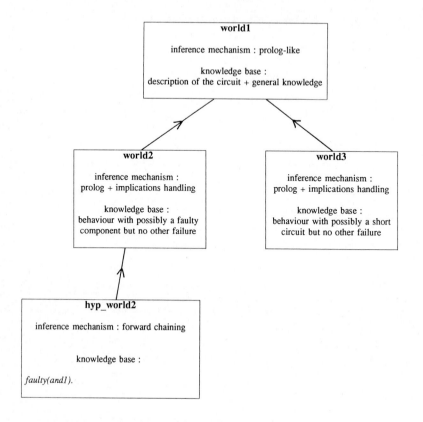

Interesting points illustrated by this example are :
- hypothetical reasoning.
- the ability to use two worlds to simulate two different types of behaviour of the circuit. For instance, the predicate "value" has not got the same definition in world2 and world3.
- the ability to use various strategies (backward chaining and forward chaining).

4. CONCLUSION

A prototype of MULTILOG has been implemented in Prolog. It runs on a VAX-780/UNIX (using C-Prolog <Pereira 84>) and on a SUN workstation (using Quintus Prolog <Bowen 85>).

On a SUN workstation, naive reverse of a 30 elements list (using a single world, whose inference mechanism is a pure Prolog inference mechanism) needs about 2.5s. As a comparison, the same example needs about 1.1s if we use interpreted Quintus Prolog.

Besides the examples presented in this paper, it has been used, for instance, for the Three Wise Men puzzle <Attardi 84> <Kauffmann 86b> and in the field of logic databases <Gallaire 84> <Kauffmann 86a>.

Some limitations arise from the impossibility of defining one´s own inheritance relations or defining the order in which clauses are inherited. It would also be useful to clarify the various ways MULTILOG worlds can be used.

Actually, thanks to the notion of local reasoning, MULTILOG allows us to handle problem solving types such as :
- cooperative reasoning, needed for example in distributed problem solving or default reasoning.
- concurrent reasoning, including hypothetical reasoning or managing different viewpoints.

REFERENCES

G. Attardi & M. Simi : "Metalanguage and Reasoning Across Viewpoints", Proc. European Conference on Artificial Intelligence, 1984.

D. Bowen et al. : "Quintus Prolog Reference Manual", Quintus Computer Systems, May 1985.

K.A. Bowen & R. Kowalski : "Amalgamating Language and Metalanguage in Logic Programming", in "Logic Programming", Clark & Tärnlund (Eds.), Academic Press, 1982.

D.R. Brough & A. Walker : "Some practical properties of logic programming interpreters", Proc. International Conference on Fifth Generation Computer Systems, 1984.

T. Chikayama : "Unique Features of ESP", Proc. International Conference on Fifth Generation Computer Systems, 1984.

A. Colmerauer, H. Kanoui & M. Van Caneghem : "Etude et Réalisation d'un système Prolog", Internal Report, University of Aix-Marseille II, May 1979.

M. Dincbas : "The METALOG problem solving system", Proc. Logic Programming Workshop, Debrecen, July 1980.

K. Furukawa et al. : "Mandala, a logic based knowledge programming system", Proc. International Conference on Fifth Generation Computer Systems, 1984.

D.M. Gabbay & U. Reyle : "N-Prolog : an extension of Prolog with hypothetical implications", in "The journal of logic programming 1/4", December 1984.

H. Gallaire, J. Minker & J.M. Nicolas : "Logic and Databases : a Deductive Approach", ACM Computing Surveys, Vol 16, No 2, pp 153-185, June 1984.

G.G. Hendrix : "Expanding the utility of semantic networks through partitioning", Proc. International Joint Conference on Artificial Intelligence, 1975.

Inference Corporation : "ART Reference Manual", 1985.

H. Kauffmann & A. Grumbach : "Representing and manipulating knowledge within worlds", Proc. First International Conference on Expert Database Systems, 1986a.

H. Kauffmann : "MULTILOG : utilisation de mondes en programmation logique pour représenter et manipuler des connaissances", Thèse de troisième cycle, University of Paris VI, June 1986b.

R. Kowalski : "Logic for Problem Solving", Artificial Intelligence series, North Holland, 1979a.

R. Kowalski : "Algorithm = Logic + Control", Communications of the ACM, Volume 22, No 7, July 1979b.

J. Mc Carthy & P.J. Hayes : "Some philosophical problems from the standpoint of Artificial Intelligence", in Machine Intelligence 4, pp 463-502, B. Meltzer and D. Michie (Eds), Edinburgh University Press, 1969.

M. Minsky : "A Framework for Representing Knowledge", in "The Psychology of Computer Vision", P. Winston (Ed.), McGraw-Hill, New York, 1975.

H. Nakashima : "Knowledge Representation in Prolog/KR", Proc. International Symposium on Logic Programming, 1984.

F. Pereira : "C-Prolog user's manual", EdCAAD, University of Edinburgh, 1984.

L.M. Pereira : "Logic Control with Logic", Proc. First International Logic Programming Conference, 1982.

P. Szeredi : "Module concepts for Prolog", Proc. Workshop on "Prolog Programming Environments", Linköping, Sweden, 24-26 March 1982.

M. Van Caneghem : "L'anatomie de Prolog II", Thèse d'Etat, University of Aix-Marseille II, October 1984.

J.M. Wright and M.S. Fox : "SRL/1.5 User Manual", Technical Report, Carnegie-Mellon University, 1983.

Advances in Artificial Intelligence - II
B. Du Boulay, D. Hogg and L. Steels (Editors)
© Elsevier Science Publishers B.V. (North-Holland), 1987

INTROSPECTION IN KNOWLEDGE REPRESENTATION.

Pattie Maes

Artificial Intelligence Laboratory
Vrije Universiteit Brussel
Pleinlaan 2
1050 Brussels
Belgium

ABSTRACT

Introspective systems are systems that reason about themselves.
They access representations of themselves and modify these in a
causally connected way. The paper tries to clarify what introspection
means and what the relationship is with concepts such as meta-
knowledge and reflection. The technical requirements of introspective
systems are discussed and previous attempts to construct such systems
are compared. The relation between the model an introspective system
has of itself and its introspective power is discussed. It is shown how a
knowledge representation language can be provided with a framework
for introspection and how a lot of functions become facilitated and
more smoothly integrated. Examples are non-monotonic reasoning,
error handling, learning and control.

1. INTRODUCTION.

Introspection has recently become an active research topic in Artificial Intelligence (AI) research. The literature abundantly argues for introspection and related
topics such as reflection, meta-knowledge and meta-reasoning. It is commonly
agreed that it is a crucial quality of intelligence and that it substantially increases the
expressive and deductive power of AI systems (Batali,1983; Aiello,1984; Barr,1979;
Davis and Buchanan,1979; Doyle,1980; Smith,1982).

A lot of intelligent functions are by nature introspective. They require an intelligent system to be able to reason about itself. Consider for example learning. The
goal of a system with learning capabilities is to improve its performance at some task
by reasoning about its own problem solving. Other examples of intelligent functions
that exhibit an introspective behavior are assumption-based reasoning, handling
inconsistent or uncertain knowledge, handling errors and control of reasoning.

Until now, these functions were implemented in knowledge representation in an
ad hoc way. Analysing these (mostly very complex) functions in terms of introspection makes them become better understood and more easily tractable. It elucidates

This research was supported by ESPRIT (project 440). The author is a
research assistant of the Belgian National Fund for Scientific Research.

design choices, facilitates the comparison and experimentation with alternative choices and the making of extensions. It is therefore important that knowledge representation languages provide a framework for the representation of introspective knowledge.

But the issues related to introspection are very complex and at the moment still badly understood. Papers by Aiello (1984), which contains a survey of meta-knowledge, and Batali (1983), which discusses computational introspection, are valuable efforts to bring some perspective to the field. An even less understood issue is that of actually building introspective systems. That is probably the reason why there exist a lot of systems with limited, compiled-in introspective abilities, but only few that provide an explicit and uniform framework for introspection. This paper tries to clarify what introspection means and identifies the problems that have to be faced in building the latter type of systems.

The structure of the paper is as follows. Section two presents some definitions related to introspection. Section three gives a survey of the important approaches to introduce some form of introspection into AI systems. Section four discusses the techniques for providing a language with a framework for introspection. Section five stresses the importance of the representations an introspective system has of itself for the introspective power that it can exploit. Section six briefly introduces an object-oriented knowledge representation language that provides a framework for introspection. Section seven demonstrates how a lot of intelligent functions that were previously supported in ad hoc ways, can be smoothly integrated into such a language. Finally section eight contains some conclusions.

2. INTROSPECTIVE SYSTEMS.

Introspection is the process of thinking about one's own thoughts. Since AI adopts the computation-paradigm to discuss aspects of thinking, this paper is concerned with computational systems that introspect or "computational systems about themselves".

The aim of a **computational system** (abbreviated "system" in the rest of the paper) is to anwer **questions** about some particular problem domain and/or to support **actions** in this domain. An accounting system, for example, is able to answer questions about financial transactions and the state of various accounts. It also supports the creation of new accounts, transfers between accounts, etc.

A **meta-system** is a computational system whose problem domain is another computational system. It answers questions about and supports actions in its **object-system**. E.g. a program optimiser answers questions about programs and supports making modifications to programs.

An **introspective system** is a meta-system whose problem domain is itself. It answers questions about itself and supports actions in itself. An example of an introspective system is a system with learning capabilities. It answers questions about itself and modifies itself in such a way that its performance at a certain task improves.

3. HOW CAN INTROSPECTIVE SYSTEMS BE BUILT?

Several approaches to build introspective systems can be identified. They can be classified according to the paradigm that is used for combining object-system and meta-system.

First, there are introspective systems that incorporate some form of introspection in a wired-in (or compiled-in) way. A limitation of this approach is that the introspective framework is not explicit and therefore not accessible to the user. For example, learning systems exhibit introspective knowledge because they are able to improve themselves. But most learning systems today are only capable of introspecting upon some predefined aspects in a predefined way. E.g. some learning systems modify themselves (e.g. the rules they use) by chunking the results of previously experienced problems (e.g. SOAR (Laird, Rosenbloom and Newell,1984)), while other systems improve themselves by making analogies the moment a new problem has to be solved, etc. The design choices, such as what situations trigger the introspective computation, what representations are manipulated during introspection or how these manipulations affect the future performance of the system, are not explicit. This makes it difficult to compare different designs or experiment with alternatives.

Second, we can identify a group of computational systems that make use of introspective facilities provided by the language by which they are implemented. These languages can be classified in two categories.

On the one hand, there are languages that provide explicit meta-constructs, i.e. constructs to access and manipulate representations of systems, in the object-level itself. Object-level and meta-level computation takes place in the same context. LISP, for example, provides meta-constructs such as quote, eval and apply. These functions can be used in the object-level computation as in:

(car '(+ 1 2)) --> +

Systems that make use of these meta-constructs have again limited possibilities for introspection, because the object-systems that are being manipulated (such as the expression "(+ 1 2)" in the above example) are not real objects in a meta-level context. In the above example it is only possible to reason about the expression "(+ 1 2)" as being a syntactic form (a list). It is not possible to reason about the denotation of this expression (the addition of numbers 2 and 3) or about the result of its evaluation (i.e. "3").

On the other hand, there are languages that provide a uniform framework for the specification of introspective knowledge. Examples of such languages are 3-LISP (Smith,1982), FOL (Weyhrauch,1980) and TORPIT (Doyle,1980). These languages allow all systems implemented in them to introspect upon themselves in an explicit and uniform way. A characteristic of these languages is that object-level systems are identical to meta-level systems: they have the same representational and computational behavior with "linking rules" between the two levels to guarantee the communication of results. Because object-system and meta-system are identical, introspection can recurse infinitely.

Figure 1 presents an example of an introspective system in 3-LISP. Divide is a procedure for dividing two numbers x and y. It specifies object-level and meta-level

computation: the procedure introspects upon itself before applying the standard procedure for dividing two numbers. It will check in the reflective lambda expression
whether the divisor is bound, and if not, take it to be "1" in the continuing object–
level computation.

```
(DEFUN divide (x y)
  (/ x
   (lambda REFLECT (arg env cont)
     (if (not (binding arg env))
         (cont (rebind arg 1 env)))
     y)))
```
                                                                         Fig. 1.

The lambda function has access to representations of itself by means of the variables
cont (representing its continuation) and env (representing the current bindings). It is
able to inspect them (e.g. checking the binding of a variable) and to modify them
(e.g. changing the continuation or changing the binding of a variable). When the
function divide is called, for example in:

$$\text{(let ((z 12))} \qquad\qquad\qquad (1)$$
$$\text{(divide z r))}$$

The continuation of the lambda function will be modified to be the result of rebind-
ing variable y to number 1. The object–level computation will continue with the
modified computation, such that (1) returns "12".

4. LANGUAGES WITH A FRAMEWORK FOR INTROSPECTION.

A lot of confusion with the term "introspection" originates from a failure to
respect the distinction between **languages with a framework for introspection** and
computational systems that actually show an introspective behavior. A language with
a framework for introspection supports the construction of potentially introspective
systems: systems implemented in it have the capability to introspect. Such a language
must have the expressive power for building introspective systems. For this it has to
fulfill the following three requirements:

First, the language–interpreter has to be able to **construct an explicit model** of a
system and its current state at any moment in time. It is on the basis of these
representations that the system will be able to introspect, i.e. to answer questions
about itself and support actions upon itself. The 3–LISP language, for example, is
able to construct a model of any procedure that is implemented in it. The model that
is built consists of two lisp–variables that represent the current environment and continuation of the computation. By accessing these variables, the procedure is able to
reason about itself and to modify its own behavior during its computation. For example, the "rebind" function call in the above example will mutate the environment,
such that "arg" is bound to "1".

A second problem is the **architecture of introspection**. The language must provide a means to specify when the object–level computation of a system should be
halted to jump to a meta–level where one can access and manipulate explicit

representations of that system and its current state. It should be possible to specify when to return to the object–level computation. Concretely, this means that there are two linking functions:

introspect, which causes a jump to the meta–level of a system,

resume[1], which continues the object–level computation.

One technique that can be used to implement the introspect–function, is the technique of "reflection". **Reflection** (Smith,1982) is a form of introspection where the jump to the meta–level is controlled by the systems themselves. They are able to specify interrupts during their own computation which bring the computational activity to a meta–level. TORPIT (Doyle,1980) presents an alternative architecture, where the introspective activities are controlled by a global "meta–agent". In SOAR (Laird, Rosenbloom and Newell,1984) the introspective activities are caused by an impasse during problem solving. E.g. when the computation cannot proceed, an introspective activity is set up which will try to resolve the impasse at a meta–level.

A third problem to be faced is the **causal connection** requirement (Batali,1983). The model of the system that is manipulated at the meta–level has to be connected to the system itself in such a way that when the meta–level computation is resumed, the object–level computation continues with a system and state that is in accord with this model. Vice-versa, the model of a system always has to be consistent with the actual state of the system. Languages such as OMEGA (Attardi and Simi,1984) incorporate a "read-only" model of systems: it is possible to answer questions about a system, but when the model is changed, the system does not change accordingly. Therefore these languages do not provide an introspective framework.

The most common technique to solve the causal connection problem is to use the explicit representations of the system to run the system, i.e. to make the language operational by means of a circular interpreter (Abelson and Sussman,1985). A necessary condition to let a language actually operate by means of a circular interpreter is that there exists a second interpreter written in another language which is able to interpret the circular one (in order not to fall into a loop of circular interpreters interpreting circular interpreters)[2]. It should be guaranteed that these two interpreters cause exactly the same behavior.

5. INTROSPECTION IS THEORY RELATIVE.

Not all languages with an introspective framework provide equal introspective possibilities. The introspective power of a language is **theory relative** (Batali,1983), which means that the model a computational system has of itself in the language determines what introspective activities become possible. This model can focus upon different aspects of the computational systems, which results into different powerful applications of the introspective framework:[3]

---

[1] The resume-function is superfluous when the introspection happens by means of a function-call.

[2] Two interpreters are necessary, but also sufficient: we can generate meta[n] interpreter-levels by recursively using the circular interpreter.

[3] The discussion is illustrated with a logic language, but the same as-

a) The syntactical aspect.

The model may focus upon the syntactical aspect of computational systems, i.e. upon the syntactic form of objects at the object-level. In such a language systems have the possibility to reason about or manipulate the syntax of the language from within the language itself. A system can for example extend this syntax by stating that:

$$Is\text{-}legal\text{-}construct("P <=> Q.").$$

From that moment on, it would be possible to use this new syntax construct (although there is not yet a meaning associated with it).

b) The semantic aspect.

The model may focus upon the semantic aspect of computational systems, i.e. upon the rules to relate the syntactic structures of computational systems to objects in their problem domain. In such a language, systems can change the semantics of the language or extend it with meaningful constructs:

$$Same("P <=> Q.","P <= Q." \text{ and } "Q <= P.").$$

An advantage of such a language is that it has local semantics (Weyhrauch, 1980), i.e. it is free of unconcealed assumptions and irrelevant associations of meaning.

c) The deductive aspect.

The model may focus upon the deductive aspect of computational systems, i.e. upon the allowable inferences one can make in a computational system. In such a language systems are able to prove properties about their own inference theory (e.g. monotonicity, provability) or to extend it, as in:

$$Is\text{-}Fact("Innocent(X).") <= Not\text{-}Provable("Guilty(X).").$$

d) The control aspect.

The model may focus upon the control aspect of computational systems, i.e. upon how it is decided what inferences are actually made at a specific moment in time. In such a language systems have the possibility to reason about and experiment with different control strategies. For example:

$$Is\text{-}goal("P.") <= Is\text{-}goal("Q.")$$
$$\text{and } Not\text{-}is\text{-}fact("Q.")$$
$$\text{and } Is\text{-}horn\text{-}clause("Q <= P.").$$

e) The operational aspect.

The model may focus upon the operational aspect of computational systems, i.e. how they are emulated by a computational medium. In such a language, systems have the possibility to reason about how they are being processed. For example, when the language is PROLOG and this PROLOG is interpreted by means of an interpreter written in LISP, then the systems can reason about the LISP computation that is being performed while processing them. They can for example reason about their own performance or modify their own interpreter such that it becomes a lazy-

---

pects can be identified in other languages.

interpreter, etc.

But the introspective power is not only determined by the aspects the language takes into account. Even two languages that focus upon the same aspect(s) of computational systems can be suited for completely different introspective activities. For example, one language can have a model of the operational aspect of systems in terms of machine concepts such as registers and instructions, which makes it suited for reasoning about the time and space requirements of systems. While another language may model the operational aspect in terms of high-level concepts such as programming cliches, which makes it suited to reason about the algorithmic aspects of the interpretation, but less for reasoning about time and space trade-offs. So there is no such thing as a complete or optimal model of computational systems.

6. INTROSPECTION IN A KNOWLEDGE REPRESENTATION LANGUAGE.

The aim of this section and the following one is to illustrate concretely how introspection can be incorporated into knowledge representation and what kind of functionalities it provides. Several valuable efforts to build introspection into procedural languages, e.g. 3-LISP (Smith,1982), logic languages, e.g. FOL (Weyhraugh,1980), and production rule languages, e.g. SOAR (Laird, Rosenbloom and Newell,1984), can be identified. Since object-oriented formalisms are increasingly used as a basis for knowledge representation languages (cfr. KEE, LOOPS, etc.), the discussion here is illustrated by means of an object-oriented language, called KRS (Steels,1985).

Computational systems in KRS consist of **concepts**. A concept is like a frame. It has **subjects** which are like the slots of a frame. Everything in KRS is a concept. The introspective model of a concept is called the **meta-concept** of a concept. It contains the methods to make an instance of the concept, to print the concept, to inherit information in the concept, to let the concept handle a message, etc. It stores information such as who created the concept, when it was created or how many time it is accessed.

Every concept in KRS has such a meta-concept. Thus also meta-concepts and meta-meta-concepts and so on. When the definition of a concept does not specify what sort of meta-concept should be constructed for the concept, the concept is given a default-meta-concept. A default-meta-concept describes the concept in a standard way. It is possible to explicitly define what sort of model should be constructed for a concept. Most of the time such a meta-concept is defined as a specialisation of the default-meta-concept, as illustrated in figure 2. The model concept foo has of itself is richer than the default model, because it also maintains how many instances of foo were constructed.

The computation of a concept always takes place at the meta-level, i.e. in the meta-concept of the concept. Whenever something should happen with a concept, e.g. if it has to be instantiated or if it has to respond to a message, the computation is handled by the meta-concept of the concept. So a meta-concept is a circular interpreter for its concept. For example, if the message bar is send to concept foo:

(send foo bar)

this will result in the sending of the following message:

```
        concept DEFAULT-META-CONCEPT
        how-to-make-instances: a procedure to make an instance
                               of the concept
        how-to-print: a procedure to print the concept
        how-to-respond-to-message (x): a procedure to let the
                               concept respond to a message x
        how-to-inherit-information (x): a procedure that delegates the
                               message x to the type of the
                               concept
            ...

        concept META-OF-FOO-CONCEPT
        type: default-meta-concept
        my-concept: foo
        number-of-instances-of-me: an integer
        how-to-make-instances: a procedure that makes an instance of
                               the concept foo and increments the variable
                               number-of-instances-of-me with one

        concept FOO
        meta: meta-of-foo-concept
                                                        Fig. 2.
```

(send meta-of-foo-concept (how-to-respond-to-message bar))

The meta-of-foo-concept will compute how its concept foo will handle this message. At this level, the concept itself (because a meta-concept has a backpointer to its concept) and an explicit model of its behavior (in terms of the meta-concept) are accessible to reason about or to make modifications. E.g. the concept can be questioned about its current state, this state can be modified, extra slots for the concept can be created, or even its meta-concept can be modified. By means of this architecture every concept has the possibility to show introspective behavior. Figure 3 shows a concept that modifies its instance-variable my-most-recent-instance when a new instance of it is created.

```
        concept DATE
        my-most-recent-instance: date-245
        meta: meta-of-date-concept

        concept META-OF-DATE-CONCEPT
        type: default-meta-concept
        my-concept: date
        how-to-make-instances: a procedure that makes an instance
                               of the concept date and that sets the
                               variable my-most-recent-instance of
                               date to the newly created instance
                                                        Fig. 3.
```

Computation in KRS can be viewed as an infinite tower of meta–concepts all reasoning about the level below. The lowest level reasons about the actual problem domain. The other levels manipulate causally connected representations of the level below. It is technically possible to implement this infinity because a specific application will only use a finite number of meta–concept levels. So one only needs to construct meta–concepts when their concept makes use of its introspective abilities.

Since all computation of concepts is handled by means of circular object–oriented interpretation, the causal connection requirement is fulfilled: the manipulations at the meta–level affect the computation of the concept. But because the meta–concept of a concept is again a concept, a second interpreter is needed to make this interpretation actually work. The trick that is used is that the default–meta–concept is emulated by an interpreter written in LISP.

When a concept has a default–meta–concept, it will be handled by this LISP–program: it is this program that will compute how the concept responds to a message, how an instance of the concept is created, etc. The jump to the introspective circular interpreter is only performed when there is a deviation, e.g. when the concept has another form of inheritance or another way to create instances. This means that in practice there will always be a finite tower of circular interpreters.

7. The use of introspection in knowledge representation.

A lot of intelligent functions exhibit an introspective behavior. Until now, they were implemented into knowledge representation in an ad hoc way. This section shows how they would be implemented in a knowledge representation that provides a uniform framework for the specification of introspective knowledge. By explicitly representing introspective knowledge, the semantics of the knowledge representation language become simplified and its expressive and deductive power enlarged.

7.1. Assumption–based reasoning.

Assumption–based reasoning is a typical example of introspection. An AI–system may decide to assume some fact when it understands that it does not have sufficient information. Examples of assumption–based reasoning are defaults, non–monotonic reasoning and some forms of inheritance. Most knowledge representation languages provide some fixed forms of assumption–based reasoning, which are wired into the interpreter of the language. They do not allow different forms unless by making modifications to the actual interpreter. By representing this knowledge as introspective knowledge, the semantics of the language become explicit and simplified. Figure 4 presents an example. The concept John shows an introspective behavior. It uses a default–value for its age if the age of John is really needed in some computation and no value can be found. E.g:

> (send john age)

will return "25". But this value is not visible when for example printing the concept John. If some concept requires a different form of default–handling (e.g. defaults should be cached), one simply gives it another default–handling meta–concept.

```
        concept JOHN
          age: no value
          meta: meta-of-john

        concept META-OF-JOHN
          type: default-handling-meta
          my-concept: john
          defaults: ((age 25))

        concept DEFAULT-HANDLING-META
          type: default-meta-concept
          defaults: a list of variables with associated default-values
          how-to-respond-to-message (x): a procedure that first tries
                                         to handle the message x in the
                                         default way and if negative
                                         returns the default-value for
                                         x if there is one
```
                                                                      Fig. 4.

7.2. Learning.

Also learning activities can most naturally be analysed in terms of the introspective architecture:

(i) What representations are manipulated and modified during learning,

(ii) What situations trigger learning,

(iii) In which way do these modifications affect the behavior of the system in future related situations.

Figure 5 presents an example of a production-program with simple learning capabilities. The system learns new rules by chunking results of previous inferences. When the message:

(send production-program-1 result)

will be sent, the result will be that first all inferences are made that can be made by applying the rules rule1 and rule2 exhaustively upon the initial working memory. And second a new rule is created, which memorizes the results of this production program:

```
        concept RULE3
          type: rule
          if-part: (q1)
          then-part: (q1 q2 q3)
```

7.3. Handling inconsistent, incomplete and uncertain knowledge.

A lot of AI-systems have to be able to handle inconsistent, incomplete and uncertain knowledge. These functions are typically introspective. They require a system to be able to reason about the limits of its own capabilities. Figure 6 presents an example of a production program that is able to identify whether its rules are inconsistent. When the message:

concept RULE
    if–part: *a list of properties that have to be true*
    then–part: *a list of properties that will be asserted*
    definition: *a procedure that checks if all properties*
                in the if–part are true and if positive,
                asserts all properties in the then–part

concept PRODUCTION–PROGRAM
    initialisation: *the initial values for the properties*
                 in the working–memory
    result: *a procedure that activates all rules upon*
          the working–memory, untill no new values can
          be derived
    working–memory: *a list of properties*
    rules: *a list of rules*
    meta: meta–of–production–program

concept META–OF–PRODUCTION–PROGRAM
    type: default–meta–concept
    my–concept: production–program
    how–to–respond–to–message (x): *A procedure that first lets*
                                the concept respond to the message
                                x in the default way, and that
                                second, if x is equal to
                                "result", creates a new
                                instance of a rule, which has
                                as if–part the initial state of
                                the working–memory and as then–part
                                the final state

concept RULE1
    type: rule
    if–part: (q1)
    then–part: (q2)

concept RULE2
    type: rule
    if–part: (q2)
    then–part: (q3)

concept PRODUCTION–PROGRAM–1
    type: production–program
    initialisation: ((q1 true) (q2 unknown) (q3 unknown))
    working–memory: (q1 q2 q3)
    rules: (rule1 rule2)

Fig. 5.

(send production–program–2 result)

is sent, it will return with an error–message telling that the combination of rule1 and rule3 causes an infinite loop.

```
concept RULE1
  type: rule
  if-part: (p1)
  then-part:(p2 notp1)

concept RULE2
  type: rule
  if-part: (p2)
  then-part: (p3)

concept RULE3
  type: rule
  if-part: (p3)
  then-part: (p1 notp3)

concept A-SPECIAL-PRODUCTION-PROGRAM
  type: production-program
  meta: inconsistent-rule-set-handling-meta

concept INCONSISTENT-RULE-SET-HANDLING-META
  type: default-meta-system
  my-concept: a-special-production-program
  rules-analysis (rule-set): a procedure that returns false,
                             unless it identifies two rules Ri
                             and Rj in the rule-set, such that Ri
                             makes (possibly indirectly) its own
                             if-part false and that of Rj true
                             and vice-versa.
  how-to-handle-message (x): a procedure that when x is
                             equal to "result", checks
                             the rules of its concept by activating
                             the rules-analysis method and if
                             negative, handles the "result" message
                             as normally, if positive gives an
                             error-message

concept PRODUCTION-PROGRAM-2
  type: a-special-production-program
  rules: (rule1 rule2 rule3)
  working-memory: (p1 p2 p3)
  initialisation: ((p1 true) (p2 unknown) (p3 unknown))
```

Fig. 6.

7.4. Demons.

Demons are a typical example of introspection. They require a system to be able to look at its own state of computation and to perform a side-effect whenever some specific action is performed. Figure 7 presents an example of a concept that mutates itself. It destroys itself once that it was asked for some information. When the concept self-destroying-concept receives the message:

(send self-destroying-message code)

```
          concept SELF-DETROYING-CONCEPT
          meta: self-destruction-meta
          code: a procedure that prints "the code is 2648"

          concept SELF-DESTRUCTION-META
          meta:  default-meta-concept
          my-concept: self-destroying-concept
          how-to-respond-to-message (x): a procedure that, if x is
                                    the message "code", returns
                                    an answer and redefines itself
                                    to be the empty-concept
```

Fig. 7.

for the first time, the string "the code is 2648" will be returned and self-destroying-concept will be redefined to be the empty-concept (a concept without information). The next time self-destruction-concept is asked for its definition the answer will be empty.

8. CONCLUSION.

An introspective system is a system that has causally connected access to representations of itself. It can answer questions about itself and is able to modify itself. Several approaches to build introspective systems can be identified. The most powerful approach is to provide introspection as a basic feature of a language. Three problems have to be faced: the construction of an explicit model, the architecture for introspection and the causal connection problem. The paper presented a concrete effort to introduce introspection into an object-oriented knowledge representation language and illustrated how a lot of intelligent functions become very naturally integrated.

9. ACKNOWLEDGEMENT.

Thanks to all members of the V.U.B. AI-lab. Especially to Luc Steels, who supported the growth of these ideas and read drafts of the paper, and to Kris Van Marcke, who assisted in the technical realisation.

10. REFERENCES.

Abelson H. and Sussman G. (1985) Structure and Interpretation of Computer Programs. MIT-Press. Cambridge, Massachusetts.

Aiello L. and Levi G. (1984) The Uses of Metaknowledge in AI Systems. In *Proceedings of the 6th European Conference on Artificial Intelligence*. Pisa, Italy.

Attardi G. and Simi M. (1984) Metalanguage and Reasoning across Viewpoints. In *Proceedings of the 6th European Conference on Artificial Intelligence*. Pisa, Italy.

Barr A. (1977) Meta-knowledge and Cognition. In *Proceedings of the 5th International Joint Conference on Artificial Intelligence*. Cambridge, Massachusetts.

Batali J. (1983) Computational Introspection. Massachusetts Institute of Technology. Artificial Intelligence Laboratory. Memo 701. Cambridge, Massachusetts.

Davis R. and Buchanan B. (1977) Meta-level: Overview and applications. In *Proceedings of the 5th International Joint Conference on Artificial Intelligence.* Cambridge, Massachusetts.

Doyle J. (1980) A Model for Deliberation, Action and Introspection. Massachusetts Institute of Technology. Artificial Intelligence Laboratory. Technical Report 581. Cambridge, Massachusetts.

Genesereth M. (1983) An Overview of Meta-level Architecture. In *Proceedings of the National Conference on Artificial Intelligence. AAAI-83.* Washington D.C., Maryland.

Laird J., Rosenbloom P. and Newell A. (1984) Towards Chunking as a General Learning Mechanism. In *Proceedings of the National Conference on Artificial Intelligence.* Austin, Texas.

Smith B. (1982) Reflection and Semantics in a Procedural Language. Massachusetts Institute of Technology. Laboratory for Computer Science. Technical Report 272. Cambridge, Massachusetts.

Steels L. (1985) The KRS Concept System. Vrije Universiteit Brussel. Artificial Intelligence Laboratory. Technical Report 85-4. Brussels, Belgium.

Weyhrauch R. (1980) Prolegomena to a Theory of Mechanized Formal Reasoning. In: *Artificial Intelligence* Vol. 13 No. 1,2. North Holland. Amsterdam. The Netherlands.

Advances in Artificial Intelligence - II
B. Du Boulay, D. Hogg and L. Steels (Editors)
© Elsevier Science Publishers B.V. (North-Holland), 1987

A PARALLEL ALGORITHM FOR CONSISTENCY MAINTENANCE IN KNOWLEDGE REPRESENTATION.

Kris Van Marcke

AI-Lab.
Vrije Universiteit Brussel
Pleinlaan 2, B-1050 Brussels, Belgium.

ABSTRACT

FPPD is a Consistency Maintenance System based on forward propagation of proposition denials. It is designed to support an automatic caching–management system for the knowledge representation system KRS and to guarantee integrity in a non–monotonically changing knowledge base. The fundamental difference with earlier Truth Maintenance Systems is that the user does not define the dependency–relations explicitly. FPPD is continuously shifting parts of the dependency–network from the implicit description (as it is defined by the user) to explicit dependency–relations and vice–versa. The implementation of FPPD on a machine which supports mass–parallelism like the connection machine significantly speeds up the performance of knowledge representation systems.

KEYWORDS: Truth Maintenance, Knowledge Representation, Problem Solving, Caching, Parallelism

1. Introduction

1.1. Truth Maintenance in Problem Solving

A Truth Maintenance System (TMS) serves three functions within a problem solving program. *(i)* It caches all the inferences made by the problem solver to avoid unnecessary recomputation. *(ii)* It supports non–monotonic inferences, i.e. inferences that cause previously valid statements to become invalid. *(iii)* It decides which statements are currently valid and which are currently invalid, making sure that no contradictions arise. More information about the services provided by a TMS can be found in [2] and [3].

Most of the existing TMS's have been based on a model introduced by Sussman [1]. They operate on an evolving set of statements. The world of current beliefs is a subset

This work was supported by Esprit project P440.

of this set. The problem solver adds and retracts statements from this world. Since the presence of a statement depends on the presence or absence of others, various kinds of truth maintenance algorithms have been developed. De Kleer [3] indicates some problems with conventional TMS's and gives an alternative mechanism that solves those problems.

1.2. Consistency Maintenance in Knowledge Representation

Since the complexity of Knowledge Representation Systems increases very rapidly – e.g. by the introduction of multiple formalisms and meta-levels [6] – techniques are needed to augment the speed of the system. One technique is caching intermediate results [7]. But because there may be changes to the knowledge-base, some mechanism is needed to keep the original data and the cached results consistent and to distinguish between current and obsolete results.

Although there are similarities between these tasks and the use of a TMS in a problem solver, the nature of the problem in both cases is quite different. A problem solver demands a lot of expensive operations over a limited set of statements. Because of the cost of these operations, the number of statements should be relatively small. This is illustrated by the way de Kleer implemented assumptions in his ATMS: Every assumption has a fixed and unique number and a set of assumptions is implemented as a bit-vector [3].

The equivalent of an assumption for a knowledge representation system is a datum of the knowledge base. Because there are thousands of these, a system is needed that can operate efficiently over tens of thousands of dependencies. The origin of dependencies between knowledge items is also far from uniform. This diversity in combination with the amount of data results in a very complex dependency graph.

1.3. FPPD: An easy way to control a complex structure.

FPPD is a Consistency Maintenance System based on forward propagation of proposition denials. It was designed to support an automatic caching-management system for the knowledge representation system KRS [6] and to guarantee integrity in a non-monotonically changing knowledge base. FPPD can be used independently to support problem solving which involves the reconsideration of assumptions.

The most important innovation of FPPD lies in the treatment of the dependency network. A TMS expects an explicit definition of the links between the nodes. The problem solver has to provide them. This would be very hard to do in knowledge representation, because of the complexity of the dependency structure. Therefore, FPPD does *not* expect an explicit dependency network from the user. The user defines the graph in an *implicit* way. He defines nodes and specifies how they should react when their value is asked. There are two possibilities: either they just return a user-defined value, or they return the result of the computation of a user–defined function. While the values are computed, FPPD constructs parts of the dependency graph explicitly. *It does this by "looking over the shoulder" as computation goes on and noticing dependency relations.*

When an operation of the user causes some computed values to become obsolete, FPPD destructs the corresponding part of the network. The next time one of these values is requested, it will be recomputed. Though the same implicit description will be used, this may result in a completely different graph.

1.4. FPPD and causal reasoning.

FPPD can be used independently to support problem solving which involves the reconsideration of assumptions. Two assumptions underly the design. The application must rely a lot on dependency–constraints and the frequency of questioning values must be notably higher than the frequency of changing them.

In [10] a causal reasoning algorithm is explained and implemented using FPPD. This algorithm is developed and discussed by Van de Velde in [8].

1.5. Mass Parallelism and Knowledge Representation.

Though parallelism is generally expected to increase the speed of knowledge representation systems, no appropriate algorithms have been developed yet. When caching is heavily used to increase a system's speed, consistency maintenance may become a time critical factor and therefore be an excellent domain to introduce parallelism.

A mass parallel machine is a machine which has theoretically an infinite number of processors. Although some doubt about their usefulness has been expressed lately (in particular about the possibility to find algorithms that take full benefit of the architecture), we think that they do open promising perspectives and that we really should try to find out how AI and in particular knowledge representation can exploit their power.

We have designed FPPD with this challenging topic in mind. It turns out that FPPD is indeed suited to be implemented on a mass parallel machine. In this paper we give the implementation of FPPD in Cmlisp, which is an extension of Lisp to program the Connection Machine.

1.6. Overview.

Section 2 describes the dependency graph. Section 3 describes how and when FPPD translates the implicit graph definition into explicit dependency relations. Section 4 describes how and when FPPD destructs these relations again to fall back on the implicit descriptions. In section 5, a new operation is added, which is used to distinguish between two "styles" of using FPPD. In section 6 finally, we describe how FPPD can be implemented on the connection machine.

2. The FPPD Dependency Graph.

2.1. Propositions.

A node in the FPPD dependency graph is called a proposition. A proposition can hold a value – which can be anything – and communicate it back when asked to do so.

There are two different types of propositions:
1: *primitive-propositions* are propositions that hold *primitive values*. These values are defined externally, and can only be changed externally.
2: *relative-propositions* are propositions that hold a value which depends on the execution of a function within a context. The function is defined when the proposition is created. The context is given whenever the value is requested. The value of a relative-proposition is computed by FPPD, and is called a *Relative Value*.

2.2. A Network of Propositions.

FPPD maintains a continuously changing graph of propositions using the direct–support and direct–dependent relations. We say that a proposition P1 is a *Direct-Support* of a proposition P2 if P2 is a relative-proposition and the value of P1 was used for computing the value of P2.[1] The inverse relation is *Direct-Dependent*. P1 is a direct-dependent of P2 if P2 is a direct-support of P1. Note that a primitive-proposition can not have direct–supports.

The transitive closure of the direct–support relation is the *Support* relation. A proposition P1 is a support of a proposition P2 if P1 is a direct-support of P2 or if P1 is a direct–support of a proposition P3 and P3 is a support of P2. The inverse relation is *Dependent*. It is the transitive closure of the direct–dependent relation.

2.3. Communicating with the Dependency Graph.

There are seven functions to interact with the dependency graph: two to create new

---

[1] The term *was used* should be interpreted as follows: If the function of a proposition P1 asks the value of a relative-proposition P2 whose function asks the value of a proposition P3, then P3 is a direct-support of P2, but not of P1!

propositions and five to communicate with existing propositions.

(*Make–Primitive* value) creates a new primitive–proposition with a given value and no direct dependents.

(*Make–Relative* function) creates a new relative–proposition with a given function. The direct–dependents list and the direct–supports list are initially empty. The relative–proposition is denied, so that the initial value is unimportant (see 4.1).

(*Proposition–Value* proposition &optional context) returns the value of a proposition. For a primitive–proposition, this is the stored value. For a relative–proposition, it is the stored value if the proposition is not denied (see 4.1), otherwise it is the result of the application of the function within the context (see 3.1).

(*Primitive–Redefine–Value* proposition new–value) changes the value of a primitive–proposition and adapts the dependency–graph. The propositions depending on the old value are denied (see 4.1). Initially no propositions depend on the new value.

(*Proposition–P* something) checks if something is a proposition. Returns T or NIL.

(*Deny–Proposition* proposition) informs a proposition that its value (and thus the values of its dependents) has become uncertain. (see 4.1)

(*Proposition–Probe* proposition &optional context) returns the value of the proposition just as Proposition–Value does. However, less dependency relations are stored. (see 5)

3. From Implicit Descriptions to Explicit Dependency Relations.

The functions in relative–propositions hold an implicit description of the dependency–graph. The graph is made explicit when the functions are applied and made implicit when the propositions are denied. This makes it possible to have very dynamical and drastical structural changes of the dependency–graph. Making the dependency relations explicit and implicit are the two crucial steps of the algorithm. In this section and in section four, these steps are elaborated.

3.1. Automatic Support Detector.

The Automatic Support Detector (ASD) makes the dependency relations explicit. It automatically finds the direct–supports of a given (relative–) proposition, i.e. the propositions that were used during the computation of the value.

ASD is invoked by the function *Proposition–Value* (figure 1) whenever the value has to be computed (thus also the first time the value is asked). ASD defines an active–

Figure 1

```
(defun PROPOSITION-VALUE (proposition context)
  (i-am-used proposition)
  (if (denied-p proposition)
      (let ((value (asd proposition context)))
        (setf (value proposition) value)
        (setf (denied-p proposition) nil)
        value)
      (value proposition))))

(defun I-AM-USED (proposition)
  (push proposition *active-support-collector*))

(defun ASD (proposition context)
  (with-new-active-support-collector
    (funcall (function proposition) context)
    (setf (direct-supports proposition) *active-support-collector*)
    (mapc #'(lambda (prop)
              (add-direct-dependent prop proposition))
          *active-support-collector*)))
```

support-collector, which is used to gather all propositions used during the computation of the function. As a matter of fact, those propositions put themselves in the active-support-collector by calling the operation I-Am-Used whenever their value is asked. Because every Apply-within-Context creates a new support-collector, not all supports of a proposition but only the direct-supports are gathered in a collector. When the computation is finished, ASD stores explicit dependency relations in both directions.

4. Forward Propagation of Proposition Denials.

In section 3, we described how implicit dependencies are made explicit. In this chapter we will describe how the external change of a primitive value causes the destruction of a part of the network and how the implicit descriptions regain their previous role.

4.1. Denying a proposition.

When the value of a relative-proposition becomes uncertain, the proposition is *denied*. A relative value becomes uncertain when either *(i)* the value of one of its primitive supports has been changed, *(ii)* when one of its supports have been denied explicitly by the user with the function *Deny-Proposition* (figure 2), or *(iii)* when it has been denied explicitly itself. When this happens, all the values of all its dependents become uncertain. Therefore, Deny-Proposition will recursively deny all direct-dependents too. This

Figure 2

```
(defun DENY-PROPOSITION (proposition)
  (if (not (deniedp proposition))
      (let ((direct-dependents (direct-dependents proposition)))
        (setf (status proposition) 'denied)
        (setf (direct-dependents proposition) empty)
        (mapcar #'deny-proposition direct-dependents)))
  :done)
```

is the origin of the expression *Forward Propagation of Proposition Denials*. While propagating proposition denials, FPPD destructs the direct-support relations. The next
time the propositions value is asked, it is recomputed and a new, possibly different
graph is built.

4.2. Lazy Constraint Propagation.

FPPD follows the principle of *Lazy Constraint Propagation*. In short, if some primitive
value changes, all its dependents are told that their value has become uncertain, but the
new value is not computed immediately.

This technique has been chosen because it gives on an average the best performance.
We assume that we are working with a system with a lot of dependency-relations. So
changing one value can influence a lot of dependent values. To inform the system that
all those values have become uncertain can be done fairly fast. (This is a simple operation which eventually can be done in parallel). However, if one event would cause the
recomputation of a few hundred values, this could take some time. When we now,
instead of recomputing immediately, recompute the values of denied propositions the
moment we need them, the system will be reinstalled gradually. Clearly the advantage
of lazy propagation diminishes for applications with a large rate of change. A lot of
changes leads to systems with more obsolete than current values, so that we lose the
benefit of precomputed values.

5. Naive use versus Sensitive use.

The ASD mechanism as described earlier on is called a *naive* algorithm. Every proposition used during the computation of a relative value becomes a support of that
relative-proposition. There are no conditions that are to be fulfilled in order to install a
dependency-relation.

For our purposes, this is the best thing to do. Since knowledge representation systems
are by definition very complex and very large, speed is a crucial factor. The overhead
of keeping track of reasons for dependencies would slow down FPPD far too much.

This does not preclude the possibility of using FPPD in a more *sensitive* way. FPPD provides an operation, *Proposition–Probe*, which returns the value of a proposition without putting the proposition in the active support collector. The computation of the value of this proposition happens exactly as with the Proposition–Value operation. This means that when the value has to be computed, a new support collector will be set up, and the supports of the proposition will be stored.

This operation allows the user to control ASD. It creates the possibility of putting sense into the dependency relations. However, it is the responsibility of the user to know when to probe for a value, and when to ask for it. The use of the probe operation is illustrated in [10].

6. FPPD on the Connection Machine.

6.1. The Connection Machine.

The connection machine [11] is a fine–grain general communication parallel machine. The currently existing prototype is a SIMD^2 machine with 65,536 cells. Each of those cells contains one processor and 4,096 bits of memory.

There are three heuristics a connection machine programmer should keep in mind:
.The connection machine has to be seen as an amount of high level memory in which very smart data–structures can be built, rather than as a machine that executes several parts of your program in parallel.
.The machine is designed to do applications which change the topological configuration of processors dynamically.
.Doing an operation on a connection machine processor or doing it on all of them, takes exactly the same time.

These heuristics suit perfectly for the development of FPPD. FPPD can be viewed as a high level cache memory. Therefore we need a data–structure that does its own dependency bookkeeping. The structure of the dependency graph changes dynamically, which involves changing the topological structure of the processing units in our high level data–structure. And finally, the bookkeeping of the dependencies can be done concurrently which means exactly that one operation has to be done on a lot of data–items simultaneously.

---

2 "SIMD" stands for "Single Instruction Multiple Data". This means that at all times, when a processor executes an instruction, all other processors are or doing nothing, or executing the same instruction (on their own data of course). Danny Hillis claims that a Simd and a Mimd (multiple instruction multiple data) machine differ by no more than a multiplicative constant in speed since any of both machines can simulate the other [11].

6.2. Implementing Propagation of Denials.

CMLisp is an extension of Commom Lisp, designed to support the parallel operations of the Connection Machine. The most important new data-structure of Cmlisp is a *Xector* (pronounced "Zek'tor"). A simplified way of viewing a Xector is as a list, of which each element is stored in a different processor on the Connection Machine so that operations over this list might happen on all elements simultaneously. The "funcall" is extended so that when it gets a Xector of functions and Xectors of arguments, all functions in the first Xector are applied concurrently to the corresponding data in the other Xectors. With the results, a new Xector is formed. *Alfa* is a Cmlisp operator that creates a constant Xector, which is a Xector where every element is equal to the argument of the alfa operator. The alfa detects itself how many copies of its argument are needed.

Figure 3

```
(defun DENY-PROPOSITION (proposition)
  (if (not (deniedp proposition))
      (let ((direct-dependents (direct-dependents proposition)))
        (setf (status proposition) 'denied)
        (setf (direct-dependents proposition) empty)
        ((alfa 'deny-proposition) direct-dependents)))
  :done)
```

The Cmlisp implementation of the algorithm to propagate proposition denials, which is in essence a simple marker propagation algorithm, is given in figure 3. As expected, this implementation is identical to a sequential Lisp implementation, except for the "mapcar" which is replaced by the operator "alfa".[3] The alfa creates a constant Xector of the function Deny-Proposition, so that all Deny-Proposition calls will be performed in parallel.

6.3. Implementing the Automatic Support Detector.

Implementing the Automatic Support Detector, either sequentially or in parallel, is not an obvious task. It must detect dependencies in a computation on which it has no control. To solve this problem, the function Proposition-Value stores some control information whenever it is used. This information can be used by ASD when control is handed back to it.

---

[3] When alfa is applied to the function of an s-expression, it can be seen as a concurrent version of mapcar.

Figure 4

```
(defun PROPOSITION-VALUE (proposition context)
  (rplaca (used proposition) t)
  (if (denied-p proposition)
      (let ((value (asd proposition context)))
        (setf (value proposition) value)
        (setf (denied-p proposition) nil)
        value)
      (value proposition)))

(defun ASD (proposition context)
  ((alfa 'push-used) *all-propositions*)
  (funcall (function proposition) context)
  (setf (direct-supports proposition)
        (remove nil
                ((alfa 'define-dependency-graph)
                 *all-propositions*
                 (alfa 'proposition))))
  ((alfa 'pop-used) *all-propositions*))

(defun PUSH-USED (proposition)
  (setf (used proposition) (cons nil (used proposition))))

(defun POP-USED (proposition)
  (setf (used proposition) (cdr (used proposition))))

(defun DEFINE-DEPENDENCY-GRAPH (support dependent)
  (if (first (used support))
      (add-dependent support dependent)))
```

In the sequential implementation (see 3.1), this information was gathered in a support–collector. This method is uncomfortable, because the only way to represent support collectors is with dynamically scoped variables. Every time a new (recursive) computation starts, a new support collector has to be defined, in order to distinguish between supports and direct–supports.

In the CM implementation (figure 4), the control information can be stored in the local memory of the CM processors. When control is handed back to ASD, we can in one step access all propositions and tell them that if this control flag is set, they should store the proposition whose value is just computed in their direct dependents list. The result of this operation is a Xector, containing those propositions for which the control bit was set, and as many NIL's as there were unused propositions. Those NIL's can be removed in one step and the resulting Xector contains the direct–supports of the proposition in question.

6.4. Analysis of the different implementations.

The Cmlisp implementation of propagation of proposition denials gives a speed up from O(exp n) to O(n). To see this consider "x" being the average length of a non-circular path in the direct-dependents graph and "y" being the average number of direct-dependents of one proposition. The sequential implementation has to visit O(y**x) nodes where the Cmlisp implementation visits the same number of nodes, but using time O(x). There cannot be a significant difference in the constants of both complexity calculations since an access to memory and an access to a CM processor takes roughly the same time.

Concerning the ASD implementation, the concurrent solution is much cleaner, because we can use the local memory of the individual processors to store the information whether a proposition is used or not. We could of course use the CM strategy also in the sequential implementation, but that would slow down this implementation far too much, while it does not slow down at all the Connection Machine implementation.

Although it is clear that the CM implementation of ASD will be faster, it is not so easy to predict how much faster that will be. Suppose P is the proposition whose value is computed. Defining P as direct-dependent of all propositions used during the computation happens now in one step, while it needs as many steps as there are used propositions in the sequential implementation. Defining the direct-supports of P happens in one step in both implementations. However, gathering the direct-supports was a little more expensive in the sequential implementation, but this difference is not too important.

There is currently another lisp-dialect (*Lisp) which communicates with the Connection machine, though at a much lower level. The difference between Cmlisp and *Lisp is like the difference between low level and high level languages. Although higher level languages are certainly to be preferred, we can wonder if we would ever need more explicit control about what happens inside a CM processor (which is possible with *Lisp). Therefore we should try to make a guess about the size of our dependency network, since applications can grow rather fast. E.g. a large krs application may contain up to 50 000 concepts. A concept may use on the average about 4 propositions. Since the direct-supports and direct-dependents lists can be very large, they should be implemented with fanin and fanout trees. Thus approximately 5 processors may be a realistic guess of the average number of processors used to represent one proposition. This implies that about 1 000 000 processors are required.

A proposition holds a value (32 bits), a function (20 bits), two pointers to trees for direct-supports and direct-dependents (2 * 20 bits) and the additional fields proposition-p, status and used (3 * 1 bit). This gives 95 bits for one proposition. Since a processor has 4K bits memory, we can have about 32 virtual processors on one physical processor. Since there are currently 64 K physical processors, we can have (32 * 64 * 2**10 = 2 ** 21) about 2 000 000 propositions. We see that this is already coming pretty close. For this kind of applications, it becomes important to be careful not to waste any processor, nor processor memory.[4]

7. Conclusion

Recent knowledge representation systems like KRS and ARLO demand an underlying consistency maintenance mechanism. In this paper, we propose such a system, based on propagation of proposition denials. The crucial innovation in comparison with related systems as truth maintenance or constraint systems, is the implicit description of the dependency-graph, which is continuously being manipulated by FPPD.

FPPD is a Consistency Maintenance System that meets the requirements imposed by a knowledge representation system, in particular KRS. It is suited to work with a very large set of propositions and a very complex dependency-graph. It is made lazy in order to avoid a computational explosion the moment some primitive values are changed. Additionally FPPD is useful for all kinds of algorithms that have to do a lot of computation and that want to avoid needless recomputation.

FPPD is designed to introduce parallelism in knowledge representation. To get full benefit of mass parallelism, we will certainly need concurrent algorithms at the knowledge representation level. However, by introducing it here, we already obtain a significant improvement in performance, and we can start thinking about it from a different angle.

Currently, FPPD is implemented on a Symbolics 3670 Lisp-Machine and integrated in the KRS programming environment, for which it has until now never caused a noticeable slow down.

8. Acknowledgments

I wish to thank all members of the Vub-AI-Lab for their helpful comments on both the paper and the system itself. I am indebted to Luc Steels and Walter Van de Velde for several careful readings and quite a few extended discussions. Many helpful suggestions were offered by Pattie Maes and Viviane Jonckers. I also wish to thank Brewster Kahle of Thinking Machines Inc. with whom I had some very interesting discussions about the Connection Machine and how to program it.

---

[4] However, the same need was expressed when the first (imperfect) high level languages for sequential machines were introduced and memory was scarce and expensive.

9. References

[1] Stallman, R.M. and Sussman, G.J. (1977) Forward Reasoning and dependency-directed backtracking in a system for computer aided circuit analysis. In *Artificial Intelligence Journal*. North Holland Pub. Amsterdam.

[2] Doyle, J. (1979) A Truth Maintenance System. In *Artificial Intelligence Journal*. North Holland Pub. Amsterdam.

[3] de Kleer, J. (1985) An Assumption-Based TMS.

[4] Steele, G. and Sussman, G.J. (1978) Constraints. MIT AI-memo 502.

[5] Steels, L. (1985) Constraints as consultants. In *Progress in Artificial Intelligence*. Ellis Horwood series in Artificial Intelligence.

[6] Steels, L. (1986) The KRS concept system. VUB AI-LAB, Technical Report 86-1.

[7] Haase, K. (1985) ARLO – Another Representation Language Offer. MIT Bachelor's Thesis, 1984.

[8] Van de Velde, W. (1985) Naive Causal Reasoning for Diagnosis". In *Proceedings of the Fifth International Workshop on Expert Systems and their applications*. Avignon.

[9] Lukaszewicz, W. (1984) Nonmonotonic Logic For Default Theories. In *Proceedings of the 6th European Conference on Artificial Intelligence*. Pisa, Italy.

[10] Van Marcke, K. (1986) FPPD : A Consistency Maintenance System based on Forward Propagation of Proposition Denials. VUB AI-LAB, AI-Memo 86-1.

[11] Hillis, D. (1985) The Connection Machine. MIT Press.

TAXONOMIC REASONING

G. Attardi, A. Corradini, S. Diomedi, M. Simi

DELPHI SpA
via della Vetraia 11
I-55049 Viareggio, Italy

Abstract. In most object centered knowledge representation systems (e.g. those based on semantic networks or frames) object descriptions are organized in conceptual taxonomies. A taxonomy defines a partial ordering relation over (classes of) objects. *Taxonomic reasoning* is a deduction process performed by traversing such taxonomies.
We explore the idea of taxonomic reasoning in the context of the Omega description system. Our ultimate goal is to show that all the deductions that are allowed in the Omega logic can be performed by a process of lattice traversal/marking/instantiation. To achieve this, a suitable representation is developed that enables statements with variables also to be embedded in the lattice. A classification algorithm is relied upon that, whenever a new description is entered into the knowledge base, builds an access structure for it and properly connects it to other descriptions related by inheritance.

Introduction. Knowledge representation systems based on frames or on semantic networks are called *object centered* systems, as opposed to *rule centered* (e.g. production systems) or *predicate centered* (e.g. those based on first order logic). In object centered representation systems object descriptions are organized in taxonomies, that is partial ordering relations among (classes of) objects. For example in semantic networks these relations are often explicitly represented with some sort of *is-a* links [Brachman 83], while in frame based formalisms they can be explicitly stated or deduced looking at the structure of the frames [Brachman-Levesque 84, Lipkis 82].

Taxonomies usually represent membership/inclusion relations between (classes of) objects, and are the basis of an inheritance mechanism. *Taxonomic Reasoning* is a deduction process which exploits the organization of objects in taxonomies.[1]

An important example of taxonomic reasoning is the determination of *subsumption*, that is the ability of the system of determining whether the partial ordering relation induced by the taxonomy holds between a pair of descriptions.

In the following discussion, we will restrict our attention to a subset of the full Omega representation language. In the next section we give a short and informal description of such subset of Omega. After a discussion of the structure of an Omega knowledge base and classification of descriptions, examples of taxonomic reasoning are presented.

The Omega Knowledge Representation Language. Omega is a representation language based on the notion of description. Descriptions provide a way to categorize objects according to their properties in a inheritance network.

A description describes a class of objects. For example:

This work was supported by ESPRIT, project P440, and is a contribution to workpackage 4 of Cost-13 project n. 21 "Advanced Issues in Knowledge Representation".

[1] The term *taxonomic reasoning* is used with a different meaning in [Tenenberg 85], where it denotes what we call *reasoning about taxonomies*.

John

describes the class containing just the individual entity denoted by 'John'

(a Man)

describes the class of men.

Descriptions like **John**, which represent a single individual, are called *individual descriptions*. A description like (a Man), representing the collection of all men, is called an *instance description* with *concept* Man.

An instance description may specify *attributions* for the objects it represents. For example:

(a Man (**with** job computer-hacking))

describes the class of men whose job is 'computer-hacking'.

More complex descriptions can be built using the description operators **and, or, not** which correspond to the set operators for intersection, union and complement. Thus the description

(a Positive-number) **and** (**not** (1 **or** 2))

describes the class of all natural numbers greater than 2.

The elementary sentence in Omega is the *predication*, relating two descriptions with our subsumption relation **is**:

(a System-engineer) **is** (a Person (**with** job computer-hacking))

A predication asserts inclusion between two classes (or *subsumption*) between descriptions.

Nothing and **Something** are special descriptions denoting the empty set and the universe respectively.

Variables can appear anywhere within statements. They are considered as universally quantified and ranging over descriptions.

Omega Logic.

Valid facts and legal deductions in Omega are defined by a set of axioms and logical inference rules.

For instance a suitable comprehension rule, together with the rule about the transitivity of **is**, allows us to deduce from the statements:

John **is** (a Man (**with** dog Fido))

(a Man (**with** dog =x)) **is** (a man (**with** friend =x))

that

John **is** (a Man (**with** friend Fido))

by instantiating =x with 'Fido'.

Several axioms define the properties of attributes. The axiom of omission states that by omitting an attribution we get a more general description:

(a c (with a_1 δ) α) is (a c α)

where α stands for a sequence of zero of more attributions. For example

(a Cat (with name Jerry)) is (a Cat)

The axiom of *Monotonicity* is states that:

δ_1 is δ_2 → (a c (with a_1 δ_1) α) is (a c (with a_1 δ_2) α)

For example:

John is (an Artist) → ((a Person (with child John)) is (a Person (with child (an Artist))))

(a Factorial (with arg 0)) is 1 →
  (a Product (with arg_1 (a Factorial (with arg 0)))) is (a Product (with arg_1 1))

Attributions of type **with-unique** are meant to have a single value for the attribute. For this kind of attributions the property of *fusing* holds, which is described by the following schema:

(a c (with-unique a_1 δ_1) (with a_1 δ_2)) is (a c (with-unique a_1 (δ_1 and δ_2)))

For example:

(a Car (with-unique owner Bob) (with owner (a Doctor))) is
  (a Car (with-unique owner (Bob and (a Doctor)))

The most common attribution type is **with-unique**. We will use the short-hand notation "[att δ]" for "(**with-unique** att δ)".

More complex statements can be built by means of logical operators like ~, ∧, ∨, →. In the subset of Omega we are considering we restrict our attention to predications (see [Attardi et al. 85b] for a treatment of more complex statements).

In Figure 1 the BNF syntax is presented of the subset of Omega that we will discuss. For a detailed description of to the full Omega logic and the formal semantics of the Omega language we refer to [Attardi-Simi 81, Attardi et al. 85a].

The Omega Knowledge Base. In an Omega knowledge base information is organized in a lattice, where the nodes are descriptions and the links represent the **is** relation. **Nothing** and **Something** are the bottom and top elements of the lattice, respectively.

Whenever a new statement of the kind (δ_1 is δ_2) is asserted, δ_1 and δ_2 are inserted in the lattice, then a **is** link is created to link the two descriptions. The insertion of a new description is the task of the classification process which will place it in such a way that all its subsumers in the network can be reached following **is** links.

In order to assist the classification process, our implementation maintains a special ordering between instance descriptions, based on the value of attributes, so that the search of the place for a description can be performed efficiently. A more detailed account of classification is given in section 4.

Statements with variables: Predications with variables are also inserted in the lattice, in order to make them accessible during deductions from descriptions matching either side of the statement. This is achieved by classifying in a suitable way the descriptions which occur in the predication. Suppose we have to insert the statement

---

<description> ::= <individual-description> |
               Nothing | **Something** |
               <instance-description> |
               <variable> |
               (<description> **and** <description>) |
               (<description> **or** <description>)

<individual-description> ::= <symbol>

<instance-description> ::= ([a | an] <concept>
          {(([with | with-unique | with-every] <attribute-name> <description>)})

<concept> ::= <symbol>
<attribute-name> ::= <symbol>
<variable> ::= =<symbol>

Figure 1. Syntax of descriptions of a subset of Omega

$\delta1[=x]$ is $\delta2[=x]$

We have to guarantee that, starting from any description above (which subsumes) the ones that match the right part of the statement, the statement itself will be reached and instantiated in the right way. Symmetrically, the statement will be reachable from any description under the ones that match the left part of the statement. This is achieved by inserting $\delta1[=x]$ at the place where it would be classified if $=x$ had value **Something** (the classification algorithm finds the place for $\delta1[=x/\text{Something}]$) and $\delta2[=x]$ at the place found by classifying $\delta2[=x/\text{Nothing}]$.[2]

Descriptions which include variables are implemented as structures (actually flavors [Moon et al. 83]) of data type *open description*, to distinguish them from ordinary descriptions. The two open descriptions are linked with a standard is link.

For example, suppose that the statements

(a Man (**with** dog =x)) **is** (a man (**with** friend =x))
John **is** (a Man (**with** dog Fido))

are asserted and we look for all descriptions above John in the Omega lattice. From John we can get the description (a Man (**with** dog Fido)). Then, thanks to the classification and the fact that, by monotonicity,

(a Man (**with** dog Fido)) **is** (a Man (**with** dog **Something**))

we reach (a Man (**with** dog =x)). But since this last description is an open description, it has

---

[2] Actually the construction of the description to classify is slightly more complex, in the sense that one has to take into account whether the variable appears inside some negation.

to be instantiated to obtain the proper description. An unification is done with the description (a Man (with dog Fido)) which produces the binding between =x and Fido; we proceed one level up the lattice to (a Man (with friend =x)), which is instantiated with the same binding just produced. Therefore (a Man (with friend Fido)) can be reached.

Notice that unification performed above always succeeds, unlike in system like PROLOG where unification is used to determine whether a clause is applicable and therefore may fail. Here the organization in the lattice, obtained by the classification, guarantees that only relevant and applicable rules are met while traversing the lattice.

Thus, during deductions, the interesting rules can be reached simply by following pointers, without the need of extensive pattern matching with rules stored in big tables, as usual in other systems.

Viewpoints. Viewpoints are a mechanism which enables to handle different views of the knowledge base, thus providing a mean to represent changes to the world we are modelling. They also provide an effective way to modularize and factor portions of knowledge.

Every assertion made by the user belongs to a specific viewpoint, and normally a deduction activity is performed in a viewpoint (but more complex deductions can span over several viewpoints, can create some new ones and kill some others).

Formally a viewpoint is a set of statements, the assumptions; what holds in the viewpoint is whatever can be deduced by the assumptions in the viewpoint, according to deductive rules of the Omega logic. We write (σ in vp) to state that σ is a logical consequence of the statements in vp. We refer to [Attardi-Simi 84] for a formal definition of viewpoints, based on a metacircular description of Omega in itself.

From the implementation point of view, any **is** link in the Omega network is viewpoint dependent. Viewpoints are organized in a structure which corresponds to inheritance relations between them. Multiple inheritance is allowed, thus the structure can be in general an acyclic graph.

The assumptions of a viewpoint include all facts asserted in the viewpoint itself and in those others from which it inherits. Thus to assert a statement in a viewpoint vp simply means to add it to vp. Omega logical axioms and theorems derivable only from such axioms hold in any viewpoint. The simplest way to implement such a behaviour is to have that every viewpoint inherits from a special one, to which all Omega logical axioms belong. Thus the inheritance structure of viewpoints is a rooted acyclic graph. The root viewpoint is called the *Tautological viewpoint*.

Access and Classification. Whenever a new predication is asserted, its subject and predicate descriptions have to be inserted in the Omega lattice, if not already present.

The classification algorithm, invoked when a new description has to be inserted, implements two different but related functionalities:

- Creates an access structure to descriptions in the lattice
- Creates a number of **is** links connecting the new description to other descriptions in the lattice, making explicit a subset of the **is** relation.

The formal semantics of Omega [Attardi and Simi 81] defines the **is** relationship between descriptions.

The problem of determining subsumption, and therefore the **is** relationship, is undecidable in Omega and complex in any language with a significant expressive power [Brachman and Levesque 84].

Therefore the classification algorithm implemented restricts the attention to that part of the **is** relation which is explicitely represented by links or paths in the lattice and which is induced by a few structural properties of descriptions. The tests for subsumption in the classification algorithm are to be viewed in this restricted sense and we will make precise later which subset of the **is** relation is made explicit with links and paths in the network.

Direct access points in the network are available to reach individual constants and the most generic representative of instance descriptions with the same concept (the one with no attributions). For instance, when trying to locate (a Man (with dog Fido)), one starts from the node (a man) which is directly accessible through the concept "man".

The most difficult task of the classification algorithm is the classification of instance descriptions. To classify an instance description δ, the classification algorithm starts from the description which is directly accessible from the concept name of δ and searches the lattice downward. For each child s of this description, a test is done to determine whether s is more general then δ (i.e. δ **is** s). In particular, given two instance descriptions:

(a C [attr1 $\delta1$] [attr2 $\delta2$] [attr3 $\delta3$])
(a C [attr1 $\delta4$] [attr3 $\delta5$])

we can prove that

(a C [attr1 $\delta1$] [attr2 $\delta2$] [attr3 $\delta3$]) **is** (a C [attr1 $\delta4$] [attr3 $\delta5$])

if the following hold:

$\delta1$ **is** $\delta4$
$\delta3$ **is** $\delta5$

That is, if two instance descriptions are compared during the classification process, the corresponding attribute values are also compared, according to the monotonicity of attributions.

If (δ **is** s) is not true, then none of the children of s could be more specific than δ either, so it remains just to consider whether the opposite **is** relation holds between s and δ, so that δ could be classified as a parent of s. On the other hand, if (δ **is** s), we recursively classify δ under s.

Since in general a description might have several children, a simple minded classification algorithm would have to search through all the children in some order and since a description could be a child (or a parent) of more than one description, all children will have to be considered.

This is a potential source of combinatorial explosion. Therefore we have devised a schema by which children of an instance description are ordered in such a way that the path to an already existing description (or to the place in which to insert a new description) can be determined without backtracking.

In addition the classification does some work in order to reduce the branching factor of the lattice: when a new child has to be inserted with common characteristics with respect to an existing one, a new description is created factoring the common characteristics of the two descriptions and this one is inserted as a child: the two descriptions become its children.

The classification algorithm links the new description to already inserted descriptions in such a way that the transitive closure of the links created by the classification itself implements the subset of the is relation specified below; that is, if (δ_1 is δ_2) according to the definition below, then after the classification there will be a path of one or more links between δ_1 and δ_2.

The subset of the is relation taken into account by the classification is defined by the following axioms:

Something
T1: δ is **Something**

Nothing
T2:   **Nothing is δ**

Transitivity
T3: $\delta1$ is $\delta2 \wedge \delta2$ is $\delta3 \rightarrow \delta1$ is $\delta3$

And elimination
T4:   (δ_1 and δ_2) is δ_i i=1,2

Or elimination
T5: δ_i is (δ_1 or δ_2)   i=1,2

Omission
T6:   (a c (with a_1 δ) α) is (a c α)

Monotonicity
T7: δ_1 is $\delta_2 \rightarrow$ (a c (with a_1 δ_1) α) is (a c (with a_1 δ_2) α)

The classification algorithm guarantees that the following properties are satisfied:

Soundness: If there is a path from $\delta1$ to $\delta2$ in a viewpoint vp, then ($\delta1$ **is** $\delta2$) can be deduced from the assumptions in vp.

Completeness with respect to axioms T1-T7: If δ1 and δ2 are descriptions in the lattice and (δ1 **is** δ2) can be deduced from the assumptions in a viewpoint vp, using axioms T1-T7, then there is a path from δ1 to δ2 in viewpoint vp.

The fact that completeness has to be considered relative to descriptions in the lattice, can be explained with the following example. Given that (John **is** (a Man)) and the description (a Man [father (a Man)]) is in the network, (a Man [father John]) is classified under (a Man [father (a Man)]), but no new assertions are made nor descriptions created. So even if, in virtue of monotonicity, (a Person [son John]) **is** (a Person [son (a Man)]) is also a consequence of (John **is** (a Man)) this assertion nor the component descriptions will appear in the network just for that reason.

Among **is** links created by the classification, the ones established in virtue of axioms T1, T2, T4, T5 and T6 are not viewpoint dependent in that they correspond to a relationship based on the structure of the descriptions, therefore they belong in the Tautological Viewpoint. The **is** links created, in virtue of axioms T3 and T7 belong in the viewpoint in which the antecedents of the implication are asserted (the current viewpoint or the Tautological viewpoint).

Taxonomic Reasoning in Omega. Algorithms for taxonomic reasoning rely upon the structure built by the classification.

As an example of taxonomic reasoning, we present here the algorithm that is used in Omega to answer existence queries.

An existence query is an interrogation of the form

(is-there? δ[=x])

where δ[=x] is any description where the variable =x appears. The semantics of this query is to find the minimal descriptions d_1, different from **Nothing**, such that:

d_1 is δ[d_2]

for some description d_2.

We present here the case where δ[=x] is of the form (a c ...).

The query (is-there? d[=x]) is processed as follows:

Step 1 First a set of candidates is selected by traversing the lattice downwards, starting from the extension of concept c, in the following way. A template for comparisons is created by making a copy of the query. Each node in the lattice that is visited, corresponding to description dl, is marked and then, to decide wheather to go further down or to stop, dl is compared with d[**Something**].

> If dl **is** d[**Something**],
>> then the template is fused with dl and added as a candidate,
>> else if d[nothing] **is** dl
>>> then
>>>> a copy of the template is made, it is fused with dl and we
>>>> go further down using the result as the new template
>>> else discard dl

When dl has no unmarked sons, then the current template is added to the set of candidates.

Step 2   Candidates are compared with each other, and arranged themselves in a hierarchy graph by means of the classification algorithm.

Step 3   Starting from each root of this graph, descend the graph, and fuse each node with its superiors. Stop when a node reduces to nothing or we reach a leaf of this lattice.

As an example, consider the following lattice, which is a simplification from that used in [Attardi et al. 1985] to describe the behavior of a hair dryer. The **is** links that appear here arise either from user assertions or from the classification.

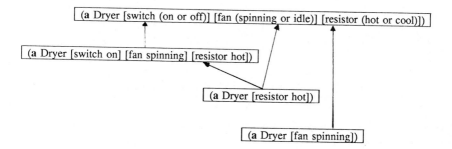

and a query like:

     (is-there? (**a** Dryer [switch =s] [fan =f] [resistor hot]))

Step 1 of the algorithm, produces three candidates, which arranged in a lattice in step 2, appear as follows:

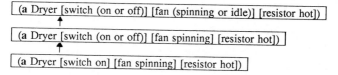

The result from step 3 is the bottom element of this tree, which provides as answer to the query with values "on" for =s, "spinning" for =f.

Conclusions. By arranging all knowledge within a lattice of description, reasoning in Omega can be performed by a process of lattice traversal/marking/instantiation. The technique appears to be promising to be amenable to concurrent execution, exploiting parallelism in the search through the lattice.

Acknowledgements. We are grateful to Maurizio De Cecco for implementing an earlier version of the classification algorithm and for many stimulating discussions.

References

Attardi, G. and M. Simi Semantics of Inheritance and Attributions in the Description System Omega. AI Memo 642, M.I.T., 1981.

Attardi, G. and M. Simi Metalanguage and Reasoning across Viewpoints. Proc. of Sixth European Conference on Artificial Intelligence, Pisa, 1984.

Attardi, G., Corradini, A., De Cecco, M., Simi, M. The Omega Primer, DELPHI Tech. Rep. ESP/85/8, 1985.

Attardi, G., Corradini, A., De Cecco, M., Simi, M. Representation and Deduction Strategies for Complex Statements, DELPHI Tech. Rep. ESP/85/9, 1985.

Brachman, R.J., What IS-A is and isn't: An Analysis of Taxonomic Links in Semantic Networks - IEEE Computer, Special Issue on Knowledge Representation, pp. 30-36, October, 1983.

Brachman, R.J., Levesque, H.J., The Tractability of Subsumption in Frame-Based Description Languages, in Proc. AAAI-84, Austin, Texas, 34-37, August 1984.

Lipkis, Thomas A., A KL-ONE Classifier, Proceedings of the 1981 KL-ONE Workshop, BBN, pp. 128-145, June 1982.

Moon, D., Stallman, R. M. and Weinreb, D. Lisp Machine Manual, 1983.

Tenenberg, J.D., Taxonomic Reasoning, in Proceedings of the Ninth Joint Conference on Artificial Intelligence, pp. 191-193, August 1985.

Advances in Artificial Intelligence - II
B. Du Boulay, D. Hogg and L. Steels (Editors)
© Elsevier Science Publishers B.V. (North-Holland), 1987

A SYNTHESIS SYSTEM MECHANIZING PROOFS BY INDUCTION *

Susanne Biundo , Universität Karlsruhe

ABSTRACT: A method to find existence proofs using techniques of deductive program synthesis is presented. An existentially quantified variable in a formula
is replaced by a skolem term. Using this new formula as a specification an algorithmic definition for the skolem function will be derived. It is shown that
a successful synthesis also represents an induction proof of the original formula. A system which under some user guidance finds existence proofs by synthesis is presented.

1. INTRODUCTION

On proving theorems by induction formulas including existential quantifiers
like $\psi = \forall x^* \exists y \forall z^*\ \varphi[x^*\ y\ z^*]$ (where x^* and z^* are lists of variables and φ is
a first-order formula without any quantifier) can cause certain problems:

One problem is to find an appropriate induction scheme for the formula. This
may be difficult because the existentially quantified variable y may be the
only 'induction candidate'. The second problem is that the existential quantification may cause some kind of inconstructiveness. Proving theorems automatically by induction means to prove theorems in constructive theories where
the objects under consideration are defined in a constructive way. In this
context existence proofs may be difficult because they require a search for a
'solving term'. Therefore the induction system has to search for a term which
after replacing the existentially quantified variable makes the formula true.
Such a search may be expensive (if it is successful at all).

In the induction proving systems of Boyer and Moore [3] and Aubin [1] these
problems are solved rather radically by prohibiting the usage of existential
quantifications. There the user is forced to replace in ψ the existentially
quantified variable y by an appropriate term, for example $f(x^*)$. If f is not
already defined the user has to support the system by giving a constructive
definition for f, i.e. an algorithm computing f.

Other approaches in mechanizing induction theorem proving are based on the
Knuth-Bendix completion algorithm [5,6,8]. There the problems of existential

---

* This research is part of the Sonderforschungsbereich 314 'Künstliche Intel-
ligenz' and supported by the Deutsche Forschungsgemeinschaft.
Author's address: Institut für Informatik I , Universität Karlsruhe , Postfach
6980 , D-7500 Karlsruhe.

quantifications do not arise because all variables are universally quantified. The step of replacing y in ψ by f(x*), called skolemization, yields a for- mula $ψ_0$ = ∀x*z* ψ[x* f(x*) z*] which can be viewed as a specification of a function f. In this context deductive program synthesis appears suitable to solve the problem of obtaining a constructive definition of f. Our idea is to mechanize existence proofs (as far as possible), i.e. to mechanize the task the Boyer/Moore - user has to perform when proving existence formulas by in- duction.

In this paper we present a system to synthesize algorithmic definitions of skolem functions. We give a formal description of the system and show that the synthesis process is sound, i.e. it represents an induction proof of the exis- tence formula (i.e. a formula containing an existentially quantified variable) initially submitted to the system. A user-guided system is described by means of an example which demonstrates the complete synthesis of a skolem function. It is an experimental system used to deal even with big examples in order to find strategies and heuristics which are hoped to lead to the implementation of a nearly automatic control component.

The synthesis system is implemented as part of the INKA-system, an induction theorem prover currently under development at the University of Karlsruhe.

2. THE LOGICAL BASIS

Given a finite set of axioms Ax and a formula φ an induction theorem prover attempts to find a proof of φ from Ax, denoted Ax ⊢$_I$ φ , using some sound first-order inference rules as well as some induction rules from an induction rule base I. The axiom set Ax consists of first-order representations of (1) the various domains under consideration (called structures), e.g. natural num- bers, lists of natural numbers, etc., and (2) algorithms computing functions which operate on these domains, e.g. subtraction of natural numbers, concate- nation of lists of natural numbers, etc. The domain of natural numbers (abbre- viated nat), for example, is defined by the following set REP$_{nat}$ of represen- tation formulas for nat.   REP$_{nat}$ = { ∀x:nat [x≡0 ∨ ∃y:nat x≡s(y)] , ∀x:nat ~s(x)≡0 , ∀x,y:nat [s(x)≡s(y) → x≡y] }, where ≡ denotes syntactic equa- lity. The subtraction of natural numbers (abbreviated sub) can be defined by the following set DEF$_{sub}$ of definition formulas for sub. For convenience we write DEF$_{sub}$ as implications, whereas the system uses clausal form to repre- sent definition and representation formulas.   DEF$_{sub}$ = { ∀x,y:nat [x≡0 → sub(x y)≡0] , ∀x,y,w:nat [x≡s(w) ∧ y≡0 → sub(x y)≡x] , ∀x,y,u,v:nat [x≡s(u) ∧ y≡s(v) → sub(x y)≡sub(u v)] }. Given, for instance, Ax = REP$_{nat}$ ∪ DEF$_{sub}$ and φ = ∀x:nat sub(x x)≡0 an induction system proves Ax ⊢$_I$ φ using the induction

rule   sub(0 0)≡0 ∧ ∀x,u:nat [x≡s(u) ∧ sub(u u)≡0 → sub(x x)≡0] ⊢
∀x:nat sub(x x)≡0. However, finding the right induction rule, i.e. a rule
which carries the proof, is crucial in induction theorem proving, cf. [3].

New domains and functions are introduced by extending the given axiom set
with new representation and definition formulas. However care has to be taken
to guarantee that the axiom set remains consistent. In the case of new domains
only trivial features like those of syntax and of unique usage of symbols have
to be tested. For a new function g it has to be guaranteed in addition that
the conditions of all definition formulas in DEF_g (1) mutually exclude each
other (uniqueness property) and (2) form a complete case analysis (completeness property). Additionally it has to be verified that (3) in each recursive
function call the arguments decrease according to some well-founded order
relation (termination property), cf. [3].

We formulate all these tests as first-order formulas the proof of which
from the original axiom set Ax constitutes the admissibility test for the new
function g. It has to be performed before the new set of definition formulas
is accepted, i.e. before Ax is extended by DEF_g. In this case we call DEF_g
admissible. E.g. given Ax = REP_{nat} the admissibility test for the function
sub consists in proving Ax $⊢_I$ ∀x,y,u,v,w:nat [~[x≡0 ∧ x≡s(w) ∧ y≡0] ∧ ~[x≡0 ∧
x≡s(u) ∧ y≡s(v)] ∧ ~[x≡s(w) ∧ y≡0 ∧ x≡s(u) ∧ y≡s(v)]]   (uniqueness) ,
Ax $⊢_I$ ∀x,y:nat [x≡0 ∨ ∃w:nat [x≡s(w)∧y≡0] ∨ ∃u,v:nat [x≡s(u)∧y≡s(v)]]   (completeness) and Ax $⊢_I$ true (termination). The termination test the system
performs presently consists in deciding whether the function terminates according to the well-founded order relation of the immediate structural prede-
cessor, cf. [1], and this is obviously satisfied in the case of sub.
Because all admissibility conditions are proved the definition of sub will be
accepted. Finally its recursion scheme will be determined: Both arguments of
function sub are recursion arguments.

3. A METHOD OF DEDUCTIVE PROGRAM SYNTHESIS

A central assumption in traditional induction theorem proving is that all
functions under consideration are defined in a constructive way, i.e. by an
algorithm computing the desired function. Hence induction base(s) and conclu-
sion(s) of a formula (which are generated by an induction rule) can be evaluated symbolically which is a central task in order to find a proof [7]. But
symbolic evaluation is only possible if the functions involved are given by
algorithms. Consequently the systems of Boyer and Moore [3] and Aubin [1] prohibit existentially quantified variables because existential quantifiers can
cause some kind of inconstructiveness, i.e. a search for a solution. Given,

for instance, $Ax = REP_{nat} \cup DEF_{sub}$ and $\psi = \forall x,y:nat \; \exists z:nat \; sub(z\;y)\equiv x$, the
user of the Boyer/Moore - system has to 'invent' a function plus by submitting
DEF_{plus} to the system which then proves $Ax \cup DEF_{plus} \vdash_I$
$\forall x,y:nat \; sub(plus(x\;y)y)\equiv x$, i.e. a theorem which is sufficient for the original one. It is our approach to 'mechanize' the Boyer/Moore - user in this
respect: Given the skolemized formula $\psi_0 = \forall x,y:nat \; sub(f(x\;y)y)\equiv x$ using techniques of deductive program synthesis we attempt to derive a definition DEF_f
satisfying $Ax \cup DEF_f \vdash_I \psi_0$.
Deductive program synthesis [2,9,10] is one of the earliest approaches to
derive constructive (algorithmic) definitions of functions. It consists in
transforming a specification of a function into an algorithm which computes
the specified function. The transformation, obtained by so-called transformation rules [9,10] is driven by several strategies and heuristics. Here we
use the techniques of deductive program synthesis for our problem of finding
existence proofs in the following way:
Given Ax and $\psi = \forall x^* \exists y \forall z^* \; \varphi[x^* \; y \; z^*]$ we start to prove $Ax \vdash_I \varphi$ by skolemi-
zing ψ in a first step yielding $\psi_0 = \forall x^* z^* \; \varphi[x^* \; f(x^*) \; z^*]$. ψ_0 can be used as a
specification of some unknown function f. It constitutes a synthesis problem,
i.e. we are looking for an algorithm DEF_f which computes f such that ψ_0 holds.
Now suppose given ψ_0 as input a synthesis system returns a set of definition
formulas DEF_f satisfying $(*)$ $Ax \cup DEF_f \vdash_I \psi_0$. Then we also have
$Ax \cup DEF_f \vdash_I \psi$ because $\psi_0 \to \psi$ is valid. But ψ does not contain f, i.e. the
axioms DEF_f can be omitted and we obtain $Ax \Vdash_I \psi$. To demonstrate in which
way our synthesis system guarantees $(*)$ for a definition DEF_f derived from ψ_0
we shall now give an abstract description of the system.
Given a set of axioms Ax and a skolemized formula ψ_0 as input various transformation rules are applied to ψ_0. An application of a rule R to a formula φ
produces a set of formulas Φ, denoted $\varphi \Rightarrow_R \Phi$. For a set of formulas Ψ we define $\Psi \cup \{\varphi\} \equiv\rangle_R \Psi \cup \Phi$ iff $\varphi \Rightarrow_R \Phi$. The transformation process terminates if
some termination criterion (cf. section 4) is encountered yielding a set of
formulas Ψ_k such that $\{\psi_0\} \equiv\rangle_{R1} \dots \equiv\rangle_{Rk} \Psi_k$.
Now by pure syntactical reasoning Ψ_k is divided into $\Psi_k^D = DEF_f \subset \Psi_k$, the
set of definition formulas for f, and into $\psi_k^R = \Psi_k \setminus \Psi_k^D$, the set of so-
called remainder formulas. In order to find a proof of our original problem ψ
we have to verify whether (1) $\Psi_k^D = DEF_f$ is an admissible definition, and
whether (2) $Ax \cup DEF_f \vdash_I \psi_0$ holds.
For (1) we simply use the admissibility test of our system. If it succeeds,
i.e. if the synthesized definition DEF_f is admissible, we attempt to verify
(2) in the following way: We require that all transformation rules R we use in

the system are sound, i.e. $\varphi \Rightarrow_R \Phi$ implies $Ax \vdash_I \wedge\Phi \to \varphi$, where $\wedge\Phi$ denotes the conjunction $\wedge_{\delta\in\Phi} \delta$. Thus with $\{\psi_0\} \equiv\!>^+ \Psi_k$ (where $\equiv\!>^+$ denotes the transitive closure of $\Rightarrow_R$ for arbitrary rules R) we also have (3) $Ax \vdash_I \wedge\Psi_k \to \psi_0$. Now it is sufficient for (2) to show that (*) $Ax \cup \wedge\Psi_k^D \vdash_I \wedge\Psi_k^R$ because then obviously $Ax \cup DEF_f \vdash_I \wedge\Psi_k$ and with (3) we finally obtain (2). ∎

Consequently, the proof of an existence formula ψ consists in a transformation $\{\psi_0\} \equiv\!>^+ \Psi_k^D \cup \Psi_k^R$, testing $\Psi_k^D = DEF_f$ for admissibility, and finally verifying $Ax \cup DEF_f \vdash_I \wedge\Psi_k^R$.

4. THE SYNTHESIS SYSTEM

The synthesis component which is implemented as a part of the INKA-system performs a user-guided synthesis of skolem function definitions. We shall now give an example to demonstrate how the transformation rules are applied to an initial formula ψ_0 in order to find a definition of a skolem function f.

All the formulas we are dealing with are represented as clauses. The transformation rules are implemented as transitions from clauses to sets of clauses. Let $Ax = REP_{nat} \cup DEF_{sub} = \{$ < $x\equiv 0$, $x\equiv s(p(x))$ > [Ax1] , <~s(x)≡0> [Ax2], < ~s(x)≡s(y) , $x\equiv y$ > [Ax3] , < ~x≡0 , sub(x y)≡0 > [Ax4] , < ~x≡s(w) , ~y≡0 , sub(x y)≡x > [Ax5] , < ~x≡s(u) , ~y≡s(v) , sub(x y)≡sub(u v) > [Ax6] $\}$. Given a formula $\psi = \forall x,y:nat\; \exists z:nat\; sub(z\;y)\equiv x$ as input the system generates a formula $\psi_0 = <$ sub(f(x y)y)≡x > by the skolemization rule (SK).

An algorithm for the skolem function f has to be given by case analysis and by recursion. The problem to find a recursion scheme for f is quite similar to the problem of generating an induction scheme for a formula φ using the recursion schemes of the functions occurring in φ [3].

One successful heuristic (which is applicable in many cases) is to use the recursion scheme of one of the most nested functions of ψ_0 [4], where a most nested function (mnf) is a function (different from the skolem function f) occurring at an innermost position in ψ_0. The mnf-heuristic applies if all recursion arguments of the occurrence of the mnf in $\psi_0 = \forall x^*z^*\varphi[x^*f(x^*)z^*]$ are elements of x^*, i.e. they are also arguments of f.

Unfortunately this heuristic does not apply for our example: The only most nested function in $\psi_0 = <$ sub(f(x y)y)≡x > is function sub. One of its two recursion arguments is the term f(x y) and therefore its recursion scheme cannot be taken as the recursion scheme for f.

Another heuristic to obtain a recursion scheme and a suitable case analysis for the definition of f is to generate so-called induction subgoals according to the method of Aubin [1]. In our system this is done by the induction rule (IND). The method of selecting the induction variables differs from that of

Aubin in that, given a formula $\forall x^* z^*\ \varphi[x^*\ f(x^*)\ z^*]$ the system takes only those variables of x^* as induction variables which are as well recursion arguments of a mnf of φ. If no such function does exist any argument of f is selected arbitrarily.

In our example with $\psi_0 = \langle\ sub(f(x\ y)y)\equiv x\ \rangle$ as input the induction rule selects y as induction variable and generates two formulas: $\psi_1 = \langle\ \sim y\equiv 0$, $sub(f(x\ y)y)\equiv x\ [G]\rangle$ and $\psi_2=\langle\sim y\equiv s(v),\ \sim sub(f(x\ v)v)\equiv x\ [H],\ sub(f(x\ y)y)\equiv x\ [G]\rangle$, where the literals are labeled according to their origin as goals [G] and as induction hypotheses [H]. The literals without labels are called conditions.

If we represent derivations like $\psi \Rightarrow_{SK} \{\psi_0\}$ and $\psi_0 \Rightarrow_{IND} \{\psi_1,\psi_2\}$ by a derivation tree as in figure 1 (see appendix) the synthesis process can be viewed as expanding the leaves in the tree (like ψ_1 and ψ_2 above) by application of any transformation rules. This process terminates if each node is closed, i.e. it is a definition formula (i.e. a clause containing only one goal literal which is of the form $f(x^*)\equiv t$, where f is the skolem function) or it is a remainder formula (i.e. either a clause to which no further transformation rule is applicable or a clause the goal literals of which do not contain the skolem function f). Before proceeding in our example the transformation rules will be described.

The evaluation rule (EV) symbolically evaluates the functions occurring in a formula.

$$EV:\quad C\ \cup\ \{L\}\ \Rightarrow_{EV}\ \{C\ \cup\ \{L\ [h(t^*)/\sigma q]\ \}\}$$

where C and D are clauses, L is a goal literal, $D\ \cup\ \{\ h(x^*)\equiv q\ \}\ \in\ DEF_h\ \subset\ Ax$, and $\sigma D \subset C$ for some substitution σ such that $\sigma(x^*)=t^*$. We let $L[p/r]$ denote (somewhat ambiguously here) the literal which results from L by replacing some subterm p of L by r. The EV-rule is sound because with $D\ \cup\ \{\ h(x^*)\equiv q\ \}\ \in\ Ax$ and $\sigma D\subset C$ we have $Ax \vdash C\ \cup\ \{L\ [h(t^*)/\sigma q]\ \}\ \rightarrow\ C\ \cup\ \{L\}$.

The splitting rule (SP) is used to add new conditions to a clause ψ_i in order to render further applications of the evaluation rule:

$$SP:\quad C \Rightarrow_{SP} \{C\ \cup\ \{\sim f(x^*)\equiv g_1(y_1^*)\}\ ,\ \ldots\ ,\ C\ \cup\ \{\sim f(x^*)\equiv g_n(y_n^*)\}\}$$

where C is a clause , $\{\ \langle\sim x\equiv g_1(y_1^*)\rangle\ ,\ldots,\ \langle\sim x\equiv g_n(y_n^*)\rangle\ \}$ is the case analysis of a structure S (the case analysis of structure nat, for example, reads $\{\langle\sim x\equiv 0\rangle,\langle\sim x\equiv s(u)\rangle\}$) and the skolem term $f(x^*)$ occurs in a goal literal of C and is of structure S. The splitting rule is sound because with $\langle x\equiv g_1(t_1^*)\rangle,\ldots,x\equiv g_n(t_n^*)\rangle\ \in\ REP_S\ \subset\ Ax$ (e.g. $\langle x\equiv 0\ ,\ x\equiv s(p(x))\rangle\ \in\ REP_{nat}$ we have $Ax \vdash C\ \cup\ \{\sim f(x^*)\equiv g_1(y_1^*)\}\ \wedge\ \ldots\ \wedge\ C\ \cup\ \{\sim f(x^*)\equiv\ g_n(y_n^*)\}\ \rightarrow\ C$

The substitution rules SUB.F and SUB.E are used to extract terms by eliminating functions and equalities .

$$SUB.F:\quad C\ \cup\ \{L\}\ \Rightarrow_{SUB.F}\ \{C\ \cup\ \{t_k\equiv t_k'\}\}$$

where $L = \{g(t_1 \ldots t_n) \equiv g(t'_1 \ldots t'_n)\}$ is a goal literal, and $t_i = t'_i$ for $i \in \{1, \ldots$
$\ldots, n\} \setminus \{k\}$. The rule SUB.F is sound because with $t_i = t'_i$ for $i \in \{1, \ldots, n\} \setminus \{k\}$ it
is $Ax \vdash C \cup \{t_k \equiv t'_k\} \to C \cup \{g(t_1 \ldots t_n) \equiv g(t'_1 \ldots t'_n)\}$.

$$SUB.E: \quad C \cup \{K,L\} \Rightarrow_{SUB.E} \{C \cup \{M\}\}$$

where $L = \{t' \equiv t\}$ is a goal literal, $K = \{\sim t'' \equiv t\}$ is a literal, and $M = \{t' \equiv t''\}$ is a
goal literal. The rule SUB.E is sound because with $Ax \vdash \langle L, \sim M, K \rangle$ we can prove
$Ax \vdash C \cup \{M\} \to C \cup \{L,K\}$. The substitution rules are very strong and therefore
(up to exceptions) applied whenever possible. Hence formulas are often transformed goal-directed to render the applicability of a substitution rule.

The implication rule (IMPL) is used to replace a goal literal by a new one
to enable further transformations.

$$IMPL: \quad C \cup \{L\} \Rightarrow_{IMPL} \{C \cup \{\sim \sigma K\} | K \in D \setminus \{L'\}\}$$

where C and D are clauses, L and $\sim \sigma K$ are goal literals, $D \cup \{L'\} \in Ax$ and
$\sigma L' = L$ for some substitution σ. The implication rule is sound because with
$D \cup \{L'\} \in Ax$ and $\sigma L' = L$ we have $Ax \vdash \Lambda_{K \in D \setminus \{L'\}} C \cup \{\sim \sigma K\} \to C \cup \{L\}$.

The last rule to be described is the elimination rule (EL) which allows to
eliminate certain conditions from a clause.

$$EL: \quad C \cup \{L\} \Rightarrow_{EL} \{C\}$$

where C is a definition formula, L is an induction hypothesis or there exists
a variable which occurs in L but not in C. This rule is sound because
$Ax \vdash C \to C \cup \{L\}$.

We now proceed in our example. The first step in expanding the node
$\psi_1 = \langle \sim y \equiv 0 , sub(f(x\ y)y) \equiv x \ [G] \rangle$ will be trying to evaluate function sub. But
to apply the EV-rule together with axiom Ax5 fails because we do not have any
information about the term $f(x\ y)$. Therefore a case analysis about that term
would be helpful. Application of the splitting rule yields: $\psi_3 = \langle \sim f(x\ y) \equiv 0 ,$
$\sim y \equiv 0, sub(f(x\ y)y) \equiv x \ [G] \rangle$ and $\psi_4 = \langle \sim f(x\ y) \equiv s(u) , \sim y \equiv 0 , sub(f(x\ y)y) \equiv x \ [G] \rangle$.
Expanding ψ_3 by the EV-rule using Ax4 gives us $\psi_5 = \langle \sim f(x\ y) \equiv 0, \sim y \equiv 0, 0 \equiv x \ [G] \rangle$.
The node ψ_5 is closed because the goal literal does not contain function f. By
expansion of formula ψ_4 whith the EV-rule using Ax5 we obtain $\psi_6 = \langle \sim f(x\ y) \equiv s(u)$
$\sim y \equiv 0 , f(x\ y) \equiv x \ [G] \rangle$, to which the elimination rule can be applied yielding
$\psi_7 = \langle \sim y \equiv 0, f(x\ y) \equiv x \ [G] \rangle$. This node is closed because it is a definition for-
formula. So far, our derivation tree looks like in figure 2 (see appendix).

Now we turn our attention to formula $\psi_2 = \langle \sim y \equiv s(v) , \sim sub(f(x\ v)v) \equiv x \ [H] ,$
$sub(f(x\ y)y) \equiv x \ [G] \rangle$. The first two transformation steps are done analoguously
to those of formula ψ_1. We first apply the splitting rule and get
$\psi_8 = \langle \sim f(x\ y) \equiv 0 , \sim y \equiv s(v) , \sim sub(f(x\ v)v) \equiv x \ [H] , sub(f(x\ y)y) \equiv x \ [G] \rangle$ and
$\psi_9 = \langle \sim f(x\ y) \equiv s(u), \sim y \equiv s(v), \sim sub(f(x\ v)v) \equiv x \ [H], sub(f(x\ y)y) \equiv x \ [G] \rangle$. Expanding ψ_8 by the EV-rule using Ax4 yields $\psi_{10} = \langle \sim f(x\ y) \equiv 0, \sim y \equiv s(v),$

~sub(f(x v)v)≡x [H],   0≡x [G]> , which is a closed node because the goal literal does not contain f. Expanding ψ_9 by the EV-rule using Ax6 yields
ψ_{11} = <~f(x y)≡s(u), ~y≡s(v), ~sub(f(x v)v)≡x [H], sub(u v)≡x [G]>. We now see
that it is possible to apply the substitution rules SUB.E and SUB.F. Rule
SUB.E yields: ψ_{12} = <~f(x y)≡s(u), ~y≡s(v), sub(u v)≡sub(f(x v)v)[G]>. Rule
SUB.F yields: ψ_{13} = <~f(x y)≡s(u), ~y≡s(v), u≡f(x v) [G]>. Now a definition
formula could be derived (by rule SUB.E) if we were able to identify the terms
u and s(u) in ψ_{13}. Such kind of problems are solved by the implication rule
together with axiom Ax3. We obtain ψ_{14} = < ~f(x y)≡s(u), ~y≡s(v),
s(u)≡s(f(x v))[G]> and finally with SUB.E ψ_{15}=<~y≡s(v), f(x y)≡s(f(x v))[G]>.

Since ψ_{15} is a definition formula all nodes in the derivation tree are
closed and the synthesis process terminates (see figure 3). ψ_7 and ψ_{15} are the
definition formulas of function f. Written as implications we have synthesized
∀x,y:nat [y≡0 → f(x y)≡x]   and   ∀x,y,v:nat [y≡s(v) → f(x y)≡s(f(x v))]. Now
this definition has to be tested for admissibility. The test succeeds, i.e.
the system proves Ax ⊢$_I$ ∀y,v:nat ~[y≡0 ∧ y≡s(v)]   (uniqueness) ,
Ax ⊢$_I$ ∀y:nat [y≡0 ∨ ∃v:nat y≡s(v)] (completeness) and the termination according to the well-founded order relation of the immediate structural prede-
cessor. Finally the induction system has to prove the remainder formulas
ψ_5= ∀x,y:nat [y≡0 ∧ f(x y)≡0 → x≡0] and ψ_{10}= ∀x,y,v:nat [y≡s(v) ∧ f(x y)≡0 ∧
sub(f(x v)v)≡x → x≡0] . Ax U DEF$_f$ ⊢$_I$ ψ_5 holds because ψ_5 is an immediate consequence of the first definition formula of f. Ax U DEF$_f$ ⊢$_I$ ψ_{10} holds because
according to the second definition formula of f the conditions y≡s(v) and
f(x y)≡0 mutually exclude each other, i.e. f(x(s(v))=s(f(x v))≠0 . Thus we
have completed the synthesis successfully and thereby ψ is proved. The algorithm the synthesis system has generated for f obviously computes the addition
of natural numbers.

Note however that the formula ψ = ∀x,y:nat∃z:nat sub(z y)≡x we used here can
be proved by our induction system without program synthesis. We have choosen ψ
only to demonstrate our method by a clear and short example. The real advantage of our method appears if the existence formulas to be proved are more
complex and the functions to be synthesized are not as natural as the addition
of natural numbers. An example for a more complex problem is the 'TAUTOLOGY:
CHECKER' (TC) of Boyer and Moore [3]. TC is a decision procedure for the propositional calculus. The completeness of TC reads:
∀e:expression [∀a:assignment value(e a)≡true → TC(e)] resp.
(*)   ∀e:expression ∃a:assignment [~TC(e) → value(e a)≡false]. To prove this
formula Boyer and Moore define a function falsify which given a propositional
expression e returns an assignment which makes e false, provided e is no tau-

tology. Replacing the existentially quantified variable a by falsify(e) their system is able to prove the completeness of TC. In our system we attempt to prove (*) by synthesizing the function falsify.

5. CONCLUSION

We have presented a method to find existence proofs using techniques of deductive program synthesis. A formal framework and several transformation rules have been specified. Many examples have been completed by hand: Among others we have synthesized the minimum- and sort-function on lists of natural numbers, the gcd-function and the function falsify (cf. section 4).

Our method has been implemented by a synthesis system which in its current implementation state performs a user-guided synthesis of some arithmetical functions like addition, difference, the remainder function etc. Additionally several non recursive function definitions have been derived automatically. We are presently working on the implementation of some additional transformation rules to enable the system to interactively derive definitions of more complex functions like, for instance, gcd, falsify etc.

The synthesis system presently works as follows: Given an existence formula ψ as input skolemization and the induction rule are carried out automatically. The system attempts to expand each node of the derivation tree, i.e. finds out which transformation rules can be applied to a node ψ_i and asks the user which one to select. According to the answer the system carries out the transformation. The process resumes with the new nodes until each node is a definition or a remainder formula. The process terminates if all nodes are closed. Then the definition formulas are picked up and tested for admissibility. Finally the remainder formulas are proved by the induction system.

The synthesis system as it is now implemented serves to obtain some experience with our method. It is used to deal with examples which are too complex to be dealt with manually. By means of those examples we intend to develop strategies and heuristics to drive and select the transformation rules. This control information will be implemented by a control component to enable the system to synthesize function definitions with as little user-guidance as possible.

ACKNOWLEDGEMENT:

I would like to thank C. Walther for his helpful criticism and support which greatly contributed to the present form of this paper.

REFERENCES:
[1] Aubin R., Mechanizing Structural Induction. Part I: Formal System.
Part II: Strategies. Theoretical Computer Science 9 (1979).
[2] Bibel W., Syntax-Directed, Semantics-Supported Program Synthesis. Artificial Intelligence 14 (1980).
[3] Boyer R.S., Moore J S., A Computational Logic. Academic Press (1979).
[4] Biundo S., Zboray F., Automated Induction Proofs Using Methods of Program
Synthesis. Computers and Artificial Intelligence 3, No.6 (1984) also: Interner
Bericht 16/84 Universitaet Karlsruhe (1984).
[5] Goguen J.A., How to Prove Algebraic Inductive Hypotheses Without Induction, With Applications to the Correctness of Data Type Implementation. Proc.
of the 5th Conference on Automated Deduction (1980).
[6] Huet G., Hullot J.M., Proofs by Induction in Equational Theories with
Constructors. 21st Ann. Symp. on Foundations of Computer Science. IEEE (1980).
[7] Hutter D., Using Resolution and Paramodulation for Induction Proofs. Interner Bericht 6/86 Universitaet Karlsruhe (1986).
[8] Musser D.L., On Proving Inductive Properties of Abstract Data Types.
Proc. of the 7th Ann. ACM Symp. on Principles of Programming Languages (1980).
[9] Manna Z., Waldinger R., Synthesis: Dreams → Programs. IEEE Transactions
on Software Engineering Vol.SE-5 No.4 (1979)
[10] Manna Z., Waldinger R., A Deductive Approach to Program Synthesis. ACM
Transactions on Programming Languages and Systems Vol.2 No.1 (1980)

APPENDIX:

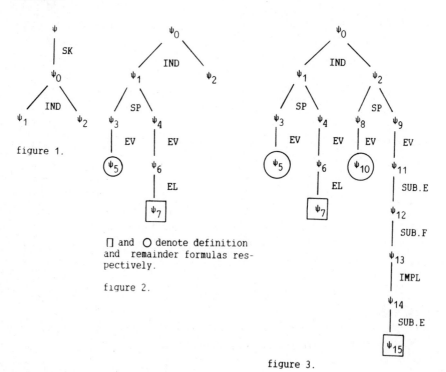

figure 1.

$\square$ and $\bigcirc$ denote definition
and remainder formulas respectively.

figure 2.

figure 3.

Advances in Artificial Intelligence - II
B. Du Boulay, D. Hogg and L. Steels (Editors)
© Elsevier Science Publishers B.V. (North-Holland), 1987

AUTOMATED DEDUCTION IN AN UNCERTAIN AND INCONSISTENT DATA BASIS.

Béatrice Duval, Yves Kodratoff
Laboratoire de Recherche en Informatique,
UA 410 du CNRS
Université Paris-Sud, Bâtiment 490,
91450 ORSAY

I. INTRODUCTION

Uncertain reasoning must deal with modalities that concern temporality, regularities, typicality (with the problem of case exceptions), uncertainty about the validity of inferences, uncertainty about data...[Doy 79, Far 82, Farre 85, Gab 84, Rei 85]. Since classical logic cannot deal with these problems, representations using modal logic, multivalued logic or fuzzy logic are at a development stage. These approaches concentrate on the study of modalities,but present two drawbacks. Firstly, at present there exists no system able to handle all these modalities. The only exception we know is L.Farrinas Del Cerro's attempt with a theorem prover in modal logic[Far]. Secondly, these systems do not really possess explicative abilities. For instance, one of the most famous expert system, MYCIN, uses a logic based on certainty factors, but the exact meaning of inferences using certainty factors has not yet been completely elucidated and the explanation ability can only be realized by complex systems like MIRLITHO [Gan 83].
Here we present a quite different approach, in the sense that we do not concentrate on the logic of modalities, but rather study which inference mechanisms are valid in the domain of uncertain knowledge.
For that purpose, we propose a model based on the resolution principle and which represents modalities as symbolic operators that are combined during inferences. Those symbolic operators, called modulations (in order to stress the difference with logic modal operators) are defined by the user and their combinations, obtained during inferences, will be interpreted in further studies. Of course, we are studying this interpretation problem but this is not expounded in this paper. On the other hand, we stress the problem of correct reasoning, especially when we have to deal with contradictory information.
We think that a system carrying out automated deduction on uncertain knowledge must compulsarily fulfil the three following requirements.
1- Inference explanation ability.
This requirement is universally accepted in the Expert Systems community, but in the field of uncertain knowledge, existing realizations use representations and deduction schemas that make this goal difficult. The method that we describe here proposes to lead inferences while keeping a trace of modulations concerned, and then to interpret this trace using a modulation solver. The writing of this future modulation solver will rely heavily on the results of Modal Logics. This approach will enable result justification to be obtained without any difficulty.
2- Contradiction handling.
Experts usually use negative information that is difficult to express and that introduces "inconsistency" in the knowledge basis. We speak of "inconsitency" or contradiction in the data basis when two reasonings leading to contradictory events, are possible in the same context. This also happens when the knowledge basis contains general laws and some of their exceptions. Even if we are able to detect such contradictory data, we cannot get rid of them because they reflect the experts' practical experience. This is why we propose a study of inferences on uncertain and "inconsistent" data basis. We think that this difficult problem is fundamentally relevant to reasoning and that it cannot be solved by only numerical means [Kod-Per 85].
3- Flexibility relative to external demands.
This distinction between reasoning and combination of plausibilities enables us to access to very improbable reasonings when conclusions of high plausibility lead to failure. Let us consider for example the following problem. Physicians know that the stings of some venimous

harvest-bugs induce a deterioration of the nervous system, and that venimous harvest-bugs are very common in Africa, but that there are no venimous harvest-bugs in France. A patient presents symptoms of tiredness and nervous trouble. This patient was never out of France, but among different remarks about his recent past, he points out that he has been stung by a harvest-bug. The diagnosis : venimous harvest-bug is so unlikely that it cannot be reached. Yet it is the right diagnosis that the physician must propose after considering that the other possible conclusions led to failure. This situation can be obtained automatically only if reasoning schemas are not embedded in plausibility evaluation. In this case, a special session should be run taking into account the information about the patient being stung by a harvest-bug, regardeless of plausibility. In this case the external demand would be: find a reasoning path which explains the symptoms and uses some argumentative information about harvest-bug. This is indeed a quite unusual demand!

II. INCONSISTENCY IN UNCERTAIN DATA BASIS.

In the following, we shall use Edinburg PROLOG convention [Clo].
A Horn clause $P_1 \lor \neg N_1 \lor ... \lor \neg N_m$
is written $P_1 :- N_1 , ... , N_m$.
A pure negative clause $\neg N_1 \lor ... \lor \neg N_p$
is written $:- N_1 , ... , N_p$.

Uncertain knowledge bases are often "inconsistent". We mean by "inconsistent" that two reasonings leading to contradictory events are possible in the same context. This often happens with uncertain knowledge bases because they are linked to problems where the expert must lead reasonings on incomplete data bases and must conclude in spite of some lack of information.
An other example is the case of exceptions. One knows a law that is generally true and an instance of it that says the contrary.
For instance suppose that one knows that, generally, birds fly and that penguin is a bird that does not fly. A possible internal representation of this information (where the "uncertainty" is neglected) is

$$fly(X) \qquad :- \quad bird(X).$$
$$bird(penguin) \quad :- \quad .$$
$$:- \quad fly(penguin).$$

which of course is contradictory.

These remarks raise a problem which is important in practice, the problem of negative information handling.
Imagine that the negation of some predicates is defined. Let us denote by $\neg A = A'$, as for instance in the case of the predicate "not-equal" which is defined as "different".
There are, in general, few such predicates.
Furthermore let us imagine that the negation of some modalities is also known. Let us note it by $\neg [mod] = [mod']$.
The contrary of "generally" can be defined as "weakly-possible".
There are also, in general, few such modulations.
The case we are considering here may therefore happen, but notice that it is only "weakly-posssible".
If it happens, it is quite obvious that, in classical logics the three following expressions should be equivalent :

$$[mod] \qquad :- \quad A.$$
$$[mod'] \quad A \quad :- \quad .$$
$$[mod] \quad A' \quad :- \quad .$$

This is no longer true when the data basis becomes inconsistent.
One must be aware that contradictions can in this way be introduced or removed by the user.
The set of clauses

$$[generally] \qquad\qquad :- \quad different(a, b).$$
$$different(X, Y) \quad :-$$

is inconsistent, but the set

[*weakly-possible*]   *different(a, b)*   :-   .
                        different(X, Y)   :-   .

which is supposed to express the same thing is no longer inconsistent.
The user must be aware that giving information about the negation of a predicate cannot be considered as being strictly equivalent to giving information about its assertion. This is the price one has to pay when dealing with inconsistency. Nevertheless, the following examples show how seldom the case occurs.
In the example about penguins, we already had predicate "fly" at our disposal, this is why internal representation of "penguin does not fly" is

$$:-fly(penguin).$$

Let us imagine that we have interesting information relative to "unflying" animals, then one could have also written

$$unfly(penguin) :-$$

together with the negative information that "fly" is the contrary of "unfly", i.e., that they cannot occur together, the internal representation of which is

$$:-fly(X), unfly(X)$$

It follows that the existence of predicate negations cannot be used to remove inconsistency. On the contrary, the existence of modulation negations can allow the removal of some inconsistencies.The decision to use one modulation or its opposite, to introduce or not two contrary predicates, is a decision that cannot be taken in advance and must be left to the expert.
In the treatment of Natural Language, extreme care should be given to the real informative content of sentences of the type : Generally A occurs, and : A does seldom not occur.
For instance, when one says "Generally, Mary is present to the meeting", one means less than when one says " Mary is seldom not present to the meeting". Usually, internal representation will use the predicate "is-present(X)" rather than its contrary "is-not-present(X)". Therefore, it is better to represent both of the above sentences by using the predicate "is-present(X)". The first sentence will be internally represented by a "generally" which is weaker than in the internal representation of the second sentence.

III. MODULATION OF UNCERTAINTY

Modal Logics introduce modal operators that give the modality of the concerned expression. Their aim is the description of the laws that govern the use of the operators.
For each modality, a specific logic is created. How to combine the different modalities is a difficult problem. Besides, in practice, **each** specific application will use its own specific modalities. For instance, the modality of generality is different in Chemistry and Metallurgy.
In the following we shall introduce operators that apply to the whole clause (and neither to its predicates nor to its variables).
In order to avoid confusion with Modal Logics, the way we express modality will be called here a *modulation*. It is an operator put inside brackets to the left of the clause. The difference with Modal Logics is that we shall use the classical first order resolution principle. The resolution process is carried out as if the clauses were not modulated, but each time a resolvent is computed, we build the modulation of the resolvent clause, which is a chain (or a pile) of the modulations of its parent clauses. The exact meaning of such a chain is not given here and is left to the user, since we believe that the combination of modalities is strongly domain dependent.
Example.
Suppose that we want to represent the knowledge included in the two following sentences.
S_1 : *If Robert is present , generally Mary is present also.*
S_2 : *Generally Robert is present.*
Let us suppose that we dispose of the predicate "is-present(X)" to give an internal representation to these sentences, and of the modulation "[generally]".
A possible internal representation is then using the two following clauses.

C_1 [generally] is-present(mary) :- is-present(robert).
C_2 [generally] is-present(robert) :-

The modulation [generally] expresses the modality of the whole clause that follows.
Suppose that one now asks the question

$Q1$: *Is Mary present ?*

This will be internally represented by the pure negative clause

$$C_3 \quad :- \quad is\text{-}present(mary).$$

Resolution leads to the empty clause with the resolution of C1 and C_3 that gives

$$C_4 \quad [generally] \quad :- \quad is\text{-}present(mary).$$

Resolution of C_4 and C2 gives the empty clause with the chain of modulations

$$[generally, generally]$$

We conclude that Mary is present and that this information is known with the modality expressed by the modulation [generally, generally].

The comma is here a composition operator which will not be further defined. The user must say what he considers as valid composition of generally during the execution of an inference.

Nevertheless, to help the reader's intuition, let us propose some examples of possible composition laws.

- As an example, one can propose that [generally, generally] = [often], but more detail depends on the topic of the inferences.

- An other example is that [generally] can be replaced by a belief coefficient, as has been done in EMYCIN, and the method reduced to EMYCIN combination of beliefs.[Bo 82, Hay 82].

- A third example would be that the combination is the EMYCIN one, with symbolic test beforehand that would decide that [generally, .., generally] reduces to [seldom] for a chain whose length might be, for example, 10. This can enables discontinuous jumps in the computation of the beliefs.

- Let us now give a final, less trivial example, suited to the case where some instantiations take place during the inference process.

Instantiating a law with variables can lead to special trouble in uncertain reasoning. We do not claim that we solve this problem here, but we propose a solution that can be very often valid.

This solution takes into account the fact that a user should always be much more aware of facts that are completely instantiated than of general laws. If one disagrees with this statement, the following solution is no longer valid.

Suppose that our knowledge includes that generally, frenchmen drink coffee and that a particular one, named Toto, seldom drinks coffee. The internal representation of this information can be as follows.

$$
\begin{array}{llll}
C_1 & [generally] & drinks\text{-}coffee(X) & :- \quad french(X). \\
C_2 & [seldom] & drinks\text{-}coffee(toto) & :- \quad . \\
C_3 & [certain] & french(toto) & :- \quad .
\end{array}
$$

Let us then ask the question;" Does Toto drink coffee? ". We therefore add to the above set of clauses the new one

$$C_4 \quad :- \quad drinks\text{-}coffee(toto).$$

During resolution, let us keep track of the instantiations that are carried out.

By resolution of C_4 and C_2, the empty clause is obtained, with the modulation [seldom]. The conclusion is that Toto seldom drinks coffee.

But another proof is also possible, by resolving C_4 and C_1 with the substitution $\{X <- toto\}$. This gives

$$C_5 \quad [generally\{X <- toto\}] \quad :- \quad french(toto).$$

where the substitution recalls that this modulation comes from a resolution with a substitution.

One can then resolve C_4 and C_5, obtaining thus the empty clause with modulation $[generally\{X <- toto\}, certain]$. Recall that "." is the modulation composition operator used in one reasoning path.

Let + be the composition operator for two modulations issuing from two different proofs of the same statement.

Combining the two proofs, one finds that Toto drinks coffee with the modulation [seldom] + $[generally\{X <- toto\}$, certain], which is certainly absurd if one does not come back to [seldom] which is a given data.

Suppose therefore that we want to put faith into the instantiated data, we shall use the combination law

$$[modulation] + [modulation\text{'}\{X <- ..\}] = [modulation]$$

An other possible solution is to refuse to give any weight at all to the general law and to use a combination law that will less drastically reduce the influence of the general law.

This example shows that our approach greatly differentiates between the composition laws "," and "+".

IV. SYMBOLIC UNCERTAIN INFERENCE.

IV-1. Uncertain resolution from a consistent set of clauses.

Obtention of one modulation chain.

Let us consider the problem of a consistent set of clauses.

Recall that each Horn clause (and not its variables nor some of the predicates it contains) is qualified by a modulation like "generally", "seldom", "often"..

To perform an uncertain inference, we want to apply PROLOG resolution strategy and build the pile formed by the modulations of the clauses used during this process. Each time a goal matches the head of a clause, the modulation of this clause is added to the list of modulations. When the empty clause is deduced, which means in PROLOG that the pile of goals to be solved is empty, the pile of modulations so obtained can be given as a chain of modulations that modulate the last solved problem.

If backtracking is necessary, the modulation pile must be handled exactly in the same way as the substitutions pile is handled by PROLOG interpreter: Modulations present in the pile up to the backtrack point are removed from the pile of modulations. So it seems that this construction can be achieved in the PROLOG interpreter itself without great effort. A new field should be added in the internal representation of a clause to describe the modulation, and traces of modulaions used during inferences are constructed by using a pile which is handled similarly to the pile of substitutuions. Finally, each chain corresponds to a different proof of the goal one started from.

The main point we should like to stress here is that inclusion of modalities should then have little effect on PROLOG execution speed.

Combination of uncertain reasonings.

It may happen that for a given question many ways of deducing the empty clause are possible. As we work with uncertain inference, we must explore all the ways which lead to the empty clause and can give different chains of modulations. At the final stage, we simply give to the user a printout of all these results without solving the problem of combining the different chains.

We are well aware that we therefore skip the difficult problem of explicitly finding the combination laws. Our opinion, already given in the introduction is that this is in any case the user's responsability. Examples of this behaviour have already be given in section III.

Our approach consists in explicitly keeping the modulation tree, and then computing it with a modulation solver built as an expert system: the combination laws are given by the user and are suited to the type of problem and the nature of uncertainty in the expert domain.

Our purpose here is only to show how one can modify the classical theory of first order resolution in order to deal with uncertainty in the PROLOG environment.

IV-2. Uncertain resolution from an inconsistent set of clauses.

We say that an uncertain data basis is inconsistent if, when forgetting the modulations, we can deduce the empty clause from the data basis alone.

In this case, it is obvious (see example below) that a classical demonstration enables both a fact and its contrary to be deduced, using different reasonings.

So we consider that in an inconsistent data basis the modulation of A and the modulation of ¬A are independent (an example follows shortly).

So the classical postulate : if A is true then ¬A is false, is no longer valid and we have to find the modulation of ¬A independently of the A's . We must point out that this is not an intuitionistic postulate (intuitionism works with consistent data basis) but a way of taking into account contradictions in the data basis.

This postulate prohibits the use of the PROLOG predicate "NOT".

Let us consider, for example, the following statements:

P_1 : *if Robert is present, generally Mary is present.*
P_2 : *if John is present, generally Mary is not present.*
P_3 : *if Mary is present, generally the meeting is not quiet.*
P_4 : *if Mary and Betty are present, often the meeting is not quiet.*
P_5 : *Robert is present.*
P_6 : *sometimes Betty is present.*
P_7 : *generally John is present.*
We want to have information about "quiet(meeting)", which means that we want to know if this fact can be deduced from this statement, and to find its modulation.

The problem expressed in natural language is translated into a set of clauses; our inconsistent data basis consists of:
     - a set S1 of Horn clauses, each of them containing one positive predicate;
     - a set S2 of negative clauses.

For our example, the sentences are represented by the two following sets of clauses.

$$S_1$$

C_1	[generally]	is-present(mary)	:-	is-present(robert).
C_5		is-present(robert)	:-	.
C_6	[sometimes]	is-present(betty)	:-	.
C_7	[generally]	is-present(john)	:-	.

$$S_2$$

C_2	[generally]	:-	is-present(john), is-present(mary).
C_3	[generally]	:-	is-present(mary), quiet(meeting).
C_4	[often]	:-	is-present(mary), is-present(betty), quiet(meeting).

Purely negative information is disjointed from the other clauses, and let us recall that we do not use the PROLOG "NOT".
To obtain information about a predicate A, we must first find the modulation of this predicate A, which means finding the modulation that qualifies the statement " A is true ". To perform this task, we apply the resolution mechanism to the set of clauses S_1 with the initial goal A. We are working on a set of Horn clauses with the question ¬A; so the uncertain inference process described in section IV-1 works and gives us all the modulation chains for A.
In our example, the clause that represents the question is:
$$:- quiet(meeting).$$
None of the clause heads of S_1 matches this goal. It follows that we have no information about the truth of that predicate "quiet(meeting)".

Because we have seen that the modulations of A and ¬A are not linked, we must now find the modulation that qualifies the predicate ¬A, i.e. the modulation that qualifies the statement "A is false".
To find the modulation of ¬A, we must compute the refutation proofs of ¬A from the data basis formed by S_1 and S_2. We propose a mechanism that enables the search for these refutation paths using PROLOG strategy.

The data basis S_1 is modified into S_1'.
S_1' contains as first clause the clause:

$$C_0: \qquad A \quad :- \quad .$$

and then all the clauses of S_1.
The set S_1' for our example is:

C_0 :		quiet(meeting)	:-	.
C_1 :	[generally]	is-present(mary)	:-	is-present(robert).
C_5 :		is-present(robert)	:-	.
C_6 :	[sometimes]	is-present(betty)	:-	.
C_7 :	[generally]	is-present(john)	:-	.

We shall run several PROLOG sessions with different questions: each clause of S_2 is a question of a PROLOG session. From the sessions which can deduce the empty clause, we only keep those which use the clause

$$A \quad :- \quad .$$

of S'_1, and the corresponding chains of modulations are printed out: those chains provide the information about the statement "A is false".

Since our set S_2 contains three clauses, we shall successively run three PROLOG sessions. The first one will try to answer the question

$$[generally] \quad :- \quad is\text{-}present(john), is\text{-}present(mary).$$

The empty clause can be deduced for this session, but the resolution path does not use the clause

$$C_0 \quad quiet(meeting) \quad :- \quad .$$

So we do not keep the modulation chain obtained during this proof.

The second session tries to answer the question:

$$[generally] \quad :- \quad is\text{-}present(mary), quiet(meeting).$$

This conjunction of goals can be proved by a resolution using clauses C_1, C_5, C_0. The resolution path uses the clause C_0 which is our subject of interest, so we notice the corresponding modulation chain $[generally, generally]$.

The third session tries to answer the question

$$[often] \quad is\text{-}present(mary), is\text{-}present(betty), \quad quiet(meeting).$$

This conjunction of goals can be proved using clauses C_1, C_5, C_6, and C_0, and the modulation chain built during this proof is $[often, generally, sometimes]$.

So the results proposed to the user would be:
- *no information about quiet(meeting).*
- *knowledge about -quiet(meeting) is affected by the modulation chain: $[generally, generally]$ + $[often, generally, sometimes]$.*

At present, the authors do not know whether the strategy underlying the above example is complete or not. We are still looking either for a proof of its completeness or for a characterization of the cases where it can be applied if it should proved incomplete.

At any rate, compared to more classical stategies[Hay 82] that directly combine the proof of a fact and of its negation, our stategy does not mix the uncertainty relative to truth and to falsity.

V. CONCLUSION.

Up to now, most of the work done in Symbolic Uncertain Inference has been referred to as Modal Logics. In this paper, we are pushing forward a practical point of view which is not part of the usual approach of Modal Logics.

Our opinion is that optimal solutions can be found only by merging the results of our approach and those obtained by Modal Logics.

Therefore, this paper does not at all claim to be the final solution to the difficult problem of Uncertain Reasoning. Rather it attempts to show that more effort than expected is necessary. An implementation of these ideas will be carried out next year and should be part of a PROLOG environment.

Other developments concerning Symbolic Uncertain Inference we are currently studying are:
- a study of modulations qualifying particular predicates, instead of the whole clause[Gan 85].
- a study of the use of modulations as a guide to the difficult problem of a "conflict resolution" as defined by the Expert System Approach.

ACKNOWLEDGEMENTS.
This paper has been partially sponsored by ESPRIT ALPES contract and by GRECO & PRC "Intelligence artificielle".

REFERENCES.

[Bo 82] Bonnet A., Harry J., Ganascia J.-G., "Un système expert inférant la géologie du sous-sol", TSI 1, 1982.

[2] Cloksin and Mellish, Programming in PROLOG, Springer Verlag.

[Doy 79] Doyle J., "A truth maintenance system". Artificial Intelligence, Vol 12 1979.

[Du 85] Dubois D, Farreny H., Prade H., "Some Problems in the Automation of Common Sense Reasoning". AFCET 1985.

[Far 82] Farinas del Cerro L., "A simple deduction method for modal logic", Information Processing Letters, Vol 14, 1982.

[Far] Farinas Del Cerro L., "MOLOG: a System that extends PROLOG with Modal Logic", to appear in New Generation Computer Journal.

[Farre 85] Farreny H., Prade H., "Mécanisation de raisonnement par défaut en termes de possibilités", TSI, 1985.

[Gab 84] Gabbay D. and Reyle U., "N-PROLOG: An extension of PROLOG with hypothetical implications.", Journal of Logic Programming, vol.1 numb. 4, 1984.

[Gan 83] Ganascia J.-G., "Mirlitho: Validation des résultats et détection de contradictions dans les systèmes de diagnostic" Thèse de Docteur Ingénieur. Université de Paris Sud. 1983.

[Gan 85] Ganascia J.-G., Kodratoff Y., "Symbolic uncertain inference: A Study of Possible Modalities", Proc. Expert Systems 85,Warrick Dec. 85.

[Haj 82] Hajek P., "Combining Functions for Certainty Factors in Consulting Systems", A. I. and Information Control Systems of Robots, Smolenice 1982, p. 107-110.

[Kod-Per 85] Kodratoff Y., Perdrix H., Franova M., "Traitement Symbolique du Raisonnement Incertain", Actes du Congres AFCET: Materiels et Logiciels pour la 5ème génération, Paris, Mars 1985.

[Kod 85] Kodratoff Y., Ganascia J.-G., "Démonstration automatique de théorèmes et systèmes experts,quelques faits élémentaires", Proc. 5th International Worksh op on Expert Systems & their Applications, Avignon 1985, pp. 69-98

[Kow 79] Kowalski R., "Logic for Problem Solving", North Holland Elsevier, New York 1979.

[Lusk 82] Lusk E., Overbeek R., "An LMA-Based Theorem Prover", Publication interne, Argonne National Laborarory, 1982.

[Derm 82] Mac Dermott D., "Non-monotonic Logic. Non-monotonic modal theories", J. of Assoc.Comp. Mach., Vol. 29, 1982.

[Rei 80] Reiter R., "A logic for default reasoning", Artificial Intelligence, Vol. 13, 1980.

[Rob 65] Robinson J.A., "A machine oriented logic based on resolution principle", J.ACM, 1965.

Advances in Artificial Intelligence - II
B. Du Boulay, D. Hogg and L. Steels (Editors)
© Elsevier Science Publishers B.V. (North-Holland), 1987

TAXONOMIC DEFAULT THEORY

Christine FROIDEVAUX

Laboratoire de Recherche en Informatique
Bat 490 University of Paris XI
91405 Orsay - FRANCE

This paper presents a new formalization of NETL-like semantic networks using Default Logic, and shows the advantages of this formalization over a previous one (Reiter & Etherington). In order to do this we introduce a new class of non-normal and non-semi-normal defaults, which constitute a so called taxonomic theory. We state that these theories have an extension. We then provide a way of translating these default rules into PROLOG clauses, yielding a hierarchical logic Data Base. We establish a link between both formalisms.

1. Introduction

Type hierarchies, like those of Semantic Networks, are a way of representing general statements about typical objects, and allowing information about individual objects to be inferred by means of simple inheritance mechanisms. A correspondence between some types of semantic networks (not compatible with any form of default reasoning) and certain classical first-order theories has been provided by Schubert (1976) [16] and Hayes (1977) [10]. The NETL system, conceived by Fahlman [6], and modified by Touretzky, Van Roggen and himself [7], is a knowledge-base system allowing inheritance with exceptions, that has interesting features, namely the heuristic power of semantic networks combined with a precise semantics due to a possible translation into default logic [14].

A first correspondence is provided by Etherington and Reiter in [4]. We give here a different interpretation using default logic for the NETL hierarchies: this formalization has the advantage of determining the translation of one link independently of that of the others and could include a handling of ambiguity.

Reiter has only established the existence of extensions for normal theories [14]. Unfortunately, the class of normal theories has turned out to be insufficient for knowledge representation problems: semi-normal default theories have been introduced by Reiter and Criscuolo [15]. Etherington and Reiter have shown in [4] that some semi-normal default theories have an extension, namely the default theories corresponding to acyclic inheritance networks with exceptions.

We propose a new class of default theories, all of whose defaults are neither normal nor semi-normal. The special form of the defaults guaranties, nevertheless, the existence of an extension for such theories. Moreover it enables us to use an algorithm that generates theorems. More precisely, the defaults translate easily into PROLOG clauses that constitute a part of a logic data base satisfying Clark's hierarchical constraint [2]. We establish a link between the default theory and the logic data base.

In the first part of the paper, we deal with the problem of the translation of the NETL-like ISA hierarchies with exceptions into default logic. In the second part we study the formal properties of the formalization that we propose.

2. Semantic networks and default logic

2.1. NETL semantic networks

We restrict the NETL network to the partial graphs which deal with IS-A hierarchies. The graphs are acyclic.

Consider the following example (*) from Fahlman [6]:
    (a) Molluscs are Shell-bearers
    (b) Cephalopods are Molluscs, but are not Shell-bearers
    (c) Nautili are Cephalopods, but are Shell-bearers

(For Fahlman these are assertions about prototypes). The resulting network is:

fig.1

Sb (Shell-bearers)   (The semantic network for example (*))
M (Molluscs)   ⟶ : ISA   : isa link (links two prototypes)
C (Cephalopods)   +++◇ : CANCEL : exception link
N (Nautili)   - - -> : UNCANCEL : counterexception link

2.2. Default Logic [14]

We propose a review of some basic definitions and properties. A detailed development can be found in [5, 14].

Definition 2.2.1

A default theory $\Delta = (D, W)$ consists of a set of closed first-order formulae W, and a set of defaults D. A default is any expression of the form: $\dfrac{\alpha(x_1, \ldots, x_n) : \beta(x_1, \ldots, x_n)}{\gamma(x_1, \ldots, x_n)}$, where $\alpha(x_1, \ldots, x_n)$, $\beta(x_1, \ldots, x_n)$ and $\gamma(x_1, \ldots, x_n)$ are well-formed formulae whose free variables are among $x_1, \ldots, x_n$ -, and are called the prerequisite, justification, and consequent of the default, respectively. Their meaning is as follows: if α is known and if β is consistent with what is known, then γ may be inferred. A default is said to be closed if it has no free variable. A default theory (D, W) is closed iff every default of D is closed. "The defaults in D can be viewed as extending the first-order knowledge, contained in W, about an incompletly specified world. An extension is then interpreted as an acceptable set of beliefs one may hold about that world." [5]. (Note that not every default theory has an extension and some have more than one.)

Examples

1) $D = \{\ \dfrac{A : B}{C}\ ;\ \dfrac{A : D}{\neg C}\ \}$; $W = \{A\}$. Then $\Delta = (D,W)$ has no extension.

2) $D = \{\ \dfrac{:C}{\neg B}\ ;\ \dfrac{:B}{\neg C}\ \}$; $W = \phi$. Then $\Delta = (D,W)$ has two extensions: $T_1 = \{\neg B\}$; $T_2 = \{\neg C\}$.

Theorem 2.2.1

Let $\Delta = (D,W)$ be a closed default theory. E is an extension for Δ iff $E = \overset{\infty}{\underset{i=0}{\cup}} E_i$, where

$E_0 = W$, and for $i \geqslant 0$

$E_{i+1} = \text{Th}(E_i) \cup \{\omega \mid \dfrac{\alpha : \beta}{\omega} \in D,\ \alpha \in E_i,\ \text{and}\ \neg\beta \notin E\}$

Definition 2.2.2

If D is a set of defaults, then CONSEQUENTS(D) is defined as: CONSEQUENTS(D) = $\{\ \omega\mid \dfrac{\alpha : \beta}{\omega} \in D\}$

Theorem 2.2.2

If E is an extension for $\Delta = (D, W)$, then E is consistent if and only if W is.

Henceforth, we will assume that formulae are in clausal form, i-e, expressed as a conjunction of disjunctions of literals.

Definition 2.2.3

- Any default of the form $\dfrac{\alpha : \omega}{\omega}$ is said to be normal.

- Any default of the form $\dfrac{\alpha : \beta\ \&\ \gamma}{\beta}$ is said to be semi-normal.

- A default theory (D, W) is normal (respectively semi-normal) iff every default of D is normal (respectively semi-normal).

Theorem 2.2.3

Every closed normal default theory has an extension.

2.3 Interpretation of NETL proposed by Etherington and Reiter [4]

Etherington and Reiter have shown that, by using the NETL inference procedure, the NETL network representation can lead to anomalous conclusions. Hence, they modify slightly the link types and propose the following link types:

(1) $A \longrightarrow B$:$(\forall x)\ (A(x) => B(x))$ (strict ISA link) ("A's are always B's")

(2) $A \longrightarrow\!\!\!\!\!\!\bullet\ B$:$(\forall x)\ (A(x) => \neg B(x))$ (strict ISN'T-A link) ("A's are never B's")

(3) $C - ->$:exception link. This link must have at its head a default link. It cannot be translated independently of this default link. There are two cases:

(i) $A \ \_{\not\!\!\!\!\!\!\!\!\!/}\!\!\!\rightarrow\ B$: $\dfrac{A(x) : B(x)\ \&\ \neg C_1(x)\ \&\ ...\ \&\ \neg C_n(x)}{B(x)}$ ($A \longrightarrow B$ is a default ISA link)

$C_1'...C_n'$

(ii) $A \ \longrightarrow\!\!\!\!\!\!\bullet\ B$: $\dfrac{A(x) : \neg B(x)\ \&\ \neg C_1(x)\ \&\ ...\ \&\ \neg C_n(X)}{\neg B(x)}$ ($A \longrightarrow\!\!\!\!\!\!\bullet B$ is a default ISN'T-A link)

$C_1'...C_n'$

Recall example (*). The corresponding default theory is:

$\Delta = (D, W);\ D = \{\ \dfrac{M(x) : Sb(x)\ \&\ \neg C(x)}{Sb(x)}\ ;\ \dfrac{C(x) : \neg Sb(x)\ \&\ \neg N(x)}{\neg Sb(x)}\ \}$

$W = \{(\forall x)\ (N(x) => C(x);\ (\forall x)\ (C(x) => M(x));\ (\forall x)\ (N(x) => Sb(x))\ \}$

Given c, a nautilus. Let W_1 be $W \cup \{N(c)\}$. $\Delta_1 = (D, W_1)$ has a unique extension that contains C(c), M(c) and Sb(c); c is a Cephalopod, a Mollusc and a Shell-bearer. Given b, a Cephalopod not known to be a nautilus. Let W_2 be $W \cup \{C(b)\}$. $\Delta_2 = (D, W_2)$ has a unique extension that contains $M(b)$ and $\neg Sb(b)$; b is a Mollusc but is not a Shell-bearer. Etherington proved the following result: the default theory corresponding to an acyclic inheritance network with exceptions has at least one extension.

An important drawback of such a formalization is that the translation of general statements explicitly mentions the exceptions. This gives rise to different problems. Either we assume that the exceptions are all known previously (an improbable assumption) or we accept to continually modify the defaults as often as new exceptions are known. An increasing number of exceptions increases the complexity of defaults. Moreover, the links of the network cannot be translated independently of each other.

We propose another formalization using default logic, that does not present such disadvantages, and that is closer to the NETL structure. This idea has been suggested by Mc Dermott's proposal for handling exceptions [13].

3. Another Formalization using Default Logic for ISA Hierarchies with Exceptions
3.1 Definition of the semantics used

The formal semantics proposed here for inheritance networks are based on the exact definition of links, nodes and wires in NETL.

In this system the ISA link between two nodes A and B is in fact identified with a node R_i - the name of the assertion -, linked by wires to nodes A and B and to a third node named ISA which specifies the nature of the assertion. R_i is called the **"justification"** of the assertion.

The IS-A link between A and B, therefore will be represented as follows: $A \longrightarrow R_i \longrightarrow B$. If A and B are type nodes, the IS-A link translates into the default : $\delta_i = \dfrac{A(x):R_i(x)}{B(x)}$ (is-a default rule) (where $A(x)$ and $B(x)$ are property predicates, and $R_i(x)$ an assertion predicate).

We can modify slightly the NETL syntax of the CANCEL link: $C \rightarrow CANCEL \leftrightarrow B$, without any drawbacks. The CANCEL link is used to prohibit the use of the ISA link $A \longrightarrow R_i \longrightarrow B$ for C. Thus the head node is no longer node B, but rather node R_i. The CANCEL link becomes analogous to the UNCANCEL link which has a link at its head - a CANCEL link moreover. Like the IS-A link, the CANCEL link is represented with a node for the name of the assertion. Its graphical representation is as follows:

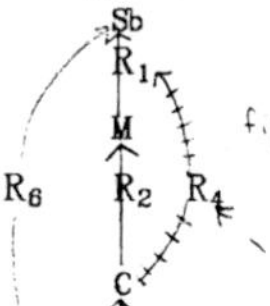

$A \longrightarrow R_i \longrightarrow B$ It translates into the default:
$$\delta_j = \frac{C(x) : R_j(x)}{\neg R_i(x)}$$
(exception default rule)

In the same manner the notation for the UNCANCEL link is: 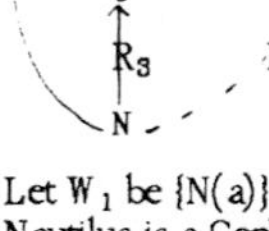
$C \leftrightarrow R_j \leftrightarrow R_i$ and the link is translated into the default:
$$\delta_k = \frac{D(x) : R_k(x)}{\neg R_j(x)}$$
(uncancel default rule)

3.2 An example

Consider the facts concerning Shell-bearers used in example (*). With our notation, we get the following semantic network:

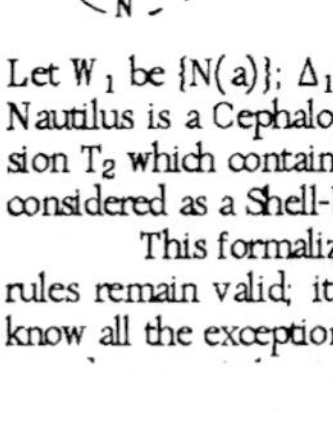

Fig 2

The corresponding default theory is:

$$D = \{ \frac{M(x):R_1(x)}{Sb(x)}, \frac{C(x):R_2(x)}{M(x)};$$

$$\frac{C(x):R_4(x)}{\neg R_1(x)}, \frac{N(x):R_3(x)}{C(x)},$$

$$\frac{N(x):R_5(x)}{\neg R_4(x)}, \frac{N(x):R_6(x)}{Sb(x)} \}$$

Let W_1 be $\{N(a)\}$; $\Delta_1 = (D, W_1)$ has a unique extension T_1 which contains $C(a)$, $M(a)$ and $Sb(a)$: a particular Nautilus is a Cephalopod, a Mollusc and a Shell-bearer. Let W_2 be $\{C(b)\}$; $\Delta_2 = (D, W_2)$ has a unique extension T_2 which contains $M(b)$ but does not contain $Sb(b)$: a Cephalopod not known to be a Nautilus will not be considered as a Shell-bearer.

This formalization has the same useful property as the NETL system: as new exceptions are added, old rules remain valid; it is only necessary to introduce new exception default rules δ_j; there is thus no need to know all the exceptions beforehand, thanks to the use of the assertion predicates $R_i(x)$. One could object to the introduction of these assertion predicates $R_i(x)$, because there are so many assertions (note). On the one hand, they correspond to elements in the NETL network (namely handle nodes), and, on the other hand, they provide means of handling ambiguities [9].

4. Existence of an extension for the taxonomic default theories

We have shown in [9] that the default theories corresponding to ISA hierarchies have an extension. We will describe briefly the principal steps.

We deal with ISA semantic networks that obviously have default-isa links and also strict-isa links which translate into universal statements, such as those of Reiter and Etherington in [4], but which have no isn't-a link. The absence of isn't-a link plays an important part in what follows. Moreover in the corresponding default theory - as defined in §3 -, we replace every assertion predicate R_i by the opposite of a new predicate Nonri. We can now specify the form of the default theories for which we will construct an extension.

Let $\Delta = (D,W)$ such a theory. Formulae of W are of the form:

i) $\alpha(a)$, where α is a unary predicate and a is a constant - (such a first-order formula corresponds to the node α that will be marked in the network) - or

ii) $\neg\alpha_1(x) \vee \alpha_2(x)$, where α_1 and α_2 are atoms, and x is a free variable.

D has defaults of the form $\dfrac{\alpha(x) : \neg\beta(x)}{\omega(x)}$, where $\alpha \in E_1$, - E_1 is the set of property predicates -, $\beta \in EE_2$, - EE_2 is the set of the new predicates Nonri, which replace the assertion predicates - , and $\omega = P$, where $P \in E_1$, or $\omega =$ Nonri, where Nonri $\in EE_2$.

Etherington [5] has pointed out an important fact with respect to the appeals to non-provability in the default theories corresponding to ISA hierarchies. "For these theories, all predicates are unary. Given an individual b, which is an instance of a predicate P, we must determine all predicates $P_1, ..., P_n$, such that $P(b)$, $P_1(b)$, ..., $P_n(b)$ belong to a common extension." For such a problem we can limit ourselves to closed defaults, because during the construction of an extension, the defaults used become instantiated by the constant b.

Finally defaults are of the form: $\dfrac{\alpha : \neg\beta}{\gamma}$, where α, β, γ are atoms such that there exists a constant b and $\alpha = P(b)$ for some $P \in E_1$, $\beta =$ Nonri(b) for some Nonri$\in EE_2$ and $\gamma = Q(b)$ for some $Q \in E_1$ or $\gamma =$ Nonrj(b) for some Nonrj$\in EE_2$. We can also assume that the formulae of W are purely propositional by keeping only the formulae of type (i) where the constant b occurs and by instantiating the formulae of type (ii) by the constant b. Henceforth, we deal only with such default theories.

Definition 4.1.

Let $\Delta = (D, W)$ be a closed default theory. The **Universe** of Δ, $U(\Delta)$ is defined as follows:
$U(\Delta) = \{ \alpha \mid \alpha$ is a positive literal and $\exists \beta$ a positive literal such that $((\neg\alpha \vee \beta) \in W)$ or $(\alpha \vee \neg\beta) \in W) \}$
$\cup \{ \alpha \mid \alpha$ is a literal and $\exists \beta, \gamma$ such that $\dfrac{\alpha : \beta}{\gamma} \in D \}$
$\cup \{ \neg\beta \mid \beta$ is a literal and $\exists \alpha, \gamma$ such that $\dfrac{\alpha : \beta}{\gamma} \in D\} \cup$ CONSEQUENTS(D).

Note that every element of $U(\Delta)$ is a positive literal.

Definition 4.2

We define the partial relations $<<<$ and $<<$ on $U(\Delta) \times U(\Delta)$ as follows:
(1) If $w \in W$ and is not an atom then $w = \neg\alpha \vee \beta$. Let $\alpha <<< \beta$.
(2) If $\delta \in D$ then $\delta = \dfrac{\alpha : \neg\beta}{\gamma}$. Let $\alpha << \gamma$ and $\beta << \gamma$

(3) The relations $<<<$ and $<<$ are transitive: $\forall \alpha, \beta, \gamma, \in U(\Delta)$,
   (i) If $\alpha <<< \beta$ and $\beta <<< \gamma$ then $\alpha <<< \gamma$
   (ii) If $\alpha << \beta$ and $\beta << \gamma$ then $\alpha << \gamma$
   (iii) If $(\alpha << \beta$ and $\beta <<< \gamma)$ or $(\alpha <<< \beta$ and $\beta << \gamma)$ then $\alpha << \gamma$

Definition 4.3

A closed default theory $\Delta = (D, W)$ whose defaults are of the form $\dfrac{\alpha : \neg\beta}{\gamma}$, where α, β, γ are atoms, is said to be **taxonomic** iff $\forall \alpha \in U(\Delta) \neg(\alpha << \alpha)$

Note : Another non-monotonic treatment of ISA hierarchies with exceptions, using circumscription, is proposed by Mc Carthy [12]. He supposes that every object is abnormal in some way and hence "wants to allow some aspects of the object to be abnormal and still assume the normality of the rest". For it he introduces a predicate ab, and as many aspect functions as there are assertions, and hence as numerous as our assertion predicates.

The default theories which we have constructed in §3 are such taxonomic default theories, because for ISA networks, the underlying partial graph obtained by considering both property nodes and assertion nodes, is a directed acyclic graph.

Definition 4.4.

Let $\Delta = (D, W)$ be a taxonomic default theory. We define the function ν on $U(\Delta)$ as follows:

1) $\forall \beta \in U(\Delta)$, if $(\exists \alpha \in U(\Delta) \mid (\neg \alpha \vee \beta) \in W)$, then $\nu(\beta) \geq \nu(\alpha)$

2) $\forall \gamma \in U(\Delta)$, if $(\exists \alpha, \beta \in U(\Delta) \mid \frac{\alpha : \neg \beta}{\gamma} \in D)$ then $\nu(\gamma) \geq (\sup(\nu(\alpha), \nu(\beta))) + 1$

3) $\forall \alpha \in U(\Delta)$, if $(\forall \beta \in U(\Delta), \neg \beta \vee \alpha \notin W)$ and if $(\forall \beta, \gamma \in U(\Delta), \frac{\beta : \neg \gamma}{\alpha} \notin D)$ then $\nu(\alpha) = 0$.

4) $\forall \gamma \in U(\Delta)$, $(\nu(\gamma) = n+1 \implies \exists \alpha, \beta \in U(\Delta) \mid \frac{\alpha : \neg \beta}{\gamma} \in D, \nu(\alpha) = n$ or $\nu(\beta) = n.)$

Note that the function ν is well defined because the default theory is taxonomic.

Example

Recall example about Molluscs. We add now the following assertion: All Shell-bearers are animals. It translates into the formula: $(\forall x) (Sb(x) \implies A(x))$ Assume that we are interested by the properties of the nautilus. We choose a constant a and add the assertion $N(a)$. Every default will be instantiated by the constant a. We get thus the default theory $\Delta = (D, W)$ where:

$$D = \{ \delta_1 = \frac{M(a) : \neg Nonr1(a)}{Sb(a)} ; \delta_2 = \frac{C(a) : \neg Nonr2(a)}{M(a)} ; \delta_3 = \frac{N(a) : \neg Nonr3(a)}{C(a)} ;$$
$$\delta_4 = \frac{C(a) : \neg Nonr4(a)}{Nonr1(a)} ; \delta_5 = \frac{N(a) : \neg Nonr5(a)}{Nonr4(a)} ; \delta_6 = \frac{N(a) : \neg Nonr6(a)}{Sb(a)} \}$$

$W = \{ w_1 = N(a); w_2 = \neg Sb(a) \vee A(a) \}$

$U(\Delta) = \{Nonr1(a), Nonr2(a), ..., Nonr6(a), N(a), C(a), M(a), Sb(a), A(a) \}$

- $\nu(w) = 0 \implies w \in \{Nonr5(a), Nonr3(a), Nonr2(a), N(a) \}; \nu(w) = 1 \implies w \in \{C(a), Nonr4(a) \}$
- $\nu(w) = 2 \implies w \in \{ M(a), Nonr1(a) \}; \nu(w) = 3 \implies w \in \{ Sb(a), A(a) \}$

Definition 4.5

- If $\Delta = (D, W)$ is a closed taxonomic default theory, then there is a partition $\{D_i\}$ ($i > 0$) for D, induced by the function ν by: $(\forall \delta \in D)$, $\delta \in D_i$ iff $(\delta = \frac{\alpha : \beta}{\gamma}$ and $\nu(\gamma) = i)$
- We construct the sets of first-order formulae (E^i) ($i \geq 0$) corresponding to the sets of defaults D_i, by induction as follows:
$\Delta_0 = (D'_0, W)$ where $D'_0 = \phi$, and for $i > 0$,
$\Delta_i = (D'_i, E^{i-1})$, where $D'_i = \{ \frac{\alpha : \beta}{\beta} \mid \exists \frac{\alpha : \gamma}{\beta} \in D_i$ and $\neg \gamma \notin E^{i-1} \}$ and E^{i-1} is an extension of Δ_{i-1}. E^{i-1} exists because Δ_{i-1} is a normal default theory (theorem 2.2.3). E^{i-1} can be constructed by following the process described in the proof of the theorem in [14].

Lemma 2.2

Let $\Delta = (D, W)$ be a closed taxonomic default theory; let $\{D_i\}$ be the partition induced by ν on D; let (E^i) be the corresponding sequence of sets of first-order formulae of the definition 4.5. Assume that W is consistent.

Let $E = \bigcup_{i=0} E^i$. Then:

- E is consistent and $\forall \omega \in$ CONSEQUENTS(D), $\neg \omega \notin E$
- Let $\Delta'_i = (D_i, E^{i-1})$. Then for $i > 0$, E^i is an extension of Δ'_i.

Theorem 4.3.

If $\Delta = (D, W)$ is a closed taxonomic default theory, then $\Delta = (D, W)$ has an extension.

Proof: Intuitively we can replace every default $\frac{\alpha : \beta}{\gamma}$ by a semi-normal default $\frac{\alpha : \beta \wedge \gamma}{\gamma}$, by lemma 2.2. This process is similar to the translation method proposed by Lukaszewicz in [12]. The formal proof succeeds - if W is consistent - by constructing an extension for Δ, using theorem 2.2., by following the same technique as in [5]. We establish that $E = \bigcup_{i=0} E^i$ is an extension for $\Delta = (D, W)$, where (E^i) ($i \geq 0$) is the sequence of the definition 4.5.

5. Construction of an extension by means of a PROLOG program

In §4 we have modified the defaults by introducing new predicates Nonri, so that their consequent is positive. All defaults have now as a justification a negative predicate of the form $\neg Nonri(x)$. If the prerequisite of the default is known, and its justification is consistent with what is known (i.e. the negation of the justification is not provable: $\neg \neg Nonri(x)$ is not provable), then the consequent can be inferred. With the negation operator **not** of PROLOG, this means that not(Nonri(x)) succeeds. This remark justifies the construction of a logic data base that has some interesting properties with respect to the taxonomic default theory.

Definition 5.1.
   We define the logic data base $DB(\Delta)$ corresponding to a taxonomic default theory Δ as follows:
(i) Let α be a positive literal such that $\alpha \in W$, then the clause $\alpha \in DB(\Delta)$.
(ii) If $\neg \alpha \vee \beta \in W$, where α and β are positive literals, then the clause $\beta \leftarrow \alpha \in DB(\Delta)$.
(iii) If $\delta = \dfrac{\alpha : \neg\beta}{\gamma} \in D$, then the clause $\gamma \leftarrow \alpha \ \& \ \neg\beta \in DB(\Delta)$.

   The intensional component of $DB(\Delta)$ is constitued by the clauses of (ii) and (iii), while the extensional component is provided by the clauses of (i).

Example
Returning to the example discussed in § 2.1.,- without taking the ISA link between N and Sb into account- , we get the following PROLOG clauses:
   $Sb(X) :- M(X), not(Nonr1(X))$.
   $M(X) :- C(X), not(Nonr2(X))$.
   $C(X) :- N(X), not(Nonr3(X))$.
   $Nonr1(X) :- C(X), not(Nonr4(X))$.
   $Nonr4(X) :- N(X), not(Nonr5(X))$.
   The extensional data base contains the clauses $N(a):-$, $C(b):-$, $M(c):-$, and $Sb(d):-$, obtained by instantiating every predicate with a different constant. For information retrieval, we can add the clauses $:-C(a)$, $:-M(a)$ and $:-Sb(a)$ or $:-M(b)$ and $:-Sb(b)$.
   Running this program yields the desired results. Note that we are sure that the program is cycle-free, for exactly the same reasons for which the corresponding default theory is taxonomic.
   We do not recall the definitions of hierarchical constraint [2] and covering axiom in logic data bases which can be found in [2] and [17].
   Because for ISA hierarchies the underlying partial graph is acyclic, we get the following result:

Proposition 5.1.
   The logic data base $DB(\Delta)$ corresponding to a taxonomic default theory Δ satisfies the hierarchical constraint and the covering axiom.

Definition 5.2
   We define a function l on the data base DB as follows:
- If w is an unit clause, then $l(w) = \nu(w)$.
- If w is a clause of the form $\beta \leftarrow \alpha$, then $l(w) = \nu(\beta)$.
- If w is a clause of the form $\gamma \leftarrow \alpha \ \& \ \neg\beta$, then $l(w) = \nu(\gamma)$.
   The clauses of the logic data base DB can be grouped into disjoint sets $\{P_i\}$ ($i \geqslant 0$) such that ($\forall i \geqslant 0$) ($w \in P_i$ iff $l(w) = i$).
   (Note that both clauses $\beta \leftarrow \alpha$, $\gamma \leftarrow \beta$ can belong to the same set P_i; hence the relations are relations of level $\geqslant i$).

   The Query Evaluation Process QEP has been defined by Clark in [2] as a linear resolution proof procedure with negated literals evaluated by a failure proof. This is the way that PROLOG handles negation. (Recall that the PROLOG selection rule is always choose the leftmost literal in a query).
   Now we want to show that the PROLOG QEP gives the theorems of the taxonomic default theories. More precisely, let $\Delta = (D,W)$ be a taxonomic default theory and let $DB(\Delta)$ be the corresponding data base. By theorem 4.3. Δ has an extension E. It can be shown that elements of E are positive literals or disjunctions of literals. These disjunctions belong necessarily to W. Let α be an element of E:
- If α is of the form $\neg P \vee Q$, then by definition of $DB(\Delta)$, the clause $Q \leftarrow P$ belongs to $DB(\Delta)$.
- If w is any positive literal, then the following theorem tells us that QEP ends in success iff $w \in E$.

Theorem 5.2.
   Let $\Delta = (D,W)$ be a taxonomic default theory. Let $DB(\Delta)$ be the corresponding logic data base. Let QEP be the PROLOG query evaluation process. Let E be an extension of Δ. Then:
   For any positive literal, QEP ends in success for the query $\leftarrow L$ iff $L \in E$.
   (Note that proposition 5.1. guaranties that QEP ends with a success or failure for every allowed query).
   Proof: We have shown in [9] by induction that : ($\forall i \geqslant 0$) ($\forall L$ a positive literal $|\nu(L) \leqslant i$) (QEP ends in success iff $L \in E^i$), where E^i is the sequence of sets of definition 4.5.

6. Conclusion

- Our formalization using default logic shows the correctness of the NETL semantics networks for the handling of hierarchies with exceptions.
- We have introduced a new class of default theories having an extension, although the defaults are neither normal nor semi-normal. We suggest calling such theories, taxonomic default theories.
- The translation of the defaults into PROLOG clauses yields an algorithm which provides the theorems of the extensions. We propose a method of translation of taxonomic defaults into logic data base clauses.

ACKNOWLEDGEMENTS

I am grateful to D.KAYSER of LIPN and to Ph.BESNARD of IRISA for their helpful comments. Ph.BESNARD has also suggested the use of the term "taxonomic" to me. This paper as been partially sponsored by PRC "Intelligence Artificielle" and by ATP "Intelligence Artificielle".

REFERENCES

[1] AI (1980), Special issue on Non-monotonic Logic, Artificial Intelligence, 13, (1,2), April.

[2] CLARK K.L., (1978), Negation as failure, in Logic and Data Bases, H.Gallaire and J.Minker (eds.), Plenum Press, New-York, pp 293-322.

[3] DOUCET A. and FROIDEVAUX C., (1985), Comparaison et Synthèse de deux méthodes de Représentation des connaissances, A.D.I. Contract Report, L.R.I, Univ. of Orsay.

[4] ETHERINGTON D.W. and REITER R., (1983), On Inheritance Hierarchies with exceptions, Proc. of AAAI-83, Washington D.C., August 24-26, pp 104-108.

[5] ETHERINGTON D.W., (1983), Formalizing Non-monotonic Reasoning Systems, Technical Report 83-1, Department of Computer Science, Vancouver, B.C.

[6] FAHLMAN S.E. (1979), NETL : A System for Representing and Using Real-World Knowledge, MIT Press Cambridge, Mass.

[7] FAHLMAN S.E., TOURETZKY D.S. and Van ROGGEN W. (1981), Cancellation in a Parallel Semantic Network, Proc. IJCAI-81, Vancouver, B.C., August 24-28, pp 257-263.

[8] FROIDEVAUX C. (1985), Exceptions dans les hiérarchies SORTE-DE, Congrès AFCET-RFIA, November 27-29, Grenoble.

[9] FROIDEVAUX C. (1986), Existence d'une extension pour les théories des Défauts taxonomiques, Research Report, L.R.I., Univ. of Orsay.

[10] HAYES P.J. (1977), In Defence of Logic, Proc. IJCAI-77, Cambridge, Mass, pp 559-565.

[11] LUKASZEWICZ W. (1985), Two results on default logic, Proc. IJCAI-85, Los Angeles, CA, August 18-23, pp 459-461.

[12] McCARTHY J. (1984), Application of Circumscription to Formalize Common Sense Knowledge in Non-monotonic Reasoning, Workshop AAAI, October, pp 295-324.

[13] McDERMOTT D. (1982), Non-monotonic Logic II : Non-monotonic Model Theories, Journal of the ACM, Vol. 29, n 1, January, pp 33-57.

[14] REITER R. (1980), A Logic for Default Reasoning, Artificial Intelligence, 13, (1,2), pp 81-132.

[15] REITER R. and CRISCUOLO G. (1980), On interacting defaults, Proc. IJCAI-81, Vancouver, B-C, August 24-28, pp 270-276.

[16] SCHUBERT L.K. (1976), Extending the Expressive Power of Semantic Networks, Artificial Intelligence 7 (2), pp 163-198.

[17] SHEPHERDSON J.C. (1984), Negation as Failure : A Comparison of Clark's Completed Data Base and Reiter's Closed World Assumption, in the Journal of Logic Programming, Vol. 1, n 1, June, pp 51-79

[18] TOURETZKY D.S. (1984), Implicit Ordering of Defaults in Inheritance Systems, Proc. of AAAI-84, University of Texas at Austin, 6-10 August, pp 322-326.

Advances in Artificial Intelligence - II
B. Du Boulay, D. Hogg and L. Steels (Editors)
© Elsevier Science Publishers B.V. (North-Holland), 1987

Transforming Logic Programs By Specialising Interpreters

John Gallagher
SCS Technische Automation und Systeme GmbH
Oehleckerring 40
D-2000 Hamburg 62
West Germany

Abstract

A method of transforming logic programs by specialising meta interpreters is described. The transformation process requires three inputs; a logic program (the object program), an interpreter for some control strategy, expressed as a logic meta-program, and a query on the object program. The transformed program simulates the action of the meta-interpreter for the given object program and query, but much more efficiently than running the meta interpreter directly. The transformation may be viewed as compiling the control strategy into the object program. The transformation method is based on program specialisation; the transformed program is a specialised version of the interpreter which interprets only the given object program and query. It is suggested that this method of transformation can be useful in a problem solving system, by compiling general strategies into problem specifications.

Program Specialisation

To specialise a program means to restrict the input output relation which it computes. The aim of specialising a program is to obtain a version which treats fewer cases, but which deals more efficiently with those cases than would the general program. It is more efficient because some parts of the general computation can be precomputed in the specialised version, and because redundant parts of the general program may be omitted.

For logic programs, program specialisation may be characterised as follows. A logic program P defines a predicate $r(x_1,...,x_n)$, which denotes a relation R consisting of the set of tuples $(a_1,..,a_n)$ such that $r(a_1,..,a_n)$ can be derived from the program. In a specialised version of P, the predicate $r(x_1,...,x_n)$ denotes a subset of R. The subset of R may be specified by giving an instance of $r(x_1,...,x_n)$ (that is, by giving some of the arguments of the predicate), or by adding constraints to $r(x_1,...x_n)$

$$r(x_1,...,x_n) \ \& \ c(x_1,...x_n).$$

Methods of specialising programs have been developed by several researchers (Chang & Lee), (Goad), (Venken), (Bloch), (Komorowski), (Takeuchi & Furukawa), (Kahn), (Jones et al). All these use some form of partial evaluation or

symbolic evaluation of the program.   As much as possible of
the program is precomputed during symbolic evaluation,   and
the remainder,   or residual program forms   the   specialised
program.

Logic programming is particularly   suitable for   partial
evaluation because of the generality of the   unification
mechanism.   For pure logic programs,   symbolic   evaluation
is no different from normal evaluation.   However,   partial
evaluation of logic programs containing arithmetic   or   meta
predicates need special   symbolic   evaluation   mechanisms,
which will be discussed below.

Although partial evaluation or symbolic evaluation are   important,   effective specialisation needs other techniques   as well
as these.   In particular,   it is sometimes necessary to construct new predicates in the specialised program;   partial or
symbolic evaluation alone cannot do this.

An Example of Specialisation

A logic program to transpose a matrix is   given   below.
The matrix is represented by a list of its rows, where each row
is a list of elements.   The query

        transpose(((1,2,3), (4,5,6)),Ans)

is solved with the substitution

        Ans = ((1,4),(2,5),(3,6))

The program is as follows.   The clauses   are   given
references which will be used later.   (X . Y) represents a list
with head X and tail Y.

T1: transpose(M, ()) :- nullrows(M).

T2: transpose(M1, (Row.M2)) :-
         makerow(M1,Row, M3),
         transpose(M3,M2).

M1: makerow((),(),()).

M2: makerow(((X.R1) . M1), (X.Row), (R1.M2)) :-
         makerow(M1, Row, M2).

N1: nullrows(()).

N2: nullrows((().M)) :-
         nullrows(M).

        Program 1

Suppose the program is to be specialised for the case where the first row contains two elements, but the number of rows is unknown (greater than zero). The program is specialised with the query,

Q1: transpose(((A,B).M1),M2)

The specialised program produced contains the clause,

```
transpose(((X,Y).M1),((X.R1),(Y.R2))) :-
    makerow(M1,R1,M2),
    makerow(M2,R2,M3),
    nullrows(M3).
```

Program 2

with the same clauses as above for makerow and nullrows.

If the number of rows is also known to be two, the query is

Q2: transpose(((X,Y),R2),M2)

This gives rise to a completely determinate computation and the specialised program is the single clause,

```
transpose(((X,Y),(Z,W)),((X,Z),(Y,W))).
```

Program 3

The method of deriving these specialised programs will be described below.

Specialising Meta-programs

The transformation method of this paper depends on specialising meta-programs, such as interpreters. In principle, specialising a meta-program is no different from specialising an object program: the data just happen to be object programs. However, due to the lack of an explicit distinction between object and meta languages in most versions of Prolog, some particular problems need to be considered, such as the treatment of "meta logical" predicates supplied in Prolog. These will be discussed later.

The analogy between specialising metaprograms and compiling was identified by Futamura (Futamura). An interpreter may be abstractly considered as a function of two arguments:

Interpreter : (Program X Input) → Output

Compiling may be considered as a partial evaluation of the interpreter with the given program but no input (in particular, the partial evaluation parses the program) leaving a residual

program which is the compiled version,   a   function   of   one
argument.

Compiled-program : Input → Output

The compiled program can be considered   as   a   specialised
version of the interpreter which interprets   just   the   one
program.

The significance of this analogy   for   logic   programming
is that there are many possible   interpreters   for   logic
programs,   corresponding to different   control   strategies.
It is prohibitively inefficient to run   many   of   these
interpreters directly,   and impractical to write a   separate
compiler for each one.   A general-purpose   specialiser   for
logic (meta-)   programs could compile any strategy for which
a logic meta-program could be written.

The Specialisation Method

The query is symbolically executed,   and a   directed   graph
is constructed which represents a trace of the   computation.

o   The nodes of the graph represent states of the computa-
      tion,   that is,   conjunctions of goals   to be solved.

o   The arcs are labelled by references   to   clauses   of
      the program.   A link from node A to node B labelled by
      clause C means that C is applied to   the   first   goal
      in node A, giving the goals at B.

Using the clause references given in   the   above   program,
the graph produced for the first query Q1 is,

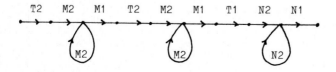

Figure 1

where the query is associated with the leftmost node.

The graph for the second query Q2 is,

```
     T2    M2    M2    M1    T2    M2    M2    M1    T1    N2    N2    N1
•→•  •→•  •→•  •→•  •→•  •→•  •→•  •→•  •→•  •→•  •→•
```

Figure 2

Construction of the Graph

An outline of how the graph may be produced now given.
A description of a program to contruct such graphs may be found
in (Gallagher). The graph is constructed by evaluating the
query, adding an arc for each clause matched. One arc leaves a
node for each clause which matches the first goal at that
node. A crucial part of the process is obviously the detection of infinite paths in the graph; the query being evaluated
may not have the required input which drives the computation towards termination. Various loop criteria are
possible, but in each case it is necessary to identify some
node in the graph with one of its predecessors (e.g. one
test is whether a goal is identical with an ancestor except
for renaming variables; this test, however, will not catch all
loops).

o   A branch node is a node with at least two arcs leaving
     it, which represent alternative course of computation.

o   A loop node is a node with at least two arcs entering it,
     from which there is a path which leads back to it. (If
     a loop contains no branch node, the program would loop
     for all queries; the branch represents an exit from the
     loop.)

From the graph, the specialised program is constructed
in two stages.

1.   Extract from the graph all the clause sequences,
     which are the longest possible paths in the graph
     which do not pass through a loop node. (That is,
     any loop node in a clause sequence must be the last
     node).

2.   For each clause sequence, construct one or more
     clauses for the specialised program.

The clause sequences are obtained by splitting the graph
into sections, by detaching from each loop node all the
arcs which lead into it. For the graph in Figure 2 this
results in the sections,

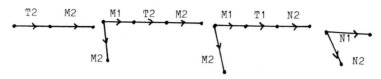

Figure 3

The graph in Figure 2 has no loop nodes, so cannot be split.

For each disjoint section of the graph, clause sequences are
obtained by starting at a node with no arcs entering it,
and tracing from it all paths ending with a node with no arc
leaving it. From the sections in Figure 2 are obtained
the sequences

        (T2,M2)
        (M2)   (M1,T2,M2)
        (M2)   (M1,T1,N2)
        (N2)   (N1)

          Figure 4

A clause sequence gives rise to one or more clauses by applying
the sequence to the most general goal which matches the
first clause in the sequence. If the sequence is

        (C1,....,Cn)   n > 0

then each Cj is applied to the head of the conjunction remaining after applying C1,...,Cj-1. It may happen that after applying some Cj in the sequence there are no more goals in the
conjunction. In this case a new clause sequence is started from Cj+1.

The clause resulting from a sequence (C1,...,Cn), if G is the
most general goal matching C1, is

        G´ :- D1,..,Dk   k ⩾ 0

where D1,..,Dk are the goals remaining after applying Cn,
and G´ is the instance of G which has arisen from the
substitutions made in the process of applying the clauses.

The clauses obtained are given an ordering induced
naturally by the clauses in the original program.

Renaming predicates

It is sometimes necessary to rename predicates in the
specialised program, to distinguish calls to the same
procedure from different places in the computation. If
two clause sequences appear in the graph,

        (...C1,......)

        (...C2,.....)

where C1 and C2 are clauses for the same predicate P, and C1
and C2 label two arcs which lead from two distinct nodes,
we produce two different predicates corresponding to the
different cases. In view of this renaming, the following
clauses are produced from the clause sequences in the graph
in Figure 3.

```
transpose(((X1.X2).X3),((X1.X4).X5)) :-
    makerow1(X3,X4,X6),
    transpose1((X2.X6),X5).

transpose1(((X1.X2).X3),((X1.X4).X5)) :-
    makerow2(X3,X4,X6),
    transpose2((X2.X6),X5).

transpose2(((().X1), ()) :-
    nullrows1(X1).

makerow1((),(),()).

makerow1(((X1.X2).X3), (X1.X4), (X2.X5) ) :-
    makerow1(X3,X4,X5).

makerow2((),(),()).

makerow2(((X1.X2).X3), (X1.X4), (X2.X5) ) :-
    makerow2(X3,X4,X5).

nullrows(()).

nullrows((().X1)) :-
    nullrows(X1).
```

Program 4

The program is refined by unfolding immediately all calls
to procedures with only one clause, that is, to transpose1
and transpose2. Also, we note that makerow1 and makerow2
are identical, so they need not be distinguished. When
these operations are done, we obtain the program given
above (Program 2).

Interpreters for Logic Programs

Many authors have shown that interpreters for logic
programs can be written concisely as logic programs
themselves, e.g. (Pereira & Monteiro), (Porto), (Bowen
& Kowalski), (Shapiro 83). The view of logic programming
as deduction is that a computation is the proof of a
theorem; that is, the goal or query is shown to be a
logical consequnce of the sentences of the program.

This may be expressed by a meta-predicate,

    provable("program", "goal", Subst)

where "program" and "goal" are the names of the program
and the goal. That is, there is a naming scheme which
represents the program and the goal as variable-free terms
of first order logic. Subst is a substitution returned

if the goal is provable.

A logic program can be written (called INT), using Horn clauses
with the standard procedural interpretation,   which   defines
the predicate "provable" (Bowen & Kowalski).   INT is an interpreter for logic programs;   there are many versions   of   INT
corresponding to different control strategies   for   the   proof
of the goal.

In fact,   interpreters written in Prolog are   often   somewhat
different from this.

1.   The   program   is   not   represented   explicitly   as   an
      argument of "provable",   but is added as   extra   clauses
      to INT, in a form such as,

          clause(Head, Body)

2.   Secondly,   there is no explicit naming of   object   level
      terms as variable-free meta-terms,   as   above.   There
      is   no   distinction   between   object   and   meta-level
      variables or terms.   This means that   the   unification
      and renaming procedures built into   the   Prolog   system
      can be used for the   object   level   terms;   otherwise
      as predicate such as

          unify(T1, T2, Subst)

      would have to be defined as   part   of   INT,   to   unify
      object level expressions.

Some anomalies may arise because of the failure to   distinguish
object and meta-level,   particularly with the so-called "meta-
-predicates" like var(X),   X==Y,   and so on.   These predicates
must be dealt with in the partial   evaluation   procedure, since
meta-interpreters tend to make   use   of   these   predicates.
However,   a predicate such as var(X)   is   not really a logical
predicate in Prolog;   since   for   example var(X) may be true,
but its instances   false.

An Example of a Logic Program Interpreter

We consider the components of   a   coroutining   interpreter.
Coroutining in this sense means that goals in   the   same   con
junction which share   variables   are   solved   cooperatively.
There are producers and consumers;   a producer is   evaluated
until one or more specified variables are instantiated   by   a
non-variable,   after which it is suspended.   A consumer   is
evaluated until one or more specified   variables   are   about
to   be   instantiated,   after   which   it   is   suspended.

First the evaluator   for   the   producer   is   defined.   The
predicate

```
produce(P1, P2, V1, V2)
```

means that the conjunction of goals P1 is solved
(depth-first) until one of the variables in the list of
variables V1 becomes instantiated by a non-variable. Then
the computation is suspended, leaving a conjunction P2
waiting to be solved, and a new list of variables V2.

```
produce((),(), V,V).

produce((G.P), NewP, V, NewV) :-
     clause(G, Body)
          (newsubstitution(V, NewV),
          append(Body, P, NewP) ;

          no_newsubst(V),
          append(Body, P, P1),
          produce(P1, NewP, V, NewV)).
```

Program 5

where newsubstitution(V, NewV) is true if V contains
non-variables and NewV is a list of the variables in V;
no_newsubst(V) is true if V is a list of variables.

The clauses for consume are similar; the predicate

```
consume(P1, P2, V)
```

means that P1 is a conjunction which is evaluated until
one of the variables in a list V is about to be
instantiated by a non-variable. The computation is then
suspended leaving a conjunction P2 remaining to be solved.

```
consume((), (), _).

consume((G.P), NewP, V) :-
     copy((G,V),(G1,V1)),
     clause(G1, Body),
          (newsubstitution(V1,_),
          NewP = (G.P) ;

          no_newsubst(V1),
          G = G1,
          append(Body, P, P1),
          consume(P1, NewP, V)).
```

Program 6

Note that the consume procedure copies the goal before
matching it, so that it can check whether a variable in V
becomes instantiated without actually performing the substitution.

A simple coroutining interpreter might then have the clause

```
coroutine(Producer, Consumer, Vars) :-
    produce(Producer, P1, Vars, V1),
    consume(Consumer, C1, V1)
    coroutine(P1, C1, V1).
```

Program 7

which calls the producer and consumer alternately.   Many
other variations are possible,   with several   producers   and
consumers;   in the example below,   two producers and   no
consumers are used.   Using components like   the   ones
sketched above,   complex interpreters can easily   be   built
up.   They sometimes carry a lot of overhead   to run them.
This is the problem at which specialisation is aimed.   It com-
piles-in the complex strategy with   the   object program,
yielding a program   which   simulates   the   complex strategy
when run under the standard control.

Comparing the Leaves of two Trees

The predicate leaves(T,L)   means that L is a   difference   list
of the leaves of binary tree T.

```
leaves( leaf(X), (X.Q) - Q).

leaves(tree( L, R), Leaves-Q) :-
    leaves(L, Leaves-LR),
    leaves(R, LR-Q).
```

Program 8

Given two trees T1 and T2,   we wish to see   whether   they
have the same leaves. A query to establish this is,

```
leaves(T1, L-()), leaves(T2, L-())
```

which succeeds if the leaves are   the   same.   If   the   two
trees differ,   it would be advantageous to find   out   before
generating the whole list for T1,   as the   standard   control
does.   A sensible strategy is for each tree to produce   one
leaf at a time,   which is then checked by the   other   tree,
which in turn produces one leaf,   and so on. Similar strategies are discussed in (Pereira & Monteiro)   and (Burstall &
Darlington).   An interpreter to implement   this   strategy
could be,

```
coroutine(( ),( ),_ ).



coroutine(P1, P2, V) :-
```

```
produce(P1, NewP1, V, V1),
produce(P2, NewP2, V1, NewV)
coroutine(NewP1, NewP2, NewV).
```

Program 9

The query to this program is,

```
coroutine((leaves(T1, L-())),(leaves(T2,L-())), (L)).
```

where T1 and T2 are the trees to be compared, and the variable controlling coroutining is L.

Specialising this program (without knowing T1 and T2), we obtain the following clauses for produce:

```
produce((),(),V,V).
produce(((leaves(leaf(X),(X.Q)-Q). G1),G2, (L), V1) :-
    var(L),
    produce(G1,G2,(L),V1).

produce(((leaves(leaf(X),(X.Q)-Q).G1),G1,(L),(Q)) :-
    nonvar(L).

produce(((leaves(tree(TL,TR),L-Q).G1),G2,(L1),V) :-
    produce(((leaves(TL,L-LR),leaves(TL,LR-Q).G1),
            G2,(L1),V).
```

Program 10

The second clause corresponds to the absorption of a leaf which has been produced by the other producer, while the third corresponds to the production of a new leaf, after which the producer is suspended.

Partial Evaluation of Meta-Predicates

As mentioned above, meta-predicates cannot be treated like any other predicate. However, in order to derive the specialised program listed above, it is necessary to be able to evaluate these predicates. The solution we suggest is to distinguish different kinds of variables during partial evaluation. For many purposes, the following two types of variables are sufficient:

o   A set C, containing variables which range over object level constant terms (i.e. containing no object level variables). These usually correspond to the "input" variables.

o   A set V, which range over object level variables; these correspond to "output" variables.

The sets C and V are disjoint. In the example above, the

set C would initially consist of (T1,T2), the trees to
be compared, and V would be (L), the output list of leaves.

After each unification, the two sets C and V may be altered.
The rules for altering the sets, and for computing the values
of meta-predicates, using these two sets, may be found in
(Gallagher).

These rules allow the predicates newsubstitution(V,V1)
and no_newsubst(V) in the produce and consume procedures
to be evaluated symbolically.

The sets V and C may also be maintained by symbolic
evaluation of arithmetic predicates like "X is Y", even
when Y is not fully instantiated. A predicate,

```
evaluate((X is Y),V,C,V1,C1) :-
    constant(Y),
    append((X),C,C1),
    delete(X, V, V1).
```

expresses the fact that after evaluating (X is Y) where
Y constains no variables, X becomes a constant and can
be added to C and deleted from V.

Applications of Program Specialisation

Several authors have discussed useful applications of
partial evaluation. It has been used for optimising
database calls in a Prolog-database interface (Venken). A
Prolog compiler has been produced by partially evaluating
a Lisp interpreter for Prolog (Kahn). It may be used for
type-checking (Bloch), and for compiling runtime checks
for deadlock in Concurrent Prolog program (Shapiro 85),
and for efficient control of expert system rules (Takeuchi
& Furukawa).

The specialising of interpreters seems likely to give the
most useful results. In particular, it can be exploited,
as in the leaf-comparison example above, to transform a
program running under the standard control strategy to one
running under a user-defined strategy which may be quite
complex and too expensive to use interpretively.

As another example, we have transformed an inefficient specification of the N-queens problem into an efficient
version which places the queens one at a time and checks
the safety of each one as it is placed (Gallagher). This
was done by specialising a coroutining interpreter with
breadth first search in the consumer. This problem has also
been tackled recently by Bruynooghe et al. in a similar
manner (Bruynooghe et al.).

Future Applications

In problem-solving, one is often required to solve a combinatorial problem whose solution requires the cooperative solution of a number of goals. Such problems are often easy to state as generate-and-test problems, but require complex strategies to solve them. It is suggested that specialisation of strategies can be a useful problem-solving technique. A problem-solving strategy sometimes uses much look-ahead to gather information about the search-space. This may often be done before run-time by specialising a strategy with a general statement of the problem to be solved. Thus general-purpose strategic knowledge can be intertwined with problem-specific knowledge.

Conclusion

A method of specialising logic programs has been described, based on partially evaluating the program, producing a graph from which the specialised program is derived. Unlike most other authors who deal with specialisation, we emphasise that partial evaluation is only part of the specialisation method; in particular it is sometimes necessary to create new predicates which were not in the original program.

The application of specialisation to meta-programs, especially interpreters, was discussed, and the analogy with compiling emphasised. Specialisation is presented as a practical method of compiling complex control strategies defined as meta-programs.

It is believed that specialisation of interpreters will be a useful method in logic problem-solving systems, by compiling a general strategy into a particular problem description.

Acknowledgements

Most of this work was done as a Ph.D. thesis in Trinity College, Dublin. I should like to thank Prof. J.G. Byrne, Hugh Gibbons and Mike Brady for useful discussions.

References

(Bloch)
C. Bloch, "Source-to-Source Transformations of Logic Programs", Weizmann Inst. of Science, Rehovot, Israel, Report CS84-22 (1984)
(Bowen & Kowalski)
Bowen, K. & Kowalski, R., "Amalgamating Language and metalanguage in Logic programming", in K. Clark and S. Tarnlund (eds.) Logic Programming, Academic Press, (1983)
(Bruynooghe et al.)

Bruynooghe, M., De Schreye, D., Krekels, B. "Compiling Control", Draft Report, Dept. of Computer Science, Katholieke Universitiet Leuven, Belgium, (1985)
(Chang & Lee)
Chang, C-L, & Lee, R.C-T., " Symbolic Logic and mechanical Theorem Proving", Academic Press (1973)
(Futamura)
Futamura, Y., "Partial Evaluation of Computer Programs, An approach to a Compiler-Compiler", J. Inst. Electronics and Communication Engineers (1971)
(Gallagher)
Gallagher, J., "An Approach To The Control of Logic Programs", Ph.D. thesis, Dept. of Computer Science, Trinity College, Dublin, Ireland (1983)
(Goad)
Goad, C., "Automatic Construction of Special Purpose programs", Proc. 6th Conf. on Automated Deduction, New York (1983), Springer Lecture Notes in Computer Science, Vol. 138
(Jones et al.)
Jones, N. et al., "An experiment in partial evaluation", Report 85-1, DIKU, Copenhagen Univ. (1985)
(Kahn)
Kahn, K. "A Partial Evaluator of Lisp Programs written in Prolog", Proc. 1st Int. Logic Progr. Conf., (1982)
(Komorowski)
Komorowski, H., "A specification of an abstract Prolog machine and its application to partial evaluation", Ph.D. thesis, Linkoping, (1981)
(Pereira and Monteiro)
Pereira, L.M., and Monteiro, L., "The semantics of parallelism and coroutining in logic programming", Colloquium on mathematical logic in computing science, Salgotarjan, Hungary (1979)
(Porto)
Porto, A., "Epilog: A language for extended programming in logic", Tech. Report, Dept. de Informatico, Univ. Nova de Lisboa, Portugal (1982)
(Shapiro 83)
Shapiro, E.Y., "A Subset of Concurrent Prolog and its Interpreter", Tech. Report, TR-003, ICOT, Tokyo, (1983)
(Shapiro 85)
Shapiro, E.Y., Lecture notes, Advanced Course in AI, Vignieu, France, (1985)
(Takeuchi & Furukawa)
Takeuchi, A., and Furukawa, K., "Partial Evaluation of Prolog programs and its application to Meta programming", ICOT Research Centre, Tokyo, Japan (1985)
(Venken)
Venken, R., "A Prolog meta-interpreter for partial evaluation and its application to source-to-source transformation and query optimisation", Proc. ECAI 84, Pisa, (1984)

Advances in Artificial Intelligence - II
B. Du Boulay, D. Hogg and L. Steels (Editors)
Elsevier Science Publishers B.V. (North-Holland), 1987

AUTOMATIC NODE RECOGNITION IN A PARTITIONING GRAPH
Restricting The Search Space While Preserving Completeness

D. GOOSSENS

Département d'Informatique
Université PARIS-8
2, rue de la Liberté
93526 St-DENIS Cedex 02 (France)

Abstract

We propose a new algorithm which solves the important problem of searching intersection, union and difference nodes of two given nodes in a partitioning graph. A related subproblem has recently been discussed by L. Schubert and M.A. Papalaskaris: checking inclusion and disjunction relationships between nodes in a partitioning graph. They developped an algorithm for a restricted class of partitioning graphs.

We view the problem solved by our algorithm as maintaining a uniqueness principle over a partitioning graph (two different nodes in a graph denote two different sets), while computing intersection, union and difference nodes. Our algorithm treats partitioning graphs as substructures of Boolean algebras. It isolates minimal generating sets and computes canonical forms.

Keywords: knowledge representation, partitioning graphs, taxonomies, many-sorted unification, Boolean lattices, Boolean algebras, recognition.

1. Introduction

Taxonomies and related inference mechanisms are a central issue in Artificial Intelligence. [10] and [11] have recently proposed and argued the use of the more discriminative *partitioning graphs* as a classification structure for knowledge representation.

The association of sorts to variables has been frequently advocated in Automatic Theorem Proving [12]. Sorts are elements of a partially ordered set used to restrict the range of variables. Sorts have been structured into:

- Complete finite lattices: Unification of two variables involves restricting their ranges to the computed inf [1]. Hierarchy is a particular case.
- Partial orders: May be viewed as taxonomies of concepts (involving one single kind of link: subset-of). Variables in symbolic expressions are sorted over a taxonomy of concepts. The inf of two nodes is not systematically provided.
- Hierarchies: The most frequent case. Unification of two variables simply involves checking if their ranges are disjoint.
- Partitioning graphs: Partial orders are augmented into partitioning graphs when, in addition to inclusion, disjunction and equality relationships are systematically used (also called *semantic graphs* in [9]).

Partitioning graphs may represent any instance of the previous orderings by replacing each occurence of the relation x≤y by the partition of y, into x and its complement relative to y. They can explicitly represent intersections and differences of generic classes. They are thus particularly adapted to understanding and reasoning processes that operate by intersecting generic classes.

If the intersection of two concepts is necessary for the performance of understanding and reasoning tasks, the same holds for their union and differences, as we have argued in [4] and [5].

This paper presents an algorithm that grows partitioning graphs by connecting two arbitrary nodes to their intersection, difference and union nodes. All algebraic structures referenced in this paper are supposed finite. We assume the reader is familiar with Boolean lattices and algebras.

2. Intersection of two nodes in a partitioning graph.

Nodes in a partitioning graph may be seen as denoting sets, and links as constraints on these sets; equality relations between a set and some of its partitions. Thus, we shall often talk of nodes as if they were sets.

Finding inclusion and disjunction relationships between nodes is a particular case of the problem of unifying two variables whose ranges are both concretised by a node. Unification first computes the intersection of the ranges. It fails if it is empty (disjunction) and differently assigns the variables if one range is included in the other (inclusion). This problem is itself a particular case of the problem of recognizing nodes and preserving the uniqueness principle [8] over a partitioning graph. We write $\boxed{x}$ for a node and **x** for the denoted set.

A straightforward approach to compute the intersection of any two nodes $\boxed{x}$ and $\boxed{y}$ in a partitioning graph is to look for the nodes derivably included both in $\boxed{x}$ and $\boxed{y}$, and then build their union. To avoid building too many irrelevant links we propose representing the intersection of two nodes as a single node. Given two variables Vx and Vy with respective ranges $\boxed{x}$ and $\boxed{y}$, unification of Vx and Vy will first compute the intersection of **x** and **y**, and should give one of the following:

-     ϕ (empty set) ; **x** and **y** are disjoint.
-     $\boxed{x}$; **x** is included in **y**
-     $\boxed{y}$; dual
-     $\boxed{x \cap y}$; a node denoting the intersection of **x** and **y** already exists in the graph. Since a representation of the intersection range needs to be kept, this recognition preserves a uniqueness principle.
-     otherwise ; the intersection of **x** and **y** is not empty. $\boxed{x \cap y}$ does not already exist and may be newly created.

Note that this result is the sparest, while allowing further recognitions of the intersection node of any other pair of nodes. The same holds for their union and difference nodes.

In the next section, we define the Y operation, which computes the intersection, union and difference nodes of two nodes. Thus, a partitioning graph which permits this Y operation is a virtual representation of a Boolean algebra.

3. Y-graphs

We first restrict partitioning graphs to Y-graphs. We use Y-graphs in order to define an algorithm which recognizes or creates intersection, union and difference nodes. We then show that any partitioning graph is isomorphic to a subgraph of a Y-graph.

Y-graphs are a subclass of binary partitioning graphs (bpgs):
definition:
   A binary partitioning graph (bpg) is a couple <N,E>, with:
   syntax: N is a set of nodes and E a set of equations $\boxed{z}=\boxed{x}+\boxed{y}$ where $\boxed{x}$ $\boxed{y}$ and $\boxed{z}$ are nodes.
   semantics: each node $\boxed{n}$ denotes a set **n**, and each equation $\boxed{z}=\boxed{x}+\boxed{y}$ stands for: **z**=**x**∪**y** and **x**∩**y**=ϕ, where ∪ and ∩ are the union and intersection operations on sets and ϕ is the empty set.

That is, + is the disjoint union of two sets, and {**x**,**y**} is a 2-elements partition of **z**.
We represent sets of equations as graphs involving the subpattern:

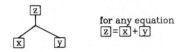

for any equation
$$\boxed{z}=\boxed{x}+\boxed{y}$$

More generally, nodes in a bpg and the symbols ∩, ∪, +, ϕ, may be understood as denoting objects and operations in a Boolean lattice.

We now define Y-graphs as a constructive subset of the set of bpgs.

definition: A Y-graph is any couple <N,E> that has been built using only rules 1 and 2. N is its set of nodes and E its set of *structures*. Each structure is a set of equations:

1. Any bpg <N,E> where E is empty is a Y-graph. N is its *generating set*. Each node in N denotes a distinct element of the generating set of the associated Boolean lattice.

2. If G is a Y-graph and $\boxed{x}$ and $\boxed{y}$ are two of its nodes, then:

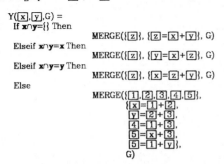

$$Y(\boxed{x},\boxed{y},G) =$$
If $\mathbf{x} \cap \mathbf{y}=\{\}$ Then
$$\text{MERGE}(\{\boxed{z}\}, \{\boxed{z}=\boxed{x}+\boxed{y}\}, G)$$
Elseif $\mathbf{x} \cap \mathbf{y}=\mathbf{x}$ Then
$$\text{MERGE}(\{\boxed{z}\}, \{\boxed{y}=\boxed{x}+\boxed{z}\}, G)$$
Elseif $\mathbf{x} \cap \mathbf{y}=\mathbf{y}$ Then
$$\text{MERGE}(\{\boxed{z}\}, \{\boxed{x}=\boxed{z}+\boxed{y}\}, G)$$
Else
$$\text{MERGE}(\{\boxed{1},\boxed{2},\boxed{3},\boxed{4},\boxed{5}\},$$
$$\{\boxed{x}=\boxed{1}+\boxed{2},$$
$$\boxed{y}=\boxed{2}+\boxed{3},$$
$$\boxed{4}=\boxed{1}+\boxed{3},$$
$$\boxed{5}=\boxed{x}+\boxed{3},$$
$$\boxed{5}=\boxed{1}+\boxed{y}\},$$
$$G)$$

is also a Y-graph. MERGE(N,S,G) adds the nodes in N to the nodes of G if and only if G does not already contain nodes with the same denotation (recognition condition). It adds the structure S (set of equations) to its set of structures, if and only if there is no structure in G containing both $\boxed{x}$ and $\boxed{y}$

- For any $\boxed{x}$ and $\boxed{y}$ in G, the generating set of $Y(\boxed{x},\boxed{y},G)$ is that of G.
- $\boxed{x}$ and $\boxed{y}$ are the *parents* of the structure added by MERGE. Its *consequents* are $\boxed{z}$ in the first three cases and $\boxed{1}$ $\boxed{2}$ $\boxed{3}$ $\boxed{4}$ and $\boxed{5}$ in the last.
- The set of *paths of structures* SPS($\boxed{n}$) associated to each node $\boxed{n}$ in N, is the set of paths leading from the generating set to $\boxed{n}$. Each path is a binary tree of structures, recursively defined as :

If $\boxed{n}$ is in the generating set, then {} is a path associated to $\boxed{n}$. Its *base* is $\{\boxed{n}\}$.
else, for any structure S with parents $\boxed{x}$ and $\boxed{y}$ and having $\boxed{n}$ as a consequent, for any path Px in SPS($\boxed{x}$) and Py in SPS($\boxed{y}$), the tree with root S and sons Px and Py is a path associated to $\boxed{n}$. Its base is the union of the bases of Px and Py.

A Y-graph is thus a bpg grown from a set of nodes $\{\boxed{b1} \dots \boxed{bn}\}$ (its generating set), using only the Y operation. It is isomorphic to a subset of the Boolean algebra generated by B=$\{\mathbf{b1} \dots \mathbf{bn}\}$ satisfying $\mathbf{x}=(\bigcup_{i=1}^{n}\mathbf{bi})\cap\mathbf{x}$ for any $\mathbf{x}$. We shall refer to this restricted Boolean algebra as RBA(B). This restrictively generated Boolean algebra may also be defined as an algebraic structure <S,∩,∪,−> freely generated by $\{\mathbf{b1} \dots \mathbf{bn}\}$, where <S,∩,∪> is a Boolean lattice and where − is defined as $\mathbf{x}-\mathbf{y}=\mathbf{x}\cap\mathbf{y'}$, where $\mathbf{y'}$ is the complement of $\mathbf{y}$.

The last call to MERGE adds the
structure :
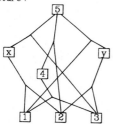
which may also be
represented as a
derivation step,
with $\boxed{x}$ and $\boxed{y}$
as parents :
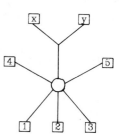

This structure is a 2-dimensional representation of the Boolean algebra generated by two free elements RBA($\boxed{x}$,$\boxed{y}$) (ϕ is not represented) : $\boxed{2}$ is $\boxed{x} \cap \boxed{y}$, $\boxed{1}$ is $\boxed{x} - \boxed{y}$, $\boxed{3}$ is $\boxed{y} - \boxed{x}$, $\boxed{4}$ is the symmetric difference of $\boxed{x}$ and $\boxed{y}$, and $\boxed{5}$ is $\boxed{x} \cup \boxed{y}$.

The structures added by the other calls to MERGE represent RBAs generated by two elements related by a disjunction or inclusion relation.

A related definition of a Y-graph G is thus as a set of Boolean expressions over the generating set of G and the operations $\cap$, $\cup$, $-$. To each node of G is associated a finite set of such Boolean expressions, each one corresponding to a path of structures from the generating set to the node. The base of the path corresponds to the base of the Boolean expression seen as its set of leaves. The recognition condition ensures that the Boolean expressions associated to a single node are all equivalent.

Theorem: *Any Y-graph verifies the uniqueness principle.*

Proof : Let G be a partitioning graph and $\boxed{n1}$ and $\boxed{n2}$ two distinct nodes in G such that n1=n2. We prove that G is not a Y-graph :
- If both $\boxed{n1}$ and $\boxed{n2}$ are in the generating set of G, then n1 and n2 are two different elements of the generating set of the corresponding RBA, which contradicts the hypothesis.
- Otherwise, the total order of construction on the structures of any Y-graph induced by the constructive definition implies that either $\boxed{n1}$ is a consequent of a structure S, that was added to G after $\boxed{n2}$ or conversely. Let G' contain $\boxed{n2}$ but not $\boxed{n1}$ such that the Y-graph G"=Y($\boxed{x}$,$\boxed{y}$,G') adds S to G' for some $\boxed{x}$ $\boxed{y}$ in G'. Now, if in G" we have n1=n2, then MERGE will have recognized $\boxed{n2}$ instead of creating $\boxed{n1}$. ∎

Theorem : *Any bpg is isomorphic to a subgraph of a Y-graph.*

In [6] we give proofs of this, based on weak and strong methods for completing a bpg into a Y-graph.

4. An algorithm for Y($\boxed{x}$,$\boxed{y}$,G)

The algorithm is based on the computation of canonical forms of Boolean expressions. It proceeds in two steps : Once the canonical form of the consequent nodes of $\boxed{x}$ and $\boxed{y}$ are computed, the **Merge** procedure has to find the consequent nodes which are already in G. This can be achieved by computing the canonical form of every node in G, but it amounts to reconstructing the whole Boolean algebra. It is thus imperative that **Y**($\boxed{x}$,$\boxed{y}$,G) finds a common base as small as possible to $\boxed{x}$ and $\boxed{y}$ in G and also restricts the set of nodes whose canonical forms must be computed for recognition while preserving completeness. This becomes apparent in the following algorithm, through the operations **Compute the canonical form** and **Merge1**. These operations consider only those nodes $\boxed{n'}$ such that there is no path in SPS($\boxed{n'}$) whose base lacks an element of the base of the canonical form of $\boxed{n}$.

$\mathbf{Y}(\boxed{x},\boxed{y},G) =$

If there is a structure in G which contains both $\boxed{x}$ and $\boxed{y}$
then solve the problem in the RBA represented by the structure.
else

1- **Compute the canonical forms** fcx and fcy of $\boxed{x}$ and $\boxed{y}$
2- **Reduce** fcx∩fcy **to canonical form** fcx∩y
3- Choose appropriate call to **Merge** :

    If fcx∩y=∅ then

    Reduce fcx∪fcy **to canonical form** fcx∪y
    Merge({<$\boxed{z}$, fcx∪y>}, {$\boxed{z}$=$\boxed{x}$+$\boxed{y}$})
    elseif fcx∩y=fcx then

    Reduce fcy−fcx **to canonical form** fcy−x
    Merge({<$\boxed{z}$, fcy−x>}, {$\boxed{y}$=$\boxed{x}$+$\boxed{z}$})
    elseif fcx∩y=fcy then

    Reduce fcx−fcy **to canonical form** fcx−y
    Merge({<$\boxed{z}$, fcx−y>}, {$\boxed{x}$=$\boxed{y}$+$\boxed{z}$})
    else

    Reduce fcx∪fcy **to canonical form** fcx∪y
    Reduce fcx−fcy **to canonical form** fcx−y
    Reduce fcy−fcx **to canonical form** fcy−x
    Reduce (fcx−y)+(fcy−x)
                to canonical form fcxΔy
    Merge({<$\boxed{1}$,fcx−y>,<$\boxed{2}$,fcx∩y>,<$\boxed{3}$,fcy−x>,
              <$\boxed{4}$,fcxΔy>,<$\boxed{5}$,fcx∪y>},

    {$\boxed{x}$=$\boxed{1}$+$\boxed{2}$,
    $\boxed{y}$=$\boxed{2}$+$\boxed{3}$,
    $\boxed{4}$=$\boxed{1}$+$\boxed{3}$,
    $\boxed{5}$=$\boxed{x}$+$\boxed{3}$,
    $\boxed{5}$=$\boxed{1}$+$\boxed{y}$})

Merge(NODES,STRUCTURE) =
Let Bxy be the union of the bases of fcx and fcy (minimal bases of x and y)
  1. Associate to every node $\boxed{n}$ in Bxy the set {$\boxed{n}$}
  2. Compute **Candidates**(Bxy)
  3. For each NODE in NODES, compute **Merge1**(NODE)
  4. Unless there is in G a structure containing the nodes in STRUCTURE
     add STRUCTURE to the set of structures of G

Merge1(<$\boxed{n}$,fcn>) =
Let B be the base of fcn (the minimal base of $\boxed{n}$)
  If B has two elements and a structure containing them both is in G
  then $\boxed{n}$ is the node in the structure determined by fcn
  else
    1- For each $\boxed{ni}$ in G with a set Bi associated by **Candidates**
         such that Bi includes or equals B
       Compute the canonical form fcni of $\boxed{ni}$
       If fcni=fcn then replace $\boxed{n}$ by $\boxed{ni}$ in Structure, and exit of **Merge1**
    2- Since $\boxed{n}$ was not found in G, add $\boxed{n}$ in G as a new node.

To **Compute the canonical form** fcx of a node $\boxed{x}$:

    If fcx was already computed then return it.
    elseif $\boxed{x}$ is in the generating set of G, then fcx=$\boxed{x}$
    else

      Choose any structure containing $\boxed{x}$ as a consequent, with parents $\boxed{a}$ and $\boxed{b}$.
      Compute the Boolean relation $\boxed{x}$=f($\boxed{a}$,$\boxed{b}$) in terms of ∩, ∪, −
      Compute the canonical forms fca and fcb of $\boxed{a}$ and $\boxed{b}$
      Reduce f(fca,fcb) **to canonical form**. The result is fcx.

To **Reduce** f **to canonical form,**

    Use any canonical rewriting set of reductions for Boolean algebras (such as those automatically
    obtained in [7][2]), or a more efficient hand-coded one such as may be found in [6].

Candidates(F) =
For any two nodes $\boxed{n1}$ and $\boxed{n2}$ in G
  - not already processed
  - such that at least one of $\boxed{n1}$ and $\boxed{n2}$ is in F
  - such that the structure S with parents $\boxed{n1}$ and $\boxed{n2}$ is in the graph G,

let B1 and B2 be the sets respectively associated to $\boxed{n1}$ and $\boxed{n2}$.
For any consequent $\boxed{i}$ in the structure S, if $\boxed{i}$ was already associated a set Bi, associate the set $(B1\cup B2)\cap Bi$ to $\boxed{i}$. Otherwise, associate the set $B1\cup B2$ to $\boxed{i}$.
Add the consequents to F and state the pair $\boxed{n1},\boxed{n2}$ already processed and compute **Candidates**(F).

We now outline the proof of correctness and completeness of **Y**: if G is a Y-graph, then $Y(\boxed{x},\boxed{y},G)$ computes a Y-graph, for any distinct $\boxed{x}$ and $\boxed{y}$ in G.

In addition to the correctness problem involved with canonical forms in a Boolean algebra, the only precision to add to the uniqueness and completeness proofs of the denotational definition of Y-graphs is the proof of completeness of the For each loop in **Merge1**: The nodes searched for are obligatorily examined by the For each loop in **Merge1** if they are present.

Just as every Boolean expression has a unique minimal base, which is the base of its canonical form (this base is included in or equal to every other of its bases), similarly, every node has a unique minimal base.

The **Candidates** procedure associates to a node $\boxed{n'}$ a set S of nodes which is the intersection of the restrictions of its bases to the set Bxy. Bxy is chosen so that it includes or equals each of the minimal bases of the nodes looked for.

Thus, if one of these minimal bases B includes a node $\boxed{b}$ which is not in S, then there is at least one base B' of $\boxed{n'}$ which lacks $\boxed{b}$. It follows that B may not be the minimal base of $\boxed{n'}$ and $\boxed{n'}$ may not equal $\boxed{n}$.

5. Relations to the work of Schubert

In [11], Schubert proposes to transform any partitioning graph into a P-graph. A P-graph is either a possibly tangled hierarchy, or a P-graph with another P-graph attached to it by one and only one of its main roots. He uses his restricted algorithm to answer part-of and disjoint-from questions.

We believe that this solution is adapted to finding inclusion and disjunction relationships between nodes. In its current state, our algorithm would do something that amounts to reconstructing a P-graph. But Schubert's solution is not adapted to the general problem of *recognizing* nodes, which requires that graphs verify the uniqueness principle. During this process of recognition, much of the canonical rewriting can be viewed as extending the graph and approaching a P-graph-like structure. The question of keeping the extensions after an invocation of the **Y** algorithm then arises. Since the temporarily added nodes are not recognized in the graph Everything must be garbaged in order to preserve uniqueness. Keeping a graph as a P-graph while new information is added would ask for too many recognitions.

The Y-graph below is not a P-graph. To the question "is $\boxed{y}$ disjoint from $\boxed{x}$?" Schubert's algorithm will answer "unknown" despite the derivable answer $\boxed{y}\cap\boxed{x}=\phi$:

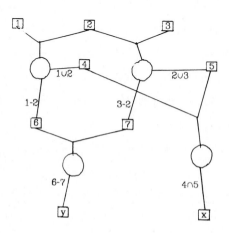

The derivation of $x\cap y=\phi$ from this Y-graph may be done simply by propagating "inclusion in $\boxed{y}$'s complement" labels, from $\boxed{y}$ [6].

Despite the restriction of the search space provided by the **Candidates** procedure, the set of nodes examined by **Merge1** may still be very large. In the spirit provided by Schubert's algorithms, it may be useful to discard nodes by a label propagation technique which marks the nodes that are explicitly different from a given node. We give in [6] a set of rules that propagate inclusion and disjunction relationships and an algorithm which recursively starts a propagation from every node involved in the computation of a canonical form. We then show that this algorithm accounts for the associativity and commutativity properties of ∩ and ∪ during comparison of Boolean expressions.

6. Relations with Knowledge Representation

- Y-graphs: The relations between Y-graphs, seen as substructures of Boolean algebras, and knowledge, appear multiple and complex. We assume in this paper that taxonomic knowledge can be embodied into Y-graphs. The same holds for sets of parts of a structure, where inclusion is replaced by the part-of relation, as is done in [10]. The Y operation computes sets of common and distinguishing parts from two given structured objects.
There is an analogy between the previous remarks and two ways of using Y-graph as classifying structures for retrieving first-order terms by the intersection, union and difference operations provided by the Y operation: terms as classes of ground terms, and terms as sets of occurences.

- Y operation: Y-graphs are built by the Y operation from generic concepts, not from ground instances, that is, from intensions rather than from extensions. The Y operation thus complements the classical mechanisms that deal with individuals and extensions, such as intersection, difference and union operations in the style of [3].

7. Conclusion

We have presented a complete algorithm for recognizing the intersection, union and difference nodes of two nodes in a partitioning graph. It is a necessary basis onto which practical realizations and argumented restrictions will be designed, in order to address an essential AI problem: recognizing intersections. If [3] outlined the significance of computing intersections of extensions, this paper assumes a similar significance for intensions.

8. Acknowledgments

We acknowledge the useful comments and insights provided by Ellen Sparer, Harald Wertz and Patrick Greussay. We wish to thank the IRCAM laboratory and LITP for their support.

References

[1] **AIT-KACI H., NASR R.** *Logic and Inheritance* ACM POPL-86, Jan. 1986, pp 219-228.

[2] **FAGES F.** *Formes canoniques dans les algèbres Booléennes et applications a la démonstration automatique en logique du premier ordre* Thèse de 3ième cycle, LITP, Univ. Paris-7, Nov. 1983.

[3] **FAHLMAN S.E.** *NETL : A System for Representing and Using Real-World Knowledge* MIT Press 1979.

[4] **GOOSSENS D.** *La méta-évaluation au service de la compréhension automatique de programmes* Thèse de 3ième cycle, Univ. Paris-6, Jan 1981.

[5] **GOOSSENS D.** *The conceptual calculus for automatic program understanding* 7th IJCAI, Vancouver 1981, pp 992-997

[6] **GOOSSENS D.** *Les Y-graphes* RT-1, Univ. Paris-8, Avril 1986.

[7] **HSIANG J.** *Topics in Automated Theorem Proving and Program Generation* Ph.D. Thesis. Univ. of Illinois at Urbana-Champaign, Nov. 1982.

[8] **MAIDA A.S. SHAPIRO S.C.** *Intensional Concepts in Propositional Semantic Networks* Cognitive Science Vol 6 n.4, Oct 1982, Ablex Pub. Corp. Norwood, New-Jersey, pp 291-330.

[9] **McSKIMMIN J.R. MINKER J.** *A Predicate Calculus based Semantic Network for Deductive Searching* In *Associative Networks* N. Findler ed. Academic Press 1979, pp 205-238.

[10] **SCHUBERT L.K.** *Problems with parts* 6th IJCAI, Tokyo 1979, pp 778-784.

[11] **PAPALASKARIS M.A., SCHUBERT L.K.** *Parts inference: closed and semi-closed partitioning graphs* 7th IJCAI, Vancouver, 1981, pp 304-309

[12] **WALTHER C.** *A Mechanical Solution of Schubert's Steamroller by Many-Sorted Resolution* Artificial Intelligence Vol 26 n.2, May 1985, North-Holland, Amsterdam, pp 217-224.

Advances in Artificial Intelligence - II
B. Du Boulay, D. Hogg and L. Steels (Editors)
© Elsevier Science Publishers B.V. (North-Holland), 1987

PROGRAM SYNTHESIS BY INDUCTIVE INFERENCE

Matthew M. Huntbach
Cognitive Studies Programme
University of Sussex
Brighton, BN1 9QN
England.

1. INTRODUCTION

In his thesis 'Algorithmic Program Debugging' [16], E.Y.Shapiro
presents a theoretical framework for program debugging using an
inductive inference mechanism. The general nature of this
framework means that, by specifying an initial empty program, it
may also be used for the inference of programs from examples of
input/output behaviour.

We have implemented Shapiro's Model Inference System, and made a
number of changes and additions to it. In particular, we no longer
regard it as specifically a tool for Prolog programmers, but as a
general program synthesis system. Our efforts have been
concentrated on producing a practical refinement operator [17].

This paper describes our system without using logic programming
terminology. We also indicate how we see this system becoming part
of a collection of tools to provide automated assistance to the
computer programmer.

2. DATA FLOW PROGRAMS

Shapiro's framework adapts most easily to the logic programming
language Prolog, and his system uses Prolog as both the
implementation and target language. The work presented here relies
on Shapiro's framework, and does in fact use a subset of Prolog as
the target language. But we find it easiest to think of our target
programs in the form of generalised data flow diagrams [4]. We are
influenced particularly by the plan notation of the Programmer's
Apprentice [19]. Our system is implemented in a combination of
Prolog and Pop-11, using the Poplog system [13].

In our notation, a procedure is shown by a set of data flow
diagrams, each representing one particular path through the
program. All diagrams for a particular procedure have the same
number of input and output ports representing that procedure's
parameters. A diagram consists of a number of segments which
themselves have input and output ports, linked by data flow lines.
A procedure may be incomplete, in which case there are possible
paths through the program for which no diagram is present.

The segments represent calls to subprocedures or tests. A
procedure segment when presented with input values or
tokens produces output tokens which are assumed to flow along the
data flow lines. A test produces no output tokens but instead
either succeeds or fails. If any test fails, the control path
represented by the diagram is the wrong one for the given input,
and another is tried, until one succeeds in which case the tokens
which arrive at the output ports of the diagram are the output of
the whole procedure. The program fails if no program path

succeeds. A program for a procedure as opposed to a test is
complete only when it never fails on any input which it is
possible for that procedure to receive. The tests and
subprocedures may themselves be represented by further data flow
diagrams, they may be recursive calls, or they may be system
primitives. Any program path on which a subprocedure fails also
fails.

A program path is said to 'cover' a given input/output pair if,
when presented with the given input, it succeeds and produces the
given output when the execution of the program path is simulated
by executing only system primitives and asking the user for the
output he would expect from the other subtests and subprocedures.
We term this 'query execution'. It is equivalent to Shapiro's
definition of 'cover' using the 'eager strategy' — we do not
consider his other search strategies here.

Figure 1 gives an example for a program which inserts an integer
in position into an ordered list of integers (the program is in
fact incomplete and contains bugs). The system primitives are
"head", "tail", "isnil", ">", "cons", and "createnil" which takes
no inputs and always returns the empty list as output. If "t" is a
test we also have "not(t)" which succeeds when t fails and vice
versa. For convenience we will assume in future that "head" and
"tail" have a built-in test for "not(isnil)".

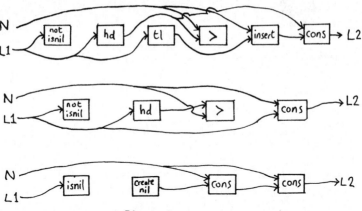

Figure 1

To test whether the first program path covers the pair
insert(2,[1,2,3]) -> [1,2,3] the program path would be executed
until it came to the recursive call 'insert(2,[2,3])'. The user
would then be asked for the result. He would enter [2,2,3] (this
is the expected result rather than the one that would be produced
were the program fully executed) and the execution would continue,
giving the output [1,2,2,3], so the input/output pair is covered
by the path.

3. PROGRAM DIAGNOSIS

Shapiro presents three algorithms to diagnose faults in three
different cases where bugs are found. Each of these will
interactively query the user during execution.

Algorithm 1 is used when the program fails on a given input where the user considers it should return a certain output. It takes the program with the input and expected output. It returns an input/output pair which the user defines as true but which is not covered by any existing path in the program.

For example, the program in figure 1 will fail when called with input insert(2,[1,2,3]), expected output [1,2,2,3], because there is no program path to cover the case of inserting an integer into a list whose head is equal to the integer. The algorithm will return insert(2,[2,3]) -> [2,2,3] as the uncovered input/output pair.

Algorithm 2 is used when the program succeeds on a given input, but the output produced is different from that expected. It takes the program with the input and incorrect output produced. It returns a program path which covers a false input/output pair.

For example, the program in figure 1 if called with input insert(4,[1,2,3]) will return [1,2,3,4,4] rather than the expected [1,2,3,4]. The algorithm will find that the third program path covers the input output pair insert(4,[]) -> [4,4] which the user indicates should be false.

Algorithm 3 is used when the program fails to terminate. It returns a program path which is looping. It works by keeping a stack of procedure calls to a fixed limit. When this limit is exceeded, the program is assumed to be looping. The stack is searched to find any point where a procedure with a given input calls itself with the same input, or where some violation of a well-founded ordering on procedure calls occurs [5]. The algorithm returns the program path responsible for the violation.

4. PROGRAM SYNTHESIS

Shapiro's diagnosis algorithms have been fairly widely implemented, not only for Prolog, but also for other languages such as Pascal [14]. Less attention has been given to his use of these algorithms in inductive program synthesis.

The basis of this system is that a series of input/output examples is presented by the user. Each of these is tested in turn against the current conjectured program. If an example indicated as true fails, or one indicated as false succeeds, the diagnosis algorithms are used to detect a bug, and the conjectured program is replaced by one with this bug corrected which also behaves correctly with respect to all other input/output examples presented previously. If the conjectured programs are restricted to be any recursively enumerable class of programs that are everywhere terminating then, using concepts introduced by Gold [7], the correct program may be identified in the limit.

The inference algorithm is incremental, that is any path which was removed for covering a false input/output example is never added again to the program. The complete algorithm is shown in figure 2.

The diagnosis algorithms generate a considerable number of queries, the answers to which are added to the list of known input/output pairs. Whenever a query is made, this list is first searched to check whether the answer has been given previously, thus cutting the number of queries made directly to the user.

```
set P to the empty program
let the set of marked program paths be empty
repeat
    read the next input/output pair
    repeat
        if the program P fails on a true example then
            use Algorithm 1 to find an uncovered input/output
                pair A
            search for an unmarked program path p that covers A
            add p to P
        endif;
        if the program P succeeds on a false example or
            produces an output different from that expected
        then
            use Algorithm 2 to detect a false program path p
            remove p from P, and add it to the set of marked
            program paths
        endif;
    until P is correct with respect to all known input/output
                pairs;
until no input/output pairs are left to read;

interrupt if the depth of a computation on some input/output
            pair A exceeds some limit
            use Algorithm 3 to find a program path p which
            is looping
            remove p from P, add it to the set of marked
            program paths
            restart the computation of A
endinterrupt
```

Figure 2

5. SEARCHING FOR NEW PROGRAM PATHS

The major part of our research has been to improve the method used
to search for a new program path to cover a given input/output
pair. In an earlier paper, we describe Shapiro's method with
respect to Prolog in detail, and suggest some improvements [10].
Here, we give a simple method of searching the space of possible
program paths using our data flow notation. Our simplifications
are due mainly to our use of separate "hd", "tl" and "cons"
operations, rather than the list templates of Prolog clauses.

We introduce the concept of an incomplete program path. This is a
program path in which there are no data flow lines leading to the
output ports of the main procedure. In the search tree for
covering program paths, the non-leaf nodes are incomplete program
paths, the leaves are complete. The root node is an incomplete
program path consisting of just the input and output ports with no
data flow lines at all.

There are three refinement operations by which children may be
generated:

1) Add a subprocedure. This involves constructing data flow lines
   either from the input ports of the main procedure or the output
   ports of existing subprocedures. The output ports of the new
   subprocedure are unconnected.

2) Add a test. This is similar to the above, except that tests
have no output ports.
3) Close the program path (producing a leaf node). This involves
constructing data flow lines to the output ports of the main
procedure from either its input ports or the output ports of
subprocedures.

No subprocedure may be added that exactly duplicates the main
procedure (as this would lead to a looping path) or exactly
duplicates a subprocedure already added. No program path may be
closed in such a way that there exists a subprocedure which has no
dataflow lines from any of its output ports (since such a
subprocedure would be superfluous).

For each procedure used, the user must declare
1) The number of input and output ports it has, and the type of
the data items each port uses.
2) The subprocedures and tests it may call.

For example, the insert procedure of figure 1 is declared to have
two input ports: N type integer, L1 type list(integer) and one
output port: L2 type list(integer). It is declared to make use of
one test ">" and one subprocedure, "insert" (that is, itself
called recursively). In addition it is assumed that each procedure
may make use of various system procedures and tests such as simple
list operations.

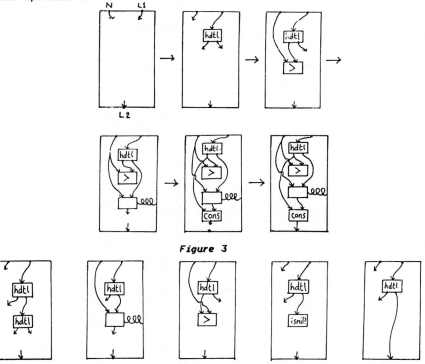

Figure 3

Figure 4

Figure 3 shows the sequence of operations needed to construct the
first program path in figure 1. Here, we treat the addition of the
"hd" and "tl" procedures as one operation. We indicate a recursive
call by a coiled line. Figure 4 shows some of the possible siblings
of the   third   node of figure 3.

Heuristic values may be assigned to program paths to guide the
search, though we do not consider this further here. When a
complete path is found during the search, it is tested to see
whether it covers the input/output pair. For example, if we are
searching for a path to cover insert(3,[1,2,4]) -> [1,2,3,4] the
fifth path in figure 4 does not cover it since it leads to
insert(3,[1,2,4]) -> [2,4]. An incomplete path may also be tested
to see if it covers a pair. It fails to cover it if it contains a
test which fails. The third and fourth paths in figure 4, for
example, fail to cover insert(3,[1,2,4]) -> [1,2,3,4] since they
lead to the tests 1>3 and isnil([2,4]) respectively. Any
descendant of an incomplete path which fails to cover a pair will
also fail to cover it, so it need not be searched and the tree can
be pruned. A complete covering path may be found which is,
however, marked, that is it has already been removed from the
program because it leads to false output for another input. In
this case, search continues for an alternative covering path.

6. GOAL DIRECTED CLOSURE

Consider the program path shown in figure 5. This might be
generated during the search for a program path to cover the pair
dbl2nd([a,b,c,d,e,f]) -> [a,b,b,c,d,d,e,f,f], "dbl2nd" being a
procedure to double every second element in a list. If this
incomplete path were query executed (resulting in the user being
queried for the result of dbl2nd([c,d,e,f])), the values shown
would be produced at each output port.

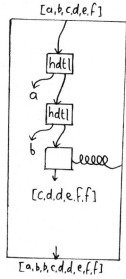

Figure 5

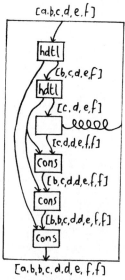

Figure 6

It can be noted at this stage that we now have the components needed to construct the output value. So we can immediately add "cons" operations and close the path as in figure 6, to produce a covering path which is conjectured to apply to all list of length 2 or more (the system would generate separate paths to cover the base cases of the empty list or a list of one element).

We add to our search algorithm an operation which query executes each incomplete program path using the input for the pair which needs to be covered. The values produced at each of the output ports are stored, and a test is made to see if these may be used to construct the output for the pair and thus produce a covering path. If there is more than one way of constructing the output, each is produced in case some are marked paths.

Using this technique, heuristic search of program paths produced by adding construction operations and closure is unnecessary.

7. CREATING AUXILIARY PROCEDURES

If, while testing for a goal directed closure, it is found that it is possible to create only part of an output value, the program path may be closed by creating an auxiliary procedure which produces the rest. Figure 7 shows such a closure for the procedure "combs" which takes a list as input and produces as output a list of all two-element combinations of items in the list.

A program path to cover the new pair aux([a,b,c,d]) -> [[a,b],[a,c],[a,d]] must now be synthesised. However, the user has not specified the use of the procedure "aux" and so cannot be expected to answer queries on it (as would be necessary if query executing a recursive path in the search for a covering path). It is however possible to use a backwards reasoning to give the answer to queries involving auxiliary procedures. In the case of figure 7, the answer to any query involving the procedure "aux" may be found by applying the same input values to the path in figure 8 and query executing it. The system procedure "bsub" takes the seconds argument from the back of the first, that is if append(A,B) = C then bsub(C,B) = A.

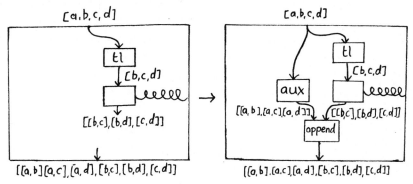

Figure 7

So to find the output of aux([a,b,c]) the user would be asked first for the output of combs([a,b,c]) then for the output of combs([b,c]) that is [[a,b],[a,c],[b,c]] and [[b,c]] respectively.

The output for aux([a,b,c]) is then shown to be [[a,b],[a,c]].

We may also generate auxiliary tests. Suppose we want a function
"addnew" which adds an element to a list only if that element is
not already a member of that list, otherwise it returns the list
unchanged. Then if we present the system with the pair
addnew(e,[a,b,c,d]) -> [e,a,b,c,d] it will produce the program
path shown in figure 9 to cover it.

However, this program path will be removed when the system is
presented with the pair addnew(c,[a,b,c,d]) -> [a,b,c,d] since it
leads to the false input/output pair addnew(c,[a,b,c,d]) ->
[c,a,b,c,d]. The system then needs to search for a new path which
covers addnew(e,[a,b,c,d]) -> [e,a,b,c,d] but not
addnew(c,[a,b,c,d]) -> [c,a,b,c,d].

One possibility is to modify the removed path by adding an
auxiliary test as in figure 10. The two input/output pairs
auxtest(e,[a,b,c,d]) -> true and auxtest(c,[a,b,c,d]) -> false are
added to the databse of pairs, and the system will search for a
program to cover them.

For any queries of auxtest(X,Y) the user is asked for the result
of addnew(X,Y). auxtest(X,Y) is defined as true when addnew(X,Y) =
cons(X,Y), false otherwise. This may be used to sythesise
"auxtest" (in fact, our system would identify it as being
equivalent to the system test "not(member)").

Although the generation of auxiliary procedures and tests may lead
to inefficient or unusually structured programs, we envisage
program transformation techniques [3] being applied to them. We
have already implemented a simple transformation which
incorporates the program path to cover some auxiliary into the
parent path if the program for the auxiliary is found to be a
single path.

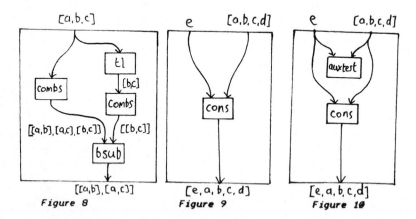

Figure 8   Figure 9   Figure 10

8. PROGRAM PATHS TO PROGRAMS

A set of program paths may be represented and executed as a set of
Prolog clauses by representing each path as a clause, and each
subprocedure and test segment in a path as a subgoal. Each output
port is represented by a new Prolog variable. A data flow line is

represented by using the Prolog variable as an input parameter in
a subsequent procedure or test. The input and output ports of a
program path are represented by the variables in the head.

However, as we have indicated, our intention is that each program
path should be thought of as one particular flow of control
through a program. Our program paths may be combined to form plan
diagrams as used by the M.I.T. Programmer's Apprentice [15]. This
plan notation is claimed to represent all the essential details of
a program while suppressing those incidental features which stem
from particular programming languages. Translators to and from the
plan notation and several standard programming languages have been
written. Thus, with the appropiate translator, our system could be
used to synthesise programs in any standard language.

We envisage our program synthesis system being incorporated as one
element in a larger programmer's assistant type system such as has
been suggested with PSI [8]. We agree with Kant [12] that
'incorporating an inductive inference capability into a program
synthesis system makes sense; expecting it to solve the entire
program synthesis problem does not'. It may best be used perhaps
for filling in gaps or correcting mistakes that inevitable arise
when programs are methodically derived from specifications [6]
especially from informal specifications [1].

9. CONCLUSIONS

Our work represents a further step from theoretical work on
inductive inference [7],[2] towards a tool which may be of
practical use to computer programmers. The link is Shapiro's Model
Inference System [16]. We have demonstrated that there is great
scope for improvemnets to be made to this system, particulalrly to
the program synthesis part.

We have also tried to separate Shapiro's work from the field of
logic programming. Although the use of Prolog was important in
allowing the construction of a demonstratable system, we feel the
work needs to be seen more in its own right.

In the field of program synthesis from examples, we have produced
a system which can cope with most of the examples dealt with by
other systems [9], [18], [11] as well as some not previously
synthesised entirely from examples.

10. ACKNOWLEDGMENTS

Financial assistance for this work was given by the Artificial
Intelligence group at the G.E.C. Marconi Research Centre. I also
thank my supervisor, Rudi Lutz, and other people in the Cognitive
Studies Programme at Sussex University for helpful comments.

11. REFERENCES

[1] R.Balzer, N.Goldman, D.Wile. Informality in program
    specification. IEEE Trans. Soft. Eng. SE-4,2 pp.94-103. 1978.
[2] L.Blum & M.Blum. Towards a mathematical theory of inductive
    inference. Information and Control 28. 1975.
[3] J.Darlington. Program transformation. In 'Functional
    Programming and its Applications', pp.193-215. Eds.
    J.Darlington, P.Henderson, D.A.Turner. Cambridge Univ. Press,
    U.K. 1982.

[4] J.B.Dennis.Dataflow supercomputers. IEEE Computer 13,11
    pp.48-56. 1980.
[5] R.W.Floyd. Assigning meaning to programs. In Proc. Symp. on
    App. Math. Ed. J.D.Schwartz. American Math. Soc. 1967.
[6] S.L.Gerhart & L.Yelowitz. Observations of fallibility in
    applications of modern programming methodology. IEEE Trans.
    Soft. Eng. SE-2,3 pp.195-207. 1976.
[7] E.M.Gold. Language identification in the limit. Information
    and Control 10 pp.447-474. 1967.
[8] C.Green. A summary of the PSI program synthesis system.
    IJCAI-77 pp.380-381. 1977.
[9] S.Hardy. Synthesis of Lisp programs from examples. IJCAI-75
    pp.240-245. 1975.
[10] M.M.Huntbach. An improved version of Shapiro's Model Inference
    System. Third International Logic Programming Conference,
    London 1986.
[11] J.P.Jouannaud and G.Guiho. Inference of functions with an
    interactive system. Machine Intelligence 9, pp.227-250. 1979.
[12] E.Kant. Understanding and automating algorithm design. IEEE
    Trans. Soft. Eng. SE-11, 11. pp.1361-1374. 1985.
[13] C.Mellish & S.Hardy. Integrating Prolog into the Poplog
    environment. In 'Implementations of Prolog', ed. J.A.Campbell.
    Ellis Horwood 1984.
[14] S.Renner. Location of logical errors in Pascal programs with
    an appendix on implementation problems in Waterloo Prolog/C.
    Internal report UIUCDCS-F-82-896. Knowledge Based Programmer's
    Assistant Project, University of Illinois, 1982.
[15] C.Rich. A formal representation for plans in the Programmer's
    Apprentice. IJCAI-81 pp.1044-1052. 1981.
[16] E.Y.Shapiro. Algorithmic Program Debugging. M.I.T. Press 1982.
[17] E.Y.Shapiro. Inductive Inference of Theories from Facts. Yale
    Univ. Dept. of Computer Science. Research Report 192. 1981.
[18] D.E.Shaw, W.R.Swartout, C.Green. Inferring Lisp programs from
    examples. IJCAI-75, pp.260-267. 1975.
[19] R.C.Waters. The Programmer's Apprentice: knowledge based
    program editing. IEEE Trans. Soft. Eng. SE-8,1 pp.1-13. 1982.

Advances in Artificial Intelligence - II
B. Du Boulay, D. Hogg and L. Steels (Editors)
© Elsevier Science Publishers B.V. (North-Holland), 1987

PROGRAM SYNTHESIS = PROOF METHOD + KNOWLEDGE

Example about Recursive Function Synthesis

Paul JACQUET and Marie-Laure POTET

LIFIA-ENSIMAG   BP 68
38402 St. Martin d'Hères cedex
FRANCE

ABSTRACT

To master the inherent complexity of deductive program synthesis we propose
an approach in which the proof of the initial specification is split up
into two parts. One constructs a program in proving the specification, the
other infers the needed theorems. We illustrate this decomposition in
developing a strategy for the synthesis of recursive functions.

1.INTRODUCTION

The idea of assimilating the construction of a program to the proof of a
theorem, expressed in a suitable logic, is now admitted [MaW 80], [Con 83],
[Nor 81]. However, among the different problems on which the automatisation
of such an approach stumbles, we can mention the combinatoric nature of the
proof and the necessity to dispose of specific knowledge useful to a proof.
A possible solution to the first problem consists in developing strategies
to guide the elaboration of a proof. Very early, the importance of such
strategies has been pointed out as well in the deductive approach [Bib 78]
as in the transformational one [ClD 78]. The aim of our work is to
characterize, in a deductive approach, the needed knowledge to apply a
strategy connected to recursive function synthesis. Moreover, showing the
link between proof strategy and the set of necessary theorems allows us to
consider the synthesis process as the result of an interaction between a
proof system (inference rules and strategies) and a deductive knowledge
base including the user. The studied strategy, based upon the notion of
decomposition algebra [BuL 69], [Kla 84], has already been proposed, in
different ways, in the field of assisted program construction [Gre 84], and
in the field of synthesis based upon the use of program schemas [Smi 85],
[BCF 85], [Per 84].

The first part of this paper briefly sets out the proof system we have
developed. The second part is dedicated to a detailed study of the
strategy. It shows the necessary information exchanges between the two
components of the system and points out the failures and their

consequences. This strategy is based on some preliminary choices, the main one being the selection of a decomposition algebra. The study of the second part allows us to find some criteria. This is illustrated in the examples of the last part.

2.THE PROOF SYSTEM

The deductive approach to program synthesis consists in proving, in some model, the initial specification of a problem, in such a way that it is possible to extract straight away, from the obtained proof, a program describing the elaboration of the result.

In our approach a problem consists of finding a function whose specification is of the form:

$$\forall x \quad (P(x) \Rightarrow Q(x, f(x)))$$

where P is a property describing the data x (one element or a vector) and Q a relation linking x and the result of the function to synthetize. We also suppose that the type of x and f(x) is supplied, such information allows us to select the model in which the proof will be carried out.

The target language, TL, in which the resulting programs are described is functional. In this language a function definition is written such as : **f(x) <- F(x)** where F(x) is a term of TL built from a set of base functions and from the following three functionals: well founded recursion, conditional and functional composition. The aim of the synthesis system is then to construct a definition of the function f in TL.

The formal system we are developing, founded on an axiomatic definition of the target language, is based on the following interpretation:

> A specification is true, if and only if, for every value of x having the property P, one can give a definition F for f in TL such that the relation Q(x, EVAL(F(x))) is true in the selected model. EVAL is the evaluating function defining the operational semantic of the target language.

This system contains four inference rules corresponding to the introduction of each construction of the target language: the three functionals and the identification of base functions. The searched function f can be described by a term t of TL if the initial specification of f can be proved using the inference rule relative to the introduction of the considered construction.

Let us now consider the rule relative to the introduction of recursion. A possible definition for f in TL is:

```
f(x) <- if C(x) then f0(x)
                 else g(f(h1(x)), ... , f(hn(x)), x)
```

where C, f0, h1, ... , hn and g are new functions to construct, if the initial specification is proved using the following inference rule. In this rule the set of premises can be split up into two parts:
- The functions f0, C, h1, ..., hn and g have to be constructed. The premises referred by (Ai) are the specifications of these functions. They have to be proved using the proposed formal system.

- The above construction must be correct regarding the initial specification. The premises, referred by (Bi), insure this correctness and they can be proved using a demonstrator of any kind: based on resolution, rewriting system ...

$$(\textit{ Premises relative to } f0 \textit{ })$$

(A1) $P(x) \quad \wedge \quad C(x) \quad \Rightarrow Q0(x, f0(x))$

(B1) $P(x) \quad \wedge \quad C(x) \quad \wedge \quad Q0(x, f(x)) \Rightarrow Q(x, f(x))$

$$(\textit{ Premises relative to } hi \textit{ for } 1 \leq i \leq n \textit{ })$$

(A2) $P(x) \quad \wedge \quad \neg C(x) \quad \Rightarrow Qi(x, hi(x))$

(B2) $P(x) \quad \wedge \quad \neg C(x) \quad \wedge \quad Qi(x, hi(x)) \quad \Rightarrow P(hi(x))$

(B3)   There is a well founded ordering, noted <, such that, for every i:

$P(x) \wedge \neg C(x) \wedge Qi(x, hi(x)) \Rightarrow (hi(x) < x)$

$$(\textit{ Premises relative to } g \textit{ })$$

(A3) $Pg(z, x) \quad \Rightarrow Qg(z, x, g(z, x))$

(B4) $P(x) \wedge \neg C(x) \wedge \bigwedge_{i=1}^{n} [Qi(x, hi(x)) \wedge Q(hi(x), f(hi(x)))]$

$\Rightarrow Pg(f(h1(x)), \ldots, f(hn(x)), x)$

(B5) $P(x) \wedge \neg C(x) \wedge \bigwedge_{i=1}^{n} [Qi(x, hi(x)) \wedge Q(hi(x), f(hi(x)))]$

$\wedge Qg(f(h1(x)), \ldots, f(hn(x)), x, f(x)) \Rightarrow Q(x, f(x))$

$$P(x) \quad \Rightarrow \quad Q(x, f(x))$$

where x is universally quantified.

The premises (Bi) express the following facts:

- In order that f(hi(x)) be well defined, hi(x) must belong to the definition domain of f and so must verify the property P (premise B2). In the same way the arguments of g must verify Pg (premise B4).
- The underlying reasoning to this inference rule is of an inductive nature and requires the use of the following hypothesis:

$$\forall x \ (P(hi(x)) \Rightarrow Q(hi(x), f(hi(x)))).$$

The correctness of this reasoning depends on the existence of a well founded ordering (premise B3).
- When the base condition C of the recursion is verified, the function f0 specified by P, C and Q0 must be a possible solution for f, and then must verify the relation Q (premise B1). In the same way the function g must be a possible solution for f (premise B5).

3. A STRATEGY FOR RECURSIVE FUNCTION SYNTHESIS

A. Notion of Decomposition Algebra.

A decomposition algebra is essentially characterized by an algebra A and a well founded decomposition mapping, noted d [Kla 84]. This function, applied to any term a of A, decomposes the term respectively into an operation F of the considered algebra, and in a sequence a1, ..., an of elements of A such that: $d(a)=(F, a1, ..., an) \Rightarrow a=F(a1, ..., an)$.

Moreover we define $<_d$ in the following manner:
  $a <_d b$ iff $d(b) = (F, c1, ..., cn)$ and $a = ci$ for some $i \in [1,n]$.
d is said well founded if an infinite decreasing chain of the following form does not exist: $x0 >_d x1 >_d x2 >_d ...$

A decomposition D is often split up into a set of **indicators** Ci which allow us to identify the operations **Fi** by which some element is generated, and into a set of **selectors** Hi,j, associated to each indicator, which select the respective arguments of the operation.

This allows using simplified decompositions such as the following:
  Cb(**a**)   :   **a** = F0
  ¬Cb(**a**)   :   **a** = F1(H1(**a**), ..., Hk(**a**))
where Cb and ¬Cb are the indicators and H1, ..., Hk the selectors. This choice is essentially made to simplify the following development. The study of the strategy for more general decompositions is no particular problem. Moreover we suppose that the decomposition function is well founded and that we get programs for indicators and selectors.

B. Description of the strategy

The considered strategy consists in first choosing a decomposition of the input x: this comes to instanciate the functions C, h1, ..., hn of the inference rule with the selectors and indicators. Then this strategy produces a specification of the functions f0 and g. Another strategy, dual of the previous one, consists in instanciating the function f0 and g using a possible construction of the result f(x), permitting a specification of C, h1, ... ,hn. In theory, this strategy, unlike the first one, doesn't always produce a program: some recursions do not need an explicit construction of the result such as the classical calculus of the GCD of two integers (the result of the function is the one of the recursive call).

We illustrate the following development with the help of a well-known example, a synthesis of a sort function whose specification is:
    int-list(**x**) $\Rightarrow$ perm(**x**,sort(**x**)) Λ int-list(sort(**x**)) Λ ord(sort(**x**))
where int-list is the type of x and sort(x). Perm(l, r) is a predicate evaluated to true if and only if r is a permutation of l and ord is the property to be ordered.

B.1. Choice of a decomposition.

For a given specification, the choice is made among the set of decompositions associated with the type of the input. The domain of a problem can be a subset of the values of the data type, this subset being characterized by the precondition P of the specification. The condition C has to describe the smallest element(s) in the well founded ordering of the decomposition having this property. Thus the knowledge base has to be able to supply such an instance of C.

Choosing the classical decomposition of lists based upon the constructors nil and cons, null(x) becomes a possible instance for C(x), the precondition P *being only the type of* x.

B.2. Selection of the recursive calls.

At this step, we determine the selectors Hi such as Hi(x) can be arguments of a recursive call. Hi(x) fits if:
- Its type is identical to the one of x. This can easily verified by simple type checking.
- It verifies the precondition P. The knowledge base must try to prove P(hi(x)). The only available hypotheses are P(x) and x=F1(H1(x), ..., Hk(x)). That amounts to proving: **P(x) ∧ ¬C(x) ⇒ P(Hi(x))**. To do that, the knowledge base must infer a recursive definition of P(x) based upon the selected decomposition.

At the end of this step we have found the number n of the recursive calls. When no Hi suits, the decomposition does not allow introduction of recursion and we have to choose a new decomposition or to reject the used strategy. Otherwise, we instanciate the functions hi using the selected Hj. As we have programs for the selectors, the relations Qi(x, hi(x)) specifying hi become superfluous. This allows us to simplify the remaining premises. In choosing for < the ordering associated with the decomposition, we obviously prove the premise B3 relative to the existence of a well founded ordering. In the following we suppose that the n retained selectors are numbered from 1 to n and we generate the induction hypothesis Q(Hi(x), f(Hi(x))) for each of them.

Among the two selectors, car *and* cdr, *we only can select* cdr. *The program schema for* sort *will be:*

   sort(x) <- **if** null(x)   **then** f0(x)
                             else g(sort(cdr(x)), x)

B.3. Elaboration of specifications for f0 and g.

When the decomposition is suitable, the functions f0 and g must still be constructed. At first, we look for instances of Q0, Pg and Qg in trying to prove the premises B1, B4 and B5 with the help of the knowledge base. In a general way, the relation Q linking the input and the output of the function can be expressed such as: **L(x, f(x)) ∧ R(f(x))** where L specifies the existing link between input and output and R the properties of the result. The elaboration of specifications for f0 and g can be done in two steps, R playing the role of a filter on the possible values of f(x) verifying the relation L(x, f(x)).

B.3.1 Specification of f0.

At first we want to find the new link, L0, between f(x) and x knowing that x verifies the property C. Then a specification of f0 will be:

   C(x) ⇒ L0(x, f0(x)) ∧ R(f0(x)).

To insure the correctness of the program, L0 must verify the following theorem: **C(x) ∧ L0(x, f(x)) ⇒ L(x, f(x))** (premise B1 simplified). Thus we ask the knowledge base about such a relation L0. If no answer is given, the chosen decomposition is questioned.

If the synthesis of f0 fails, we deduce that we cannot resolve the initial
problem for x having the property C either because of the incompetence of
the knowledge base or because no solution effectively exists for these x.

*We suppose that the knowledge base can supply the following instance of
L0(x, f0(x)): [f0(x)=nil]. Recall that we want L0(x, f0(x)) ⇒ perm(nil,
f0(x). A possible specification for f0 is:*

$$null(x) \Rightarrow f0(x)=nil \wedge ord(f0(x)).$$

From this specification we obviously obtain the program f0(x)<-nil.

B.3.2 Specification of g.

For the sake of legibility, yi denotes now the intermediate result f(Hi(x))
and r the result of the call g(y1, ..., yn, x). A first step consists in
finding the new relation Lg linking x, y1, ..., yn and r. The only available
hypotheses are the existing links between yi and x and between r and x, that
is to say L(Hi(x), yi) (inductive hypotheses) and L(x, r). To guarantee the
correction of the program (premise B5 simplified) Lg(x, y1, ..., yn, r) must
verify the following theorem:

$$Lg(x, y1, ..., yn, r) \wedge P(x) \wedge \bigwedge_{i=1}^{n} L(Hi(x), yi) \Rightarrow L(x, r).$$

In order to get this theorem the knowledge base must be able to infer a
recursive definition of L based on the selected decomposition. If no
relation Lg is found, the choice of the decomposition is called into
question. On the contrary we get the following specification of g:

$$P(x) \wedge \neg C_B(x) \wedge \bigwedge_{i=1}^{n} R(yi) \Rightarrow Lg(x, y1, ..., yn, r) \wedge R(r).$$

The relations L(Hi(x), yi) are kept outside the specification because they
can allow to infer properties of yi from those of x.

Now, if this synthesis succeeds there are two possibilities: either the
properties R(yi) have been used and the synthesis of f is completed, or the
introduced recursive calls are questioned. These properties not being
necessary, the recursive calls can be replaced by function calls ki which
don't require recursion and whose possible specifications are: P(x) ⇒
L(x, ki(x)). If g cannot be synthetized, we must question the choice of
the decomposition.

We suppose that the knowledge base is able to infer the theorem:

$$perm(cdr(x), sort(cdr(x))) \wedge$$
$$[elim(sort(x), car(x)) = sort(cdr(x))] \Rightarrow perm(x, sort(x))$$

*elim(x, n) is a function defined only if n occurs in x, the result is then x
from which one occurrence of n has been removed. Thus one obtain the
instance of Lg(x, sort(cdr(x)), sort(x)): elim(sort(x), car(x)) =
sort(cdr(x)). The specification of g is then:*

$$list\text{-}int(x) \wedge list\text{-}int(y) \wedge \neg null(x) \wedge ord(y) \Rightarrow$$
$$[elim(g(y, x), car(x)) = y] \wedge ord(g(y, x)) \wedge list\text{-}int(g(y, x))$$

*One can say that a specification of a function which inserts an integer in
a sorted list is obtained.*

From this development, we conclude that this strategy succeeds at the first
level if the knowledge base is able to supply a decomposition D associated
to the data type of the input, a recursive definition of P and L using D and
a simplification of L knowing C. Therefore one obtain programs describing C,
h1, ... ,hn and specifications for f0 and g. If these specifications are of
the form f(x)=T(x), where T(x) is a term of the target language, then we can
generate the program f(x) <- T(x). Otherwise we have to synthesize f0 and g
from these specifications.

The requests to the knowledge base are essentially of two kinds.
  1) Recursive definitions based upon a given decomposition.
    We only consider two cases:
    a) This request focuses on a single predicate: either the knowledge base
    directly contains such a definition or, the knowledge base must contain
    a specification of this predicate. To obtain a recursive definition, we
    have then to synthesize this predicate using the same strategy and the
    same decomposition.
    b) This request focuses on a conjunction of predicates: We suppose that
    it is only necessary to find a recursive definition of each of these
    predicates. This hypothesis, although simplifying, is satisfactory in
    most cases.
  2) Simplifying knowledge.
    When this request focuses on a predicate, the knowledge base takes
    advice from the theorems concerning this object and tries to find such a
    formula. When the request focuses on a conjunction, the same work is
    done for each element of this conjunction.

4.CHOISE CRITERIA FOR DECOMPOSITION.

The idea we develop consists in basing the choice of a decomposition on the
recursive definitions available in the knowledge base. Such a process can be
decomposed into three steps:

  1) For each variable xi (input or output) occuring in the specification,
  we ask the knowledge base about recursive definitions for the predicates
  of the specification having xi as one of its arguments. The decomposition
  must focus on this variable.

  2) For each of these xi, we look for a possible common decomposition D
  from the definitions given in the previous step.
    - either a recursive definition of each predicate based upon a same
    decomposition (D) exists.
    - Or we must first select D among the given decompositions. The
    selection criterion notably takes into account the knowledge linking the
    operators appearing in the different decompositions. On the other hand,
    we must find recursive definitions based upon D when the knowledge base
    doesn't provide them.

  3) We choose the object(s) which will be split up. Then we apply one of
  the strategies (the one presented in part 2 or its dual) depending on
  whether the select objets are input or output variables. Notice that we
  don't choose a priori one or the other of these strategies.

A.Research example for recursive definitions.

Let the specification of the insertion function be:

$$int(n) \wedge int\text{-}list(x) \wedge ord(x) \Rightarrow [elim(r, n) = x]$$
$$\wedge \; ord(r) \wedge int\text{-}list(r)$$

where r denotes the result of insertion(n, x). This specification is a generalization of the one obtained in B.3.2.

Requests to the knowledge base:
  1) Recursive definitions of elim based upon a decomposition of n.
  2) Recursive definitions of elim and ord based upon a decomposition of x.
  3) Recursive definitions of elim and ord based upon an explicit construction of r.

We suppose that the knowledge base contains the following programs for elim and ord:

```
ord(x)    =   if null(x) then true
              else ord(cdr(x)) and less(car(x), cdr(x))

elim(x, n) =  if in(n, x) then
                  if car(x)=n then cdr(x)
                  else cons(car(x), elim(n, cdr(x)))
              else undefined
```
The definitions of in and less are obvious.

From these definitions we deduce that x can be decomposed using car and cdr and that the result can be constructed using cons. On the other hand, since none of these definitions are based upon a decomposition of n, we cannot decompose this variable.

Finding the "good" induction for a proof is a problem which is being study in the field of automatic deduction [BiC 85], [Fra 85]. As for our work this part needs a deeper understanding of the nature of the requests, depending on the form of the specification, asked to the knowledge base.

B. Examples of search for common decompositions

Now we consider non-determinist decompositions for which several sets of selectors exist.

B.1 We suppose that, in the previous example, the knowledge base cannot supply the definition of ord depending on nil and cons but only the following one:

```
ord(x) =  if null(x) or unit(x) then true
          else ord(h1(x)) and ord(h2(x)) and less2(h1(x), h2(x))
```
with append(h1(x), h2(x))=x and h1(x)≠nil and h2(x)≠nil. less2 is a predicate which holds if and only if every element of h1(x) is less than or equal to every element of h2(x).

We can choose a decomposition between nil and cons (supplied by the definition of elim) and nil, unit and append (supplied by the previous definition of ord). We favour the first one because of its deterministic nature. We have now to infer a recursive definition of ord using this decomposition. In order to do this, the system asks the knowledge base for a

definition of cons using the function append at the top level. For instance:
```
cons(a, nil) = unit(a)
cons(a, l) = append(cons(a, nil), l).
```

We want to obtain: ord(x) = **if** null(x) **then** r1 **else** r2 with r1=ord(nil) and r2=ord(cons(car(x), cdr(x)). Using the previous relations and the definition of ord depending on nil, unit and append, we obtain:

```
ord(nil) = true
ord (cons(car(x), cdr(x)))= if null(cdr(x)) then ord(unit(car(x)))
                                else ord(append(cons(car(x), nil), cdr(x)))
```
That is to say:
```
ord(x) = if null(x) then true
            else if null(cdr(x)) then true
                    else ord(cons(car(x), nil) and ord(cdr(x))
                    and less2(cons(car(x), nil), cdr(x))
```

This can be simplified to:
```
ord(x) = if null(x) or null(cdr(x)) then true
            else ord(cdr(x)) and less2(cons(car(x), nil), cdr(x))
```

The necessary definition being found, we can apply the strategy.

B.2 We now consider a more complex example. Let f be a function whose specification is:
$$a>0 \ \Lambda \ \ n > 1 \ \Rightarrow f(n) = a^n \ * \ \Sigma \ (\text{decomp}(n)).$$
decomp is a function which constructs the list of all the prime factors of its argument and Σ the function which computes the sum of all the elements of an integer list. Suppose we dispose of the following definitions:

(a) x^m = **if** m=0 **then** 1 **else if** m=1 **then** x **else** $x^{m1} \ * \ x^{m2}$
with m1+m2=m and m1≠0 and m2≠0. m1 and m2 are the result of non-determinist selectors.

(b) decomp(n) = **if** prime(n) **then** unit(n)
                    else append (decomp(n1), decomp(n2))
with n1 $*$ n2 = n and n1 < n and n2 < n.

If we dispose of programs for m1, m2, prime ... we obviously get a program for f. However we want to find a recursive definition of f using a unique decomposition of n. To do that, we can use either a definition of * according to + or a definition of + according to *. For instance:

(1)   0 $*$ n = 0

n1 $*$ n2 = (n1-1) $*$ n2 + n2

(2)   divide(n1, n2) $\Rightarrow$ n1 + n2 = (n1/n2 +1) $*$ n2
where divide(n, m) is true if and only if m divides n.

We choose the first one because it is always applicable, thus obtaining:
n1 $*$ n2 = m1 + m2   with   m1 = (n1-1) $*$ n2 and m2 = n2.

This provides the following definition of the exponentiation:
$\neg$ (prime(n)) $\Rightarrow$ $x^{n1*n2} = x^{m1+m2} = x^{(n1-1)*n2} \ * \ x^{n2}$

Using this new definition, we can transform the initial definition of f(n), when n isn't prime, in the following way:

$f(n) = a^{n1*n2} * \Sigma \, (\text{decomp}(n1*n2))$

$= a^{(n1-1)*n2} * a^{n2} * \Sigma \, [\text{append}(\text{decomp}(n1), \text{decomp}(n2))]$

And using the distributivity of $*$ on $+$ and the fact that $\Sigma \,(\text{append}(l1, l2))$

$= \Sigma\,(l1) + \Sigma\,(l2)$:

$= a^{(n1-1)*n2} * a^{n2} * \Sigma \,(\text{decomp}(n1)) + a^{(n1-1)*n2} * a^{n2}$

$* \Sigma \,(\text{decomp}(n2))$

A recursive call of the form f(n2) can be introduced. But, to obtain f(n1), a new theorem has to be used, for instance:

$x^{(n1-1)} * n2 = x^{(n2-1)*n1-n2} * x^{n1}$.

Then we obtain:

$\neg\,(\text{prime}(n)) \Rightarrow f(n) = a^{(n2-1)*n1-n2} * a^{n2} * f(n1) + a^{(n1-1)*n2} * f(n2)$

And the following program:

$f(n) = \mathbf{if}\ \text{prime}(n)\ \mathbf{then}\ a^{n} * n$
        $\mathbf{else}\ a^{(n2-1)} * n1 * f(n1) + a^{(n1-1)} * n2 * f(n2)$

The procedure followed in this step coincides with existing works on data types representation, among which we can quote [Sri 82].

5. CONCLUSION

To conclude we emphasize two main ideas presented in this paper. The first one relates to the proposed deductive approach for program synthesis. In order to master its inherent complexity, the proof process is split up into two distinct parts. The first one corresponds to the construction of the program and is run using the four inference rules mentioned. The aim of the other part is to infer, in specific models, the theorems justifying this construction. For one strategy, we have shown the necessary interaction between these two parts. It remains now to define more precisely the form of this dialogue. The second point deals with the strategy used to introduce recursion. In its first presentation (§2) the idea is to ba.. the definition of new functions on the underlying inductive definition of input's domains. This approach is closely akin to the one associated with the formalism of algebraic abstract data types [Hen 75]. It leads, when it succeeds, to a restricted class of algorithms. The approach developed in the last part allows us to broaden the notion of decomposition by using the properties of the objects of the specification. The chosen decomposition then depends not only on input's domain, but also, on the problem (through its specification) to be resolved. Therefore, this allows a suitable decomposition to be found more easily.

REFERENCES

[Bib 78] W. BIBEL
           On strategies for the synthesis of algorithms.
           Proc. on Artificial Intelligence and Simulation of Behavior,
           Hambourg, July 1978.

[BCF 85]   R. BRENA, R.CAFERRA, B. FRONHOEFER, C. GRESSE, P. JACQUET,
              M-L. POTET
              Program synthesis through problem splitting: a method for
              subproblem characterization.
              Computers and Artificial Intelligence, vol 4, no 5, pp 421-429,
              1985

[BiC 85]   M. BIDOIT, M-A. CHOQUER
              Preuve de formules conditionnelles par recurrence.
              5e congrès AFCET "Reconnaissances des formes et Intelligence
              Artificielle" , GRENOBLE, 27-29 november 1985

[BuL 69]   R. M. BURSTALL, P. J. LANDIN
              Programs and their Proofs: an Algebraic Approach.
              Machine Intelligence, no 3, pp 17-43, 1969

[ClD 78]   K. L. CLARK, J. DARLINGTON
              Algorithm classification through synthesis.
              The Computer Journal, vol 23, no 1, june 1978.

[Con 83]   R.L. CONSTABLE
              Mathematics as Programming.
              TR 83-565 Cornell University Ithaca, New York, 1983.

[Fra 85]   M.FRANOVA
              Preuves constructives dans des domaines constructibles.
              5e congrès AFCET "Reconnaissances des formes et Intelligence
              Artificielle" , GRENOBLE, 27-29 november 1985

[Gre 84]   C. GRESSE
              Contribution à la programmation automatique. CATY: un système de
              construction assistée de programmes.
              Thèse de Docteur d'Etat, Université de PARIS, march 1984.

[Hen 75]   F. W. von HENKE
              On generating Program From Data Types: An approach to Automatic
              Programming.
              Colloques INRIA sur la construction, l'amélioration et la
              vérification de programmes.
              Arcs et Sénans, 1975.

[Kla 84]   H.A. KLAEREN
              A Constructive Method for Abstract Algebraic Software
              Specification.
              Theoritical Computer Science, pp 139-204, August 1984.

[MaW 85]   Z. MANNA, R. WALDINGER
              A deductive approach to program synthesis.
              ACM Transactions on Programming Languages, vol 2, no 1, january
              1980.

[Nor 81]   B.NORDSTROM
              Programming in Constructive Set Theory: Some Examples.
              Proc. 1981 Conf. on Functional Prog. Lang. and Computer Archi.
              Portsmouth, pp 141-153, 1981.

[PER 84]   H. PERDRIX
            Synthèse de programmes à partir de leurs spécifications.
            Rapport de recherche no 187, Université de PARIS, september 1984.

[Smi 85]   D. R. SMITH
            The design of divide and conquer algoritms.
            Science of Computer Programming, no 5, pp 37-58, 1985.

[Sri 82]   M.K. SRIVAS
            *Automatic Synthesis of Implementation for Abstract Data Types
            from Algebraic Specifications.*
            MIT/LCS/Tech. Rep-276, Laboratory for Computer Science, MIT, June
            1982.

Advances in Artificial Intelligence - II
B. Du Boulay, D. Hogg and L. Steels (Editors)
© Elsevier Science Publishers B.V. (North-Holland), 1987

GRAPHOIDS: GRAPH-BASED LOGIC FOR REASONING ABOUT RELEVANCE RELATIONS *
or
When would x tell you more about y if you already know z ?

Judea Pearl
Computer Science Department
University of California, Los Angeles
Los Angeles, California 90024

and

Azaria Paz
Computer Science Department
Technion, Israel Institute of Technology
Haifa, Israel

ABSTRACT: We consider 3-place relations $I(x, z, y)$ where, x, y, and z are three non-intersecting sets of elements (e.g., propositions), and $I(x, z, y)$ stands for the statement: "Knowing z renders x irrelevant to y." We give sufficient conditions on I for the existence of a (minimal) graph G such that $I(x, z, y)$ can be validated by testing whether z separates x from y in G. These conditions define a GRAPHOID. The theory of graphoids uncovers the axiomatic basis of information relevance (e.g., probabilistic dependencies) and ties it to vertex-separation conditions in graphs. The defining axioms can also be viewed as inference rules for deducing which propositions are relevant to each other, given a certain state of knowledge.

1. INTRODUCTION

Any system that reasons about knowledge and beliefs must make use of information about relevancies. If we have acquired a body of knowledge z and now wish to assess the truth of proposition x, it is important to know whether it would be worthwhile to consult another proposition y, which is not in z. In other words, before we consult y we need to know if its truth value can potentially generate new information relative to x, information not available from z. For example, in trying to predict whether I am going to be late for a meeting, it is normally a good idea to ask somebody on the street for the time. However, once I establish the precise time by listening to the radio, asking people for the time becomes superfluous and their responses would be irrelevant. Similarly, knowing the color of X's car normally tells me nothing about the color of Y's. However, if X were to tell me that he almost mistook Y's car for his own, the two pieces of information become relevant to each other. What logic would facilitate this type of reasoning?

In probability theory, the notion of relevance is given precise quantitative underpinning using the device of conditional independence. A variable x is said to be independent of y given the information z if

$$P(x, y \mid z) = P(x \mid z) P(y \mid z)$$

However, it is rather unreasonable to expect people or machines to resort to numerical verification of equalities in order to extract relevance information. The ease and conviction with which people detect relevance relationships strongly suggest that such information is readily available from the organizational structure of human memory, not from numerical values assigned to its components. Accordingly, it would be interesting to explore how assertions about relevance can be tested in various models of memory and, in particular, whether such assertions can be derived by simple manipulations on graphs.

Graphs offer useful representations for a variety of phenomena. They give vivid visual display for the essential relations in the phenomenon and provide a convenient medium for people to communicate and reason about it. Graph-related concepts are so entrenched in our language that one wonders whether peo-

* This work was supported in part by the National Science Foundation, Grants DCR 83-13875 & 85-01234.

ple can in fact reason any other way, except by tracing links and arrows and paths in some mental representation of concepts and relations. Therefore, if we aspire to use non-numeric logic to mimic human reasoning about knowledge and beliefs, we should make sure that most derivational steps in that logic correspond to simple operations on some graphs.

When we deal with a phenomenon where the notion of neighborhood or connectedness is explicit (e.g., family relations, electronic circuits, communication networks, etc.) we have no problem configuring a graph which represents the main features of the phenomenon. However, in modelling conceptual relations such as causation, association and relevance, it is often hard to distinguish direct neighbors from indirect neighbors; so, the task of constructing a graph representation then becomes more delicate.

This paper studies the feasibility of devising graphoid representations for relational structures in which the notion of neighborhood is not specified in advance. Rather, what is given explicitly is the relation of "in betweenness." In other words, we are given the means to test whether any given subset S of elements *intervenes* in a relation between elements x and y, but it remains up to us to decide how to connect the elements together in a graph that accounts for these interventions.

The notion of conditional independence in probability theory is a perfect example of such a relational structure. For a given probability distribution P and any three variables x, y, z, while it is fairly easy to verify whether knowing z renders x independent of y, P does not dictate which variables should be regarded as direct neighbors. Thus, many topologies might be used to display the dependencies embodied in P.

The theory of graphoids establishes a clear correspondence between probabilistic dependencies and graph representation. It tells us how to construct a unique edge-minimum graph G such that each time we observe a vertex x separated from y by a subset S of vertices, we can be guaranteed that variables x and y are independent given the values of the variables in S. Moreover, the set of neighbors assigned by G to each x coincides exactly with the boundary of x, i.e., the smallest set of variables needed to shield x from the influence of all other variables in the system. This construction is further extended by the theory of graphoids to cases where the notion of independence is not given probabilistically or numerically. We now ask what *logical* conditions should constrain the relationship: $I(x, z, y) =$ "knowing z renders x irrelevant to y" so that we can validate it by testing whether z separates x from y in some graph G. We show that two main conditions (together with symmetry and subset closure) are sufficient:

weak closure for intersection: $I(x, z \cup w, y) \ \& \ I(x, z \cup y, w) \Rightarrow I(x, z, y \cup w)$ (1)

weak closure for union: $I(x, z, y \cup w) \Rightarrow I(x, z \cup w, y)$.   (2)

Loosely speaking, (1) states that if y does not affect x when w is held constant and if, simultaneously, w does not affect x when y is held constant, then neither w nor y can affect x. (2) states that learning an irrelevant fact (w) cannot help another irrelevant fact (y) become relevant. Condition (1) is sufficient to guarantee a unique construction of an edge-minimum graph G that validates $I(x, z, y)$ by vertex separation. Condition (2) guarantees that the neighborhoods defined by the edges of G coincide with the relevance boundaries defined by I. These two conditions are chosen as the defining axioms of graphoids, and are shown to account for the graphical properties of probabilistic dependencies.

This paper is organized as follows: In Section 2 we exemplify a graphoid system using probabilistic dependencies and their graphical representations. Section 3 introduces an axiomatic definition of graphoids, and states (without proofs) their graph-representation properties; the proofs can be found in [Pearl and Paz 1985]. Section 4 discusses a few extensions and outlines open problems.

2. PROBABILISTIC DEPENDENCIES AND THEIR GRAPHICAL REPRESENTATION

Let $U = \{\alpha, \beta, \cdots\}$ be a finite set of discrete-valued random variables characterized by a joint probability function $P(\cdot)$, and let x, y, and z stand for any three subsets of variables in U. We say that x and y are conditionally independent given z if

$$P(x, y \mid z) = P(x \mid z) P(y \mid z) \qquad \text{when } P(z) > 0 \tag{3}$$

Eq.(3) is a terse notation for the assertion that for any instantiation z_k of the variables in z and for any instantiation x_i and y_j of x and y, we have

$$P(x{=}x_i \text{ and } y{=}y_j \mid z{=}z_k) = P(x{=}x_i \mid z{=}z_k) P(y{=}y_j \mid z{=}z_k) \tag{4}$$

The requirement $P(z) > 0$ guarantees that all the conditional probabilities are well defined, and we shall henceforth assume that $P > 0$ for any instantiation of the variables in U. This rules out logical and functional dependencies among the variables a case which would require special treatment.

We shall use $(x \perp z \perp y)_P$ or simply $(x \perp z \perp y)$ to denote the independence of x and y given z. Thus,

$$(x \perp z \perp y)_P \iff P(x, y \mid z) = P(x \mid z) P(y \mid z) \iff P(x \mid y, z) = P(x \mid z) \tag{5}$$

Note that $(x \perp z \perp y)$ implies the conditional independence of all pairs of variables $\alpha \, \varepsilon \, x$ and $\beta \, \varepsilon \, y$, but the converse is not necessarily true.

The relation $(x \perp z \perp y)$ satisfies the following logical independent properties:

Symmetry:	$(x \perp z \perp y) \iff (y \perp z \perp x)$	(6.a)
Closure for Subsets:	$(x \perp z \perp y, w) \Longrightarrow (x \perp z \perp y) \,\&\, (x \perp z \perp w)$	(6.b)
Weak Closure for Intersection:	$(x \perp y, z \perp w) \,\&\, (x \perp y, w \perp z) \Longrightarrow (x \perp y \perp z, w)$	(6.c)
Weak Closure for Union:	$(x \perp y \perp z, w) \Longrightarrow (x \perp y, z \perp w)$	(6.d)
Contraction:	$(x \perp y, z \perp w) \,\&\, (x \perp y \perp z) \Longrightarrow (x \perp y \perp z, w)$	(6.e)

While the properties in (5) characterize the numeric representation of P, those in (6) are purely logical, void of any association with numerical forms and can be viewed, therefore, as an axiomatic definition of conditional independence. A graphical interpretation for properties (6.c) through (6.e) can be obtained by envisioning the chain $x - y - z - w$ and associating the triplet $(x \perp z \perp y)$ with the statement "z separates x from y" or "z intervenes between x and y."

Ideally, dependent variables should be displayed as connected nodes in some graph G and independent variables as unconnected nodes. We would also like to require that if the removal of some subset S of nodes from the graph renders nodes x and y disconnected, written $<x \mid S \mid y>_G$, then this separation should correspond to conditional independence between x and y given S, namely, $<x \mid S \mid y>_G \Longrightarrow (x \perp S \perp y)_P$ and conversely, $(x \perp S \perp y)_P \Longrightarrow <x \mid S \mid y>_G$.

This would provide a clear graphical representation for the notion that x does not affect y directly, that its influence is mediated by the variables in S. Unfortunately, we shall next see that these two requirements might be incompatible; there might exist no way to display all the dependencies and independencies embodied in P by vertex separation in a graph.

Definition: An undirected graph G is a *dependency map* (D-map) of P if there is a one-to-one correspondence between the variables in P and the nodes of G, such that for all non-intersecting subsets, x, y, S of variables we have:

$$(x \perp S \perp y)_P \Longrightarrow <x \mid S \mid y>_G \tag{7}$$

Similarly, G is an *Independency map* (I-map) of P if: $(x \perp S \perp y)_P \Longleftarrow <x \mid S \mid y>_G \tag{8}$

A D-map guarantees that vertices found to be connected are indeed dependent; however, it may occasionally display dependent variables as separated vertices. An I-map works the opposite way: it guarantees that vertices found to be separated always correspond to genuinely independent variables but does not guarantee that all those shown to be connected are in fact dependent. Empty graphs are trivial D-maps, while complete graphs are trivial I-maps.

Given an arbitrary graph G, the theory of *Markov Fields* [Lauritzen 1982] tells us how to construct a probabilistic model P for which G is both a D-map and an I-map. We now ask whether the converse construction is possible.

Lemma: There are probability distributions for which no graph can be both a D-map and an I-map.

Proof: Graph separation always satisfies $<x \mid S_1 \mid y>_G \implies <x \mid S_1 \cup S_2 \mid y>_G$ for any two subsets S_1 and S_2 of vertices. Some P's, however, may induce both $(x \perp S_1 \perp y)_P$ and NOT $(x \mid S_1 \cup S_2 \perp y)_P$. Such P's cannot have a graph representation which is both an I-map and a D-map because D-mapness forces G to display S_1 as a cutset separating x and y, while I-mapness prevents $S_1 \cup S_2$ from separating x and y. No graph can satisfy these two requirements simultaneously. Q.E.D.

An example illustrating the conditions of the proof is an experiment with two coins and a bell that rings whenever the outcomes of the two coins are the same. If we ignore the bell, the coin outcomes are mutually independent, i.e., $S_1 = \varnothing$. However, if we notice the bell (S_2), then learning the outcome of one coin should change our opinion about the other coin.

Being unable to provide a graphical description for *all* independencies, we settle for the following compromise: we will consider only I-maps but will insist that the graphs in those maps capture as many of P's independencies as possible, i.e., they should contain no superfluous edges.

Definition: A graph G is a *minimal I-map* of P if no edge of G can be deleted without destroying its I-mapness.

Theorem 1:   Every P has a (unique) minimal I-map G_0 (called the *MARKOV-NET* of P) constructed by connecting *only* pairs (α, β) for which

$$(\alpha \perp U - \alpha - \beta \perp \beta)_P \quad is \quad FALSE \qquad (9)$$

(i.e., deleting from the complete graph *all* edges (α, β) for which $(\alpha \perp U - \alpha - \beta \perp \beta)_P$).

Definition: A *Markov boundary* $B_P(\alpha)$ of variable α is a minimal subset S that renders α independent of all other variables, i.e.,

$$(\alpha \perp S \perp U - S - \alpha)_P, \, \alpha \notin S \qquad (10)$$

and simultaneously, no proper subset S' of S satisfies $(\alpha \perp S' \mid U - S' - \alpha)_P$. If no S satisfies (10), define $B_P(\alpha) = U - \alpha$.

Theorem 2:   Each variable α has a unique Markov boundary $B_P(\alpha)$ that coincides with the set of vertices $B_{G_0}(\alpha)$ adjacent to α in the Markov net G_0.

The usefulness of Theorem 2 lies in the fact that in many cases it is the Markov boundaries $B_P(\alpha)$ that define the organizational structure of human memory. People find it natural to identify the immediate consequences and/or justifications of each action or event, and these relationships constitute the neighborhood semantics for inference nets used in expert systems [Duda et al. 1976]. The fact that $B_P(\alpha)$ coincides with $B_{G_0}(\alpha)$ guarantees that many independencies can be validated by tests for graph separation at the knowledge level itself [Pearl 1985].

3. GRAPHOIDS

Definition: A *graphoid* is a set I of triplets (x, z, y) where x, z, y are three non-intersecting subsets of elements drawn from a finite collection $U = \{\alpha, \beta, \cdots\}$, having the following four properties. (We shall write $I(x, y, z)$ to state that the triplet (x, y, z) belongs to graphoid I.)

Symmetry	$I(x, z, y) \Longleftrightarrow I(y, z, x)$	(11.a)
Subset Closure	$I(x, z, y \cup w) \Longrightarrow I(x, z, y) \ \& \ (x, z, w)$	(11.b)
Intersection	$I(x, z \cup w, y) \ \& \ I(x, z \cup y, w) \Longrightarrow I(x, z, y \cup w)$	(11.c)
Union	$I(x, z, y \cup w) \Longrightarrow I(x, z \cup w, y)$	(11.d)

For technical convenience we shall adopt the convention that I contains all triplets in which either x or y are empty, i.e., $I(x, z, \varnothing)$.

If U stands for the set of vertices in some graph G, and if we equate $I(x, z, y)$ with the statement: "z separates between x and y," written $<x \mid z \mid y>_G$, then the conditions in (11) are clearly satisfied. However, not all properties of graph separation are required for graphoids. For example, in graphs we always have $[<\alpha \mid z \mid \beta>_G \ \& \ <\alpha \mid z \mid \gamma>_G]$ iff $<\alpha \mid z \mid \beta \cup \gamma>_G$ while property (11.b) requires only the "if" part. Similarly, graph separation dictates $<x \mid z \mid y>_G \Longrightarrow <x \mid z \cup w \mid y>_G, \quad \forall w$, while (11.d) severely restricts the conditions under which a separating set z can be enlarged by w.

Definition: A graph G is said to be an I-*map* of I if there is a one-to-one correspondence between the elements in U and the vertices of G, such that, for all non-intersecting subsets x, y, S we have:

$$<x \mid S \mid y>_G \Longrightarrow I(x, S, y) \tag{12}$$

Theorem 3: Every graphoid I has a unique edge-minimum I-map G_0. $G_0 = (U, E_0)$ is constructed by connecting *only* pairs (α, β) for which the triplet $(\alpha, U-\alpha-\beta, \beta)$ is not in I, i.e.,

$$(\alpha, \beta) \notin E_0 \quad \textit{iff} \quad I(\alpha, U-\alpha-\beta, \beta) \tag{13}$$

Definition: A *relevance sphere* $R_I(\alpha)$ of an element $\alpha \in U$ is any subset S of elements for which

$$I(\alpha, S, U-S-\alpha) \text{ and } \alpha \notin S \tag{14}$$

Let $R_I^*(\alpha)$ stand for the set of all relevance spheres of α. A set is called a *relevance boundary* of α, denoted $B_I(\alpha)$, if it is in $R_I^*(\alpha)$ and if, in addition, none of its proper subsets is in $R_I^*(\alpha)$.

$B_I(\alpha)$ is to be interpreted as the smallest set that "shields" α from the influence of all other elements. Note that $R_I^*(\alpha)$ is non-empty because $I(x, z, \varnothing)$ guarantees that the set $S = U-\alpha$ satisfies (14).

Theorem 4: Every element $\alpha \in U$ in a graphoid I has a unique *relevance boundary* $B_I(\alpha)$. $B_I(\alpha)$ coincides with the set of vertices $B_{G_0}(\alpha)$ adjacent to α in the minimal graph G_0.

Corollary 1: The set of relevance boundaries $B_I(\alpha)$ forms a *neighbor system*, i.e., a collection $B_I^* = \{B_I(\alpha) : \alpha \in U\}$ of subsets of U such that (i) $\alpha \notin B_I(\alpha)$, and (ii) $\alpha \in B_I(\beta)$ iff $\beta \in B_I(\alpha)$, $\alpha, \beta \in U$

Corollary 2: The edge-minimum I-map G_0 can be constructed by connecting each α to all members of its relevance boundary $B_I(\alpha)$.

Thus we see that the major graphical properties of probabilistic dependencies are consequences of the intersection and union properties, (11.c) and (11.d), and will therefore be shared by all graphoids.

4. SPECIAL GRAPHOIDS AND OPEN PROBLEMS

4.1 Graph-induced Graphoids

The most restricted type of graphoid is that which is isomorphic to some underlying graph, i.e., *all* triplets (x, z, y) in I reflect vertex-separation conditions in an actual graph.

Definition: A graphoid I is said to be *graph-induced* if there exists a graph G such that

$$I(x, z, y) <\!=\!=\!> < x \mid z \mid y >_G \tag{15}$$

Theorem 5: A necessary and sufficient condition for a graphoid I to be graph induced is that it satisfies the following five independent axioms:

$$
\begin{array}{lll}
I(x, z, y) <\!=\!=\!> I(y, z, x) & \text{(symmetry)} & (16.\text{a}) \\
I(x, z, y \cup w) =\!=\!> I(x, z, y) \ \& \ I(x, z, w) & \text{(subset closure)} & (16.\text{b}) \\
I(x, z \cup w, y) \ \& \ I(x, z \cup y, w) =\!=\!> I(x, z, y \cup w) & \text{(intersection)} & (16.\text{c}) \\
I(x, z, y) =\!=\!> I(x, z \cup w, y) \ \ \forall w \subset U & \text{(strong union)} & (16.\text{d}) \\
I(x, z, y) =\!=\!> I(x, z, \gamma) \ \text{ or } \ I(\gamma, z, y) \ \ \forall \gamma \notin x \cup z \cup y & \text{(transitivity)} & (16.\text{e})
\end{array}
$$

Remarks: (16.c) and (16.d) imply the converse of (16.b), The union axiom (16.d) is unconditional and therefore stronger than the one required for general graphoids (11.d). It allows us to construct G_0 by simply deleting from a complete graph every edge (α, β) for which a triplet of the form (α, S, β) appears in I.

4.2 Probabilistic Graphoids

Definition: A graphoid is called *probabilistic* if there exists a probability distribution P on the variables in U such that $I(x, z, y)$ iff x is independent of y given z, i.e.,

$$I(x, z, y) <\!=\!=\!> (x \perp z \perp y)_P \tag{17}$$

In other words, probabilistic graphoids capture the notion of conditional independence in Probability Theory (see Section 2).

Theorem 6: Every graph-induced graphoid is probabilistic.

Since every probabilistic-independence relation satisfies (6.a)-(6.e), a necessary condition for a graphoid to be probabilistic is that, in addition to (11), it also satisfies the contraction property (6.e), i.e.,

$$I(x, y \cup z, w) \ \ \& \ \ I(x, y, z) =\!=\!> I(x, y, z \cup w) \tag{18}$$

(18) can be interpreted to state that if we judge w to be irrelevant (to x) after learning some irrelevant facts z, then w must have been irrelevant before learning z. Together with the union property (11.d) it means that learning irrelevant facts should not alter the relevance status of other propositions in the system; whatever was relevant remains relevant and what was irrelevant remains irrelevant.

Conjecture: The contraction property (18) is sufficient for a graphoid to be probabilistic.

Unlike the sufficiency condition for graph-induced graphoids, we found no way of constructing a distribution P that yields $I(x, z, y) =\!=\!> (x \perp z \perp y)_P$ for every I that satisfies (18).

4.3 Correlational Graphoids

Let U consist of n random variables $u_1, u_2, \ldots, u_n$, and let z be a subset of U such that $|z| \leq n-2$. The *partial correlation coefficient* of u_i and u_j with respect to z, denoted $\rho_{ij \cdot z}$, measures the correlation between u_i and u_j after subtracting from them the best linear estimates using the variables in z (Cramér, 1946). In other words, $\rho_{ij \cdot z}$ measures the correlation that remains after removal of any part of the variation due to the influence of the variables in z.

Definition: Let x, y, z be three nonintersecting subsets of U. A relation $I_c(x, y, z)$ is said to be *correlation-based* if for every $u_i \in x$ and $u_j \in y$ we have:

$$I_c(x, z, y) <\!=\!=\!> \rho_{ij \cdot z} = 0 \tag{19}$$

In other words, x is considered irrelevant to y relative to z if every variable in x is uncorrelated with every variable in y, after removing the (linear) influence of the variables in z.

Theorem 7: Every correlation-based relation is a graphoid which, in addition to axioms (11), also satisfies the contraction property (18) and the converse of (11.b), i.e.,

$$I(x, z, y) \text{ and } I(x, z, w) =\!=\!> I(x, z, y \cup w) \tag{20}$$

Conjecture: Every graphoid satisfying (18) and (20) is isomorphic to some correlation-based relation.

5. CONCLUSIONS

We have shown that the essential qualities characterizing the probabilistic notion of conditional independence are captured by two logical axioms: weak closure for intersection (6.c), and weak closure for union (6.d). These two axioms enable us to construct an edge-minimum graph in which every cutset corresponds to a genuine independence condition, and these two axioms were chosen therefore as the logical basis for graphoid systems — a more general, nonprobabilistic formalism of relevance. Vertex separation in graphs, probabilistic independence and partial uncorrelatedness are special cases of graphoid systems where the two defining axioms are augmented with additional requirements.

The graphical properties associated with graphoid systems offer an effective inference mechanism for deducing, in any given state of knowledge, which propositional variables are relevant to each other. If we identify the relevance boundaries associated with each proposition in the system, and treat them as neighborhood relations defining a graph G_0, then we can correctly deduce irrelevance relationships by testing whether the set of currently known propositions constitutes a cutset in G_0.

REFERENCES

Cramér, H. (1946), *Mathematical Methods of Statistics,* Princeton University Press, Princeton, N.J.

Duda, R. O., Hart, P. E., and Nilsson, N. J., (1976), Subjective Bayesian Methods for Rule-Based Inference Systems, *Proceedings, 1976 NCC (AFIPS),* 45, 1075-1082.

Lauritzen, S.L. (1982), *Lectures on Contingency Tables,* 2nd Ed., U. of Aalborg Press, Aalborg, Denmark.

Pearl, J. (1985), Fusion, Propagation and Structuring in Bayesian Networks, Technical Report CSD-850022, June 1985.

Pearl, J. & Paz, A., (1985), GRAPHOIDS: a Graph-Based Logic for Reasoning about Relevance Relations, *Technical Report CSD-850038,* December 1985.

Advances in Artificial Intelligence - II
B. Du Boulay, D. Hogg and L. Steels (Editors)
© Elsevier Science Publishers B.V. (North-Holland), 1987

UNIFICATION THEORY

Jörg H. Siekmann
Universität Kaiserslautern
FB INFORMATIK
Postfach 3049
D-6750 Kaiserslautern
WEST GERMANY

ABSTRACT: This article surveys what is presently known in Unification Theory and records its early history.

1.INTRODUCTION

Überhaupt hat der Fortschritt das an sich, daß er viel größer ausschaut, als er wirklich ist.

J.N.Nestroy, 1859

Unification theory is concerned with problems of the following kind: Let f and g be function symbols, a and b constants and let x and y be variables and consider two *first order terms* built from these symbols, for example:

$$s = f(x \ g(a \ b))$$
$$t = f(g(y \ b) \ x)$$

The problem is whether or not there exist terms which can be substituted for the variables x and y such that the two terms thus obtained from s and t become equal: in the example g(a b) and a are two such terms. We shall write

$$\sigma = \{x \mapsto g(a \ b), y \mapsto a\}$$

for such a unifying substitution: σ is a *unifier* of s and t since $\sigma s = \sigma t = f(g(a \ b) \ g(a \ b))$. In addition to the above *decision problem* there is also the problem of finding a *unification algorithm* which enumerates the unifiers for a given pair s and t

Consider a variation of the above problem, which arises when we assume that f is commutative:

$$(C) \quad f(x \ y) = f(y \ x)$$

Now σ is still a unifying substitution and moreover $\delta = (y \mapsto a)$ is also a unifier for s and t since $\delta s = f(x \ g(a \ b)) =_C f(g(a \ b) \ x) = \delta$.

But δ is more general than σ since σ is an instance of δ obtained as the composition $\lambda \circ \delta$ with $\lambda = (x \mapsto g(a \ b))$; hence a unification algorithm only needs to compute δ.

In some cases there is a single and essentially unique least upper bound on the generality lattice of unifiers, called the most general unifier.

Under commutativity however, there are pairs of terms which have more than one most general unifier, but they always have at most finitely many. This is in contrast for example to the above situation of free terms, where every pair has at most one general unifying substitution.

The problem becomes entirely different when we assume that the function denoted by f is associative:

$$(A) \quad f(x \ f(y \ z)) = f(f(x \ y) \ z)$$

In that case σ is still a unifying substitution, but $\tau = \{x \mapsto f(g(a\ b)\ g(a\ b)), y \mapsto a\}$ is also a unifier: $\tau s = f(f(g(a\ b)\ g(a\ b))\ g(a\ b)) =_A f(g(a\ b)\ f(g(a\ b)\ g(a\ b))) = \tau t$.

But $\tau = \{x \mapsto f(g(a\ b)\ f(g(a\ b)\ g(a\ b))), y \mapsto a\}$ is again a unifying substitution and by iteration of this process it is not difficult to see that there are infinitely many unifiers, all of which are most general.

Finally, if we assume that both axioms (A) and (C) hold for f then the situation changes yet again and for any pair of terms there are at most finitely many most general unifiers under (AC).

The above examples as well as the many practical applications of unification theory quoted in the following paragraph share a common problem, which in its most abstract form is as follows: Given a formal language L with variables and two words s and t in that language. For a given relation $\approx$ in $L \times L$ find a substitution σ such that $\sigma s \approx \sigma t$ (provided σs and σt are welldefined).

If for example the relation can be axiomatized by some equational theory T and L is the language of first order terms, unification of s and t under T amounts to solving the equation s = t in the variety defined by T. If T is an axiomatization of the natural numbers and s and t are as before, the unification of s and t amounts to solving Diophantine equations.

The mathematical investigation of equation solving however is a subject as old as mathematics itself and, right from the beginning, very much at the heart of it: It dates back to Babylonian mathematics (about 2000 B.C.) and has dominated much of mathematical research ever since.

Unification theory carries this activity on in a more abstract setting: just as universal algebra abstracts from certain properties that pertain to specific algebras and investigates issues that are common to all of them, unification theory addresses problems, which are typical for equation solving as such.

Just as traditional equation solving drew much of its impetus from its numerous applications (for example the - for those times - complicated division of legacies in Babylonian times and the application to physics in more modern times), unification theory derives its impetus from its numerous applications in Computer Science, Artificial Intelligence and in particular in the field of Computational Logic.

Central to unification theory are the notion of a *set of most general unifiers* $\mu U\Sigma$ (traditionally: the set of base vectors spanning the solution space) and the *hierarchy of equational theories* based on $\mu U\Sigma$. Both are defined in the second paragraph, where we denote a *unification problem* under a theory T by

$$<s = t>_T.$$

In many practical applications unification is too general, but it is of interest to know for two given terms s and t if there exists a *matcher* (a one-way-unifier) μ such that $\mu(s)$ and t are equal under T.

We denote a *matching problem* under a theory T by

$$<s \geq t>_T.$$

In other words, in a matching problem we are allowed to substitute into one term only (into s using the above convention) and we say s *matches* t with *matcher* μ.

1.1. Applications

There is a wide variety of areas in Computer Science and Artificial Intelligence where unification problems arise.

Databases

A deductive database [GM78] does not contain every piece of information explicitly. Instead it contains only certain facts from which other information can be deduced by some inference rule. Such inference rules (deduction rules) heavily rely on unification algorithms.

Also the user of a relational database [Da76] may logically AND the properties he wants to retrieve or else he may be interested in the NATURAL JOIN [Co70] of two stores relations. In neither case, would he appreciate if he constantly had to take into account that AND is an associative and commutative operation or that NATURAL JOIN obeys an associative axiom, which may distribute over some other operation [SH85].

Information Retrieval

A patent office may store all recorded electric circuits [BC66] or all recorded chemical compounds [Su65] as some graph structure, and the problem of checking whether a given circuit or compound already exists is an instance of a test for graph isomorphism [Ul76], [Un64], [Cr68]. More generally, if the nodes of such graphs are labelled wtih universally quantified variables ranging over subgraphs, these problems are practical instances of a graph matching problem.

Computer Vision

In the field of computer vision it has become customary to store the internal representation of certain external scenes as some net structure [BB82], [Wn75]. The problem to find a particular object -also represented as some net - in a given scene is also an instance of the graph matching problem [Rl69]. Here one of the main problems is to specify as to what constitutes a successful match (since a test for endomorphism is too strict for most applications): matching is carried out with respect to some distance function.

Natural Language Processing

The understanding of natural language by a computer [Wn72] [Wn83] [Te81] is based on transformation rules to change the syntax of the input sentence into a more appropriate one. Inference rules are used to manipulate the semantics of an input sentence and to disambiguate it.The knowledge about the external world a natural language understanding system must have is represented by certain (syntactic) descriptions and it is paramount to detect if two descriptions describe the same object or fact.

Transformation rules, inference rules and the matching of descriptions are but a few applications of unification theory within this field.

The meaning of a natural language utterance has to be represented in some internal representation language [BL85]. Recently developed representation languages such as PATR [SK84] have but one basic operation for their manipulation, namely unification with respect to certain constraints. Also special functional grammars have been designed for the parsing of natural languages, called unification grammars [SK85] [Ka84] [Ka85].

Expert Systems

An expert system [BS85] is a computer program whose performance largely depends on its ability to represent and manipulate the knowledge of its field of expertise. Commonly this knowledge is represented in the form of productions such that if the conditions of a production are fulfilled its action part will be executed. Special languages such as OPS5 [Fo81] and others have been developed for the implementation of expert systems. In OPS5 the condition part of a production is matched against the entries of the knowledge base and if the match succeeds, the condition is considered true.

The efficiency of the matching process is of crucial importance and special techniques (e.g. the Rete-algorithm [Fo82]) and their hardware realisation have been proposed [RZ85], which are very similar to the strive for efficient implementations of the unification algorithm in logical programming languages (see below).

Textmanipulation Languages

The fundamental mode of operation for programming languages like SNOBOL [FG64] is to detect the occurrence of a substring within a larger string of characters (which may be a program or some other text) and there are methods known, which require less than linear time [BM77]. If these strings contain the SNOBOL 'don't-care'-variable, the occurrence problem is an instance of the stringunification problem mentioned below.

Patterndirected Programming Languages

An important contribution to programming language design is the mechanism of pattern-directed invocation of procedures [BF77], [Ht76], [RD72], [BM82]. Procedures are identified by patterns instead of procedure identifiers as in traditional programming languages and these invocation patterns are usually designed to express goals achieved by executing the procedure. Incoming messages are tried to be matched against the invocation patterns of procedures in a procedural data base, and a procedure is activated after having completed a successful match between message and pattern. So, matching is done (1) for looking up an appropriate procedure that helps to accomplish an intended goal, and (2) transmitting information to the involved procedure.

For these applications (often called demons, censors,, agents, etc.) it is particularly desirable to have methods for matching objects belonging to high level data structures such as strings, sets, multisets and others.

A little reflection will show that for very rich matching languages, as it has e.g. been proposed in MATCHLESS for PLANNER [Ht72], the matching problem is undeciable. This presents a problem for the designer of such languages: on the one hand, very rich and expressive matching languages are desirable, since they form the basis for the invocation and deduction mechanism. On the other hand, drastic restrictions will be necessary if matching algorithms are to be found. The question is just how severe do these restrictions have to be.

Knowledge Representation Languages

Based on recently developed framelike techniques to structure and represent knowledge [Mi75] special purpose programming languages such as KRL [BW77] or KLONE [BS85] have been designed for this task.

Apart from their respective commitment to the representation and structuring issue they all support but one central operation: "matching of descriptions". In a sense unification theory relates to these new kind of programming languages - and hence to knowledge based systems - as formal language theory   relates to traditional programming languages.

Logic Programming Languages

The discovery of the close relationship between logical deduction and computation, which makes logic enjoy a role in computer science quite similar to the role of analysis in physics, is certainly one of the outstanding scientific achievements of this late century.

However there is a more specific point to this namely that predicate logic itself can be viewed as a programming language [Ko79] given a suitable machine to execute it: predicate logic relates to a deduction system as for example LISP relates to EVAL. This insight opened up a new technology race for appropriate machines [Wa77] [IM83] [GL84], for which the Japanese coined the name "Fifth Generation Computers" [FG84]. The central computation performed in logic programming is unification: in fact the unification algorithm - being it implemented in software or in silicon - is the "CPU" of these machines. Hence the speed of these machines is not expressed in MIPS (million instructions per second) as for conventional machines, but in KLIPS (2^{10} logical inferences per second), which is a measure of the number of unifications performed per second.

Term Rewriting Systems

The manipulation of terms subject to equationally defined theories, traditionally called demodulation [WR67], has always played an important role in deduction systems. However if in addition the directed equations are confluent and finitely terminating [HO80] they can be used to compute a unique normal form. The test for confluence can be carried out by a procedure known as the Knuth-Bendix completion procedure [KB70], which uses a unification algorithm as its central component.

Certain equational axioms are notoriously difficult to handle, but sometimes they can advantageously be built into special purpose unification algorithms [PS81].

Term Rewriting Systems are of considerable interest for computer science [Bu85] and have found their place in most computer science curricula today. Not the least important among the many applications these systems have is their being a basis for a new kind of programming languages that elegantly combine functional programming with logical programming style [DL86].

Computer Algebra

In computer algebra [Ng79] matching and unification algorithms also play an important role: for example the integrand in a symbolic integration problem [Mo71] may be matched against certain patterns in order to detect the class of integration problems it belongs to and to trigger the appropriate action for its solution (which in turn may involve several quite complicated matching attempts [Bl71], [Fa71]). Hence most computer algebra systems like REDUCE [Hn71], MACSYMA [Mo74] or MATHLAB [MB68] make extensive use of unification or matching algorithms.

Algebra

A famous decidability problem, which inspite of many attacks remained open for over twenty five years, has been solved: the monoid problem (also called Löb's Problem in western countries, Markov's Problem in eastern countries and the Stringunification Problem in Automated Deduction [Hj64], [Hj67], [LS75], [Ma54], [SS61], [Pl72]) is the problem to decide whether or not an equation system over a free semigroup possesses a solution. This problem has been shown to be decidable [Ma77]. The monoid problem has important practical applications inter alia for Deduction Systems (stringunification [Si75] and second order monadic unification [Ht76], [Wn76]),for Formal Language Theory (the crossreference problem for van Wijngaarden Grammars [Wi76]) and for pattern directed invocation languages in Artificial Intelligence as mentioned above.

Without surveying classical equation solving as such, one "unification problem" that should be mentioned is Hilbert's Tenth Problem [Da73], which is known to be undecidable [Ma70].

The problem is whether or not a given polynomial $P[x_1,x_2,...,x_n] = 0$ has an integer solution (a Diophantine solution). Although this problem was posed originally within the framework of traditional equation solving, unification theory has shed a new light upon this problem (see 3.1.1).

Semigroup Theory [CP61] [Ho76] is the field traditionally posing the most important unification problems, i.e. those involving associativity. Although scientifically more established than unification theory is today, some interesting semigroup problems have been solved using techniques of unification theory and term rewriting systems (see e.g. [SS82], [La80], [La79]), for a survey on Semithue Systems see [Bo85].

Deduction Systems

All present day theorem proving or deduction systems - based on resolution [Ro65] or not - have a unification algorithm for first or higher order terms as their essential component.

Also for almost as long as attempts at proving theorems by machines have been made, a critical problem has been well known [GO67], [SI72], [Ne71]: Certain equational axioms, if left without precaution in the data base of the deduction system, will force the system to go astray. In 1967 A.Robinson [Ro67] proposed that substantial progress ("a new plateau") could be achieved by removing these troublesome axioms from the data base and building them into the deductive machinery.

One central idea is to build these axioms - which often define common data structures - into the unification algorithm. G. Plotkin has shown in a pioneering paper [Pl72] that whenever a deduction system is to be refutation complete, its extended unification procedure must generate a set of unifiers satisfying the three conditions completeness, correctness and minimality, which today are used to axiomatically define $\mu U\Sigma$, the set of most general unifiers.

It is the field of Automated Deduction [Lo80], where unification problems became historically first of general importance and it is this field that contributed most to unification theory as it is known today.

1.2. Early History (*)

The visionary thoughts about the nature of mathematics, symbols and human reasoning that Emil Post recorded in his diary and notes - partially published in [Da65] - contain the first hint as early as the 1920s to the concept of a unification algorithm that computes a most general representative as opposed to all possible instantiations (p.370 in [Da65]).

(*) Allowing for some exceptions we draw the not entirely arbitrary line that work until 1976 is considered "early history", whereas the later contributions are recorded in the third section under the heading "results".

A more concrete account of a unification algorithm, although far from our present notation, is given in J. Herbrand's celebrated thesis "Recherches sur la theorie de la demonstration" in 1930 [He30], where he introduced three concepts with respect to the validity of formulas. He called them A, B and C. Concept B and C were the basis for the wellknown Herbrand Theorem, whereas concept A was by and large consigned to oblivion. In order to calculate if property A holds for a formula, he gave an algorithm which computes it: the first published unification algorithm.

Based on Herbrand's idea of a finite counterexample, i.e. only a finite number of instantiations are necessary in order to show the unsatisfiability of a set of formulas, early theorem proving programs were developed, but it was not until 1960 when D.Prawitz [Pr60] suggested a way out of these "British Museum Techniques" as they were called later on: the computation of a most general representative for the albeit finite but still abundant number of instantiations that are possible otherwise. However as his logic did not contain any function symbols there was little to compute in fact.

In 1963 M.Davis published [Da63] a proof procedure that combined the virtues of Prawitz`s procedure and of the Davis-Putnam procedure. The implementation of this new proof procedure on an IBM 7090 at Bell Labs used a unification algorithm to compute the "linked conjuncts" and was the first fully implemented unification algorithm in actual use.

It was not until 1965 however when the seminal paper on the resolution principle by A.Robinson was published that the first explicit account of a unification algorithm for first order terms which computes an essentially unique, single representative (i.e. the most general unifier) appeared in print.

This was the most influential paper that firmly established the concept of unification for all automated deduction systems (including the nonresolution based systems) henceforth. The work for this paper was done essentially in 1963 at Argonne National Lab, a time when a different group headed by J.R. Guard at the Air Force Cambridge Lab developed a deduction system based on a Gentzen-style sequent logic that also incorporated a unification algorithm. The work was published in some internal reports [Gu84] and later in [GO69]; although their algorithm was correct and complete, it was however not formally shown so. They also suggested extensions of the algorithm to higher order logic as well as first order extensions to incorporate axioms like commutativity and associativity. The algorithms used for these latter extensions were heuristically motivated (reordering of terms, rebracketing etc.) and were incorrect and incomplete in general.

The basic unification algorithm was discovered again by D.Knuth and published in a paper [KB70] that became a classic in the field of term rewriting systems: in order to turn a given set of equations into a canonical system a completion process is described that heavily depends on a unification algorithm, whose theoretical properties (computation of the most general unifier) were recognised and shown.

In 1967 A. Robinson proposed to build certain troublesome axioms directly into the deductive machinery of an automated theorem paper and in 1972 G. Plotkin showed in a pioneering paper [Pl72] how this can be done without losing completeness. From the point of view of unification theory this paper contained two major contributions: firstly the definition of a set of most general unifiers, which became - in particular through the work of G. Huet [Ht76] - a central notion of the field. And secondly the discovery that there are equational theories (e.g. the associativity axiom) which induce an infinite set of most general unifiers.

This work was taken up in my own thesis [Si75], which described several special purpose unification algorithms for the axioms of associativity, commutativity and idempotence and their combinations. Unification theory as a field worthy of its own existence - rather than an arbitrary collection of special algorithms - was suggested, centering around the concept of the Unification Hierarchy, which was introduced here along with some preliminary results about this hierarchy.

While this track of developments is viewed under its contributions towards first order unification there was important work on higher order unification around the same time: Based on the above mentioned theorem proving system of Guard et al, W.F. Gould [Go66] investigated the most general common instance of two higher order terms and discovered that there are infinitely ascending chains of most general unifiers (i.e. a minimal set of most general unifiers does not exist for ω-order-logic). Influenced by A. Robinson [Ro69] and in particular by P.Andrews [An71], whose work was most influential for higher order deduction systems, G. Huet developed a socalled "constrained resolution method" [Ht72] for higher order theorem proving, based on an ω-order unification algorithm. This work was then further developed in his "thèse d'état" [Ht76], which became of foundational importance for shaping the field of first and higher order unification theory.

2. NOTIONS AND NOTATION

Unification Theory rests upon two notational pillars: Universal Algebra (see e.g. [Gr79]) and Computational Logic (see e.g. [Lo78], [HO80] of which we shall now give a brief account.

As a starting point let us take the familiar concept of an algebra $\mathbf{A} = (A,F)$ where A is the carrier and F is a family of operators (the signatur of $\mathbf{A}$) given with their arities.For a given congruence relation ρ the quotient algebra modulo ρ is written as $\mathbf{A}_{/\rho} = (A_{/\rho}, F)$.

Assuming that there is at least one constant (operator of arity O) in F and a denumerable set of variables V, we define TERM, the set of first order terms, over F and V, as the least set with (i) $V \subseteq$ TERM, and if arity (f) = 0 for f $\in$ F then f$\in$ TERM and (ii) if t_1, ..., $t_n \in$ TERM and arity (f) = n then f(t_1... t_n)$\in$ TERM.

Let Var(t) be the variables occuring in term t. A common trick is to let **T** denote the algebra with carrier TERM and the operators are the term constructors corresponding to each operator of F. **T** is called the absolutely free (term) algebra, i.e. it just gives an algebraic structure to TERM. If the carrier is ground it is called the initial algebra [GT77] or Herbrand universe [Lo78].

Given any set Σ with elements σ, δ, τ, ... and a partial order $\leq$ on Σ. Then $\mu\Sigma$, the base of Σ or the μ-set of Σ is defined as:

(i)	$\mu\Sigma \subseteq \Sigma$	(correctness)
(ii)	$\forall\delta\in\Sigma$ there exist $\sigma\in\mu\Sigma$ with $\delta\leq\sigma$	(completeness)
(iii)	$\sigma,\tau\in\mu\Sigma$: $\sigma\leq\tau$ implies $\sigma=\tau$.	(minimality)

We are interested in the existence, uniqueness and cardinality of such sets in the more specific context of unification.

2.1 Unification

A substitution $\sigma\colon \mathbf{T} \to \mathbf{T}$ is an endomorphism on $\mathbf{T}$, which is identical almost everywhere on V and hence can be represented as a finite set of pairs $\sigma = \{x_1\to t_1,..., x_n\to t_n\}$. The restriction $\sigma|_V$ of a substitution to a set of variables is defined as $\sigma|_V x = \sigma x$ if $x \in V$ and $\sigma|_V x = x$ otherwise.

Σ is the set of substitutions on $\mathbf{T}$ and ε the identity. The application of a substitution σ to a term t is written as σt. The composition of substitutions is defined as the usual composition of mappings: $(\sigma\circ\tau)t = \sigma(\tau t)$ for $t\in\mathbf{T}$.

Hence we have the substitution monoid $\Sigma:=\Sigma(F,V)$ of a term algebra as the set of finitely representable endomorphisms on the term algebra:

(i)	$\varepsilon\in\Sigma$ and $\sigma,\tau\in\Sigma \Rightarrow \sigma\tau\in\Sigma$	(identity and composition)
(ii)	$c\in F_0$, $f(t_1,...,t_n)\in\mathbf{T} \Rightarrow \sigma c = c$, $\sigma f(t_1,...,t_n) = f(\sigma t_1,...,\sigma t_n)$	(homomorphism)
(iii)	$\sigma\in\Sigma \Rightarrow \mathrm{card}(\{v\in V\colon \sigma v \neq v\}) < \infty$	(finite domain).

Define
$$DOM\sigma = \{x\in V\colon \sigma x\neq x\} \qquad \text{(domain of }\sigma\text{)}$$
$$COD\sigma = \{\sigma x\colon x\in DOM\sigma\} \qquad \text{(codomain of }\sigma\text{)}$$
$$VCOD\sigma = Var(COD\sigma) \qquad \text{(variables of codomain of }\sigma\text{)}$$
If $VCOD\sigma = \varnothing$ then σ is a **ground** substitution.

An equation $s = t$ is a pair of terms. For a set of equations T, the equational theory presented by T (in short: the equational theory T) is defined as the finest congruence $=_T$ on $\mathbf{T}$ containing all pairs $\sigma s = \sigma t$ for $s = t$ in T and σ in Σ, i.e. the Σ-invariant congruence relation generated by T.

Two terms s,t are T-equal if $s =_T t$. We extend T-equality in $\mathbf{T}$ to the set of substitutions Σ by:

$$\sigma =_T \tau \quad \text{iff} \quad \forall x\in V \quad \sigma x =_T \tau x.$$

If T-equality of substitutions is restricted to a set of variables W we write

$$\sigma =_T \tau \, [W] \quad \text{iff} \quad \forall x \in W \quad \sigma x =_T \tau x$$

and say σ and τ are **T-equal in W**.

A term s is a **T-instance** of t, $s \leq_T t$, iff there exist $\lambda \in \Sigma$ with $s =_T \lambda t$; s is T-equivalent to t, $s \equiv_T t$, iff $s \leq_T t$ and $s_T \geq t$.

A substitution τ is **more general** than σ on W (or σ **is a T-instance of** τ on W):

$$\sigma \leq_T \tau \, [W] \quad \text{iff} \quad \exists \lambda \in \Sigma \quad \sigma =_T \lambda \tau \, [W].$$

Two substitutions σ, τ are called T-equivalent on W

$$\sigma \equiv_T \tau \, [W] \quad \text{iff} \quad \sigma \leq_T \tau \, [W] \text{ and } \tau \leq_T \sigma \, [W].$$

Given two terms s,t (built up over a welldefined signature) and an equational theory T a unification problem for T is denoted as $<s = t>_T$. Note that a unification problem is characterized by the equational theory T and also by the signature out of which s and t are built.

We say $<s = t>_T$ is T-unifiable iff there exists a substitution $\sigma \in \Sigma$ such that $\sigma s =_T \sigma t$ and we call σ a T-unifier of s and t. For the set of all T-unifiers of s and t we write $U\Sigma_T(s,t)$ which is a left ideal in the substitution monoid Σ, since $U\Sigma =_T \Sigma \cdot U\Sigma[W]$. Without loss of generality we can assume the unifiers of s and t to be idempotent, since if not we can always find equivalent ones which are. For a given unification problem $<s = t>_T$, it is unnecessary to compute the whole set of unifiers $U\Sigma_T(s,t)$, which is always recursively enumerable for a decidable theory T, but rather a smaller set useful in representing $U\Sigma_T$. Therefore we define $cU\Sigma_T(s,t)$, the **complete set of unifiers** of s and t on W = Var(s,t) as:

(i) $cU\Sigma_T \subseteq U\Sigma_T$ (correctness)

(ii) $\forall \delta \in U\Sigma_T \; \exists \sigma \in cU\Sigma_T : \; \delta \leq_T \sigma[W]$ (completeness)

The set of most general unifiers $\mu U\Sigma_T(s,t)$ is defined as the μ-set of $U\Sigma_T(s,t)$. A set of substitutions $\Sigma \subseteq \Sigma$ is said to be **based on W away from Z** $\supset$ W iff the following two conditions are satisfied:

- $DOM\sigma = W$ for all $\sigma \in \Sigma$
- $VCOD\sigma \cap Z = \emptyset$ for all $\sigma \in \Sigma$.

For substitutions σ based on some W we have $DOM\sigma \cap VCOD\sigma = \emptyset$, which is equivalent to the idempotence of σ, i.e. $\sigma \cdot \sigma = \sigma$. This property is often very useful and we usually require $\mu U\Sigma_T$ to be based on W = V(s,t) away from Z $\supset$ W [Pl72].

The set $\mu U\Sigma_T$ does not always exist [FH83] [Sch86] [Ba86]; if it does then it is not unique. However it is unique up to the equivalence $\equiv_T$ (see [Ht76] [FH83]) and for that reason it is sufficient to generate just one $\mu U\Sigma_T$ as a representative of the equivalence class $[\mu U\Sigma_T]_{\equiv_T}$.

Based on the cardinality of $\mu U\Sigma$ we can classify unification problems and equational theories according to the following hierarchy, which turned out to be the backbone of unification theory.

A given unification problem $<s = t>_T$ is of type

(i) **unitary** if $\mu U\Sigma(s,t)$ exists and has at most one element
(ii) **finitary** if $\mu U\Sigma(s,t)$ exists and is finite
(iii) **infinitary** if $\mu U\Sigma(s,t)$ exists and is infinite
(iv) **nullary** (or of type **zero**) if $\mu U\Sigma(s,t)$ does not exist

Similarily we say an equational theory T is unitary (finitary) if for all $s,t \in T$ $\mu U\Sigma_T(s,t)$ is unitary (finitary) and it is infinitary (nullary) if there exists a pair of terms s,t such that $\mu U\Sigma_T(s,t)$ is infinitary (nullary).

A **unification algorithm** for a given theory T is an algorithm that takes two terms s and t as input and generates some subset of $U\Sigma_T(s,t)$. A complete unification algorithm generates $cU\Sigma_T(s,t)$ and a minimal unification algorithm generates the base $\mu U\Sigma_T(s,t)$. For many practical applications the notion of a minimal algorithm is not strong enough, since it does not imply that the algorithm terminates even for a finite $\mu U\Sigma$. On the other hand for a finitary theory the minimality requirement is often too rigid, since an algorithm which generates a (comparatively small) superset of $\mu U\Sigma$ may be far more efficient than a minimal one and hence preferable.

For that reason we say a unification algorithm is **type conformal** if it generates a set Ψ such that:

(i) $\mu U\Sigma \subseteq \Psi \subseteq cU\Sigma$
(ii) If T is finitary then Ψ is finite and the algorithm terminates
(iii) If T is infinitary then $\Psi \equiv_T \mu U\Sigma$

The three mayor problems of unification theory can now be stated as:

PROBLEM ONE:
For a given equational theory T, is it decidable whether s and t are unifiable for any s and t ?

PROBLEM TWO:
Given an equational theory T, what is its type in the unification hierarchy ?

PROBLEM THREE:
For a given non-nullary equational theory T find an (efficient) unification algorithm that enumerates $\mu U \Sigma_T$.

2.2 EQUATIONAL LOGIC

Although unification theory is not restricted to equationally defined theories most results have been obtained within this frame.

A finite set T:= {(s,t): s,t∈ T} of term pairs is called an **axiomatization** of an equational theory, the elements are called **axioms**. The equational theory is the least Σ-invariant congruence relation $=_T$ on **T** containing the set T:

(i) $=_T$ is an equivalence relation with: if (s,t)∈ T then s $=_T$ t

(ii)   if $s_1 =_T t_1$, ... , $s_n =_T t_n$, f∈ F_n then $f(s_1,...,s_n) =_T f(t_1,...,t_n)$
(congruence)

(iii) if $s =_T t$, σ∈ Σ then σs $=_T$ σt
(Σ-invariance)

We are only interested in consistent theories, i.e. theories, which do not collapse into a single equivalence class. A theory is **consistent** if for all v,w∈ V: v $=_T$ w implies v = w.
Frequently the axiomatization T itself is called a theory, and we write s = t instead of (s,t) for the axioms.

An equation s $=_T$ t is **regular**, iff Var(s) = Var(t) [PL69]. Equations t $=_T$ v with v∈ V, t∉ V are called **collapse** equations and equations $f(v_1,...,v_i,...,v_n) =_T v_i$ (for some i with 1≤i≤n) with pairwise different $v_1,...,v_n∈ V$ are called *projection* equations; in this case f∈ F_n is called a **projection** symbol.

A collapse equation of the form f(v) $=_T$ v is called a monadic collapse equation. A theory is called **regular**, iff all equations are regular. A theory without collapse equations is called **collapse free**. Both properties are inherited from the axiomatization to the whole equational theory:

An equational theory is regular, iff all axioms are regular.
An equational theory is collapse free, iff no axiom is a collapse axiom.

The above axioms (i) to (iii) are in fact Birkhoff's axioms. Writing T ⊢ s = t instead of the abbreviation s $=_T$ t (since starting from T there is a finite sequence of operations taken from (i), (ii) or (iii) that will lead to s = t) we obtain Birkhoff's theorem [Bi35]:

T ⊢ s = t   iff   T ⊨ s = t

where $T \models s = t$ denotes that $s = t$ is valid in all models of T. For a survey on classical equational logic see e.g. [Ta79], sequences of replacement are used in [Mc76]. Since neither $\models$ nor $\vdash$ are particularly convenient for a computational treatment of $=_T$, two computer oriented techniques for equational axioms called paramodulation [WR73] and demodulation [WR67] are extensively used in the field of automated deduction. Suppose the equational theory is actually presented as $T = \{l_1 = r_1, l_2 = r_2, ..., l_n = r_n\}$. A term s is said to be **demodulated** to t, $s \to t$, if there is a subterm $\hat{O}$ s in s and a pair $l_i = r_i$ in T such that $\hat{O}$ s $= \mu l_i$ for some matcher μ; term t is obtained from s by replacement of $\hat{O}$ s by μr_i.

A term is said to be **paramodulated** to t, $s \dashrightarrow t$, if there is a subterm $\hat{O}$ s in s and a pair $l_i = r_i$ in T such that $\sigma \hat{O}$ s $= \sigma l_i$ for a unifier σ ; term t is obtained from σs by replacement of $\sigma \hat{O}$ s by σr_i. Note that this is only a special case of paramodulation, in the context of full predicate logic a little extra machinery is required [Lo78].

If for example $T = \{g(x,0) = 0\}$ we have for $s = f(g(a,y), y) \dashrightarrow f(0,0) = t$ with $\sigma = \{x \leftarrow a, y \leftarrow 0\}$ but not $s \to t$, since we are not allowed to substitute into s. The strength of the best current theorem proving systems can be largely attributed to an exploitation of these two rules: e.g. the Argonne National Lab System uses demodulation and paramodulation, also the induction prover of R.Boyer and J.Moore heavily depends on demodulation. The idea of demodulation has been taken further in a paper by D.Knuth [KB70] , which is now a classic in the field called Term Rewriting Systems. The essential observation is that it is often possible to find an equivalent set of equations, which is directed from left to right $l_i \Rightarrow r_i$, $1 \leq i \leq m$, with $Var(r_i) \subseteq Var(l_i)$; this is then called a **term rewriting system** (TRS). If there are no infinite sequences $s_1 \to s_2 \to ...$ the relation $\to$ (based on the TRS) is said to be finitely terminating or **Noetherian**. The relation $\to$ is called **confluent** if for every r, s, t with $r \to s$ and $r \to t$ there exists a term u such that $s \to u$ and $t \to u$; a confluent, Noetherian relation (a TRS) is called **canonical**. Canonical relations are an important basis for a computational treatment of equational logic, since they define a unique normal form ‖t‖ for every term t given by: $t \to$ ‖t‖ and there does not exist a term s with ‖t‖ $\to$ s. ‖t‖ exists because of the finite termination property and it is unique because of confluence; hence $s =_T t$ iff ‖s‖ = ‖t‖. Because of the great importance of TRS for computer science there is intensive research now on methods of how to obtain a canonical TRS from a given set of equations (see [HO80] [Bu85] for a survey).

If the paramodulation relation is based on a directed set of equations it is sometimes called **narrowing** [Hu80] or directed paramodulation and becomes of importance for universal unification algorithms (see 3.2.2.) as well as for the design of recent programming languages that combine functional with logical programming style [DL86].

3. RESULTS (*)

The development of unification theory into a field of its own is hallmarked by the emergence of a theory that addresses the three basic problems of unification theory as introduced above in a more general setting: How and under which conditions can unification algorithms be combined ? Why is the combination of a finitary and an infinitary theory sometimes finitary and sometimes infinitary ? Is it possible to give a universal unification algorithm (similar to a universal Turing machine as opposed to a particular Turing machine), which takes as input a pair of terms and an equational theory ? What is the exact relationship between matching and unification ? Is it possible to develop a general theory in order to classify equational theories with respect to the unification hierarchy ?

For this and other reasons this section is divided into two main paragraphs: special results and results of the general theory.

3.1 The Special Theory *"... a general comparative study necessarily presupposes some previous separate study, comparison being impossiblewithout knowledge."*

N.Whitehead, 1898

This paragraph is divided into three parts giving a separate account of first and higher order unification as well as of unification in sorted logics.

3.1.1 First Order Unification

Unification of Free Terms.

The historical experience with the first deduction systems revealed hat "the unification computation occurs at the very heart of most deduction systems. It is the addition and multiplication of deduction work. There is accordingly a very strong incentive to design the last possible ounce of efficiency into a unification program. The incentive is very much the same as that for seeking maximally efficient realizations of the elementary arithmetic operations in numerical computing - and the problem is every bit as interesting." ([Ro71], p.64)

A first and influential paper in this direction appeared in 1971 by A.Robinson [Ro71] and a proposed table-driven implementation technique that derived its strength from an ingenious manipulation of a pointer structure, which is - with some improvements - still at the heart of current techniques.

(*) For space limitations this section is abbreviated and some paragraphs had to be omitted. A complete version is to appear in the "Journal of Symbolic Computation".

The manipulation of pointers - instead of the objects themselves - was also proposed by R.Boyer and J.Moore and became known as structure sharing.

The final race for the fastest algorithm however started in 1973 with a proposal by L.D.Baxter [Ba73], that was further improved by M.Venturini-Zilli [VZ75] in 1975, by G.Huet [Ht76] in 1976 and by A.Martelli and U.Montanari [MM79] in 1979, who proposed an almost linear algorithm: it is a well-known fact that the original unification algorithm is exponential as a worst case. The first linear unification algorithm was designed in 1976/77 and finally published in a celebrated paper by M.Paterson and W.Wegman [PW78], who used a particular data structure (directed acyclic graphs, dag) to represent the terms. Linearity is achieved by moving an additional pointer structure through these dags.

Although this work appeared to settle the problem once and for all the issue was taken up again, when it became apparent that maintaining the dags and the pointer structure can be expensive and for most practical cases (i.e. short and usually not deeply nested terms) too inefficient.

A most recent improvement was published by D.Kapur, M.S.Krishnamoorthy and P.Narendsan [KK82] in 1982. A first comparison of several algorithms in terms of empirical findings was carried out by G.Winterstein [Wn77]; a more recent comparison by H.J.Bürckert [Bü85] shows again that the issue is far from being finally settled.

Unification in Equational Theories.
The following table summarizes the results that have been obtained for unification problems $<s = t>_T$ with s, t $\in$ **T** and special equational theories T.
The special theories consist of combinations of the following equations:

A	(associativity)	$f(f(x,y), z) = f(x, f(y,z))$
C	(commutativity)	$f(x,y) = f(y,x)$
D	(distributivity)	$D_R: f(x, g(y,z)) = g(f(x,y), f(x,z))$
		$D_L: f(g(x,y), z) = g(f(x,z), f(y,z))$
H, E	(homomorphism, endomorphism)	$\varphi(x \circ y) = \varphi(x) \circ \varphi(y)$
I	(idempotence)	$f(x,x) = x$
T	(transitivity)	$f(g(x,y), g(y,z)) = f(g(x,y), g(x,z))$
$C_{R,L}$	(right, left commutativity)	$f(f(x,y), z) = f(f(x,z), y)$
		$f(x, f(y,z)) = f(y, f(x,z))$

Theory T	Type of T	Unifiability decidable	A_T	References
Ø	1	Yes	Yes	[He30] [Ro65] [Ro71] [KB70] [Gu64] [Pr60] [Ba73] [Ht76] [MM79] [PW78] [KK82]
A	∞	Yes	Yes	[Hj67] [Pl72] [Si75] [LS75] [Ma77] [Si78]
C	ω	Yes	Yes	[Si76]
I	ω	Yes	Yes	[RS78] [Hu80]
A+C	ω	Yes	Yes	[St81][LS76][Hu79][Fa83][Ht78][HS85][Bü85]
A+I	0	Yes	?	[SS82] [SCH86] [BA86]
C+I	ω	Yes	Yes	[RS78] [JK83]
A+C+I	ω	Yes	Yes	[LS76] [Bü86]
D	∞	?	Yes	[Sz82] [AT85] [Mz86] [SU78]
D+A	∞	No	Yes	[Sz82]
D+C	∞	?	Yes	[Sz82]
D+A+C	∞	No	Yes	[Sz82]
D+A+I	?	Yes	?	[Sz82]
H, E	1	Yes	Yes	[Vo78]
H+A	∞	Yes	Yes	[Vo78]
H+A+C	ω	Yes	Yes	[Vo78]
E+A+C	∞	?	?	[Vo78]
T	ω	Yes	Yes	[Ki85]
T+C	ω	Yes	Yes	[Ki85]
T+C+C	ω	Yes	Yes	[Ki85]
$C_{R,L}$	ω	Yes	Yes	[Je80]
QG	ω	Yes	Yes	[Hu80]
AG	ω	Yes	Yes	[LA79] [LBB84]
H10	?	No	?	[MA70] [DA73]
FPAG	ω	Yes	Yes	[LA80] [KR85]
HF	0	Yes	?	[FH83]
MINUS	∞/ω	Yes	Yes	[Ki85]
ABS	∞/ω	Yes	Yes	[Ki82]
BR	1	Yes	Yes	[MN86]

Abbreviations:

FPAG:	Finitely Presented Abelian Group	type 1 :	unary
QG:	Quasi-Groups	ω :	finitary
AG:	Abelian Groups	∞ :	infinitary
H10:	Hilbert`s 10th Problem	0 :	nullary
FH:	$1 * x = x$, $q(x * y) = q(y)$		
MINUS:	$-(-x) = x$; $-(x * y) = (-y) * (-x)$		
ABS:	Signed binary trees		
BR:	Boolean Rings		

The column under A_T indicates whether or not a type conformal algorithm is known.

Except for Hilbert's tenth problem, we have not included the classical work on equation solving in "concrete" structures such as rings and fields, which is well known. The relationship of universal unification to these classical results is similar to that of universal algebra to classical algebra.

Let us comment on a few entries in the above table: The **Robinson Unification Problem**, i.e. unification in the free algebra of terms or unification under the empty theory Ø has attracted most attention so far.

Unification under associativity is the famous monoid problem mentioned in paragraph 1.1. G.Plotkin gave the first unification algorithm for this theory [Pl72] and used it to demonstrate the existence of infinitary equational theories. Completeness, correctness and minimality proofs are presented in [SI78]. Makanin showed the decidability of this unification problem [Ma77].

Unification under commutativity has a trivial solution, whereas minimality presents a hard problem; a type conformal algorithm is presented in [Si76]. The main interest in this theory however derives from its finitary nature in contrast to the infinitary theory of associativity. A nice characterization of this difference is possible in terms of the universal unification algorithm to be presented below. However a deep theoretical explanation of why two seemingly very similar theories belong to entirely different classes is still an open research problem.

Terms under **associativity and commutativity** closely resemble the datastructure multisets (sets which may contain multiple occurrences of the same element), which is used in the matching of patterns (pattern directed invocation) in many programming languages of Artificial Intelligence. This pattern matching problem for multisets (often called **bags** in the AI-literature) was investigated by M.Stickel in [St75], [St76], who observed that this problem can be reduced to the problem of solving homogeneous linear diophantine equations over the positive integers with the additional proviso that only *positive* linear combinations of the solution set are admissible. His results were finally published in [St 81] .

Building upon the work of G.Plotkin [Pl72], Livesey and Siekmann [LS76] [LS78] investigated the axioms of associativity (A) and commutativity (C), since they so frequently occur in applications of automated theorem proving. Independently of M.Stickel they also observed the close relationship between the AC-unification problem and the solving of linear diophantine equations. They proposed a very different reduction (among other differences a reduction to *inhomogeneous* linear diophantine equations) which appears to have some advantages over the combinatorics of the "variable-abstraction" process in the Stickel algorithm.

However an important problem remained open: the extension of the AC-unification algorithm to the whole class of first order terms turned out to be more difficult than anticipated. The suggestions for such an extension in [St76] as well as the naive sketch of an extension proposed in [LS76] were missing a crucial point namely that the subformulas of a term to be

AC-unified can become longer, i.e. have more symbols, than the original term. Hence the termination of the extended AC-unification procedure became a major problem, which remained open for many years. It was finally positively solved by F. Fages [Fa83] using an ingenious complexity measure on AC-terms.

G.Huet [Ht78] , A.Fortenbacher [Fo83] , D.Lankford [La85] and W.Büttner [Bü85] give efficient methods to solve homogeneous linear equations where only positive linear combinations are admissible, a problem originally investigated in [G1873] . This is an important component of every AC-unification algorithm. A comparison of the algorithms of Huet and Fortenbacher and an extension of these algorithms to the case of inhomogeneous equations can be found in [GH85].

J.M.Hullot [Ht80], F.Fages [Fa84] and Fortenbacher [Fo83] [Fo85] discuss computational improvements of the original Stickel-algorithm. Recently another approach to AC-unification was proposed in [Ki85].

G.E.Peterson and M.E.Stickel [PS81] present a generalisation of the Knuth-Bendix completion algorithm for term rewriting systems [KB70] based inter alia on AC-unification. The practical advantage of a special purpose AC-unification algorithm is particularily well demonstrated for term rewriting systems in [St84].

Apart from interest in a practical and fast algorithm, which computes the set of unifiers there is the main theoretical observation that the set of most general unifiers is always *finite* for AC-unification problems. This fact was independently discovered in [St75] and [LS76]. However, since the set of most general unifiers (mgu) corresponds to the set of nonnegative solutions of certain linear diophantine equations, the finiteness of the set of mgu's follows immediately from a theorem of Dickson [DI13].

Two recent papers by A.Herold, J.Siekmann [HS86] and W.Büttner [Bü85] improved on the original work of [LS76] [LS78]. In [HS86] an extension of the algorithm to the whole class of first order terms is presented using a modification of the Fages-complexity measure in the proof of termination.

The AC-unification algorithm has become just as important for practical work as the original Robinson Algorithm, since the axioms of associativity and commutativity so often occur in practice.

Apart from its practical relevance, however, AC-unification poses an important theoretical problem: why is it that the combination of an infinitary theory (A) with a finitary theory (C) results in a finitary theory (A+C), whereas the combination of an infinitary theory (D) with the finitary (C) results in infinitary theory (D+C) ?

Unification under **distributivity and associativity** provides a point in case that the combination of two infinitary theories is an infinitary theory. Is this always the case ? The D+A Unification Problem is also of theoretical interest with respect to Hilbert`s Tenth Problem, which is the problem of Diophantine solvability of polynomial equation. An axiomatization of Hilbert`s Tenth Problem would involve the axioms A and D plus additional axioms for integers, multiplication, etc. Calling the union of these axioms HTP, the famous undecidability result [Da73] shows the undecidability of the unification problem under HTP. Now the undecidability of the D+A-Unification Problem demonstrates that all Hilbert axioms in HTP can be dropped except for D and A and the problem still remains undecidable. Since A-unification is known to be decidable, the race is open as to whether or not A can be dropped as well and D on its own presents an undecidable unification problem.

More generally: it is an interesting and natural question for an undecidable problem to ask for its "minimal undecidable substructure". Whatever the result may be, the D+A problem already highlights the advantage of the abstract nature of universal unification theory in contrast to the traditional point of view, with its reliance on intuitively given entities (like integers) and structures (like polynomials).

It is important to realize that the results recorded in the above table do not always hold for the whole class of first order terms, which is but a special case of the Combination Problem of Theories:

From the above table we already have

A	infinitary,	I	finitary	and	A+I	nullary
D	infinitary,	A	infinitary	and	D+A	infinitary
D	infinitary,	C	finitary	and	D+C	infinitary
A	infinitary,	C	finitary	and	A+C	finitary
C	finitary,	I	finitary	and	C+I	finitary
H	unitary,	A	infinitary	and	H+A	infinitary
H	unitary,	A+C	finitary	and	H+A+C	finitary
D_L	unitary,	C	finitary	and	D_L+C	infinitary
D_L	unitary,	D_R	unitary	and	D_L+D_R = D infinitary	

Using a more informal notation we can write: $\infty + \infty = \infty$, $\infty + \omega = \infty$, $\omega + \omega = \omega$, $1 + \infty = \infty$, $1 + \omega = \omega$, $1 + \omega = \infty$ and even $1 + 1 = \infty$, $\infty + \omega = 0$ for these results.

Here we assume that for example C and A hold for the same function symbol f and the combination of these axioms is denoted as C+A. But what happens if C and A hold for two different function symbols, C for f and A for g ? Even the most trivial extension in this spirit, which is the extension of a known unification result to additional "free" functions (i.e. the empty theory for every function symbol which is not part of the known unification result) as mentioned above is unsolved in general. The results known so far are recorded in section 3.2.1.

Summarizing we notice that unification algorithms for different theories are usually based on entirely different techniques. They provide the experimental laboratory of Universal Unification Theory and it is paramount to obtain a much larger experimental test set than the one recorded above.

Unification in Logic Programming Languages

Terms like f(x, g(x)) and f(y,y) are not unifiable in the classical sense: although both terms are "standardized apart" (i.e. have different variables), once the first arguments of f are unified the second arguments share the same variable in y and g(y) and the socalled "occur-in-check" reports failure.

In order to avoid this (expensive) checking two approaches are possible: either to admit infinite terms [Mu83] or else to accept the occasional error as for example in most PROLOG implementations [CM81].

Since unification is the central operation of logic programming languages and the CPU of Fifth Generation Computers more elaborate schemes have been designed for speed up. Most prominent is currently the WARREN-Machine [GL84], which consists of machine instructions into which a logic programming language can be compiled. This set constitutes an abstract machine and each instruction can then either be supported by actual hardware or else by some sequence of microcode instructions of a more or less conventional machine (like e.g. in the SYMBOLICS LISP-Machine).

Unification Chips

Anticipating the upcoming technology race for ultrafast unification there were early attempts to "compile the unification algorithm into silicon" and to design a special unification processor called the SUM [Ro85].

Similarly if the Warren instruction set is directly supported by suitable hardware this can be viewed as a unification machine.

Current experiments use a pipeline of unification processors or else try to marry the Warren machine with a (set of) special unification processor(s) [FG84].

3.1.2   Unification in Sorted Logics

This section is excluded for space limitations. Most recent work (with appropriate back references) is reported by Ch.Walther [Wa86] and M.Schmidt-Schauss [Sch86].

3.1.3   Higher Order Unification

This section is excluded for space limitations. A recent article with appropriate back references is by P.Andrews [An84].

3.1.4   Unification Grammars

This section is again excluded for space limitations. A recent collection of papers with current references is [SK84] [SK85].

3.2 The General Theory   *" However to generalize, one needs experience ..."*
G.Grätzer, 1968

3.2.1 Combination of Unification Algorithms

Given a unification algorithm for an equational theory T_1 and another algorithm for a theory T_2: how can we obtain an algorithm for the theory $T = T_1 \cup T_2$?

There are at least two cases to be distinguished: if the axioms in T_1 and T_2 involve the same function symbol there is little hope for a general recipe of how to obtain a unification algorithm for T out of the separate algorithms for T_1 and T_2. For example if T_1 is the associativity axiom (A) a complete and minimal unification algorithm is known that is infinitary. Suppose now T_2 is the commutativity axiom (C) for the same function symbol: again a type conformal algorithm is known which is finitary. But the finitary AC-algorithm for the union of A and C is completely different. Even taking the separate algorithm as a heuristic guideline in order to find the algorithm for the union would be utterly misleading in this case (however sometimes it may not): it was the distrust in the obvious combination of the C-algorithm and the A-algorithm that lead to the A+C-algorithm.

This situation is to be expected in general: solving equations in an algebra defined by T_1 and T_2 respectively may have nothing to do with solving equations in the algebra defined by $T = T_1 \cup T_2$.

However if T_1 and T_2 involve different function symbols the situation is different and under certain preconditions the separate algorithms for T_1 and T_2 can indeed be combined just as decision procedures for different theories can sometimes be combined into a decision procedure for their union [NO80].

There are currently three approaches:

Building upon the variable abstraction of M.Stickel and F.Fages, that was successfully used for the AC-unification problem, K.Yelick [Ye85] and E.Tidén [Ti85] independently gave algorithms for a combination of finitary theories. Essentially these algorithms are a generalization of the AC-unification idea by abstracting those subterms to variables that do not belong to the theory of the top function symbol. K.Yelick restricts the problem to regular finitary collapse free theories whereas E.Tidén presents a combination for collapse free theories without the regularity restriction.

A second approach was presented by A.Herold [He85], whose technique is a generalization of the constant abstraction used for the AC-unification algorithm of M.Livesey and J.Siekmann. Again his technique is restricted to finitary collapse free theories.

A third approach is given by C.Kirchner in [Ki85], who tackles the problem by a decomposition of the terms to be unified. Currently his combination only works for a more restrictive class than the regular finitary collapse free theories (however this may be generalized).

3.2.2   Universal Unification

As unification algorithms for different theories are usually based on entirely different methods it would be interesting to have a universal unification algorithm for a whole class of theories: a universal unification algorithm (a universal matching algorithm) for a class of theories $\mathbb{T}$ is an algorithm which takes as input a pair of terms (s,t) and a theory $T \in \mathbb{T}$ and generates a complete set of unifiers (matchers) for $<s = t>_T$ (for $<s \geq t>_T$). In other words just as a Universal Turing Machine takes as its input the description of a special Turing Machine and its arguments, a universal unification algorithm accepts an (equational) theory T <u>and</u> two terms to be unified under T.

To show the essential idea behind the universal algorithms suppose $<s = t>_T$ is the unification problem and R is a rewrite system for T. Let h be a "new" binary function symbol then h(s,t) is a term. Using these conventions we have the following consequence of Birkhoff's theorem as a basis for all universal unification algorithms:

There exists $\sigma \in \Sigma$ with $\sigma s =_T \sigma t$ iff there exist terms p,q and $\delta \in \Sigma$ such that $h(s,t) \supset\!\!\to_R h(p,q)$
with $\delta p = \delta q$.

A first step towards an application of this result is a proper organization of the paramodulation steps $\supset\!\!\to$ into a tree, with the additional proviso that we never paramodulate into variables.

For a given term t the labeled paramodulation tree P_t is defined as:

  (i)   t (the root) is a node in P_t
  (ii)   if r is a node in P_t and $r \supset\!\!\to s$, then s (the successor) is a node in P_t
  (iii)   the edge (r,s) , where $r \supset\!\!\!-\!\!\!-\!\!\!-\!\!\to s$, is labeled with the triple $[\pi,i,\theta]$.
                                          $[\pi,i,\theta]$

Using the above result we have: if h(p,q) is a node in $P_{h(s,t)}$ such that p,q are Robinson-unifiable with σ then $\delta = s \circ \theta$ is a correct T-unifier for s and t, where θ is the combination of all the paramodulation substitutions obtained along the path from h(s,t) to h(p,q).

And vice versa for every T-unifier τ for s and t there exists a node h(p,q) in $P_{h(s,t)}$ such that p and q are Robinson-unifiable with σ and $\tau \leq \sigma \circ \theta$.

Of course the set of unifiers obtained with this tree is far too large to be of any interest and the work of D.Lankford [La79] and G.Hullot [Hu80], based on [Fa79], is concerned with prunig this tree under the constraint of maintaining completeness. G.Hullot [Hu80] shows the close correspondence between $\to$ (rewrite) and $\supset\!\!\to$ (paramodulation, narrowing) steps and [JK83] investigate an incremental universal unification algorithm by separating the given theory T into two constituent parts $T = R \cup E$, where only R must be E-canonical.

Since the set of unifiers $U\Sigma_T$ is trivially recursively enumerable for any decidable theory T there is the important requirement that a universal unification algorithm generates the minimal set $\mu U\Sigma_T$ or is at least type conformal. Since such a result is unattainable in general, there is a strong incentive to find classes of theories, such that a universal unification algorithm is minimal for every theory T within this class. Such a class should be large enough to contain most theories of practical interest and show that the universal unification algorithm based on P_t is correct, minimal and complete for this class. J.Siekmann and P.Szabo propose such a class (called ACFM-class) [SS81]. A.Herold [He82] gives an extension of this class, which is the widest currently known.

The next 700 Unification Algorithms.

These theoretical results can be applied in practice for the design of an actual unification algorithm. So far the design of a special purpose algorithm was more of an art than a science, since for a given theory there was no indication whatsoever of how the algorithm might work. In fact the algorithms recorded in the table of 3.1.1 all operate on entirely different principles.

Using the universal unification algorithm as a starting point this task is now much easier by first isolating the crucial parts in the universal algorithm and then designing a practical and efficient solution. A collection of canonical theories [Hu80] is a valuable source for this purpose and has already been used to find the first unification algorithms for Abelian group theory and quasi group theory [La79], [Hu80].

Logic Programming.

Universal unification is the basis of an interesting new approach to programming languages that combines the virtues of functional programming [Bacus] with logical programming.

The idea is to have a logical programming language with equality and to use the (directed) equations in just the same way as they are used in the universal unification algorithm. This technique is called **narrowing** or directed paramodulation and interest is in finding equational classes where this can be done effectively. A collection of papers centered around this approach is contained in [DL86].

3.2.3 Matching and Unification

An equational theory that is finitary with respect to unification is of course finitary matching, but not vice versa: for example stringunification is finitary matching but infinitary with respect to unification.

What is then in general the relationship between matching and unification and more specifically: how are the two respective hierarchies related?

The problem is that a matcher is in general not just a special unifer. For example the substitution $m = \{x \longmapsto f(x)\}$ is a matcher for the problem $<f(x) \leq x>_\emptyset$ but not a unifier for the corresponding unification problem $<f(x)=x>_\emptyset$. Matching and semi-uification [HT76] are but special cases of the general notion of a V-restricted unification problem, which is a unification problem $<f(x)=x>_T$, where the unifier is allowed to move only a subset of Var(s,t).

Some general results are shown in [Bü86], in particular it is shown how the most general restricted unifiers can be computed from the unrestricted most general unifiers (for the special case of collapse free equational theories).

3.2.4. Classification of Equational Theories

This section is again omitted for space limitations. Some results are summarized in [SI84].

3.2.5. Unification Hierarchy

In the 1970`s many **unitary, finitary** and **infinitary** equational theories were discovered. It was also wellknown that for higher order logics the minimal set of unifiers $\mu U\Sigma$ does not always exist: i.e. for certain problems there are infinitely ascending chains of unifiers $\sigma_1 \leq \sigma_2 \leq \sigma_3 \leq ...$ with no upper bound. Hence the natural problem, which was open for several years: are there first order equational theories with th esame unpleasant feature or is the class of nullary first order theories empty?

G.Huet and F.Fages showed that unfortunately this is the case: in [FH83] they construct a special equational theory, which even admits a canonical rewriting system, of **type zero**. Recently it was shown independently by M.Schmidt-Schauss [Sch86] and A.Baader [Ba86] that idempotent semigroups (called bands in semigroup theory) are of type nullary, thus opening up a whole class of "natural" theories (varieties) all of which are of type zero.

Similarly we may ask if the unification hierarchy is the finest possible structure or else is it possible to refine the hierarchy into subclasses? A natural candidate might be the class of finitary theories that could be decomposed into **bounded** theories. An equational theory T is bounded by N if for every pair of terms s,t the cardinality of $\mu U\Sigma(<s=t>_T)$ is less than N. While it is easy to find special unification problems that are bounded by some N (for certain subclasses of terms) it is shown in [BS86] that equational theories which are not unitary are unbounded. Hence this notion can _not_ be used to refine the hierarchy. In particular it can not be used to clarify the borderline between unitary and finitary theories nor - by considering the limes - the borderline between finitary and infinitary theories.

Both of these questions are still major open research problems. There are results and hard open problems similar to the compactness theorems or Ehrenfeucht Conjecture. These are tied to the concept of local subclass of a class of equational theories.

Let term(T) := {l,r: l=r ∈ T} be the set of terms in the axiomatization of T and let I(T) be the set of instances of these terms:

$$I(T) := \{\sigma t: t \in term(T), \sigma \in \Sigma\}.$$

Similarly we define G(T) as the finite set of all generalizations of these terms:

$$G(T) := \{\sigma t: t \in term(T), \sigma = [\pi \leftarrow x], \pi \in \Pi(t), x \in X\}.$$

We assume terms equal under renaming to be discarded, i.e. $G(T)/_{\sim}$. With these two sets we obtain the characteristic set of an equational theory T as:

$$\chi(T) := I(T) \cup G(T)$$

and the finite local-characteristic set as:

$$\lambda(T) := term(T) \cup G(T).$$

Let E(T) be some first order property of T. If the property E is only considered with respect to a subset TS of **T**, we write $E(T)|_{TS}$. For a theory T E(T) is χ-reducible iff $E(T)|_{\chi(T)}$ implies E(T). Similarly theory T is λ-reducible iff $E(T)|_{\lambda(T)}$ implies E(T).

For certain theories it may even be possible to reduce E(T) to a finite test set loc(T)$\subset$**T** such that $E(T)|_{loc(T)}$ implies E(T).

A typical result, shown in [Sz82] is:

Theorem: The matching problem for admissible, canonical and regular theories is χ-reducible.

This theorem greatly simplifies the test for finitary or infinitary matching since we only have to show that it holds for matching problems on $\chi(T)$; i.e. for all problems $<s \geq t>_T$ with s,t$\in \chi(T)$.

A major research problem of the field is to λ-reduce (or at least to χ-reduce) the property of a theory to be unitary, finitary or infinitary. A first result in this respect is the λ-reducibility of unitary matching theories [Sz82]:

Theorem: The test for unitary matching is λ-reducible.

Theorems of this nature are of considerable practical importance since they allow an immediate classification of a given theory: usually it is not too hard to find some unification algorithm for a given theory - however it can be very tricky to ensure that it is complete, i.e. that it generates all unifiers. But if we already know that the given theory is unitary or finitary this task is greatly simplified.

The following results are concerned with the reducibility of unitary unification theories.

In 1975 P.Hayes conjectured that Robinson's unification algorithm for free terms may well be the only case with at most one most general unifier.

Unfortunately this is not the case: for example let $T_{a,b} := \{a=b\}$ for any constants a,b then $T_{a,b}$ is unitary.

But the problem turned out to be more complex than anticipated at the time: for example let $T_{aa} := \{f(a,a) = a\}$ for any constant a, then T_{aa} is unitary.

We first observe that the unitary unification theories are a proper subset of the unitary matching theories and in [Sz82] it is shown that

Theorem: The unitary unification theories are χ-reducible.

To illustrate the use of the above theorems let us consider the empty theory $T_\varnothing$, i.e. the Robinson unification problem for free terms. In order to show that $T_\varnothing$ is unitary, in the stone age of unification theory one had to invent a special algorithm and then prove its completeness and correctness [Ro65], [KB70].

A more elegant method is contained in [Ht76]: factoring $\mathbf{T}$ by $\approx$, it is possible to show that $\mathbf{T}|_\approx$ forms a complete semi-lattice under $\leq$. Hence if two terms are unifiable there exists a common instance and hence there exists a l.u.b., which is the most general such instance: thus follows $T_\varnothing$ is unitary.

However using the above theorem, this result is immediate: Since the absolutely free algebra of terms is in particular Ω-free: $T_\varnothing$ is finitary matching [Sz82]. Now since $\chi(T_e)$ is empty every TEST set is empty. Hence there does not exist a pair in TEST with more than one mgu, thus follows $T_\varnothing$ is finitary.

Although the comparative study of theories and classes of theories has uncovered interesting algebraic structures this is without doubt nothing but the tip of an iceberg of still unknown results.

5. Bibliography

[An71]   P.Andrews: "Resolution in Type Theory", J. of Symbolic Logic, vol.36, 1971

[An84]   P.Andrews: "Automating Higher Order Logic", in: Contemporary Mathematics, American Math Soc., 1984

[AT85]   A.Arnberg, T.Eiden;: "Unification Problems with One-Sided Distributivity", Proc. of Conf. on Rewriting Techniques, Springer Lecture Notes on Comp. Sci., 1985

[BA72]   Barrow, Ambler, Burstall: "Some techniques for recognizing Sructures in Pictures", Frontiers of Pattern Recognition, Academic Press Inc., 1972.

[Ba78]   L.D.Baxter: "The Undecidability of the Third Order Dyadic Unification Problem", Information and Control, vol.38, no.2, 1978

[Ba73]   L.D.Baxter: "An efficient Unification Algorithm", Rep. CS-73-23, University of Waterloo, Dept. of Analysis and Computer Science, 1973

[Ba86]   A.Baader: "Unification in Idempotent Semigroups is of Type Zero", J. of Automated Reasoning, to appear 1986

[BB82]   D.Ballard, Ch.Brown: "Computer Vision", Prentice Hall, New Jersy, 1982

[BC66]   H.Bryan, J.Carnog: "Search Methods used with Transistor Patent Applications", IEEE Spectrum 3, 2, 1966

[BF77]   H.P.Böhm, H.L.Fischer, P.Raulefs: "CSSA: Language Concepts and Programming Methodology", Proc. of ACM, SIGPLAN/ART Conference, Rochester, 1977

[Bi35]   G.Birkhoff: "On the Structure of Abstract Algebras", Proc. Cambridge Phil. Soc., vol.31, 1935

[Bl71]   F.Blair et al.: "SCRATCHPAD/1: An interactive Facility for Symbolic Mathematics", Proc. of the 2nd Symposium on Symbolic Manipulation, Los Angeles, 1971

[BL77]   A.Ballantyne, D.Lankford: "Decision Procedures for simple Equational Theories", University of Texas at Austin, ATP-35, ATP-37, ATP-39, 1977

[BL85]   Brackmann, Levesque: "Readings in Knowledge Representation", Will. Kaufmann Inc., 1985

[BM77]   R.Boyer, J.S.Moore: "A Fast String Searching Algorithm", CACM vol.20, no.10, 1977

[BM82]   Ch.Beilken, F.Mattern, M.Spenke: "Entwurf und Implementierung von CSSA", vol.A-E, SEKI-Memo-82-03, University of Kaiserslautern, 1982

[Bo68]   D.G.Bobrow (ed.): "Symbol Manipulation Languages", Proc. of IFIP, North Holland Publishing Comp., 1968

[Bo85]   R.Book: "Thue Systems as Rewriting Systems", in: Proc. of Rewriting Techniques, Springer Lecture Notes in Comp. Sci., vol.202, 1985

[BS85]   Brachmann, Schnolze: "An Overview of KL-ONE", Cognitive Science, vol.9, no.2, 1985

[BS85]   B.Buchanan, R.Shortliffe: "Rule Based Expert Systems", Addison Wesley, 1985

[BS86]   R.Book, J.Siekmann: "On the Unification Hierarchy", to appear in J. of Symbolic Computation, 1986

[Bu85]   B.Buchberger: "Basic Features and Development of the Critical Pair Completion Procedure", Proc. Rewritung Techniques and Applications, Springer Lecture Notes is Comp. Sci., vol.202, 1985

[Bü86]   H.J.Bürckert: "Some Relationship between Unification and Matching", Proc. 8th Conf. on Autom. Deduction , Springer Lecture Notes Comp. Sci., 1986

[Bü85]   W.Büttner: "Unification in the Datastructure Multisets", SEKI-Report, Univ. Kaiserslautern, 1985

[Bü86]   W.Büttner: "Unification in the Datastructure Sets", Proc. of 8th Conf. on Automated Deduction, Springer Lecture notes, 1986

[BW77]   D.Bobrow, T.Winograd: "An Overview of KRL", Cognitive Science, vol.1, no.1, 1977

[CK71]   C.Christensen, M.Karr: "IAM, A System for Interactive Algebraic Manipulation", Proc. of the 2nd Symposium on Symbolic Manipulation, Los Angeles, 1971

[CM81]   W.Clocksin, C.Mellish: "Programming in PROLOG", Springer 1981

[Co70]   E.F.Codd: "A Relational Model of Data for Large Shared Databanks", CACM, 13, 6, 1972

[Co72]   E.F.Codd: "Relational Completeness of Data Base Sublanguages", in Data Base Systems, Prentice Hall, Courant Comp. Science Symposia Series, vol.6, 1972

[CP61]   A.Clifford, G.Preston: "The Algebraic Theory of Semigroups", vol.I and vol. II, 1961

[Cr68]   D.G.Corneil: "Graph Isomorphism", Ph.D.Dept. of Computer Science, University of Toronto, 1968

[Da71]   J.L.Darlington: "A Partial Mechanization of second Order Logic", Mach. Int.6, 1971

[Da76]   C.J.Date: "An Introduction to Database Systems", Addison-Wesley Publ. Comp. Inc., 1976

[Da63]   M.Davis: "Eliminating the Irrelevant from Mechanical Proofs", Symposia of Applied Math., vol.15, American Mathematical Society, 1963

[Da65]   M.Davis: "The Undecidable", Raven Press, New York, 1965

[Da73]   M.Davis: "Hilbert`s Tenth Problem is Unsolvable", Amer. Math. Monthly, vol.80, 1973

[DL86]   D.Degroot, G.Lindstrom: "Logic Programming: Functions, Relations and Equations", Prentice Hall, 1986

[Fa71]   R.Fateman: "The User-Level Semantic Matching Capability in MACSYMA", Proc. of the 2nd Symposium on Symbolic Manipulation, Los Angeles, 1971

[Fa79]   M.Fay: "First Order Unification in an Equational Theory", Proc. 4th Workshop on Automated Deduction, Texas, 1979

[Fa83]   F.Fage: "Associative Commutative Unification", INRIA report CNRS-LITP4, 1983

[FG64]   D.J.Farber, R.E.Griswald, I.P.Polonsky: "SNOBOL as String Manipulation Language", JACM, vol.11, no.2, 1964

[FG84]   Proc. of Conf. on Fifth Generation Computer Systems, ICOT, North Holland, 1984

[FH83]   F.Fage, G.Huet: "Complete Sets of Unifiers and Matchers in Equational Theories", Proc. CAAP-83, Springer Lec. Notes Comp. Sci, vol.159, 1983

[Fo81]   C.Forgy: "OPS5 User Manual", CMU Techn. Report, CMU-CS-81-135, 1981

[Fo82]   C.Forgy: "Rete: A Fast Algorithm for the Many Pattern/Object Match Problem", J. of Art. Intelligence, vol.19, no.1, 1982

[Gi73]   J.F.Gimpel: "A Theory of Discrete Patterns and their Implementation in SNOBOL4", CACM 16, 2, 1973

[Gl84] J.Gabriel (et al.): "A Tutorial on the Warrren Abstract Machine", Argonne National Lab., ANL-84-84, 1984

[GM78] H.Gallaire, J.Minker: "Logic and Databases", Plenum Press, 1978

[Go66] W.E.Gould: "A Matching Procedure for ω-Order Logic", Scientific Report no.4, Air Force Cambridge Research Labs., 1966

[GO67] J.R.Guard, F.C.Oglesby, J.H.Benneth, L.G.Settle: "Semi-Automated Mathematics", JACM 1969, vol.18, no.1

[Go81] D.Goldfarb: "The Undecidability of the Second Order Unification Problem", Journal of Theor. Comp. Sci., 13, 1981

[Gr79] G.Grätzer: "Universal Algebra", Springer Verlag, 1979

[GT77] J.Goguen, J.Thatcher, E.Wagner, J.Wright: "Initial Algebra Semantics and Continuous Algebras", JACM, vol.24, no.1, 1977

[Gu64] J.R.Guard: "Automated Logic for Semi-Automated Mathematics", Scientific report no.1, Air Force Cambridge Research Labs., AD 602 710, 1964

[He82] A.Herold: "Universal Unification and a class of Equational Theories", Proc. GWAI-82, W.Wahlster (ed.) Springer Fachberichte, 1982

[He82] A.Herold: "Some Basic Notions of First Order Unification Theory", Univ. Karlsruhe, Interner Report, 1983

[He86] A.Herold: "Combination of Unification Algorithms", Proc. 8th Conf. on Autom. Deduction, Springer Lecture Notes on Comp. Sci., 1986

[He30] J.Herbrand: "Recherches sur la Théorie de la Démonstration", Travaux de la Soc. des Sciences et des Lettres de Varsovie, no.33, 128, 1930

[He75] G.P.Huet: "A Unification Algorithm for Typed λ-Calculus", J. Theor. Comp. Sci., 1, 1975

[Hj64] J.I.Hmelevskij: "The Solution of certain Systems of Word Equations", Dokl. Akad. Nauk SSSR, 1964, 749 Soviet Math. Dokl.5, 1964, 724

[Hj66] J.I.Hmelevskij: "Word Equations without Coefficients", Dokl. Akad. Nauk SSSR 171, 1966, 1047 Soviet Math. Dokl.7, 1966, 1611

[Hj67] J.I.Hmelevskij: "Solution of Word Equations in three Unknowns", Dokl. Akad. Nauk SSSR 177, 1967, no.5, Soviet Math. Dokl.8, 1967, no.6

[Hl80] J.M.Hullot: "A Catalogue of Canonical Term Rewriting Systems", Research rep. CSL-113, SRI-International, 1980

[Hn71] A.Hearn: "REDUCE2, A System and Language for Algebraic Manipulation", Proc. of the 2nd Symposium on Symbolic Manipulation, Los Angeles, 1971

[Ho76] J.Howie: "Introduction to Semigroup Theory", Acad. Press 1976

[HO80] G.Huet, D.C.Oppen: "Equations and Rewrite Rules", in "Formal Languages: Perspectives and Open Problems", Ed. R.Book, Academic Press, 1980

[Hr73] S.Heilbrunner: "Gleichungssysteme für Zeichenreihen", TU München, Abtl. Mathematik, Ber. Nr.7311, 1973

[HS85] A.Herold, J.Sekmann: "Unification in Abelian Semigroups"

396   J.H. Siekmann

[Ht72]   C.Hewitt: "Description and Theoretical Analysis of PLANNER, a Language for Proving Theorems and Manipulation Models in a Robot", Dept. of Mathematics, Ph.C. Thesis, MIT, 1972

[Ht76]   C.Hewitt: "Viewing Control Structures as Patterns of Passing Messages", MIT, AI-Lab., Working Paper 92, 1976

[Ht72]   G.P.Huet: "Constrained Resolution: A Complete Method for Theory", Jenning's Computing Centre rep. 1117, Case Western Reserve Univ., 1972

[Ht73]   G.P.Huet: "The Undecidability of Unification in Third Order Logic", Information and Control 22 (3), 257-267, 1973

[Ht75]   G.Huet: "Unification in Typed Lambda-Calculus", in λ-Calculus and Comp. Sci.Theory, Springer Lecture Notes, No.37, Proc. of the Symp. held in Rome, 1975

[Ht76]   G.Huet: "Résolution d` Équations dans des Langages d`ordre 1,2,...,ω", Thèse d`État, Univ. de Paris, VII, 1976

[Ht78]   G.Huet: "An Algorithm to Generate the Basis of Solutions to Homogenous Linear Diophantine Equations", Information Proc. Letters 7, 3, 1978

[Ht80]   G.Huet: "Confluent Reductions: Abstract Properties and Applications to Term Rewriting Systems", JACM vol.27, no.4, 1980

[Hu79]   J.M.Hullot: "Associative Commutative Pattern Matching", 5th Int. Joint Conf. on AI, Tokyo 1979

[Hu80]   J.M.Hullot: "Canonical Forms and Unification", Proc. of 5th Workshop on Automated Deduction, Springer Lecture Notes, 1980

[IM83]   N.Ito, K.Masuda, H.Shimizu: "Parallel PROLOG Machine", ICOT Research Centre, TR-035, 1983

[Je80]   J.Jeanrond: "Deciding Unique Termination", Proc 5th Conf. on Autom. Deduction, Springer Lecture Notes in Comp. Sci., vol.87, 1980

[JP73]   D.Jensen, T.Pietrzykowski: "Mechanizing λ-Order Type Theory through Unification", Rep. CS73-13, Dept. of Applied Analysis and Comp. 4, 1972

[JK83]   J.Jouannaud, C.Kirchner, H.Kirchner: "Incremental Construction of Unification Algorithms in Equational Theories", Proc. Int. Colloq. on Automata, Languages and Programming, 1983

[JKK82]   J.Jounnaud, C.Kirchner, H.Kirchner: "Incremental Unification in Equational Theories", Université de Nancy, Informatique, 82-R-047, 1982

[Ka84]   M.Kay: "Functional Unification Grammars", Proc. of COLING, Stanford, 1984

[Ka85]   L.Karttunen: "Helsinki Unification Grammars", SRI-International and CSLI, 1985

[KB70]   D.E.Knuth, P.B.Bendix: "Simple Word Problems in Universal Algebras", in: Computational Problems in Abstract Algebra, J.Leech (ed), Pergamon Press, Oxford, 1970

[Ki85]   C.Kirchner: "Methodes et Outils de Conception Systématique d`Algorithmes d`Unification (thèse d`état), Univ. Nancy, 1985

[KK82]   D.Kapur, M.S.Krishnamoorthy, P.Narendran: "A New Linear Algorithm for Unification", General Electric, Rep. no. 82CRD-100, New York, 1982

[KM72]   Karp, Miller, Rosenberg: "Rapid Identification of Repeated Patterns in Strings, Trees and Arrays", ACM Symposium on Th. of Comp. 4, 1972

[KM74]   Knuth, Morris, Pratt: "Fast Pattern Matching in Strings", Stan-CS-74-440, Stanford University, Comp. Sci. Dept., 1974

[KM77]   S.Kühner, Ch.Mathis, P.Raulefs, J.Siekmann: "Unification of Idempotent Functions", Proceedings of 4th IJCAI, MIT, Cambridge, 1977

[Ko79]   R.Kowalsky: "Logic for Problem Solving", North Holland, 1979

[La79]   D.S.Lankford: "A Unification Algorithm for Abelian Group Theory", Rep. MTP-1, Louisiana Techn. Univ., 1979

[La80]   D.S.Lankford: "A New Complete FPA-Unification Algorithm", MIT-8, Louisiana Techn. Univ., 1980

[LB79]   D.S.Lankford, M.Ballantyne: "The Refutation Completeness of Blocked Permutative Narrowing and Resolution", 4th workshop on Autom. Deduction, Texas, 1979

[LBB84]   D.S.Lankford, G.Butler, B.Brady: "Abelian Group Unification Algorithms for Elementary Terms", Contemporary Mathematics, American Math. Soc., 1984

[Lc72]   C.L.Lucchesi: "The Undecidability of the Unification Problem for Third Order Languages", Rep. CSRR 2059, Dept. of Applied Analysis and Comp. Sci., Univ. of Waterloo, 1972

[Lo78]   D.Loveland: "Automated Theorem Proving", North Holland, 1978

[LS75]   M.Livesey, J.Siekmann: "Termination and Decidability Results for Stringunification", Univ. of Essex, Memo CSM-12, 1975

[LS76]   M.Livesey, J.Siekmann: "Unification of Sets and Multisets", Univ. Karlsruhe, Techn. Report, 1976

[LS79]   M.Livesey, J.Siekmann, P.Szabo, E.Unvericht: "Unification Problems for Combinations of Associativity, Commutativity, Distributivity and Idempotence Axioms", Proc. of Conf. on Autom. Deduction, Austin, Texas, 1979

[LS73]   G.Levi, F.Sirovich: "Pattern Matching and Goal-Directed Computation", Nota Interna B73-12, Univ. of Pisa, 1973

[Ma54]   A.A.Markov: "Trudy Mat. Inst. Steklov", no.42, Izdat. Akad. Nauk SSSR, 1954, NR17, 1038, 1954

[Ma70]   Y.Matiyasevich: "Diophantine Representation of Rec. Enumerable Predicates", Proc of the Scand. Logic Symp., North Holland, 1978

[Ma77]   G.S.Makanin: "The Problem of Solvability of Equations in a Free Semigroup". Soviet Acad Nauk SSSR, Tom 233, no.2, 1977

[MB68]   Manove, Bloom, Engelmann: "Rational Functions in MATHLAB", IFIP Conf. on Symb. Manipulation, Pisa, 1968

[Mi75]   M.Minsky: "A Framework for Representing Knowledge" in: P.Winston: "The Psychology of Computer Vision", McGraw Hill, 1975

[MM79]   A.Martelli, U.Montaneri: "An Efficient Unification Algorithm", University of Pisa, Techn. Report, 1979

[MN86]   U.Martin, T.Nipkow: "Unification in Boolean Rings", Proc. 8th Conf. on Autom. Deduction , Springer Lecture Notes, 1986

[Mo71]   J.Moses: "Symbolic Integration: The Stormy Decade", CACM 14, 8, 1971

[Mo74]   J.Moses: "MACSYMA - the fifth Year", Project MAC, MIT, Cambridge, 1974

[Mu83]   K.Mukai: "A Unification Algorithm for Infinite Trees", Report ICOT, 1983

[Mz86]   J.Mzali: "Matching with Distributivity", Proc. of 8th Conf. on Automated Deduction, Springer Lecture Notes, 1986

[Ne71]   A.Nevins: "A Human Oriented Logic for ATP", JACM 21, 1974 (first report 1971)

[Ng79]   W.Ng (ed): "Proc. Conf. Symbolic and Algebraic Computation", Springer Lecture Notes in Comp. Sci., 1979

[NO80]   G.Nelson, D.Oppen: "Fast Decision Procedures Based on Congruence Closure", JACM, 27, 2, 1980

[Pl72]   G.Plotkin: "Building in Equational Theories", Machine Intelligence, vol.7, 1972

[Pr60]   D.Prawitz: "An Improved Proof Procedure", Theoria 26, 1960

[PS81]   G.Peterson, M.Stickel: "Complete Sets of Reductions for Equational Theories with Complete Unification Algorithms", JACM, vol.28, no.2, 1981

[PW78]   M.Paterson, M.Wegman: "Linear Unification", J. of Comp. and Syst. Science, 16, 1968

[RD72]   Rulifson, Derksen, Waldinger: "QA4: A Procedural Calculus for Intuitive Reasoning", Stanford Univ., Nov. 1972

[Rl69]   J.Rastall: "Graph Family Matching", University of Edinburgh, MIP-R-62, 1969

[Ro67]   J.A.Robinson: "A Review on Automated Theorem Proving", Symp. Appl. Math., vol.19, 1-18, 1967

[Ro65]   J.A.Robinson: "A Machine Oriewnted Logic Based on the Resolution Principle", JACM 12, 1965

[Ro69]   J.A.Robinson: "Mechanizing Higher Order Logic", Machine Intelligence, vol.4, Edinburgh Univ. Press, 1969

[Ro71]   J.A.Robinson: "Computational Logic: The Unifiction Computation", Machine Intelligence, vol 6, 1971

[Ro85]   P.Robinson: "The SUM: An AI Coprocessor", Byte, vol.10, no.6, 1985

[RS78]   P.Raulefs, J.Siekmann: "Unification of Idempotent Functions", Universität Karlsruhe, Techn. Report, 1978

[RSS79]   P.Raulefs, J.Siekmann, P.Szabo, E.Unvericht: "A short Survey on the State of the Art in Matching and Unification Problems", SIGSAM Bulletin, 13, 1979

[RZ85]   R.Ramnarayan, G.Zimmermann: "PESA, A Parallel Architecture for OPS5 Production Systems", 19th Annual Hawaii International Conference on Systems Sciences, 1985

[Sz79]   P.Szabo: "Undecidability of the D_A-Unification Problems", Proc. of GWAI, 1979

[Sch86]   M.Schmidt-Schauss: "Unification under Associativity and Idempotence is of Type Nullary", J. of Automated Reasoning, to appear 1986

[Sch86]   M.Schmidt-Schauss: "Unification in Many-Sorted Equational Theories", Proc. of 8th Conf. on Autom. Deduction, Springer Lecture Notes Comp. Sci., 1986

[Sh76]   E.H.Shortliffe: "MYCIN: Computer Based Medical Consultations", North Holland Publ. Comp., 1976

[SH75]   B.C.Smith, C.Hewitt: "A Plasma Primer", MIT, AI-Lab., 1975

[Sh84]   R.Shostak: "Deciding Combinations of Theories", JACM, vol.31, no.1, 1984

[SH85]   G.Snelting, W.Henhapl: "Unification in Many Sorted Algebras as a Device for Incremental Semantic Analysis", Internal Report PU2R2/85, Techn. Univ. Darmstadt, FB Informatik, 1985

[Si75]   J.Siekmann: "Stringunification", Essex University, Memo CSM-7, 1975

[Si76]   J.Siekmann: "Unification of Commutative Terms", Univ. Karlsruhe, 1976

[Si78]   J.Siekmann: "Unification and Matching Problems", Ph.D., Essex Univ., Memo CSA-4-78

[SK84]   S.Shieber, L.Karttunen, F.Pereira: "Notes from the Unification Underground", SRI-International, TN327, 1984

[SK85]   S.Shieber, L.Karttunen, F.Pereira: "More Notes from the Unification Underground", SRI-International, TN361, 1985

[Sl72]   J.R.Slagle: "ATP with built-in Theories including Equality, Partial Ordering and Sets", JACM 19, 120-135, 1972

[Sl74]   J.R.Slagle: "ATP for Theories with Simplifiers, Commutativity and Associativity", JACM 21, 1974

[SO82]   J.Siekmann, P.Szabo: "Universal Unification and a Classification of Equational Theories", Proc. of Conf. on Autom. Deduction, 1982, New York, Springer Lecture Notes Comp. Sci., vol.87

[SS81]   J.Siekmann, P.Szabo: "Universal Unification and Regular ACFM Theories", Proc. IJCAI-81, Vancouver, 1981

[SS82]   J.Siekmann, P.Szabo: "A Notherian and Confluent Rewrite System for Idempotent Semigroups", Semigroup Forum, vol.25, 1982

[SS61]   D.Skordew, B.Sendow: "Z. Math. Grundlagen", Math.7 (1961), 289, MR 31, 57 (Russian) (English translation at Univ. of Esex, Comp. Sci. Dept.)

[St81]   M.Stickel: "A Unification Algorithm for Assoc. Commutative Functions", JACM, vol.28, no.3, 1981

[St74]   G.F.Steward: "An Algebraic Model for String Patterns", Univ. of Toronto, CSRG-39, 1974

[Su65]   E.Sussenguth: "A Graph-theoretical Algorithm for Matching Chemical Structures", J. Chem. Doc.5, 1, 1965

[SU78]   P.Szabo, E.Unvericht: "The Unification Problem for Distributive Terms", Univ. Karlsruhe, 1978

400   *J.H. Siekmann*

[Sz82]   P.Szabo: "Theory of First Order Unification" (in German, thesis) Univ.
            Karlsruhe, 1982

[Ta68]   A.Tarski: "Equational Logic and Equational Theories of Algebra", Schmidt et al
            (eds), Contributions to Mathematical Logic, North Holland, 1968

[Ta79]   W.Taylor: "Equational Logic", Houston J. of Math. , 5, 1979

[Te81]   H.Tennant: "Natural Language Processing", Petrocelli Books, 1981

[Ti84]   E.Tiden: "Unification in Combination of Collapse Free Theories with Disjoint Sets
            of Function Symbols", Proc. 8th Conf. on Autom. Deduction, Springer Lecture
            Notes on Comp. Sci., 1986

[Ul76]   J.R.Ullman: "An Algorithm for Subgraph Isomorphism", JACM, vol.23, no.1,
            1976

[Un64]   S.H.Unger: "GIT - Heuristic Program for Testing Pairs of Directed Line Graphs
            for Isomorphism", CACM, vol.7, no.1, 1964

[Va75]   J.van Vaalen: "An Extension of Unification to Substitutions with an Application
            to ATP", Proc. of 4th IJCAI, Tbilisi, USSR, 1975

[Vo78]   E.Vogel: "Unifikation von Morphismen", Diplomarbeit, Univ. Karlsruhré, 1978

[VZ75]   M.Venturini-Zilli: "Complexity of the Unification Algorithm for First Order
            Expression", Clacolo XII, Fasc IV, 1975

[Wa77]   D.H.D.Warren: "Implementing PROLOG", vol.1 and vol.2, D.A.I. Research
            Rep., no.39, Univ. of Edinburgh, 1977

[Wa84]   Ch.Walther: "Unification in Many Sorted Theories", Univ. Karlsruhe, 1984

[Wa86]   Ch.Walther: "A Classification of Many Sorted Unification Problems", Proc. of 8th
            Conf. on Automated Deduction, Springer Lecture Notes Comp. Sci., 1986

[WC76]   K.Wong, K.Chandra. "Bounds for the String Editing Problem", JACM vol.23,
            no.1, 1976

[We73]   P.Weiner: "Linear Pattern Matching Algorithms", IEEE Symp. on SW. and
            Automata Theory, 14, 1973

[Wi76]   van Wijngaarden (et al.): "Revised Rep. on the Algorithmic Language
            ALGOL68", Springer Verlag, Berlin, Heidelberg, N.Y., 1976

[Wn75]   Winston: "The Psychology of Computer Vision", McGraw Hill, 1975

[Wn72]   T.Winograd: "Understanding Natural Language", Edinburgh Univ. Press, 1972

[Wn83]   T.Winograd: "Language as a Cognitive Process", vol.1, Addison Wesley, 1983

[Wn76]   G.Winterstein: "Unification in Second Order Logic", Bericht 3, Univ.
            Kaiserslautern, 1976

[WR67]   L.Wos, G.A.Robinson, D.Carson, L.Shalla: "The Concept of Demodulation in
            Theorem Proving", JACM, vol.14, no.4, 1967
[WR73]   L.Wos, G.A.Robinson: "Maximal Models and Refutation Completeness:
            Semidecision Procedures in Automatic Theorem Proving", in: Word Problems
            (W.W.Boone, F.B. Cannonito, R.C.Lyndon, eds), North Holland, 1973
[Ye85]   K.Yelick: "A Generalized Approach to Equational Unification, MIT/ LCS/TR-344,
            1985

PART III

NATURAL LANGUAGE

Advances in Artificial Intelligence - II
B. Du Boulay, D. Hogg and L. Steels (Editors)
Elsevier Science Publishers B.V. (North-Holland), 1987

WEP (WORD EXPERT PARSING) REVISED AND APPLIED TO DUTCH (1).

GEERT ADRIAENS
DEPT OF LINGUISTICS
UNIVERSITY OF LEUVEN AND N.F.W.O.
BLIJDE-INKOMSTSTRAAT 21, B-3000 LEUVEN

1. Introduction

When the Word Expert Parser was first introduced (Small 1980) its view of parsing as a distributed word-based sense discrimination process made it an "enfant terrible" among the existing parsing systems. Though its ideas have since inspired the development of related word-based systems (see e.g. Hirst 1983, Cottrell & Small 1983) WEP itself was not developed any further. In the meantime, however, the rapidly growing shift of attention from syntax to lexicon in linguistics, psycho- and neurolinguistics, the emergence of interactive models of natural language understanding (NLU) in psycholinguistics and the neurosciences (Marslen-Wilson & Tyler 1980, Just & Carpenter 1980, Feldman & Ballard 1982), and the continued attempts to develop parallel NLU systems (partly inspired by the interactive models) in AI (see e.g. Pollack & Waltz 1985, Cottrell 1985) have revived interest in the model. Elsewhere the merits and flaws of the system as a model of human natural language processing have been discussed (Small & Lucas 1983, Adriaens & Small forthcoming), as well as the linguistic approach ("process linguistics") partly inspired by the model (Adriaens 1985 and forthcoming). In this paper I will briefly describe how WEP works, and discuss how it was revised and successfully applied to some challenging phenomena of the Dutch language.

2. WEP briefly described

2.1 General principles

Two observations that formed the point of departure for the development of WEP are 1) the highly idiosyncratic nature of linguistic elements, and 2) the belief that natural language understanding is a word-by-word, expectation-based, interactive process ("interactive" meaning that different knowledge sources are available at all times during comprehension and used efficiently whenever needed; cp. Marslen-Wilson & Tyler 1980, Just & Carpenter 1980). Most existing parsing systems seem to ignore the riches of individual words and the problem of selecting a contextually appropriate meaning, advocating instead an approach that captures generalities about language in syntactic and/or semantic rules, treating the words as tokens that simply participate in comprehension by virtue of their inclusion in these rules (cp. Rieger & Small 1981). The apparent incompatibility of the sense selection problem and the rule-based approaches led to a radically different model organization: instead of having a number of com-

---

(1) This research was made possible by an IBM grant allowing me to spend the summer of '85 at the University of Rochester New York; I am grateful to Steve Small who helped me understand and revise his program.

ponents (morphological, syntactic, semantic,...) consisting of
static rule structures spanning sentence constituents or complete
sentences, with some central interpreter taking care of the
application of these rules to the input, the words themselves are
considered as active agents (word-experts) triggering processes
that idiosyncratically control the whole parsing process. This
process involves continuous interaction of a word with a number of
knowledge sources in memory: the words in its immediate context,
the concepts processed so far or expected locally, knowledge of
the overall process state, of the discourse, and real-world
knowledge. These knowledge sources are not invoked uniformly by a
general interpreter, but are accessible at all times by the word-
expert processes throughout the overall process of sense discrimination in order to enable the experts to eventually agree on a
context-specific semantic interpretation of a fragment of text.
This overall parsing process makes crucial use of (word-based)
expectations and memory.

2.2 Representation and implementation

Informally, word-experts can be viewed as sense discrimination
networks consisting of nodes of context-probing questions and arcs
corresponding to the range cf possible answers; each of the leaves
of the network represents a specific contextual meaning of the
word in question reached after network traversal during sentence
processing. Formally, their declarative representation uses
graphs composed of designated subgraphs without cycles. Each sub-
graph consists of question and action nodes that are interpreted
procedurally during the WEP process: word-experts are coroutines
of which the subgraphs form subprocesses ("entry points"). When it
is executing, such a coroutine temporarily controls the whole
parsing process until it suspends itself (passing control to
another expert) or stops executing. The questions and actions constitute the formal representation language that makes WEP a working NLU system. The questions probe the multiple knowledge sources
mentioned in 2.1; the actions (taken depending on the answers to
the questions or taken independently) serve two functions. They
build and refine the concepts that will eventually form the output
structure of the WEP process, and they take care of the exchange
of information within the distributed environment: they allow
experts 1) to make concepts (e.g. an action (verb) concept)
and/or signals (e.g. about the process state) available for use by
other experts and 2) to wait for concepts and/or signals sent by
other experts. Awaiting and receiving information implies suspension of execution while waiting and resumption of execution upon
reception; this basic aspect of the distributed control is taken
care of by restart demons, data structures created automatically
by the WEP action AWAIT which specifies the nature of the awaited
information and the point at which to continue execution upon
arrival of the awaited data. It should be noted here that execution of the AWAIT action does not necessarily imply complete
suspension of a word-expert since the different entry points of an
expert are designed to be executed concurrently; as such, one part
of the process may temporarily be suspended, but other parts can
go on, even initiating other restart demons in turn (several outstanding AWAITs are possible). Yet, an expert cannot wait forever
for some piece of information as there is no certainty about
arrival; therefore, each restart demon is accompanied by a timeout
demon specifying both how long the expert is willing to wait for

the information it desires (2) and the point at which to continue
processing if the restart demon times out (see Small 1981 for a
full discussion of timeouts).

3. WEP revised and applied to Dutch

3.1 Introduction

For the application of WEP to Dutch the overall system implementation (the coroutine regime) did not require any changes at
all; on the contrary, as will be discussed below, it proved very
handy for parsing the numerous discontinuities of linguistic elements in Dutch. The changes that have been made pertain to morphology, syntax and semantics ; they involve the questions and
actions of the representation language and the way specific
linguistic phenomena are dealt with.

3.2 Morphology

In WEP (as in most NLU systems) a morphological segmentation
subprogram consisting of afffix-stripping rules is invoked at an
early stage of analysis (i.e. as soon as a word is read from the
input); the exact nature of the relationship between stem and
affixes is then determined by lexical interaction among them (i.e.
affixes are modelled as word-experts too). In the application to
English a side-effect of the morphological segmentation is that
the order of stem and suffix is reversed and execution happens in
that order for reasons of ease of analysis: when a suffix runs, it
can assume that the word to its right is its stem, which makes
interaction less complicated. Because of the cognitive implausi-
bility of this approach and additional problems with words containing prefixes (or pre- and suffixes) the order of execution of
stem and affixes is their order of occurrence in the application
to Dutch. In order to enable the experts to find out whether they
are part of a complex word or not (remember that each expert coordinates the parsing process in turn and independently) a new question was introduced in the representation language (QPARTOFWORD).
An expert can ask this question to the morphological analysis component whenever it needs to know whether it is part of a morphologically complex word or not. If it is, it can start interacting
with the next expert with the certainty that it belongs together
with it; if it is not, it leaves the next expert alone. This
allows for a more flexible and decentralized use of the morphological information.

A serious problem for the "segmentation first, interpretation
after" approach in morphological analysis is formed by multiply
segmentable words such as kwartslagen: it means "quarter beats" if
segmented as kwart+slagen and "quartz layers" if segmented as
kwarts+lagen. Correct segmentation is only possible by considering the context; yet, in WEP the words are the only active

---

(2) The units of measurement for timeouts are based on certain
model events, including (a) the number of syntactic groups created
(by the specific WEP actions taking care of this), (b) the number
of words read, (c) the number of sentence breaks encountered, and
(d) the termination of particular word-experts.

processes, and no interaction between the morphological analysis
subprocess on the one hand and the context on the other ("over the
heads of the experts") is possible. Thus, the segmentation process
cannot decide which experts will have to be initialized. The only
possibility left is to have kwartslagen as a word in its own right
in the dictionary; the process associated with it can then easily
disambiguate the word through interaction with the context.
     The main disadvantage of fully listing words is the enormous
duplication of (processual) information in the lexicon; trying to
avoid this implies the necessity of closely examining the internal
structure of the lexicon (grouping together words that are morphologically related and trying to have them share information).
Since WEP does not (yet) have a fully developed semantic network
relating words phonologically, morphologically and semantically,
little can be done about the organization of such a network now.
However, the problems with words like kwartslagen, taken together
with the many idiosyncrasies of derivational morphology and the
sometimes unnecessarily complicated interactions between stem and
affixes suggest the following non-uniform treatment of morphology
in the further development of WEP. The segmentation-rule component can be removed, and all morphemes (words and affixes) are
"listed", be it in different ways. Stems and affixes trigger their
processes as they do now; in cases where lexical interaction can
handle the relationship between stem and affixes of complex words
(disambiguating multiple possibilities if necessary), these words
are listed with their component parts (i.e. morphology is present
in the lexicon); these parts are executed in the order they occur
in (i.e. no separate process is needed for a complex word of this
kind). However, in cases where segmentation is problematic, or
where lexical interaction between stem and affixes may look like
"processual overkill", the words are listed without internal morphemic marking, and they have their own process associated with
them. Which words are to be listed without morphemic marking and
which with marking is a matter of further application of WEP to a
larger subset of Dutch (and also of results of research in psycholinguistics dealing with on-line morphological analysis).

3.3 Syntax and semantics

3.3.1 Introduction

     Some English example sentences the Word Expert Parser can
analyze correctly (i.e. lexically disambiguate and assign a semantic concept structure) are:

The man eating peaches throws out a pit.
The man eating tiger growls.
The man eating spaghetti growls.
The deep philosopher throws a peach pit in the deep pit.
The man has thrown in the towel.
The case was thrown out by federal court.

     From these examples it will be clear that WEP does not handle a
wide variety of syntactic structures for English. All the sentences are of the NP(Subject)-VP-(NP) (PP) variety; no questions,
imperatives or declaratives starting with a PP are analyzed. The

most interesting syntactic phenomenon that WEP can handle nicely
are passive sentences, in which the lexical encoding of processual
information in the -ed morpheme and the interaction of this morpheme with the rest of the verb group leads to correct interpretation of the sentence (see Small 1980 or Adriaens forthcoming for a
more detailed description). Thus, the challenge was to try to
enhance the scope of syntactic structures parsed without giving up
the view of language analysis as a lexically-based decentralized
process: can the words themselves take care of the correct
analysis of declaratives (with or without inversion, see 3.3.2),
questions and imperatives without the imposition of "extraneous"
rules ? In 3.3.2 we will see that the semantic notion of dynamic
caseframes can easily deal with varied syntactic structures.

Beside the scope of syntactic structures, the problem of
discontinuous lexical sequences (common in Dutch with its "pincers
construction", see 3.3.3) has received extra attention; in 3.3.3 I
will show that specific cases of discontinuous sequences can
easily be dealt with in a highly interactive, context-bound,
expectation-based system like WEP.

Finally, in 3.3.4 I will go into the relationship between concepts and lexical sequences (constituents), suggesting that the
latter can be shown to "fall out" of the way the former are processed.

3.3.2 Dynamic caseframes

As was to be expected, in a lexically-based system it is the
verb that is responsible for overall sentence understanding.
Dynamic caseframes are a processual encoding of the attempt of a
verb to "catch" concepts processed before it (if any) and to be
processed after it into possible frames (though "frame" is not
such a good term here, since it suggests a fixed structure). As an
example I take the verb eten ("to eat"); Figure I below shows what
happens when the verb enters the comprehension process. For easy
understanding it is rendered in an informal way; to make it more
concrete I give the possible ordering of constituents in simple
sentences in Dutch (they are referred to by number in Figure I):

1) De man eet een appel.   (declarative without inversion)
   (The man eats an apple)
2) 's Morgens eet de man een appel. (declarative with inversion)
   (In the morning the man eats an apple)
3) Eet de man een appel ?   (yes-no-question)
   (Does the man eat an apple ?)
4) Waarom eet de man een appel ?   (question-word-question)
   (Why does the man eat an apple ?)
5) Eet een appel !   (imperative)
   (Eat an apple)

i) if   no concepts have yet been processed ((3) and (5))
    then refine sentence structure as question or imperative
    else if   the concept is an interrogative word (group) ((4))
         then refine sentence structure as question
         else refine sentence structure as declarative

ii) try to find a concept of type entity in active memory
    (viz. an animate entity) that can fill the agent role

    if   found ((1))
    then a) refine sentence structure as declarative without inversion
         b) try to find a concept of type entity in active memory
            that can fit the object role (viz. something edible)

            if   found
            then refine sentence structure as imperative ((5))
                 unless it was refined as declarative with inversion earlier ((2))
            else wait for such a concept

                 if   it arrives then OK
                 else (if it does not arrive before the end of the sentence) refine
                      eten as having an implicit object (e.g. "De man eet")

    else (i.e. agent not found ((2) (3) (4) (5)) wait for a possible agent

         - if   agent arrives in time ((2) (3) (4))
           then refine sentence structure as decarative-with-inversion
                unless it was refined as a question earlier (which it remains then)
         - goto b) above

Figure I. Dynamic caseframe process of a verb.

Some interesting linguistic aspects of this approach (3) are:

1) It is semantic in nature: the search triggered by the verb
   looks for semantically specified agents, objects or complements. Note that syntactic structure specification falls out
   of discrete points in the semantic search process. It can of
   course not be denied that observation of linguistic structure
   (sentence types and their frequencies) has influenced the ordering of the search (i.e. an agent is looked for first), but
   these structures do not guide the search process; on the contrary, they can be retrieved as a side-effect of the process.

2) Related to 1): dynamic caseframes do not assume structurally
   fixed positions (as put down in rules, for instance) for the
   different cases revolving around the verb; the verb is seen as
   an active "case catcher" that finds its cases at specific
   points in the process (i.e. time-bound processes dominate over
   space-bound structures). This also implies that verbs -- when
   present -- are considered as the most important process-
   triggering lexical elements in understanding.

_____
(3) Note that no new actions or questions were needed to implement dynamic caseframes ; the memory probing questions and
await actions of WEP proved powerful enough to do this.

3) Note also that posssible different caseframes are related to each other; for <u>eten</u> the transitive frame and the implicit-object frame are related through the expectation for the object: if it does not arrive it time, the implicit-object frame is automatically chosen; the application of the latter frame depends on the failure of application of the former.

4) Expectations play a central role in dynamic caseframes: the whole process is one of either catching concepts in memory or else waiting for them. As we will see in 3.3.4, for preposi- tional or noun phrase processing, expectations also play a cru- cial role; the scope differences between the verb expectations and those involved in the processing of these phrases will be discussed in that subsection.

A remark is in order about passive sentences. In Dutch the verb <u>worden</u> is the auxiliary of the passive; it uses a (different) dynamic caseframe for the analysis of passives: instead of waiting for an agent first, it looks/waits for an "object-or-affected" first, and then for a possible by-agent ("door-bepaling"). The "object-or-affected" expectation is a consequence of the ambiguity of <u>worden</u>. In "De appel wordt door de man opgegeten" (The apple is eaten by the man), "de appel" is finally refined as object after lexical interaction between <u>wordt</u> and <u>opgegeten</u> ; in "Een appel wordt rood in de zomer" (An apple turns red in summer), on the contrary, "een appel" is refined as affected. The latter refinement is a matter of waiting (by <u>word-</u>, the verb stem word- expert) for the signal *predicative* which (in "Een appel wordt rood etc.") will be sent by <u>rood</u> when it finds out in context that it is used predicatively and not attributively; when <u>word-</u> catches this signal, it refines "een appel" as affected.

3.3.3 <u>Discontinuous constituents</u>

Sentences 1) and 2) contain examples of discontinuous consti- tuents (the parts belonging together are underlined):

1) De appel <u>wordt</u> op maandag door Hilde <u>opgegeten</u>.
   (The apple is eaten by Hilde on Monday)

2) Geert <u>belt</u> Hilde op maandag <u>op</u>.
   (Geert calls up Hilde on Monday)

1) contains a discontinuous verb group and 2) a discontinuous compound verb (<u>opbellen</u>, "to call (up)"). The occurrence of these discontinuous constituents is an essential characteristic of Dutch; it has been dubbed the "pincers construction" (<u>tangconstructie</u>) because the discontinuous elements are like the sharp edges of a pair of pincers holding other constituents in between them. Discontinuous linguistic elements offer serious problems for linguistic theories that deal with syntax through context-free rules; thus, a parsing system based on these theories or on context-free rules in general needs extra machinery to interpret

sentences like 1) or 2) correctly. In Small 1980 and 1983 it is claimed that WEP should have no trouble analyzing those sentences because of its powerful wait-and-see mechanism and its stress on contextual interaction; the Dutch pincers construction was an ideal testcase to see if these claims were correct. It proved very easy indeed to deal with discontinuous constituents by having the words of such a sequence interact through the sending and awaiting/receiving of signals. For the verb opbellen ("to call up"), for instance, bel- (the stem) contains an entry that waits for a possible *particle* signal from a particle, and op sends this signal when it has found out in the course of its process that it is not a preposition but a particle; a new action (ADDLEX) added to the WEP representation language takes care of bringing together discontinuous elements in one lexical sequence in the final WEP output structure.

The discontinuity of verb groups is handled in the same way: a potential auxiliary (such as wordt in "De appel wordt door Hilde opgegeten") waits for a signal form a verbal element (viz. a past participle) arriving later in the comprehension process. This participle figures out in the context whether it is used as an adjective or not. In the latter case, it sends the signal *complete-action* (meaning that a verbal element was found in context), the auxiliary catches this signal, and both parts of the group pair up nicely; in the former case no such signal is sent and the expectation of the potential auxiliary times out.

A final remark about syntactic discontinuities: beside the fairly simple cases of split constituents discussed here and handled easily by WEP, one could consider "filler-gap sentences" (long-distance dependencies) like "Who <=filler> do you think I saw <gap> ?" or "He wondered who <=filler> his sister had been seeing <gap>" as complex cases of syntactic discontinuities. Though no attempts have yet been made to make WEP analyze such sentences, I believe that the wait-and-see strategy and the signal/concept communication of WEP can handle these cases without great difficulties. An analysis of "Wie denkt hij dat je gezien heb ?" ("Who does he think you have seen ?") in WEP would not be a matter of trying to fill gaps (a spatial or structural view of the phenomenon) but of the dynamic caseframes of the verbs trying to catch concepts in memory at specific points in the process. The dynamic frame of denk- could be written in such a way that it does not immediately assume that a potential agent concept processed earlier (viz. "Wie") is its agent, but that it checks the concept following it first; if this is also an agent candidate (as in the example, hij), Wie will be left uninterpreted by the denk- expert. When ge- and zie- run later on and zie- tries to bind a concept into the object role, Wie is still available and is correctly caught by it. This interpretation process is a matter of concepts being rejected for certain roles and remaining available for others; as such, in the sentence "Wie denkt hij dat je gezien hebt ?" Wie is not seen as a constituent "moved" from a position further down in the sentence, but as a concept left uninterpreted by the denk- caseframe running before the zie- caseframe. In structural terms this means that "...denkt hij dat..." is seen as an interposed clause even though it is the main clause syntactically; I believe that "Wie heb je gezien ?" is the more important part of the requested information. Now, if we consider this last question as a sentence in its own right with a specific word order (no "movement" of constituents whatsoever), all that happens in the sentence "Wie denkt hij dat je gezien hebt ?" is the enlargement of the distance between "Wie" and "gezien hebt" (in spatial terms) or the temporary uninterpretability of "Wie" (in temporal terms), as reflected in the suggested parsing by WEP.

3.3.4 Lexical groups and concepts

In WEP the processing of (semantic) concepts and of (syntactic) constituents (lexical sequences) goes hand in hand, with the former dominating the latter. CREATEC/BUILDC, REFINEC and REPORT/STOREC are the concept building actions; OPENG, DECLAREG and CLOSEG build lexical groups; LINK and ADDLEX (see 3.3.3) take care of the incorporation of a lexical sequence into a concept. An interesting feature of an interactive process model like WEP is that lexical sequence building and concept building are considered as asynchronous activities: the former happens in a strict left-to-right order (i.e. the words are put in a lexical sequence as they enter the comprehension process), whereas the latter is a matter of interactions among experts (interactions whose nature is not always predictable, i.e. the order of execution of the experts is not fixed; correct semantic interpretation of "a very good boy", for instance, implies the following sequence of expert execution: a - very - good - very - boy - good - a).

In Small 1980 little importance is attached to the lexical sequences "corresponding to" the concepts, which receive the correct refinements by the words contributing to them without these words necessarily showing up in the LEXICAL slot that is part of the structure of the concepts. The most important function of the lexical groups is their use as units of measurement for the restart demons at the heart of the coroutine regime (see 2.2); as such, they are indispensable.

During the development of the Dutch experts, I was in two minds about the sequences. On the one hand, the OPENG, DECLAREG and CLOSEG actions proved a nuisance when writing experts: it is not always clear where to put them in the expert process, the more so as they have no function in the main WEP process of sense discrimination. Moreover, leaving out the DECLAREG and CLOSEG actions altogether and retaining only the OPENG action to make sure the word-group counter is set correctly (for the restart demons) led to no problems for the analysis process. On the other hand, however, the cinderella treatment of lexical sequences is linguistically unsatisfactory. One would expect a prepositional phrase to have its preposition included in the LEXICAL slot of the concept it contributes to or at least that a preposition starts a new lexical sequence since its function as constituent boundary cannot be ignored (in the application to English, prepositions are not included in the lexical sequence of PPs, nor do they start a new lexical sequence). Thus, two opposite revisions of the system suggested themselves: one, try to do away with lexical sequence building altogether and two, try to introduce more lexical sequencing than in the original system. Both revisions have been designed, and the second one has been implemented as well; I will discuss them both, starting with the second.

In the original WEP system there could only be one "active"

lexical sequence at any point in the process, which made it impossible to have sequences within other sequences. For a prepositional phrase like "in the morning" this means that if <u>in</u> is made
to start a prepositional phrase sequence, and then <u>the</u> starts a
noun phrase sequence, the PP sequence is lost The following
changes made it possible to have several active sequences:

1) the introduction of a special data structure, a "chartlike
   stack".

2) the convention that a word that starts a lexical sequence (with
   OPENG) also closes the sequence it started (with CLOSEG).

   Whereas a "pure" stack only allows access of its top element, a
chartlike stack allows simultaneous access of all its elements.
For the stack of lexical sequences in the making, this means that
a new input word is added to <u>all</u> active lexical sequences simultaneously when it triggers the DECLAREG action. The second change
was needed to make sure that all sequences pushed on the stack
would eventually be popped: if a word <u>ending</u> more than one active
sequence were to have a CLOSEG action in it, it would be unclear
which sequence or sequences to remove from the stack. Note also
that the second change makes lexical sequencing more dependent on
concept building. As I said above, lexical sequencing normally
happens in a strict left-to-right order, whereas concept building
is a matter of moving to and fro between experts (interaction);
with the convention in 2) the strict left-to-right order for lexical sequencing is given up since the <u>first</u> word of the sequence
closes it and not the last. That the first word can do this is a
consequence of the feedback of a concept (e.g. created by a noun)
to the words waiting for it (e.g. an article and/or a preposition)
during semantic processing. An additional advantage of the convention in 2) is that it is easier to put the OPENG and CLOSEG
actions in the right place: if a word has an OPENG action, it must
also have a CLOSEG action.
   A question that arises from this approach to lexical sequences
is how they relate to their possible concept counterparts: do all
the sequences correspond to concepts ? if so, do all these concepts have to be included in the output structure ? (In the
course of the execution of the word-experts in "van de erg lekkere
appels" ("of the very tasty apples"), for instance, three
sequences one can ask this question about are built: "erg lekkere", "de erg lekkere appels", "van de erg lekkere appels".) I
will not answer this question in a definitive way here, but only
point out that the creation of lexical sequences is non-committal
as far as concept building is concerned: if no LINK action is
taken by some expert, a sequence will be removed from the stack
without incorporation into a concept. Concept building still dominates lexical sequencing, but the revision suggested here offers
a more powerful mechanism for the user of the WEP system.
   The other possible revision of lexical sequencing is an attempt
at doing away with it altogether. As I mentioned earlier, the
fact that semantic understanding does not seem to need the
sequences suggests that they are at least less important and possibly even derivable from the semantic comprehension process. Note
that in the first revision discussed, the sequences were already

made more dependent on the interaction process, with CLOSEG being done by the word-expert awaiting a concept upon arrival of this concept. And indeed, a closer look at the AWAIT actions taken by the word-experts shows that lexical sequences (constituents) can be retrieved as a side-effect of the treatment of these AWAITs by the WEP process. Figure II shows this for the lexical sequence "de erg lekkere rode appel" ("the very tasty red apple"). In this second revision I assume a minimum of lexical sequences, with the example being only one sequence. In Figure II the stress is on the AWAIT actions taken by the words and the resolution of these AWAITs when concepts are created and reported. The point is that no lexical sequence is started as long as there are AWAITs on the small stack representing part of the WEP process state; a word starts a lexical sequence only when the AWAIT stack is empty, which means that lexical sequences are derived from an important aspect (expectations) of the semantic comprehension process.

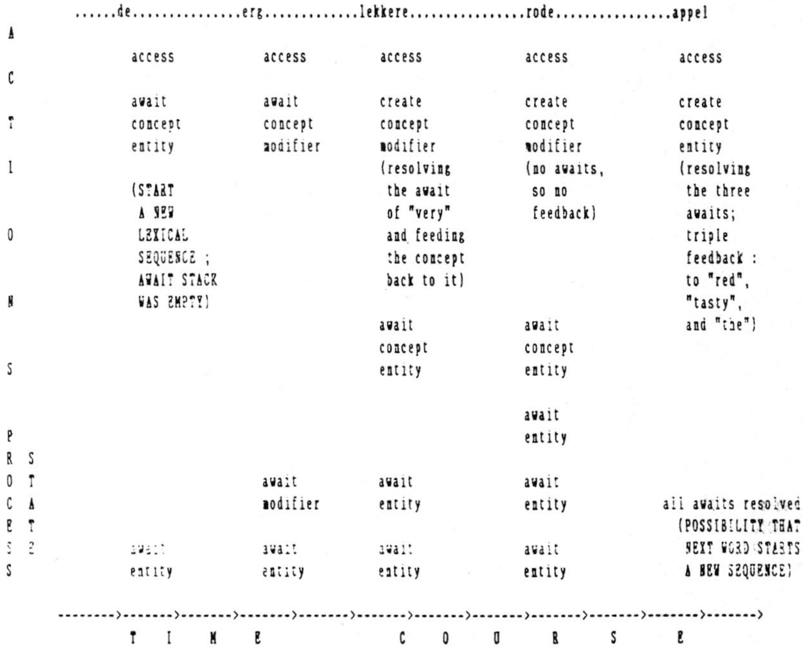

```
        ......de...............erg..............lekkere................rode................appel
A
          access         access         access          access         access
C
          await          await          create          create         create
T         concept        concept        concept         concept        concept
          entity         modifier        modifier         modifier        entity
I                                       (resolving      (no awaits,     (resolving
                          (START        the await       so no          the three
                          A NEW         of "very"       feedback)      awaits;
O                         LEXICAL       and feeding                    triple
                          SEQUENCE ;    the concept                    feedback :
                          AWAIT STACK   back to it)                    to "red",
N                         WAS EMPTY)                                   "tasty",
                                        await           await          and "the")
                                        concept         concept
                                        entity          entity
S
                                                        await
P                                                       entity
R  S
O  T                      await         await           await
C  A                      modifier      entity          entity         all awaits resolved
E  T                                                                   (POSSIBILITY THAT
S  2      await           await         await           await          NEXT WORD STARTS
S         entity          entity        entity          entity         A NEW SEQUENCE)

        -------->------->------->------->------->------->------->------->------->------->------->
              T   I   M   E              C   O   U   R   S   E
```

Figure II. Noun phrase processing through expectations.

A couple of remarks about Figure II are in order. The first question that may have arisen is what the difference is between the AWAITs used by the verb in dynamic caseframes (see 3.3.2) and the AWAITs used in concept processing here. The two types of AWAIT have a different scope: expectations attached to determiners, prepositions or adverbs are local, whereas those projected by

verbs are global. Verbs wait for completely pre-processed concepts, whereas determiners etc. take care of this pre-processing
through local expectation resolution (see Adriaens forthcoming for
a more detailed discussion of expectation types and their constraints). Another question is of course: what if one assumes that
there are more lexical sequences ? Do the sequences still "fall
out" of the local AWAITs ? The answer is yes, provided the local
AWAITs for concepts of specific types are kept separate. In the
example, this would mean that de starts a sequence (no AWAITs for
concepts of type entity) and erg starts one (no AWAITs for concepts of type modifier), with "erg lekkere" being a sequence
within the "de erg lekkere rode appel" sequence. Note that the
problem of how many sequences to have arises again (is "erg lekkere" a sequence by virtue of the presence of "erg" ? if not, why
is "rode" not a one-word sequence ?). A more serious problem is
that the typing of the AWAITs does not distinguish between prepositional phrases and noun phrases: both prepositions and determiners wait for the same entity concept, which would not allow an
NP sequence within a PP (the "await entity" stack is not empty
when the determiner starts executing). An easy solution would be
to change the type of a concept waited for by a preposition, but
this would mean that for the sequences "in summer" and "the summer" "summer" is a different concept depending on whether in
awaits it or the; the combination of the words certainly gives
rise to a different concept, but it would be "cheating" to put
information that can only be obtained by interaction in the expectations beforehand. Another solution would be to reduce the importance of the AWAITs as determiners of the lexical sequences and
simply have certain words start them unconditionally. The advantage of this approach is that it is in accord with the proven
psychological reality of constituent boundaries in psycholinguis-
tic research (see Fodor et al. 1974).

4. Conclusion and future research

     In this paper I have described how a lexically-based natural
language analysis system works (for English) and how it has been
revised in an application to Dutch; several issues pertaining to
linguistic and parsing matters have been discussed: morphology,
dynamic caseframes, discontinuous constituents and lexical groups
versus concepts. Some issues for future research are listed below
(others occurred in the course of the discussion); most of them
pertain to aspects of one general question, viz. "How far can
lexical-contextual interaction go ?"

1) Through corpus research it should be possible to find out how
   much left and right context is needed in order for specific
   words to be understandable (disambiguatable); especially the
   words considered to be global sentence modifiers (such as
   negating elements) are worth looking at: can WEP interaction
   correctly interpret words that seem to need the complete sentence they occur in as context ? Useful tools for this kind of
   research are the QUERY and PARSPAT programs developed at the
   University of Amsterdam for linguistic research with precoded
   corpora.

2) As far as the right context is concerned: as yet, WEP does not analyze postmodifying phrases (e.g. relative clauses or postmodifying prepositional phrases). The question here is how the use of lookahead (viz. having an expert run only for the purpose of helping its left neighbours in the understanding process) can be restrained so as not to create too much "noise" in the interaction processes (cp. 3.2). Postmodifiers will also put more strain on the interaction with concepts reported to the active memory.

3) Of course, the implementation of more words is a research issue that will help the further development of the representation language and that will further show the strong and weak sides of the system. Experts under development are die ("that/who"; relative and demonstrative pronoun), het ("the" (article) or "it" (pronoun)), niet ("not"), and en ("and").

4) Finally, two issues relating to the computational aspects of the system are worth mentioning. WEP now runs in Franz Lisp on a VAX750 at the computer science department of Leuven; an attempt will be made to develop a Prolog version of the system. At the same time, research will be conducted into the possible implementation of the parallellism that is part of the WEP design (the concurrent executability of subprocesses ("entry points") of one expert and/or of two or more experts); though this is a hard problem to deal with due to the complexity of interactions of the experts (symbol-passing) and the sequential ordering of discrimination networks, a closer examination of the experts implemented may show that parts of their process (possibly across the entry points as defined now) are independent of one another and thus executable in parallel.

All in all, it looks like the Word Expert Parser still offers a lot of interesting research possibilities for the fields of linguistics and artificial intelligence.

REFERENCES
ADRIAENS, G. (1985) - Process linguistics: missing link between linguistics, psychology and artificial intelligence (AI) ? University of Rochester Cognitive Science TR-28.
id. (1986) - WEP revised and applied to Dutch. In Leuvense Bijdragen 75(1). (long version of this short paper).
id. (forthcoming) - Process linguistics: the theory and practice of a cognitive science approach to natural language. University of Leuven dissertation.
id. & S.L. SMALL (forthcoming) - Word Expert Parsing: lexical ambiguity resolution and its implications for cognitive science. To appear in Small, Cottrell & Tanenhaus (eds) "Lexical Ambiguity Resolution in Human Language Understanding".
COTTRELL, G.W. (1985) - A Connectionist Approach to Word Sense Disambiguation. University of Rochester Computer Science PhD (TR-154). Rochester, NY.
id. & S.L. SMALL (1983) - A Connectionist Scheme for Modelling Word Sense Disambiguation. In Cognition and Brain Theory 6(1), 89-120.

FELDMAN, J.A. & D.H. BALLARD (1982) - Connectionist Models and
    Their Properties. In Cognitive Science 6, 205-254.
FODOR, J.A. et al. (1974) - The Psychology of Language. An
    Introduction to Psycholinguistics and Generative Grammar.
    McGraw-Hill, New York.
HIRST, G. (1983) - A Foundation for Semantic Interpretation. In
    Proceedings ACL 21 (Cambridge, Mass), 64-73.
JUST, M.A. & P.A. CARPENTER (1980) - A Theory of Reading: From
    Eye Fixations to Comprehension. In Psycholinguistic Review
    87(4), 329-354.
KING, M. (ed) (1983) - Parsing Natural Language. Academic Press,
    London.
MARSLEN-WILSON, W.D. & L.K. TYLER (1980) - The Temporal
    Structure of Spoken Language Understanding. In Cognition 8,
    1-71.
POLLACK, J. & D. WALTZ (1985) - Massively parallel parsing: A
    strongly interactive model of natural language interpreta-
    tion. In Cognitive Science 9, 51-74.
RIEGER, C.J. & S.L. SMALL (1981) - Toward a Theory of Distri-
    buted Word Expert Natural Language Parsing. In IEEE Transac-
    tions on Systems, Man, and Cybernetics 11(1), 43-51.
SMALL, S.L. (1980) - Word Expert Parsing: A Theory of Distri-
    buted Word-Based Natural Language Understanding. Computer
    Science Technical Report Series. University of Maryland PhD.
id.   (1981) - Demon timeouts: limiting the life span of
    spontaneous computations in cognitive models. In Proceedings
    3rd Annual Conference of the Cognitive Science Society,
    Berkeley CA 1981.
id.   (1983) - Parsing as Cooperative Distributed Infer-
    ence: Understanding through Memory Interactions. Chapter 12
    in King 1983, 247-276.
SMALL, S.L. & M.M. LUCAS (1983) - Word Expert Parsing: A Com-
    puter Model of Sentence Comprehension. University of Roches-
    ter Cognitive Science TR-1.

Advances in Artificial Intelligence - II
B. Du Boulay, D. Hogg and L. Steels (Editors)
© Elsevier Science Publishers B.V. (North-Holland), 1987

A GENERALIZED WORD EXPERT MODEL OF LEXICALLY DISTRIBUTED TEXT PARSING[*]

Udo Hahn

Universitaet Konstanz
Informationswissenschaft
Postfach 5560
D-7750 Konstanz 1, F.R.G.

Abstract

Adequate computational models for text analysis must account for textuality on
the level of text cohesion and text coherence, i.e. for local texture and
global well-formedness, by text grammars on a semantic basis. Considering the
requirements of corresponding text parsing devices a distributed lexical text
grammar is suggested in the format of word experts. The generalizations
proposed concern linguistic generality and methodological requirements of the
formal specification of word expert parsers. The approach is illustrated by an
informal account of word experts applying to nominal anaphora and lexical
cohesion phenomena. Repeated application of corresponding cohesion devices
yields regular text coherence structures in a frame knowledge base in terms of
basic patterns of thematic progression.

1. Introduction

This paper gives an outline of a word expert approach to text parsing. In
order to provide adequate representation structures for unrestricted expository
texts (journal and magazine articles, research papers, etc.) a lexically distributed text grammar has been developed which takes into consideration

* the conceptual structure of the underlying domain of discourse and corresponding constraints derived from a formally specified knowledge representation model [REIMER/HAHN 1985] (semantic restrictions applying to the
  internal frame structure, conceptual relations among frames, integrity rules
  guiding the slot filling processes, etc.)
* structural restrictions imposed by the text model of expository prose in
  terms of text cohesion and text coherence properties

These constraints have been incorporated into a model of lexically distributed
text parsing which considerably generalizes the standard word expert model as
described in RIEGER/SMALL 1979 or SMALL/RIEGER 1982.

In this paper, the discussion of text cohesion phenomena concentrates on
anaphoric and lexical cohesion properties of texts. These phenomena refer
directly to features common to many knowledge representation models:

* the specialization hierarchy of concepts for the purpose of anaphora resolution;

---

* This work is currently supported by BMFT/GID under contract 1020016 0. The
paper has benefited greatly from the stimulating support provided by U.
Reimer and the suggestions made by D. Soergel.

* the aggregation relations of concepts with respect to lexical cohesion among
  them

Repeated application of these text cohesion devices yields textual connectivity
on a macro level of text representations. Again, the exposition is restricted
to a major type of text coherence - basic patterns of thematic progression (cf.
DANES 1974) which are characterized by constant theme, linear thematization of
rhemes, and derived themes. These types of thematic progression typically
occur in written discourse (texts), and thus supplement the coherence relations
which have been studied with respect to conversational dialogues (cf. REICHMAN
1978, HOBBS 1983).

Text parsing is here considered as a semantic process where text knowledge is
directly represented in a frame knowledge base without considering intermediate
linguistic representations. As a consequence, disregarding textual structures
of either type during text analysis inevitably results in invalid (text cohesion) and understructured (text coherence) text representations which might
then be characterized as mere sentence level accumulations of (partially
illegal) knowledge structures. Therefore, there should be no question that
specially tuned text grammars are needed. Unfortunately, the overwhelming
majority of grammar specifications currently available is unable to provide
broad coverage of textual phenomena on the level of text cohesion and
coherence, so that the format of text grammars and corresponding parsing
devices is still far from being settled.

2. Motivating the Need for a Lexically Distributed Text Grammar

Since major linguistic processes provide textual cohesion by immediate
reference to conceptual structures of the world knowledge, and since even many
of the text coherence relations can be attributed to these semantic sources, a
semantic approach to text parsing has been adopted which primarily incorporates
the conceptual constraints inherent to the domain of discourse as well as
structural properties of the text class considered (for an opposite view of
text parsing, primarily based on syntactic considerations, cf. POLANYI/SCHA
1984). The result of a text parse are knowledge structures in terms of the
frame representation model, i.e. valid extensions of the semantic representation of the applicational domain in terms of text-specific knowledge.

Text parsing, although crucially depending on semantic knowledge, demands that
additional knowledge sources (focus indications, parsing memory, etc.) be
accessible without delay. This can best be achieved by highly modularized
grammatical processes (actors) which take over/give up control and communicate
among each other as well as with other knowledge sources depending on a
data-driven control schema. Since the semantic foundation of text understanding is most evidently reflected by the interaction of the sense(s) of the
various lexical items that make up a text, these modular elements themselves
provide the most natural point of departure to propose a lexical distribution
of grammatical knowledge when deciding on the linguistic organization of a
semantic text grammar (ALTERMAN 1985 argues in a similar vein).

Lexically oriented modeling efforts in the area of natural language parsing are
quite in agreement with current theoretical developments intended to lessen the
importance of syntactic specifications in favor of the lexical component of
grammars. The growing tendency of lexicalization of grammatical knowledge
reaches from moving complete rule components to the lexicon, i.e. distributing
that knowledge over corresponding lexical entries and elaborating complex lexical insertion criteria with respect to phrase structure trees (as in the case
of lexical functional grammar [KAPLAN/BRESNAN 1982]), or schematizing lexical
co-occurrence patterns (as in case grammars and case frame parsers [HAYES
1984]). The dominant role of lexical specifications is even more apparent in
semantic parsers [RIESBECK 1975, GERSHMAN 1982] while a lot of cognitive
evidence for lexically based text processing comes from human text understanding experiments and corresponding computer simulations [THIBADEAU et al. 1982].

However, semantic approaches to natural language parsing have serious deficiencies with respect to methodological, linguistic, and architectural considerations. There is no common description format agreed upon, dealing satisfactorily with linguistic generalizations presents problems, and the issue of clearly separating linguistic and domain-specific knowledge is far from being settled. Thus, we emphasize the development of a semantic text parsing model that exhibits appropriate theoretical generality.

3. An Outline of a Generalized Word Expert Model

The major revision of the generalized word expert model as compared to the original one (cf. SMALL 1980) concerns linguistic generalization: We do not assign a specific word expert to each individual word, but instead assign generalized word experts to a fairly restricted subset of the words which will occur in a text.

Selection of a suitable subset is currently guided by the intended depth of text understanding. The performance of TOPIC [HAHN/REIMER 1986], the text understanding system into which the word expert parser has been integrated, currently focuses on the production of indicative abstracts, and thus only provides the information of what the original text basically is about. This kind of information is carried predominantly in domain-specific keywords as designators of contents (cf. SMETACEK/KOENIGOVA 1977 for the task-domain of abstracting) – in linguistic terminology: nominals or nominal groups. Accordingly, TOPIC's parsing system is essentially based on a noun phrase grammar adapted to the requirements of text phenomena so that its shallow text parsing performance can be attributed to the exhaustive recognition of all relevant keywords and the semantic and thematic relationships holding among them.

Thus, word experts have been designed which reflect the specific role of nominals in the process of making up connected text. The following section illustrates this idea through a discussion of word experts for anaphoric and lexical cohesion processes. Both processes provide for a continuous cohesion stream and a corresponding thematic development in (expository) texts. Exceptions to this basic rule are due to special linguistic markers in terms of quantifiers, connectors, etc. As a consequence, supplementary word experts have to be provided which reflect the influence these markers have on the basic text cohesion and text coherence processes in texts: experts applying to quantifiers and comparative expressions typically block simple text cohesion processes, experts for conjunctions trigger them, and experts referring to negation particles provide appropriately modified assignments of properties to frames.

This kind of selective parsing is based on strategic considerations which, however, do not affect the linguistic generality of the approach at all. On the contrary, due to the high degree of modularization inherent to word expert specifications a corresponding grammar can easily be extended to incrementally cover more and more linguistic phenomena. Moreover, the partial specifications of grammatical knowledge in the format of word experts leads to a highly robust parsing system, while full-fledged text grammars accounting for the whole range of propositional and pragmatic implications of a comprehensive understanding of texts are simply not available (even in sublanguage domains). In other words, current text analysis systems must cope with linguistic descriptions that will reveal specification lags in the course of text analysis if ´realistic texts´ [RIESBECK 1982] are being processed. Therefore, the text parser carries the burden of recovering even in cases of severe under-specification of lexical, grammatical, and pragmatic knowledge. Unlike question-answering systems, this problem cannot be side-stepped by asking a user to rephrase unparsable input, since the input to text understanding systems is entirely fixed. Distributing knowledge over various interacting knowledge sources, then, allows easy recovery mechanisms since the agents which are executable take over the initiative while those lacking of appropriate information shut down.

Summing up, each of the word expert specifications supplied (those for nominals, quantifiers, conjunctions, etc.) is not bound to a particular lexical item and its idiosyncrasies, but reflects functionally regular linguistic processes (anaphora, lexical cohesion, coordination, etc.). Accordingly, a relatively small number of general grammatical descriptions encapsulated in highly modularized communities of agents form the declarative base of lexically distributed text parsing (cf. SMALL 1980 for a word expert model that definitely focuses on linguistic particularities and, by and large, neglects linguistic generalizations).

Parsing methodology, on the other hand, clearly demands description mechanisms which should provide clean specification tools, be natural to use, and flexible enough to capture all relevant empirical generalizations. Based on a reformulation of the generalized word expert model in terms of a graph grammar, the corresponding meta grammar states which word expert structures are valid ones and which are not. At the same time, the basic vocabulary is clearly fixed according to which query expressions, messages, and readings can be formed (similar to the word expert Sense Discrimination Language described in SMALL/RIEGER 1982). Among the graph structures derivable is an interesting subset constituted by intermediate subgraphs which factor out structural properties common to many word experts (similar to higher-order constituents of standard linguistic phrase structure grammars). These mechanisms, altogether, assign a great deal of internal structure to word experts which has been lacking so far. On the other hand, the high degree of generalization which characterizes the semantic definitions of the basic vocabulary makes the current word expert specifications independent of specific knowledge representation models and thus provides a clear separation of world knowledge and linguistic knowledge.

4. More Details on the Generalized Word Expert Model – the Declarative Structure of Word Experts

By word experts (consider the word expert prototypes provided in sec.5) we refer to a declarative organization of linguistic knowledge in terms of a decision net whose root is assigned the name of a lexical class or a specific word. Appropriate occurrences of lexical items in the text prompt the execution of corresponding word experts. Non-terminal nodes of a word expert's decision net are constructed of boolean expressions of query predicates or messages while its terminal nodes are composed of readings. With respect to non-terminal nodes word experts

- query the frame knowledge base, e.g. testing for semantic relations to hold (is-a, instance-of, is-slot, etc.), for the existence of concepts in the knowledge base, or for integrity criteria that restrict the assignment of slot values
- investigate the current state of text analysis in a working memory called cotext, e.g. the types of operations already performed in the knowledge base (activation, slot value assignment, creation of new concepts, etc.)
- consider the immediate textual environment, e.g. testing co-occurrences of lexical items under qualified conditions: within sentence or noun phrase boundaries etc.
- have message sending facilities in order to force direct communication among the active experts, e.g. for blocking, canceling, or re-starting companion experts

According to the path actually taken in the decision net of a word expert, readings are worked out which either demand various actions to be performed on the knowledge base in order to keep it valid in terms of text cohesion (incrementing/decrementing activation weights of concepts, assignment of slot values, creation of new frames as specializations of already existing ones, etc.), or which indicate functional coherence relations (e.g. contrast, classificatory relations, not considered here) and demand overlaying the knowledge base by the corresponding textual macro structure. Apparently, the basic constructs of the generalized word expert model (query predicates, messages, and readings) do not refer to any particular domain of discourse. This guarantees a high degree of transportability of a corresponding word expert grammar.

The word expert collection currently comprises about 15 word expert prototypes, i.e. word experts for lexical classes, like frames, quantifiers, negation particles, etc. Word expert modules encapsulating knowledge common to different word experts amount to 20 items. The word expert system is implemented in C and running under UNIX. Grammatical knowledge is represented using the high-level word expert specification language outlines above, and it is inserted and modified using an interactive graphical word expert editor.

5. Informal Specification of Word Experts Accounting for Nominal Anaphora and Lexical Cohesion - a Sample Parse

For illustration purposes the following section gives a sketchy specification of word experts (for a more formal specification, cf. HAHN/REIMER 1985) accounting for two major phenomena of the textual analysis of nominal expressions - the case of nominal anaphora which refers to the specialization hierarchy of concepts and lexical cohesion which is mainly due to associations between a frame, its slots and slot values. Consider the following example

{01} ... der PC-1985 wird mit Tastatur, Bildschirm sowie einem Matrixdrucker guter Qualitaet angeboten. Darueber hinaus verfuegt dieser Rechner ueber eine Vielzahl von Textverarbeitungsprogrammen, die auch von PC Inc. entwickelt worden sind ....

[... the PC-1985 is offered with a keyboard, a display, and a matrix printer of good quality. In addition, the machine has a number of text processing packages which have also been developed by PC Inc. ...]

Fig 3 shows a sample parse of {01} which gives an impression of the way text parsing is realized by word experts incorporating the linguistic phenomena just mentioned (the procedural premises inherent in the word expert text parser are dealt with more detailed in HAHN/REIMER 1985). Its results are based on the specification of a word expert which handles nominal anaphora (given in Fig 2a), while Fig 2b provides a word expert for lexical cohesion. The structure of the word experts, particularly the one pertaining to lexical cohesion, is extremely simplified (for a more detailed account cf. HAHN 1986).

With respect to the following parse a fragment of the underlying domain of discourse is introduced below. Synonyms are enclosed in round brackets, slots have angular brackets while permitted slot values can be specified two-fold. Either implicitly by means of integrity constraints inherent in the frame representation model (cf. REIMER/HAHN 1985) in which cases any subordinate frame and instance frame related to a slot is included (as an example, consider the slot <peripheral devices> of ´computer´ to which can be assigned ´keyboard´, ´display´, and ´matrix printer´ as actual slot values). Or permitted slot values can be explicitly specified by special symbolic or numerical value ranges, as illustrated, e.g. by the corresponding <price> slot whose lower and upper bound of actual slot values is indicated in square brackets.

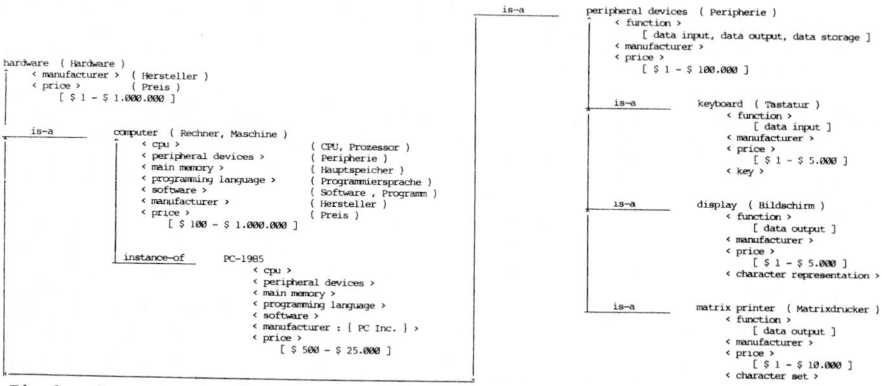

Fig 1: Frame Representation Fragment of the Underlying Domain of Discourse

With respect to text summarization (cf. HAHN/REIMER 1984) it is an important point to determine the part of the world knowledge actually considered in a text as well as its conceptual foci. These considerations lead to a functionally motivated extension of the frame representation model in that each conceptual item (frame, slot, and slot value) was assigned an activation counter. Each occurrence of a corresponding knowledge base item in the text then causes the incrementation of its activation weight (this default activation process is denoted DA in Fig_3). In order to guarantee valid activation values their assignment must be independent from linguistic interferences. As an example for a process which causes illegal activation values consider the case of nominal anaphora. They are a stylistic means to refer to the same concept through different designations; a rather specific concept introduced at the beginning of a text is referred to by more general terms in the remainder of the text. The expert for nominal anaphora mirrors exactly these regularities; cf. Fig_2a and Fig_3 with respect to the anaphoric process between [19] and [10.1] (cf. HIRST 1981 for other solutions to that problem incorporating pronominal anaphora). The shift of activation weights among the frames involved is the reading worked out by the corresponding word expert and readjusts the validity of the activation values in the knowledge base.

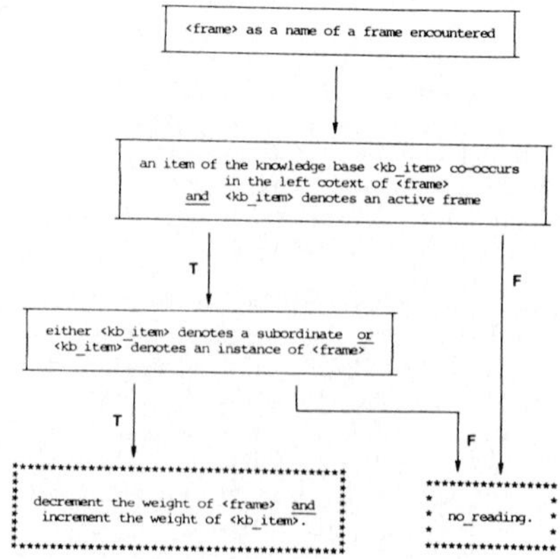

Fig 2a: Word Expert for Nominal Anaphora (= NA)

Next, lexical cohesion phenomena are considered. If these processes were not taken into account, various concepts would be activated properly although the immediate conceptual closeness (associativity) were not represented at all. To prevent the knowledge base from this kind of bias a word expert has to be devised which provides for the recognition of the conceptual aggregation relations (is-slot, is-actual-slot-value, is-permitted-slot-value, parts) which may hold among adjacent lexical items in a text; cf. Fig 2b and Fig 3 with respect to the lexical cohesion processes between [05/02], [07/05.1], [10/07.1], [24/19.1], [29/24.1], and [29.2/29.1] (cf. ROSENBERG 1980 for an alternative approach to frame-based analysis of lexical cohesion).

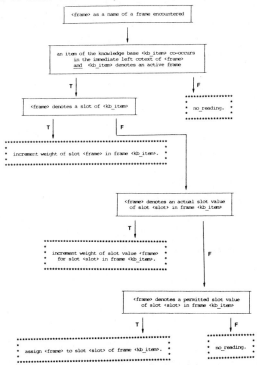

Fig 2b: Word Expert for Lexical Cohesion (= LC)

The sample parse with respect to text fragment {01} given in Fig 3 includes all actions taken with respect to nominal anaphora resolution and lexical cohesion recognition according to the specifications given in Fig 2a/b:

[02]	PC-1985	DA: 'PC-1985': Ø ---> 1
[05]	Tastatur (keyboard)	DA: 'keyboard': Ø ---> 1
[05.1]		LC: PC-1985 < peripheral devices : { keyboard } >
[07]	Bildschirm (display)	DA: 'display': Ø ---> 1
[07.1]		LC: PC-1985 < peripheral devices : { display } >
[10]	Matrixdrucker (matrix printer)	DA: 'matrix printer': Ø ---> 1
[10.1]		LC: PC-1985 < peripheral devices : { matrix printer } >
[19]	Rechner (computer)	DA: 'computer': Ø ---> 1
[19.1]		NA: 'computer': 1 ---> Ø, 'PC-1985': 1 ---> 2
[24]	Textverarbeitungsprogramm	en (text processing package)
		DA: 'text processing package': Ø ---> 1
[24.1]		LC: PC-1985 < software : { text processing package } >
[29]	PC_Inc.	DA: 'PC_Inc.': Ø ---> 1
[29.1]		LC: text processing package-Ø1 < manufacturer : { PC_Inc. } >
[29.2]		LC: PC-1985 < software : { text processing package-Ø1 } >

Fig 3: Sample Parse of Text Fragment {01} Applying the Experts LC and NA

424 U. Hahn

6. Deriving Common Text Coherence Patterns from Repeated Application of Text Cohesion Readings

The application of the word experts pertaining to frames guarantees the development of activation patterns and characteristic configurations of property assignment in the knowledge base which reflect quite regular patterns of thematic progression. Thus, viewed from the more global point of text coherence three basic modes of thematic progression in (expository) texts (cf. DANES 1974) can be distinguished in text knowledge bases:

Fig 4: Basic Patterns of Text Coherence in a Text Knowledge Bases

Taking, as an example, the parse from Fig 3 we get the following text coherence pattern for text {01}:

Fig 5: Sample Text Coherence Patterns of Text Fragment {01}

7. Conclusions

Starting from the assumption that text analysis demands particular methodological devices in order to account for textuality on the local level of text cohesion and the more global level of text coherence, an outline of a distributed lexical text grammar/parser based on the format of word experts has been given. As examples, nominal anaphora and lexical cohesion were considered as significant text cohesion phenomena. Repeated application of corresponding linguistic means produces a kind of texture which is directly reflected in the text representation structures resulting from the text parse and correspond to regular modes of thematic progression. In this way, the conceptual structures of the underlying domain of discourse and the text model based on recurrent cohesion and coherence features in expository texts highly constrains the operation of the word expert text parser.

Beside further experimental validation of the word expert approach to text parsing, three issues are of major importance to the future work:
* first of all, the further elaboration of the linguistic coverage of those forms of text cohesion phenomena actually relevant for the analysis of semantic and thematic relations of nominal structures in texts
* the consideration of additional forms of text coherence (coherence relations, cf. HOBBS 1983, REICHMAN 1978, ALTERMAN 1985)
* beside the purpose to extend the empirical scope equal attention is given to the development of a concise formal description of the distributed text grammar combining the actor model of computation and formal graph grammar specifications

REFERENCES

Alterman, R. [1985]: A Dictionary Based on Concept Coherence. In: Art. Intell. 25. 1985, pp.153–186.

Danes, F. [1974]: Functional Sentence Perspective and the Organization of the Text. In: F. Danes (ed): Papers on Functional Sentence Perspective. Prague: Academia, 1974, pp.106–128.

Gershman, A.V. [1982]: A Framework for Conceptual Analyzers. In: W.G. Lehnert / M.H. Ringle (eds): Strategies for Natural Language Processing. Hillsdale/NJ: L. Erlbaum, 1982, pp.177–197.

Hahn, U. [1986]: On Lexically Distributed Text Parsing: A Computational Model for the Analysis of Textuality on the Level of Text Cohesion and Text Coherence. In: F. Kiefer (ed): Linking in Text. Dordrecht: D. Reidel, 1986.

Hahn, U. / U. Reimer [1984]: Computing Text Constituency: An Algorithmic Approach to the Generation of Text Graphs. In: C.J. van Rijsbergen (ed): Research and Development in Information Retrieval. Cambridge: Cambridge U.P., 1984, pp.343–368.

Hahn, U. / U. Reimer [1985]: The TOPIC Project: Text–Oriented Procedures for Information Management and Condensation of Expository Texts. Final Report. Konstanz: Univ. Konstanz, Informationswissenschaft, May 1985, 155pp. (= Bericht TOPIC-17/85)

Hahn, U. / U. Reimer [1986]: TOPIC Essentials. In: Proc. COLING 86. ACL 1986.

Hayes, P.J. [1984]: Entity–Oriented Parsing. In: Proc. COLING 84. ACL 1984, pp.212–217.

Hirst, G. [1981]: Discourse–Oriented Anaphora Resolution in Natural Language Understanding: a Review. In: Amer. J. Comput. Linguistics 7. 1981, pp.85–98.

Hobbs, J.R. [1983]: Why is Discourse Coherent? In: F. Neubauer (ed): Coherence in Natural-Language Texts. Hamburg: H. Buske, 1983, pp.29–70.

Kaplan, R.M. / J. Bresnan [1982]: Lexical-Functional Grammar: A Formal System for Grammatical Representation. In: J. Bresnan (ed): The Mental Representation of Grammatical Relations. Cambridge/MA: MIT P., 1982, pp.173–281.

Polanyi, L. / R. Scha [1984]: A Syntactic Approach to Discourse Semantics. In: Proc. COLING 84. ACL 1984, pp.413–419.

Reichman, R. [1978]: Conversational Coherency. In: Cog. Sc. 2. 1978, pp.283–327.

Reimer, U. / U. Hahn [1985]: On Formal Semantic Properties of a Frame Data Model. In: Comput. & Art. Intell. 4. 1985, pp.335–351.

Rieger, C. / S. Small [1979]: Word Expert Parsing. In: Proc. IJCAI-79, pp.723–728.

Riesbeck, C.K. [1975]: Conceptual Analysis. In: R.C. Schank: Conceptual Information Processing. Amsterdam: North-Holland, 1975 (1984), pp.83–156

Riesbeck, C.K. [1982]: Realistic Language Comprehension. In: W.G. Lehnert / M.H. Ringle (eds): Strategies for Natural Language Processing. Hillsdale/NJ: L. Erlbaum, 1982, pp.37–54.

Rosenberg, S.T. [1980]: Frame-Based Text Processing. In: D. Metzing (ed): Frame Conceptions and Text Understanding. Berlin etc.: W. de Gruyter, 1980, pp.96–119.

Small, S. [1980]: Word Expert Parsing: a Theory of Distributed Word-Based Natural Language Understanding. College Park/Maryland: Dept. of Computer Science, Univ. of Maryland, Sept. 1980.

Small, S. / C. Rieger [1982]: Parsing and Comprehending with Word Experts (a Theory and its Realization). In: W.G. Lehnert / M.H. Ringle (eds): Strategies for Natural Language Processing. Hillsdale/NJ: L. Erlbaum, 1982, pp.89–147.

Smetacek, V. / M. Koenigova [1977]: Vnimani odborneho textu: experiment [The perception of specialized texts: an experiment]. Ceskoslovenska Informatika 19. 1977, No2., pp.40–46.

Thibadeau, R. / M.A. Just / P.A. Carpenter [1982]: A model of the time course and content of reading. In: Cog. Sc. 6. 1982, pp.157–203.

Advances in Artificial Intelligence - II
B. Du Boulay, D. Hogg and L. Steels (Editors)
© Elsevier Science Publishers B.V. (North-Holland), 1987

427

The KING Natural Language Generator [1]

Paul S. Jacobs

Knowledge-Based Systems Branch
General Electric Corporate Research and Development
Schenectady, NY 12301 USA

Abstract

The development of natural language interfaces to Artificial Intelligence systems is dependent on the representation of knowledge, particularly of the knowledge which relates linguistic and conceptual structures. The *Ace* framework applies knowledge representation fundamentals to the task of encoding knowledge about language. Within this framework, linguistic and conceptual knowledge are organized into hierarchies, and *structured associations* are used to join knowledge structures that are metaphorically or referentially related. These structured associations permit specialized linguistic knowledge to derive partially from more abstract knowledge, facilitating the use of abstractions in generating specialized phrases.

A natural language generator called *KING* (Knowledge INtensive Generator) has been implemented to apply the basic knowledge representation framework of Ace to the task of producing utterances. The design of KING allows for a simple, knowledge-intensive and incremental mechanism to be used to perform the generation task and promotes the extensibility and adaptability of the generation system.

1 Introduction

The Ace knowledge representation [10] was designed to alleviate knowledge representation problems that limit the extensibility and adaptability of language processing systems. The idea behind Ace was to construct a uniform knowledge network in which relationships among linguistic and conceptual structures alike are explicitly represented in the form of *structured associations*. Knowledge representation fundamentals such as those implemented in a number of systems [2,15,3,4] are supplemented in Ace by *explicit referential knowledge*, that is, knowledge that associates language and meaning.

The processes of language analysis and generation may both be modeled as mappings between linguistic and conceptual structures within this framework. The first Ace prototype is described in [10], and the design of the knowledge representation and generator are extensively covered in [8]. This paper outlines the process by which Ace knowledge is applied to the generation task. The processing framework described here is fundamental to the design of KING (Knowledge INtensive Generator), a system built to produce natural language output from a conceptual representation using a knowledge base in the Ace form.

In the spirit of PHRED[9], KING is meant to share a declarative knowledge base with a language analyzer, and to produce linguistic output in real time. KING is also geared toward facilitating the utilization of new knowledge, to make adaptation and extension easier. While the problems with PHRED and other generation systems are primarily issues in knowledge representation, the design of the mechanism that organizes and applies the knowledge is an important consideration. Two important goals for such a mechanism are that it be *knowledge-intensive* and *incremental*. The knowledge-intensive aspect of a generator is important because knowledge is easier to adapt than program. Incrementality is an asset because it helps to make the knowledge of the system more versatile, taking advantage of modularity of knowledge representation. The process described here, and realized in KING, utilizes an incremental, knowledge-intensive means of exploiting the power of the

---
[1] This paper is based on the thesis research conducted while the author was at the University of California, Berkeley. The research was supported in part by the Office of Naval Research under contract N00014-80-C-0732, the National Science Foundation under grants IST-8007045 and IST-8208602, and the Defense Advanced Research Projects Agency (DOD), ARPA Order No. 3041, Monitored by the Naval Electronic Systems Command under contract N00039-82-C-0235.

Ace representation.

2   Ace

Ace makes use of a notation in which there are two types of entities: *objects* and *structured associations*.[2] A structured association is a relation among two or more objects which also relates corresponding objects associated with the related objects. Structured associations with ROLE-PLAYs are the basic mechanism for organizing knowledge in Ace. The most common structured associations in Ace, taken from the KODIAK representation [3], are the *DOMINATE*, or "D", relation, which associates a subcategory with its parent category, and the MANIFEST or "m" relation, which associates a category with an *aspectual* or role. Two other structured associations, called VIEW and REF, are used to join structures that may be used in describing one another. REF links a linguistic structure to its meaning, and VIEW links conceptual structures that are metaphorically or referentially related. VIEWs, inspired by work such as [14,2], are used represent metaphorical and analogical relationships [12,6]. Examples are the VIEW between *transfer-event* and *action*, as expressed in "John gave Mary a hug", and the relationship between *selling* and the concept of a *commercial-transaction* [5], as expressed in "John sold Mary a book". These examples, in particular the knowledge used by KING to build the dative verb phrases, will be considered in detail here. For clarification, the reader is urged to consult [10,8,16].

We classify *commercial-transaction* as a *complex-event*, composed of at least two simpler events, *ct-merchandise-transfer* and *ct-tender-transfer*. Each of these two sub-events is a kind of *transfer-event*, and is thus used to associate roles of the *commercial-transaction* with roles of *transfer-event*. This knowledge is captured in figure 1: The *merchant* receives the *tender* from the *customer*, and the *customer* receives the *merchandise* from the merchant.

The *commercial-transaction* event is generally described using the verbs "buy", "sell", and "pay". "Sell" and "pay" behave similarly to the verb "give"; "buy", behaves more like "take". For example, "John sold Mary a book", and "Mary paid five dollars for the book" both use the dative form, and "John bought the book from Mary" exhibits a structure identical to "John took the book from Mary". The representation of the concepts *buying* and *selling* in Ace relates these concepts to *giving* and *taking* so that knowledge about expressing *giving* and *taking* may be used also for *buying* and *selling*. This is accomplished by having a hierarchy of VIEW associations, as shown in figure 2.

The representation in figure 2 demonstrates on a small scale how the hierarchical arrangement of VIEWs is used in the encoding of structured associations. Structured associations such as *view1* between *transfer-event* and *giving* DOMINATE other more specific relations, such as *view3*, between *ct-merchandise-transfer* and *selling*. Note that this makes the explicit representation of ROLE-PLAY relations for *view3* unnecessary, as the relationship between *merchant* and *seller* in *view3* is specified by the relationship between *source* and *giver* in *view1*.

The representation of the *selling* concept is a simple example of how Ace encodes abstractions that may be used in language processing. The abstraction here is the relationship between a general category *giving* and a general category *transfer-event*. There are two ways in which this abstraction may be used: (1) A more specific association may be represented as a subcategory of the abstract association. This is the case in the *selling* example presented here. In this case, knowledge about the abstract association may be used in applying the specific association, thus knowledge about expressing an abstract concept may be used in expressing a more specific concept. This allows much of the same knowledge to be used for phrases involving "giving" and "selling". (2) A concept that is associated by another VIEW with the abstract concept may then also be expressed using the abstract VIEW. This is the case with expressions such as "give a punch", which takes advantage of the abstract

---

[2]This term, and the idea of using general structured associations as a language processing tool, are due to Wilensky.

[3]These associations, as well as many of the ideas here, have evolved during a series of seminars among the Berkeley Artificial Intelligence Research group, led by Robert Wilensky. Other participants in these discussions were: Richard Alterman, Margaret Butler, David Chin, Charley Cox, Marc Luria, Anthony Maida, James Martin, James Mayfield, Peter Norvig, Lisa Rau, and Nigel Ward.

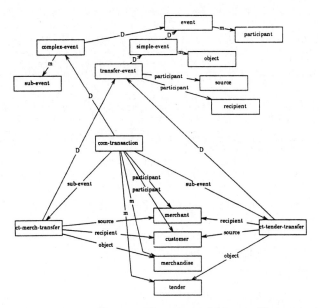

Figure 1: The *commercial-transaction* event

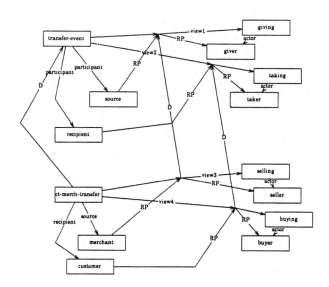

Figure 2: The hierarchy of VIEWs

action as transfer-event view in combination with the *transfer-event as giving* VIEW. The processing aspects of both of these cases will be discussed in section 3.

Linguistic knowledge in Ace is organized into a hierarchy of linguistic *patterns* and *relations*[8]. Patterns represent syntactic orderings, and relations represent linguistic structures that may be realized in a variety of patterns. The knowledge essential for realizing linguistic structures that describe concepts such as *commercial-transaction* is contained in the correspondence between linguistic relations and conceptual entities. The principal tool for representing these correspondences is a structured association called *REF*. REF links linguistic relations to conceptual relations within the Ace hierarchy. An example of this type of association is presented in figure 3: The dative verb phrase is composed of a verb part *dvp-verb* followed by two noun phrases, the first of which is linked to the verb by *ivp-pattern.* The verb part and noun phrase in the *ivp-pattern* pattern belong to the *verb-indir-relation*, which associates with the indirect object the concept of *recipient.*

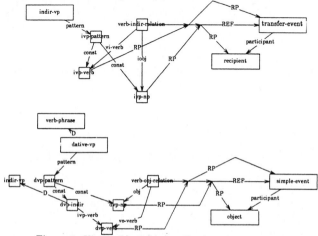

Figure 3: Knowledge linking verb phrases to events

The structured association between the *verb-obj-relation* and the *simple-event* concept in the lower diagram of Figure 3 links the object of the verb in the dative verb phrase to the object of the simple event. In this association, as in the association of the *verb-indir-relation* with the *transfer-event*, the verb part *dvp-verb* is associated via ROLE-PLAY with the event itself, rather than with any aspectual of the event.

Like the pattern-concept pair [9] or the unification grammar template [11,1], REF is a means of associating linguistic structure with conceptual structure. The template, however, is replaced with an explicit structural link in the knowledge network. This makes it easier to perform the knowledge-driven aspects of generation because no querying or complex matching is necessary. The use of the REF association also facilitates incremental generation by encoding knowledge about referential relationships as structured associations at various levels in the Ace hierarchy. [4]

This section has presented the principal knowledge representation tools used by the KING generator. The next section describes the process of constructing an utterance and shows how Ace knowledge is applied in producing phrases such as "sold Mary a book" and "gave Mary a kiss".

---

[4] Those familiar with KL-ONE and other similar representation languages will observe that the Ace representation tends to avoid matching by assuming that the concept being generated from is assigned to a specific category. Thus some of the work done by template matching in systems such as PHRED is done during the classification of a concept in Ace.

3   The Generation Process

The process of constructing an utterance in KING may be broken down into three basic phases:[5] *Mapping* is the process of retrieving and applying structured associations that relate the concept to be expressed to other conceptual structures and ultimately to linguistic structures. *Pattern selection* is the task of accessing templates specifying linguistic patterns from the knowledge base of the system, and of selecting the pattern that best fits the input constraints and the structures derived from mapping. *Restriction* consists of applying a set of constraints to a selected pattern, thereby producing a pattern whose constituents are further specified using the constraints that have led to the selection of the pattern.

For example, consider the problem of producing a sentence such as "John sold Mary a book". The input to KING in this case is the conceptual representation of a particular *commercial-transaction* event. The mapping process results in the application of structured associations between *commercial-transaction* and *ct-merchandise-transfer* and between *ct-merchandise-transfer* and the *buying* or *selling* action, and identifies linguistic relations needed to express these concepts in a surface structure. These relations, obtained from REF associations with concepts DOMINATing *ct-merchandise-transfer* and *selling*, including *verb-indir-relation* and *verb-obj-relation*. Pattern selection results in the choice of a basic sentence pattern and a dative verb phrase, *i. e.*, the means for combining these relations in a sentence. Restriction results in the insertion of aspectuals of these relations in the appropriate places in the surface structure. For example, the use of a *dvp-pattern* to realize the *verb-indir-relation* results in the restriction that the first noun phrase of the pattern be filled by the indirect object.

Figure 4 shows the input to KING for the generation of the sentence "John gave Mary a hug", discussed in [10].

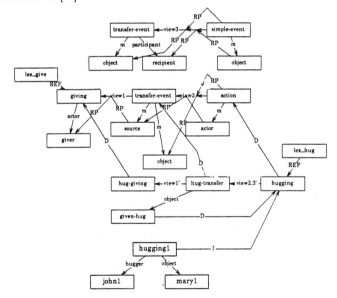

Figure 4: Input to KING for "John gave Mary a hug"

The sections that follow give an overview of each of the three phases of the generation process, referring to the representation in figure 4 and to the *commercial-transaction* example given earlier. Further implementation details are presented in [8].

---

[5]For various reasons, the process described as *concretion* in [10] is referred to here as *restriction*, and the *instantiation* process is not considered.

3.1   Mapping

The mapping phase of KING utilizes structured associations to produce new instances of knowledge structures from instances of other knowledge structures. In generation, this process can produce a variety of new structures from a conceptual input; for example, a new conceptual structure, a lexical category, a linguistic relation, or a linguistic constraint. These are derived by traversing different types of structured associations. New conceptual structures may be produced by utilizing DOMINATE, MANIFEST, and VIEW associations. New linguistic structures are generally produced from REF associations.

In the *commercial-transaction* example, the input concept may be mapped into *ct-merchandise-transfer* and *selling* using MANIFEST and VIEW associations. This use of an aspectual of the complex *commercial-transaction* event to describe the event is due to the lack of any direct means of referring to the *commercial-transaction*. REF associations are used to map into linguistic structures, including relations, constraints, and lexical categories. Linguistic relations, such as the *verb-obj-relation* and *verb-indir-relation* described earlier, are instantiated by mapping across REF structured associations.

When a VIEW association is applied in KING, the result is an instantiation of a new concept. The mapping process continues from the new concept, thereby initiating an indirect reference to the original concept. When a REF association is applied, the result is an instantiation of a linguistic structure. In this case, KING continues to attempt to apply REF associations from the same concept and then passes control to the pattern selection mechanism. No further VIEWs are used unless the process of building a linguistic pattern fails at this point. The mapping process thus applies VIEWs only until it reaches a point where it has derived enough referential knowledge for the building of the required pattern.

The discussion below considers the selection of associations in KING's mapping phase.

3.1.1   Choosing Structured Associations

Given the instantiation of a concept and its aspectuals, a new concept is instantiated using the ROLE-PLAYs of the structured association to determine the fillers of the new aspectuals. To select these associations, KING employs a strategy that replicates many of the heuristics embedded in other generation programs. This strategy may be summarized by the following principles:

* *Principle 1. Favor "horizontal" associations over other associations.*
  The explicit referential associations recognized by KING are VIEW and REF. I refer to these as "horizontal" associations. Typically, these are explored before more "vertical" associations such as DOMINATE and MANIFEST. This is similar to the "choose the most specific match" rule obeyed by BABEL [7] and PHRED: "Sell" is generally favored over "give" for a *selling* concept because it is associated with *selling* via a REF, while "give" may only be reached by first following a DOMINATE link to *giving*.
* *Principle 2. Favor "upward" associations over other vertical associations.*
  DOMINATE is an "upward" association. This principle means that in producing language one derives linguistic constructs using supercategories of the concept to be expressed, rather than attributes of the concept to be expressed. Thus indirect reference by supercategory is generally favored over reference by component.
* *Principle 3. Favor associations that yield linguistically appropriate structures.*
  The generator prefers associations that produce linguistic structures, but it is also biased towards those that produce linguistic structures that are likely to be useful. REF associations are favored over all other structured associations, provided that the linguistic structures that they produce are usable. For example, actions are often referred to using verb phrases, but in some contexts they produce nouns or modifiers. The generator should then be biased towards the appropriate structure. The phrases "John's selling the book", "John sold the book", and "the selling of the book by John", may all result from the same conceptual structure but depend on the linguistic constraints that propagate from linguistic structures already selected.

The first two principles illustrate some of the processing aspects of the interaction of specialized and generalized knowledge in KING. The idea of *preemption*, favoring specialized knowledge over more general knowledge, is behind the first principle. Because structured associations in Ace may inherit their structure from more abstract associations, this specialized knowledge may depend on more general knowledge, but it may also override or *preempt* more general knowledge. The second principle specifies that where there is no specialized knowledge about referring to a particular concept, it is acceptable to apply knowledge about a more general concept. This principle would apply, for example, in referring to the *ct-tender-transfer* concept: The verb "pay" refers to a concept that DOMINATEs *ct-tender-transfer*, as "paying" is associated with the concept with paying for anything, while *ct-tender-transfer* as used here designates an event performed in exchange for *merchandise*.

The third principle keeps the process of applying maps from producing structures that will not be useful in constructing the required phrase. This applies mainly to structured associations that yield linguistic relations. The use of these relations may be subject to a variety of constraints. For example, the *verb-obj-relation* and *verb-indir-relation* relations may be realized only in *verb-phrase* constructs; if some other construct is being produced it is necessary to refer to recipient and conceptual *object* using other relations, as in "the sale of the book to Mary". This principle has the following corollary:

- *Corollary A. Avoid redundant and semantically inconsistent expressions.* Structured associations may not be applied that involve more than one concept in the same role or involve the same concept in multiple roles. For example, "John kissed Mary's cheek" realizes the role of Mary's cheek as a conceptual *object*, but if "Mary" has been used in that role the generator finds another relation to express the cheek's role, as in "John kissed Mary *on the cheek*." This corollary also avoids sentences such as "John was kissed the cheek" and "Mary kissed John's cheek on the cheek".

Like PHRED, KING is designed to incorporate as much as possible into *predisposition* mechanisms; *i. e.* the heuristics above predispose the generator towards certain mappings and thereby influence the language produced. The generator will not produce a structure for "John sold Mary a book", another for "Mary bought a book from John", and evaluate the structural choices. Rather, it will map from *commercial-transaction* to *ct-merchandise-transfer* and then to either *buying* or *selling*, and will complete its work based on the result. In this way the biasing of the mapping process has a substantial effect on the output of the generator. This is similar to predisposition in PHRED and to the indelibility realized in MUMBLE [13], but is generalized to conceptual structures: A VIEW of a conceptual structure, once applied by KING, is not evaluated with respect to other VIEWs. If the generator applies a VIEW to obtain the *buying* concept from a *ct-merchandise-transfer*, it will not consider a *selling* VIEW.

The process of mapping using structured associations in the "hugging" example in figure 4 results in the instantiation of the *hug-giving* concept by the application of a VIEW, and proceeds by applying REF links at successively higher levels. The first such REF association produces *lex-give*, the lexical category associated with *hug-giving*. Further up in the hierarchy, the *transfer-event* concept is reached. This results in the instantiation of the *verb-indir-relation* with indirect object referring to *mary1*, and verb corresponding to *hug-giving1*. Still further up the hierarchy, the REF association between *simple-event* and the *verb-obj-relation* establishes *hugging1* as the *obj* or direct object referent in this relation.

The output of the mapping phase at this point is the following set of constraints and relations: [6] *(lex-give) (voice-active) (verb-indir-relation (iobj mary1)) (verb-obj-relation (obj hugging1))* The pattern selection phase, considered below, determines how the linguistic knowledge derived from mapping can be combined into a grammatical utterance.

3.2 Pattern Selection

Potential patterns in KING are retrieved in an ordered stream, biased by the constraints to be satisfied and the relations to be expressed by the pattern. The pattern selection mechanism has three potential outcomes: If its input specifies a lexical category, it may produce a lexeme. Otherwise, it can produce a template, including a pattern that satisfies the necessary constraints. Otherwise, it will fail, generally passing control back to the mapping mechanism.

---

[6] The constraint *voice-active* is produced via a REF association from the *giver* role, as described in Chapter 6 of [8].

The following principles describe the process of selecting patterns:

- *Principle 4. Consider only patterns from the most specific pattern category.*
  The input to the pattern selection phase may include pattern categories such as noun phrase or verb phrase. Such categories are always in the pattern that the generator is working from; for example, if KING is in the process of using an NP-VP pattern, the first constituent must be a noun phrase and the second a verb phrase. More specific categories may be given, such as *question-sentence* or *postnominal-modifier*. These categories may also be derived in the mapping process. The linguistic pattern being produced must necessarily belong to the most specific of these categories.
- *Principle 5. Favor patterns that are associated with contextual structures.*
  This principle distinguishes contextual biases from strict constraints. An element of the context may be used to derive a pattern category, but the generator can if necessary select a pattern not in that category.
- *Principle 6. Favor patterns that subsume as many relations as possible.*
  Among the candidates of equal status from Principles 4 and 5, patterns may be ordered according to the number of linguistic relations that they express. Patterns that express relations not derived from the mapping process are discarded.

Principles 4 and 5 above are relatively simple. The fourth principle dictates that only patterns that satisfy external constraints should be considered. The fifth dictates that contextual knowledge should be used where possible. Principle 6 is the basic rule for selecting among a number of valid patterns.

As an example of the pattern selection process, consider the production of the verb phrase part of "John sold Mary a book." The generator will at this point have obtained a variety of constraints such as *form-finite* and *voice-active*, and will have determined that it must produce a *verb-phrase* referring to a particular *selling* concept. The mapping process, furthermore, will have produced the relations *verb-indir-relation (iobj = mary1)* and *verb-obj-relation (obj = book1)*.

As suggested by Principle 4, the pattern selection mechanism first retrieves all templates with patterns in the *verb-phrase* category (about a dozen in the current knowledge base). It then applies Principle 6, ordering these templates according to the number of derived relations that they express. In this case, KING chooses the pattern that subsumes the *verb-indir-relation* and *verb-obj-relation*, the dative verb phrase pattern, shown in figure 5.

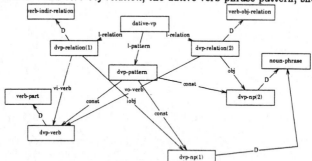

Figure 5: The instantiated *dative-vp*

Each time a pattern is selected by the generator, it is passed along to the restriction mechanism, which performs the bulk of KING's linguistic grunt work. This mechanism is described in the following section.

3.3 Restriction

Restriction is the process of applying constraints to a selected pattern, matching it with the relations it is to subsume and preparing the constituents of the pattern for completion. This role is often played by unification in systems such as those of Appelt (1983) and McKeown (1982). In PHRED the restriction process was divided into three components: *unification,* which matched the attributes of the input to the features of a pattern template, *elaboration*, which added constraints to individual constituents of the pattern, and *combination*, used to combine ordering patterns with flexible-order patterns. Restriction in KING embodies a simpler mechanism. Unification is avoided by applying simpler checks to perform constraint matching. As in PHRED, the system depends on the pattern selection mechanism to ensure that constraints are satisfied. Elaboration makes use of ROLE-PLAY relationships rather than variable binding. For example, attributes such as person, number, tense, and form are used to specify constraints on verbs, and they may be grouped into a common category, *verb-constraint*. Associated with verb-phrase constructs, then, is a ROLE-PLAY which indicates that all *verb-constraints* are constraints on the *verb-part* constituent of the verb phrase construct. This knowledge is then inherited by all verb phrase constructs.

The result of the restriction of the dative verb phrase pattern given earlier might be the following:

First constituent:
      V-P Concept=selling, Constraints=(lex sell, voice active, form finite, person third,
            number singular)

Second constituent:
      NP (1) Concept=mary1, Constraints = (case objective)

Third constituent:
      NP (2) Concept=book1, Constraints = (case objective)

The *lex sell* constraint on the verb part, produced by mapping across the REF association between the *selling* concept and the corresponding lexical category, is assigned to the first constituent by virtue of the knowledge that all *verb-constraints* on verb phrases are assigned to their verb parts. The *voice active* constraint derives in much the same manner. The *form finite* constraint is an inherent constraint on the *finite-verb-phrase* category, which is the subclass of verb phrase constructs with finite verbs. The *person* and *number* constraints are passed along from earlier stages. After each constituent is produced, the generator fills in the appropriate constraints on the dependent constituents. The case constraints on the noun phrases derive from constraints on the object and indirect object of the relations.

The output of the restriction process, as shown above, consists of a set of constituents for which concept, constraints, and category are specified. These serve as input to the generator for further refinement of the structure. The generation process thus proceeds by recursively invoking the mapping - pattern selection - restriction sequence, starting, in this case, with the verb part constituent.

This section has presented an overview of the process by which KING constructs an utterance. Because structured associations are applied repeatedly to a concept to derive linguistic structures, a variety of loosely related concepts may be described using the same linguistic knowledge. In this way "gave Mary a hug" and "sold John the book" may be realized using the same knowledge about dative verb phrases.

4   Summary and Conclusion

At the time of this writing, KING is a fully implemented tactical language generator with the ability to produce utterances that form a useful and exemplary subset of natural English. The system is incorporated in a new version of the UNIX Consultant, which is still under development. Written in Franz Lisp and compiled, the code of the generator, exclusive of indexing and knowledge representation tools, is slightly more than 20K, about one-fifth the size of the analogous code of PHRED. The Ace implementation takes up another 15K. The knowledge base includes about 50 basic linguistic patterns, 75 linguistic relations, several hundred Ace assertions describing these structures, 150 concepts, and 200 "horizontal" structured associations. The typical running time of the program is about two seconds for a sentence of 10-15 words.

In a variety of ways KING has proven to be a strong qualitative success. The most obvious successes are in alleviating the difficulties in making use of new knowledge in the system. Because the representation of the system allows new information to be easily linked to existing knowledge, extending the power of the system is far easier than it was in PHRED.

For example, the addition of a new concept related to the *transfer-event* enables the use of the dative construct. The encoding of metaphorical and referential relationships, such as that used in producing the "giving a hug" expression, is accomplished by using structured associations, thereby facilitating the representation of knowledge about similar constructs. In this way the *knowledge intensive* aspect of KING permits a simple generation mechanism to be applied to a range of utterances.

One of the major technical problems to be overcome in language generation systems is the consideration of many possible linguistic choices that are not applicable or have little chance of success. Unification-based generators tend to perform selection among these choices within the unification mechanism; others utilize queries or other matching methods to test the applicability of a pattern. The pattern selection process in KING is much simpler because it takes advantage of the relations derived from mapping. Thus it is the *incremental* nature of the generation mechanism that eliminates many of the frivolous possibilities.

The KING implementation seems to support the idea that a representation such as Ace enables the use of a simple mechanism to achieve substantial generation capabilities. The ease with which the generator is extended and adapted suggests that the use of structured associations to encode abstract knowledge about language is a powerful tool in designing a natural language generation system.

References

[1] D. Appelt. TELEGRAM: a grammar formalism for language planning. In *Proceedings of the 21st Annual Meeting of the Association for Computational Linguistics*, Cambridge, Massachusetts, 1983.

[2] D. Bobrow and T. Winograd. An overview of KRL, a knowledge representation language. *Cognitive Science*, 1(1), 1977.

[3] R. Brachman. *et. al. Research in Natural Language Understanding*. Technical Report 4274, Bolt Beranek and Newman, 1979.

[4] M. Deering, J. Faletti, and R. Wilensky. PEARL: an efficient language for artificial intelligence programming. In *Proceedings of the Seventh International Joint Conference on Artificial Intelligence*, Vancouver, British Columbia, 1981.

[5] C. J. Fillmore. Topics in lexical semantics. 1977.

[6] D. Gentner. Structure-mapping: a theoretical framework for analogy. *Cognitive Science*, 7, 1983.

[7] N. M. Goldman. Conceptual generation. In R. C. Schank, editor, *Conceptual Information Processing*, American Elsevier Publishing Company, New York, 1975.

[8] P. Jacobs. *A knowledge-based approach to language production*. PhD thesis, University of California, Berkeley, 1985. Computer Science Division Report UCB/CSD86/254.

[9] P. Jacobs. PHRED: a generator for natural language interfaces. *Computational Linguistics*, 11(4), 1985.

[10] P. Jacobs and L. Rau. Ace: associating language with meaning. In *Proceedings of the Sixth European Conference on Artificial Intelligence*, Pisa, Italy, 1984.

[11] M. Kay. Functional Unification Grammar: a formalism for machine translation. In *Proceedings of the Tenth International Conference on Computational Linguistics*, Stanford, California, 1984.

[12] G. Lakoff and D. Johnson. *Metaphors we Live By*. University of Chicago Press, Chicago, 1980.

[13] D. D. McDonald. *Language Production as a Process of Decision-making Under Constraints*. PhD thesis, MIT, 1980.

[14] J. Moore and A. Newell. How can MERLIN understand? In L. Gregg, editor, *Knowledge and Cognition*, Erlbaum Associates, Halsted, New Jersey, 1974.

[15] R. B. Roberts and I. P. Goldstein. *The FRL Manual*. Technical Report AIM-408, MIT AI Lab, 1977.

[16] R. Wilensky. KODIAK - a knowledge representation language. In *Proceedings of the Sixth Annual Conference of the Cognitive Science Society*, Boulder, Colorado, 1984.

Advances in Artificial Intelligence - II
B. Du Boulay, D. Hogg and L. Steels (Editors)
© Elsevier Science Publishers B.V. (North-Holland), 1987

THE PROSPECT OF MACHINE TRANSLATION

Margaret King
I S S C O
University of Geneva
54,   route des Acacias
CH-1227   Genève

This paper considers the current state of affairs in machine
translation, describing briefly some typical current systems.
It then argues that the need for machine translation is such that
work on "development" systems will increase, despite there being
no immediate prospect of research results which would allow the
production of perfect translations.

Keyword : machine translation

INTRODUCTION

It is rather a common belief amongst workers in artificial intelligence that machine translation received its kiss of death with
the publication of the Alpac report (ALPAC, 1966). They frequently argue that machine translation has been shown not to be feasible, and are often surprised to discover that not only do
machine translation systems exist, one can even buy them. This
paper argues that this common misunderstanding rests on a confusion concerning the nature of machine translation systems, the
market needs and the aims of system constructors.

To set the stage for discussion, the first major section will be
devoted to a fairly brief survey of the current state of affairs.
This will then be expanded by a somewhat more detailed description of one system currently under development. In the final section we shall turn to the prospects for the future.

THE CURRENT STATE OF AFFAIRS

The history of machine translation is fairly well known, and will
not be reviewed here. The interested reader is referred to
(Buchmann, 1986, Warwick, 1986). For our present purposes, we
shall look only at current work, distinguishing three main classes of activity : commercially available translator's aids systems, more ambitious systems intended to function with no significant human intervention other than relatively limited pre- or
post-editing and long-term research activity. In a paper of this
length, even within these limits, an exhaustive account is impossible. Fuller accounts can be found in King (1986), Slocum (1984,
and 1985).

a. Machine aided human translation

Over the last few years a number of machine translation systems

have come on the market. Nearly all of them - no matter what
claims their manufacturers may make - can best be classified as
systems intended to help the human translator in his work rather
than as the primary means of producing translations which then
need limited post-editing before use. (It is perhaps worth remar-
king in passing that those manufacturers who make exaggerated
claims, suggesting that their system is based on advanced AI techniques ("the first translation system which thinks") and therefore
produces high quality output do nothing but a disservice to the
field, to AI in general, and ultimately to their own products :
such claims should not be taken seriously.) In general, such systems are based on a fairly limited syntactic analysis, concentra-
ting on establishing part of speech disambiguation taking into
consideration a limited local context.

Semantic feature information is sometimes used, but the features
tend to be either very general, of the ± animate, ± physical
object variety, or very particular, e.g. ± chemical process.
(This should not be taken as severe criticism : it may be in the
nature of semantic features that no single unifying theory useful
in all applications can be found : for discussion see (Wilks,
1975). Deep case information (of the sort described in, e.g.
(Fillmore, 1968)) is usually limited to predicting the complement
cases which may occur with a predicate, and the notorious problems of circumstantials are ignored. Such systems rely very
heavily on the use of category-level dictionary information, and
relatively little on the expression of what one linguistic tradition would call "significant generalisations", either about
syntax or about semantics.

Despite their obvious limitations, such systems are beginning to
meet with considerable commercial success. To see why this is so,
let us look at one of them, the ALPS system, in slightly more
detail.

ALPS is embedded in a highly sophisticated text processing environment within which the translator composes his translation on
the screen. He can ask for three levels of help in doing so. The
first two of these are variations on dictionary look-up : both
involve user-defined dictionaries, and are primarily useful for
technical terminology. Selective dictionary look-up is rather
like a computerized version of a translator's card files : the
dictionary can be consulted and up-dated on-line whilst the
translation is being done. Automatic dictionary look-up provides
automatic word-by-word dictionary look-up for user-defined technical terminology. Morphological processing is used to identify
the base form of the term. When more than one translation is
available, the translator is asked to choose the appropriate one.
For example, in the sentence

    "The required chip is a dual-input tri-state NAND gate"

the translator would be asked to choose between the following
sets of translations (which would be offered to him depends, of
course, on the target language).

French	Spanish	German
fiche	micropastilla	Chip
micro-plquette	microplaquetta	Mikrobaustein
micro-chip	recorte	Stanzabfall
	ficha	Schuppe

The third level of help is to ask for a rough first draft translation. The translation program will handle most aspects of
inflection, word-order and agreement. In case of ambiguity, the
system once again interacts with the human translator to obtain
the correct choice.

Even from this very cursory description (more detailed description of ALPS and of similar systems can be found in (Ananiadou,
1986)), it can be seen that the quality of translation produced
is unlikely to be high except in the case of very particular
types of text.

The primary advantages of such systems are in ensuring consistency of terminology (especially when more than one translator is
working on the same text) and in facilitating the (human) work of
translation through the provision of specially-designed text
processing facilities as well as through the use of the translator's aids.

Nevertheless, such systems are quite successful, much to the surprise, usually, of the academic community. Here is our first sign
of the conflict between real commercial needs and intellectual
expectations. The systems are successful because they will increase a translator's productivity by a considerable factor :
indeed, it is sometimes possible to negotiate a contract with the
manufacturer whereby he will return the selling price if productivity has not doubled by the end of six months. An intellectual
purist, on the other hand, would probably count them as failures,
since the linguistic analysis performed is primitive, by modern
standards, the issue of ambiguity is avoided by the use of interaction, and such problems as pronoun reference are simply ignored.

b.   Human aided machine translation systems

Unlike the systems described in the previous section, in these
systems the machine carries the main burden of translation, with
human intervention being limited to restricted pre- or post-
editing. The two systems we shall use to exemplify this approach
are METAL (German-English, English-German), developed by the
Linguistics Research Center of the University of Texas, and
recently introduced as a commercial system under the name LITRAS,
and the Japanese national project, Mu (Japanese-English, English-
Japanese), which is a collaborative effort between Kyoto University, Electronical Laboratories, the Japan Information Center for
Science and Technology and the Research Information Processing
System under the Agency of Engineering Technology. Further information on METAL can be found in (Slocum, 1986, Slocum et al, 1985)
and on Mu in (Nagao et al, 1985, Nagao, 1986).

The two systems have several common aspects. Both systems are
intended for the bulk production of translations, and therefore
foresee no human intervention during processing and seek to

minimize post-editing. Both analyse the sentential structure of
the input text, rather than relying on local context of individual words, both are transfer based systems, both show a concern
for allowing the linguist involved in constructing the system
to express generalizations about his language. GRADE, the basic
software tool of Mu, is a tree-to-tree transducer, allowing
arbitrary transformations over the trees. METAL rules (for the
German analysis) take the form of phrase structure rules, thus
allowing the use of a context free parsing algorithm, but the
phrase structure grammar is augmented by procedures with facilities for, among other things, arbitrary transformations. Thus
both systems provide the linguist developing the system with a
very general tool.

The main point of contrast between the two systems is in their
use of semantics. METAL makes limited use of a set of simple
semantic features during transfer in order to improve the quality
of the translation, but relies primarily on syntax during analysis. The analysis results are a constituent structure parse of
the input.

As might be expected, given that Japanese and English come from
quite different language families, Mu relies more heavily on
semantic information. For nouns, around fifty semantic primitives
are used, grouped into eight independent hierarchies. One of these, reproduced from (Nagao et al, 1985), is shown below as an
example

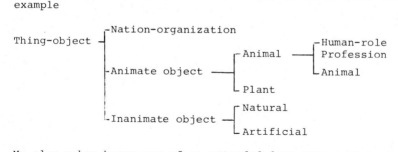

Mu also makes heavy use of an extended deep case system. Each
verb in the dictionary is coded with a set of case frame descriptions, where each description corresponds to a use of the verb.
The frame gives mapping rules between surface case markers (post-
positional case particles for Japanese) and their deep case interpretations. The analysis results are dependency trees which
show the semantic relationships between the input words. The
cases used for English are listed below (Japanese uses one extra
case).

Agent	Content	Range	Time-from
Causal Potency	Partner	Comparison	Time-at
Experiencer	Opponent	Tool	Time-to
Object	Beneficiary	Purpose	Duration
Recipient	Accompaniment	Space-from	Cause
Origin	Role	Space-at	Condition
Source	Degree	Space-to	Result
Goal	Manner	Space-through	Concession

One point to make about both these systems is, again, that both are quite successful. Slocum (1986) quotes experiments carried out by METAL's sponsors, Siemens, in order to assess cost-effectiveness. The most interesting figure is that for revision. Professional post-editors (i.e., not people who had been involved in developing the system : this tends to be important) were able to revise around 29 pages a day. This is in contrast to the average daily output of a human translator, which is around 5 to 8 pages a day. Nagao (1985) devotes an entire section to evaluation, which cannot be easily summarized here, but quotes results which suggest that around 80 % of input sentences (over a sample of around 8000 scientific abstracts) were being satisfactorily translated.

These results should come as something of a surprise to those AI workers who insist that nothing can be done without extensive use of semantics, of world-knowledge and of inferencing. Neither system makes use of world-knowledge or inferencing techniques, and only Mu makes extensive use of semantics. Nonetheless, METAL is considered to be a viable commercial product, and its sponsors seem satisfied with Mu (which was designed as a pre-commercial investigatory system).

The reason for such systems being considered viable is not, however, very obscure. The needs of the end-users are such that they are more concerned with having "nearly right" translation in bulk than in having perfect translation in limited quantity. We shall return to this point in the conclusion.

c. Eurotra

Eurotra is a research and development programme of the European Community, aimed at producing a multi-lingual machine translation system capable of dealing with translation between all of the official languages of the Community (currently seven : Danish, Dutch, English, French, German, Greek, Italian, to be augmented from January 1st, 1986, by Portuguese and Spanish). The system to be produced should cover about 20'000 lexical entries, and will be a pre-commercial system, like Mu.

It has been picked out for special attention here not only because of the author's evident prejudice, but because it reflects the effect on the design of machine translation systems of current work in computer science and in linguistics.

When Eurotra planning began, in 1978, the initial system design shared much in common with the two systems described in the last section. The underlying software was to be a tree-to-tree transducer, allowing the expression of arbitrary transformations. Not surprisingly, since both the Japanese government project and Eurotra of that time were heavily influenced by work done in Grenoble by the GETA group (Vauquois & Boitet, 1985), Eurotra, like Mu, proposed a single homogeneous data structure which was to be used throughout the system to store intermediate results, and which would, at the input to transfer, contain information coming from a variety of different dimensions of linguistic description : morpho-syntactic, surface syntactic, deep syntactic and semantic.

One of the disadvantages of such a design became quite quickly
apparent : the underlying algorithmic model was too general.
This had disadvantages both computationally and for the linguist
whose job it was to develop the system. Computationally, excessive generality leads quite quickly to extreme slowness. In terms
of linguistic expression, if the user language allows the linguist to say anything he wishes, first he must understand a rather
large and clumsy animal, and then, since the burden of control
falls on him, he must quite soon resort to tricks to make the
machine actually do what he wants.

Eurotra's first attempts to ameliorate this, under the influence
of work on expert systems and on controlled production systems
(Georgeff, 1982), consisted in splitting control away from the
statement of linguistic facts. The linguist then wrote primitive
processes (often somewhat misleadingly called grammars) which
could be combined together into larger processes as specified by
control statements. Parameters could be imposed on the processes
to govern, for example, whether execution was to proceed in sequence or in parallel, and mechanisms provided whereby unwanted
side effects could be avoided.

A further insight came from the realisation that if the system
architecture were such that the syntax and semantics of the
language used to express linguistic facts were externally defined,
then it would be possible to experiment with different user languages, allowing the linguist developing the system to interact
with software developers in order to produce an expressive tool
fitted to his needs and to the problem domain, rather than imposing on him a very general tool simply because it was difficult
to decide in advance what the appropriate specific tool would be.
This led to the type of system architecture described in (Johnson et al, 1984 and Johnson & Rosner, 1986).

A second source of over-generality was the homogeneous data structure. If all possible kinds of linguistic information are captured
in a single data structure, it becomes difficult to interpret any
single piece of information with security. As a tiny example,
consider a sentence like "Spain and Portugal are expected to join
the Community", where "Spain and Portugal" are surface subject of
"expect" but deep subject of "join", whilst the deep subject of
"expect" is missing. In a structure where both surface and relational syntactic information are simultaneously present, this
becomes extremely difficult to express in any clean and coherent
way.

This, and similar considerations, led to an attempt to separate
out a series of dimensions of linguistic description, each captured by its own representation. Translation is then seen as a
set of mappings between representations. Current Eurotra belief,
as reported in (Arnold et al, 1985) and (Des Tombe et al, 1985),
is that these mappings are compositional, in the Fregean sense
that the translation of a complex object in one representation
into an object in another representation is a function of the
translation of the simpler objects making up the complex object
and of the way their translations are combined. As an over- simplified example, consider the translation from French into English
of "le chat noir". The individual translations are straightforward.

If we take the mode of combination to be simply following the same sequence we would get "the cat black", which is wrong. Therefore, to account for this case, the definition of compositionality must be such as to allow for the transposition of elements when the translations of the elementary objects are put together.

The current hypothesis within Eurotra is that there are compositional mappings (in both directions, although the definition of compositionality is not necessarily the same in both directions) between the following pairs of representations :

a) a normalized text representation, which abstracts away from contingent text processing characteristics, e.g. formatting codes and a morphological representation, capturing the results of morphological analysis;

b) the morphological representation and a surface syntactic representation based primarily on configurational syntax;

c) the surface syntactic representation and a relational syntax representation;

d) the relational syntax representation and a semantic representation, containing, for example, semantic relations similar to the extended set of deep cases used by Mu and time indicators independent of morphological tense;

e) the semantic representation derived by analysis from an input text and a semantic representation adequate to allow generation of a translation into the target language.

It should be emphasized that the word "hypothesis" was not lightly chosen. It is only a hypothesis that these different representations can be defined for each of the Eurotra languages and that the mappings between them will be compositional. It may even turn out to be the case that different representations must be distinguished for different languages.

This brings us back to the question of experimentation and of defining appropriate tools. The current experimental software implementation uses a version of unification (Kay, 1983) as its primary mechanism. Within the software philosophy described above, it proved very quick (about 4 man weeks) to implement the current prototype in order to allow the linguists to do some first experimentation in defining the representations and the mappings between them. This is the fundamental notion underlying Eurotra's development philosophy : the problem of machine translation is not yet thorougly understood. In order to develop a system as ambitious as Eurotra, it is necessary to provide tools which allow for the rapid devlopment of prototypes and for the exploration of possible solutions.

It is too early to judge whether Eurotra will be a success. But the earlier point about the existence of real need pushing work on machine translation is illustrated here too. Eurotra is the largest machine translation project in the Western world, with an initial investment of 27 m. ECU foreseen and around a hundred research workers involved. The European Community has enormous translation problems, aggravated by the fact that it is difficult to find translators with particular language combinations, like

Danish-Greek : it is therefore worth-while for the Community to
invest directly in research on machine translation.

  d. Research activities

In this survey of the current state of affairs, Eurotra sits somewhat on the borderline between development and research, in that
it sees the problem to be solved as a research problem, and tries
to provide tools with which to do the research, yet nonetheless
aims at producing a working system (a final prototype, not a commercial system) before the end of the programme period (late 1988).
A substantial number of projects exist which are more purely
research oriented, most of them not aimed primarily at producing
systems even of the Eurotra prototype size, but at solving problems not attacked by the systems described so far.

Most of the "pure" research projects concentrate on what might be
styled the AI approach : an attempt to "understand" the text,
produce a conceptual representation of some kind, which is intended to be language independent, and to "generate" a version of
the text in the target language. The result will not be a translation in the standard sense, but a (more or less) meaning preserving paraphrase.

The most common approaches are to follow up on work started in
AI circles with reference to language understanding in general.
Thus, a popular current approach in Japan is closely related to
the frames/script approach advocated by the Yale School in, for
example (Carbonell et al, 1981) and (Lytinen & Schank, 1982).
(Interestingly though, a recent paper by Lytinen (Lytinen, 1985)
argues for an integration of semantic and syntactic parsing,
which suggests that the total repugnance once created by the use
of syntax may be weakening.) Similarly, several projects (e.g.
Uchida, 1985, Kiyono, 1985) use semantic networks as their primary knowledge representation tool, sometimes embedding them in
PROLOG in order to facilitate inferencing (Tanaka, 1985). The
most adventurous project known to the present author uses an
interactive model between memory structure and the text as the
language understanding model. The text invokes knowledge stored
as memory, where the memory structure can be organized into
long-term memory, discourse memory and episodic memory. The long-
term memory stores knowledge such as common sense knowledge, linguistic knowledge, past experience and procedural knowledge
concerning how to infer a fact from a set of facts. Discourse
memory stores knowledge concerning the situation and the history
of understanding the text, for example, knowledge of the author,
the topic, the purpose of the discourse segment. The episodic
memory stores the meaning structure of the ongoing segment of
the text. As understanding proceeds, knowledge from the episodic
memory is assimilated into discourse memory and knowledge from
the discourse memory into the long-term memory (Nomura, 1985).

Another classical approach is the attempt to develop an interlingua : the interlingual approach described in (Nirenburg et al,
1985) has much in common with knowledge representation techniques
developed in AI.

Very little more will be said here about research oriented activity, except to insist that it is long term, and that it is very
difficult indeed to predict what may come out of it. Earlier work
in AI on semantic networks, on knowledge representation languages
and on frame based systems ran into what are by now quite well-
known problems. It is difficult to see that shifting the application to machine translation will help to avoid those same problems, especially when the systems in question reach a realistic
size rather than being small experimental systems. However, most
of this work is in too early a stage for any reasonable prediction
to be made.

e. Prospects of MT

The essence of this section can be deduced from the earlier sections on existing systems. All of the systems described fulfill
a need. ALPS primarily serves the needs of free-lance translators
and of fairly small translation services. It runs on small machines, costs little, and yet will ensure consistency of terminology
and considerably speed up output. Its use, and that of similar
systems, is of obvious benefit to the individual translator.

METAL exemplifies a different kind of need being fulfilled. It
has primarily been developed for translating technical material
for use by a big organisation. More and more, a manufacturer
who wants to sell his product cannot insist that the potential
customer learn the manufacturer's language in order to read the
relevant documentation. (How many raeders of this would be prepared to buy a personal computer with documentation only available in Japanese ?) Thus, as the drive to export grows, so does
another need for machine translation.

Mu illustrates two areas of need. First, it has been developed as
a system for translating scientific abstracts. Secondly, the languages involved are rather remote from each other, and the difficulty for a speaker of one to learn the other thereby increased.
Thus we have the double need of the specialist who needs to keep
up with the literature in his field, no matter whether it is his
own or another language, and the needs of communication between
language communities whose languages are very different but who
yet have strong economic or cultural ties.

Eurotra's is the case of a multi-lingual community where for both
political and cultural reasons a conscious decision has been made
to avoid one language being used as a lingua franca and thus
dominating all the others. In such communities (Canada and Swit-
zerland are two other examples), it is normally the case that
official agencies will encourage, or even insist on, the translation of working documents into all the languages of the community.
Here too is a need that will not go away.

The astute reader will ask why these needs cannot be fulfilled by
human translators. Are machines not, after all, once again putting
people out of work ? There are three primary reasons why machines
will increasingly be called upon to play a role. The first if the
sheer volume of translation involved. A colleague who runs a
translation service pointed out that if his office were to translate all the material they are supposed to translate, the size

of the staff would have to be multiplied by twelve - which would
create as many problems as it would solve, even if that number
of appropriately qualified people could be found. The second is
precisely the problem of finding appropriately qualified people :
particular language pairs remain exotic, and the problem is aggravated when technical specialisations are involved. The final
reason is more cynical : after an initial investment, machines
(and machine translation) cost less than people, work faster,
and, if necessary, are prepared to work all night - and translations are often needed in a hurry.

This is not to suggest that machine translation will replace human translation : present day systems are not that good, and
there is no immediate prospect of them getting dramatically
better. Thus, the texts suitable for machine translation will
remain the relatively straightforward, every day material. Texts
where absolute precision is necessary, where nuance or deliberate
ambiguity are important will need to be translated by people for
a long time yet.

Nonetheless, it seems a reasonable prediction that machine translation systems will become increasingly common as those currently
available find acceptance and as the community as a whole reali-
ses their usefulness.

REFERENCES

1. ALPAC, 1966. Languages and Machines : Computers in Transla-
        tion and Linguistics. Washington D.C., Publication 1416,
        National Academy of Sciences.

2. Ananiadou, S., 1986. A Brief Survey of Some Current Operatio-
        nal Systems. In King (1986).

3. Arnold, D., Jaspaert, L., Johnson, R., Krauwer, S., Rosner,
        M., Des Tombe, L., Varile, N. and Warwick, S., 1985.
        A MU$_1$ View of the $\langle$C,A$\rangle$,T Framework in Eurotra. Proceed.
        of the Conference on Theoretical and Methodological Issues
        in Machine Translation of Natural Languages. Colgate, N.Y.

4. Buchmann, B., 1986. Early History of Machine Translation.
        In King (1986).

5. Carbonell, J.G., Cullingford, R.E., and Gershman, A.V., 1981.
        Steps towards Knowledge-Based Machine Translation.
        IEEE Transactions on Pattern Analysis and Machine Intel-
        ligence (PAMI), 3, 4.

6. Des Tombe, L., Arnold, D., Jaspaert, L., Johnson, R., Krau-
        wer, S., Rosner, M., Varile, N. and Warwick, S., 1985.
        A Preliminary Linguistic Framework for Eurotra, June 85.
        Proceed. of the Conference on Theoretical and Methodolo-
        gical Issues in Machine Translation of Natural Languages.
        Colgate, N.Y.

7. Fillmore, C., 1968. The Case for Case. In Bach & Harms,
        Universals in Linguistic Theory. N.Y.

8. Georgeff, M.P., 1982. Procedural Control in Production Sys-
        tems. Artificial Intelligence, 18:2.

9. Johnson, R.L., Krauwer, S., Rosner, M.A. and Varile, G.B., 1984. The Design of the Kernel Architecture for the Eurotra Software. COLING, 1984.

10. Johnson, R.L. and Rosner, M.A., 1986. Machine Translation and Software Tools. In King (1986).

11. Kay, M., 1983. Unification Grammar. Unpublished Memo, Xerox Palo Alto Research Center.

12. King, M. (ed.), 1986. Machine Translation To-day : the State of the Art. Edinburgh University Press. To appear.

13. Kiyono, M., 1985. Macine-aided Document Generation System. Second Joint Eurotra Japanese Workshop, Geneva.

14. Lytinen, S.L., 1985. Integrating Syntax and Semantics. Proceed. of the Conference on Theoretical and Methodological Issues in Machine Translation of Natural Languages. Colgate, N.Y.

15. Lytinen, S.L. and Schank, R., 1982. Representation and Translation. Yale Research Report 234.

16. Nagao, M., 1986. Machine Translation in Japan. IEEE Special Edition on Machine Translation, ed. G. Ferrari, to appear.

17. Nagao, M., Tsujii, J-I., Nakamura, J-I., 1985. The Japanese Government Project for Machine Translation. Computational Linguistics, Vol. II, Numbers 2-3.

18. Nirenburg, S., Raskin, V. and Tucker, A.B., 1985. Interlingua Design for TRANSLATOR. Proceed. of the Conference on Theoretical and Methodological Issues in Machine Translation of Natural Languages. Colgate, N.Y.

19. Nomura, H., 1985. Language Understanding (draft). Second Joint Eurotra Japanese Workshop, Geneva.

20. Slocum, J., 1984. Machine Translation : its History, Current Status and Future Prospects. Invited Paper, COLING '84.

21. Slocum, J. (ed.), 1985. Computational Linguistics Special Editions on Machine Translation. Computational Linguistics Vol. 11, numbers 1, 2, 3.

22. Slocum, J., 1986. METAL : the LRC Machine Translation System. In King (1986).

23. Slocum, J., Bennett, W.S., Whiffin, L. and Norcross, E., 1985. An Evaluation of METAL : the LRC Machine Translation System. Proceed. of the Second Annual Conference of the European Chapter for Computational Linguistics, Geneva.

24. Tanaka, H., 1985. DCKR - Knowledge Representation in Prolog and its Application to Natural Language Processing. Second Joint Eurotra Japanese Workshop, Geneva.

25. Uchida, H., 1985. Fujitsu Machine Translation System : ATLAS. Second Joint Eurotra Japanese Workshop, Geneva.

448   *M. King*

26. Vauquois, B. and Boitet, C., 1985. Automated Translation at
    Grenoble University. Computational Linguistics, Vol. 11,
    Numbers 2-3.

27. Warwick, S., 1986. An Overview of Post-Alpac Developments.
    In King (1986).

28. Wilks, Y., 1975. Primitives and Words. In : Seven Theses on
    Artificial Intelligence and Natural Language. ISSCO
    Working Paper no. 17.

Advances in Artificial Intelligence - II
B. Du Boulay, D. Hogg and L. Steels (Editors)
© Elsevier Science Publishers B.V. (North-Holland), 1987   449

DYNAMIC UNIFICATION IN LEXICALLY BASED PARSING

Oliviero Stock

I.P. - Consiglio Nazionale delle Ricerche
Via dei Monti Tiburtini 509, 00157 Roma, Italy

Introduction

The best machines that actually parse NL (human beings) are able to dynamically disambiguate a sentence and to make sense of partial parsings, and they take advantage of this ability in their normal activities. Machines that do not do that: a) are bound to have problems in communicating with the machines cited above b) will give a limited support to our understanding of those machines.

In recent years work on a number of languages other than English, a renewed interest in non-transformational grammars and the taking into account of the experience in working with parsers have influenced the appearance of new linguistic theories, such as Lexical-Functional Grammar [Bresnan & Kaplan 1982], GPSG [Gazdar 1981], Unification Grammar [Kay 1979], DCG [Pereira & Warren 1980], TAG [Joshi & Levy 1982]. Though for some authors there is an explicit interest in the human dynamics of parsing, for most of them the main effort is devoted towards the descriptive power of the formalism and to building clean mechanisms that are able to associate syntactic descriptions to input sentences.

In Rome we have developed a parser, for the purpose of: 1) understanding better and experimenting with our ideas on the nature of language understanding and 2) having an adequate tool for processing Italian language.

For point 1), our view of syntax is twofold. It consists of :

a) originating the search for and the linking together of pieces of semantic representation, in accordance with certain specifications. All this comes directly from impulses and specifications present in the lexicon.

b) imposing restrictions on the spaces of search for pieces to be linked together , possibly taking into account general criteria of linear precedence.

As far as point 2) is concerned, Italian is a freer word order language than English (e.g. Subject-Verb-Object is only the most likely order in simple declarative sentences - the other five permutations of Subject Verb and Object may occur as well, even in written Italian) and it has a richer morphology. Therefore the role of syntax specified in b) above is somehow reduced, while constraints and specifications due to the lexicon, of the kind specified in a) above are richer. Of course, also, morphological analysis is an inescapable aspect to which must be combined with syntax.

As mentioned before, we see syntactic knowledge as being largely distributed through the lexicon. This allows for an easier treatment of word idiosyncracies (very common in Italian in particular) and for linking the syntactic work to the semantic information carried by words (this is also emphasized in Small's work [1982], even though he attributes less importance to a general syntactic framework). Coming to parsing, we see it as a nondeterministic process governed by data and stimuli brought in, basically, by words. The main problem in parsing is building some internal representation of a sentence, while disambiguating in local conditions of uncertainty. Our point is that at any stage of this process, the state of our parser would not, in principle, be irreconcilable with a model of human behaviour. And naturally, through experimentation, refinement of the system and the introduction of heuristics, we aim at getting closer to this model.

1. Linguistic knowledge for WEDNESDAY 2

We shall outline the aspect of linguistic knowledge used by WEDNESDAY 2, a system we have implemented in INTERLISP-D on a XEROX Dandelion. A previous parser built with similar purposes [Stock 1982], [Stock, Castelfranchi & Parisi 1983] gave support to our ideas, but it was inappropriate for experimentation as, among other things, it had control buried in the system.

We shall first show briefly the linguistic knowledge that goes along with words in the lexicon, assuming for the moment that the latter consists of complete words. (Actually a morphological analyzer connected to WEDNESDAY 2 makes use of a dictionary of roots and structures of affixes, as we shall see in a later paragraph).

Each lexical entry may have many "readings" depending on the associated semantic interpretation. For one reading we may have:

- *sem-units*, i.e. a representation of the meaning of the word, in the form of a semantic net shred (the meaning is usually semantically decomposed)

- the category of the word

- if required, specification of the verb mood and tense

- syntactic data such as: a) the indication of a node (in the net) that would be referred to as the main node of the superspace (the first syntactic space that includes the word). Arbitrary features and a mark may be specified. Note that there may be a disjunctive set of values for any of features or marks (e.g. a noun may be marked as nominative or accusative). b) Specification of linguistic functions with indication of nodes referred to and specifications as in a).

- *impulses* to perform mergings of nodes, specifying: one node to be referred to explicitly or indirectly through a linguistic function, that is to be merged with another node (a filler), for which a series of alternatives are specified. An alternative includes: a contextual condition of applicability, a category, features, marking, side effects (through which, for example, coreference between subject of a subordinate clause and a function of the main clause can be indicated). Impulses may also be directed to a different space search than the normal one (see below).

- impulses to set markings or forcing features on the value of linguistic functions or of the main or of other nodes .

Furthermore, measures of likelihood can be specified a) for one alternative to be considered, b) for which relative position the filler should be in respect to the present word c) for the overall necessity of finding a filler. These measures processed together with other ones will give a quantitative account of the likelihood of an analysis, and dynamically will play an heuristic role.

The part concerned with opening, closing and maintaining of search spaces (and the only centralized linguistic knowledge here) is made of very simple space management transition networks (SMTNs), in which $EXP, a distinguished symbol on an arc, indicates that only the occurrence of something expected by preceding words (i.e. for which an impulse was set up) may allow the transition. The SMTNs can impose generalized linear precedence on labelled substrings. In Italian, however, this is trivial Only locally do they impose an ordering (for instance, propositions come before what they mark). More often they only exclude intraposition of a component not belonging to the current space. It should be noted also that a set of acceptable verbal moods and tenses may be specified on entry points in the SMTNs. For instance a (main) sentence needs a verb in a finite tense. (The required presence of a verb is indicated by a non cyclic arc that must be transited before reaching to an exit state). These expected verbal behaviours will be checked for dynamically.

The SMTNs are converted into an internal format that includes also a table of "First Transition Cross References", i.e. for each space type T, F(T), the set of initial states that allow for transition on T, or, recursively on a space type subsumed by a state in F(T).

For example, F(Det) = {NP,S},

at least.

Of course, left recursion is taken care of and termination is guaranteed. The concept of First Transition Cross References is the inverse of the one that M. Kay [1980] calls *reachability*.

2. WEDNESDAY 2 : the parser

We shall first give an account of the general data structure and the restrictions on the search spaces in WEDNESDAY 2. The system uses an extension of the idea of chart parsing [Kay 1980, Kaplan 1973]. Chart parsing is a very general concept for nondeterministic parsing [see for instance Thompson 1981 and Ritchie and Thompson 1984] historically inspired by Earley's work on CFL parsing [1970]. We shall briefly review here the main concepts.

A *chart* is a directed graph that represents the state of the parser. Given the input string, the junctures between words are called *vertices* and are represented as nodes in the chart. Each vertex has an arbitrary number of arcs, called *edges*, coming in and out of it. An edge is therefore a link between two vertices. In the classic chart definition an edge may be of two types: *inactive* or *active*. An inactive edge stands for a recognized constituent (the edge spans the words that are included). An active edge represents a partially recognized constituent. In both cases there is a specification of the category of the constituent. In the case of an active edge, a position in the right hand side of a rewriting rule in the grammar is provided, thus indicating what is missing yet to complete the recognition of the constituent. For a rule $R: L \to C_0 . . . C_n$ there would be an indication $(R . i)$, with $0 < i < n$, where i is the position in the rule. A word in the string is itself represented as an inactive edge connecting two adjoining vertices. An *empty* active edge is an active edge that spans no words and is therefore represented in the chart as a link cycling over one vertex. It means, at least in top-down parsing, a prediction of the application of a rule.

It is important to note that edges are only added to the chart, never removed. A new edge may be added in the following ways:

1) Given an active edge A spanning from V_a to V_b and an inactive edge I spanning from V_b to V_c, where A refers to the rule position (R . i), and the category of I is just C_i, as indicated in R, then a new edge A' is added to the chart, which will span from V_a to V_c, and, if C_i was the last symbol in R, A' will be an inactive edge, if not it will be an active one with rule position (R . i + 1).

2) Empty active edges are placed in the chart at particular points, according to the general strategy used. Usually the parser is a top-down one and an empty edge is introduced on a vertex V if there is a rule that has, on the left hand side, the nonterminal symbol that follows the current position in an active edge reaching V.

The whole process of parsing aims at getting one inactive edge, with category S (or more if the sentence has to be considered ambiguous) to span the whole string.

One of the great advantages of chart parsing is that whatever the strategy adopted work is never duplicated. E. g. if after backtracking the analysis is continued by extending a different active edge and a vertex is reached from where an inactive edge starts, and if the edge addition rule 1) may be applied, then the analysis take advantage of that partial analysis previously done. In other words the parser relies on a table of well-formed substrings, in the form of inactive edges and of working hypotheses in the form of active edges.

In WEDNESDAY 2 the chart is the basic structure in which search spaces are defined. An active edge defines an operational environment for impulses.

Some notable overall aspects in WEDNESDAY 2 chart are:

- instead of referring to a set of rewriting rules, edges refer to positions which are states in SMTNs (see above). This makes for an easy treatment without duplications of permutation phenomena, indicated with cycles in a SMTN. The case of the \$EXP arc will be discussed in further detail later. A final position here is a state with an EXIT arc departing from it. On reaching a state in a SMTN, depending on the presence of an EXIT arc, and/or of any other arc leaving the state, an inactive edge, an active edge or both edges are proposed for addition to the chart (but see also later).

- parsing goes basically bottom-up, with top-down confirmation. When a word edge with category C is added to the chart, its First Left Cross References F(C) are fetched and, for each of them, an edge is introduced in the chart. These particular edges are called *sleeping edges*. A sleeping edge S at a vertex V_S is *awakened*, i.e. becomes a normal active edge iff there is an active edge arriving at V_S that may be

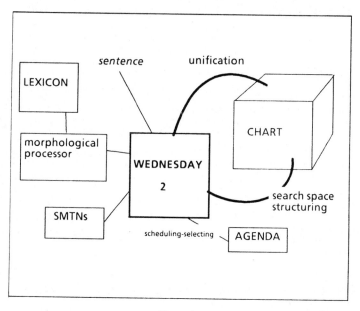

Figure 1

extended with an edge with the category of S. If they are not awakened, sleeping edges play no role at all in the process.

- An agenda is provided. Tasks are of two kinds: *extension tasks* and *insertion tasks*. An extension task specifies an active edge and an inactive edge that can extend it (together with some more information). Two functions, WHEN.ACTIVE.ADDED and WHEN.INACTIVE.ADDED, may cause the introduction of such tasks on the agenda. Insertion tasks will be explained later. At each stage the the next task chosen for execution is the value of the application of a scheduling-selecting function (Trivially, depth-first control is implemented with a simple POP, breadth-first control as a removal of the element that was inserted first in the agenda).

A diagram of WEDNESDAY 2 is shown in Figure 1.

3. Unification

Let us now focus on the actual problem of unification. First let us describe the aspect of an edge in WEDNESDAY 2 (Figure 2). Besides the specification of a provenience vertex, a destination vertex, a space type (corresponding to a category) and a state in a SMTN, the following may be specified: the main node together with its features and mark: verb tense and mood specification: the set of expected values and the actual value; a set of linguistic functions with their values as for the main node; a list of subedges (inactive edges that were used in extending the edge); a list of *heads*, i.e. references to nodes, with their characteristics, that can be picked as fillers; a list of expectations (i.e. *impulses* to *merge* items); a list of impulses to *mark* an item; a list of impulses to modify an item to an edge "above"; a list of impulses imported from an edge "below"; a measure of likelihood for this analysis. Associated with all this there is the specification of the current state of the semantic network.

Word edges are characterized by having no edges below. Their contents are established and instantiated by the lexicon (or, more exactly, by a morphological processor and the lexicon). When a word edge W is used to extend a given edge A, to produce the edge A' based on the configuration of A, then (without considering further processing described below) its contents are inserted in the corresponding slots of A' , appended to lists or smashed. as required by each case. When any other inactive edge I is used to extend an active edge A, then (without considering further processing described below) some of its contents are inserted in A' in this way: if I "plays an argumental role" in that space, information that comes from the SMTN arc, then the value of its Main is placed among the Heads of A'. If there are impulses in the Modabove field of I, they are inserted among the Modifiers in A' . The likelihood figure of A' is the result of the application of a numeric function to the likelihoods of A' and I. The semantic net shred of I is copied to A'.

What we shall call the Principle of the Good Clerk governs the unification activity:

Before the arrival of th- Main (the "Boss") the processor adopts a lazy attitude , when the Main arrives all possible (unification) activity is done, when the Main is already there an (unification) action is performed as soon as a new event occurs.

Accordingly, before the Main is arrived, an extension of an edge causes almost nothing more than the copying actions indicated above. The only check is for a verb tense to be in accordance with what was expected.

On the arrival of the Main, all the present marking and modifying impulses are "unleashed" and must find satisfaction and, for each head in Heads an expectation matching its characteristics must be found. If all this does not happen then the new edge A' supposedly to be added to the chart is not added: the situation is recognized as a failure.

After the arrival of the Main, each new head must find an impulse to merge with , and each incoming impulse must find satisfaction. Again, if all this does not happen, the new edge A' will not be added to the chart.

What are the effects of merging? The value of the linguistic function or the head that is referred to, gets "more precise" with a reference to the filler node, a category (if not yet specified), a mark as

---

an edge:
  Structural aspect
    from *a vertex*
    to *a vertex*
    spacetype *a SMTN state*
    tnstate *a SMTN state*
  Syntactic Aspect
    main *a head*
    verbtense *expected . actual*
    lingfunctions *a set of linguistic functions*
    belowedges *a list of edges*
    heads *a list of heads*
    expectations *a list of impulses*
    mark-expectations *a list of impulses*
    modabove *a list of impulses*
    modifiers *a list of impulses*
  Extimational Aspect
    likelihood *a measure*
  Semantic Aspect
    net *a semantic network*

Figure 2

prescribed by the considered alternative in the impulse and features of the two contractors merged together. If for one feature there is a set of values for one or both contractors then the intersection of the values is considered as the value. (Of course, if the intersection is empty, and/or if any of the characteristics do not match, the merger is precluded). Changes are always performed in the active edge, nothing is changed in the inactive one. Therefore if the action consists of s a modifying merging, it is the filler that actually gets "more precise". A marking instead only smashes a new mark (and, possibly, new features).

The actual unification happens in the semantic network. For a greater clarity, let us say that the semantic network is represented as a set of labelled propositions, where the arguments of a predicate can also be referred to using *reference pairs*: proposition label and ordinal number. With every entity x (variable or proposition label), R_x, a list of of reference pairs, is associated. In this way, merging x with y causes the substitution of all the occurrences of x, desumed from R_x, with y and the assignement to R_x of the union of R_x and R_y. Should there be specified side effects of a merging type (see paragraph 1), they are carried · ut in the same way.

Each reference to a semantic entity in heads and linguistic functions is in the form of a reference pair (and a proposition label gets never changed), therefore no reference needs to be changed in the syntactic aspect of the edge. A simple example, showing only some aspects of what was discussed is given in Figure 3.

With a semantic network with a more complex defining semantics, things are somehow more complex, but the substance is thesame as that outlined above.

In languages with a variable order, or, for instance, if subject gapping is admitted, possible mergings are not univocally determined by structure or position. Therefore, actually, there may be more than one complete mergings' combination for a tentative new edge A'. In this case more new edges must be added to the chart. This establishes the second kind of tasks mentioned before: an insertion task with self-explanatory execution behaviour.

4. Nondeterminism and disambiguation

Various kinds of ambiguities can be present in the linguistic knowledge. a word may be semantically ambiguous; an impulse may have a number of alternatives; a head may be ambiguously marked. And then of course, the SMTNs express an infinite set of configurations. Dynamically, apart from the general behaviour of the parser, there are some particular restrictions for its nondeterministic behaviour, that put into effect syntactic dynamic disambiguation.

1) the $EXP arc allows for a transition only if the configuration in the active edge includes an impulse to link with the Main of the proposed inactive edge.

2) The sleeping edge mechanism prevents spaces not approporiate to the left context from being established.

3) A search space can be closed only if no impulse that was specified as having to be satisfied remains. In other words, if in a state with an outgoing EXIT arc, an active edge can cause the establishing of an inactive edge only if there are no obligatory impulses left.

4) A proposed new edge A' with a verb tense not matching the expected values causes a failure, i.e. that A' will not be introduced in the chart.

5) As set out in greater detail in the previous paragraph, failure is caused by inadequate mergings, with relation to the presence, absence or ongoing introduction of the Main.

Comparing to the criteria established for LFG for functional compatibility of an f-structure [Kaplan & Bresnan 1982], the following can be said of the dynamics outlined here *Incompleteness* recognition performs as specified in 3), and furthermore there is an earlier check when the Main arrives, in case there were obligatory impulses to be satisfied at that point (e.g. an argument that must occur before the Main). *Incoherence* is completely avoided after the Main has arrived, by the $EXP arc mechanism. Before this, it is recognized as specified in 5) above, and causes an immediate failure. *Inconsistency* is detected as indicated in 4) and 5). As far as 5) is concerned, though, the attitude is to "activate" impulses

```
  ┌──────────────────────────────────────────────────────┐
  │   .                                                    │
  │                                                        │
  │  MAIN: P101                                            │
  │  LINGFUNCTIONS:                                        │
  │        SUBJECT : (P101 . 1)                            │
  │              features: nu sing                         │
  │  EXPECTATIONS:                                         │
  │        MERGE SUBJECT . .                               │
  │          1) condition: T        2) condition: T        │
  │             label: NP              label: S/Infinitive  │
  │             mark: nominative       mark: nominative     │
  │             features: nu sing          . .              │
  │                    . .                                 │
  │                                                        │
  │   .                                                    │
  │  NET:   P101: (shine x102)                             │
  │                                                        │
  └──────────────────────────────────────────────────────┘
```

```
  ┌ ─ ─ ─ ─ ─ ─ ─ ─ ─ ─ ─ ─ ─ ─ ─ ─ ─ ─ ─ ─ ─ ─ ─ ─ ─ ─ ┐
  : a head: (P105 . 1)                                    :
  :       label NP                                        :
  :       mark: nominative or accusative                  :
  :       features: ge fem                                :
  :                 nu sing                               :
  :            . .                                        :
  : &                                                     :
  :                                                       :
  : net: P105: (moon x110)                                :
  └ ─ ─ ─ ─ ─ ─ ─ ─ ─ ─ ─ ─ ─ ─ ─ ─ ─ ─ ─ ─ ─ ─ ─ ─ ─ ─ ┘
```

```
  ┌──────────────────────────────────────────────────────┐
  │   .                                                    │
  │                                                        │
  │  MAIN: P101                                            │
  │  LINGFUNCTIONS:                                        │
  │        SUBJECT : (P101 . 1)                            │
  │              label: NP                                 │
  │              mark: nominative                          │
  │              features: ge fem                          │
  │                        nu sing                         │
  │  EXPECTATIONS: NIL                                     │
  │  HEADS: NIL                                            │
  │                                                        │
  │   .                                                    │
  │  NET: P101: (shine x110)                               │
  │       P105: (moon x110)                                │
  │                                                        │
  └──────────────────────────────────────────────────────┘
```

Figure 3. The sentence is *splendente e' la luna* ("shining is
the moon"). The first frame shows the situation in the S edge
before the NP edge contribution (shown in the second one).
The last frame shows the situation after merging.

when the right premises are present and to "look for the right thing" and not to "check if what was done
is consistent".

Now an important aspect to work at is finding appropriate syntactic heuristics that should apply to the
parsing process. In this regard we proceed in three directions:

a) To take advantage of measures that are introduced in the system, while integrating them with other overall information on the state of the chart. In this context we must find data on human performance to better specify the measures in the lexicon and on the SMTNs.

b) To consider information that comes from failures in unifying, and to use this information in selecting what to do next.

c) To reconsider in the present framework work done before on strategy selection with an ATN system [Ferrari & Stock 1980].

One hitherto fundamental, but only partially implemented, aspect is a mechanism for semantic disambiguation that would interact with WEDNESDAY 2. In fact some aspects of the parser have been designed just in view of such interaction.

5. Implementation and environment

WEDNESDAY 2 is implemented in Interlisp-D and runs on a Xerox 1108 (Dandelion). It takes advantage of the Interlisp data type facility at all levels.

We have built an environment that allows easy experimentation with WEDNESDAY 2 (fig. 4). All kind

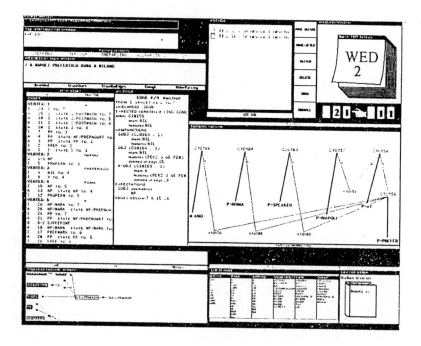

Figure 4

of data are interactively displayed in perspicuous format and a stepper allows the user the state of the system at any point. A graphic agenda manipulator has been built: when in "stepping mode" this interactive device allows the user to schedule tasks This is a basic resource for experimenting with heuristics.

A morphological processor is connected to WEDNESDAY 2. This device is based on a lexicon of roots and several lists of affixes, with various links connecting one to the other. In Italian, for instance there are no less than four dozen forms for each verb. We are not going to discuss here the internal behaviour of the morphological processor. Still it should be clear that the morphological processor here is not only finding the proper segmentations of the word but it also connects in a non trivial way separate information that is linked to the root and to the affixes. For the user there is a two-level interface. On one level one can introduce a word from scratch and, by simple menu interaction, set its characteristics, or introduce a new word by modifying an existing one, or change a whole class of words by specifying a prototype. No LISP, but informal WEDNESDAY 2 lexicon characteristics knowledge is necessary. On the other level no WEDNESDAY 2 knowledge at all is necessary: the program goes through queries in natural language *a la* TEAM [Grosz 1983] . The result of course is less accurate: this modality is conceived only for encouraging the use of the system and may be useful for future applications.

6. Conclusions

We have focussed on an important feature of a parser: being able to perform unification while working on structures. The parser we have introduced is based on linguistic knowledge distributed through the lexicon and uses a chart with unification activity developed when new edges are established. The so called "Principle of the Good Clerk" regulates the unification process. Our purpose is now to experiment on two aspects (beyond the obvious linguistic coverage aspect): a) to work on psycholinguistically motivated heuristics to be introduced as scheduling functions b) to work at an integration of WEDNESDAY 2 with a knowledge based disambiguation system, and more generally to place all this in the framework of a theory of memory in parsing.

Acknowledgments

The author is greatly indebted to Ron Kaplan for his helpful criticism of a previous version of the parser and for many technical discussions as well as to Cristiano Castelfranchi and Domenico Parisi together with whom some basic ideas of this work have been conceived. Yet, obviously, for all *incompleteness, incoherence* and *inconsistencies* credit goes to the author.

REFERENCES

Earley, J. An efficient context-free parsing algorithm. *Communications of the Association for Computing Machinery.* 13(2): 94-102 (1970)

Ferrari,G. & Stock,O. Strategy selection for an ATN syntactic parser. *Proceedings of the 18th Meeting of the Association for Computational Linguistics,* Philadelphia (1980)

Gazdar, G. Phrase structure grammar. In Jacobson and Pullman (Eds.), *The Nature of Syntactic Representation.* Dordrecht: Reidel (1981)

Grosz, B. TEAM, a transportable natural language interface system. In *Proceedings of the Conference on Applied Natural Language Processing,* Santa Monica (1983)

Joshi, A., & Levy, L. Phrase structure trees bear more fruits then you would have thought. *American Journal of Computational Linguistics, 8; 1-11 (1982)*

Kaplan, R. A general syntactic processor. In Rustin, R. (Ed.), *Natural Language Processing.* Englewood Cliffs, N.J.: Prentice-Hall (1973)

Kaplan,R. & Bresnan,J. Lexical-Functional Grammar: a formal system for grammatical representation. In Bresnan,J., Ed. *The Mental Representation of Grammatical Relations.* The MIT Press, Cambridge, 173-281 (1982)

Kay, M. Algorithm Schemata and Data Structures in Syntactic Processing. Xerox, Palo Alto Research Center (October 1980)

Kay, M. Functional Grammar. In *Proceedings of the 5th Meeting of the Berkeley Linguistic Society,* Berkeley, 142-158 (1979)

Pereira, F. & Warren, D., Definite Clause Grammars for language analysis. A survey of the formalism and a comparison with Augmented Transition Networks. *Artificial Intelligence,* 13; 231-278 (1980)

Ritchie, G. & Thompson, H. Implementing Natural Lnguage Parsers. In O'Shea, T. & Eisenstadt, M. (Eds.), *Artificial Intelligence: Tools, Techniques and Applications*, New York: Harper & Row (1984)

Small, S. Word expert parsing: a theory of distributed word-based natural language understanding. (Technical Report TR-954 NSG-7253). Maryland: University of Maryland (1980)

Stock, O. Parsing on WEDNESDAY: A Distributed Linguistic Knowledge Approach for Flexible Word Order Languages. (Technical Report No.312) Roma: I.P. - Consiglio Nazionale delle Ricerche (1982)

Stock, O., Castelfranchi, C. & Parisi, D. WEDNESDAY: Parsing flexible word order languages. In *Proceedings of the First Meeting of the Association for Computational Linguistics, European Chapter*, Pisa (1983)

Thompson, H.S. Chart parsing and rule schemata in GPSG. In *Proceedings of the 19th Annual Meeting of the Association for Computational Linguistics*. Alexandria, Va. (1981)

PART IV

EXPERT SYSTEMS

Advances in Artificial Intelligence - II
B. Du Boulay, D. Hogg and L. Steels (Editors)
© Elsevier Science Publishers B.V. (North-Holland), 1987

Knowledge Representations for Diagnosis and Test Planning in the Domain of Electromyography
-o-

S.K.Andersen°, S.Andreassen°, M.Woldbye°

Nordjydsk Udviklings Center
Badehusvej 23
DK-9000 Aalborg, Denmark

ABSTRACT

In electromyography (EMG) - the diagnosis of disorders of muscles and peripheral nerves by electrical measurements - 13 main types of knowledge are needed for an expert EMG-assistant. These include knowledge about the manifestations of the diseases to be diagnosed, a topological understanding of neuroanatomy, and procedural knowledge about EMG-tests. An EMG-examination consists of an iterative cycle of 1) planning of the sequence of EMG-tests, 2) collection of information by execution of the tests, and 3) diagnosis based on the presently available information. A causal multilayer network linking diseases and their manifestations is proposed as a unified approach to diagnosis, planning and explanation. Each node in the network has local capability to support diagnosis, explanation of test plans and report generation.

1. INTRODUCTION

The performance of an expert system depends on how well the chosen knowledge-representations reflect the underlying structure of the domain knowledge. This paper discusses knowledge-representations in an expert system for electromyography and electroneurography (EMG). The expert system will assist in the tasks of diagnosis and planning of test sequences. Section 2 will outline the functionality of the system to the extent that it is relevant for the discussion of the domain knowledge representations. In section 3 the types of knowledge are identified. Section 4 will focus on a proposed causal network for representing the relations between diseases and their manifestations (findings). Each node in the network has local capability to support diagnosis, planning, and explanations.

Causal models have been included in several recent medical expert systems, starting with CASNET and with increasingly more sophisticated structures, to ABEL and CADUCEUS. In CASNET, a system for diagnosis and treatment of eye diseases [Weiss et. al. 78], the disease process is modelled as a causal-associational network consisting of three levels of states, observations, pathophysiological states, and disease categories, with causal links between states within a level and associational links between states at different levels. The network is restricted to being acyclic and uses simple 1:1 link mechanisms with weights resembling conditional propabilities. In ABEL, an expert consultant for acid-base disturbances [Patil 81], the causal links are treated as multi-attributed objects and the states are given a multilevel description. In CADUCEUS which assists the physician to make multiple diagnoses in internal medicine [Pople 82], the causal network is part of a network with several other types of links as planning, constrictor, and classification links.

°Affiliation: Institute of Electronic Systems
Aalborg University
Strandvejen 19,
DK-9000 Aalborg, Denmark

Our analysis of the types of knowledge in the EMG-domain lead us to propose a simple multilevel causal network with only one type of links. Despite its simplicity we will argue that the network is an efficient tool for the main reasoning tasks in an EMG-examination, primarily diagnosis, test planning, and explanations to the user of its line of reasoning, leading either to a diagnosis or to a proposed test plan.

2. SYSTEM FUNCTIONALITY

In order to justify the proposed knowledge representations the functionality of the system will be described briefly.   The main function of the system is to be an expert assistant to a physician during an EMG-examination.The man-machine interface is an important aspect of functionality, which is a determining factor in the acceptability of the system. The details of the interface are not settled yet, but for the purpose of this paper the system will be assumed to have the functionality described below. The main task is incremental diagnosis based on the presently available data, and incremental planning, i.e. deciding which sequence of EMG-tests to perform next. The expert assistant must also be able to explain its reasoning and to report findings and conclusions. In addition to the problem-solving tasks itself, attention should be paid to providing the expert with a cooperative system i.e. the system must contain knowledge about how to be a good assistant [Worden et al. 86].

Three things will be done to facilitate communication and to reduce the necessary amount of communication between the physician and the expert assistant during the examination. 1) Graphical input/output will be the preferred mode of interaction. 2) The system contains an integrated EMG measurement system that automatically transfers test results to the other parts of the system, thus eliminating the need for manual input of the test results. In other expert systems, PUFF [Aikins et al. 83] the advantage following from integration of a measurement system has been crucial for user acceptance. 3) The expert assistant will interfere minimally during the course of the EMG examination, thus reducing the time and effort the physician has to spend on communication.

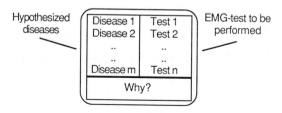

Fig. 1 Sketch of user interface

The main components of the user interface for the diagnostic and test planning tasks may be visualized as a split screen (fig 1) in which the left half is dedicated to a ranked list of the diagnoses or groups of diagnoses that the system at present believes to be most likely. The right half of the screen is dedicated to a ranked list of the EMG-tests that the system believes are most likely to support or reject the top ranked diagnoses.

At the bottom of the screen there is a "query button". The physician may at any time point to one of the diagnoses and query the expert assistant to explain its line of reasoning leading to its present belief in the diagnosis. Alternatively the physician may query any of the EMG-tests suggested by the system. The expert assistant must then the explain how the suggested test is expected to contribute to the diagnosis. At all times the physician chooses the next test, following or disregarding the expert assistants suggestions as he pleases.

The last aspect of the functionality to be mentioned is report writing. This can be regarded as a special case of explanation of diagnostic reasoning, which is performed at the end of the examination, when the physician and hopefully also the expert assistant is satisfied that the repeated cycle of hypothezising diagnoses and performing EMG-tests has been exhausted.

3. DOMAIN DESCRIPTION

In this section we shall try to identify which types of domain knowledge and which types of patient data are needed during the course of an EMG-examination, and we shall try to indicate appropriate choices of knowledge representations. The EMG-domain has a number of characteristics that must be taken into account:

1) The domain is large. Of the order of 4000 individual measurements distributed over a number of muscles and nerves are potentially relevant to diagnose at least a couple of hundred neuro-muscular disorders. This leads to a demand for economy in the expression of domain knowledge.

2) An EMG-examination is time-consuming and moderately uncomfortable for the patient. Typically 5 to 20 EMG-tests are performed, each yielding 1 to 5 numbers, giving 5 to 100 measurements out of 5000 possible. This has two major consequences: Planning of the sequence of EMG-test becomes very important, in order to get the relevant data from the patient within a reasonable time, and the system has to be able to operate efficiently in a situation where the input data is very sparse.

3) The range of EMG equipment used, the repertoire of EMG-tests available and the way in which they are carried out differs widely between countries and even between individual laboratories in one country. The conceptual description of EMG-domain thus has to be general enough to encompass these differences.

3.1 Types of Domain Knowledge

3.1.1 Diagnosis

To illustrate the types of domain knowledge, we consider the diagnosis of Duchenne dystrophy, a hereditary progressive muscle disease (myopathy) with fatal outcome [Kimura 83]. Its heredity and severity makes an exact diagnosis important. The system's disease specific knowledge is illustrated in fig 2.

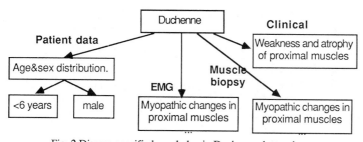

Fig. 2 Disease specific knowledge in Duchenne dystrophy

Duchenne dystrophy is a sex-linked recessive disease with onset in early childhood as
expressed in the frame "Age & sex distribution". Clinically the patient presents with "Weakness
and atrophy (reduced muscle volume) of proximal muscles". The typical myopathic changes in the
proximal muscles, e.g. most prominent in the hip muscles and the muscles of the shoulder girdle,
can be assessed by microscopic examination of a sample of the muscle (muscle biopsy) or by an
EMG-examination.

Pursuing the EMG-examination the next step is to determine which muscles qualify as
proximal. This requires a knowlege of <u>neuroanatomy</u>. In this case a very restricted knowledge ,
but in other cases where the disease may be a local lesion of a peripheral nerve the diagnosis is
basically a topological puzzle. This requires a comprehensive knowledge of the relations between
nerves and the muscles they innervate (fig 3.). In Duchenne dystrophy the expert assistant only
uses the neuroanatomy to compile a list of the proximal muscles that are expected to show
myopathic changes (fig 4.).

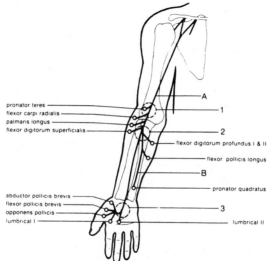

Fig. 3 Diagram of the median nerve, its nerve branches and
the muscles innervated by it. From[Kimura 83]

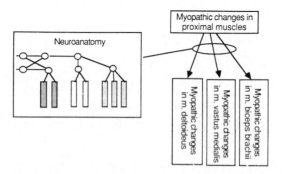

Fig. 4 List of proximal muscles obtained
from the neuroanatomy.

The next type of knowledge required is a <u>knowledge of pathophysiology</u>, in order to express the pathophysiological changes caused by Duchenne dystrophy. We propose that all changes in a muscle can be described through combinations of only 8 pathophysiological states (fig 5.), The links indicate that Duchenne dystrophy will cause changes in " Motor unit structure" and will lead to "Ongoing denervation" and "Ongoing reinnervation".

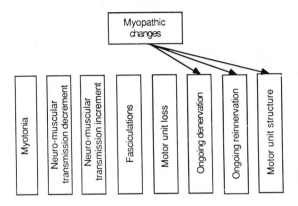

Fig. 5 Pathophysiological concepts used to describe the state of a muscle. Myopathic changes are expected to cause changes of "Motor unit structure", to cause "Ongoing denervation" and "Ongoing reinnervation".

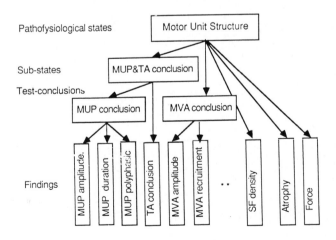

Fig.6: Findings related to "Motor unit structure". Prefix on findings indicate the EMG-test: MUP = Motor Unit Potential analysis, TA = Turns& Amplitude, MVA = Maximal Voluntary Activity, and SF = Single Fiber

Introducing the concept pathophysiological states has two main advantages:

1) Although conclusions about pathophysiological states are derived from findings extracted from different EMG-tests, either directly or through test conclusions and substates (fig 6), the states themselves are general enough to be described without requiring specific EMG-tests to be done in certain ways. They should, therefore, be able to encompass national differences in EMG-traditions.

2) The pathophysiological states provide an economical expression of the changes in a muscle. Once, for example, the description of myopathic changes of a certain type and severity is generic. The same description can be applied to all other muscles in the body. The states can be instantiated for all relevant muscles as indicated in fig 7.

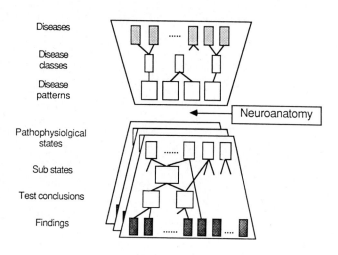

Fig .7 Overall structure of the network linking findings and
diseases

3.1.2 Planning of sequences of EMG-tests

Knowledge requirements for performing the diagnostic task has been identified. Test planning re-uses some of the knowledge but additional knowledge is necessary. For example, a generalized cost of an EMG-test must be calculated. Some of the cost components are:

1) The cost of the supplies spent to do the test
2) The time it takes to do the test in a given muscle
3) The inconvenience and risk involved for the patient
4) Is the test available and routinely used in this laboratory ?

Apart from deciding how much pain (for the patient) is equivalent to 10 minutes (of the physicians time) the calculation is complicated by interaction between different tests. While doing a test that requires insertion of a needle electrode into a muscle, the additional cost of doing other tests that also require a needle in the muscle is reduced. The planning of the sequence of

EMG-tests can be done by balancing the cost of the EMG-tests against their importance. The importance must be estimated from the capacity of a test to supply data that may influence the diagnosis. Knowledge about importance or diagnostic capacity is therefore needed. The importance of a given test changes throughout the course of an examination, and at the end of a successful examination all tests should have a low importance/cost ratio.

3.1.3 Execution of EMG-tests

A new iteration in the hypothesize and test cycle is initiated by choosing an EMG-test from the suggested test plan. To execute the chosen EMG-test procedural knowledge about the EMG-test is needed. The nerves or muscles must be located and electrodes placed appropriately. This requires test specific knowledge of neuroanatomy. Next step in performing an EMG-test is to set the system up to do a specific test e.g. "recording spontaneous muscle activity by concentric needles" This involves adjusting amplifiers, filters, timebases etc. Thus, the expert assistant needs knowledge of test set-up. After recording of the electrical activity of the muscle or nerve, signal processing e.g. digital filtering or averaging, may be required. Diagnostically interesting features of the processed signal must be extracted, i.e. knowledge of EMG-measurements is required. The knowledge may be simple, e.g. "measure the amplitude of the electrical activity in this particular way", or it may involve complicated pattern recognition methods [Andreassen 83]. To be useful the measurement must be converted to an EMG-finding. This implies comparing of the measurement with a normal value from a reference material and assessing if the measurement is normal and if not, the degree of abnormality. Knowledge of reference values is not trivial and must incorporate strategies for extrapolating non-existing reference values: "What is the reference value in a similar muscle" or "Compare with the same measurement in the opposite (normal) side of the body".

3.1.4 Explanations and report generations

The knowledge needed for explanation and report generation tasks has not yet been identified. To generate explanations the expert assistant must have knowledge for explanation of diagnoses and knowledge for explanation of test plans. In addition the expert assistant must have knowledge about report writing. In principle the report contains three types of information: The likely diagnoses, the EMG-findings, and an outline of how well the EMG-findings support one or more diagnoses.

3.2 Representations of domain knowledge.

The different types of knowledge needed to perform the five tasks of the expert assistant i.e. diagnosis, planning, explanation of diagnosis and planning respectively, and report generation, are now established. They are listed in fig. 8 together with a suggestion of an appropriate knowledge representation for each of them.

The neuroanatomy that the expert assistant is going to use for anatomical reasoning (2a in fig. 8) may be represented as an object with entry points of the type: "Generate a list of proximal muscles" or "List all muscles innervated by nerve x". In the representation of the neuroanatomy inside the object a graph with nodes representing nerve segments or muscles is convenient (fig 4.)

To assist the physician's reasoning a graphical schematic representation (2b) may be helpful (fig 3). Part of the test specific neuroanatomical knowledge may also be represented graphically (6a). Cost of EMG-test (4), EMG-test set up (7), and reference values (10) are also naturally represented as objects. An entry point for the reference values may be: "Produce the mean and standard deviation for the measurement x in EMG-test y in muscle z".

The knowledge about signal processing (8) and extraction of EMG-measurements (9) is mainly of algorithmic nature, naturally expressed as a procedure. All the remaining types of knowledge can be represented in the nodes of one and the same causal network as exemplified in section 4.

	Knowledge type	Knowledge representation
1	Disease specific	Causal network
2a	Neuroanatomy	Object
2b	Neuroanatomy	Graphical
3	Pathophysiology	Causal network
4	Cost of EMG-tests	Object
5	Importance (diagnostic capability)	Causal network
6a	Test specific neuroanatomy	Graphical
6b	Test specific neuroanatomy	Causal network
7	EMG-test set up	Object
8	Signal processing	Algorithmic
9	EMG-measurements	Algorithmic
10	Reference values	Object
11	Explanation of diagnoses	Causal network
12	Explanation of test plan	Causal network
13	Report generation	Causal network

Fig. 8 Types of knowledge and associated knowledge representations.

4. A UNIFIED APPROACH TO DIAGNOSIS, PLANNING AND EXPLANATION

The discussion of the domain knowledge to be included in the expert assistant made it clear that a considerable part of the knowledge can be represented in a causal network. The network consists of nodes representing EMG-concepts ranging from findings at the lower end through convenient clusters of findings over pathophysiological states to diseases. The causality is in the direction from diseases to findings. The domain description represented by the causal network forms a unified knowledge representation within which local reasoning for the purpose of diagnosis, planning, and explanation can take place. This is done by assigning to each EMG-concept scores, importance and explanations and by ensuring that this information propagates coherently to neighbouring elements in the network.

To illustrate the reasoning principles we will focus on one of the nodes (MUP.conclusion) contained in the EMG-example discribed earlier, to see which information it is necessary to store in order to perform local reasoning concerning the EMG-concept which the node represents. MUP.conclusion is a clustering of three of the findings extracted from Motor unit potential analysis. Figure 9 visualizes the causal links from MUP.conclusion towards findings.

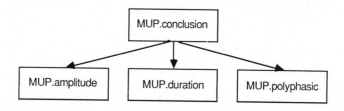

Fig. 9 The test conclusion MUP.conclusion and its causal links to lower level EMG-concepts, the findings MUP.amplitude, MUP.duration, and MUP.polyphasic.

4.1 Diagnosis

MUP.conclusion provides a quantitative evaluation of the motor unit structure within the muscle under examination expressed in terms of the following possible outcomes: severe myogenic, moderate myogenic, normal, mild neurogenic, moderate neurogenic, severe neurogenic, and inconclusive. The evaluation is based on the findings: MUP.amplitude, MUP.duration, and MUP. polyphasic. MUP.amplitude and MUP.duration are given in the unit of standard deviations from the reference value while MUP.polyphasic has a binary outcome, namely either polyphasic (more than 12% polyphasic potentials) or non-polyphasic.

In the case of Duchenne dystrophy the expected result of the evaluation of MUP.conclusion is either severe myogenic or moderate myogenic.

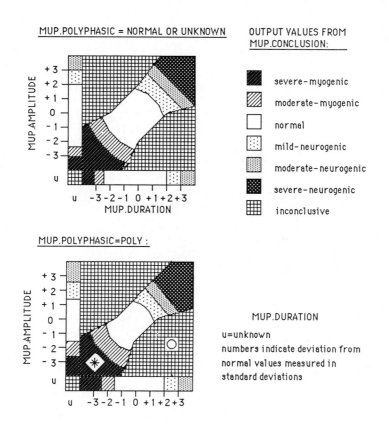

Fig. 10 An example of a graphical representation of the scoring rule for MUP.conclusion

To evaluate MUP.conclusion based on the input available at any given moment, the node must contain enough neurophysiological knowledge to compute the outcome from the inputs. This knowledge of how to map inputs onto outputs can be stored in what will be referred to as a scoring rule. An example of a representation of the scoring rule is given in fig 10.

In a scoring rule not all inputs are given the same weight. This is because some of the inputs to the node are known to be more reliable and objective, or to give stronger evidence than others. This type of knowledge about the inputs must be built into the scoring rule of that node.

For example, the MUP.amplitude and MUP.duration give stronger evidence to the evaluation of MUP.conlusion than does MUP.polyphasic. These facts are reflected in the scoring rule illustrated in fig 10 in the following ways, 1) if both amplitude and duration is known then the result of MUP.polyphasic has little influence on the result of the scoring of MUP.conclusion, (for example MUP.duration and MUP.amplitude corresponding to the asterisks in fig 10 gives the outcome severe myogenic, irrespective of the value of MUP.polyphasic) and 2) if only MUP.polyphasic is known then the actual score of the node is inconclusive.

The outcome "inconclusive" has two possible interpretations. An actual score "inconclusive" of a node can express lack of known input as descibed above, or a contradiction between two or more of the known inputs. In our case, the latter interpretation of "inconclusive" would be used if simultaneously MUP.amplitude is above normal (pointing at neurogenic motor unit structure) and MUP.duration is below normal (pointing at myogenic motor unit structure) corresponding to the circle in fig 10.

The actual score or belief of a node must be contained in the node itself and can be represented either as categorical belief in one of the possible outcomes, or as a belief factors linked to each of them. The scoring rules may be of a non-probabilistic type, as in INTERNIST or CADUCEUS [Pople 82], or may be probabilistic [Cheeseman 83, Spiegelhalter & Knill-Jones 84, Pearl & Kim 83].

The above discussion of the scoring mechanism demonstrates the need to store in each node the information listed in fig. 11a

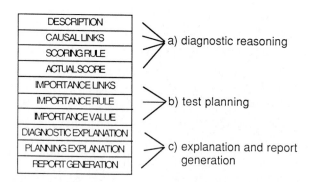

Fig. 11 A list of the information contained in each node to deal with a) diagnostic reasoning b) test planning and c) explanations and report generation.

4.2 Planning

For the purposes of test planning an importance value is associated with each EMG-concept (node) in the network. The importance of a node reflects how diagnostically useful the node is, i.e. the extent to which it affects the score of the nodes from which it receives causal links. Concider, for example, MUP.conclusion (fig 10). MUP.conclusion has a causal link from MUP&TA.conclusion, meaning that it contributes to the outcome of MUP&TA.conclusion. MUP.conclusion therefore receives importance from MUP&TA.conclusion. It redistributes the recieved importance to the findings MUP.amplitude, MUP.duration, and MUP.polyphasic by multiplying it with a local importance factor assigned to each of the findings. The importance factors can be derived by reading the scoring rules "backwards". Consider again the example, where MUP.amplitude and MUP.duration have the values corresponding to the asterisks in fig .10. Then, look up the diagnostic score for each of the two outcomes of MUP.polyphasic. Compare the two results. As the value of MUP.polyphasic does not affect the outcome of MUP.conclusion, set the importance to zero. Figure 11b summarizes the knowledge that must be contained in a node to deal with the planning task.

4.3 Explaning diagnosis, planning, and report generation

To fulfil the required tasks the causal network must be able to handle explanations of both diagnosis and test planning during the course of an EMG-examination, and at the end of the examination to generate a report. Generation of explanations and reports is done in similar ways. Together with score and importance, explanations of diagnosis and planning respectively flow through the network. Within a node the explanations input to that node are summarized and connected to the explanation of the node itself and then sent off.

Returning to the EMG-example, the diagnostic explanation in MUP.conclusion transferred to higher level EMG-concepts with causal links to the conclusion could be "MUP.conclusion shows a severe myogenic organisation of the motor units. This is based on reduced amplitude (- 2.2 SD), reduced duration (- 3 SD), and a normal (8 %) percentage of polyphasic potentials (non-polyphasic)". The explanation is formed from a standard phrase filled in with the explanations from MUP.amplitude (reduced amplitude (- 2.2 SD)), from MUP.duration (reduced duration (- 3 SD)), and from MUP.polyphasic (normal (8 %) percentage of polyphasic potentials (non-polyphasic)). An similar example could be constructed to illustrate explanation of test planning. It is easily seen that complexity of the explanation tasks increases with the number of nodes in the path on which the explanation passes through the network.

A report is a list of all results obtained during an EMG-examination and the diagnostic explanation of the hypothesized diseases. Thus, this task is easily performed by picking up test results and findings at the lower edge of the network and explanations of diseases at the upper edge of the network.

Figure 11c illustrates a list of the knowledge to be contained in a node in order to perform explanation tasks and report generation.

5. CONCLUSION

Analysis of the types of knowledge required in an EMG-examination led us to propose a causal network to represent the relations between diseases and EMG-findings. Some of the intermediate nodes in the network represent pathophysiological states. The pathophysiological states make it possible to give a description of the EMG-domain that is general enough to encompass local or national EMG-traditions. At the same time the pathophysiological states can be used for generic description of pathological changes of a muscle. This generic description can then be instantiated for all desired muscles, resulting in a very economic and compact domain description.

The causal network is conceptually simple with only one type of links, yet it proved possible to use it for the main reasoning tasks, diagnosis, test planning, and explanations. The causal network is a domain description, and does not in itself impose any restrictions on the inference mechanisms - both probabilic and non-probabilistic inference can be used.

Acknowledgement

This work was supported in part by the ESPRIT programme of the European Community under project P599: An expert assistant for electromyography. We thank the members of the ESPRIT project team for many encouraging discussions concerning the ideas presented in this paper.

References

Aikins,J.S.,Kunz,J.C., and Shortliffe,E.H.: PUFF: an Expert System for Interpretation of Pulmonary Function.Data, Computers and Biomedical Research, vol. 16, pp.199-208,1983.

Andreassen,S.:Computerized analysis of motor unit firing. In: Progress in Clinical Neurophysiology, vol. 10. (ed J.E.Desmedt), pp.150-163, Karger,Basel,1983.

Cheeseman,P.C.: A Method of Computing Generalized Bayesian Probability Values for Expert Systems. Proc. 8th Int. Conf. Artificial Intelligence, Karlsruhe, pp198-202, August.1983.

Kimura,J.: Electrodiagnosis in Diseases of Nerve andMuscles: Principles and Practice. F.A.Davis Company, Philadelphia 1983.

Patil,R.S.: Causal Representation of Patient Illness for Electrolyte and Acid-Base Diagnosis. Laboratory for Computer Science,MIT, PhD Thesis, 1981.

Pearl,J. and Kim, J.H.: A Computational Model for Causal and Diagnostic Reasoning in Inference System.Proc. 8th Int. Conf. Artificial Intelligence, Karlsruhe, pp190-193, August,1983.

Pople,Jr.,H.E.: Heuristic Methods for Imposing Structure on Ill-Structured Problems: The Structuring of Medical Diagnostics, pp119-190 in Artificial Intelligence in Medicine (ed P.Szolovits) Westview Press, Boulder Colorado ,1982. AAAS Selected Symposium Series 51.

Spiegelhalter, D.J. and Knill-Jones R. P.:Statistical And Knowledge-based Approach to Clinical Decision-support Systems, with an Application in Gastroenterology. J.R.Statist.Soc.A,147,35-77,1984.

Weiss,S.M.,Kulikowski,C.A.,Amaral,S., and Safir,A.: A Model-Based Method for Computer-Aided Medical Decision making, Artificial Intelligence 11, pp 145-178 ,1978.

Worden,R.P.,Foote,M.F.,Knight,J.,Andersen,S.K.:Co-operative Expert Systems, Proc. European Conf. Artificial Intelligence, Brighton, July 86.

Advances in Artificial Intelligence - II
B. Du Boulay, D. Hogg and L. Steels (Editors)
© Elsevier Science Publishers B.V. (North-Holland), 1987

Qualitative Control

W.F. Clocksin and A.J. Morgan
Computer Laboratory, University of Cambridge
Corn Exchange Street, Cambridge CB2 3QG, England

Abstract

*We introduce the issues of qualitative control, the control of plant by means of non-numerical
techniques rather than by conventional mathematical modelling. The approach of qualitative control is
to represent the semantics of the plant; this approach is in contrast to expert systems, which employ a
shallow model in the form of heuristic rules. Other researchers have used qualitative modelling for the
analysis of systems rather than for the synthesis of control methods. We derive a number of qualitative
controllers and compare their performance with conventional controllers. The controllers are
demonstrated on the coupled-tanks plant, a standard control theory example.*

1. Introduction

Qualitative reasoning systems model a particular domain by incorporating fundamental knowledge
about its structures and functions. Previous results have been concerned with the *analysis* of systems
[5]. A further possibility which has received less attention is to consider whether the techniques used
for qualitative analysis can be used for *synthesis*. As an example of a synthesis problem, we examine
the task of building qualitative automatic controllers for a simple physical system. A controller is
taken to be *qualitative* if it can operate without the precise numerical parameters required for a
conventional automatic controller. Here we shall design some conventional and qualitative
controllers. Space permits only a brief comparison of the controllers; the full paper [15] gives a
detailed comparison on the basis of standard criteria such as robustness (behaviour in response to drift
in plant characteristics), speed of response, and accuracy.

Our motivation for considering qualitative control stems from the challenges presented to
conventional control methodology by the demands of industrial plant. In particular, we suspect that
many control failures are due to inadequacies in modelling the full range of plant parameters and
relating plant components to the model. These problems come to the attention of an operator when
acceptable operating limits are exceeded owing to plant malfunction or model inaccuracy.

The roots of qualitative control are in the field of qualitative modelling, and in the application of
Prolog programming [2] to control [9,10] and diagnosis of reactor plant faults [17]. We have also been
influenced by our current investigations of the qualitative control of a small petrochemical plant and
the qualitative analysis of CMOS transistor networks [1].

2. Conventional Control

Automatic control provides a good domain for investigating qualitative techniques because of the
wealth of example problems and the availability of techniques for the design of controllers. The latter
can be used to judge a qualitative design. We shall now outline a typical control problem to be used in
the subsequent examples. Figure 1 shows a simple physical system known as the "coupled tanks".
Variants of this problem are frequently found in control engineering texts [13,16]. A pump moves
liquid from a sump into Tank 1. Liquid flows between Tanks 1 and 2 via Pipe 1. Liquid flows out of
Tank 2 through Pipe 2 and returns to the sump. The problem is to design a control system which
adjusts the level of liquid in Tank 2 to match a required level setting.

A quantitative model of the coupled tanks forms the basis of a conventional controller which we derive
for the purposes of comparison in [15], where we use a fourth-order Runge-Kutta simulation of the
state-space equations. Although this representation is commonly used in conventional control, it is
important for our purposes to recognise that it does not correspond exactly to a real physical system
because of the simplifying assumptions made:

(a) The numerical parameters are assumed to be known exactly, and to be time-invariant.

(b) Physical limits are not included. For example, the arrangement of the input pipe at Tank 1 will
    only allow fluid to flow into the system (*i.e.* no liquid can be withdrawn from Tank 1). Also, the
    finite capacity of the tanks is ignored.

(c) Relationships are assumed to be linear. This does not necessarily hold: as, for example, in the case of the relationship between pressure and flow in a pipe where it depends on whether the flow is laminar or turbulent.

In spite of these simplifications, the conventional linear model can provide a good representation of a plant for the purpose of designing a controller, provided that the plant will always be operated within the limits for which it has been designed. The response of the plant with a conventional PID controller to a step input is shown in Figure 2. It is important to recognise that the plant and controller equations represent tightly compiled knowledge about the plant. This has two side-effects. First, because the equations are derived from the plant parameters, it is assumed that the plant's characteristics do not change during its operation. Second, although the equations offer an efficient and accurate way of calculating a control effort (given the assumptions above), the knowledge they represent cannot be used in any other way, for example, to ask the controller to explain an action.

We see that the plant has been modelled using standard methods, but at the risk of making simplifying assumptions and by not using information that relates the controller to components of the plant. This can be acceptable provided the plant does not exceed its operating limits. However, this presents two challenges. The first challenge arises when, owing to plant malfunction or model inaccuracy, operating limits are overstepped. It is very likely that at this time at least one control function will be attempting control in a region in which the assumptions are not valid, thus compounding the problem. The other challenge is that the plant operator is given no way to diagnose the failure, because the plant model is not expressed in terms easily related to components of the plant. Conventional control theory gives no guidance on plant that has gone out of control. This problem is compounded when more sophisticated mathematical methods are used to model highly nonlinear and discrete systems.

3. Qualitative Reasoning

A theme common to qualitative modelling [4-8,11,12] is the use of a *qualitative mathematics* to describe system quantities with limited information. We shall use the notation of de Kleer, in which $[Q]_a$ and its qualitative derivatives $[\delta Q]_a, [\delta^2 Q]_a$ (relative to reference value a) take on values drawn from the set of signs $\{-, 0, +\}$. Where de Kleer uses the qualitative function (**sum** A_1 A_2) which may return problematical undefined results, we shall introduce the functions (**invert** A), which reverses the sign of its input, and (**vote** $A_1,...,A_n$), which returns the majority sign of its n inputs.

4. Qualitative Control

4.1 Simple Policies

We now consider a qualitative controller. The aim is to control the plant without requiring an accurate numerical representation of the system. The starting point is a qualitative description of the influences acting on and within the plant. We should not expect that a qualitative controller will perform as accurately as a conventional controller. Perfect knowledge of the plant parameters will always allow a superior controller to be built. However, there will be practical situations where the benefits of a qualitative approach are significant, and these are discussed in [15].

Considering the coupled tanks, if L_2 is the error in level in Tank 2 then the qualitative value $[L_2]$ can take the following values: $[L_2] = +$ if the level in Tank 2 is above the required level; $[L_2] = 0$ if the level in Tank 2 is correct; $[L_2] = -$ if the level in Tank 2 is below the required level. Similarly, if the control action is designated by U, then its qualitative value can be expressed as: $[U] = +$ if the pumping rate is to increase; $[U] = 0$ if the pumping rate is to remain steady; $[U] = -$ if the pumping rate is to decrease. Note that $[U]$ is the difference between the current value of U and the required value at the next sample instant. The qualitative value is therefore more properly described as a rate, and written $[\delta U]$.

Both $[L_2]$ and $[\delta U]$ are values which exist at sample intervals. There is no way to detect the values of $[L_2]$ or $[\delta U]$ between sample instants. We could, however, adopt different policies for U depending on the interpretation of $[\delta U]$. For example, given $[\delta U] = +$, the pumping rate must obviously increase before the next sample instant. This could be achieved by increasing the value of U by some fixed amount, or by increasing U at a steady rate between sample instants. In this paper we shall assume that an incremental step size is defined for U and that $[\delta U] = +$ is interpreted as "increase the value of U by one increment" (and similarly, $[\delta U] = -$ indicates a decrease by one increment).

The notation used here for the qualitative value of a variable, say Q, at a particular sample instant k is $[Q]_{(k)}$. This should not be confused with the notation introduced by De Kleer for the qualitative value of Q relative to a specified value, (say a), which is $[Q]_a$. Finally, $[L_2]$ may be obtained by taking the difference between the actual and required levels at the same sample instant $[L_2]_{(k)} = [actual\_level_{(k)} - required\_level_{(k)}]$.

A straightforward controller can now be defined (called controller Q1 for reference). Q1 simply examines the value of $[L_2]$ and forces the value of $[\delta U]$ in the opposite sense. With this definition, controller Q1 may be defined as $Q1 \equiv_{def} [\delta U]_{(k)} = (\textbf{invert}\,[L_2])_{(k)}$. The response of this controller to a step input is shown in Figure 3. Clearly, its dynamic performance is very poor compared with the digital PID controller. The response to a step change in required value takes some time to reach the necessary level, and then oscillates around the required value. Changing the control increment size in U does not help. If the increment size is increased, the required level is reached faster but with greater overshoot and oscillation. A small increment size reduces the magnitude of the oscillations, but makes the system slow to respond. The problem lies in the simplicity of the controller. Only one qualitative value is used: the relative level of liquid in Tank 2.

4.2 Improved controllers

The coupled-tank system has been used as an example by Francis and Leitch [9,10] to test the performance of a real-time expert system shell called ARTIFACT. Although linguistic terms such as *pump_increasing* or *level_steady* are used rather than the notation given here, it is clear to us that the ARTIFACT controller example is based on qualitative variables. The controller uses measurements and estimates of the plant variables in a state-space defined by the error in level at Tank 2, the rate of change of level in Tank 2, and the rate of change of level in Tank 1. As each of these three state variables takes one of the three values {+, 0, -}, the system is in one of 3^3 states. For each of these 27 states there is a corresponding control action. Francis and Leitch express a set of control rules governing the controller actions, which appear to be derived empirically by considering the action required for each state in turn. The controller actions are given in [9] as a set of Prolog clauses. The inference procedure works from the current system state by constructing a derivation leading to the desired goal state in which Tank 1 and Tank 2 are stable and Tank 2 is at the required level. Examination of the controller actions show that they are much as would be expected from common sense, although there is room for some argument over the most appropriate action to take in situations such as "Tank 2 is above the required level and steady, and the level in Tank 1 is falling".

We may now define a qualitative controller (called Q2 for reference) which corresponds to the ARTIFACT example. The plant variables are now expressed as the qualitative values $[L_2]$, $[\delta L_2]$, and $[\delta L_1]$, which become the *qualitative state variables* for the system. To maintain compatibility with the ARTIFACT example, the rate of change of level in Tank 1 (δL_1) is derived from the Tank 2 measurements: $\delta L_1 = (L_{2_{(k)}} - L_{2_{(k-1)}}) - (L_{2_{(k-1)}} - L_{2_{(k-2)}})$. In fact this value is more properly described as $\delta^2 L_2$ (the second difference of the level in Tank 2). Controller Q2 can now be expressed as: $Q2 \equiv_{def} [\delta U]_{(k)} = (\textbf{invert}\,(\textbf{vote}\,(\textbf{vote}\,[L_2]_{(k)}\,[\delta L_2]_{(k)})\,[\delta L_1]_{(k)}))$, which gives the same result as the ARTIFACT shell. The behaviour of controller Q2 is detailed in [15]. Controller Q3, a simplified version using a three-argument vote function, is defined as $Q3 \equiv_{def} [\delta U]_{(k)} = (\textbf{invert}\,(\textbf{vote}\,[L_2]_{(k)}\,[\delta L_2]_{(k)}\,[\delta L_1]_{(k)}))$, and performs in a very similar way to controller Q2 despite differences in its steady-state cycle. The response of this controller is given in Figure 4. Extensional representation of these controllers are shown in Figure 5.

In [15] we derive and give detailed performance characteristics of improved controllers that take account of temporal information. Controller Q4 varies the step size in response to changes in the rate of error, using variable slope delta modulation to choose a step size drawn from the Fibonacci sequence. Controller Q5 uses extended precision, where a three-sign qualitative value is used to partition the measurement space of Q into subranges. The results obtained from this controller correspond to existing results using fuzzy logic [14]. Controller Q6 uses the function **weight**, which is a voting function for extended precision qualitative values. Controllers Q7 and Q8 are "target controllers" of the general form (for coefficients α, β, γ):

$$Q7 \equiv_{def} [(L_2) + \alpha(\delta L_2) + \beta(U)]_{(k)} = 0$$
$$Q8 \equiv_{def} [(L_2) + \alpha(\delta L_2) + \beta(U) + \gamma(e)]_{(k)} = 0.$$

Observe that Q8 is in fact a qualitative representation of a PID controller, as can be seen from the proportional (L_2), integral (error sum e), and derivative (δL_2) terms present. Results obtained from this controller show a similarity to the conventional PID controller derived earlier.

5. Discussion

This paper has presented a number of different methods of implementing qualitative control. No particular attempt has been made to create the "best" qualitative controller from the various methods presented. In practice, the designer of a qualitative control system is likely to use a combination of methods. The qualitative control algorithms derived here have been regular in the sense that they can be expressed by simple finite-state machines which deal with system quantities in a regular way. A qualitative controller offers potential freedom from the need to obtain numerical information on plant values. For example, an influence diagram [3] can be an adequate specification of the plant [15]. On the other hand, a conventional system must be specified in numerical terms before a conventional design can proceed.

In the case of a nonlinear plant, a conventional PID controller may need re-tuning for different output levels, where a qualitative controller can operate over a wide range without being re-tuned. The experiments reported in this paper do not deal with non-linear regions of operation, (such as the square-root law governing flow through an orifice), but the results reported in [9,10] appear to confirm that qualitative controllers are less sensitive to nonlinearities in laws governing flows and other influences. The requirement is for *monotonicity* rather than *linearity*. We are currently investigating this further by applying these techniques to the control of a small petrochemical plant.

As suggested by the simulation results in [15], some care is needed in the implementation of a qualitative controller for a particular case. The use of a simple control policy alone such as Q1 is unlikely to produce a satisfactory controller. Controllers which have a more complex decision space can work well but care is needed in their application. There is a complicated relationship between the controller parameters (δU increment size, the qualitative decision space, the sampling rate, and the control algorithm), and the plant parameters (loop gain and time constants).

Comparing the synthesis task in this paper with the qualitative analysis used in "envisioning" [5] shows one clear difference. The control systems considered here, and probably any systems which have to interwork with the real world, operate on <u>samples</u> of the plant (or world). The analytic "envisioning" systems emphasise the importance of recognising the special time points at which the system reaches a distinguished value. However, in the case of a sampled system, there is no guarantee that these special points will fall at sample instants (generally, of course, they will not). Consequently, it is not possible to take a simple view of a control system triggered by these points. If their recognition is necessary, some additional inference procedures must be used to reconstruct their positions from the available sampled data.

In complex plant, any human operator of the system is greatly assisted by an explanation facility. A conventional controller uses a tightly compiled representation of the system, allowing only a "surface" interrogation of a controller. No explanation is possible outside of a re-statement of the control algorithm used. An explanation facility can be added to a qualitative controller, so that an operator can query what control policy is currently in operation, why the selected control action is preferred to others, and which components of the plant are being influenced. We intend to investigate this in future work, particularly explanation by relating operating characteristics to plant components.

Acknowledgements

A.J.M. is supported by a studentship from his employer Systems Designers Ltd. We are grateful to Edwin Gorczynski of BP Research for his encouragement of this project.

7. References

[1]   Clocksin W.F. and Leeser M.E. Automatic determination of signal flow through MOS transistor networks, *Integration*, in press.
[2]   Clocksin W.F. and Mellish C.S. *Programming in Prolog*, Springer-Verlag, 1981.
[3]   Coyle R.G. *Management System Dynamics*, John Wiley & Sons, 1977.
[4]   De Kleer J. and Brown J. S. The origin, form, and logic of qualitative physical laws, *Proceedings of the Eighth International Joint Conference on Artificial Intelligence*, 1158-1169, 1983.
[5]   De Kleer J. and Brown J. S. A qualitative physics based on confluences, *Artificial Intelligence* 24, 7-83, 1984.

[6]   Forbus K. Qualitative reasoning about physical processes, *Proceedings of the Seventh International Joint Conference on Artificial Intelligence,* 326-330, 1981
[7]   Forbus K. Measurement interpretation in qualitative process theory, *Proceedings of the Eighth International Joint Conference on Artificial Intelligence,* 315-320, 1983
[8]   Forbus K. Qualitative process theory, *Artificial Intelligence* 24, 85-168, 1984.
[9]   Francis J.C. and Leitch R.R. ARTIFACT: A real-time shell for intelligent feedback control, in *Research and Development in Expert Systems.* ed. M. Bramer: 151-162, Cambridge University Press, 1985.
[10]   Francis J.C. and Leitch R.R. Intelligent knowledge-based process control, *Proceedings of IEE International Conference on Control Engineering,* 1985.
[11]   Kuipers B. Commonsense reasoning about causality: Deriving behaviour from structure, *Artificial Intelligence* 24, 196-203, 1984.
[12]   Kuipers B. The limits of qualitative simulation, *Proceedings of the Ninth International Joint Conference on Artificial Intelligence,* 128-136, 1985
[13]   Kuo B.C. *Digital Control Systems,* Holt, Rinehart, and Winston Inc., 1980
[14]   Mamdani E.H. and Gaines B.R. *Fuzzy Reasoning and its Applications,* Academic Press, 1981.
[15]   Morgan, A.J. and Clocksin, W.F. Qualitative modelling in control systems, submitted for publication.
[16]   Palm W.J. *Modeling, Analysis, and Control of Dynamic Systems,* John Wiley & Sons, 1977.
[17]   Wos L., Overbeek R., Lusk E., and Boyle, J. *Automated Reasoning.* Prentice Hall, 1984.

Figure 1

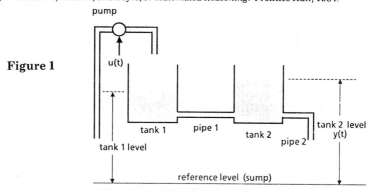

Figure 2

step response of

conventional

PID controller C2

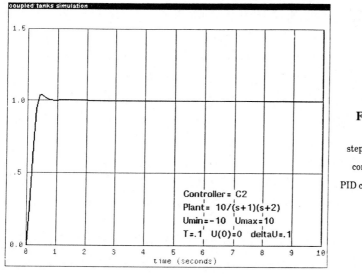

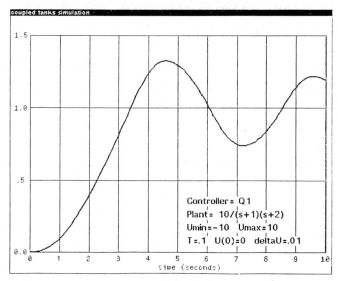

Figure 3

step response of naïve qualitative controller Q1

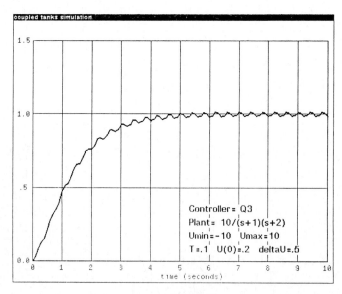

Figure 4

step response of improved qualitative controller Q3

row	State			Controller (see text)		
	[L2]	[δL2]	[δL1]	Q1	Q2	Q3
1	+	+	+	-	-	-
2	+	+	0	-	-	-
3	+	+	-	-	0	-
4	+	0	+	-	-	-
5	+	0	0	-	-	-
6	+	0	-	-	0	0
7	+	-	+	-	-	-
8	+	-	0	-	0	0
9	+	-	-	-	+	+
10	0	+	+	0	-	-
11	0	+	0	0	-	-
12	0	+	-	0	0	0
13	0	0	+	0	-	-
14	0	0	0	0	0	0
15	0	0	-	0	+	+
16	0	-	+	0	0	0
17	0	-	0	0	+	+
18	0	-	-	0	+	+
19	-	+	+	+	-	-
20	-	+	0	+	0	0
21	-	+	-	+	+	+
22	-	0	+	+	0	0
23	-	0	0	+	+	+
24	-	0	-	+	+	+
25	-	-	+	+	0	+
26	-	-	0	+	+	+
27	-	-	-	+	+	+

Figure 5

extensional representation of three qualitative controllers

Advances in Artificial Intelligence - II
B. Du Boulay, D. Hogg and L. Steels (Editors)
© Elsevier Science Publishers B.V. (North-Holland), 1987

EXPLOITING PHYSICAL AND DESIGN KNOWLEDGE IN THE
DIAGNOSIS OF COMPLEX INDUSTRIAL SYSTEMS

Massimo Gallanti (*)
Luca Gilardoni (*)
Giovanni Guida ($)
Alberto Stefanini (*)

(*) CISE s.p.a., P.O. Box 12081, 20134 Milano, Italy
($) Politecnico di Milano, Dipartimento di Elettronica,
Progetto di Intelligenza Artificiale, Milano, Italy

ABSTRACT

Malfunction diagnosis of complex industrial systems involves, in addition to empirical knowledge,
formal knowledge about the design principles and physical laws underlying system operation. This paper
presents the results obtained in a research effort
focused on a case study of industrial relevance: on-
line fault detection and diagnosis of the condenser
subsystem of a thermal power plant. A novel representation paradigm and an inference mechanism are proposed, that utilize both qualitative and quantitative
techniques for generating causal explanations of an
observed malfunction. The main features of the proposed paradigm include the use of explicit fault
models and the consideration of cost and reliability
of the possible measurements that drive the diagnostic
process. The proposed approach is presently being
tested on a running prototype and is illustrated in
the paper through a diagnosis example worked out in
detail.

1. Introduction

Knowledge-based system applications in real problem environments
often require representation and use of knowledge about physical
systems that is in nature structured, formal, relying on established theories, certain, and complete. For example, physiological and biochemical knowledge in medical diagnosis (Kuipers,
1985b; Escaffre, 1985), knowledge about macro-economic laws in
financial forecasting (Iwasaki and Simon, 1985), and knowledge
about solid state physics, semiconductor technology, and
integrated electronic circuit design principles in circuit
testing (Brown, Burton, and De Kleer, 1982; Davis, 1984).

The exigency of modelling complex physical systems is specially
relevant in a class of applications of increasing importance in
the knowledge-based system field, namely, expert system applications to industrial process environments, including fault

detection and diagnosis, on-line monitoring, maintenance, and safety (Gallanti and Guida, 1985). In this field, an adequate representation of the physical system (e.g., a plant, a component, a complex machinery, etc.) that is the subject of the knowledge-based system activity is needed. This representation should encompass a detailed description of (Guida, 1985):

- the structure of the system in terms of components and connections among them;

- the operation of each component (both normal and faulty), based on the identification of the causal relationship existing between its parameters and variables;

- the basic physical laws that rule the processes occurring in the system and the technical principles used for system design;

- the global external behaviour of the system and its expected normal mode of operation.

A description of this kind is often referred to as a deep model, (Hart, 1982; Michie, 1982) as it accounts for the physical structure and operation of the system, which are behind its surface observable performance. Thus, a deep model can be used to investigate system behavior on the basis of the internal mechanisms that, according to some physical theory, can provide a justification of the external behaviour. In recent years several research efforts have been devoted to the topic of deep modelling, both from the theoretical perspective and from the point of view of applications, and several interesting results have been achieved (see, e.g., Bobrow, 1984; Chandrasekaran and Milne, 1985).

The purpose of this paper is to explore a new approach to deep system representation, based on physical equations, where qualitative and quantitative methods are used in an integrated way to reason about system behaviour. This approach has been implemented in a prototype system based on a constraint propagation algorithm (Steele, 1980), and it has been tested on a case study concerning fault diagnosis of a component of a thermal power plant, namely the steam condenser. This is in fact a reasonably simple system, whose operation is based on well known physical laws and design principles, that maintenance experts usually exploits when analyzing a malfunction situation. Moreover, the diagnosis method followed by the expert is committed to exploit the minimum set of directly observable parameters, as every measurement has an associated cost, thus imposing precise constraints to the fault diagnosis strategy. Finally, the deductive process of the expert strongly relies on heuristics, and it therefore offers a good example of integration of empirical reasoning and deduction based on deep knowledge about structure and behaviour

The paper is organized as follows. Section two describes the case study, focusing on the structure of the system and on the physical equations that rule its behaviour. Moreover the diagnostic process is illustrated, introducing a fault model for each of the considered malfunctions. In section three the representation formalism adopted is outlined and a model of the condenser is introduced. The inference procedures used to implement the diagnostic process are then illustrated. An extensive example of fault diagnosis is reported and discussed in section five. Section six concludes the paper.

2.   The case study: the condenser in a thermal power plant

2.1.   Basic description

The role of the condenser in the water-steam cycle of a thermal power plant is to cool the steam coming from the turbine to bring it back to the liquid state. A simplified schema of a condenser is reported in Figure 1.

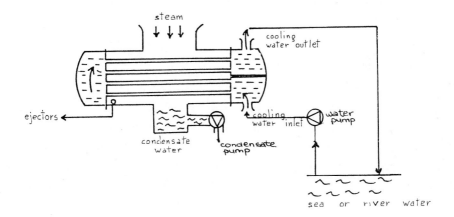

Figure 1 - Simplified schema of a condenser.

Condensation is obtained using surface condensers (i.e., without mixing the cooling water with the steam), in order to keep the chemical characteristics of the cycle water unaffected. The cooling fluid is open-loop water taken from a river or from the sea. In order to increase cycle efficiency, fluid condensation occurs in depressurized conditions, i.e. the pressure inside the condenser is kept lower than the outside atmospheric pressure. The cooling water is circulated by a water pump through a tube bundle located inside the condenser, where steam condensation takes place. The condensate water is gathered at the basis of the condenser (hot well), from which it is removed by a condensate pump.

Since the pressure inside the condenser is lower than outside, air infiltrations can occur. Air can be extracted from the condenser by means of special pumping devices, called ejectors. Two main processes take place in the condenser: heat exchange between the the two fluids, and cooling water circulation. We focus on each of them in turn in the following section.

2.2. Physical equations

The two processes occurring within the condenser can be adequately described using classical fluid mechanics and thermodynamics principles. The following sets of equations can be given (*).

The hydraulic circuit

Let us first consider the geometrical relations among the parameters of the hydraulic circuit.

Let D be the outer diameter of a tube, l its length, and n the number of tubes in the tube bundle. The exchange surface S can then be expressed as:

$$(1) \qquad S = n*pi*l*D.$$

If delta is the average thickness of a tube, and d its internal diameter, then:

$$(2) \qquad D = d + delta,$$

and the equivalent cross section A of the cooling circuit is given by:

$$(3) \qquad A = n*pi*(d^2)/4.$$

The flowrate G is related to the fluid velocity v and the cross section A of the cooling circuit by the equation:

$$(4) \qquad G = v*A.$$

The presence of the water pump in the cooling circuit imposes that:

$$(5) \qquad G*H = P,$$

where P is the power and H the head provided by the pump. H is equal, apart from an additive constant, to the load loss Dp of the cooling water through the tube bundle :

$$(6) \qquad H = Dp + const.$$

Dp is in turn a function of v, l, n, and d according to the empirical relation:

$$(7) \qquad Dp = f * \frac{l}{n*d} (v^2),$$

where f is a factor depending on the motion type.

_____

(*) For the sake of brevity some of the equations are reported here in a simplified form.

The heat exchange process

The amount of heat removed by the cooling water (Q) is proportional to the difference of the cooling water temperatures at the cooling circuit inlet (t1) and outlet (t2), according to the following equation:

$$(8) \qquad Q = G*(t2-t1).$$

The relation among t1, t2, and the steam temperature inside the condenser (ts) is expressed by:

$$(9) \qquad \frac{K*S}{G} = \log \frac{ts-t1}{ts-t2} ,$$

where K is a thermal exchange coefficient which obeys the following equation:

$$(10) \qquad \frac{1}{K} = \frac{1}{alfa\_s} + \frac{delta}{lambda} + \frac{1}{alfa\_w} ,$$

where alfa_s is the thermal transmission coefficient between the external tube wall and the steam, delta is the tube wall thickness, lambda is the thermal conductivity of the tube material, and alfa_w is the thermal transmission coefficient between the internal tube wall and the cooling water, which is related to the water velocity v through the equation:

$$(11) \qquad alfa\_w = const*e^{(1.3*v)}.$$

Finally, the heat Q is monotonically increasing with the steam temperature ts:

$$(12) \qquad Q = f\_inc(ts)$$

and the pressure (ps) and temperature (ts) inside the condenser are also bounded by a monotonically increasing function:

$$(13) \qquad ps = f\_inc(ts).$$

2.3. The diagnostic task

Only few parameters, among those mentioned above, can be directly measured. Moreover, the measurement instrumentation installed on the condenser can be subject to decalibration, so as the quantitative information supplied by the instruments is not always reliable and it is significant only as far as it concerns deviations from the expected values (the design working point of the condenser). Furthermore, some measurements require specific instrumentation to be installed on the plant. Therefore, each measurement has a precision and a cost.

The parameters that can be directly measured are:

-   internal pressure of the condenser (ps): this measurement is always available and reliable;

- steam temperature in the condenser (ts): this measurement is less reliable than the previous one but not so important, as ts can be derived from ps;

- inlet and outlet temperature of the cooling water (tl, t2): these measurements are carried out through thermocouples (subject to decalibration) and are not very accurate;

- load loss of the water through the tube bundle (Dp): this measurement is quite accurate but it requires installation of a special instrumentation on the cooling circuit;

- flowrate of the cooling water (G): this measurement is poorly reliable and very costly, as it requires a special equipment to be installed on the cooling circuit.

Condenser malfunctions cause the condensation process to take place under conditions different from those defined by the design. Representing equation (9) in the plane ts-t2, taking tl as a parameter, a family of curves is obtained (see Figure 2), that represent the working point of the condenser in design conditions. When the values of tl, t2, and ts do not fit the curves in Figure 2, the condenser does not work according to the design conditions because of some malfunction.

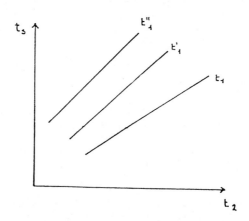

Figure 2 - Condenser working points in design conditions.

Five main malfunction causes are considered:

a)   the water pump does not work correctly;

b)   air infiltration in the condenser can not be removed by the ejectors;

c)   a portion of the cooling circuit tube bundle is clogged by obstructions (e.g., plastic bags, mussels, etc.);

d) the cooling circuit tubes are crusted on the internal wall because of impurities of the cooling water;

e) the cross section of the cooling circuit is augmented because of erosion of the internal wall of the tubes.

These malfunctions directly affect some parameters (e.g., K, S, n, etc.) that cannot be directly measured but have an associated nominal value defined by the project:

+ the product between cooling water flowrate and head of the water pump (G*H) decreases in case of pump malfunction;

+ the thermal transmission coefficient between the external tube wall and the steam (alfa_s) decreases because of air infiltration;

+ the number of tubes of the tube bundle (n) decreases because of tube clogging;

+ the average thickness of a tubes (delta) can vary because of crusts (increasing), or because of erosion (decreasing);

+ the thermal conductivity of the tube material (lambda) decreases because of crusts.

With reference to equations (1) to (13) of section 2.2, the diagnosis problem can be stated in the following way: using the lowest cost set of measurements determine:

- the presence of a system malfunction (fault detection);

- which cause, among the possible five above mentioned, is responsible for it, under the assumption that only one of them is present at a time - single fault assumption (fault diagnosis).

As far as fault detection is concerned, according to the relations presented in Figure 2 the measurement of t1, t2, and ts is sufficient, at least in principle, to determine the presence of a malfunction.

For what concerns fault diagnosis, we note that human experts carry out this task by discriminating among the previously mentioned malfunction causes that one which best complies with the observed symptoms. Their activity relies more on qualitative reasoning than on evaluation of quantitative data, and it is based on a deep model of the structure and function of the condenser.

3. A model of the condenser

On the basis of the analysis developed in the previous sections we can represent the behaviour of the condenser as illustrated in Figure 3. Measurable parameters are underlined and parameters directly affected by some malfunction cause are circled. The formalism adopted aims at providing a natural and workable representation of the physical equations (1) to (13). Each one of the operators defined in the schema of Figure 3 has a twofold meaning:

- qualitative: in this case the operator is used to identify how the variations of parameters (increasing, decreasing, steady) are propagated through the system (Kuipers 1984);

- quantitative: the operator is used to determine the value of one of the involved parameters once the other are known.

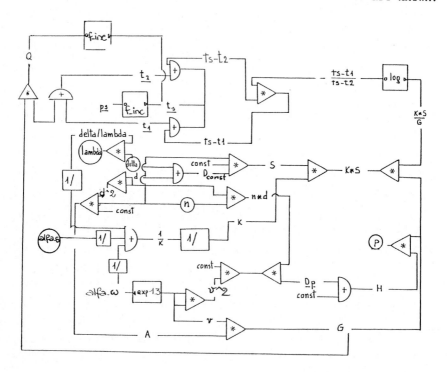

Figure 3 - Condenser behaviour model.

The model of Figure 3 is moreover based on equilibrium equations and, therefore, it is not adequate for modelling dynamic situations.

This model applies both when the condenser is operating correctly and when it is malfunctioning, as it relies on a physical description that is valid in any steady state. In this sense, it is a deep model capable of covering both normal and abnormal situations and of expressing valid causal relationships also when the system does not operate according to the design data. In fact, it incorporates both design knowledge, useful for reasoning about the normal operation of the system (and for discovering abnormal situations), and physical knowledge valid in any situation.

4. The diagnostic process and its implementation

We can analyze now the basic features of the inference mechanisms used to exploit the deep knowledge embedded in the condenser model above illustrated in the process of fault diagnosis.

The diagnosis process starts from the assumption that a malfunction is occurring. Each one of the five possible malfunction causes is considered in turn with the aim of disproving it.
Each malfunction cause determines a set of known variations of a set of directly affected parameters, namely:

	n	delta	lambda	alfa_s	P
pump malfunction	std	std	std	std	dec
air infiltration	std	std	std	dec	std
tube clogging	dec	std	std	std	std
tube crusts	std	inc	dec	std	std
tube erosion	std	dec	std	std	std

For each possible cause three main diagnosis steps are performed:

1. Step one starts from the qualitative variations observed on the measured parameters t1, t2, and ts, and propagates them through the model of the condenser using a constraint propagation method derived from (Steele, 1980).
    In addition, the qualitative variations implied by the currently considered malfunction cause are propagated as well.
    This step ends when:

    a) either some input parameters to an operator are unknown or propagation through some operators of the model gives ambiguous results thus making further propagation impossible (the unknown parameters that prevent further propagation are called the propagation border);

    b) a contradiction between parameter values propagated from the measured parameters and from those implied by the considered malfunction cause has been found.

In case b) the currently considered malfunction cause is rejected. In case a) the qualitative reasoning process can continue only if new measurements are taken that allow propagation to overcome the current border. Measurements,

however, have an associated cost: it is not always
appropriate to blindly choose to invest in this task if
other opportunities are possible (which must, of course,
rely on quantitative reasoning). Furthermore, it may be the
case that no more measurements are possible. In order to
explore further these possible choices, step two is
entered.

2.   Step two is devoted to choose which is the most suitable
     measurement to take next. The unknown parameters identi-
     fied in the previous step (the propagation border) are con-
     sidered together with equations where they are referred
     to, and the measurable parameters referenced in these equa-
     tions are identified. The choice of the most appropriate
     measurement to do is then taken according to heuristic cri-
     teria, including, for example:

     -    computational cost of the path from a measurable
          parameter to one of the unknown parameters;

     -    cost and precision of the measurement.

     After the most appropriate parameter to measure next has
     been identified, it has to be decided between two possibil-
     ities:

     a)   actually operating this measurement, and then continu-
          ing with qualitative propagation returning to step
          one;

     b)   giving up with the measurement, e.g., as it is too
          much expensive, and resorting to quantitative reason-
          ing in order to overcome the difficulty that caused
          step one to be stopped, thus entering step three.

3.   Step three is based on quantitative reasoning: the opera-
     tors previously used in a merely qualitative way, are now
     used in their quantitative meaning, in order to actually
     compute the values of the parameters in the propagation
     border. The computed values are then compared with the
     nominal ones, and the variation thus obtained are used to
     resume the refutation process based on the qualitative pro-
     pagation, returning to step one.

Steps of qualitative propagation and quantitative computation
are thus alternated until insulation of a single malfunction
cause is eventually obtained, or until propagation (both qualitative and quantitative) is completed. In this case, different
parameter values are obtained, each one corresponding to a possible malfunction cause, and the malfunction hypothesis that
best matches the values directly derived from measurements
should be preferred. However, the uncertainty of the measurements does not allow, in general, the exact malfunction cause to
be precisely identified; plausible causes can only be ranked
according to appropriate certainty factors.

5. An example

In this section we illustrate through a detailed example the process of fault diagnosis. Let us suppose that the condenser is malfunctioning as a consequence of a fault in the pump. Qualitative propagation (step one) is first started. From the temperature measurements we observe that ts and t2 are increased, whereas tl is steady. Qualitative propagation of these observations (see Figure 3) yields that ts-tl increases, while nothing can be decided about ts-t2. Thus the propagation cannot proceed further from this side. Considering now in turn all possible malfunction causes and propagating their effects we obtain (see section 2.3):

a)   Pump malfunction causes P to decrease. Such a variation cannot be further propagated because both G and H are unknown. Being lambda, delta, n, and alfa_s steady, d, n*d, S, and A are steady too. The variations of 1/K, G, H, v^2, alfa_w, and Dp represent the propagation border.

b)   Air infiltration causes alfa_s to decrease. Being n, lambda, delta, and P steady, also d, n*d, S, and A are steady. The propagation border is once again 1/K, G, H, v^2, alfa_w and Dp.

c)   Tube clogging causes n to decrease, while lambda, delta, P and alfa_s are steady. Propagating these variations we obtain that d and S are steady, while n*d and A decrease. The propagation border is the same as in the previous cases.

d)   Tube crusts cause lambda to decrease and delta to increase, while n, alfa_s, and P are steady. Propagating these variations we obtain that delta/lambda increases, d, A, and n*d decrease, and S is steady. The propagation border is the same as in the previous cases.

e)   Tube erosion causes delta to decrease, while n, lambda, alfa_s, and P are steady. Propagating these variations we obtain that d, n*d, and A increase. The propagation border is the same as in the previous cases.

Therefore, no further qualitative propagation being possible, step two is entered. The propagation border parameters 1/K, G, H, v^2, alfa_w and Dp, with the addition of ts-t2, which is the propagation border from the side of the measured variables tl, t2, and ts, are considered.
Dp is directly measurable at low cost. Let us assume that a Dp decrease is observed. This qualitative information will be further propagated, resuming step one. Reconsidering the five cases above introduced, we now obtain that:

a)   Dp decreases, therefore H decreases. Since also G*H decreases, G cannot be determined this way. On the other hand, n*d is steady so that v^2 decreases. Since A is steady, from equation (4) we have that G decreases. Finally, we have that alfa_w decreases and, being alfa_s and lambda/delta steady, 1/K increases and K decreases. This implies that, being S steady, K*S decreases. K*S/G cannot be determined and constitutes the new propagation border (in addition to ts-t2).

b)   Dp decreases, therefore H decreases. Since G*H is steady,
      then G increases. On the other hand, n*d is steady, there-
      fore v^2 decreases. Since A is steady, from equation (4)
      we have that G must decrease. We therefore obtain a con-
      tradiction concerning G that leads to rejecting this
      hypothesis of malfunction.

c,d) These hypotheses are also rejected, as contradictions simi-
      lar to that one discussed in the above case are discovered.

e)   Dp decreases, therefore H decreases. Since G*H is steady,
      then G increases. On the other hand, n*d is steady,
      whereas Dp decreases, therefore v cannot be determined.
      Finally, G increases but also A increases and again v can-
      not be determined. The new propagation border includes v,
      alfa_w, 1/K, and K*S (in addition to ts-t2).

Therefore, at the end of step two, two malfunction causes remain
plausible, namely a) and e). These two causes lead to opposite
conclusions concerning the variation of flowrate G. They might
therefore be discriminated by measuring G. However this measurement is very expensive. There are not, on the other hand, other
parameters directly measurable, therefore it is possible to
avoid measuring G only resorting to quantitative propagation
(step three):

a)   The propagation border includes K*S/G and ts-t2.   Both of
      them can be quantitatively determined, but ts-t2 has a
      lower computational cost. The system chooses therefore to
      compute ts-t2 and finds that it is increased. Since also
      ts-t1 is increased, then (ts-t2)/(ts-t1) cannot be qualita-
      tively determined, and quantitative propagation must be
      instantiated again, starting from the new border that
      includes K*S/G and (ts-t1)/(ts-t2).
      The latter involves the least computational cost and is
      evaluated.   Let us suppose that it is increased. Resorting
      again to qualitative reasoning, we obtain that log((ts-
      t1/ts-t2)) is also increased. As it equals K*S/G by virtue
      of equation (9), there is no propagation border left,   so
      qualitative propagation is concluded. Since no contradic-
      tion has been found, the current hypothesis is still valid.

e)   As in the previous case, we can derive that   K*S/G is
      increased.   But in the frame of the current hypothesis we
      already found that G is increased and, therefore, resorting
      to qualitative reasoning, we have that K*S is increased
      too. Since S is supposed to be steady, K is increased and
      1/K decreased. But K cannot be qualitatively evaluated
      because it depends on alfa_w, whose value is not known.
      Therefore, also this hypothesis cannot be rejected through
      qualitative propagation.

If we still want to avoid measuring G, the only way to proceed
is quantitatively propagating the measured value of Dp. Thus:

a)   Using the value of Dp and the nominal value of n*d, accord-
      ing to equation (7), the value of v is obtained and from it
      the value of all other parameters involved (including
      K*S/G) is computed.

e)   From the measurement of Dp and from the   nominal   value   of
     G*H,   the   value of G is obtained. From equations (7), (3),
     and (4) we have:

     (I)   Dp*n*d = const*(v^2)

                            G
     (II)   v = -------------.
                     cost*n*(d^2)

     Since n has the nominal value, from the above two equations
     the values of d and v can be computed and, therefore, being
     the value of 1/alfa_w known, it is possible to calculate K.

If the value of K does not exceed the nominal one, hypothesis e)
must   be   discarded,   as   it   has previously been deduced that K
should have been increased, in contradiction   with   the   present
result.   So   hypothesis a) only is not rejected and the problem
is solved.
On the contrary, if the value of K is increased beyond its nominal value, the ratio K*S/G has to be calculated. Again, if K*S/G
is not increased a contradiction with previous results has   been
found   and   hypothesis   e)   is   rejected. If K*S/G is increased,
quantitative propagation in the cases a) and   e)   leads   to   two
different quantitative evaluations of K*S/G that can be compared
against the value computed using only measured   parameters   (tl,
t2   and   ts).   This   allows   the   credibility   of the remaining
hypotheses a) and e) to be ranked according   to   the   difference
between the two estimated values of K*S/G and the value computed
from the temperature measurements.

6.   Conclusions

In the previous sections we have   briefly   discussed   the   basic
features   of   a   mechanism   for   representing   and   using   deep
knowledge, both qualitative and quantitative,   in   the   diagnosis
of   a complex system. The proposed approach has been implemented
and tested in a prototype system written in Lisp   running   on   a
SUN-2 workstation.

Our proposal, although   basically   inspired   to   the   works   of
(Kuipers,   1984   and   1985a; De   Kleer   and   Brown, 1984), shows
several significant differences   from   these   approaches.   Here,
starting from a quantitative model of a physical system, a qualitative   model   is   obtained   and   used   for   predicting   system
behaviour   from   a partially known initial state towards a final
steady state.   We face instead a different task, as   we   aim   at
identifying   which   variations of the independent variables that
characterize the system can explain the transition from a   known
initial   state   (the   design working point) to a partially known
steady state (the faulty state).   This   goal   cannot   be   always
reached using only qualitative considerations.
For   instance,   if   both   the   differences   ts-tl   and   ts-t2
increase, it is impossible to predict anything about their ratio
(ts-tl)/(ts-t2) using qualitative reasoning only. It is   instead
necessary   to   compute   the values of ts-tl and ts-t2 in order to
assess whether their ratio is increased, decreased, or   steady.
Our proposal also shares some features with the work of   (Yamada
and   Motoda,   1983;   Motoda,   Yamada   and   Yoshida,   1984).   Both

models analyze malfunction causes, but our approach includes, in addition to modeling the normal behavior of the system, an explicit representation of its behavior in faulty conditions. However, a complete enumeration of all possible malfunction causes is needed to start the propagation/refutation process. Moreover, our approach is essentially based on a description of the system in terms of closely interacting physical processes, rather than of loosely connected components. Also, it always prefers, whenever possible, qualitative reasoning rather than quantitative computations.

Among the main points that deserve further investigation, we mention:

-   the integration of physical modeling with shallow and heuristic knowledges, (e.g., frequencies of faults, naive expectations on possible faulty behaviors, empirical associations between symptoms and diagnosis, etc.) which is expected to have a major role in making the propagation/refutation process more effective and natural;

-   the possibility of removing the single fault assumption, taking into account the fact that our model based on physical equations is valid both in normal and faulty situations.

ACKNOWLEDGMENTS

The development of the case study reported in the paper has required several technical meetings and discussions about the condenser behaviour and diagnosis with the problem experts L. Donzelli and A. Cavanna of Ansaldo Divisione Impianti (Genova, Italy). We would like to acknowledge their mostly appreciated contribution and to thank Ansaldo Divisione Impianti for the support offered.
We would also like to thank B. Meltzer for his suggestions concerning the formulation of the general lines of this work and J. F. Allen, J.S. Brown and B. Kuipers for many enlightening remarks.
This work has been partially funded by the Commission of European Communities in the frame of ESPRIT Project P256.

REFERENCES

Bobrow D.G. (Ed.) (1984) Special Volume on Qualitative Reasoning about Physical systems. Artificial Intelligence 24 (1-3).

Brown J.S., Burton R.R. and De Kleer J. (1982). Pedagogical, natural language and knowledge engineering techniques in SOPHIE I, II and III. In Intelligent Tutoring Systems, D. Sleeman and J.S. Brown (Eds.). Academic Press, New York, N.Y., 227-282.

Chandrasekaran B. and Milne R. (Eds.) (1985). Special Section on "Reasoning about structure, behavior and function". ACM SIGART Newsletter 93, 4-55.

Davis R. (1984). Diagnostic reasoning based on structure and behavior. Artificial Intelligence 24, 347-410.

De Kleer J. and Brown J.S. (1984). A qualitative physics based on confluences. Artificial Intelligence 24, 7-83.

Escaffre D. (1985). Qualitative reasoning on physiological systems: The example of the blood pressure regulation. In Artificial Intelligence in Medicine, I. De Lotto and M. Stefanelli (Eds.), North-Holland, Amsterdam, NL, 51-63.

Gallanti M. and Guida G. (1985). Intelligent decision aids in process environments: An expert system approach. Proc. NATO Advanced Study Institute on Intelligent Decision Aids in Process Environments, San Miniato, Italy, G. Mancini, E. Hallnagel, and D. Woods (Eds.), Springer-Verlag, Berlin, FRG.

Guida G. (1985). Reasoning about physical systems: Shallow versus deep models. Proc. UNICOM Seminar on Expert Systems and Optimization in Process Control, London, UK, The Technical Press, Aldershort, UK.

Hart P.E. (1982). Direction for AI in the eigthies. ACM SIGART Newsletter 79, 11-16.

Iwasaki Y. and Simon H.A. (1985). Causality in device behavior. Report CMU-CS-85-118, Carnegie-Mellon University, Pittsburgh, PA.

Kuipers B. (1984). Commonsense reasoning about causality: Deriving behavior from structure. Artificial Intelligence 24, 169-203.

Kuipers B. (1985a). The limits of qualitative simulation. Proc. 8th Int. Joint Conf. on Artificial Intelligence, Los Angeles, CA, 128-136.

Kuipers B. (1985b). Qualitative simulation in medical physiology: a Progress Report. Report MIT/LCS/TM280 Massachusetts Institute of Technology, Cambridge, MA.

Michie D. (1982). High-road and low-road programs. The AI Magazine 3(1), 21-22.

Motoda H., Yamada N., and Yoshida K. (1984). A knowledge based system for plant diagnosis. Proc. Int. Conf. on Fifth Generation Computer Systems, ICOT, Tokyo, Japan, 582-588.

Steele G.L. (1980). The definition and implementation of a computer programming language based on constraints. Report MIT AI-TR 595, Massachusetts Institute of Technology, Cambridge, MA.

Yamada N. and Motoda H. (1983). A diagnosis method of dynamic system using the knowledge on system description. Proc. 8th Int. Joint Conf. on Artificial Intelligence, Karlsruhe, FRG, 225-229.

Advances in Artificial Intelligence - II
B. Du Boulay, D. Hogg and L. Steels (Editors)
© Elsevier Science Publishers B.V. (North-Holland), 1987

Models of Expertise

B.J. Wielinga and J.A. Breuker

Department of Social Science Informatics, University of Amsterdam
Herengracht 196, 1016 BS Amsterdam, The Netherlands

Abstract

This paper presents methods for describing expert knowledge in such a way that the resulting model preserves the possibilities of the extreme flexibility that experts have when performing a task. The knowledge of the expert is modelled at several levels: the domain level, where mainly objects and relations are represented, and a number of higher levels which contain descriptions of the ways in which the domain knowledge can be used. Generic models at the various levels can be used to make the interpretation of verbal data from experts more effective.

1. The Nature of Expertise

One of the more striking manifestations of expertise is the flexibility with which domain knowledge can be used. Depending on the goals that an expert has in a particular situation -be it problem solving, teaching, explaining, finding bugs in reasoning patterns, or communicating new insights- the wealth of knowledge of the domain can be applied in a variety of ways. The expert is able to structure different types of tasks in such a way, that in all circumstances effective use is made of the domain knowledge. Experts use different strategies for different types of problems. There is 'graceful degradation' at difficult, atypical problems.

There is a second manifestation of the flexibility of experts, one that comes up in knowledge acquisition. Experts tend to formulate their knowledge in a declarative way; they rarely speak in rules. The presentation of such declarative knowledge may vary widely, depending on the circumstances and the viewpoint that the expert has. Moreover experts have difficulty in explicating their problem solving strategy. The reason is almost obvious: they do not have detailed strategies explicitly represented as knowledge structures. Experts are able to organise their performance in a very efficient way, but this performance is usually not a fixed pattern, it is created. So, strategies are the result of knowledge rather than knowledge structures themselves. The problem for the knowledge engineer is to envisage a structure in the elements of knowledge that the expert has produced, and to mold these elements into a working system, i.e. to add control information.

The goal of this paper is to sketch a framework which can serve as a basis for description of expertise in its full glory, i.e. a description which maintains the flexibility of expert behaviour. Such a framework serves three purposes: 1) it allows in principle a full description of the expert's knowledge, 2) it can be used as a starting point for the implementation of more flexible systems than we currently see, and 3) it provides strong support for the analysis of expert knowledge during the knowledge acquisition stage of building expert systems. This last point may need some explaining. A descriptional framework can be augmented with templates for generic tasks or task components. Such templates -which we have called *interpretation models* elsewhere (Wielinga & Breuker, 1984)- can be used as a guide during the interpretation of verbal data obtained from an expert. Indeed, such template models are a conditio sine qua non, since the interpretation of verbal data is virtually impossible without some prior assumptions about the processes and knowledge that underly the data (see section 5).

A framework which serves these purposes must be at the epistemological level. The current techniques and vocabulary of AI at the implementation level do not suffice to describe the types of knowledge we are aiming at. Moreover, when we use a particular descriptional framework during the analysis stage, we do not want to be biased towards a particular implementation formalism.

Two basic premises underly the ideas presented here. First, we assume that it is possible and useful to distinguish between several generic types of knowledge, corresponding to different roles that knowledge can play in reasoning processes. Second, we assume that these types of knowledge can be organised in several layers, which have only limited interaction. Both in recent AI work (Davis, 1980; Clancey, 1983; 1985b) and in psychological theories on problem solving (Sternberg, 1980) there is ample evidence that a separation between object level knowledge and meta level knowledge is both plausible and useful. Here we will take such a separation of knowledge in two layers one step further, and will argue for a refined distinction of different types of knowledge at various levels.

In the next section we will pursue the question what different types of knowledge underlying flexible expert problem solving. Subsequent sections will elaborate the different types of knowledge, give examples and describe the role that the descriptional framework can play in knowledge acquisition.

2. Layers of Knowledge

The layers at which the knowledge of experts can be analysed and described are based on epistemological distinctions: they contain different types of knowledge. We distinguish between static knowledge describing concepts and relations, knowledge of different types of inferences that can be made, knowledge representing elementary tasks, and strategic knowledge. Each of these categories of knowledge is described at a separate level. The separation reflects different ways in which the knowledge can be viewed and used. The first layer contains the static knowledge of the domain: domain concepts, relations and complex structures, such as models of processes or devices. The second layer is the inference layer. In this layer we describe what inferences can be made on the basis of the knowledge in the static layer. Two types of entities are represented at the inference layer: meta-classes and knowledge sources. Meta-classes describe the role that domain-concepts can play in a reasoning process. For example, a domain concept like *infection* can play the role of a *finding* in a consultation process, but it may also play the role of *hypothesis*. Knowledge sources describe what types of inferences can be made on the basis of the relations in the domain layer. Examples are refinement and generalisation knowledge sources, which both make use of a subsumption relation in the domain layer.

The third layer is the task layer. At this level the basic objects are goals and tasks. Tasks are ways in which knowledge sources can be combined to achieve a particular goal. The fourth layer is the strategic layer in which knowledge resides which allows a system to make plans- i.e. create a task structure-, control and monitor the execution of tasks, diagnose when something goes wrong and find repairs for impasses. The four layers are schematically presented in figure 1.

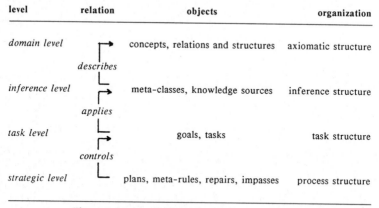

Figure 1. Layers of description of expert knowledge

Each layer has its own organisational principles which reflect the constraints that apply to the ways in which the objects on a particular level can be combined. These organisational principles will be discussed in subsequent sections.

The distinction between different types of knowledge is -of course- not a novel idea. Several authors have reported ideas which pertain on the separation of domain and control knowledge, and ways to increase the flexibility of control in expert systems. The seminal work of Davis (1977; 1980) introduced meta knowledge as a means to control inference processes in a flexible way. In the NEOMYCIN system (Clancey, 1985b), different functions of knowledge are explicated by separating domain knowledge and control knowledge and introducing a meta level description of the strategies that a system uses. Pople (1982) has stressed the problem of the right task formulation. He considers it as a fundamental challenge for AI research to model the meta-level reasoning process of expert diagnosticians which determines the optimal configuration of tasks to perform in order to solve a problem.

In the area of logic programming considerable work has been performed on meta level reasoning and control. Early work by Hayes (1973) introduced the idea of controlling inference processes by means of logic. This idea has been further pursued by Gallaire and Lasserre (1982). They discuss a number of ways to control inference processes from a meta level: control by annotating the program, control by meta rules which influence the operation of the inference mechanism, and control by means of a special -domain specific- meta interpreter. This latter approach -although dismissed by Gallaire and Lasserre on the grounds that such meta interpreters must be based on principles for structuring world knowledge- has been the basis of work of Bundy on controlling problem solving processes by using meta knowledge which is domain specific (Bundy et al., 1979; Bundy & Sterling, 1981). Sterling (1984) further elaborates this approach, arguing that meta level knowledge embodies a theory of a particular domain, and such a theory is precisely what is needed for flexible and powerful problem solvers, such as expert systems.

In this paper we elaborate the latter point of view further, and use the task-level and strategy-level descriptions as a vehicle to generalise from one particular task domain to classes of tasks and classes of domains. Such a generalisation not only creates the elements to capture flexibility, but is also the basis of a model-driven knowledge acquisition methodology.

3. Descriptional Vocabulary

3.1. Concepts, relations and structures

In the lowest layer knowledge is represented as concepts, relations between concepts and structures build from relations. For example, in a medical domain objects at the domain level can be the various disorders, causes of these disorders, complaints, laboratory data. Relations in a domain represent facts, empirical associations, structural relations and attributive relations. In a medical domain, we may have subsumption relations between disorders, causal relations between causes and complaints, or between causes and disorders, and empirical associations between data and disorders. The knowledge in this layer is *task neutral*, i.e. it is not represented in a special way in order to support a particular task. Knowledge at the domain level permits some problem solving processes, but does not contain facilities to control such problem solving. In other words, we could think of the domain level as a competence model of expertise: all the knowledge is there, but it still has to be made to work.

The knowledge at the domain level usually has organisational principles underlying its structure. We have called this the axiomatic structure to indicate that at this level the only constraints on the choice of concepts and relations come from the axiomatisation chosen for a particular domain. These choices may be dependent on known formalisms to interpret relations or known structures to represent domain knowledge. One may for instance decide to include time-related concepts and relations in the domain layer only in a rudimentary way. Current practice in building expert systems does not distinguish between 'not known' and 'not required'. The latter constraints are to be derived from the requirements of the inference layer; not from (assumed) limits of representation formalisms and knowledge modelling.

3.2. Meta classes and Knowledge Sources

The knowledge at the domain level does not constrain the potential inferences that can be made. The inferences are not controlled. Even if a very simple inference engine is defined to interpret the relations in the domain, inferences may expand the knowledge in all directions. Problem solving is characterised by directed inferences. The role that concepts, relations and structures can play in a particular reasoning process is (partially) specified by descriptions of these objects at the inference level by *meta classes* and *knowledge sources*.
Meta classes
Meta classes describe what role(s) a concept can play in a reasoning process: how it is to be used, and what its status can be during various stages of a problem solving process. A particular infection can play the role of explanatory object of certain facts, it can be seen

as a hypothesis to be verified, and it can play the role of solution in a problem solving process. In NEOMYCIN two meta classes are distinguished: findings and hypotheses. In a more general model of diagnostic reasoning, a more elaborate set of meta classes will be needed. Table 1 represents a set of meta classes in a diagnostic domain, with examples from medicine:

Table 1: meta classes in a medical domain

meta class	examples	role
symptom	complaints fever pallor headache	in triggering hypotheses
manifestation	hypotension fever	in verification of hypotheses
factor	alcohol consumption medication age	as supporting evidence
hypothesis	pathological state causal object	in finding a diagnosis
clinical diagnosis causal diagnosis	syndrome disorder	solution

Note that concepts may belong to more than one meta class: fever can be a symptom that is part of initial observations, but may also be derived as a manifestation, the presence of which has to be verified. Similarly, disorders may play the role of hypothesis in the initial states of the problem solving proces, but may also be the final result of that same process, in which case they play the role of diagnosis. Meta classes may themselves form a sub/super class hierarchy: e.g the meta class *data* subsumes meta classes such as observable, symptom etc. Figure 2 gives an example of a hierarchy of meta classes.

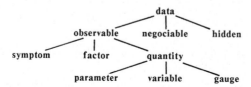

Figure 2. Example hierarchy of meta classes of data

Meta classes provide a means to talk about sets of domain concepts, without enumerating these, or having to rely on hierarchies at the domain level. By assigning a domain concept, e.g. *age*, to a meta class, e.g. *factor*, we know that it can be asked in a consultation, that it can be used as supporting evidence during inferencing, but also that it can never be a manifestation of a disorder.

Knowledge Sources

Knowledge sources are descriptions of the way in which a domain relation can be used to make inferences. For example, the domain relation *subsumes* can be used in a variety of ways, depending on the meta class of the objects in the subsumes relation, and depending on the ways in which the relation is to be used. Figure 3 gives some knowledge sources which describe the different uses of the subsumes relation in a diagnostic context. The notation of the example is in Prolog with the additional convention that O(i) denotes a concept at the domain level.

Domain relations	*Meta Classes*
subsumes(O(i),O(j)).	hypothesis (O(i)).
has-attribute(O(i),A(i,k)).	attribute(A(i,k)).

Knowledge Sources

%*refinement-by-specialisation*
refines(O(j),O(i)) :-
    hypothesis(O(i)),
    hypothesis(O(j)),
    subsumes(O(i),O(j)).
%*generalisation*
generalises(O(i),O(j)) :-
    hypothesis(O(i)),
    hypothesis(O(j)),
    subsumes(O(i),O(j)).

%*specification-by-inheritance*
inherits(O(j),A(i,k),O(i)) :-
    attribute(A(i,k)),
    subsumes(O(i),O(j)).

%*specification-by-inheritance*
inherits(O(j),A(i,k),O(i)) :-
    consists-of(O(i),O(j))),
    attribute-type(A(i,k),part-transitive).

Figure 3
Some knowledge sources describing ways of using domain relations

The 'inherits' examples illustrate how the same type of inference (specification by inheritance of attributes) can be made on the basis of different domain relations.

With respect to referencing to domain relations, knowledge sources have a similar role as typologies of relations such as in CADUCEUS (Pople, 1982), where relations are distinguised such as caused-by, planning, constrictor, ellipsis and subclassification. In NEOMYCIN there are similar types of domain relations: causal, subsumption, trigger, factual. In both systems the typing of the domain relations is represented as a simple classification of the way in which the domain relations are to be used. The way we propose to describe the possible inferences that can be made on the basis of domain relations allows more complex inferences relations to be defined. The following example knowledge source infers that a particular attribute (A) differentiates between two hypotheses (H1, H2) which are part of a subsumption hierarchy:

    differentiates(H1,H2,H0,A):-
        hypothesis(H1), hypothesis(H2),
        subsumes(H0,H1), subsumes(H0,H2),
        attribute(H0,A),
        value(A,H1,V1), value(A,H2,V2),
        not-equal(V1,V2).

The example shows how complex inference patterns can be defined using the meta classes and domain relations. Knowledge sources describe types of inferences. Inferences can be characterised by their effects. A tentative classification of these effects the following:

value of attribute
    compare
    change value
    instantiate (gives values to all attributes of a concept)
attribute of concept
    specify (gives new attribute(s) to concept)
    classify (attributes class to concept)
    abstract (deletes attributes from concept)
    generalise (attributes superclass to concept)
structure concepts
    collect (forms set of concepts)
    order (forms ordered list of concepts)
    assemble (form part-whole structure)
    match (compare structures of concepts)
change structure
    sort (change order of concepts)
    transform (change type of structure)

This classification is by no means complete. For instance, many effects are the inverse of other effects (e.g. abstract vs specify; assemble vs disassemble, etc). A typology of knowledge sources can be further refined by specifying the *inference methods* that are used to achieve the effects. Examples of inference methods are: inheritance (cf Figure 3), value propagation, empirical association, version space, resolution, etc. For instance, heuristic matching consists of matching by use of empirical associations (Clancey, 1985a; see also figure 6). Analyses in a number of domains has shown that in particular knowledge sources which affect the attributes of concepts occur invariably (e.g. Wielinga & Breuker, 1984; De Greef & Breuker, 1985).

The definition of knowledge sources does not fixate a particular strategy of use. The knowledge sources are *handles* for the strategic knowledge on the domain knowledge (cf. section 3.4 and 3.5). Clancey (1983) puts forward that structures in the domain knowledge can be used as handles for strategies. Taking the view that knowledge sources are a generalised way of structuring the domain knowledge along a functionality dimension, Clancey's observation can be generalised.

3.3. Inference Structure
The inference structure relates in a network the meta classes and knowledge sources, indicating what inferences can be made in a domain and implicitly what inferences cannot be made. For example the inference structure embodied in NEOMYCIN has the following form:

data --(abstraction)->evidence --(association)-> hypothesis --(refinement)-> diagnosis

The relationships represented in the inference structure, are in a sense constraints on the reasoning process. The inference strcuture describes *what* inferences can be made, but it does not specify in what order inference steps are made, i.e. it is a static structure that does not specify a strategy.

3.4. Fixed Strategies
Once we have defined the meta-classes, knowledge sources and the inference structure, we can define the strategy which determines how and when certain inference steps will be made. A common way to represent such a strategy is a *goal-tree* and a corresponding task decomposition. In NEOMYCIN for example the diagnostic strategy is represented as a tree representing subtasks of the diagnostic task. Similarly in PDP, a physics problem solving program (Jansweijer & Wielinga, 1984), the task decomposition represents strategic information. Once a task has been decomposed in noninteracting subtasks search is sufficiently constrained to solve even difficult problems. Figure 4 represents as an example part of the task hierarchy for physics problem solving as used by PDP.

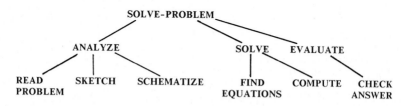

Figure 4.
Static task decomposition for physics problem solving

The actual satisfaction of a goal is achieved by *task rules*. For example the following task rules represent methods to rule out hypotheses.

if the goal is to rule out hypothesis(H)
and there are KS's that refute H on the basis of attribute A
and A of H has been obtained
then put on the agenda refute(H,A).

if the goal is to rule out hypothesis(H),
and there are generalisation KS's for H,
then attempt to rule out a generalisation of H.

if there are two competing hypotheses (H1,H2),
and the goal is to establish one hypothesis
and there are differentiation KS's differentiates(H1,H2,H0,Attribute)
then put on the agenda obtain(Attribute),
and rule out one of H1,H2.

In NEOMYCIN Clancey uses similar meta rules, but these rules refer directly to classes of domain rules. In our approach we refer to domain knowledge through the inference level. This approach makes the knowledge at the task level less dependent on the particular domain. All actions at the task level refer to types of knowledge sources and meta classes. Tasks are different from knowledge sources because tasks are goal directed, while knowledge sources are not. Tasks can be organised in hierarchies, from general to more specific. Depending on the generality of the goal a range of tasks may be applied to achieve a goal. For instance the following hierarchy shows tasks which obtain a particular datum:

```
task
|   obtain_datum
|   |   findout
|   |   |   look_up
|   |   |   |   look_up_in_memory
|   |   |   |   look_up_in_database
|   |   |   |   look_up_in_table
|   |   |   infer
|   |   |   |   infer_by_definition
|   |   |   |   infer_by_computation
|   |   |   |   infer_by_chaining
|   |   |   measure
|   |   |   ask_user
|   |   |   ask_expert
|   |   estimate
|   |   |   interpolate
|   |   |   extrapolate
|   |   |   qualitative_estimate
|   |   |   prognostic_estimate
|   |   |   estimate_by_analogy
|   |   |   statistical_estimate
|   |   |   random_guess
|   |   negociate
|   |   assume
|   |   |   assume_default
|   |   |   assume_zero
|   |   |   assume_average
```

In combination with hierarchies of meta classes (e.g. the meta class *datum*, as shown in figure 2) several tasks can easily be selected that attempt to obtain certain data in an optimal way.

3.5. Strategic Reasoning

Although models of fixed strategies are very powerful tools for problem solving they do not account for the flexibility of expert behaviour that we have described above. A fixed-strategy model may solve problems in a way that is similar to human experts, but it is not flexible: it will always pursue similar issues, ask similar questions, and fail in the same ways. Models of real expertise need to be more flexible.

The solution we propose here is to equip the model with a planning component which dynamically generates the goal tree. Such a planner uses knowledge about general problem solving methods, such as means ends analysis, heuristic classification etc., and adapt its behaviour on the basis of the task environment and the modality of the system i.e. the way the system has to communicate with the user. An example of a rule that could be part of such a planner:

    if top-goal is finding(solution)
    & modality is consultation
    & there are KS's relating findings to hypotheses
    & there are KS's to refine hypotheses
    then
      decompose the top goal in:
        gather findings,
        generate hypotheses,
        refine hypotheses.

In general planning a solution is not sufficient for flexible problem solving behaviour. When a plan is being executed, its progress has to be monitored, and possible difficulties have to be remedied. Figure 5 gives a structure for flexible strategic reasoning.

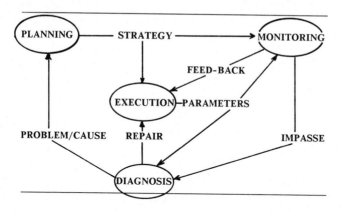

Figure 5. Structure of a strategic reasoning process

4. An example analysis

An analysis of the expertise involved in assessing the risks of providing commercial loans shows how the ideas from the previous sections can be applied in a practical domain.

A client (a company) requests for a(n additional) loan at the local branch of a bank. The commercial loans officer interviews the client and when he believes this request is acceptable, he sends a proposal to a commercial loans expert at the main office of the bank. The task of the expert is to check this proposal, i.e. to decide whether the risks and earnings involved in granting a loan to the client are acceptable to the bank. The proposal consists of two parts. The first part contains necessary data, in particular on the financial position of the client and on securities to support the requested loan(s). The second part consists of an explanation. In the explanation the problem is stated, i.e. why a client needs a loan. Further, it contains a description of the client's company, detailed balance sheet data, marketing reports, and more data that may be relevant.

The domain *concepts* are attributes of companies and loans. Some of these are translated into parameters that are compared to norms which indicate the maximum risk the bank is willing to take and reflect the experience and policies of the bank. The major attributes of companies are quantitative (financial) ones. These can be read or inferred from balance sheet data and marketing studies. Some qualitative data play also an important role like legal status, marketing sector, etc. The loan attributes refer to types of loans and the terms for granting the loans. The major domain *relations* are: subsumption (e.g. classifications of balance sheet data, types of loans and types of property), quantitative (e.g. in formulas to calculate parameters), empirical (e.g. between market sector and financial attributes), consist-of (e.g. between company property and securities).

At the inference level these domain concepts can be mapped onto *meta class* objects. This requires an analysis of the roles these concepts play in the problem solving process. The proposal sent by the local branche has the role of a proposed solution; the data in the proposal are used as evidence that this solution is both adequate (i.e. solves the client's problem) and acceptable. The task of the expert is to assess this evidence, i.e. to find falsifying or insufficient evidence. This (sub)task is similar to a diagnostic task in which potential sources of error ('malfunction') have to be checked. The inferences required are to classify data for (re)calculating parameters, and to compare these with the norms. The major parameters can be summarised as follows. The risk is acceptable when the client can comply with the terms of the loan, i.e. has sufficient property to secure the loan at 100%, and has a sufficient earning capacity to pay the interest, installments, etc. An additional risk factor that has to be assessed as well is the client's solvability (>10%). Solvability is an indicator of the survival capacity of a company. The diagnostic inferences are made on the basis of knowledge about potential sources of error. The 'remedies' (conclusions) consist of corrections of parameter values. The major metaclass objects and their domain references are:

Table 2: meta classes for decision making domains

meta class	domain concept
parameter	solvability, earning capacity, securities,
norm	loan terms
data	company attribute, loan attribute
solution	type of loan
problem	need for loan
decision class	yes/no/defer
hypothesis	unreliabiliy of data; incompleteness of data
conclusion	correction value

The required *knowledge sources* (KS) can be read from the following inference structure.

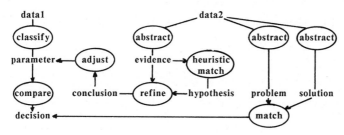

Figure 7. Inference structure for commercial loans assessment.

There are three lines of inference. Some data are used to calculate parameters. This mostly involves simple classification (via subsumption hierarchies), but sometimes heuristic associations have to be used (e.g. to correct for 'hidden capital'). Other data are used to abstract the client's problem and to check the solution. The third line of inference is similar to Clancey's (1985) inference structure for diagnosis by classification. The conclusion (i.e. the remedy) is some estimate of error, by which a parameter can be adjusted accordingly.

At the third level the tasks and goals are described. From thinking aloud protocols a standard strategy was deduced. The explanation is read and the client's problems are identified. Then the expert assesses whether the solution (type and amount of loans) is indeed an answer to the client's needs. Inadequate solutions are also a risk for the bank. The assessment of the risks involved in the solution is performed in two steps. First, the parameter values are taken at face value and this is taken as a rough estimate of the actual risks. If the values indicate a clear 'yes' or a clear 'no' decision the diagnosis process is executed at a superficial level, because potential corrections will not have a significant influence on the outcome. There is rather a process of weirdness scanning than deep diagnosis. This occurs in about 50% of the cases. For borderline cases the checking of the correctness of the data is much less superficial, and there is a heavy reliance on the diagnostic line of inference (Figure 6). The expert tries to find potential sources of errors, particularly those that may have inflated a parameter value. The reliability and assumptions of prognostic data are carefully scrutinised (find (error) task in Figure 7). This may even involve obtaining data from independent 'sources': the expert may compare data which are given with estimates that are inferred by running mental models of company economics (estimate [] task in Figure 7).

The error finding task is a classical diagnostic one in which each hypothesis is successively evaluated. As a consequence the proposal is not read from start to finish, but first the explanation is read and whenever some datum triggers a hypothesis the expert searches for other relevant data that can be used as evidence. This seemingly chaotic reading behaviour is easily explained by the task structure in Figure 7. In Figure 7 the deepest subtasks are performed first (e.g. in the assess(risk) task the read(data) task is the first one to be performed); tasks at the same level are executed in top to bottom order.

```
decide (yes/no)
    assess (solution), *construct (new_solution)
        obtain (solution)
        obtain (problem)
    assess (risk)
        estimate (risk)
        calculate (parameters)
            correct (data)
                obtain (data)
                    read (data), *estimate [(data)], *request (data)
                find (error)
                    collect (data2), *reinterpret (data)
                    generate (hypothesis)
                        focus (reliability, assumptions)
                    obtain evidence
                apply (correction)
    apply (norms)
```

Figure 7: major task structure for commercial loans assessment. (* = next option)

This task structure constrains and combines the use of inferences as described in figure 6. For instance, this same inference structure can also be used to describe the inference competence of a completely different task in the same domain, i.e. the task of the loans officer at the local branch who interviews the client and draws up the proposal.

The task structure represents a fixed strategy that is applied by most experts in both simple and difficult cases. In the difficult cases processing is deeper and involves more data. If deeper processing still leads to parameter values around the yes/no threshold optional tasks are performed by some experts leading to flexibility within the fixed strategy. The expert may try to reinterpret the data by abstracting new 'circumstantial' evidence (cf *reinterpret (data2),

Figure 7). For instance, the potential loss of the bank by not granting a new loan to a client who is credited already some loans can be taken into account. Sometimes a decision is reached by constructing a new solution that consists of a less risky combination of types of loans. In such case the expert performs one of the tasks of the officer at the local branch. This flexibility by weaving options into the fixed strategy are sometimes standard practice and can be viewed as available repairs (Figure 5); sometimes these are newly planned strategies.

Another flexible strategy was observed with a 'super' expert. The 'correct (data)' task, i.e. diagnose and remedy, was not performed by evaluating one hypothesis after the other. Different from other experts he read the data from left to right. Each data was interpreted to some extent which might lead to generating new hypotheses, to evaluative evidence for already generated hypotheses or to a rejection as irrelevant data. As this superexpert proceeds the number of simultaneously active hypotheses grows, and decreases finally when most have been confirmed or falsified. From a thinking aloud protocol we could deduce that halfway reading a proposal the number of active hypotheses was at least 7. At the end of the reading and simultaneous hypothesis generation and verification process the superexpert wraps up the results, points to missing data (evidence), to confirmed hypotheses, corrects the data, etc. In other words, he uses at the top level the same task structure as the other experts, but his diagnostic strategy is different.

This flexibility in pursuing more than one hypothesis at a time requires a large amount of information management. We may assume that this flexibility is not due to planning new courses of action when the fixed strategy fails and the options within this strategy are exhausted. This strategy appears to be enabled by a well organised structure of potential hypotheses. This structure supports the information managament that is required to keep track of the various active hypotheses. This is reminiscent of the observation by De Groot (1966) that differences in well structured and detailed knowledge rather than differences in strategies explains differences in performance between master and experienced chessplayers. This is not to say that we have drawn a full circle now and that flexibility is ultimately embedded in domain knowledge. The point is that flexibility by information management support is different from flexibility that comes from strategic reasoning. In the latter the expert is trying to get as much as possible out of available knowledge by taking new points of view of its inference potentialities, i.e. applying new constraints to the inference structure.

5. Models for Knowledge Acquisition

The description of meta level knowledge in problem solving may also serve other purposes than the description of flexible use of domain knowledge. In knowledge acquisition for building expert systems, in particular for the analysis stage, there is a need for tools and models to analyse (verbal) data which are elicited from domain experts. Elsewhere (Wielinga & Breuker, 1984; Breuker & Wielinga, forthcoming) we have described how *interpretation models* provide such support in the KADS methodology. *) The analysis of the commercial loans expertise is presented as a bottom up one. In reality this analysis was supported by the KADS methodology so that important parts could be analysed in a top-down way. This was particularly the case for the diagnostic reasoning for which ready made inference structures and hypothesis checking strategies are available in the form of interpretation models.

Interpretation models are *generic models* of the problem solving processes in classes of tasks and types of domains. An interpretation model provides an initial structure to the data, and allows for a data analysis process that has a strong top down refinement component. Experiences with the specification and use of interpretation models has shown that the ingredients of such models cannot be straightforward generalisations of objects and inference procedures at the domain level. In describing interpretation models at meta levels a functional view is installed that enables the knowledge engineer to look at the domain knowledge in terms of types of inferences, tasks and the handles it provides for hooking up this knowledge to strategies, and strategic reasoning.

---

*) KADS refers both to a methodology and to a knowledge based support system for for knowledge acquisition for the design and implementation of expert systems.

An interpretation model is a kind of catalogue of types of ingredients the knowledge engineer can look for in the data, and thus functions as an organiser that provides coherence to these data. For instance, in the commercial loans example concepts about sources of unreliability are spread all over the various structures of financial data. These structures of financial data are excellent for explaining the nature of these data -and can be used as 'support' knowledge (Clancey, 1983)-, but from a functional point of view these sources should also be accessable to play the role of hypotheses in the problem solving process. Such points of view are not self evident from descriptions at the domain level. In particular they can hardly be deduced from written documentation and interviews. They were obtained by assuming that a diagnostic process was going on and carefully looking in thinking aloud data which domain concepts played the role of hypotheses.

The analysis of data at the epistemological level should not be confused with designing the architecture of an expert system. The result of the analysis is a process structure of the problem solving in a domain. This process structure is the functional specification of an expert system. In designing the system many practical decisions may be taken, so that it is not impossible that the highly articulate structure that is the result of the analysis, is transformed into an almost flat architecture of an expert system. The advantage of this analysis is that the mapping of epistemological categories onto implementation formalisms is considerably easier than directly from verbal data and that moreover the choice of implementation formalisms can be justified and guided by what is required instead of the other way around. Available formalisms (shells) may act as Procrustian beds in which the expertise is molded, deformed, fixed and sometimes killed. In figure 8 we present a summary of the dependencies in the analysis of expertise and the design of an expert system, as specified in KADS.

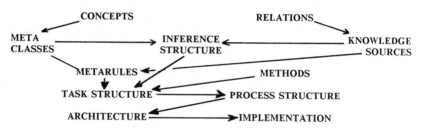

Figure 8: Development of a knowledge based system in the KADS methodology.

6. Discussion

The methods to represent expert knowledge are to a large extent similar to the model that is the basis of NEOMYCIN (Clancey, 1985b). Our model is more explicit in two respects. First, in NEOMYCIN the separation of domain concepts, and their role in the inference process, is made only to a limited extent. The introduction of complex specifications of the way in which domain relations can be used, allows a much greater flexibility of use of domain knowledge than is possible with fixed and limited meta classifications of domain relations. A second difference between our model and that of Clancey is the introduction of a strategic planning level. Admittedly, we have not worked out this level in detail, but our analyses of expert behaviour in various domains clearly show that experts adapt the way in which they decompose a task to the problem environment in a very flexible way.

A potential weakness in the approach presented here is that at the domain level no strong semantics are imposed. The user of the methods has full freedom of defining objects and relations without defining the meaning of these knowledge elements. The meaning is specified by means of the structures at other levels. We feel that -in particular during the early stages of knowledge acquisition- some of this is unavoidable: the knowledge engineer has to have the freedom to define objects and relations which may not have a clearly defined meaning as yet, but which are important and will find there place in the model later on. On the other hand, however, this freedom at the domain level shows that a more top-down, model-driven approach can be a powerful way to focus the knowledge acquisition process. When we start knowledge acquisition with a well specified inference or task structure, the analysis of the domain concepts and relations can be much more focussed. This is precisely the function of interpretation models.

We have attempted to show that the distinction between a number of different levels of knowledge description enhances the possibilities of 1) describing flexible strategies, and 2) abstracting from the domain at hand. From the examples it will be clear that the knowledge at each layer higher up is more general. At the domain layer the knowldge is very domain specific. At the inference level the knowledge is generalised to types of inferences and their interactions, while at the task and planning level the knowlege is applicable to classes of task and types of domains. This observation implies that models at the higher levels can be used as templates in knowledge acquisition. The general categories of knowledge guide the knowledge engineer in the process of interpreting the data obtained from experts.

In summary, we have attempted to proceed one step further in developing a theory of expert problem solving processes, by further separating out the different types of knowledge involved, and by sketching possible ways of representing the different types of knowledge. We are convinced that this approach has strong implications for knowledge acquisition, and can be a basis for developing more flexible expert systems than are currently available.

Acknowledgements
This research was supported in part by the ESPRIT program of the Commission of the European Community, under contract P1098. Partners in this project are: STC, Scicon, SCS, KBSC and Cap Sogeti. Maarten van Someren and Hank Kahney have made helpful comments

7. References

Breuker, J.A. & Wielinga, B.J. Use of models in the interpretation of verbal data, In A. Kidd (ed) *Knowledge Elicitation for Expert Systems* New York: Plenum Press, forthcoming.
Bundy, A., & Sterling, L., Metalevel inference in algebra, Edinburgh, Dep. of Artificial Intelligence, Paper, 164, 1981
Bundy, A., Byrd, L., Luger, G., Melish, C., Milne, R., & Palmer, M. Solving mechanics problems using meta level inference, *Proceedings of the IJCAI-6*, 1979, p 1017-1027
Clancey, William J., The Epistemology of a Rule-Based Expert System - a Framework for Explanation (1983) *Artificial Intelligence*, 20, 215-251.
Clancey W.J. Heuristic Classification, *Artificial Intelligence*, 1985a, 27, 215-251
Clancey W.J. Acquiring, representing and evaluating a competence model of diagnostic strategy. Stanford Knowledge Systems Laboratory, KSL 84-2, 1985b (to appear in: Chi, Glaser and Farr, *Contributions to the nature of expertise*).
Clancey, W.J. Representing control knowledge as abstract tasks and metarules. Stanford Knowledge Systems Laboratory, KSL 85-16, 1985c (to appear in M. Coombs & L. Bolc (eds) Computer Expert Systems, Springer Verlag).
Davis, R. and Buchanan, B. Meta level knowledge. Proc. of the IJCAI, 1977.
Davis, R. Metarules: reasoning about control. *Artificial Intelligence*, 1980, 15, 179-222
Gallaire, H. and Lasserre, C. Metalevel control for logic programming. In: K.L. Clark and S.A. Taernlund (Eds.) Logic Programming, London: Academic Press, 1982.
De Greef, P. & Breuker, J.A. A case study in structured knowledge acquisition *IJCAI*, 1985
De Groot, A.D. Perception and memory versus thought. In B. Kleinmuntz (ed) *Problem Solving: research, method and theory* New York, Wiley, 1966
Hayes, P. Computation and deduction. *Proceedings of MFCS Symposium*, Czech Academy of Sciences, 1973
Pople, H.J., Heuristic methods for imposing structure on ill-structured problems: the structure of medical diagnosis. In: Szolovits, P. (Ed.) *Artificial Intelligence in medicine*. Boulder: Westview Press, Inc. 1982.
Sterling, L. Logical Levels of problem solving, Weizman Institute, Rehovot, CS84-03, 1984
Sternberg. R.J. Reasoning, problem solving and intelligence, In R. J. Sternberg (ed) *Handbook of human intelligence*, Cambridge MA, Cambridge University Press, 1982
Wielinga, B.J. & Breuker, J.A. Interpretation of verbal data for knowledge acquisition. *Proceedings of ECAI-84*, 1984, p41-50

Advances in Artificial Intelligence - II
B. Du Boulay, D. Hogg and L. Steels (Editors)
© Elsevier Science Publishers B.V. (North-Holland), 1987

CO-OPERATIVE EXPERT SYSTEMS

R.P.Worden [*]
M.H.Foote [*]
J.A.Knight [*]
S.K.Andersen [+]

Abstract : Many expert systems under development are intended to be assistants rather than autonomous problem-solvers, yet little attention has been paid to what it means to be an assistant - to co-operate on a task where two agents have incomplete and overlapping knowledge, and to use the best of each agent's knowledge. Expert systems are built using knowledge of how to do the job, not of how to be an assistant. This will put an unacceptable load on the user of making the co-operation work.

We present a framework for building expert systems which can co-operate in something of the manner we would expect a human assistant to co-operate - accepting advice from the user when he knows best, not repeating mistakes unnecessarily, attempting to understand the reasons behind user interventions, and sometimes knowing when it is out of its depth. In this framework, knowledge of how to do the job is separated from knowledge about how to be an assistant.

The ideas are illustrated by an example from the field of Electromyography, which runs on a prototype version of the framework.

1. INTRODUCTION AND SUMMARY

The work of this paper was motivated by the following practical problem : a person performs a task with a computer expert assistant. The assistant offers a piece of advice which the person overrides, for some good reason. How can the assistant behave 'sensibly ' while helping with the remainder of the same task? In particular, if the task involves repetition of the same step with slightly changed data, how can the assistant avoid giving the same bad advice time and time again ? This problem, which has received little attention so far, will be of great importance for the acceptability of many expert systems to their users.

Expert systems are currently being built for a very wide range of task domains, and in many of these domains it is recognised that an expert system will not have the breadth of knowledge, the available data or the inference methods to perform the task autonomously. The task may occasionally require common sense or perceptions that we cannot hope to computerise for some time. So these expert systems are presented as 'assistants' rather than as autonomous problem-solvers.

However,most of the effort in expert system development is put into knowledge of how to do the job, not of how to be an assistant. Being a competent assistant involves many non-trivial skills and some tacit knowledge which we take for granted in humans, and are not building into computers. Many expert systems will fail simply because they are not good assistants, even if they are quite good at their jobs.

* Logica Cambridge Ltd.,Betjeman House,104 Hills Road, Cambridge CB2 1LQ, England

+ Nordjysk Udviklings Center, Badehusvej 23, DK-9000 Aalborg, Denmark

Early expert systems acted as though they were solving the problem single-handed, treating the user merely as a source of information. The later development of the 'critiquing' style of expert system (1,2) allows the user to make his own decisions, while the expert system 'shadows' him or her, only intervening when it detects significant disagreement ; then it 'critiques' the user's choice, which may persuade him to change his mind. This style of interaction appears to be less obtrusive and overbearing, and to be more acceptable to many users, particularly in medical applications. However, this is only one step along the road to effective assistance. The purpose of this paper is to discuss the other functions required for a co-operating expert assistant, and to describe a prototype expert system which embodies some of these functions.

The essential problems of assistance are : how can two agents with incomplete and overlapping knowledge co-operate effectively on a task as a team to make the best use of their knowledge? Specifically, how can the assistant properly take account of those things which the user knows best? Many tasks involve some short-term repetition of similar sub-tasks in slightly varying circumstances; when the user corrects a mistake made by the assistant, how can it avoid making the same mistake again?

We believe that there are some useful and general answers to these questions, which can be embodied in heuristics for interacting with the user, supported by a suitable framework (or shell). They are modelled on the way human assistants perform co-operative tasks. However, they require special mechanisms to be built in to the shell to keep track of information flows and dependencies. We have built a prototype system which has these mechanisms, and we are currently experimenting with its use in an assistant for certain aspects of an electromyography (EMG) examination.

Section 2 is a discussion of the kinds of behaviour we expect from human assistants, based on observation and introspection, and a comparison with what we currently get from expert systems. Section 3 discusses what kinds of knowledge are needed to support co-operative assistant behaviour. Section 4 illustrates these ideas by an example from the electromyography assistant which we are building, and section 5 gives some details of our current (Prolog - based) prototype . Section 6 concludes, and relates our approach to other work.

2. WHAT WE EXPECT FROM AN ASSISTANT

When we perform a cognitive task such as running an industrial plant, filling in a set of forms, diagnosing a disorder or planning a budget, with a human assistant, what kinds of behaviour do we expect from the assistant ?

In what follows, we shall use the term 'leader' to refer to the person who has overall responsibility for successful completion of the job and who generally knows more about it - even though he may sometimes delegate responsibility for parts of it to the assistant, who then in some sense 'leads' those parts. The assistant may know more than the leader about some aspects of the task; in those cases, the leader usually knows that the assistant knows more . We describe initially the case of human leader, human assistant (our eventual aim is to build computer assistants for human leaders).

- The leader expects to agree some sort of division of the task into sub-tasks, then to work an adaptive **dynamic division of labour** with the assistant on different sub-tasks ; the leader may do some entirely by himself,with or without comment from the assistant,and he may delegate others to the assistant, with or without checking his answers. The distribution of sub-tasks is often not rigid or pre-defined.

- The leader expects to know,or to be able to observe, things which are unknown to the assistant; then he expects to be able to **override** his recommendations.The leader **considers the consequences of a disagreement** when deciding whether or not to override.

- The assistant should to be able to **follow through the consequences** of the leader's overriding interventions ; he should also have some idea of, or find out, how long theoverrides are valid for.

- Since many tasks are repetitive in nature, when once the leader   has overridden a decision of the assistant, he expects him **not to   make the same mistake again** on re-doing that sub-task.

- In order to avoid repeating his mistakes, an assistant will   **attempt to understand the leader's interventions** ; the   leader is prepared to spend some time explaining why he overrides the assistant's decisions in order to help him perform better in future.

- When a decision has been overridden for reasons the assistant does not understand,and the same decision is required to be made in altered circumstances, the assistant should **know when he is out of his depth** and ask the leader for his decision again.

- The assistant should be able to **explain his decisions** and **criticise the leader's decisions,** both to help the leader do the job and to help the leader explain things to him.

- Underlying all this behaviour, the assistant is expected to   **maintain a co-operative working store** which embodies the best joint understanding of the leader and the assistant about the current state of the task.

These capabilities are so fundamental that we take most of them for granted in any human assistant . Yet apart from explaining and criticising, current expert systems have essentially none of them. Where they do, they have been built in essentially ad hoc ways at some expense.

3. KNOWLEDGE REQUIRED FOR CO-OPERATIVE BEHAVIOUR

What knowledge structures might human assistants use to achieve the behaviour described in section 2? It appears that in general, **effective co-operation depends on knowledge about the structure and extent of our own knowledge, and of our partner's knowledge.** The relative importance of self-knowledge and partner-knowledge depends on the context :-

When acting as a teacher,we assume that our own knowledge of the subject is near-perfect, and concentrate on the structure and extent of the student's knowledge,in the 'student model'.

When we act as an assistant, ultimate responsibility for the success of the task lies with our partner. We may point out things to him which he may not know, but if he chooses to override us, there is nothing else we can do about it. Therefore our main responsibility is to recognise and act sensibly in situations where the user knows best.For this reason,the most important meta-knowledge required by an effective assistant is **a knowledge of the structure and extent of his own knowledge**.

In particular,for repetitive tasks with a non-trivial time-structure (which include many monitoring and re-planning tasks),an assistant needs knowledge about the structure of his own knowledge in time. These points will be illustrated with reference to the kinds of assistant behaviour described above, in the case of human leader, human assistant.

- To support the **dynamic division of labour** between leader and assistant, the assistant knows about the division of the task into sub-tasks, and he knows which sub-tasks he cannot do.

- To **follow through the consequences** of overrides by the leader,an assistant will often use a rough meta-knowledge about what depends on what ; in particular he will know what does not depend on a change imposed by the leader, and what therefore need not be reassessed.

- To **attempt to understand the leader's interventions**, an assistant will again use his knowledge of 'what depends on what' to reason about their causes. In particular when a difference of opinion between leader and assistant could be understood by abandoning one of several pieces of the assistant's knowledge,the assistant will tend to abandon the least reliable of these. For this he needs knowledge about the reliability of parts of his own knowledge,including both facts and rules.

- To **avoid repeating mistakes** often requires knowledge about the time-structure of knowledge to know how long a leader's interventions are valid for. The leader says 'A', which the assistant knows depends on B and C, although he may not know in detail how. The next time A is required, if B and C have not changed then the old value of A can be used.

- To **know when he is out of his depth** an assistant must know about the quality of different pieces of his own knowledge. He must know what depends on what, to spot things which depend on things he does not know. In the example above,if B or C are no longer what they were when the leader said 'A', then the assistant knows that he no longer knows A.

- To **explain his decisions and criticise the leader's decisions**, an assistant requires some model of the leader's knowledge ; also, as criticism involves analysing a difference between leader's and assistant's views, the reliability of parts of the assistant's knowledge is relevant.

Therefore in addition to meta-knowledge about subtasks and the knowledge required for them (as identified, for instance, in Clancey's work (3)), we have identified three kinds of knowledge about his own knowledge which an assistant requires :

- He must know **what depends on what**
  (even though he may not know in detail how it depends)

- He must know **how reliable different pieces of his knowledge are**
  (even knowing of the existence of knowledge which he does not have)

- He must know **what has changed when**
  (even though he may not know how or why it changed).

To make the discussion more concrete, we shall consider an example from the prototype Electromyographer's assistant which we are currently building in an ESPRIT project.

4. AN EXAMPLE IN ELECTROMYOGRAPHY

Electromyography (sometimes abbreviated to EMG) is a technique for examining the electrical activity of nerves and muscles, measuring parameters such as nerve conduction velocities to help in the diagnosis of peripheral nerve disorders.

In the 45 minutes typically allotted for an EMG examination it is possible to perform about half a dozen separate tests, each one of which can give several different pieces of diagnostically interesting information. The EMG examiner aims to send back a one-page report to the referring neurologist, which either satisfies his 'reasons for referral' (a typical reason for referral is 'Confirm diabetic neuropathy' or 'Exclude Motor Neuron Disease'), or else gives him a useful basis on which to proceed.

Because of the range of different tests which can be done,and the wide range of anatomical locations at which a test can be done, a novice EMG examiner may often spend time doing redundant tests which do not add to the picture, or fail to do important tests so that the patient has to be recalled later.

We are currently building a prototype expert 'EMG assistant' whose main aims are to advise the examiner on the choice of tests (what test to do next,and where to do it), and to help him prepare the final report.

To do this it must know how to interpret the test results at any stage of the exam, because if these rule out a favoured diagnostic hypothesis the goals of the exam may change.

In this paper we shall discuss only one small sub-problem for the EMG assistant - that of <u>choosing which anatomical site to use</u> for a test such as measuring the muscle action potentials. The choice of a muscle for one of these tests is basically a **tradeoff** involving a number of factors, such as:-

- **anatomical appropriateness**; for instance, if you are trying to confirm a lesion of a particular spinal nerve root, choose a muscle which is fed by a nerve from that spinal root

- **the quality of 'normal data'** for that muscle in healthy patients, to show the existence of an abnormality

- **the sensitivity of the test** in that muscle for the disorder in question ; how often it can give false positives or false negatives

- **what has been done already** in that examination (don't repeat a test ; left-right comparisons can be useful)

The choice of a muscle for a test may be done repeatedly for the same test during one examination ; the circumstances change slightly from one choice to the next,but many factors remain the same.

We represent this tradeoff in the assistant by the following sequence of steps :-

(S1) Of all the muscles in the body, produce a shortlist of those which are basically eligible for use in the test.

(S2) Eliminate those for which the test has been adequately performed already.

(S3) For each of a number of relevant 'Factors' (e.g. patient discomfort, quality of control data) work out or look up a 'Rating' A...E for each remaining eligible muscle.

(S4) Use heuristic rules (or even arithmetic) about the current importance of the different factors to combine the factors into an overall rating for each eligible muscle.

(S5) Order the muscles by their overall rating and choose the best.

The information flow in this tradeoff process is illustrated in figure 1.

Obviously this general approach to making a tradeoff could be applied to other aspects of the EMG examination or to many other tasks.

It is a good example of a co-operative task because there are some factors which the assistant may be expected to know better (or look up more reliably) than the user, and there are other factors, particularly those involving the clinical picture or observation of the patient, which the user may be expected to know better than the assistant. Some will change with time, others will be constant through the examination. **The assistant's job is to point out those things it knows well and which are relevant, to accept the user's overrides where he makes them, to work out their consequences, and to try to understand them so it can behave sensibly in future.**

In a typical interaction,the assistant recommends that the next test be done on the Deltoid muscle, but the user chooses the Biceps. (This may take the form of the assistant displaying its recommendation and the user disagreeing, or it may involve the user inputting his choice first and the assistant critiquing it.) In either case the assistant will give some kind of 'explanation' of its own reasoning and critique of the user's presumed reasoning. The user may do one of three things :

- accept the assistant's recommendation

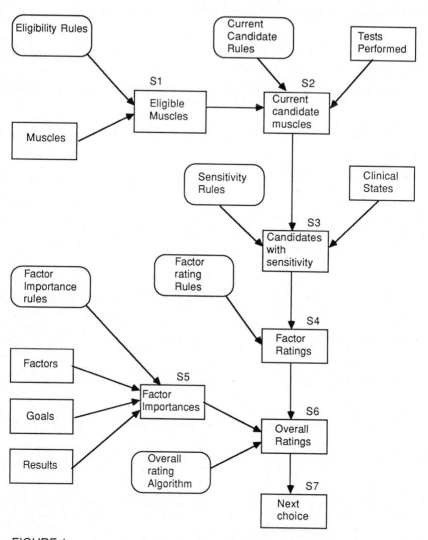

FIGURE 1

- override it without explaining why

- override the recommendation and explain why he is doing so.

In this case the patient is showing some signs of distress (which the assistant did not know), so the factor 'Patient Discomfort' assumes added importance. Doing the test in the Deltoid is significantly more painful than doing it in the Biceps, but the Deltoid test is more sensitive. The user 'explains' his choice to the assistant by directly modifying the importance rating of the 'Patient Discomfort' factor, which ensures that the assistant will not recommend any uncomfortable muscles again during this examination.

Had the user not explained his choice in this way, the assistant would have been at a loss to recommend the next test for the same examination ; it would not know whether the user's choice followed from some unknown factor which made the biceps better than expected for the test, or some factor which made the deltoid worse than expected. It would simply have to ask the user for his choice again.

This example illustrates the use of 'what depends on what' knowledge and knowledge of time dependencies to guide the assistant's actions. The assistant knows that the result 'Biceps is best' depends on all sorts of factors, many of which may change from one test to the next. Therefore when recommending the next test the user's choice can neither be blindly re-used nor blindly overridden. However it also knows that the input datum 'Patient discomfort is very important' is unlikely to change from one test to the next (if it does change,it is the user's responsibility to say so). Therefore the assistant can re-use this piece of information from the user without re-consulting him.

5. DESIGN OF A CO-OPERATIVE EXPERT SYSTEM

We intend the EMG assistant expert system to be capable of the kinds of co-operative behaviour described in preceding sections. A major design aim is that the knowledge of how to assist and co-operate should not be intermingled in an ad hoc manner with the knowledge of how to do the job.

To explore this issue, and to explore the underlying capabilities required for co-operative interaction, we have built a prototype system in Prolog which handles the muscle trade-off problem in certain cases. It has limited knowledge of anatomy,and of many of the factors involved in choosing a test site, such as patient discomfort,sensitivity,and reproducibility of results. As well as these, it has the meta-knowledge required for sensible co-operative behaviour of the kind described in previous sections. It can make a recommendation, give an elementary explanation of its reasoning, accept an override by the user and continue to use it for as long as appropriate, critique the user's choices where they differ from its own, and hold an exploratory dialogue with the user to understand the reasons for his interventions.

The design of the system has been influenced by NEOMYCIN (3) in a number of ways. First, in an attempt to separate declarative domain knowledge from procedural 'how to do the job' knowledge we have embodied the latter in a structure of tasks and subtasks which does not depend closely on specific domain knowledge (the same task structure would be appropriate for many tradeoff decisions). Second,we have adopted a relational formalism for the knowledge base, including particularly the 'working storage' where details of the current case are stored. We differ from NEOMYCIN in trying to build in a third kind of knowledge, of 'how to be an effective assistant' which is based on self-knowledge.

The relational model has been used for the KB in preference to richer structures such as frames , because the sparseness and precision of the relational model keeps the issues clear when the knowledge base is being updated by two separate agents (the user and the assistant) - for instance when the user removes an item of data and the assistant wants to re-instate it. However, the main results of this paper do not depend on the relational model and could in principle be applied using any data model ; so we will not use relational terminology in describing the system, but will use general terminology which can be mapped onto other data models .

The data relevant to the problem is divided into a number of **data sets** - some static (unchanging in the course of an examination) and others dynamic. Each data set is a collection of **data items**. The rectangular boxes in figure 1 each represent a data set - for instance the data items in the data set 'Current Candidate Muscles' are the names of muscles which are currently candidates to be the site of the next test. A data item is the smallest unit which can be modified by the user or the assistant - for instance the user may wish to override the assistant by removing one of the current candidate muscles.

Computation is done by a calling hierarchy of **tasks** and **subtasks.** A task is a subdivision of the overall job which is meaningful to the user and which may therefore figure in discussions with him as 'We are now doing task X .....'. Subtasks go down to a smaller subdivision of labour. Each subtask takes its input data from a number of data sets in the KB, and updates a number of data sets. It consists typically of doing a simple piece of arithmetic, or of forward-chaining on some small local ruleset.

The data sets and the subtasks define a **coarse dependency graph** which is a kind of data flow diagram showing which data set depends, directly or indirectly, on which other data sets. The dependency graph for the muscle tradeoff example is shown in figure 1. It will be seen that the KB includes several 'static' data sets which will not change during a single examination.

The coarse dependency graph could be used to run a kind of dataflow-driven computation, of the form 'If data set R changes then you must re-run subtasks S1 and S2, which in turn may change data sets U,V....'. However,the assistant needs to make use of more specific dependency information, in the form of **fine-grained dependency rules** which state more precisely which data items in a data set depend on which data items in other data sets. An example of a fine-grained dependency rule is that all the ratings of a particular muscle (its rating for data quality, patient discomfort,etc.) depend only on facts about that muscle ; they do not depend on facts about any other muscle.

The assistant has knowledge of what tasks and subtasks need to be done, and in what order, to complete the job . It also needs a set of **task division rules** to define which tasks shall be done by whom (user or assistant). We can currently support four different points on the spectrum of subdivision of labour :

- user does task
- user does task, assistant critiques
- assistant does task, user vets result
- assistant does task.

The first of these is uninteresting ; it essentially only requires facilities for the user to input the results into the affected data sets. The fourth is the way in which most current expert systems operate. The middle two are the interesting cases, because they are typical of the way most people use an assistant, and they require ways of handling differences of opinion between user and assistant.

When the user disagrees with the assistant, he may add, modify or delete data items from certain data sets. Usually the assistant must take these modified data sets as the definitive versions in future ; but to be a good assistant, it must do much more. We shall illustrate the kinds of things it must do - and can do in our current prototype - by means of an example. We shall also use the example to show the underlying mechanisms used by the prototype.

When the assistant has calculated a preferred site for the next test, it displays the results of its calculation in a table as shown in figure 2. This table,and the recommendation below it, contain information from several of the data sets in figure 1. The muscles in the left-hand column come from the data set 'Current candidate muscles' ; the bulk of the table from the data set 'Factor ratings' consisting of ratings A..E of individual muscles against tradeoff factors such as patient discomfort,sensistivity and so on ; the right-hand column comes from the data set 'Overall ratings'; and the recommendation is the data set 'Next choice'.

Muscle name	Data	Sensitivity	Difficulty	Discomfort	Reproducability	**Overall**
DELTOID	A	A	D	E	D	C
TRAPEZIUS	E	B	D	C	E	E
QUADRICEPS	E	B	D	C	E	E
BICEPS	B	D	D	C	B	D
ORIS	A	B	D	E	E	D

> The recommended site is the Deltoid

FIGURE 2

The ratings A..E used by the assistant correspond to verbal ratings of quality used by people ; A= excellent, B=good, C=average, D=bad, E=very bad. Users soon adapt to the translation and appreciate the conciseness of the letters, for instance in tabular displays.

The user is then free to query or modify any of the information displayed. Since most data items were derived by forward chaining on small rulesets, the assistant will usually 'explain' an item by simply displaying in pseudo-english the rule which gave it ; for instance :-

" The Deltoid has a Sensitivity Rating A, because
      (1) The Deltoid is currently a candidate test site
  and (2) The Deltoid is a muscle with high or very high sensitivity. "

(In fact the overall ratings are derived not by rules , but by an empirically derived function from individual factor ratings and factor importances to an overall rating. This function can be regarded as a kind of shorthand for many rules of the form "If the importance of the factor 'Sensitivity' is 'high' and a muscle has sensitivity rating A and the importance of the factor 'Patient discomfort' is 'low' and..... then the overall rating of the muscle is B". The same kind of 'explanation' can be given for this function, by simply quoting the input values which gave the result.)

When the user overrides any value given by the assistant, then the assistant must obviously work out the consequences of the override, by re-doing all calculations 'downstream' in the dependency graph of figure 1. For instance, if the user changes an individual factor rating of a muscle, the assistant must re-calculate its overall rating which may in turn affect the choice of best test site. This our prototype can do using its knowledge of data dependencies.

More interesting questions arise 'next time round' when the assistant is asked to recommend another test site in slightly altered circumstances. We must first ensure that the assistant does not blindly undo an override made by the user, be re-applying the rule which gave the 'wrong' result in the first place. This is done by marking each data item with a flag, which says whether the assistant or the user supplied the current value ; the assistant will never blindly modify a use-supplied value. However, it is not a priori obvious whether the user-supplied value can simply be re-used next time round ; circumstances may have changed to make it invalid.

Consider the case where the assitant recommends the Deltoid and the user actually wants to use the

R.P. Worden et al.

Biceps. He can make this override in one of two ways :-

- He can change the data item in data set 'Next choice' from Deltoid to Biceps, thus simply altering the final result.

- He can change the factor rating for 'Patient Discomfort' of the Deltoid from C to E ; then the assistant recalculates 'downstream' from this, finds the Deltoid is no longer such a good idea, and elects the Biceps as first choice.

The consequences at the time of the override are the same in both cases ; the test is done on the Biceps. However , the consequences next time round are very different in the two cases.In the first case, the assistant is nonplussed ; it knows that the user chose the Biceps last time, but the Biceps can no longer be the best choice because it has now been used for the test. Should it go back to the Deltoid? In the second case it knows very well it should not go back to the Deltoid; because of the high expected patient discomfort in that muscle, the Trapezius is preferable. When the user explains the reasons for his override (i.e. puts it in as far 'upstream' as possible) the assistant is less likely to be at a loss in future.

To answer the question 'Is this data item which the user gave me still valid?' the assistant asks itself two further questions :-

- What other data items should this data item depend on ?

- Have any of them changed since the user gave me this data item ?

The first question is answered by the use of the detailed dependency rules, which are roughly of the form 'Data item X depends on data item Y if .....' . In the prototype these are expressed as Prolog rules , allowing unification of variables within X and Y. Prolog backchaining produces a list of data items which any user-changed data item should depend on. The second is answered by storing a timestamp with each data item, showing when it last changed. By examining these timestamps, the assistant establishes whether anything has changed,which might affect the value of a data item X, since the user supplied a value for X. If it has not, the assistant assumes that the user-supplied value is still valid, and uses it. If something has changed, the assistant has to re-ask the user for a new value.

To return to the two possible overrides in the example ; the data item 'Biceps' in the data set 'Next choice' depends on the data item 'Biceps = not used yet' which obviously changes when the Biceps is used; so the assistant must re-ask the user for a next choice. But the data item 'Rating of Deltoid for Patient discomfort = E' depends on various static data items about the Deltoid, which do not change ; so the assistant knows it can re-use it.

It appears that items 'upstream' in the dependency graph are more stable and less subject to change than downstream items. Therefore the assistant always encourages the user to input his changes as far upstream as possible. It does this by 'critiquing' any user -supplied change through a contradiction-backtracing mechanism,which relates the change to 'upstream' changes which might have caused it,and inviting the user to choose one of these.

Contradiction backtracing is a way of analysing some user-supplied value (which the assistant cannot derive from the current state of the knowledge base). The assistant examines all rules or functions which could in principle have given the user-supplied value, and finds all the ways in which one other data item could be changed to make the rule fire appropriately or the function give the required value. Thus it tries to explain a fact by changing one 'upstream' fact (not by changing a rule). For instance , if the user changes the overall rating of a muscle, the assistant will produce a 'critique' of this change in the form :

" You have stated that the ADM has an overall rating C. I can only only find a reason for this if one of the following is true :

(1) the ADM has a Patient discomfort rating D

(but at the moment the ADM has a patient discomfort rating A)

(2) the ADM has a Difficulty rating D
(but at the moment the ADM has difficulty rating A)

(3) etc.

Which , if any, of these is the reason behind your statement? "

The user may then select one of these to confirm (in which case his override has been 'moved' one step upstream in the dependency graph), withdraw his override because the critique convinces him that he is wrong, or simply insist on the override without providing any justification for it. If he accepts one of the explanations of his change, this in turn is critiqued, so moving the change further upstream until either the user changes a static data item (which cannot be traced back further) or he insists on an unjustified change. Users know that the further back they 'explain' their changes , the better is the assistant able to cope without intervention in future.

One further piece of information is stored with each data item (or at least defined for each data item by Prolog rules) : that is a crude measure of the reliability with which the assistant expects to know that data item . Then when presenting possible upstream data changes to the user for his confirmation, the assistant can present them with the most plausible changes first (i.e. with changes to least reliable data items first), and need not consider changes to highly reliable data items. In cases when there is only one plausible explanation of a user's override, the assistant may even do the backtracing automatically without asking for confirmation by the user.

That concludes the overall description of the methods used by our prototype EMG assistant to take account of user overrides (both when they are made and subsequently), to know how long they are valid for and to trace them back to 'upstream' changes so as to perform better in future. The mechanisms are domain-independent, so can be applied to any expert system application provided that the necessary meta-data (on data dependencies, reliability and so on) can be supplied and the underlying shell is built to use them in the manner described above.

There follow a number of detailed points which are optional reading.

The possibility exists that the user changed a data item (or inserted it or deleted it) because of some factor unknown to the assistant, which then changes unknown to the assistant . The assistant assumes that in this case the user will make the change again when appropriate. We believe that this behaviour corresponds to an accepted division of responsibility between people and their human assistants ; when you bring to a problem information which your assistant cannot access, you then take responsibility for subsequent changes in that information.

Note that the answer to 'When might this data item change?' must be derived from permanent **dependency rules** rather than **dependency records** of the data items which a data item actually depended on at the time it was changed. This is because new data items may subsequently be created (which the changed data item also depends on). Dependency rules will catch these ; dependency records will not. For instance, the statement 'ADC is the best current candidate muscle' depends on all candidate muscles, not just on those which were candidates when the statement was first made.

The update algorithm must be implemented carefully to handle all cases correctly, particularly not to let the assistant re-insert a data item which the user has just deleted. This requires keeping 'shadow' records of deleted data items. Also the handling of timestamps is not as simple as one might expect.

An alternative to keeping timestamps is to keep 'dependency records' of everything a data item depended on at the time the user changed it, as well as the general dependency rules. Then one can check whether the dependency set has changed by direct comparison of old and new values. This would have the advantage of avoiding re-consulting the user in some cases where a data item changes and then changes back to its old value, but at a cost of extra complexity and storage. Our current implementation uses only timestamps.

Often the user's explaining a change reveals 'collateral' consequences which may be of interest to him. For example, the assistant may believe that eligible muscles must be fed from the C5 spinal cord root and so recommends the brachialis ; the user chooses the triceps. The assistant critiques this choice on the grounds that the triceps is fed from C7, and the 'understanding' process then reveals that the user is actually interested in muscles fed from C5,C6 or C7. The assistant then re-calculates, revealing several other muscles fed by C6 and C7 which are actually better than the triceps.

We can now list the different kinds of knowledge in the system, and how they are used.

- **Declarative domain knowledge** stored as rules and facts in data sets in the KB, the facts subject to change by the user. Used by subtasks for calculation and inference.

- **Dynamic Knowledge** about the current case, stored in data sets.
Also subject to change by the user.

- **Procedural Knowledge** about how to do the job (independent of who is doing it) stored in tasks and subtasks.

- **Task Division Knowledge** stored as rules defining when the assistant does a task,when the user does it, and with what input from the other

- **System Self-knowledge** about the structure and quality of its own knowledge ; consisting of dependency rules, timestamps, sources of updates and measures of reliability . Used as described above to handle user interventions.

- **'How to be an assistant' Knowledge** ; some of this is built into the basic algorithms for updating the KB,and the rest consists of the methods to detect a disagreement with the user and do something about it; how to critique his choices, how and when to trace them back to earlier changes,how to re-consult the user.

The prototype is implemented in LPA MacProlog (Edinburgh dialect) and uses the windowing and menu facilities of the Macintosh for user interactions. It has general facilities for maintaining the co-operative KB as described above, for implementing subtasks as forward-chaining rulesets, for tabular output of the contents of any data sets in the KB , rules to define which parts of the KB can be modified by the user and when, menu-driven user update of the KB, English-like explanation of any fact in the KB or any rule-firing, contradiction backtracing for user-assistant disagreement, generating a critique and allowing the user to explain his intervention in terms of the critique.

The prototype demonstrates the close relationship between explanation, critiquing and the 'understanding' process whereby the assistant finds out what it can about the basis of the user's interventions. A critique consists of a number of possible explanations of a change put in by the user, in terms of possible 'earlier' changes in the dependency graph ; the user may select one of these possible changes in order to 'explain' to the assistant why he made the change,and thus to help it understand and perform more effectively in future.

Our experience from this implementation shows that :

(1) Mechanisms to support a co-operative Knowledge Base (embodying the best consensus of user and assistant) can be built into the shell at a basic level.

(2) These mechanisms use meta-knowledge about data dependencies, reliability of data, and time dependence in domain-independent ways.

(3) Once the general mechanisms are built, heuristics for user interaction and assistant behaviour

can be separated fairly cleanly from the 'performance' knowledge. Building in the performance knowledge is no harder than in a conventional expert system.

(4) There is commonality of function between explanation, critiquing and the process of understanding user interventions, so that they can be built with common underlying mechanisms.

6. DISCUSSION AND RELATION TO OTHER WORK

Expert systems will be incomplete, imperfect artefacts for some time to come, perhaps always. Therefore their ability to function as assistants, accepting corrections from their users and acting sensibly on them, will be essential for their operational use. In particular for repetitive tasks, where the same sub-task is repeated with slightly differing data over short timescales, an expert assistant will be expected not to keep repeating the same mistakes, or to keep asking for user input unnecessarily.

This problem has not yet received much attention in the expert systems literature. This is not because it is an unimportant problem; it has not received attention because so few expert systems have been taken to the point of routine repetitive use (particularly in continuous monitoring and re-planning problems) that it has not yet become a visible problem. If expert systems succeed, it will become highly visible . Most expert systems and expert system-building tools are not equipped to handle it.

We have built a small prototype system in the domain of electromyography which demonstrates the basic elements of responsible assistant behaviour . It will accept overrides from the user, critique these overrides, try to understand them in order to perform better in future, and avoid repeating its mistakes. The mechanisms which achieve this behaviour are of general applicability, and are based on the assistant's self-knowledge about the structure, extent and quality of its own knowledge.

The prototype is a first step towards an expert system which truly knows how to be a good assistant . Much work remains to be done in exploring and implementing the wide range of concious and tacit knowledge which people use when acting as assistants or delegates. This work is closely related to work in a number of fields within AI, in particular to :

- Reason maintenance systems

- Rule learning programs

- Expert systems based on deep knowledge

- Intelligent tutoring systems

It is instructive to discuss how our work relates to these fields in order to see the problems which will be encountered, and the solutions which may be enlisted, in taking this work further.

The underlying mechanism which we have used for updating the 'co-operative knowledge base' can be regarded as a simple form of reason maintenance system. Essentially the assistant regards every conclusion it reaches as provisional (an 'assumption' in the sense of Doyle (4)), and subject to contradiction by the user. When the user contradicts a conclusion, the assistant will draw the implied consequences from this new input, and will not later try to deny it. It will also do a form of dependency-directed backtracking to try to find the source of the user's change. These are all standard functions of a RMS, but our implementation differs in style from most RMS implementations because of the nature of our use of the RMS.

Many reported applications of RMS, such as causal reasoning, circuit diagnosis and planning, are in some sense 'precise' applications where the problem is well understood and the system makes assumptions only to fill in essentially unknown information - what is wrong with the circuit, how a physical system evolves, or what plan is chosen. It then finds contradictions and uses these to narrow down the set of possibilities to a smaller set which are each logically self-consistent. This requires elaborate mechanisms to achieve logical consistency by a single, perfectly rational agent.

In contrast an expert assistant in a messy real-world task will often employ rules which are known to be convenient fictions. When a contradiction occurs, it is not as a result of rational deduction from precise assumptions, it is a bolt from the blue - because the user decrees it. Therefore 'patching up' a system of beliefs to accommodate the new information is much more a matter of pragmatic exploration, guided by the user, than of logical deduction.

In Doyle's RMS, the meta-knowledge used to guide belief revision is a precise structure of justifications which are explicitly stored at each node ; it is assumed that when a new justification for a node becomes available, it can be computed and stored. In our system we do not store the precise justification of each node, but store rules defining which other nodes could in principle figure in its justifications - all the nodes which a node could depend on. These rules may be less fine-grained than reality - sometimes making the system think that A depends on B when it actually does not - but can be more robust for that.

Because contradictions (differences of opinion between the user and the assistant) can arise for a great variety of reasons, the effectiveness of our belief revision methods will depend not so much on their logical adequacy as on pragmatic factors about what data tend to be more reliable, what questions the user can be expected to answer, and so on. These are embodied in heuristics and approximate meta-knowledge whose precise form must be refined by experiment for each application domain. Nevertheless, issues of negation, circularity, and logical consistency will sometimes be important, so we would expect the more elaborate mechanisms built into other RMS to be relevant to many applications.

An alternative treatment of reason maintenance consists of maintaining multiple possible 'viewpoints' or 'hypothetical worlds' in which differents sets of beliefs are held, rather than withdrawing beliefs in one world (de Kleer (12)). This approach has a number of advantages - for instance in explanation and in allowing the assistant to maintain an opinion of its own - which we have not had time to explore.

There is a considerable body of work on rule-learning programs (5-9) which work by tracing contradictions back to a faulty or missing rule, and then trying to amend the rule. The aim of this is to achieve a long-term improvement in performance of the system. This contrasts with the system described here, in which contradictions are traced back to faulty facts, which are then amended to achieve a short-term performance improvement.

One may ask - how do you know whether it is the rules or the facts which should be altered ? Surely the system can only accumulate faulty 'facts' by applying faulty rules or being fed erroneous data, so it would be better always to try to amend the rules. There are several reasons why this is not so.

In general, full contradiction backtracing will always go back through one or more facts to an erroneous or missing input fact, or an erroneous rule. However, in operational use it will not always be possible to trace back this far, principally because the user wants to get on with the job. Even partial tracing back is useful, because you will trace back to less time-dependent facts, so will need to re-consult the user less often.

Even if you do trace back to a faulty rule (which will often happen), it is much more difficult and time-consuming to correct a rule than to correct a fact, and the user will probably not want to do this in mid-task. Finally, there are many cases in which even though a rule was at fault, it should not be corrected. Many of the most useful 'surface' rules in expert systems are convenient approximations which hold most of the time, but which occasionally break down; the 'exact' rules would cater for all imaginable exceptions but would be too cumbersome for practical use.

Therefore there is an important distinction between a good assistant and a good apprentice. An apprentice tries to learn pragmatically correct rules from selected training cases, in order to be effective in the long-term future. An assistant has to make pragmatic adjustments to its understanding of the facts of the present (unselected,difficult) case to be effective over the next few minutes. While there is some overlap in methods, there are large differences of emphasis.

While one may not want to modify a rule in an expert system every time it gives the wrong answer, it may be useful to know why it gave a wrong answer for that case. The way to do this is shown by the work of Smith et al (9) whose Learning Apprentice System stores a 'justification structure' for each individual rule. This shows how a 'surface' rule used for everyday performance is justified in terms of deeper knowledge and (usually correct) approximations, much as in Swartout's XPLAIN system (10). When a rule fails, it is then possible to trace back to the underlying deep knowledge and approximations, to see which one is wrong for the particular case. Our contradiction traceback mechanism would be capable of this tracing back to deeper knowledge, but it has not yet been used in that way. Given the importance of deep knowledge for explanation (10), and the close relationship between explanation and the assistant's 'understanding' process, this seems an important avenue to explore.

Throughout this paper we have taken the somewhat extreme position of a 'servile' assistant which believes that its master is always right. While this may be a good way of avoiding litigation, it may not always be the best way of doing the job. If an expert assistant,like an intelligent tutoring system (11), had a good model of its user's knowledge - knowing about areas where the user knew less than itself - then it could persist in critiquing some user decisions in order to push him towards the right answer. Thus a good assistant must ultimately have a model of the user's knowledge as well as a model of its own. However, handling both together will be a complex task. In this work we have emphasised only the assistant's self-knowledge, which we believe is the more important of the two when co-operating with a user who is ultimately responsible for the success of the task, and whose own self-knowledge should tell him when to accept the advice of the assistant.

Acknowledgements

We would like to thank the Commission for the European Communities for part-funding of ESPRIT project P599, on which this work was done, and our colleagues on the project for many stimulating discussions and ideas; also our colleagues at Logica and elsewhere for helpful comments and criticism.

REFERENCES

(1) P.L.Miller : A Critiquing Approach to Expert Computer Advice; ATTENDING . Pitman,1984.

(2) C.P.Langlotz, E.H.Shortliffe in: Developments in Expert Systems, Academic Press 1984

(3) W.J.Clancey, The epistemology of a rule-based expert system: A framework for explanation. Artificial Intelligence 20, 1983 215-251

(4) J.Doyle, A Truth Maintenance System, Artificial Intelligence 12, No. 3, 1979, 231-272

(5) J.R.Quinlan, Discovering rules by induction from large collections of examples in: D.Michie (Ed), Expert Systems in the Micro-electronic age, Edinburgh University Press 1979, 168-201.

(6) R.M.Young, G.D.Plotkin and R.F.Linz, Analysis of an extended concept- learning task, in: R.Reddy (Ed), Procs. fifth IJCAI, 1977, 285.

(7) T.M.Mitchell, P.E.Utgoff and R.Banerji, Learning by

Experimentation: acquiring and modifying problem-solving
heuristics, in R.S.Michalski, J.G.Carbonell and T.M.Mitchell
(Eds), Machine Learning (Tioga, Palo Alto, CA, 1983) 163-190.

(8)   A.Bundy, B.Silver and d.Plummer, an Analytical Comparison of
      Some Rule-Learning Programs, Artificial Intelligence 27,
      (1985) 137-181

(9)   R.G.Smith, H.A.Winston, T.M.Mitchell and B.G.Buchanan,
      Representation and Use of Explicit Justifications for
      Knowledge Base Refinement, Proceedings of the ninth IJCAI
      (1985), 673-680

(10) W.R.Swartout, XPLAIN: a System for Creating and explaining
      expert Consulting Programs, Artificial Intelligence 21
      (1983) 285-325

(11) D.H.Sleeman and J.S.Brown, Intelligent Tutoring Systems, New
      York, Academic Press, 1982.

(12) J. de Kleer, choices without backtracking, Proc. national conference
      on AI , AAAI, (1984), 79-85.

Advances in Artificial Intelligence - II
B. Du Boulay, D. Hogg and L. Steels (Editors)
© Elsevier Science Publishers B.V. (North-Holland), 1987

NUMERIC AND SYMBOLIC REASONING
IN EXPERT SYSTEMS

Paul R. Cohen
Department of Computer and Information Science
University of Massachusetts
Amherst, MA 01003

Abstract

This paper is about qualification of reasoning due to ambiguity, lack of evidence, poor quality data, and the many other factors that are usually associated with uncertainty. A broad distinction is often made between unqualified, categorical, or definite reasoning; and qualified, or uncertain reasoning. We start this paper from the position that all reasoning is subject to qualifications, though they may seem insignificant. Indeed, we are concerned with how people come to view qualifications as insignificant — how people can act as if certain under uncertainty.

This paper discusses ways to represent and reason about qualifications. Our goal is to provide these abilities for expert systems and other artificial intelligence (AI) programs, so that they can reason intelligently under uncertainty. [1]

In overview, we will discuss the sources of uncertainty in reasoning, and the responses to uncertainty that, in people, we call intelligent. Then we survey current AI approaches to uncertainty. We find that few of our criteria for intelligent reasoning under uncertainty are manifested by AI programs. We assess the reasons for these deficits, and discuss three AI programs that, collectively, lay the groundwork for a new technology for reasoning under uncertainty. In the course of the paper, we find that reasoning under uncertainty is closely related to two other persistent problems for expert systems. One is the problem of controlling the behavior of large, knowledge-based systems; the other is the issue of explanation. The control problem, as we see it, is how to select a course of action that is responsive to one's uncertainty. Should the program pursue one hypothesis at a time, or all together, or postpone this decision and search, instead, for more discriminating evidence? Which of several evidence-gathering plans is best? To answer these questions properly, we need to know the qualifications on reasoning — the reasons for uncertainty. Since these qualifications are the impetus for control decisions, they are also the basis for explanations of reasoning.

Our emphasis is on representing knowledge about uncertainty to facilitate reasoning under uncertainty. This is a common perspective in AI, where representing knowledge adequately is understood to be a prerequisite for intelligent reasoning. Thus, the current reliance on inadequate numeric representations is puzzling. One explanation is that

---

[1] Our use of the word "qualification" is not incongruent with that of McCarthy (1980). His "qualification problem" refers to the need to act despite the fact that the conditions for action can not be stated completely. McCarthy asks, as we do, how we decide that we know enough to act.

probability and uncertainty are so closely associated that the one is mistaken for the
other. The situation is analogous to mistaking a reproduction of a painting for the
painting itself. A reproduction allows us to make *some* inferences about the painting,
maybe enough inferences to tempt us to say, incorrectly, that we know what the painting
looks like. And as the distinction between the original and the reproduction fades, we
loose sight of the fact that different *kinds* of reproductions support different kinds of
inferences about the original: any representation supports some kinds of inferences at
the expense of others. Probabilities support inferences about the *degree* of uncertainty
at the expense of inferences about the *reasons* for uncertainty. This paper suggests
reversing these priorities.

1.   Sources of Uncertainty

Uncertainty is a state of mind that arises during reasoning. By asking what aspects
of reasoning give rise to uncertainty, we focus on its causes and consequences, not on
the mental phenomenon itself. The sources of uncertainty are many but they can be
discussed under three headings (see Cohen and Gruber, 1984, for more detail). First,
uncertainty is introduced by evidence that is errorful, irrelevant, insufficient, and so on.
Second, reasoning about evidence depends on heuristic knowledge, which can sometimes
lead to a wrong conclusion. Third, the organization of knowledge, and the methods by
which it is accessed, can introduce uncertainty.

Uncertainty due to evidence is especially problematic for systems that rely on sensory input. These include vision, robotic, and speech understanding systems. Evidence
is typically *noisy*, meaning that parts of the evidence have been deleted or are obscured.
The transducers that make evidence available to the system that interprets it can also
introduce uncertainty. Most transducers have a limited bandwidth — they reproduce
only some evidence faithfully; for example, sound transducers limit the frequencies they
pass. Even if evidence is not noisy, and is not degraded by its transducers, its *relevance*
may be uncertain. Most of the sensory data available to humans and other organisms
is filtered by attentional processes. AI programs require procedures to select evidence
from masses of information; these procedures introduce uncertainty. Finally, relevant,
noise-free evidence may still be *inadequate*. Many tasks are uncertain not because
the quality of evidence is poor but because there isn't enough evidence to complete the
task. Sometimes the needed evidence is too expensive, sometimes it just isn't available.

Uncertainty in evidence can be managed if one knows its source. For example,
high spatial frequency noise is common in vision systems, and the common remedy is
to run the noisy image through a bandpass filter that cuts off the high frequencies.
This eliminates the noise but introduces another kind of uncertainty: sharp intensity
gradients (edges) become blurred. The remedy here is often edge enhancement of some
kind. If the source of uncertainty is known, it can be managed. This argues for explicit,
informative knowledge about uncertainty; it argues against limiting our knowledge of
uncertainty to our degree of belief.

Once an expert system acquires evidence, the next step is to interpret it. Expert
systems, more than other kinds of AI programs, rely on heuristic knowledge to interpret

evidence; knowledge acquired from experts who will not always vouch for its accuracy. Expertise is experiential and pragmatic, and is sometimes unsupported by theory. Most tools for building expert systems allow the expert to qualify his or her knowledge with a degree of belief; but these rarely express qualifications satisfactorily (e.g., Gadsden, 1984). One kind of qualification has to do with *exceptions*. Since expert heuristics are *compilations* of expert experience, some aspect of the experience will be left out. A heuristic will "work" most of the time; uncertainty is introduced because a situation could arise in which the heuristic won't work. Doyle (1983) has suggested making these exception cases explicit when they are known. Then heuristics could be used with certainty in the standard cases and with caution at other times. Again, we see that uncertainty can be managed if its source is known.

But one cannot know, ahead of time, *all* the situations in which an expert heuristic should *not* be used. This source of uncertainty is unavoidable, but not necessarily unmanageable. Heuristics have applicability conditions which, in rule-based expert systems are the clauses in the *condition-part* of an inference rule. If the condition-part is satisfied, the action-part is asserted. Yet most rule-based systems do *not* execute all applicable rules, but select among them according to a *control strategy*. If the control strategy exploits some uncertainty-reducing aspect of a domain, such as redundancy, then the rules selected for execution are more apt to be those that *should* be accepted. This technique for managing uncertainty is discussed further in the section on control approaches, below.

Uncertainty is introduced in evidence and the knowledge that interprets evidence, and also in the *strategies* that control the use of the knowledge. For example, the question often arises, how long should one wait, or how much effort should one expend, to find some evidence? Some strategies cut off the waiting or search for evidence, thus introducing the uncertainty that a little more time or effort would have provided it. Many strategies are based on assumptions about the organization or extent of our knowledge. For example, the *closed world assumption* supports the conclusion that a fact is false if an exhaustive search of a knowledge base fails to turn it up (Reiter, 1980). The idea of a closed world is that we know all relevant facts; this is usually false, so inferences based on the assumption are uncertain. A similar assumption underlies *lack-of-knowledge* inferences, described by Collins (1978). Asked, "Is the Mekong River very long?" I reason that if it were, I would know it, and since I don't, it isn't. Similar knowledge is used to assess subjective probabilities. One method, called *availability*, is used by humans to estimate probability based on the ease of calling something to mind. Concepts that are "available" in memory are judged relatively probable; unavailable concepts are judged improbable (Tversky and Kahneman, 1982). We overestimate the probability of publicized events, such as winning lotteries; and students, for example, underestimate the probability of dying of heart disease, since few instances come to mind. Availability introduces uncertainty about the accuracy of our assessments of probability.

These heuristic methods for controlling access to our knowledge, like other heuristics, introduce uncertainty. But, as we noted above, if the source of uncertainty is known, it can be managed. The source of uncertainty in the Mekong River example is the assumption, "If the Mekong was long, I would know it." If I mistrust the assumption, then I can consult an authority – a person for whom the assumption is true. The credibility of a lack-of-knowledge inference is directly proportional to the amount one knows about the topic. Once one knows the source of uncertainty – in this case an assumption – and the factors that affect credibility, then the uncertainty is manageable. Assumptions play a major role in managing uncertainty, since they are explicit records of uncertain "stepping stones" in lines of argument. The assumption above is *needed* to answer the question, "Is the Mekong a long river?" Doyle (1983b) has developed *reason maintenance* mechanisms for managing the uncertainty represented by assumptions. This work, and the endorsement-based methods described below, recognize the need for explicit knowledge about uncertainty. For Doyle, assumptions are explicit records of the deliberate introduction of uncertainty, and, as such, pinpoint the source of uncertainty and provide a basis for its management.

2.   Desiderata for Intelligent Reasoning About Uncertainty

This section asks what behaviors we should require of expert systems that reason intelligently about uncertainty. The requirements are of two kinds: first, we discuss what an expert system ought to *do* about uncertainty, then we focus on the representation of knowledge required to reason as we desire. It is striking that contemporary expert systems do very little about uncertainty besides measuring it. Some expert systems assess degrees of belief for hypotheses, but they do not use these numbers except to rank hypotheses and for some rudimentary control decisions. What more should an expert system do? We focus on two behaviors: planning (or control) and explanation.

Intelligent behavior under uncertainty requires a plan for the management of the uncertainty. Here are some examples of plans:

1. Confronted with uncertainty about which of two diseases afflict a patient, try to rule out the most serious one. Specifically, order relatively inexpensive, non-invasive tests before more costly ones, and give the patient a therapeutic trial of medication for the more serious disease. See the patient again after the test results are known and after the therapeutic trial has an opportunity to alleviate symptoms.

2. Since I am uncertain whether my weekday bus runs on the weekend, I decide to drive my car.

3. I am going to visit my parents, who say they have a birthday present for me. They won't tell me what it is, so just to be safe, I put the roof-rack on my car.

The first case is taken from a series of interviews with a physician on the problem of diagnosing chest pain. Two causes of pain, angina and esophageal spasm, can have identical manifestations, but one is more serious than the other. Thus, physicians will try to *rule out* angina first, and may prescribe therapy for angina on a trial basis. The angina/esophageal spasm differential is not usually resolved by ruling *in* esophageal spasm, since it is difficult to get direct, physical evidence of spasm. However, this plan is appropriate if less costly tests fail to resolve between the disease hypotheses. In contrast, one can sometimes quickly rule out angina by demonstrating that the pain is due to damage to the muscles of the chest. This "rule-out by ruling-in" plan may not be appropriate, however, if the patient is at risk for heart disease because of smoking, age, family history, and so on, since this patient may have *both* heart disease and some other cause of chest pain.

Thus, intelligent reasoning under uncertainty involves selecting a plan appropriate to the nature of the uncertainty. The "rule-out by ruling in" plan may be appropriate in some cases but not to the angina/esophageal spasm differential if the patient is at risk for heart disease and if less difficult tests have not yet been tried.

If one knows enough about the nature of one's uncertainty to intelligently select a plan, then this knowledge can be used to explain one's behavior:

- Why did you try to rule out angina before esophageal spasm?

- Because the consequences of my uncertainty about angina are more serious; and because it is difficult to find direct evidence for or against esophageal spasm; and because there is evidence that the patient is at risk for heart disease, so ruling in esophageal spasm would not rule out heart disease.

Many plans for managing uncertainty are much simpler than this one. The second example, above, is a case of sidestepping uncertainty. Instead of facing the uncertainty of whether a bus is running, the question is made irrelevant by deciding to drive a car. The third case is similar: it involves anticipating possible outcomes and preparing for the most extreme. When uncertain about the size of a birthday present, one prepares for the worst (best?) case by arranging transportation for the biggest possible object.

One characteristic of these examples is that the *probability* of the various uncertain outcomes is both insufficient to determine a response to the uncertainty, and further- more, it is largely irrelevant. In the medical example, provided there is "enough" evidence for angina, the physician pursues the angina hypothesis not because it is more likely than esophageal spasm but because it is more dangerous. In the second case, if there is "not enough" evidence that the bus is running, the commuter decides to drive. The extent of the uncertainty in these cases, and the third case, is not the salient factor in deciding on a plan to manage the uncertainty.

Yet, the probability of outcomes plays a *small* role in these examples, and a greater role in other cases, such as this one:

An airplane has crashed in dense jungle. Searchers superimpose a grid on a map of the area and calculate, for each square in the grid, the probability that the plane crashed in that square. They search the high-probability areas first.
Here, the appropriate plan for managing uncertainty depends on knowing the likelihood of outcomes. Thus, in addition to planning and explanation, we need the ability to believe one proposition more than another. This, in turn, requires the ability to update degrees of belief in light of evidence.

In summary, the behaviors that make for intelligent reasoning about uncertainty are: the ability to plan a course of action appropriate to one's uncertainty, the ability to explain one's actions, and the ability to determine degrees of belief in alternatives given evidence. We now consider the conceptual tools required to build expert systems with these abilities.

An expert system requires a representation of knowledge about its uncertainty and methods for manipulating this knowledge to plan and explain actions, and to modify its belief in propositions. A good representation supports all the concepts one wishes to reason about, and all the methods one uses to reason about them. A good representation makes important distinctions explicit. One should not have to struggle to represent a situation — the representational techniques should make the "translation" between a situation and its representation easy. If these representational criteria are met, then we will be able to represent the knowledge required to achieve the three performance criteria outlined above. Table 1 summarizes the performance and representational criteria. We now survey current AI approaches to reasoning under uncertainty from the perspective of these criteria.

TABLE 1

Performance Criteria

Planning:	Plan actions that are appropriate to uncertainty
Explanation:	Explain plans for managing uncertainty
Measurement:	Modify degree of belief in light of evidence

Representational criteria

Adequacy:	Support all interesting concepts and methods for reasoning about them
Explicitness:	Make important distinctions explicit
Ease-of-use:	Make the "translation" between situation and representation easy

---

3. AI Approaches to Uncertainty

Many techniques for reasoning under uncertainty have been adopted or invented for AI programs. We group them according to how they represent uncertainty, and, thus, by the extent to which uncertainty is actively managed.

Parallel Certainty Inferences. The *parallel certainty inference* approach divides reasoning under uncertainty into parallel streams: one is a stream of domain inferences; the other, a stream of calculations of the credibilities of the domain inferences (Cohen,

1983). This is shown in Figure 1. Along the top of the figure is a chain of domain inferences – if a person is on fixed income then he or she has low risk tolerance, and if a person has low risk tolerance, then he or she ought to buy bonds. Along the bottom of the figure is a series of calculations of the credibilities of the data and conclusions. The first inference rule (fixed income implies low risk tolerance) is not entirely credible; its degree of belief is only 0.8. Moreover, the finding that this client is on fixed income is not entirely credible; its degree of belief is just 0.6. How credible is the conclusion of low risk tolerance, given the credibilities of the inference rule and the data? A *combining function* calculates, by multiplication, the degree of belief in the conclusion to be 0.48.

Among the parallel certainty inference methods we find strict probabilistic methods (e.g., Pearl, 1982), subjective probability techniques that are more or less distantly related to Bayesian updating (Shortliffe and Buchanan, 1975; Duda, Hart, and Nilsson, 1976), Dempster-Shafer calculi (Ginsberg, 1984; Strat, 1984; Gordon and Shortliffe, 1984; Lowrance and Garvey, 1982), and fuzzy logic (e.g., Zaheh, 1975) Though the proponents of the individual methods argue about their relative merits, for our purposes they may be grouped as the techniques that keep domain inferences and credibility calculations in separate compartments, using numbers to represent credibility.

The parallel certainty inference approach, though common, is unsatisfactory in terms of our performance and representation criteria. The good news is that degrees of belief are easily adjusted in light of evidence. But this advantage is not unqualified, since, in practice, we cannot assume that the numbers evoked from experts and propagated through chains of inferences are accurate. Nor can we guarantee that the combining functions used by the more subjective methods preserve the meanings of the numbers they combine. The bad news is that this approach denies to expert systems the ability to *plan* actions to manage their uncertainty; degrees of belief serve no purpose other than to find the highest-ranking conclusion, and sometimes to throw away conclusions with very low degrees of belief. The chains of logical and numerical inferences in Figure 1 are parallel in the sense that degree of belief has little or no effect on which domain inferences are made, when they are made, how they are corroborated, and so on. Since degrees of belief have no role in planning actions, they cannot be used to *explain* behavior. Furthermore, it is difficult to explain what a degree of belief means, since it is a poor representation of the complex mental processes that evoke it. Degrees of belief fail the *representational adequacy* criterion because they represent only the extent of one's belief, not the reasons for believing and disbelieving. They fail the criterion of making important distinctions *explicit*, because the degree of belief is a summary the many factors that contribute to uncertainty, including probability and utility. Finally, experts and others generally dislike the process of trying to quantify all aspects of their uncertainty, so degrees of belief fail the *Ease-of-use* criterion.

Control Strategies. A second category of techniques, the *control* methods, manage uncertainty actively by *ordering* problem solving actions or sequences of actions. For example, I want to buy my wife a birthday present and a colorful box in which to wrap it. Since I haven't bought the present yet (and I'm not sure what I will buy), I am uncertain how big the box should be. The "obvious" solution is to buy the box after the present. So obvious, in fact, that it obscures an important conclusion: uncertainty is often due to the *timing* of evidence, and it can therefore be minimized by ordering one's actions so that the timing of evidence is most facilitative. This principle underlies *least-commitment planning* and related techniques (Sacerdoti, 1977; Stefik, 1980).

Other control approaches exploit characteristics of a domain to order problem-solving actions. For example, when building a jigsaw puzzle, it is best to start with "border" pieces, and then extend in from the border. This is because the border pieces are easily recognized, and once placed, constrain the placement of the other pieces. Redundancy is an important characteristic of some domains, and is exploited by control approaches to problems such as speech understanding. This problem is uncertain due to the noise and ambiguity inherent in the speech signal, but because speech is redundant, it is possible to work on the relatively certain parts of a speech signal first, then use them to constrain work on the uncertain parts. This approach was used in the HEARSAY-II speech understanding system (Erman, Hayes-Roth, Lesser, and Reddy, 1980).

Control approaches satisfy several of our performance and representation criteria. First, systems like HEARSAY-II actively plan which of several uncertain hypotheses to work on next. Unfortunately, they typically use numeric *evaluation functions* to decide where to direct their attention. The terms of evaluation functions represent, as numbers, factors relevant to managing uncertainty. In HEARSAY-II these include measures of the validity of data, the cost-effectiveness of actions, the desirability of understanding a particular segment of the speech signal, and so on. These numbers are combined into summary measures that control focus of attention. HEARSAY-II is thus able to select from among the many tasks it *might* do those which reduce its uncertainty about the speech signal. Its representation of knowledge about uncertainty supports productive reasoning methods (the *representational adequacy* criterion). But the factors that determine focus of attention are summarized in a single measure of worth, violating the *explicitness* criterion; and, since the requisite knowledge is not explicit, the *explanation* criterion. Roughly, the system works but it doesn't know why. HEARSAY-II is typical of systems that use control strategies to manage uncertainty.

Endorsement-based Reasoning. We turn now to four efforts to reason symbolically about uncertainty that, collectively, represent stages in the development of *endorsement-based* reasoning. Endorsements are explicit records of reasons to believe and disbelieve propositions. Endorsement-based reasoning satisfies most of the criteria in Table 1. Since it relies on reasons for uncertainty, it can plan and explain its plans to manage uncertainty. But since reasons for uncertainty are not *quantities*, precise reasoning about degrees of belief is awkward. This tradeoff is acceptable if one's emphasis is actively managing uncertainty instead of just measuring it.

Our first endorsement-based program, called SOLOMON for the wisdom we wished it had, attached mnemonic endorsements to propositions in place of numeric degrees of belief (Cohen and Grinberg, 1983; Cohen, 1983). Each endorsement was used to select a course of action appropriate to the kind of uncertainty it represented. For example,

we endorsed the rule

$$\text{IF age} > 65 \text{ THEN risk-tolerance} = \text{low}$$

with the mnemonic **overgeneralization**, meaning that, for some individual, the conclusion *could* be false when the premise is true. Now, one can imagine adding clauses to the premise to pinpoint more certainly the criteria for low risk tolerance. The same effect can be had by finding another rule with a different premise but the same conclusion. Thus, given a conclusion endorsed as an **overgeneralization**, SOLOMON searched for a corroborating conclusion, that is, a rule with the same conclusion but a different premise. If this succeeded, SOLOMON endorsed the conclusion as **corroborated**.

The theme of the SOLOMON program is familiar: a system must respond appropriately to its uncertainty. Endorsements characterize uncertainty and are the key to intelligent responses. But this early work considered relatively few endorsements and responses to uncertainty. Nor did we modify the endorsements associated with propositions in the light of evidence. This became the focus of our next study.

Numeric approaches to uncertainty modify the degrees of belief in propositions as evidence becomes available. The "running total" belief for a hypothesis is increased or decreased in response to evidence pro or con. Endorsements do not represent degrees of belief, but rather, reasons for belief. We explored how these reasons are adjusted by evidence in the context of a plan recognition program called HMMM (Cohen, 1984; Sullivan and Cohen, 1985). Imagine a simple device that can execute one of two plans, each composed of 3 steps:

plan		steps
plan 1	:	a b c
plan 2	:	b d e

If the device takes step **a**, what plan does it have "in mind"? Since step **a** is unique to plan 1, the device either has made a mistake, or it intends plan 1. Assume the device now takes step **b**. This provides no evidence to discriminate the interpretations of the first step: the device may be pursuing plan 1 or it may have recovered from its mistake and started plan 2. If the next step is **c**, then it looks as though plan 1 was intended all along; if it is **d**, then apparently plan 1 was started and abandoned for plan 2. The question we want to answer is, if the endorsement of the plan 1 interpretation of **a** is **may be a mistake**, what happens to this endorsement as more evidence — subsequent plan steps — becomes available? Answering this question is analogous to finding a combining function for numeric representations of uncertainty.

We do not believe that all kinds of evidence should be combined with the same combining function. That is one of our complaints against numeric approaches. We devised several *combining schemas* for endorsements that captured the flux of our reasons for uncertainty in the plan recognition problem. We noted above that the evidence **b** cannot reduce our concern that **a** was a mistake, since **b** is ambiguous with respect to plan 1 and plan 2. On the other hand, the input **c** is unique to plan 1 and "finishes off" the plan, and seems to reduce the concern that **a** was a mistake. This kind of reasoning is captured in the following combining schema, in which the endorsements

— the reasons to believe and disbelieve interpretations of plan steps — are shown in uppercase.

> IF   step I IS-UNIQUE-TO plan N, and
>   step J IS-UNIQUE-TO plan N, and
>   step J FOLLOWS-IN-THE-PLAN step I, and
>   the plan N interpretation of step I
>   is endorsed by MAY-BE-A-MISTAKE
> THEN erase the endorsement

By eliminating the second clause of this schema, the negative endorsement on the plan 1 interpretation of **a** is erased as soon as the evidence **b** becomes available. This seems premature, as we said, since **b** is ambiguous, but we give the example to raise a point: Our goal in this work was not to provide a *prescriptive* theory of how endorsements should combine, but rather, to give a framework for subjectively combining endorsements.

Clearly, erasing endorsements is a degenerate form of combining them, and loses valuable information about the interrelationships between pieces of evidence. A more realistic scheme would reduce the weight of the **may be mistake** endorsement as subsequent, consistent evidence becomes available; alternatively, one endorsement might be made dependent on another, as in Doyle's (1983b) work on reason maintenance.

Before implementing such a scheme, however, we were diverted by a difficult question: Where do endorsements come from, and what do they mean? The mnemonic value of endorsements like **may be a mistake** disguises the fact that endorsements are arbitrary symbols, whose meaning comes from the rules by which they are combined with other endorsements. We were concerned that, for complex domains, dozens of endorsements and combining schemes would have to be acquired. Although we had no objection in principle to acquiring this knowledge from an expert (much as other domain knowledge is acquired), we wondered whether the endorsements and combining schemas of a domain could be derived from other knowledge about the domain, such as inference rules. If so, we would worry less about whether we had the "right" endorsements and combining schemas.

We focused on the uncertainty inherent in a single problem-solving task, namely classification, to pinpoint the sources of uncertainty (and thus endorsements) of all classification tasks. Classification is the problem solved by many or most expert systems (Clancey, 1984): Given data, find the conclusion (or classification of the data) that fits the data best. Uncertainty in classification tasks is due, primarily, to mismatch between evidence and its various classifications. Degree of belief in a conclusion given evidence reflects the degree of fit between the evidence and the classification. For example, if the flu is characterized by fatigue, nausea, and aching limbs, then one's certainty in a diagnosis of flu depends on the degree of fit between symptoms and this characterization. Does a midafternoon nap constitute evidence for fatigue? Is skipping lunch evidence for nausea? Is a headache evidence for aching limbs? To the extent that these findings correspond to the symptoms of flu, the diagnosis of flu is credible. The chief source of uncertainty in classification tasks is partial matching between the evidence one needs and the evidence one has. Endorsements ought to describe these partial matches, and ideally should be derived from knowledge about the classification task.

Consider the evidence for flu: is a midafternoon nap evidence of fatigue? Fatigue is good cause for a nap, quite possibly the *only* cause. In contrast, there are many reasons to skip lunch, of which nausea is only one. Given this, it seems reasonable to suggest that the midafternoon nap is stronger evidence of fatigue than the skipped lunch is of nausea. Finally, headache seems to be very weak evidence for aching limbs because the head and the limbs are different parts of the body. Figure 2 shows how evidence and conclusions are associated for each of these cases. Figure 2a shows a causal relationship between fatigue and taking a nap; Figure 2b shows that nausea is one of several phenomena associated causally with skipping lunch; Figure 2c shows the head and limbs as *siblings* in a *part-of* hierarchy.

Path endorsements reflect the associations between pieces of domain knowledge, such as those shown in Figure 2. *The credibility of a conclusion such as "the patient has aching limbs" depends on the associations that form a path between the conclusion and the evidence.* The *sibling* path between head and limbs is, in general, not the basis for credible inferences: something that is true of an object is not necessarily true of its siblings. A headache is not evidence that the rest of the body aches. On the other hand, the single causal association between fatigue and taking a nap is the basis for credible inferences; given that a person takes a nap, it is credible to infer fatigue. But it is not credible to infer nausea given that a person skips lunch, because of the many possible causes for skipping lunch. Path endorsements describe typical patterns of associations between evidence and conclusions. Inferences based on these associations are more or less credible, as we discussed, so path endorsements are the basis for judging the credibility of inferences. Note that path endorsements are derived from knowledge about how objects in a domain are associated. They are not "made up" by knowledge engineers to represent suspected sources of uncertainty.

We developed an expert system, called GRANT, based on path endorsements. Its task is to match researchers with funding agencies that are likely to support their work (Cohen, Davis, Day, Greenberg, Kjeldsen, Lander, and Loiselle, 1985). This is a classification problem in which the evidence is a research proposal, and the conclusions are the funding agencies that best fit the proposal. The chief source of uncertainty is partial matches between the interests and requirements of funding agencies and the interests and needs of researchers. To the extent that the match between an agency and a researcher is good, the agency is likely to support the researcher. Path endorsements are used to find matches between the respective research interests of the parties. For example, an agency interested in neurological diseases is unlikely to fund a researcher interested in osteopathic diseases, because the path between neurology and osteopathy includes the sibling relationship between the head and the limbs, shown in Figure 2c.

All endorsements in GRANT were derived *after* the knowledge for performance of the matching task was in place. The endorsements literally "come from" the associations that are needed to encode a large semantic network of research topics. The network contains over 4500 concepts that describe the research interests of about 700 funding agencies. The interests of researchers are described by the same concepts, and GRANT finds agencies to fund researchers by following well-endorsed associative pathways between concepts. So far, the path endorsements are discerning enough that less that 1/3rd of the agencies found by GRANT are judged, by our expert, unlikely to fund the researcher's proposal. Moreover, GRANT finds over 80% of the agencies judged acceptable by our expert (Cohen, Stanhope, Kjeldsen, 1986).

Our fourth effort at reasoning with endorsements is currently in progress. We are developing an expert system for diagnosing the causes of chest pain. This problem was selected because it gives us an opportunity to study intelligent responses to uncertainty. Although we started to explore how endorsements could select responses in the SOLOMON project, the range of responses was small. The issue lay dormant in the HMMM and GRANT projects. But in diagnosing chest pain, a physician has access to a rich source of actions, and must select the appropriate ones based on his or her uncertainty. Many factors influence this choice. For example, the amount of time it takes to get evidence from tests must be weighed with the time course and seriousness of the disease, to decide whether to prescribe therapy or wait for evidence.

MUM (Cohen et al, 1986) is a knowledge-based consultation system designed to manage the uncertainty inherent in medical diagnosis (the acronym stands for Management of Uncertainty in Medicine). Managing uncertainty means planning actions to minimize uncertainty or its consequences. Thus it is a control problem – an issue for the component of a knowledge system that decides how to proceed from an uncertain state of a problem. Uncertainty can be managed by many strategies, depending on the kind of problem one is trying to solve. These include asking for evidence, hedging one's bets, deciding arbitrarily and backtracking on failure, diversification or risk-sharing, and worst-case analysis. The facility with which a consultation system such as MUM manages uncertainty is evident in the questions it asks: it should ask all necessary questions, no unnecessary questions, and it should ask its questions in the right order. These conditions, especially the last one, preclude uniform and inflexible control strategies. They prompted the development of the MUM architecture in which control decisions are taken by reasoning about features of evidence and sources of uncertainty.

4.   Conclusion

Our research in medical problem-solving is now at the stage that we have a prototype program. The architecture of the system is guided by principles that, together, summarize the themes of this paper: Reasoning about uncertainty is knowledge-intensive, so one's representations of knowledge about uncertainty should be informative and explicit, not summary in nature. From these representations, plans to manage uncertainty can be formulated and explained. Uncertainty has many sources; intelligent management of uncertainty responds to them differently. But however responses are selected, uncertainty must be actively managed instead of passively measured.

REFERENCES

Clancey, W.S., 1984. Classification problem solving. *Proceedings of the AAAI, 1984,* p. 49.

Cohen, Paul R., Stanhope, Philip M., and Kjeldsen, Rick, 1986. Classification by semantic matching. *COINS Technical Report 86-13,* Department of Computer and Information Science, Amherst, MA.

Cohen, Paul R., Day, David, Delisio, Jeff, Greenberg, Michael, Kjeldsen, Rick, Suthers, and Berman, Paul, 1986. Management of uncertainty in medicine. *COINS Technical Report 86-12,* Department of Computer and Information Science, Amherst, MA.

Cohen, P.R., 1984. A progress report on the theory of endorsements. *Proceedings of the IEEE Workshop on Principles of Knowledge-based Systems,* Denver, CO, p. 139.

Cohen, P.R., 1983. *Heuristic reasoning about uncertainty: An artificial intelligence approach.* London:Pitman Advanced Publishing Program.

Cohen, P. and Gruber, T., 1984 Reasoning about uncertainty: a knowledge representation perspective. *Pergamon state of the art report: expert systems.*

Collins, A.M., 1978. Fragments of a theory of of human plausible reasoning. *TINLAP-2,* 194-201.

Doyle, J., 1983a. The ins and outs of reason maintenance. *Proceedings IJCAI-83,* August 1983, 349-351.

Doyle, J., 1983b, Some theories of reasoned assumptions: Some essays in rational psychology. *CMU-CS-83-125,* Carnegie-Mellon University, 1983b.

Duda, R.O., Hart, P.E., and Nilsson, N., 1976. Subjective bayesian methods for rule-based inference systems., *Technical Note 124,* Artificial Intelligence Center, SRI International, Menlo Park, California.

Erman, L.D., Hayes-Roth, F., Lesser, V.R., and Reddy, D.R. The HEARSAY-II speech understanding system: integrating knowledge to resolve uncertainty. *Computing Surveys,* 12, 1980, 213-253.

Gadsden, J.A., 1984. An expert system for evaluating electronic warfare tasking plans for the royal navy. *Proceedings of the First Conference on Artificial Intelligence Applications.,* IEEE Computer Society Press.

Ginsberg, M.L., 1984. Non-monotonic reasoning using Dempster's Rule. *Proceedings AAAI-84,* August, 1984.

Gordon, J., and Shortliffe, E.H., 1984, The Dempster-Shafer theory of evidence. B.G. Buchanan and E.H. Shortliffe, (eds.) *Rule-Based Expert Systems,* 272-292.

McCarthy, J. 1980. Circumscription – A form of nonmonotonic reasoning. *Artificial Intelligence* 13 (1,2) 27-39.

Pearl, J., 1982a, Reverend Bayes on inference engines: a distributed hierarchical approach. *Proceedings of the National Conference on Artificial Intelligence,* 133-136, Pittsburgh, PA.

Reiter, R., 1980. A logic for default reasoning. *Artificial Intelligence,* 13, 1980, 81-132.

Sacerdoti, E.D., 1977. A structure for plans and behavior. New York: American Elsevier.

Shortliffe, E.H. and Buchanan, B.G., 1975. A model of inexact reasoning in medicine. *Mathematical Biosciences,* 23, 351-379.

Stefik, M.J., 1980. Planning with constraints. (Doctoral Dissertation), Department of Computer Science Report 80-784, Stanford University, 1980.

Strat, T.M., 1984. Continuous belief functions for evidential reasoning. *Proceedings of the National Conference on Artificial Intelligence,* Austin, Texas, August, 1984, 308-313.

Sullivan, M., and Cohen, P.R., 1985. An endorsement-based plan recognition program. *COINS Technical Report 84-33,* Department of Computer Science, University of Massachusetts, Amherst. Also *Proceedings of the International Joint Conference on Artificial Intelligence..*

Tversky, A. and Kahneman, D., 1982. Availability: a heuristic for judging frequency and probability. Kahneman, Slovic, and Tversky (Eds.), *Judgment under uncertainty: Heuristics and Biases,* Cambridge.

Wesley, L.P. Reasoning about control: the investigation of an evidential approach. *Proceedings IJCAI-83,* August 1983, 203-206.

Zadeh, L.A., 1975b. Fuzzy logic and approximate reasoning. *Synthese,* **30**, 407-428.

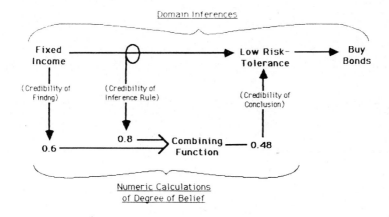

Figure 1: Parallel Certainty Inference Approach

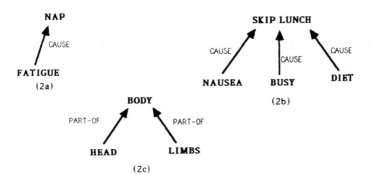

Figure 2: Deriving "Path Endorsements" from Associations
between Evidence and Conclusion

Advances in Artificial Intelligence - II
B. Du Boulay, D. Hogg and L. Steels (Editors)
© Elsevier Science Publishers B.V. (North-Holland), 1987

Steps towards Integrating Natural Language and Graphical Interaction for Knowledge-based Systems

Philip J. Hayes
Carnegie Group Inc.
650 Commerce Court at Station Square
Pittsburgh, PA 15219, USA

Abstract

Both natural language and graphical interfaces have been advanced as the best way to provide intelligent and user-friendly interfaces to knowledge-based systems. However, neither approach is sufficient on its own. This paper outlines the design[1] of a generic set of interface facilities that integrate the two modalities and allow each to contribute its relative strengths to the interface as a whole. A more detailed account is given of how the framework interprets in an integrated manner references to entities of the underlying application. The interpretation is done with respect to both the dialogue and visual contexts and for both natural language phrases and pointing events. As the detailed account of reference processing makes clear, the interface framework described in this paper depends in an essential way on the fact that the underlying application is knowledge-based.

1. Introduction

Through the use of AI techniques, intelligent knowledge-based systems are now helping people get their job done in an enormous variety of applications, including systems from manufacturing, medical, financial, and many other domains. However, the interfaces through which people interact with these expert systems often do not display a similar level of sophistication, either in intelligence or in their ability to interact (from a purely human-factors point of view). This has meant that the users have not been able to derive the maximum advantage from the expert systems, or in the worse cases, not derived any benefit at all. This is particularly true in those knowledge-based systems in which the initiative and responsibility for problem solving is divided between user and system. For such mixed initative systems, poor interfaces mean that the user cannot understand enough about what the system knows and is doing, and is also unable effectively to communicate his goals to the system. We believe that this mismatch of capability between interface and application is a major hindrance to the wider acceptance of knowledge-based systems.

The work described here is the beginning of an effort to remedy that mismatch. The work starts from the following assumptions about desirable characteristics of interfaces to mixed-initiative knowledge-based systems:

- *The interfaces should use graphical displays to convey information whenever appropriate.* Well-designed graphical output can give the user a much clearer overall picture of the system's view of the world than a scrolled dialogue (even a natural language dialogue). For instance, if the system is concerned with scheduling machining orders through various machines on a factory floor, then a graphical depiction of the machines, their layout, the current and planned location of orders, etc. would give the user a much clearer overall picture of the current state of planning than a textual description of the same information ever could.

---

[1]Nothing in this document should be interpreted as a committment to nor an announcement of specific product enhancements by Carnegie Group Inc.

- *The user should be able to access and modify the system's data and knowledge through direct manipulation of the graphical display whenever possible.* For instance, a user might be able to obtain and edit a table giving further information about a specific machine (its capacity, scheduled down-times, etc.) by clicking on the icon the scheduling system uses to represent it. Direct manipulation of this kind is often more efficient and usually easier to learn than any other kind of interaction.

- *The user should also be able to access and modify data and knowledge through a natural language dialogue.* Not all questions or updates can conveniently be made by direct manipulation. For instance, it might be quite hard to devise a piece of direct manipulation that allowed the user to find out if all scheduled orders could still be processed with any three (out of the current five) milling machines. Yet, as the previous sentence shows, it is straightforward to pose that question in natural language.

- *The natural language dialogue should integrate as closely as possible with the graphical display.* In particular, the resolution of anaphoric references should take account of what is on the screen. For instance, if the user says "the grinding machine" and only one is visible on the screen, then that should be interpreted as the one the user means, even if the system knows about four other milling machines related to the topic under discussion. Also the user should be able to point at the representation of an object on the screen instead of giving a natural language description of it. It may be a lot faster to point at an icon than to type "grinding machine number 4".

2. Overall Interaction Model

With these assumptions in mind, we are investigating generic support for a class of user interfaces suitable for a wide variety of knowledge-based applications. Individual interfaces built using this support would have two conceptually distinct, but highly integrated parts:

- **graphical display of the application domain**: The interface continuously displays a two dimensional view of the knowledge-based application's world. The view will not be fixed, but will be variable in the amount of detail shown and whether all or just a part of the world is shown. If specific entities in the world have internal structure, that may be displayed in overlaying windows. The main display may itself be split into windows for simultaneously displaying different parts of the world. Aids to locate a detailed view within its larger, containing scope will also be provided. The user is always free to alter the view of the world along any of the available dimensions. However, the system may also alter the display based on the dialogue in the dialogue window.

- **dialogue window**: The interface will also maintain a single thread dialogue with the user in natural language. The user's side of the dialogue may be conducted either through typed or spoken input. In either case, the complete dialogue thread will appear in a scrollable dialogue window. The user may refer to entities that are visible on the screen by pointing at them instead of speaking or typing out descriptions. Output from the application may also involve references or modifications to the display. In both cases, display references will appear explicitly in the dialogue transcript.

The overall feel of the interface is intended to be one where the user's main picture of what the application is doing and what information it is dealing with is provided by the display of the application's world. Navigation (in terms of both location and level of detail) around this world will be an important way for the user to obtain information that is not immediately visible. The dialogue window allows the user to ask for information that is inconvenient (or impossible) to obtain through navigation around the visual world, to make requests that he finds more natural in natural language, to discuss the world at a meta-level, etc.. We believe an interface of this kind will be extremely natural and productive to use. The style of interaction is analogous to that between two people poring over a diagram or having a discussion while writing on a blackboard - a very effective and natural form of communication. Moreover, unlike a paper diagram or blackboard, the application world display is active and can modify itself under control of the user or the interface/application system. This allows a very high bandwidth of communication and hence a highly productive interaction.

This kind of interface is highly appropriate to situations where spatial relationships between domain entities and movements of the entities through the space are an important aspect of the application's world. Factory job-shop scheduling is an example of such a domain; the paths from machine to machine and the distribution of orders around the shop are important features of the domain for the scheduling task. In addition, work by Negroponte [8] and the general success of the desktop metaphor in user interface design [10, 11] have shown that distributing information spatially is a useful information access aid, even if the spatial distribution does not correspond to any actual spatial relationships. Thus, there is every chance that the kind of interface envisaged here will also be useful in domains without a specific spatial orientation, such as a personnel database. This kind of information distribution is also useful for non-spatial information in worlds with a high degree of spatial information. For instance, in a factory scheduling application, it might be convenient for the user if he could find out about the scheduled down-time for a particular machine by "zooming in" on the icon that normally represents the machine. Such zooming could overlay the icon with a window in which scheduled down-time and other detailed information about that machine was displayed in a tabular fashion.

The dialogue component of the interface is intended to allow the user to access information (or issue commands) that is inconvenient to get at by navigation through the domain world display. For instance, in a factory scheduling system, the user might want to know whether one machine could take over the orders scheduled for another (perhaps because the first one had broken down). Since this question involves a dynamically constructed relationship between two machines, there is no obvious "place" to find it in the domain world. Instead, the dialogue facilities would allow the user to say (or type) something like "Can this machine *<point at one machine>* take over the orders scheduled for that one *<point at other machine>*". The answer could be displayed in text in the dialogue transcript, or as an overlay window on the graphical display, or as both. Note how intimately the displayed world and the dialogue interact to specify this information retrieval. The display is acting analogously to the physical context immediately surrounding human participants in a dialogue, i.e. something that can be referred to by abbreviated language or gesture in the knowledge that the other participant in the dialogue can see the same thing as you.

To support the construction of interfaces of this kind, we have designed a set of generic interface facilities for knowledge-based systems. The design views the facilities as extensions to the Knowledge Craft[TM] and Language Craft [TM] products of Carnegie Group. Knowledge Craft is a knowledge engineering tool based on a schema-oriented knowledge representation language, called CRL[TM], and incorporating OPS-5 and Prolog inference engines and a powerful graphics system. Language Craft [7] is a tool system for building natural language interfaces based on case frame parsing techniques. These techniques make Language Craft a very robust language analyser, as is appropriate to deal with the user errors that inevitably arise with interactive dialogue. The specific capabilities that the design adds to these existing systems include:

- **representation and display of domain world**: This is a generic facility for mapping the world of objects, events, and states of a knowledge-based system onto a graphical display which could be browsed by the interface user at varying levels of detail. The facility is an extension to Knowledge Craft, and its existing powerful graphics system.

- **natural language analysis**: The dialogue window needs to be supported by a robust natural language analysis system of the type provided by Language Craft. This component of the design would extend Language Craft by integrating it more fully with Knowledge Craft. This will allow the natural language analysis to communicate properly with the underlying knowledge-based system and the world display system.

- **dialogue management**:   The facilities in this area allow natural language input to the system to be interpreted with respect to the context built up during interaction in the dialogue window and the visual context of the world display. In addition to the interpretation of ellipsis already provided by Language Craft, the design would support a wide variety of anaphoric reference with respect to both kinds of context through an extension to Language Craft. The dialogue context can be altered by things that the user or system say and will be represented graphically in the domain world display. The display will be managed so that the complete dialogue context is always displayed.

- **integration of natural language and speech input**:   While natural language is a highly expressive and natural form of input, it can be tedious to input via a keyboard. Spoken input is much more convenient.   Our design integrates the natural language interpretation capability of the interface system with a speech recognition device.   In other words, Language Craft will derive the meaning of the word sequences reported by the speech recognition device. Since speech recognition is inherently error-prone, Language Craft will be used to improve the overall recognition rate of the speech device. We will do this by making all the various word hypotheses considered by the speech device (with their associated certainties) available to Language Craft and let it make the final decision using its syntactic and semantic knowledge.

- **integration of natural language and pointing input**:   Given the explicit graphical representation of context, and natural language input capability, particularly in its spoken form, it will be natural for the user to mix natural language and pointing input (e.g. "move that *<point>* from here *<point>* to there *<point>*"). Our design modifies Language Craft to deal with such pointing input.

Space does not permit us to go into detail on all these facilities. Instead in the remainder of this paper, we will focus on the way the design allows the user to refer to objects from the application domain. This will involve descriptions of the underlying natural language facilities, the way they handle anaphoric reference, and the way in which graphical pointing events can be substituted for ordinary linguistic anaphors. Before proceeding, we should reemphasize that the descriptions that follow refer to the design of a system, rather than one that is fully implemented.

3. Interpreting References to Application Domain Entities

When people engage in a dialogue, they share a context of past events, objects and events mentioned in the conversation, mutual assumptions about each other's goals and motivations, etc.. This shared context allows them to communicate intelligently with each other: by resolving pronouns or other abbreviated forms of reference into objects just mentioned, by completing elliptical questions by analogy to previous utterances, by recognizing that a statement is inconsistent with the speaker's assumed goals or beliefs and (internally) correcting it so it is consistent, etc.. For a machine to appear to communicate intelligently with a person, it needs to share context in a similar kind of way. Moreover, an ability to deal with anaphora and ellipsis allows the natural language input to be much more terse. It is much quicker to say or type "it" or "the machine" than always to have to say "grinding machine number 4".

The dialogue management facilities of the interface framework we are building are currently restricted to support for anaphora and reformulation ellipsis, though we hope in the future also to add more sophisticated facilities driven by a representation of the user's goals. This paper focuses on the way we deal with anaphora, i.e. the way we use context to interpret abbreviated descriptions of domain entities. Given the integration of graphical and natural language modalities in our interface model, we need to use two kinds of context to resolve anaphoric references:

- **dialogue context**: the set of entities mentioned or implied by the recent dialogue.

- **visual context**: the set of entities visible on the screen, plus perhaps other entities closely associated with them.

Moreover, the two modalities allow two kinds of anaphoric reference:

- • standard natural language anaphora (pronouns, definite noun phrases, etc.)
- • reference to objects by pointing at their images on the screen. Naturally, this kind of reference is resolved only against (a localized subset of) the visual context.

The following two subsections describe how each of these kinds of anaphor are handled by our design for interface facilities.

3.1. Natural language anaphora

In this section, we turn to the anaphoric interpretation capabilities we have designed as an extension to Language Craft. There is already a substantial body of work on the resolution of anaphora with respect to dialogue context (e.g. [4, 5, 6, 9]). Our approach does not represent a significant departure from this tradition. It uses techniques developed in the previous work to produce an anaphora capability suitable for restricted domain interfaces, rather than one that is completely general. In particular, we expect to make maximum use of the restricted domain semantics and not to use any techniques that would lead to noticeable (by the interface user) processing times. The novel aspects of our approach relate to the addition of visual context (though see [1, 5]).

Many current treatments of dialogue anaphora (e.g. [5, 9]) use the concept of a set of entities that are in the immediate *focus* of the context, plus others that are outside the immediate focus, but may become focussed. The focus may change through nesting (subtopics or digressions) or by moving to related topics. Entities in the immediate focus may be referred to by pronouns. Entities that are outside the immediate focus may be referred to by abbreviated descriptions. We have adopted this kind of approach. The focus of the dialogue context is represented as a set of domain world entities. These entities may be referenced by pronouns or other abbreviated descriptions. There is a second set of entities, those related to the focussed entities by one of a (domain-specific) class of relationships, that may also be referenced by definite noun phrases, but not by pronouns. These entities form the *potential focus* [9]. Referring to an entity in the potential focus adds it the focus.

We can see how this works in the following dialogue fragment with a hypothetical factory scheduling system:

> User: *Do any grinding machines have less than 80% utilization?*
> System: *Yes, grinding machine 4 has only 65% utilization.*
> User: *Has it had unscheduled downtime since Monday?*
> System: *No.*
> User: *Preventive maintenance?*
> System: *No. It is not scheduled until Friday.*
> User: *Who is the maintainer?*
> System: *Albert Smith.*
> User: *Ask him to do the preventive maintenance today.*

Here the grinding machine mentioned by the system becomes part of the focus and is referred to via the pronoun "it" by the user (and the system) in the question about utilization. The next question relies on Language Craft's current ability to handle reformulation ellipsis [3]. The system uses the context of the previous question to interpret the user's input as though he had said "Has it had preventive maintenance since Monday?". The user then goes on to refer to an entity that has not been mentioned in the dialogue so far, but is in the potential focus, viz. the maintainer of grinding machine 4, by the incomplete description "the maintainer" (the system would presumably know about lots of maintainers). There is only one maintainer in the potential focus, so the anaphoric noun phrase can be resolved correctly and unambiguously. Mentioning the maintainer entity adds it to the focus, so that the "him" in the next input can be interpreted correctly.

Integration between Language Craft and Knowledge Craft is important for the implementation of this anaphora mechanism. We represent the dialogue focus as a set of domain entities represented as Knowledge Craft schemas. The process of resolving an anaphoric referent against such a context involves integrating the constraints provided by the pronoun (e.g. "he" is a male person, "there" is a location) or noun phrase ("maintainer" is an entity in a maintaining relationship with some other entity) with the constraints provided by sentential context (e.g. in "ask him to do the preventive maintenance today", "him" must be an entity that can be asked to do maintence - an maintenance employee), and then finding items in the context that match the integrated description. Both the integration and the matching require the support of an inheritance mechanism which Knowledge Craft provides. For instance, in the above example, "him" has the constraint of being a male person inherent in the pronoun, and the constraint of being a maintenance employee from the sentential context. These two constraints are consistent since a maintenance employee ISA person and may be either gender. So the integrated description is a male maintenance employee. In the dialogue given above, this description would match (again through an inheritance process) with the focussed entity representing Albert Smith.

Knowledge Craft inheritance is also useful in specifying the relationships which define the potential focus (e.g. the relationship between a machine and its maintainer). Knowledge Craft relations are represented by user definable and modifiable schemas. This makes it convenient to attach such information to the relations.

The kind of interface we are considering here is unusual for natural language in that it has a representation of the world separate from the dialogue itself. This allows us to provide some interesting capabilities that have only been touched on in earlier work, in particular the work by Grosz [5] on task-oriented dialogues and Bolt [1] on an integrated natural language/graphical interface. First, we allow the user to refer to any entity visible in the world display by the minimum description necessary to distinguish it. For instance, if only one milling machine is shown on the display at any given time, the user would be able to refer to it by "the milling machine" rather than by typing its full name. The entities in the world display thus play a similar role to the potential focus and are treated in the same way by the anaphora resolution mechanism. In other words, the system will look for referents for definite noun phrase descriptions both among the entities in the potential focus and among the entities currently displayed on the screen.

The second useful capability opened up by the existence of the world display is an explicit representation of the dialogue focus through highlighting on the display. This allows the user to be clear at all times on what is the system's focus of attention, and helps prevent the kind of reference problems that could arise if the user thinks he has made a shift of focus, but the system fails to pick up on it. An even more intriguing possibility is to allow the user to edit the dialogue context explicitly. In this way, he could make up for any deficiencies in the system's focus tracking. He could also, as a part of browsing through the world display, explicitly set up the dialogue focus. For instance, if he set the focus of attention to include only a particular machine, then on the next natural language input, he would be able to refer to that machine by "it". The human factors of such an interface feature have never been examined and are hard to predict in advance. We, therefore, plan to determine its usefulness empirically.

In order to maintain a visual representation of the dialogue focus, the interface system will, when necessary, adjust the domain display in such a way that the dialogue focus remains a subset of the visual context. For instance, in the above dialogue example, when the user starts to ask about details of the grinding machine (utilization, unscheduled downtime, preventive maintenance, maintainer), the display of the machine (which we will assume was a named icon) would be expanded to or overlayed by a display of its attributes. The attributes that the user focusses on would be highlighted appropriately. Again, this is breaking largely unexplored ground from a human factors point of view. And we anticipate changes to the design based on experience with an implementation. The obvious danger is that the user might become confused or annoyed by changes to the display that he did not request directly. In addition, there is the potential for overly cluttered displays if this mechanism only ever displays additional entities and never removes any. The issue of when a defocussed entity can safely be removed from the display is a tricky one, involving unresolved research issues in dialogue management. Our current design does not address it.

3.2. Anaphora by pointing

One of the most interesting capabilities opened up by the kind of interface we are discussing is intermixing natural language input with pointing input. This would allow the user of a factory scheduling system to input, for instance, "Can this machine *<point at one machine>* take over the orders scheduled for that one *<point at other machine>*", where the pointing was done to the world display. We will call this kind of pointing *natural language pointing* and treat it as a kind of anaphoric reference. Natural language pointing is extremely useful in combination with speech input, allowing a very efficient combination of gesture and speech - the most natural way for people to communicate. Its effectiveness in an interface has already been demonstrated by work at MIT [1, 8]. It is somewhat less attractive for typed input because of the overhead involved in moving the hand from keyboard to pointing device and back again. However, work on the Scholar project [2] has shown that pointing can be used effectively with typed input in the context of maps in geography lessons.

Natural language pointing can be more efficient than speech alone because it is often faster to point at something than to identify it verbally (particularly when it is not in the immediate focus of the dialogue and so cannot be referred to by a pronoun). Moreover, pointing is a more direct form of identification than speech, so that its processing is likely to be faster and less error prone, considerably reducing the need for clarification dialogues, and hence enhancing communication efficiency still further. There are even some circumstances where pointing can communicate information that is very difficult to communicate through speech. For instance, pointing at a position on a map is very much easier and probably more accurate than trying to give the same information by speaking map coordinates into the system. In such circumstances, natural language pointing would also be convenient to use with typed input, particularly if all the pointing can be done after the entire sentence has been entered.

Though there are numerous advantages to natural language pointing, there are several issues which make its inclusion in an interface less than straightforward. In particular, it is necessary to:

- determine when pointing events are natural language pointing events;
- determine where the entities pointed at fit within the overall interpretation of the natural language input;
- identify which entity was actually pointed to (an issue when the visual representations of entities are nested within each other on the screen).

The difficulty of identifying pointing events as natural language pointing events stems both from ambiguity inherent in the use of the pointing device and in ambiguity in natural language as to whether a given phrase implies that a natural language pointing event will occur. In the kind of interface we are discussing, the pointing device will have other uses besides natural language pointing. In particular, it will figure prominently in the interface that allows the user to navigate around the world display. Pointing events are then potentially ambiguous between natural language pointing and these other uses of pointing. There are several potential solutions, none of which seems ideal:

- Make natural language pointing events identifiably different from others, for instance, by dedicating one mouse button (assuming there are several) to natural language pointing. This has the advantage of being clear, but the disadvantages of being fragile and difficult to learn (use of the wrong mouse button could produce highly unexpected and unintuitive results), and of reducing the options available for the world navigation interface.

- Overload some kind of neutral pointing event from the navigation interface - one that does some kind of selection without causing any specific action to happen. This has the same disadvantages in being fragile and hard to learn, and has the additional disadvantage of not being totally unambiguous, but the constraints it places on the navigation interface are different.

- Poll for the position of the pointing device when a deictic phrase is used. This avoids the disadvantages of the other alternatives, but runs into serious trouble because it is not always possible to identify deictic references in natural language just from the words involved. For instance, "there" may indicate a deictic reference or be a reference to an item in the dialogue context ("Order 17 is in the queue for ginding machine 4". "How long has it been *there*?"). It also reduces the freedom of the user in terms of the relative ordering of pointing and the deictic reference.

- Assume that all pointing events during (or close to, see below) natural language input are natural language pointing events. This has the advantages of simplicity, robustness, and lack of ambiguity. Its main disadvantage is making world navigation impossible during natural language input (even during a pause for thought during type in).

Our design currently calls for us to use the final alternative, but we regard the choice as an empirical matter and expect to experiment with several possibilities.

Once we have determined that a pointing event is a natural language pointing event, there is still the problem of matching it up with a phrase or hole in the natural language input. The co-occurrence of words and pointing events is useful information here, but does not give the whole story. All of the following examples and many other possibilities are plausible:

> *Can this machine <point at one machine> take over the orders*
> *scheduled for that one <point at other machine>*

> *Can this <point at one machine> machine take over the orders*
> *scheduled for that <point at other machine> one*

> *Can this machine take over the orders*
> *scheduled for that one <point at one machine> <point at other machine>*

The last of these is most likely in a typed input situation where the user wishes to cut down on the overhead of moving between keyboard and pointing device. The only real invariant seems to be that the natural language pointing events will occur in the same order as the phrases (or holes[2]) in the natural language input to which they correspond. Moreover, the pointing events usually come during or immediately before or after the corresponding phrase. This latter fact means that information on the start and end time of words in the natural language input is important for the analysis of natural language pointing input. This information is naturally available for speech input, and our design calls for us to extend Language Craft to make it available for typed input.

There are thus two kinds of indication, neither of them conclusive, that a phrase in the natural language input corresponds to a natural language pointing event: the temporal co-occurrence of the phrase with the pointing event, and the actual form of the phrase itself. For instance, phrases with a demonstrative determiner ("this machine") are more likely to correspond to natural language pointing than phrases with a definite determiner ("the machine"). Once a candidate correspondence has been established between a phrase and a pointing event, it must be verified that the two are compatible. This process is very similar to

---

[2]Our current design requires some form of deictic expression and does not allow the user just to leave a gap in the input corresponding to the pointing event as in "Can <point at one machine> take over the orders scheduled for <point at other machine>". The semantic caseframe approach used by Language Craft is already quite capable of skipping over gaps and producing a partial analysis of the input. The additional ability required to match up gaps with natural language pointing would be for Language Craft explicitly to recognize that there is a gap in the input and to determine where in the input that gap is.

anaphoric reference determination, except that the candidate referent is known in advance. It involves determining the constraints on the candidate phrase both instrinsically ("this machine" must be a machine) and from the sentential context (in the above examples "that one" must be a machine since orders are scheduled for it), and then checking if the entity pointed at met those constraints.

Since there is no conclusive way to determine which phrases in the natural language input correspond to pointing events, we have designed the following heuristic procedure for finding the correspondence.

1. list in left to right order all schemas representing phrases in the input that could potentially correspond to natural language pointing events;

2. list in left to right order all natural language pointing events;

3. form all lists of pairings between schemas and pointing events, such that:

     a. the left to right ordering is preserved for both schemas and pointing events;

     b. paired schemas and pointing events are compatible in the way described above;

4. if more than one list of pairings remains, choose those with the maximum number of schemas that correspond to phrases that are linguistically likely to be deictic (including all pronouns and noun phrases with demonstrative determiners);

5. if more than one list of pairings still remains, choose those with the shortest time mismatch between the pointing events and the phrases corresponding to the schemas;

6. if there is still more than one, ask the user to decide.

In the example above, little of the complexity of this algorithm is needed. There are only two pointing events and three schemas (corresponding to "this machine", "the orders", and "that one"), and hence there are three possible list of pairings, of which only the correct one satisfies all the constraints. More complex sentences could, however, require all the steps in the algorithm to find the correct pairings.

The final major issue in dealing with natural language pointing is that there can even be uncertainy as to which entity is being pointed to. In particular, if one entity has some kind of containment or subset relation with another, then the graphical representation of the contained entity may be nested within the graphical representation of the containing entity, so that pointing at the contained entity would be ambiguous between the two. For instance, an icon representing an individual machine may be graphically contained within an area which represents the factory shop of which it is a part, so that pointing at the machine icon might mean the machine or the shop. Sometimes, the corresponding natural language phrase or its sentential context can disambiguate. For instance, if the corresponding phrase was "this machine", there would be no confusion. If such disambiguation is impossible, then the system must query the user to resolve the issue. Modifying the above algorithm to use this approach means creating, for each potentially ambiguous natural language pointing event, copies of the pairing lists which differ only in the entity referred to by the ambiguous pointing event. There would be as many copies as there were alternative interpretations.

A final complication arises if the user desires to identify a group of objects or an area of the display through natural language pointing. For instance, he might want to ask about the average utilization of a group of machines. Conventional graphics applications provide ways of making group selections by incremental selection or selection by (usually rectangular) area. A similar approach could be used for natural language pointing, but it would eliminate some of the naturalness that we hope to achieve. Instead, our design allows freehand area designation by closed curves. In addition to being natural, this allows arbitrarily shaped areas to be designated as well as being able to select groups of individual entities. As in ordinary natural language pointing, all such line drawing during or temporally close to a natural language input will be interpreted as a natural language pointing event corresponding to some deictic phrase in the input.

4. Conclusion

Although natural language is an important component of intelligent interfaces to knowledge-based systems, it is not in general adequate as an interface in and of itself. Modern AI workstations provide sophisticated graphical capabilities, which can communicate many kinds of information much better than natural language dialogue. Moreover, direct manipulation of graphical interfaces is often a convenient, natural, and efficient way for the user to access and update a system's information.

Fortunately, it is not necessary to make a either/or choice between natural language and graphical interaction. This paper has outlined a set of generic facilities for constructing combined graphical/natural language interfaces for a broad class knowledge-based systems. We discussed in greater detail the aspects of those facilities that deal with the interpretation of references, both natural language and pointing, to entities in the application's world. In particular, we showed how standard dialogue anaphora resolution techniques can be integrated with the presence of a visual context and with pointing events into that visual context.

Unless interfaces to knowledge-based systems display a level of intelligence similar to the underlying systems themselves and make full use of the capabilities of the available I/O hardware, then the systems as a whole will fall far short of their potential impact. We believe that the way to construct interfaces that satisfy these goals lies in the direction we have outlined in this paper, and that this direction represents the future of user interfaces to knowledge-based systems.

References

1. Bolt, R. A. "'Put-That-There': Voice and Gesture at the Graphics Interface". *Computer Graphics 14*, 3 (1980), 262-270.

2. Carbonell, J. R. Mixed-Initiative Man-Computer Dialogues. 1970, Bolt, Beranek, and Newman, Inc., Cambridge, Mass., 1971.

3. Carbonell, J. G. and Hayes, P. J. "Recovery Strategies for Parsing Extragrammatical Language". *Computational Linguistics 10* (1984).

4. Charniak, E. C. Toward a Model of Children's Story Comprehension. TR-266, MIT AI Lab, Cambridge, Mass., 1972.

5. Grosz, B. J. The Representation and Use of Focus in a System for Understanding Dialogues. Proc. Fifth Int. Jt. Conf. on Artificial Intelligence, MIT, 1977, pp. 67-76.

6. Hayes, P. J. Anaphora for Limited Domain Systems. Proc. Seventh Int. Jt. Conf. on Artificial Intelligence, Vancouver, 1981, pp. 416-422.

7. Hayes, P. J., Andersen, P., Safier, S. Semantic Case Frame Parsing and Syntactic Generality. Proc. of 23rd Annual Meeting of the Assoc. for Comput. Ling., Chicago, June, 1985.

8. Negronponte, N. "Media Room". *Proceedings of the Society for Information Display 22*, 2 (1981), 109-113.

9. Sidner, C. L. Towards a Computational Theory of Definite Anaphora Comprehension in English Discourse. TR-537, MIT AI Lab, Cambridge, Mass., 1979.

10. Smith, D. C., Irby, C., Kimball, R., Verplank, W., and Harslem, E. "Designing the Star User Interface". *Byte 7*, 4 (April 1982), 242-282.

11. Williams, G. "The Lisa Computer System". *Byte 8*, 2 (February 1983), 33-50.

Advances in Artificial Intelligence - II
B. Du Boulay, D. Hogg and L. Steels (Editors)
© Elsevier Science Publishers B.V. (North-Holland), 1987

A BLACKBOARD SHELL IN PROLOG

John Jones, Mark Millington, Peter Ross

Department of Artificial Intelligence, University of Edinburgh
80 South Bridge, Edinburgh, EH1 1HN

Abstract

We discuss the design and implementation in Prolog of an expert system shell embodying the main features of the blackboard architecture. Issues arising include providing a clear definition of the consistency mechanism to be employed and identifying subsumption as an important concept underlying amendment.

1. The blackboard architecture

The blackboard architecture is a problem-solving framework developed for the HEARSAY-II speech recognition system ([Erman75]). It has since been used in a range of other domains including planning ([Hayes-Roth85]), plan recognition ([Carver84]), signals and data interpretation ([Engelmore79, Nii82]) and vision ([Williams77]) and considered as a general problem-solving framework ([Hayes-Roth83]). Elsewhere ([Ross85]), we have proposed the blackboard architecture for user modelling in command-driven systems, where consistent subsets (see section 3.4) of the blackboard form candidate user models.

In this paper we describe a blackboard shell that runs under C-Prolog (and NIP) on a Vax 11/750 under UNIX* (4.2). All aspects of the system described, except multiple contexts (section 3.4), have been implemented. We begin with a distillation of the notion of a blackboard system. In section 2 we present our design and in section 3 discuss several implications of it. Several blackboard architecture shells, HEARSAY-III and AGE, have also been created ([Erman81, Nii79]) and where appropriate we shall relate our design to these.

1.1. Principal features

The principal ingredients of a blackboard architecture expert system are:

Entries:
> intermediate results generated during problem solving which are interrelated by notions including support, competition and aggregation.

Knowledge sources:
> independent, event_driven, generalised condition-action rules which embody problem solving knowledge and create and modify entries.

Blackboard:
> a multi-dimensional, partitioned global data structure which mediates the communication between knowledge sources and imposes an overall relationship amongst the entries.

Scheduler:
> an intelligent control mechanism which decides which task is performed next.

---

* UNIX is a trademark of Bell Laboratories.

With the above ingredients, the behaviour of such a system is as follows. After the addition of one or more entries to the blackboard, the system selects which knowledge sources (KSs) can possibly utilise the new information. The task of deciding if a selected KS can utilise this information (it will in general require other conditions to hold also) is not performed yet, but put onto an agenda of pending tasks.

The scheduler then selects a task from the agenda to perform. If this is the evaluation of the condition of a KS, then if it evaluates to true on the current blackboard a new task is added to the agenda. This agenda entry, called a knowledge source activation record (KSAR), documents the satisfaction of the condition of the KS, its intended action, and user defined measures of reliability, usefulness and confidence of the KS. Should the task the scheduler chooses be a KSAR, then the KS is executed, provided it has remained valid, and in general new entries are created in the blackboard.

It is this separation of KS execution from initial activation which allows for intelligent scheduling and distinguishs blackboard architecture systems from simple production rule systems. This separation may also play a role in the overall efficiency of the system. For example, the computationally cheap initial activation of a KS may occur several times before the possibly computationally expensive creation of a KSAR.

1.2. Aspects of the reasoning

The blackboard architecture allows the use of diverse, independent, potentially inaccurate sources of knowledge. In the presence of uncertainty, in the KSs and the data, a solution is found (if at all) by converging on the highest rated candidate explanation. A key feature of this convergence is the incremental emergence of 'islands' in the solution space, regions of the blackboard where a coherent part of the problem has been solved. As the problem-solving continues, these 'islands' grow and merge to form an overall solution.

Key control aspects of this solution process are provided by an intelligent scheduling mechanism (possibly user defined). Each task on the agenda has associated with it various user defined measures of the reliability, usefulness and correctness of the task to be performed. The scheduler uses this information to select the best task to perform at the moment by applying some criteria, typically fixed. In more sophisticated systems ([Hayes-Roth85]), these criteria themselves are amenable to reasoning in the blackboard.

An early hope for the blackboard architecture, not yet fully realised (an initial design is described in [Ensor85]), was that it could be implemented on a parallel processor. Several aspects of the basic control cycle seem amenable to parallel computation (the evaluation of conditions of KSs, for example), although there seems to be a need to maintain some serial aspects. This mix of serial and parallel processing is one of the claims for the psychological validity of the architecture. Others include its production-like nature and the overall style of reasoning. Some evidence to support these claims and further discussion of them is given in [Hayes-Roth85].

2. Implementing the blackboard architecture

Our overriding design aim was that of simplicity both in terms of ease of description and ease of use. To achieve this aim we tried to keep the system very close to Prolog and make full use of its pattern matching facilities. Since this is an experimental tool, the question of efficiency is not considered.

2.1. Implementing the principle features

The principal blackboard features are implemented in the shell as follows:

Entries –

are Prolog unit clauses of the form

bb(Tag,Status,Index,Fact,Cf)

related by an explicit support relation of unit clauses

supports(Supporting_Tag,Supported_Tag).

The components of an entry may be summarised by:

Tag is an integer supplied by the system to uniquely identify this entry.

Status
> is one of the atoms 'in', 'inout' or 'amended' and denotes the current status of this entry. The basic status is 'in' which is given to all entries as they are inserted into the blackboard; knowledge sources can be triggered only on 'in' entries. The status 'amended' is only given to users entries that have been amended by users rules and are to be regarded as defunct. Entries of status 'inout' belong to the system, though all status components are created and maintained by the system.

Index
> is a Prolog term representing the 'position' of this entry in the blackboard; if the term is non-ground then this entry can be regarded as occurring at all indices it matches. This component is supplied by the user and a judicious choice can provide the desired dimensional structure to the blackboard. It should be noted that at no time does the system need to be told what the possible indices are, the dimensional structure of the board is completely determined by the user's use of indices and patterns by which the entries are retrieved in the conditions of rules.

Fact is an arbitrary Prolog term representing the 'content' of the entry as defined by the user.

Cf is a Prolog term representing the 'degree of belief' in this entry. These certainty factors are definable by the user (in which case a total ordering must be supplied, usually in procedural form) though a default integer scheme is provided.

Knowledge sources –
are rules of the form:

if Condition then Body to Effect est Est.
> where

Condition
> is some test of the entries present in (or absent from) the blackboard. Tests are constructed as boolean combinations of 'atomic' tests for the presence (absence) of certain [Index,Fact,Cf] combinations. Tags, status and support relationships cannot be tested for. Further details follow in section 3.

Body is the computation, a Prolog goal, to determine the desired effect. It is intended that the Body, Condition and Effect all share variables so that the exact conditions of this invocation are bound in the Body by the Condition before it is called, and the action of the Body is to instantiate variables present in the Effect. For example a mechanism for calculating the certainty factor of an entry from the certainties of its supports must be supplied by the user in the Body if required.

Effect
> is the intended effect of the rule to either create a new entry (Effect = 'add [Index,Fact,Cf]'), amend an old one (Effect = 'amend [Index,Fact,Cf]') or call some Prolog goal (Effect = 'action Goal').

Est arises because during a cycle of the system there will usually be a choice of KSARs to execute; the estimate Est is used to resolve the conflict. The user may supply his own total ordering of estimates or adopt the integer scheme as provided by the system.

The independent event–driven nature of knowledge sources is captured in the way that they are activated solely by the scheduler on the basis of changes to the blackboard entries.

Blackboard –

in this shell the blackboard does not exist as an explicit data structure per se but rather is defined implicitly by the users use of indices. The system makes use of its own blackboard entries. In particular it constructs a 'shadow' board from the users rules to record, for each index employed, which rules are interested in changes at that index. Further, the current agenda is kept in the blackboard, each KSAR being an entry of the form

bb(Tag,in,agenda,ksar(body(Body,Effect,_),Evaluated_Est),sure).

supported by those entries from which it was constructed. Unlike the most general possible blackboard scheme (where any form of task may be on the agenda) the agenda is composed solely of KSARs; this is merely a simplification which assumes that KSARs are relatively cheap to build and could easily be changed to the more general scheme outlined in section 1.1. It should be noted that because the agenda is composed of ordinary entries the consistency mechanism (see section 3.3) will remove any newly invalid KSARs automatically.

Scheduler –

the basic shell is equipped with a simple scheduling scheme wherein changes in the board are used in conjunction with the shadow board to create new entries on the agenda. By putting the agenda and shadow board in the blackboard we have made it possible for users to write their own 'smart' schedulers as ordinary knowledge sources which manipulate the agenda. Presumably such schemes would make use of the definability of KSAR estimates.

2.2. An example KS

Before going into further detail on some aspects of the shell in section 3, we finish this brief description with an example KS taken from our existing application in user modelling.

We are investigating methods of modelling users of command-driven systems, in particular of UNIX ([Ross85]), and it seems that a blackboard architecture is an appropriate framework in which to do this. The example KS proposes corrections for typing errors and comes from the initial analysis of the most recent users command. Other KSs have been implemented which carry out lexical, syntactic and some semantic analysis of the input.

We present the KS both in its form in the blackboard system and paraphrased in English. In indices we use the Prolog operator '/' as a separator. We use a Strips-like representation for UNIX commands, including incorrect usages and commands which simply provide information to the user.

```
if    [strips/A/version(X), [pre:Errors, _ _ _stderr:unpaged([_])], Cf >0]
   and [parse/full/A/version(X), Parse, Cf1 > 0]
   and [parse/partial/A/version(X), Partial_parse, Cf2 > 0]
   and [input/full/A/version(X), problems(_, []), Cf3 > 0]
then   (do_correction(Partial_parse, Parse, Errors, Answer, Rating),
        confidence(Cf, Cf1, Cf2, Cf3, Rating, Certainty),
        Y is X+1)
to add [input/partial/A/version(Y), Answer, Certainty]
est    25.
```

In our user modelling system we interpret this to mean:

if   the representation for version X of line A of the users input
        produces an error message with preconditions Errors
and   the parse of version X of line A in terms of full UNIX path names
        is Parse
and   the parse of version X of line A in terms of the path names the
        user employed is Partial_parse
and   all the fragments of the path names in version X of line A of the
        users input refer to existing directories
then   use Parse, Partial_parse, Errors, knowledge about the users file
        store and UNIX commands to select the best correction for the
        incorrect element in the input with rating Rating and calculate
        the confidence in the hypothesis
to add an entry recording version X+1 of the users input on line A
est   and rate this KS at 25.

3. The interface between KSs and the blackboard

An important consideration in designing the shell which has significant implications, both for the user and the implementation, is the exact nature of the interface between KSs and the blackboard. Exactly what kinds of tests can a KS apply to the blackboard, and what can it propose to do to the blackboard should those tests succeed? On the whole, the blackboard literature is unhelpful on this point in that KSs are often paraphrased in English to avoid presenting code. We have made several decisions in this area, and in this section we describe them and their implications in some detail.

3.1. Applying Conditions

In section 2.1 we indicated that a KS can test for the presence or absence of entries. To test for the presence of a certain kind of entry requires the user to specify a pattern for the index, a pattern for the fact and a test to apply to the certainty of the entry (of the form $Cf < X$, $Cf > Y$ or $X < Cf < Y$, where '$<$' is globally user definable, or, by default, arithmetic comparison). This is achieved in a KS by the atomic test '[Index_pattern, Fact_pattern, Cf_test]'. Such a test succeeds for each entry in the blackboard which matches the patterns and has an appropriate certainty. Consideration has to be given to how a KS should interpret the success of an atomic test in its condition. Due to the nature of unification, a general test may succeed on a specific entry or a specific test on a general entry, for example. The interpretation of this is left to the user through the usual Prolog notion of sharing variables.

There are two methods of testing for the absence of entries. A test of the form 'not Atomic_test' succeeds if no entry in the blackboard passes the test. Further, the entry made by a KS applying such a test is considered to depend on this absence. If in the future such an entry appears in the blackboard, the supported entry is invalidated, and is removed (see section 3.3). In effect, such a KS makes a default assumption. The second absence test is of the form 'notnow Atomic_test'. The distinction between this and the previous test is that the dependency described for 'not' does not apply. The motivation for this was initially pragmatic, as a means of getting data into the blackboard. However, this is a simple (if naive) way of avoiding the need for a temporal or topological logic with which to reason about such dependencies in support structures. In line with the Prolog operator 'not', no bindings are made by any test for the absence of entries.

There is also provision to attach arbitrary Prolog goals to the condition of a KS, for whatever purposes the user requires, in the form 'holds Goal'. As far as the logic of the blackboard goes, such goals are considered to simply qualify the success of the remainder of the condition.

3.2. Making amendments

As observed in section 2.1, a KS can add an entry or amend an entry already present. Problems posed to the system in doing these two effects and our solution will be discussed in section 3.3. In this section we concentrate on a restriction placed on KSs which amend an entry.

The restriction is motivated by our interpretation of an entry being amended to mean that in the proceeding inference process the amended version should be used in preference to the original (this touchs on the notion of contexts, see sections 3.3 and 3.4). The problem is in determining under what conditions it is appropriate for the new entry to supplant the old entry.

In general, an atomic test succeeding selects an entry in the blackboard. When a KS proposes to make an amendment, since its condition may select several entries in the blackboard the user must indicate which is to be amended, by prefixing the appropriate part of the condition by the symbol '@'. As observed in section 3.1 atomic tests can match entries in a variety of ways, some of which would be problematical when making an amendment. For the purposes of illustration, we consider the particular case of a ground atomic test matching a non-ground entry to be amended.

We interpret a non-ground entry to embody some generality or indefiniteness in the partial solution generated so far. A ground test selects this entry simply on the basis of a particular subcase. If amendment were allowed, how could we carry it out faithfully? We would wish to exclude from further consideration the particular subcase, but leave the remainder of the non-ground entry intact. Sometimes the subcase to be excluded may be entirely describable as a particular combination of bindings to variables in the non-ground entry and it would be sufficient to redefine unification for that entry to exclude that combination of bindings as a success. However, typically the condition of the KS will contain other tests and arbitrary Prolog goals which form part of the definition of the subcase so that this naive fix is inadequate.

Hence, if we are to be able to faithfully make an amendment as proposed we must invalidate the whole entry selected. To ensure that this is a reasonable action, the test selecting the entry must embody at least the generality of the entry it selects. Fortunately, this concept is readily definable in Prolog as subsumption. In Prolog, a term t1 subsumes a term t2 if t1 and t2 unify without instantiating any variables in t2.

Thus, the restriction on amendments is that the test which selects an entry in the blackboard to be amended must subsume that entry.

3.3. Maintaining Consistency

We have seen that the user may have KSs which make default assumptions or amend other entries. Both of these possibilities mean that some effort is required to extract a logically consistent solution to a problem from the blackboard. One approach is the contexts mechanism of HEARSAY-III ([Erman81]).

HEARSAY-III allows KSs which conclude entries documenting explicit choice points in the solution and KSs which make such choices. In HEARSAY-III, all entries are interpreted in one of a hierarchy of 'contexts' parameterised on which such choice points have been temporarily resolved in the inference process up to that point. Further, HEARSAY-III allows KSs which make such choices in two ways. One form replaces the choice entry with one of the choices creating a new context which is a subcontext of the present one. Should pursuing this choice turn out to be undesirable reasoning returns to the parent context and a new choice can be made. The second form makes the choice permanently in the current context. In HEARSAY-III the effort required to select logically consistent sets of hypotheses is expended in managing the creation of contexts.

We do not have entries which document explicit choices, but do have KSs which make default assumptions as the basis for further reasoning. This suggests that some form of contexts mechanism may be appropriate, so that if some other KS creates an entry which invalidates this default, consequences of these two entries could be pursued in distinct contexts. Similarly with amendments, the original entry and its amended version could be pursued in distinct contexts.

At present the blackboard system does not support contexts although we shall describe in section 3.4 a scheme which introduces similar capabilities. In effect the present system has only one context and the work required to obtain logically consistent solutions is expended in maintaining the consistency of this context. In this section we elaborate on how this is performed. This and the mechanism of section 3.4 are conceptually similar to those described by McDermott ([McDermott83]).

In order to clarify the presentation, we introduce some definitions. An entry C in the blackboard (written C:c) is said to follow from a set of justifications c, where c is defined inductively on the form of the condition of the KS which concluded C. While considering the following definition bear in mind that if an atomic test selects an entry in the blackboard then that entry will already have a well-defined set of justifications.

The simplest conditions are those which do not select an entry at all or select precisely one entry, in which case the justifications are:

Condition	Justifications
notnow A	{}
not A	{not(A)}
A	{A*:a}
@A	{amends(A*):a}

where A is an atomic test, A* is the entry it selected (where appropriate) and 'a' its justifications.

For complex conditions involving conjunctions the justifications are defined as the set union of the justifications of the conjuncts. For these purposes, KSs with conditions of the form 'A and B or D' ('A and @B or D') are rewritten as two KSs with conditions 'A and B', 'A and C' ('A and @B', 'A and @D').

We next introduce a non-symmetric relation between two entries and their justifications as follows. U:u is incompatible with V:v if

1) not(X) is a member of u, where V passes the atomic test X
2) amends(U):u is a member of v
3) there is a member W:w of u such that W:w is incompatible with V:v

This definition of incompatibility does not preclude the possibility that an entry is incompatible with itself (because of loops in the supports relationship).

Finally, the blackboard is consistent if no pair of 'in' entries are incompatible.

Now, maintaining the consistency of the blackboard is implemented as follows. View each cycle as the application of a KS to generate an entry to be put into the blackboard. Prior to adding the new entry, every entry that would be incompatible with it is removed from the blackboard. In the case of self-incompatibility, detected by a simple non-destructive loop check, the entry is not made.

Maintaining consistency in the present system may result in entries being removed from the blackboard. Such entries are never reinstated, although, should the user's scheduling not exclude it, such entries may possibly be reinferred. There is nothing in the blackboard architecture which dictates this approach, so it would also be possible to use a reasoning maintenance system which 'unouted' such entries (see [Brown85] for a formal method of defining the behaviour of such systems). In blackboard systems with multiple contexts, reasoning maintenance is subsumed by the handling of contexts.

3.4. Implementing multiple contexts

The current consistency scheme may be simply extended to multiple contexts by defining contexts relative to the incompatibility relation as follows:

U is incompatible with V if and only if U and V are in different contexts.

This implicitly involves treating incompatibility as a symmetric relationship and would be reflected in the implementation by regarding all entries incompatible with a new entry as being in an equally good but distinct context rather than as inferior 'old' versions to be removed.

As we saw earlier the generators of incompatibility are not-tests and amendments so we will have no explicit choice entries as in the HEARSAY-III scheme. If, however, we allow the user to define a domain specific notion of incompatibility between entries (for example by defining two entries of the same index but non-unifiable facts to be inconsistent) then a choice–points mechanism will implicitly be provided by the system. This mechanism differs from that of HEARSAY-III by never adopting or retracting contexts; all contexts have equal status in the eyes of the (basic) system. If for the users particular application it is required that some contexts be favoured over others then it is up to the user to reflect this in their 'intelligent' scheduling of tasks which favour the 'current' context.

A simple mechanism to implement the scheme described is to explicitly maintain the incompatibility relationship in the same way as the supports relationship. Though this means there are potentially n squared incompatibilities between n entries we feel that in many applications the choice points are 'isolated' enough that the incompatibilities will interact very little and many fewer than n squared will be generated. Maintaining an explicit incompatibility relation makes it easy to implement a scheme whereby KSARs can only be constructed on the basis of a set of compatible supports, i.e. entries which are in the same context.

Acknowledgement

The research described here is funded by SERC grant GR/C/35967.

References

[Brown85]   Brown, A. L., Modal propositional semantics for reasoning maintenance systems, IJCAI 85, 178-184.

[Carver84]   Carver, N. F., V. R. Lesser and D. L. McCue, Focusing in plan recognition, AAAI 84, 42-48.

[Engelmore79]   Engelmore, R. and A. Terry, Structure and function of the crysalis system, IJCAI 79, 250-256.

[Ensor85]   Ensor, J. R., and J. D. Gabbe, Transactional blackboards, IJCAI 85, 340-344.

[Erman75]   Erman, L. D. and V. R. Lesser, A multi-level organisation for problem solving using many, diverse, cooperating sources of knowledge, IJCAI 75, 483-490.

[Erman81]   Erman, L. D., P. E. London and S. F. Fickas, The design and an example use of hearsay-III, IJCAI 81, 405-415.

[Hayes-Roth83]   Hayes-Roth, B., The blackboard architecture: a general framework for problem solving?, HPP-83-30, Stanford University, 1983.

[Hayes-Roth85]   Hayes-Roth, B., A blackboard architecture for control, A. I. 26, 251-321, 1985.

[McDermott83]   McDermott, D., Contexts and data dependencies: a synthesis, IEEE Transactions on pattern analysis and machine intelligence 5, 237-246, 1983.

[Nii79]   Nii, H. P. and N. Aiello, AGE (attempt to generalise): a knowledge-based program for building knowledge-based programs, IJCAI 79, 645-655.

[Nii82]   Nii, H. P., E. A. Feigenbaum, J. J. Anton and A. J. Rockmore, Signal-to-symbol transformation: HASP/SIAP case study, A.I. Magazine, Spring 1982, 23-35.

[Ross85]   Ross, P., J. Jones and M. Millington, User modelling in command-driven systems, University of Edinburgh, Department of Artificial Intelligence, D.A.I. Research Report 264, 1985.

[Williams77]   Williams, T., J. Lowrance, A. Hanson and E. Riseman, Model-building in the VISIONS system, IJCAI 77, 644-645.

Advances in Artificial Intelligence - II
B. Du Boulay, D. Hogg and L. Steels (Editors)
© Elsevier Science Publishers B.V. (North-Holland), 1987   563

MULTIPLE WORLDS WITH TRUTH MAINTENANCE
IN AI APPLICATIONS

Bonnie A. Nardi and E. Anne Paulson
IntelliCorp, Knowledge Systems Division
1975 El Camino Real
Mountain View, CA 94040
U.S.A.

Abstract

We describe a new problem solving technique: multiple worlds with truth
maintenance. We discuss the advantages of multiple worlds and truth
maintenance compared to other problem solving methods, and go through
an example of problem solving using this new paradigm.

1. Background

Multiple worlds is an Artificial Intelligence (AI) technique for simultaneous exploration
of alternative assumptions leading to possible problem solutions. In general, when
there is uncertainty in determining a solution to a problem, the use of a multiple
worlds facility may be helpful. The essence of the technique is that a separate
"world" is created for each set of assumptions. A world is a label for a set of
assumptions and the facts that are entailed by the assumptions. Worlds can be
compared. When it is desirable to consider more than one solution to a problem, the
use of multiple worlds provides the capability of saving the states of each solution for
easy comparative analysis.

The availability of multiple worlds technology for commercial applications is quite
recent. Potential applications include scheduling and checkpointing in simulation
[Fikes et al. 7]; contingency analysis [Kunz et al. 8]; and planning, diagnosis and time-
state representation [Faught 6], [C. Williams 13].

The objective of this paper is to describe a commercially available implementation of a
multiple worlds facility, illustrating its use with a simple scheduling problem.

The invention of truth maintenance facilities grew out of the work on truth
maintenance systems conducted by Doyle [4], McAllester [9,10] McDermott [11], and
deKleer [2,3]. Truth maintenance systems are designed to enhance the efficiency of
problem solving by sharing information across regions in a search space of solutions or
partial solutions. Results obtained in one region are cached and made available to
other regions in the search space. A rule (or its programmatic equivalent) is run once
(in one part of the space) and a data structure with *a fact and its justifiers* is
created. For example, the rule "If A then B" establishes that when A is true in a
world, then B is true. B is justified by A. The truth maintenance system remembers
the fact's justification, which need never be re-computed and which is available to
other regions in the search space.

Multiple worlds facilities can be combined with the truth maintenance concept, to produce truth-maintained multiple worlds (TMS-based multiple worlds). But instead of having one world with perfect consistency among facts, many worlds are created. The facts within each world are internally consistent, but facts across worlds may be contradictory. In fact, that is precisely the point of creating many worlds - to explore the implications of contradictory facts in an orderly way.

When TMS-based multiple worlds are used, gains in efficiency are possible in two ways: (1) facts and justifications are cached and shared as in traditional truth maintenance, and (2) worlds that violate constraints established by the problem solver are invalidated, reducing the number of worlds to be searched.

To reduce the number of worlds created, the problem solver establishes constraints that prevent the exploration of unsuitable worlds. For example, in a scheduling application, a constraint could be that a job cannot be started if the number of hours it takes exceeds the hours remaining in the day. A world in which this constraint was violated would be marked as inconsistent.

2. Using multiple worlds

The examples prepared for this paper were implemented using the IntelliCorp™ Knowledge Engineering Environment™, (KEE™), a frame-based AI tool with rules, graphics, object-oriented programming and active values, truth maintenance, and multiple worlds.

In the KEE system the multiple worlds facility may be used to solve problems either using production rules or through a programmatic interface.

The KEE system's multiple worlds facility is interactive. Worlds are visually displayed in a directed graph with mouseable nodes. Each world can be moused to show the facts associated with the world, the facts that have changed with respect to a parent world, how the world compares to other worlds, the cause of failure in an inconsistent world. The world can be moused to add or delete a fact, create a descendant world or destroy the world.

The information available through the graphic interface is also available programmatically. A great deal of very detailed information is thus easily accessed by the user for explanation, debugging and re-formulation of the problem. The ease of re-formulating the problem with a multiple worlds approach cannot be over-emphasized; in fact Doyle [5] argues that one of the chief advantages of AI techniques is that they foster rapid re-formulation of problems.

In the KEE system, a world represents a set of facts said to be true in that world. There is also a set of facts true in the *background* that are true in every world created, unless specifically deleted from a world. A world can represent a collection of changes over time or a hypothetical situation. Once a world is created, facts can be added to or deleted from the world. A world can generate descendant worlds that inherit all of the facts true in the parent world. Descendant worlds may selectively delete inherited facts if desired.

Facts and their justifications are recorded in the KEE system in an assumption-based truth maintenance system (ATMS) based on deKleer's work [deKleer 3]. KEE's TMS-based multiple worlds facility is described in Morris and Nado [12].

3. Example

A world W1 is created. The background contains an object PUMP1 with slots (attributes) STATUS, CAPACITY and INPUT whose values are initially unspecified. Each slot may be restricted to only one value at any given time.

The fact "The STATUS of PUMP1 is ON" is added to W1.

Worlds W2, W3, W4 are created as descendants of W1. Facts may be added to or deleted from worlds W2, W3, and W4. The set of facts true in each descendant world is the set of facts true in the background, plus all the facts added in world W1 that are not deleted in the descendant worlds.

"The INPUT of PUMP1 is VALVE2" is added to W2. "The STATUS of PUMP1 is ON" is deleted from W3. "The STATUS of PUMP2 is ON" is added to W3. "The INPUT of PUMP1 is VALVE3" is added to W4. The set of facts true in W2 is: "The STATUS of PUMP1 is ON." "The INPUT of PUMP1 is VALVE2." The set of facts true in W3 is: "The STATUS of PUMP2 is ON."

4. Merging worlds

Worlds can be merged. When several worlds are merged to create a new world, the new world inherits all the changes (the additions and deletions) of its ancestors, instead of inheriting all the facts true in its parents. In the example above, worlds W2 and W3 could be merged to get world W5. W5 would have the following set of facts true: "The STATUS of PUMP2 is ON." and "The INPUT of PUMP1 is VALVE2."

A graph showing the worlds would look like:

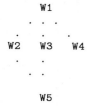

Worlds W2 and W4 cannot be merged, however, because there are two inconsistent assertions about the INPUT of PUMP1, as the pump can have only one input. The ATMS will detect the inconsistency and mark the merge as inconsistent.

The detection of inconsistencies is basic to the concept of TMS multiple worlds. Worlds represent partial solutions to a problem, and inconsistent worlds correspond to failed attempts at solutions. An inconsistent world violates some constraint. Examination of inconsistent worlds is useful in detecting the cause of a failure or bad solution. In the KEE system, inconsistent worlds can be examined graphically to ascertain the reason for failure (as will be shown in the example below).

There are many interesting possibilities for world merges. For example, this approach could be useful in diagnostic problems. The various fault hypotheses with their symptoms would be contained in top-level worlds. A merged world would represent the hypothesis that there was more than one fault, and would show the symptoms that would result from all the faults.

In planning and simulation applications, sibling worlds could be used to represent the results of independent, simultaneous actions. If sibling worlds were merged, the new world would represent the results of all the simultaneous actions. If the sibling worlds turned out not to be mergeable, then the actions were not, after all, independent; rather, they conflicted.

World merges could be used with possibly conflicting sets of facts, hypotheses, or interpretations. For example, nuclear, power, and electrical engineers may each have a different opinion or interpretation of an event. The opinions of each of the engineers could be represented in a world. The worlds would then be merged, with contradictions being pointed out. This would be a way to determine where the three engineers were not in agreement.

5. Justifications

The ATMS is explicitly told what facts are dependent upon what other facts. When the rule interpreter (or a programmatic equivalent) is run, it will tell the ATMS what conditions were used for the conclusion that is generated by a rule, and the ATMS will store this *justification* with the conclusion.

6. A scheduling application

Conventional methods for solving allocation problems include linear programming, trial-and-error (by hand or using a simulation to test results), exhaustive search through the entire space of possibilities, and use of a fixed "dispatching" rule; *e.g.*, do the job with the earliest due date, shortest processing time, longest processing time, etc.

Linear programming techniques are useful and efficient for a certain class of resource allocation problems. However, they provide no capability for explaining why a solution wasn't found, or why the solution found was optimal.

Simulation can be extremely helpful in some allocation problems. For many problems, it may be more efficient to combine a TMS multiple worlds approach with simulation by using worlds to "checkpoint" the simulation. States of the system during selected points in a run of the simulation (*e.g.*, after so many events or so much time) are recorded in worlds (or checkpoints). The worlds can be analyzed and the simulation re-run with different parameters from a particular world which is a point of interest in the simulation, (*e.g.*, a problem occurred) rather than re-initializing and re-running the entire simulation. Simulations can be run "in parallel"; that is, the simulation can be run for a while from a given world and then a switch can be made to another world (representing a different state of the system) and run from there. Results of the runs can be analyzed and compared. Experimentation with using TMS multiple worlds to checkpoint simulations is underway in both academic and corporate research environments.

Exhaustive search has the virtue of generating all candidate solutions but is intractable except for the simplest applications.

The use of a fixed dispatching rule is helpful in reducing search. However, only one measure is optimized and superior solutions that optimize more than one measure are not necessarily generated.

The use of a multiple worlds facility for some allocation applications has strong advantages. Because the problem can be expressed in rules, domain experts who are not mathematically or computationally sophisticated can model their scheduling problem by simply writing rules. The user has access to detailed information that permits insights into the implications of the choices made for scheduling and the causes of failures. Constraints are easily expressed as rules that automatically eliminate solutions that violate specified conditions. The rules need only be invoked once and the truth maintenance system records them and applies them appropriately. Search is reduced because worlds that violate user-established constraints are not further examined, but good solutions are not lost in the service of complying with fixed dispatching rules.

7. The machine shop problem

To illustrate the use of multiple worlds for allocation, we describe an example of a "machine shop scheduling problem" worked out with TMS-based multiple worlds. The problem is as follows: There are five jobs that must go through the machine shop. Each job has a set of tasks to be performed. Each task is performed at a single machine. There are four machines: a drill, a lathe, a mill, and a grinder.

Task sequence and times (in hours) for the 5 jobs:

JOB1		JOB2		JOB3		JOB4		JOB5	
Drill	1	Lathe	2	Grind	2	Drill	1	Mill	2
Lathe	2	Mill	2	Drill	2	Grind	2	Drill	2
Grind	1	Grind	1	Mill	2	Lathe	2	Lathe	1
Mill	2	Drill	2	Grind	1			Grind	1
				Lathe	1				

The problem is to assign a start time for each job's tasks so that two measures are optimized: minimum idle time for each machine and maximum number of jobs completed in 8 hours.

A schedule for the jobs that optimizes these two measures would use all four machines and finish all five jobs in 8 hours.

The MACHINESHOP knowledge base models the problem. (See Figure 1.)   The knowledge base represents the objects of interest in the machine shop and the rules that reason about the behavior of the objects.

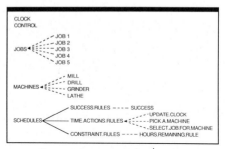

Figure 1: MACHINESHOP
Knowledge Base

The objects in the machine shop environment -- machines, jobs and a clock -- are represented as *units*. A unit is a data structure that provides a description of an object in terms of *slots* (attributes) that may be assigned values. For example, the JOB1 unit has attributes NEXT.TASK, PENDING.TASKS. (See Figure 2.)

Figure 2: JOB1 Unit

Units are organized into a taxonomy where some units are *members* of other units. In Figure 1, the relationship between member units and the classes of which they are members is shown with dashed lines. *Subclass* relationships represent a subset relationship to higher level classes, and are shown with unbroken lines. (See Figure 1.) Units allow for inheritance so that slots (and possibly their values) are passed from classes to subclasses and members. For example, the members of the JOBS unit (JOB1, JOB2, JOB3, JOB4, JOB5) inherit their slots from the JOBS unit.

The knowledge about how to generate the schedule is contained in rules. For the text of the rules see Figure 3. The overall goal of the rules is to break the scheduling problem down into subproblems so that solutions are generated hour by hour. When a viable solution to scheduling an hour is found (such that no machine has more than one job assigned to it and the time constraint is not violated) then solutions to the next hour are generated.

The reasoning uses two types of rules, action rules and deduction rules. Action rules create and modify worlds. Deduction rules establish facts that are true in any world in which the conditions of the deduction rule are true. (Deduction rules are identified

```
(Rules (HOURS.REMAINING.RULE (WHILE (THE HOUR OF CLOCK IS ?HOUR)
                                    (THE NEXT.TASK OF ?JOB IS ?NEXT)
                                    (NOT (LISP (NULL ?NEXT)))
                                    (THE PENDING.TASKS OF ?JOB IS ?TASKS)
                                    (LISP (GREATERP (PLUS (LENGTH ?TASKS)
                                                    ?HOUR)
                                    7))
                              BELIEVE FALSE))
         (PICK.A.MACHINE (IF (THE HOUR OF CLOCK IS ?HOUR)
                             (?MACHINE IS IN CLASS MACHINES)
                          THEN IN.NEW.AND.WORLD (PICK A JOB FOR ?MACHINE)))

         (SELECT.JOB.FOR.MACHINE (IF (PICK A JOB FOR ?MACHINE)
                                     (THE HOUR OF CLOCK IS ?HOUR)
                                     (THE NEXT.TASK OF ?JOB IS ?MACHINE)
                                     (LISP (NOT (NULL ?MACHINE)))
                                     (THE PENDING.TASKS OF ?JOB IS ?PENDING)
                                     (EQUAL ?NEXT.PENDING (CAR ?PENDING))
                                     (EQUAL ?REST.PENDING (CDR ?PENDING))
                                     (EQUAL ?CURRENT.JOB (LIST ?HOUR ?JOB))
                                  THEN IN.NEW.WORLD
                                     (CHANGE.TO (THE NEW.NEXT.TASK OF ?JOB
                                                 IS ?NEXT.PENDING)
                                            USING NO.RULES)
                                     (CHANGE.TO (THE PENDING.TASKS OF ?JOB
                                                 IS ?REST.PENDING)
                                            USING NO.RULES)

                                     (THE CURRENT.JOB OF ?MACHINE IS
                                                 ?CURRENT.JOB)
                                     (A JOB.SCHEDULE OF ?MACHINE IS
                                                 ?CURRENT.JOB)
                                     (DELETE (THE NEXT.TASK OF ?JOB IS ?ANY)
                                     )
                                     (DELETE (PICK A JOB FOR ?MACHINE))))
         (SUCCESS (IF (THE HOUR OF CLOCK IS (THE STOP.HOUR OF CONTROL))
                   THEN DO (DELETE (THE HOUR OF CLOCK IS ?X))
                     (ASSERT (THIS WORLD IS A SUCCESS))
                     (LISP (printout T $WORLDS "is a successful solution"
                          T))))
         (UPDATE.CLOCK (IF (THE CURRENT.JOB OF LATHE IS (LIST.OF (?CLOCKTIME
                                                 ?LJOB)))
                           (THE CURRENT.JOB OF DRILL IS (LIST.OF (?CLOCKTIME
                                                 ?DJOB)))
                           (THE CURRENT.JOB OF MILL IS (LIST.OF (?CLOCKTIME ?MJOB)
                                                 ))
                           (THE CURRENT.JOB OF GRINDER IS (LIST.OF (?CLOCKTIME
                                                 ?GJOB)))
                           (THE HOUR OF CLOCK IF ?CLOCKTIME)
                           (= ?ONE.MORE (ADD1 ?CLOCKTIME))
                        THEN IN.NEW.AND.WORLD
                           (CHANGE.TO (THE HOUR OF CLOCK IS ?ONE.MORE))
                           (FOR (THE NEW.NEXT.TASK OF ?MACHINEX IS ?JOBX)
                            ALWAYS (THE NEXT.TASK OF ?MACHINEX IS ?JOBX))
                           (DELETE (THE CURRENT.JOB OF ?MACHINE IS ?JOB)))))
```

Figure 3: MACHINESHOP Rules

by the keyword *Believe* and action rules by other keywords; here *In.New.World* , *Do* and *In.New.And.World*).

Action rules can be used in a "merge-mode" where an action rule creates a new world that is a merge of every world in which any of its conditions is true (provided the new world is internally consistent). Note that the merged world will contain all the changes made in each of its parent worlds.

For the Machine Shop problem, the first world is initialized to assign PENDING.TASKS and a NEXT.TASK to each job. The HOURS.REMAINING.RULE constrains the schedule so that a world where the remaining tasks for a particular job exceed the hours remaining in the day is marked as inconsistent. The PICK.A.JOB rule generates the worlds representing the choice points - one choice point per machine. The SELECT.JOB.FOR.MACHINE rule makes a choice by allocating some job to a machine. It assigns a CURRENT.JOB to a machine and moves the PENDING.TASKS and NEXT.TASK of each job ahead to the appropriate values for those slots. The UPDATE.CLOCK rule moves the scheduler on to the next hour. The cycle begins again as the hour has been advanced by the UPDATE.CLOCK rule. Forward chaining continues since the conclusion of the UPDATE.CLOCK rule matches the condition of the SELECT.JOB.FOR.MACHINE rule.

Worlds marked as inconsistent can be examined (see Figure 5) to ascertain causes of failures.

Worlds are created until a terminating condition is reached (here the clock stops after 8 hours). Several good solutions to the problem are generated. One solution is shown below (see Figure 6).

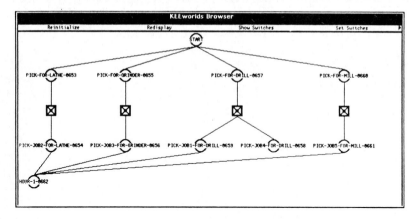

Figure 4:   MACHINESHOP worlds graph

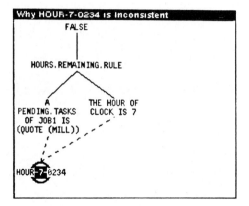

Figure 5:   An Inconsistent World

This scheduling problem using TMS-based multiple worlds was modeled with five simple rules, provides detailed graphic and textual depiction of each state of the problem, and has explanation facilities for failed solutions.

8. Summary

The use of a TMS multiple worlds facility allows for the maintenance of models of multiple hypothetical situations. Because states are saved as worlds, they can be analyzed in detail and compared. When undesirable states are generated, the user can return easily to previous states and analyze them to decide where to go next. Causes of failure can be identified. Constraints are automatically propagated across worlds, so bad search paths are immediately pruned.

Multiple worlds facilities provide good access to information, gains in efficiency due to information sharing and reduction in search, and ease of use.

Figure 6: Solution: Schedule for
World Hour-8-0405

References

[1] Bock, Conrad, Notes on the (A)TMS. IntelliCorp, Knowledge Systems Division, Mountain View, California, 1985.

[2] deKleer, Johan, Choices without Backtracking. <u>Proceedings of the National Conference on Artificial Intelligence</u>, 1984.

[3] deKleer, Johan, An Assumption-based TMS. <u>Artificial Intelligence</u>, Vol. 28, No. 1, 1986.

[4] Doyle, J., A Truth Maintenance System. <u>Artificial Intelligence</u>, Vol. 12, No. 3, 1979.

[5] Doyle, J., Expert Systems and the "Myth" of Symbolic Reasoning. <u>IEEE Transactions on Software Engineering</u>, Vol. SE-11, No. 11 1985.

[6] Faught, William, A Few Comments on the Context Mechanism/ATMS/KEEworlds. IntelliCorp, Knowledge Systems Division, Mountain View, California, 1985.

[7] Fikes, Richard, Philip McBride and Marilyn Stelzner, An Introduction to KEEworlds in KEE 3.0. Talk presented to IntelliCorp, Mountain View, California, September 20, 1985.

[8] Kunz, John, Thomas Bonura, Raymond E. Levitt, and Marilyn Stelzner, Contingent Analysis for Project Management Using Multiple Worlds. IntelliCorp, Knowledge Systems Division, Mountain View, California, 1985.

[9] McAllester, D., A Three-valued Truth Maintenance System, S.B. Thesis, Department of Electrical Engineering, Cambridge: M.I.T., 1978.

[10] McAllester, D., An Outlook on Truth Maintenance. Artificial Intelligence Laboratory, AIM-551 Cambridge: M.I.T., 1980.

[11] McDermott, Drew, Contexts and Data Dependencies: A Synthesis. IEEE Transactions on Pattern Analysis and Machine Intelligence, Vol. 5, No. 3, 1983.

[12] Morris, Paul H. and Robert A. Nado, Representing Actions with an Assumption-Based Truth Maintenance System. IntelliCorp, Mountain View, 1986.

[13] Williams, Chuck, ART The Advanced Reasoning Tool - Conceptual Overview. Inference Corporation, Los Angeles, 1984.

Advances in Artificial Intelligence - II
B. Du Boulay, D. Hogg and L. Steels (Editors)
© Elsevier Science Publishers B.V. (North-Holland), 1987

THE MACHINE FOR ARTIFICIAL INTELLIGENCE
APPLICATIONS : MAIA

J.P. Sansonnet

LABORATOIRES de MARCOUSSIS, CR-CGE
Route de Nozay
91460 Marcoussis - FRANCE

ABSTRACT

The CNET at Lannion together with the CGE at Marcoussis are currently designing a Machine for Artificial Intelligence Applications : MAIA. This is a single-processor single-user computer supporting both LISP and PROLOG; MAIA is equipped with a real-time multitasking operating system, based upon the SCEPTRE real-time kernel. It is completly integrated with LISP and specially dedicated to robotics and industrial process control. It features the conventional functions of professional workstations : bitmap screen, mouse, local network etc. The machine is based upon a symbolic processor which is interfaced with the outside world by the VME-32 standard bus. The architecture of the symbolic processor is dedicated to tree structures and lists processing. It allows MAIA to satisfy the growing requirements of Artificial Intelligence : high level software environments, powerful symbolic computation, large memory space.

1. INTRODUCTION

1.1 The situation in the USA

The development of Artificial Intelligence during the 1970s gave rise to new needs for specialised hardware. These demands on hardware were accompanied by a pressing need to develop written applications in symbolic computing languages : LISP and its different dialects, PROLOG, etc; The complexity of the data processed made evident almost immediately that the engineer would need a programming environment with high-order functions allowing for non-dissuasive response times. Thus were born the first Artificial Intelligence workstations, featuring four essential caracteristics: machine availability, a sophisticated programming environment, high-order interactive means, and, above all, powerful symbolic computing capacity. At MIT in 1973 was designed a machine specialised in the execution of LISP. Many models – CONS, CADR, LM2 – have been built and marketed by SYMBOLICS and LMI. From its beginnings, MIT's LISP machine was designed as a top-of-the-line personal professional computer, possessing a data path of 32 bits. There is also a virtual memory management system that uses high-performance disks. Single users communicate by using a bitmap screen and a mouse.

At about the same time researchers at XEROX were taking a similar route, but their goal was to build a microprogrammable computer for general use. A powerful workstation, the DORADO, was developed, into which several independent software environments were built for different languages : MESA, SMALLTALK, LISP, etc. The LISP-related environment developed by XEROX took advantage of the company's long experience with the dialect INTERLISP. It is available on 1108 stations, derived from DORADO, and more modest in performance.

Workstations experienced real success in the USA at the beginning of the 1980s. Several firms : PERK, SUN, APOLLO, etc. offered hardware prossessing, to different degrees, those of an Artificial Intelligence workstation's essential elements. Yet even if these companies offered LISP or PROLOG in their catalogues, the machines, admittedly, were not specifically designed for Artificial Intelligence. Their performance in this domain are often merely passable with regard to the integration of Artificial Intelligence systems and languages and to rapid execution.

1.2. The Fifth generation

In 1980 the Japanese challenged the West in two ways. The first challenge is technological. Japanese companies that took large market shares in electronics seek to make their supremacy permanent. The second challenge is, above all, cultural, for Japan is keen to show that it is the country of the "new frontier", on which its scientists and industrialists are willing to work together. Artificial Intelligence was chosen as the battlefield, and quite rightly so, considering its importance in the next ten years of technological development. ICOT, grouping together researchers and industrialists, launched a project to develop fifth-generation computers, designed entirely as a function of Artificial Intelligence. Any examination of the ICOT researchers' guidelines reveals that the four elements of Artificial Intelligence workstations are included and transcended. Already such "first-generation" machines as the PSI are being developed in Japanese universities with operational characteristics not unlike MIT's LISP machine. However, true fifth-generation machines, those capable of parallel unification, await the new technologies needed to build them.

1.3. The M3L Project

Europe's wait-and-see attitude towards Artificial Intelligence has disappeared with the advent of the ESPRIT project, designed to pick up the gauntlet thrown by the Japanese. For many years France and Europe had been out of the running in the race to build Artificial Intelligence computers. One of the exceptions to this situation occurred at Toulouse's University with the achievement of a LISP-machine called M3L.This project began in 1977, and in 1980 a model incorporating a microprogrammed LISP interpreter had been built. In 1982, the machine included a kernel system, and a small environment based on the Université de Vincennes' VLISP design. Although a small machine with a 16-bit data path, M3L long held the speed record for LISP interpretation. Indeed, the architecture of its CPU and the organisation of its central memory are remarkable for their originality and specially-designed capability to handle trees and lists. His qualities enabled M3L to rival many of the best American and Japanese research projects. Still, the M3L's operational limitations have presented its being developed directly for commercial marketing.

The successful work completed on the M3L led the CNET in Lannion, and the CGE, at its research laboratory in Marcoussis, to work together on developing MAIA (Machine for Artificial Intelligence Applications) as a way to respond better to Artificial Intelligence's growing needs. While MAIA takes up the ideas of M3L, it differs fundamentally in both hardware and software as a result of different choices made during the period of operational specifications.

2. THE STANDARDS OF THE MAIA SYSTEM

2.1 Software Standards

2.1.1 Common-LISP

The Common LISP standard was retained as the base for the software environment of MAIA. The Common LISP standard is made up of a set of hundreds of functions that go together to form an accounting kernel. All software written with these functions can be used on all the sites supporting Common LISP. Thus, all the software written in Common LISP are directly transferable to MAIA. Another interesting feature is this standard's high-level compatibility with such developed software as MacLISP (MULTICS) an the widely-used Franz LISP (UNIX). Of course Common LISP is not without its critics. First, some users feel the kernel is too large. Admittedly, certain implementations, on conventional machines are quite awkward. They overwork the machines, making multiple-user work difficult. With several workstations this shortcoming disappears, for all the resources of the machine are at the disposal of a single user. The Zeta LISP system (SYMBOLICS 3600), much more powerful than Common LISP with its system extensions, editor, graphics, etc., is a good example of this, a complex system functioning with ease. A second criticism arises from the power of the functions and their generality. In effect, most Common LISP functions make extended use of genericity and work as far as it is possible with the concept of typed data. Applying this concept to conventional machines can often rise serious problems, leading, in part, to the unwieldiness of existing implementations. Once again, new machines have an advantage here, being generally microprogrammable and equipped with mechanisms enabling management of class descriptors and, consequently, the integration of class check directly into the hardware. It is clear that Common LISP, at its inception, was designed to be useful for Artificial Intelligence machines. This consideration reinforced our decision to adopt it.

2.1.2. MAIALOG

The LISLOG model, developed by the CNET, served as the basis for the definition of PROLOG for MAIA : MAIALOG. As in LISLOG, the sucessful coupling of LISP and PROLOG can be found in MAIALOG. Thus any LISP expression can be inserted in MAIALOG, enabling the latter to be used with great flexibility. Movement from MAIALOG to LISP is done through the intermediary of a predicate : *LISPEVAL*. Conversely, MAIALOG is accessible to LISP through the intermediary of a predefined function : *LOGIC*.

Although MAIALOG has a good degree of originality, we wanted it to be entirely compatible with the main implementations of PROLOG. Therefore, MAIALOG has a C-PROLOG mode and PROLOG-II mode. Moreover, to ensure easy compatibility between LISP and PROLOG, MAIALOG programs use also a LISP syntax in the LISP mode. Further, the objects of MAIALOG – constants, variants, terms – are built from LISP objects. Yet another important feature of MAIALOG implementation lies in the representation by uniform structure in clauses, literals, and terms. To take but one example : the representation of functional symbols and literal lists by terms and literals, thus enlarging the unification procedure.

Aside from its *LISPEVAL* predicate that offers MAIALOG users the entirety of the Common LISP world, the MAIALOG system possesses evaluative predicates for its own input/output, resolution control (e.g. slash), clause manipulation, class testing, arithmetical operations, and many other features. It also includes an interpreter and a compiler, as well as a programming environment containing a range of tools – clause editor, manipulating and debugging of programs. The clause editor enables the user to perform operations of clause creation, modification, or deletion on the basis of the system's knowledge. The trace module allows users to follow program execution in detail and, if need be, to alter the execution by inducing a sub-goal failure or reactivating an already resolved sub-goal.. MAIALOG programs are structured as Knowledge bases. The operations performed by the user on these knowledge bases are subject to strict control in order to reduce to the minimum possible errors of syntax or non-defined references before program execution.

2.1.3. The system Extensions

LISP lends itself very well to the integration of new functions. It is easy to define extensions and add them on to the standard functions in order to create a new, larger system. This property has given rise to the numerous dialects now in existence. The Common LISP standard takes into account this particularity of LISP by allowing for a mode of integration of a wide range of extensions. Three parts comprise all Common LISP systems :

– The Core (Kernel), made up of standard functions, common to all systems. The core ensures the portability of LISP programs, written in terms of the core, to other systems.

– Language Extensions vary from system to system. They allow the inclusion of new objects and access functions to these objects in the definition of special purpose over-languages. For example : these extensions will be used to instal the object-oriented language of MAIA : LORE.This language is written in Common-LISP and is already running on several Common-LISP sites : VAX, SUN, SYMBOLICS.

– System Extensions vary as well. They influence all the software tools helping the user. On a machine already equipped with a traditional operating system, such extensions are few in number. They only ensure the relay between LISP and the system's control (cf. Franz VAX-UNIX). On LISP machines or those in which the environment system is directly integrated with the language (rather than left up to a traditional operating system), extensions play a greater part.

In many type of specialised workstations (e.g. MIT's LISP-machine, XEROX's MESA-machine), the environment system is completely developed in high-level language. This concept has proved very successful for several reasons. In a single-user station, numerous operating system functions have been radically simplified or eliminated altogether. High-level language eases the writing of basic service functions, usually simple interfaces between resources – editor, files , local networks, bitmap screens – and the programmer. As a result, the writing of specific tools is often easier than the adaptation of a traditional system both to hardware resources and to a high-level language system . The result if far more homogeneous, and the integration of system primitives into the language allows the user to include tools of his own making. This makes environment-building completely incremental and is the reason why, in MAIA, service functions are developed in LISP and defined as system extensions of Common LISP. MAIA's software consists of, aside from interpreters and compilers for LISP and PROLOG, a complete interactive graphic system : Window Manager, Video Editor with menus and designation by a mouse, file manager with directories, a local network manager, an interactive debugging system, and, most importantly, a real-time multitasking execution kernel.

Our main objective in laying out MAIA's operational specifications was to create a station that could be used for Artifical Intelligence applications which have real-time constraints, such as intelligent control in the industrial area. Today LISP-based workstations were designed for a single user. Later, multitasking functions were developed in high-level language, over and above the original system. However, it is not always possible to make certain functions within the heart of the system work properly, unless the means of their inclusion were foreseen and built into the hardware. On these machines the occurrence of a page fault, for example, does not commute with the task undertaken ; the machine must wait for the page's reappearance from the disk or for the time-slice to be finished. As a result, these machines adequately meet the multitasking needs of programmers but fail in such constrained real-time situations as robotics or production control. With MAIA, multitasking influenced the hardware architecture and the system's implementation. MAIA's multitasking manager is written directly in the assembly-language, and it is based on the *SCEPTRE standard* for real-time applications. It contains a task scheduler and interruptions handlers. It features also a virtual memory manager integated with a garbage collector. Garbage collecting capacity should also meet real-time constraints. With these it is impossible to use conventional garbage collecting algorithms because the recycling of objects can shut down the operation for more than an hour. This is why we have chosen an *ephemeral incremental Baker-based* algorithm that can be actived periodically by the task commutator.

2.2. Hardware Standards

2.2.1. A back-end Symbolic Processor

On the operational level, MAIA is organised as a back-end symbolic processor. The machine is made up of two entirely different worlds : the world of symbolic processing and the outside world. The former is based on the "Processeur SYmbolique" (PSY). PSY is the part of MAIA specialised in the data processing operations found in Artificial Intelligence. It contains many unconventional characteristics, such as a 40-bit datapath. Compared to the world of traditional computers, PSY is a completly special architecture ; hence we wanted a very good communication between the symbolic processor and the outside world. For this purpose the VME standard bus has been chosen.

2.2.2. The VME Bus

MAIA can be viewed as a VME processor. The European VME-16/32 bus offers an extremely close link between PSY and any system using the VME standard. It supports looser links as well : V24 lines, local networks, etc. A certain number of places are reserved in the back-plane for VME standard cards : So great advantage is taken of the numerous standard products available in OEM. For example, the first place is reserved for the SBC 68000 front-end card which manages the bus, starts up the symbolic processor, makes diagnostics and maintenance, and performs physical inputs / outputs. Other places are available for different types of configurations : anything from simple V24 lines to a complete system supporting UNIX. In this manner it is possible to propose a large number of operational configurations for MAIA, all based on the same symbolic processor.

2.2.3. Local network

A single-user workstation must necessarily be linked to a community. The commonest way to do this is to link the station to a local area network. MAIA will use a local network of the Ethernet type, (with the tcp-ip standard) supported by a VME card in hardware and integrated in the form of a Common LISP extension into the software system. Thanks to this network, MAIA will be able to be closely connected to traditional systems, in particular to those supporting UNIX. Thus it will be able to benefit from central services included in a network.

THE STANDARDS OF THE MAIA SYSTEM

MAIALISP is an implementation of **Common-LISP**
MAIALOG is compatible with **C PROLOG, PROLOG-I**
EMILE is like **EMACS video editor**

ETHERNET using the protocole **TCP-ip**
SCEPTRE normalised real-time kernel
VME Bus normalised European Bus

3. THE EXECUTION MODEL

3.1. The Representation of Programs

3.1.1. A Language-Machine

As with many specialised workstations, MAIA is a language-machine. With a language-machine the user has the impression that the hardware is directly executing the high-level language he is using. He no longer need take into consideration internal representations that are always dependent on the hardware and that must be re-learned at every modification. For the user, machine and language are one; hence, the tendency to speak of BASIC-machine, PASCAL-machine, etc. From their inception, Artificial Intelligence computers have adopted this strategy. Already LISP-machines exist (SYMBOLICS 3600, LMI lambda, XEROX 1108, TEXAS EXPLORER...), and soon PROLOG-machines will make their appearance. Some language-machines such as MAIA, are both LISP-machines and PROLOG-machines.

In an ordinary computer the strategy for executing programs never varies. The programmer establishes his algorithms and then writes them out in a high-level language. Thus, the resulting text is the external representation of his program. To enable execution this text must be compiled in assembly language. In a language-machine the execution model is different, relying on an intermediate level of language, which is internal and called macrocode. Its semantics are far more powerful than traditional assembly languages. In this model the compilation phase, which consists of translating the source language into macrocode, still exists, but it is very simplified. The macrocode is then totally handled by the hardware, the macrodode primitive being directly interpreted by microprograms. Recent strides in microprogramming have made possible the development of increasingly powerful micro-interpreters, which in turn can use more complex and powerful semantics. This property is of particular interest in the field of Artificial Intelligence, which is availing itself of these new possibilities. Indeed, Artificial Intelligence languages use very high-level concepts, and the semantic gap separating them from assembly languages is far greater than for numeric processing languages.

3.1.2. The return to the compiling scheme

The M3L machine built at the Université de Toulouse represents an extreme cas of language-machine. As a matter of fact, M3L's macrocode is, quite simply, the internal representation of LISP programs (i.e. a binary tree). As a result, the microprogrammed interpreter is none other than the LISP interpreter itself. This strategy was largely influenced by the Vincennes school, which defended the choice of the *interpretative mode* and developed, in the 1970s, the fastest LISP interpreters. During this time in the USA, compilers were being built that improved on the LISP-machines by an order of magnitude. For this reason we put aside the totally interpretative scheme and adopted for MAIA a more traditional machine-language scheme : the source text, LISP or PROLOG, is translated into **LEM**, the MAIA's macrocode. This language is composed of about seventy instructions whose fixed format, on 40 bits, resembles that of an assembly code. However, LEM's instruction semantic is far more powerful and the functions it handles are specially chosen for the manipulation of primitive objects that make up the structures of symbolic data.

In MAIA's execution model, the emphasis is placed on the Common LISP compiler, the normal LISP program execution mode being a compiled mode. Needless to say, for those applications requiring a dynamic execution mode, the compiler calls directly on the evaluator. In fact, the total interpenetration of the two modes offers great speed for traditional computing functions and dynamic execution for functions common in Artificial Intelligence operations. The compiler's prime rôle can be shown by the fact that the interpreter is not hand-coded in LEM assembly code but is written in Common LISP and compiled. The execution model is the same for PROLOG, but the interpreter is hand-coded in LEM. This is possible because PROLOG's interpreter can take advantage of the LISP environment and is not weighted down by numerous service functions, as is Common LISP's. The hand-coding of the PROLOG interpreter enables better use to be made of MAIA's hardware characteristics, thus improving its performance.

3.2. Representation of Data

In both LISP and PROLOG a certain number of primitive data structures are used to build the objects of the language. In LISP, for example, cells are needed for lists, fixed structures for atoms . in MAIALOG, cells are needed to represent clauses, fixed structures for variables. From the very first implementation of LISP and PROLOG on a MAIA simulator, two things became apparent : first, the primitive structures used by LISP and PROLOG are very similar ; second, they can be classified into three categories :

◊ **The MAIA Pointer** is the basic element, composed of a 40-bit word organised in four main fields :

39	37	31		0
M	D	TAG	VAL	

- **M** (1 bit) serves as a mark for certain objects
- **D** (1 bit) is reserved for activating daemons
- **TAG** (6 bits) is the descriptor of objects of LISP, PROLOG, system, etc.
- **VAL** (32 bits) is a value that is considered either as a virtual address or an immediate data (integer number, real number, character) according to the descriptor.

There are further sub-fields in MAIA's pointer : bytes, 16-bit half-words, and of course, the 40 bits can be manipulated as a whole. In the CPU of MAIA there is a specialised hardware operator that provides access to reading, writing, and modifying all of these sub-fields independently.

◊ **The Frames,** or boxed vectors in MacLISP terminology, are MAIA pointer vectors, of arbitrary size. They are accessed by a traditional indexed addressing.

◊ **The Binary Blocks** are special frames. Their size is 2, 4, 8, or 16 words. They serve to pave areas containing fixed-size objects. For example : the cell-area is composed of binary boxes of two elements ; the atom-area, of binary blocks of eight elements. MAIA's hardware favors such structures, making great use of their ability to offer instant access for each of the fields of each of the words in a binary block.

4. ARCHITECTURE OF THE SYMBOLIC PROCESSOR

4.1. Synoptic

The symbolic processor is made up of three processing units. The symbolic computing unit executes LISP and PROLOG. The virtual memory manager takes care of the disk and page changes along with the main memory. Finally the graphic operator controls the bitmap screen, the keyboard, and the mouse. These three units are linked to the main memory by point to point connections : address/data/control. The main memory is composed of one to four banks, each having a complete controller, thus enabling total interconnection among the three processing units.

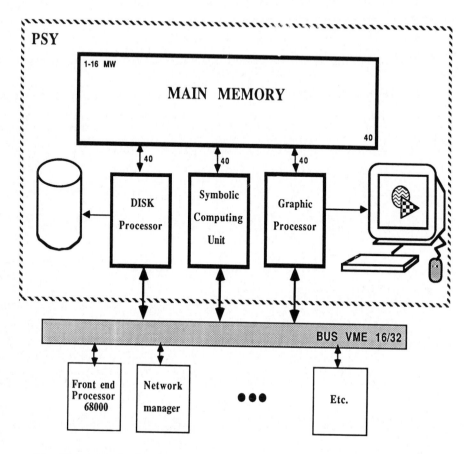

4.2. The symbolic Computing Unit

The symbolic computing unit is the heart of MAIA. It executes the LEM language. Our wish to make this unit powerful led us to build it through rapid TTL technology. It is constructed from microprocessor in AMD (8 bit) slices that use the TTL/ECL technology known as IMOX.

The symbolic computing unit is itself composed of two subunits that possess their own clocks and work in an asynchronous manner. The processing unit performs actions on objects while the control unit seeks subsequent LEM instructions. This capacity for anticipation contributes to a pipeline level within the symbolic computing unit. The processing unit and control unit are microprogrammed. The type of microprogramming is horizontal, approximately 200 bits for the processing unit and 100 bits for the control unit. This is made possible by the closeness of the LEM concepts and the material operators supporting them : the ratio is 2.7 micro-instructions for one LEM instruction. This characteristic offers the great advantage of allowing parallel control of the multiple data paths of the two units, thus notably fastening the execution time of LEM instructions.

4.3. The Hierarchy of Memories

The memory architecture of MAIA is organised around the MAIA pointer ; the memory formats and datapaths are 40 bit wide. MAIA's adressing capacity is 2^{32} words of 40 bits (more than 21 billion of bytes). To support this addressing space, MAIA has a memory hierarchised on three levels : disk, main memory, and caches.

The memory is structured into 512-word pages. A mapping table is situated in the symbolic computing unit. It is manged in part by a microcode which enables rapid computation of the real iaddress in relation to the virtual address to be effected and allows for determination of page faults. These page faults are taken into account by MAIA's kernel system. This system is helped by a disk manager that takes care of all exchanges between the disk and the main memory and of the disk itself. The main memory's size varies from1 to 16 mega-words ; the size of the standard disk is 470 megabytes.

There are two specialised caches in the symbolic computing unit. The program cache contains the LEM instructions undergoing execution. It is organised into 64-word pages and uses a mapping table that is read by the microcode for page swapping with the main memory. Part of PROLOG and LISP primitives, as well as the system's kernel, reside in the program cache. With an access time of about 35 ns, these primitives are as good as microprogrammed. The data cache contains the heads of stacks. It doesn't have a mapping table, but it is managed by a rotating algorithm : the top four pages of the stacks are always maintained in the cache. Many LISP and PROLOG programs use only these permanently-maintained pages in the data cache.

4.4 The Bitmap

MAIA has a bitmap graphic operator of its own. This choice might a first seem surprising, for the simple reason that it is easy to use a commercially available graphic operator on a VME bus. However, the setting up for the user of a highly-interactive integrated LISP environment precludes the easier solution. In effect, to make graphic objects-windows, character polices, LISP objects, the graphic operator must have knowledge of these objects in the virtual memory space of MAIA. Graphic interaction, in a MAIA-like environment, represents a sub-group peculiar to the world of graphic processing : the basic objects are windows and characters ; the manipulation of windows together with the *draw-char* functions represents the 90 percent of primitives required to the graphic operator. These objects and functions are defined as an extension language of Common LISP. They are therefore totally integrated into the language, just as cells or integer numbers are. Once this is realised the function of graphic interaction should be seen as indissociable from the symbolic processor. However, it should be said that this in no way excludes a processor specialised in image processing being placed on the VME bus for intelligent applications in that area.

The graphic operator runs the black-and-white high-resolution screen (1024 x 1024 pixels), the keyboard, and the mouse. It is organised around a 16-bit AMD 29116 microprocessor. This microprogrammable unit has a very rapid cycle time (120 ns), allowing it to perform traditional drawing and *bitblt* functions very efficiently. As for hardware, the operator runs MAIA's windowing system. Exceptional performance is the outcome, making different operational characteristics attractive to the user : a window *along with its contents* can be rapidly displaced ; writing in several windows at once, even if partially or completely hidden, is also possible, which notably improves the workings of stations for control in real time.

5. CONCLUSION

The design and writing of the basic software and the hardware for MAIA were entirely done in LISP. At first it was coded in Franz LISP on VAX, while it is now operational on both VAX-UNIX and SYMBOLICS. It is made up of an emulator of the hardware portion of the symbolic computing unit and of a complete development environment for the LEM language. This development process is entirely based in the macro-expansion in LISP. It is also used in the Common LISP compiler for generating the microcode. A large portion of MAIA software is already written or in the debugging stage.

Both dynamic and static measures have been taken on small, but significant, samples to validate, one by one, some architectural features. It should be noted that the computing power afforded by LISP on VAX or SYMBOLICS is already adequate to effect non-trivial simulations. the measures taken thus far clearly justify the choices made regarding symbolic processing and foreshadow a marked improvement over the performance of existing LISP machines. As for PROLOG, the gain in speed is even greater, since conventionnal implementations are still done on non-directly dedicated hardware.

Presently, MAIA's hardware is achieved. Four prototypes have been constructed and have been running since October, 1984. For the moment these prototypes are executing simplified software composed of a monitor into which a LISP interpreter containing 150 functions and modified for multitasking experimentation has been built. These prototypes have allowed us to validate critical parts of MAIA's architecture : the asynchronicity of the symbolic computing unit and the main memory's buses. In 1986, several new machines of the second generation are expected. The basic software of MAIA is written and has been validated on the development environment and will be installed on the prototypes.

REFERENCES

[1]   J.P. SANSONNET, M. CASTAN and C. PERCEBOIS, *"M3L : A list-directed Architecture"*, pp. 105-112 in ACM-IEEE International Symposium on Computer Architecture, La Baule (France) (May 1980).

[2]   J.P. SANSONNET, C. PERCEBOIS, D. BOTELLA and J. PEREZ, *"Direct Execution of Lisp on a List-Directed Architecture"*, pp. 132-139 in Symposium on Architectural Support for Programming Languages and Operating Systems, Palo Alto (USA) March 1982).

[3]   A. BAWDEN, R. GREENBLATT, J. HOLLOWAY, T. KNIGHT, D. MOON, D. WEINREB, " *LISP-Machine Progress report"*, MEMO 444 MIT, August 1977.

[4]   T.F. KNIGHT, Jr. D.A. MOON, J. HOLLOWAY, G.L. STEELE Jr., *"The CADR micro-processor"*, Symbolics inc., 1981.

[5]   E.A. FEUSTEL, *"On the advantages of tagged architecture"*, IEEE Transactions on computer vol. C-22 n° 7, July 1973.

[6]   L.W. HOEVEL, *"Ideal - directly executable languages - An analytical element for emulation"*, IEEE Transactions on computer vol C-23 n° 8, 1974.

[7]   T. MOTO OKA, *fifth generation computer systems*, North Holland - 1982.

[8] H. NISHIHAWA et al. *The personal sequential inference machine : PSI ; its design philosophy and machine architecture* - ICOT TR-013, 1983.

[9] S. BOURGAULT, M. DINCBAS and J.P. LEPAPE, *"The LISLOG System"*, NT/LAA/SLC186, CNET Lannion - France (1984).

[10] F. BROWAEYS, H. DERRIENIC, P. DESCLAUD, H. FALLOUR, C. FAULLE, J. FEBVRE, J.E. HANNE, M. KRONENTAL, J.J. SIMON and D. VOJNOVIC, *"Sceptre : Proposed Standard For a Real-Time Executive Kernel"* TSI 3 (1) pp. 45-62 (1984).

[11] G.L. STEELE Jr., *Common LISP Reference Manual*, Digital Press (1984).

[12] D.A. MOON and D. WEINREB, *LISP Machine Manual*, MIT, Cambridge, Mass (January 1979).

[13] R.A. BROOKS, R.P. GABRIEL *"A critique of Common Lisp"*, Conference Records of the 1984 Symposium on Lisp and Functional Programming, pp. 1-8 (August 1984).

[14] R.A. BROOKS, R.P. GABRIEL and G.L. STEELE Jr., *"S-1 Common Lisp Implementation"* Conference Records of the 1982 Symposium on Lisp and Functional Programming, pp. 108-113 (August 1982).

[15] J. COHEN, *"Garbage Collection of Kinked Data Structures"* Computing Survey 13 (3) pp. 341-367 (1981).

[16] H.G. BAKER, *"List Processing in Real Time on a Serial Computer"* Communications of the ACM 21 (4) pp. 280-294 (April 1978).

-oOo-

PART V

VISION and ROBOTICS

Advances in Artificial Intelligence - II
B. Du Boulay, D. Hogg and L. Steels (Editors)
© Elsevier Science Publishers B.V. (North-Holland), 1987   587

Weak continuity constraints generate uniform
scale-space descriptions of plane curves.

A. Blake, A. Zisserman, A.V. Papoulias[*].

Department of Computer Science,
King's Buildings, Mayfield Rd,
Edinburgh, Scotland.

ABSTRACT
Scale-space filtering (Witkin 83) is a recently developed technique,
both powerful and general, for segmentation and analysis of signals.
Asada and Brady (84) have amply demonstrated the value of
scale-space for description of curved contours from digitised
images. Weak continuity constraints (Blake 83a,b, Blake and
Zisserman 85,86) furnish novel, powerful, non-linear filters, to use
in place of gaussians, for scale-space filtering. This has some
striking advantages (fig 1). First, *scale-space is uniform*, so that
tracking across scale is a trivial task. *Structure need not be
preserved* to indefinitely fine scale; this leads to an enrichment of
the concept of scale - a rounded corner, for example, can be
represented as a discontinuity at coarse scale but smooth at fine
scale. And finally boundary conditions at ends of curves are handled
satisfactorily - it is as easy to analyse open curves as closed ones.

---

[*]Currently with: TEMA SpA (ENI), Viale Aldo Moro 38, 40217 Bologna, Italy.

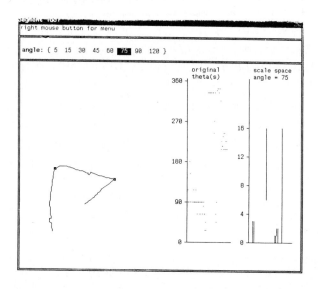

Fig. 1. Curve segmentation by weak continuity constraints. From left to right: a hand drawn curve; angle/arc-length data (note quantisation noise); scale-space, at angle sensitivity of 75° - note: 1. vertical lines (uniformity) 2. the rounded corner disappears from scale-space at fine scale (non-preservation of structure) and 3. structure near curve ends causes no problems for segmentation (there are no spurious discontinuities near the ends).

1. Weak continuity constraints

Weak continuity constraints are a principled and effective treatment of the localisation of discontinuities in discrete data. Detailed discussions are given in (Blake 83a, Blake83b, Blake and Zisserman 85, Blake and Zisserman 86). Applications in computer vision include curve description, edge detection, reconstruction of $2\frac{1}{2}$D surfaces from stereo or laser-rangefinder data, and others. This paper deals with the application of weak continuity constraints to description of plane curves. First a brief summary of weak continuity constraints is given for problems like curve description, in which the data is a 1D array. Data may be obtained from a plane curve as an array θ_i of tangent angle values at equal spacings in arc-length s.

The problem is to localise discontinuities in noisy, discrete data. The notion of a discontinuity applies to functions, not to discrete arrays, so the problem is ill-posed, and this is exacerbated by the presence of noise. One solution is to interpolate the data by a smooth function such as a gaussian, whose 1st derivative can then be examined. Of course this is common practice in edge detection and in spline interpolation (e.g. de Boor 78). Such smoothing can be regarded as fitting a function $u(s)$ which tends to seek a minimum of some elastic energy P. Energy P is traded off against a sum of squares error measure D, defined as:

$$D = \Sigma_i \, (u(s_i) - \theta_i)^2$$

by minimising variationally the total energy (or cost) $P+D$. The result is a function $u(s)$ that is both fairly smooth and is a fair approximation to the data θ_i. The simplest form of the energy P is that of a horizontal stretched string (approximately):

$$P = \lambda^2 \int (u')^2 \, ds \, ,$$

where the parameter λ governs the stiffness of the string. If λ is large then the tendency to smoothness overwhelms the tendency (from D) to approximate the data well. In the extremes, if λ is very large, the fitted function is simply $u = const$, the least squares regression of a constant function to the data θ_i; but if $\lambda \sim 0$ then u interpolates the data, linking the θ_i by straight lines.

Weak continuity constraints can be applied to a scheme like the one above, to incorporate discontinuities *explicitly* into the fitting of u above. Rather than fitting a u that is smooth everywhere and then examining the gradient u', the function u is allowed to break (at knots, in spline jargon) - it is piecewise continuous. The number and position of the discontinuities is chosen optimally, by using an augmented form of cost function $E = D + P + S$, where the additional term S embodies weak continuity constraints:

$$S = \alpha \times (\text{number of discontinuities})$$

- a fixed penalty α is paid for each discontinuity allowed. This has the effect of discouraging discontinuities; u is continuous "almost everywhere". But an occasional discontinuity may be allowed if there is sufficient benefit in terms of smoothness (P) and faithfulness to data (D) in so doing. Clearly α is some kind of measure of reluctance to allow a discontinuity.

In fact the two parameters α, λ interact in a rather interesting way. Far from being "fudge factors" that must be empirically set, they have clear interpretations in terms of scale and sensitivity (Blake and Zisserman 85,86). Here is what they signify, in the context of plane-curve segmentation:

  $\phi_0 = \sqrt{(2\alpha/\lambda)}$ is a measure of angular sensitivity. If plane curve data θ_i contains an isolated discontinuity of magnitude ϕ (e.g. two long straight line segments, joined at a vertex, making an exterior angle ϕ) then the fitted function $u(s)$ will have a discontinuity there if and only if $\phi > \phi_0$.

  λ is a characteristic scale. "Events" (e.g. steps) in the data that are separated by more than λ are treated as effectively independent by the fitting process. But events spaced less than λ apart may interact and small "glitches" in the data whose total extent is much less than λ may well be ignored - filtered out. This mechanism removes both noise and small-scale structure.

$\kappa_0 = \phi_0 / 2\lambda$ is a curvature limit. If an extended arc in the data has curvature $\kappa > \kappa_0$ then there will be a discontinuity in the fitted function u somewhere on that arc. This can be regarded as a limitation on performance - the inability to discriminate between high curvature arcs and angular discontinuities - to be traded off against the previous 2 performance measures ϕ_0, λ.

α itself is a measure of resistance to noise. If α is large compared with the variance σ^2 of the noise in the angle data, then there will be no spurious discontinuities due to noise.

2. Algorithms: graduated non-convexity (GNC) and dynamic programming.

Given a curve as a stream of coordinates (x_i, y_i), the first step is to convert it to $\theta_i(s)$ form. This is best done by dividing the stream of (x_i, y_i) into a sequence of strokes (Perkins 78) of equal lengths Δs. A stroke is formed by least squares fitting a straight line segment to the (x_i, y_i) that fall within the particular stroke. Length Δs should be chosen as short as possible to avoid blurring, but just long enough to avoid undue quantisation error. In practice, quantisation errors around $\pm 10°$ may be acceptable. The θ_i are not restricted to the range $[0°, 360°]$ but include a "winding number", so that curves with loops can be correctly represented (fig 2).

Of course, it is not quite possible in practice to fit a function $u(s)$ to the data, but only a discrete representation of $u(s)$. So $u(s)$ is approximated, in accordance with the usual practice of finite elements (see (Terzopoulos 83) for applications of finite elements to computer vision). For the simple stretched string energy P above, linear elements are sufficient. The function $u(s)$ is represented by a sequence of points u_i (at positions along the curve corresponding to the θ_i), interpolated linearly. The variational problem of the previous section becomes a discrete optimisation problem, to minimise:

$$F = \Sigma_i (u_i - \theta_i)^2 + \Sigma_i g(u_i - u_{i-1})^2$$

where the function

$$g(t) = \lambda^2 t^2 \text{ if } |t| < \sqrt{\alpha}/\lambda, \ \alpha \text{ otherwise}$$

is an interaction function between neighbouring u_i (see fig 3a) that incorporates both the membrane energy and weak continuity constraint penalties. The term $\Sigma_i g(...)^2$ above is the discrete representation of the functional $S + P$ above. Details of the discretisation, and derivation of g are given in (Blake and Zisserman 85,86).

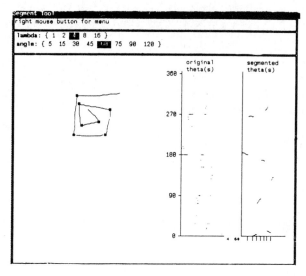

Fig 2. The θ-s representation of a curve includes winding number, so that even spirals can happily be segmented.

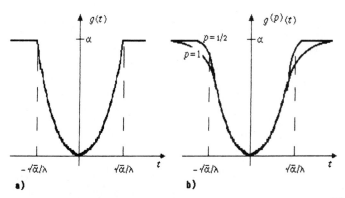

Fig 3. Neighbourhood interaction functions: (a) g for the cost function F ; (b) $g^{(p)}$ for the sequence of functions $F^{(p)}$ that approximate F.

Now a fundamental property of F is that it is non-convex, and so may have many local minima. Its global minimum cannot generally be found by naive downhill search over the u_i. A rather general way of dealing with such non-convexity is to use "simulated annealing" (Metropolis et al. 53), a stochastic method, which works for cost functions like F above (Geman and

Geman 84) but is rather expensive computationally (Marroquin 84). Here two efficient algorithms are described; both have been implemented successfully on modest serial machines.

Graduated non-convexity

"Graduated non-convexity" (GNC) is fully described in (Blake 83a,83b, Blake and Zisserman 85,86). Whereas simulated annealing uses random processes to jump out of local minima, GNC constructs a function F^* which is convex (and hence is free of spurious local minima) and approximates F well. Then a family of functions $\{F^{(p)} \, p\in[0,1]\}$ is constructed with $F^{(1)}=F^*$ and $F^{(0)}=F$, and $F^{(p)}$ varying gradually between the two as p varies from 1 to 0. The function $F^{(p)}$ is defined as F above, but with $g^{(p)}$ in place of g, where

$$g^{(p)}(t) = \alpha - c(|t|-r)^2/2 \text{ if } q \leq |t| < r, \ g(t) \text{ otherwise,}$$

where $c = 1/2p, r = \sqrt{\alpha}\sqrt{(2/c + 1/\lambda^2)}$ and $q = \alpha/(\lambda^2 r)$

- see fig 3b. The algorithm is to minimise a sequence of $F^{(p)}$ by direct descent on each one, starting with $F^{(1)}$ and ending with $F^{(0)}$. A sequence of 11 values of p {1.0,0.9,..0} proves to be more than adequate in practice. In fact, less work is needed for small λ (e.g. $\lambda \leq 4$, where the finite element between u_i, u_{i+1} has unit length) and it may be sufficient to use the convex approximation $F^* = F^{(1)}$ without bothering to descend on the remaining 10 $F^{(p)}$. But for large λ (e.g. $\lambda = 20$) the whole sequence is needed. GNC is an approximate method - it finds u_i close to the optimum of F. It has been shown, however, to be exact under certain conditions (Blake 83b, Blake and Zisserman 86). Although execution times are relatively long for large λ, multigrid methods (Terzopoulos 83) might effect a considerable improvement.

Dynamic programming

An alternative to GNC is to treat the minimisation of F as an integer programming problem, by quantising angle measures as a range of M values u_i (say to 1° or 2° accuracy), and applying dynamic programming (Bellman and Dreyfus 62). Details of this method are given in (Papoulias 85). It is applicable because the 1D vector u_i can be expressed, for all i, as a union of two sets $\{u_0,..u_i\}$ and $\{u_i,..u_N\}$ which have precisely *one* element u_i in common. Note that no equivalent family of simple decompositions exists for 2D arrays u_{ij} and hence dynamic programming is not usable for applying weak continuity constraints to 2D data, as in edge detection or surface reconstruction. Although a dynamic programming algorithm for the 2D problem could be defined, in theory, it would involve the use of tables with up to M^N entries! For similar reasons, it is not practicable to use dynamic programming for higher order energies F, involving 2nd or higher derivatives of u. Tables of size $O(M^2)$ would be required (for P involving u''). GNC is quite usable, however, both for 2D data and for 2nd order F.

Following normal dynamic programming practice, the algorithm consists largely of constructing a pair of tables (the return function f_i and the policy function p_i) for each i, each of length M. Total storage required is therefore $O(NM)$ units. The value of $f_i(u_{i+1})$ is the minimal partial cost for $u_0..u_i$, for a given value of u_{i+1}, and $p_i(u_{i+1})$ is the value of u_i at that minimum. Having constructed the tables, there remains the task (requiring relatively insignficant computation time) of tracing back through the tables, from f_N down to f_0, to recover the optimal u_i. The complexity of the algorithm is $O(NM^2)$ -so extra precision in angle quantisation (large M) is expensive. The expense can be mitigated to some degree by "table reduction" (Papoulias 85), which works as follows. For the cost function F for the weak elastic string, it transpires that each table f_i contains a non-constant interval flanked by entries all of the same constant value. Those constant entries can be treated for computational purposes as one entry. This effectively reduces the value of M. The effective M appears, in practice, to be proportional to $\sqrt{\alpha}$ (independent of λ); so the reduction may be effective even at large λ, when GNC is least efficient. In practice, reduction by a factor of up to 4 was obtained, reducing execution time by a factor of up to 16.

Comparision of GNC and dynamic programming

It has been mentioned that GNC is an approximate method, whereas dynamic programming is exact. In practice, no qualitative difference between solutions obtained from the two methods is observed; this is, in itself, a confirmation that solutions from GNC are good approximations. As for efficiency, each method has its advantages. For large values of λ GNC is slow, but (for a given α) dynamic programming continues to work well. Finally, GNC requires high precision arithmetic, unlike dynamic programming. In practice (for modest values of λ) it seems that GNC is faster on a Motorola 68000, for example, if it has adequate hardware floating-point support. For smaller values of λ, GNC runs in about 1 second (SUN 2, SKY floating point, vector length N=50, λ=2). This could be expected to improve by an order of magnitude with the new 68000 floating point co-processor.

3. Scale-space properties

This section discusses the properties of scale-space descriptions of curves, under weak continuity constraints. An example was displayed in fig 1. Several notable properties are illustrated: the most striking is the uniformity of the scale space - the locus of each discontinuity in scale space is plumb vertical. Moreover, in this scale-space, unlike gaussian scale space (Witkin, 83) in which the fingerprint theorem holds (Yuille and Poggio 84), structure is *not* preserved - discontinuities *may* be created as scale increases. We argue here that this *lack* of structure preservation is a desirable property. Four other issues are considered: how to achieve an invariant parametrisation of the curve, detection of curvature discontinuities and how to treat the "curvature limit" described in section 1, and boundary conditions for open-ended curves. Finally it is worth noting that the new scale-space has an extra parameter in addition to scale, namely angular sensitivity (ϕ_0 in section 1.). Plots of scale-space shown here are at fixed values of ϕ_0 (e.g. $75°$ in fig 1.).

Uniformity

It is apparent in fig 1 that the locus in scale-space of an individual feature (corner) is uniformly vertical, unlike gaussian scale spaces. This is a consequence of the theoretically predicted, spatial stability with respect to scale, that is inherent in optimal function fitting under weak continuity constraints (Blake and Zisserman 86). It arises because the extra cost in F, if a corner were slightly misplaced, is very large - far greater than the relatively modest extra costs introduced by spatially incoherent noise, or by extended but gentle curves (figure 4). Hence corners do not get misplaced.

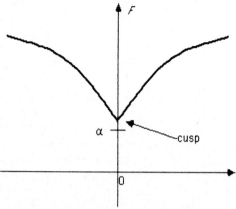

Fig. 4. The uniformity property is a consequence of the sharp, cusp-like minimum in the energy F, plotted as a function of edge position. For a displacement ϵ in edge position it can be shown (Blake and Zisserman, 86) that the corresponding F is as plotted above. Hence there is a strong attraction towards $\epsilon=0$, the true edge position.

Alternatively, in the terms of Canny's (83) performance measures, the *localisation* is very good – as good, in fact, as a difference of boxes operator. (But it doesn't have that operator's multiple response problem!) A consequence of uniformity is that any one connected contour in scale-space must belong to only *one* physical feature on the curve. This is untrue of gaussian scale-space, as fig 5. shows.

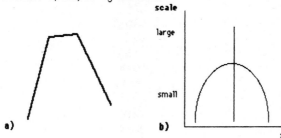

Fig. 5. The gaussian scale-space generated by a polygonal contour (a), contains a bifurcation (b) which is unstable (non-transverse). It is therefore uncertain to which fine scale zero-crossing the single coarse scale zero-crossing belongs.

Preservation of structure

Under weak continuity constraints, structure is not preserved as scale increases. There is an example of this in figure 1, in which a rounded corner is represented in scale space by a line that is present at large scale, but absent at small scale ($\lambda \in [0,6]$). This is absolutely as it should be. The rounded corner appears smooth at small scale, but as a tangent discontinuity when viewed at large scale. It seems that the ability to represent this fact is important. Whereas structure preservation is a must with gaussian filters because it guarantees a successful tracking algorithm – tracking from fine to coarse scale picks up all zero-crossings – it is redundant under weak continuity constraints. Tracking is trivial, due to uniformity.

Invariant parametrisation

A problem with any scheme that uses arclength s to parametrise curves is that the parametrisation is defined with respect to the data rather than the *interpreted* curve $u(s)$. At small scale, this could mean extreme sensitivity to sensor and quantisation noise; in a practical vision system, this would result in curve descriptions that were unstable over time. A simple solution to this is adopted by Asada and Brady (84): they obtain their data from images, by means of an edge detector that inherently supresses noise. However there remains the lesser problem, that intermediate structure could generate distortions of scale (fig 6). An elegant solution to this problem, in the context of gaussian scale space filtering, proposed by Porril (85), subjects the curve to a simulated diffusion process. Under weak continuity constraints, an invariant scheme could conceivably be attainable by fitting a curve to data supplied as a sequence of coordinate vectors $\mathbf{X}_i$, minimising curvature. Further work may be needed here.

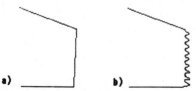

Fig 6. Non-invariance in s-parametrisation of curves. Curve (a) has two corners. Curve (b) is very similar "at large scale", but has some detail between the two corners. As a result it acquires a great deal of extra arc-length between those corners, which distorts its scale-space diagram.

Curvature limit and detection of discontinuities

It was explained in section 1 that $\kappa_0 = \phi_0/2\lambda$ is a curvature limit, such that curves of curvature $\kappa > \kappa_0$ are segmented, even if there is no curvature maximum (fig 7).

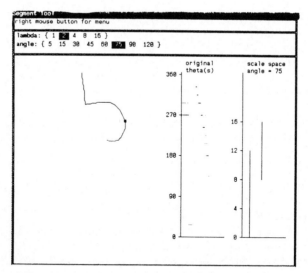

Fig 7 The gradient limit: arcs above a certain threshold curvature $\kappa_0 = \phi_0/2\lambda$ may be segmented spuriously at larger scales.

Moreover the actual point of segmentation need not be particularly spatially stable. This seems to be a limitation of the scheme, for which two partial remedies are proposed. One is to note that such segmentation points exist only at large scale - but of course there may be "genuine" structure too that exists only at large scale. A better remedy is to use a higher order scheme, in which $F = \int u''^2$. This allows both *tangent* and *curvature* discontinuities to be detected, rather than tangent only. It also pushes the "spurious" segmentation problem to higher order (i.e. spurious curvature discontinuities) - but at some extra computational expense.

Boundary conditions

A very attractive property of the proposed scheme is that boundary conditions on open-ended contours are dealt with naturally. Naive gaussian filtering generates spurious discontinuities near ends of contours, which may mask genuine features near ends. Cures are of course possible, such as using modified convolution masks near ends (thus losing the gaussian's time-saving factorisability) or a diffusion process as above. Fig 1 illustrates the correct handling of boundary conditions: the small feature near the end is treated much like the one in the middle.

Acknowledgments

The authors thank the University of Edinburgh for provision of facilities, and the SERC for funding. A. Blake is grateful for the support of the IBM Research Fellowship from the Royal Society.

References

1. Asada,H. and Brady,J.M. (1984). The curvature primal sketch. *IEEE PAMI, 8, 1,* 2-14.
2. Bellman,R. and Dreyfus,S. (1962). *Applied dynamic programming.* Princeton University Press, Princeton, USA.
3. Blake,A. (1983a). The least disturbance principle and weak constraints. *Pattern Recognition letters,* 1, 385-391.
4. Blake,A. (1983b). *Parallel computation in low-level vision,* PhD thesis, University of Edinburgh.
5. Blake,A. and Zisserman,A. (1985). Using weak continuity constraints. Report CSR-186-85, Dept. Computer Science, University of Edinburgh. Also *Pattern Recognition Letters,* in press.
6. Blake,A. and Zisserman,A. (1986). Weak continuity constraints in computer vision. Report CSR-197-86, Dept. Computer Science, University of Edinburgh.
7. Canny,J.F. (1983). *Finding edges and lines in images.* S.M. thesis, MIT, Cambridge.
8. de Boor,C. (1978). *A practical guide to splines.* Springer-Verlag, New York.
9. Geman,S. and Geman,D. (1984). Stochastic relaxation, Gibbs distributions and the Bayesian restoration of images. *IEEE trans. PAMI-6,* 6, 721-741.
10. Marroquin,J.L. (1984). Surface reconstruction preserving discontinuities. Memo 792, AI Laboratory, MIT, Cambridge, USA.
11. Metropolis,N., Rosenbluth,A.W., Rosenbluth,M.N., Teller,A.H. and Teller,E. (1953). Equation of state calculations by fast computing machines. *J. Chem. Phys.,* 6, 1087.
12. Papoulias, A. (1985). *Curve segmentation using weak continuity constraints.* M.Sc. thesis, Dept. Computer Science, University of Edinburgh.
13. Perkins, W.A. (1978). A model-based system for industrial parts. *IEEE trans. Comp.,27,* 2, 126-143.
14. Porril,J., Mayhew,J.E.W. and Frisby,J.P. (1986). Scale-space diffusion: plane and space curves. Research Memo 018, AIVRU, Sheffield University.
15. Terzopoulos, D. (1983). Multilevel computational processes for visual surface reconstruction. *CVGIP,* 24, 52-96.
16. Witkin,A.P. (1983). Scale-space filtering. *Proc. IJCAI conf. 1983,* 1019-1022.
17. Yuille,A. and Poggio,T. (1984). Fingerprints theorems. *Proc. AAAI,* 362-365.

Advances in Artificial Intelligence - II
B. Du Boulay, D. Hogg and L. Steels (Editors)
Elsevier Science Publishers B.V. (North-Holland), 1987   599

APPLICATIONS OF A FAST PARALLEL ALGORITHM
FOR THE EXTRACTION AND INTERPRETATION OF OPTICAL FLOW

Hilary Buxton and Nick Williams,
Department of Computer Science and Statistics,
Queen Mary College, London E1 4NS.

Abstract
The implementation of the SM-8-point algorithm for simultaneously solving the structure from motion and aperture problems on an SIMD parallel machine is reviewed. The computational steps and mapping of the algorithm onto the SIMD architecture is then discussed and results given illustrating the performance of the algorithm on both simulated and real image sequences. It is shown that for the ideal 1-1 mapping of the image data onto the processor array, the algorithms run at near real-time video rates. Some interesting applications of this algorithm for tracking, segmentation and scene structure and motion determination are outlined. Also, experiments are described on the integration of interpretation over time for a dynamic scene representation.

1. Introduction
There has been an increasing amount of work on the computation and description of optical flow in time varying imagery. The two main reasons for this are, first, that the characterisation of motion is important for the coding, transmission and restoration of image sequences, and second, that the optical flow field describing the motion in the image plane contains information about the three-dimensional structure of the scene. This second, important aspect of the use of visual motion was realised long ago by von Helmholtz (1925) and emphasised by Gibson (1966) among others in their work on human vision and perception. More recently, the importance of optical flow for computer vision became apparent when it was demonstrated how the three-dimensional structure could be recovered from the flow field. This means that optical flow can be used as an alternative to, or in conjunction with, binocular stereo in calculating the depth and orientation of the visible surfaces in a scene. In addition, optical flow is important for segmentation, tracking and motion analysis in computer vision.

The application of vector and parallel processors to image processing is now fairly commonplace and a number of architectures have been suggested for pattern recognition tasks (see Reeves, 1984 for a recent review). However, the use of parallel processors for three-dimensional interpretation in computer vision work is not so widespread, although SIMD machines have been used for some low-level visual tasks. Brady (1983) gives a brief survey of parallelism in computer vision including some dedicated hardware implementations. In this paper, we will describe some applications of a recently derived algorithm for obtaining three-dimensional information from visual motion (Buxton, Buxton, Murray and Williams, 1984) and its implementation on an SIMD machine, the ICL DAP at Queen Mary College.

The following section contains a brief description of how 'optical flow' or visual motion contains information about the depth and orientation of the visible surfaces and their motion relative to the sensor. The use of edge motion which can usually be accurately measured in an image sequence, rather than the full optical flow field, means that the 'aperture problem' must be solved in addition to reconstructing the missing depth information. An outline of the mathematical derivation of the solution is given in Section 3 and the implementation of a global version of the algorithm on the DAP is given in Section 4. Sections 5 and 6 describe results for reconstructing the structure and motion of the scene and a local version of the algorithm used for segmentation. Finally, some experimental results concerning the integration of interpretations over time are discussed with respect to tracking and dynamic scene representation.

2. Optical Flow
Optical flow is the motion of points in the image plane due to motion of corresponding object points relative to the sensor. The velocity of an image point $\dot{r}$ depends on the position $\underline{R} = (X,Y,Z)$ and velocity $\underline{\dot{R}}$ of the object point. In detail,

$$\dot{r} = -l\,\underline{\dot{R}}/Z + l\,\underline{R}\,\dot{Z}/Z^2 \qquad (2.1)$$

if we use the perspective transform $\underline{r} = -l\,\underline{R}/Z$ to model the geometry of the sensor which is assumed to have an effective camera length l. A number of papers have described details of the 'optical flow field' $\dot{r}(r)$ or motion over the whole of the image plane, in particular, Koenderink and van Doorn (1975), Lee (1980) and Longuet-Higgins and Prazdny (1980) and it has been shown that, in principle, the optical flow field contains enough information to allow reconstruction of structure of rigid bodies moving relative to the sensor (Ullman, 1979 and Longuet-Higgins, 1981).

Here, a slight variant of the classical 'structure from motion' problem discussed above is tackled in order to reconstruct the position and orientation of the visible surfaces in a scene. It is useful to assume that the object points lie on a planar facet $\underline{R} \cdot \underline{N} = 1$ moving with translational velocity $\underline{V}$ and angular velocity $\underline{\Omega}$ with respect to the sensor. The optical flow field $\dot{\underline{r}}(\underline{r})$ is then given by

$$\dot{\underline{r}} = \underline{V}(\underline{r} \cdot \underline{N}) + \underline{r}(\hat{\underline{z}} \cdot \underline{V})(\underline{r} \cdot \underline{N})/l + (\underline{\Omega} \times \underline{r}) + \underline{r}[\hat{\underline{z}} \cdot (\underline{\Omega} \times \underline{r})]/l \qquad (2.2)$$

In this equation, the terms involving $\underline{V}$ and $\underline{N}$ always occur as products which indicates an inherent ambiguity of the flow field, namely that small objects close by moving slowly can give rise to the same flow as large objects far away moving quickly. Given the optical flow at a small number of image points, it is possible to determine the direction of translation $\hat{\underline{V}}$ and surface orientation $\hat{\underline{N}}$, the angular velocity $\underline{\Omega}$ and the value of the product $\underline{V} \cdot \underline{N}$. In general, four interpretations may be inferred from (2.2) essentially by interchanging $\hat{\underline{V}}$ and $\hat{\underline{N}}$ or $-\hat{\underline{V}}$ and $-\hat{\underline{N}}$ etc, although only two, or sometimes one of these is compatible with the observed data. Even the residual two-fold ambiguity, if present, can be resolved by interpreting data from a subsequent frame (Longuet-Higgins, 1984). This is one of the reasons for integrating the interpretation over time (Section 7).

Before these algorithms can be used, the optical flow $\dot{\underline{r}}$ has to be calculated from the observed image irradiance $E(\underline{r},t)$. The approach used here is based on the motion constraint equation $\partial E / \partial t = -\dot{\underline{r}} \cdot \nabla E$ where ∇ is the gradient operator $(\partial/\partial x, \partial/\partial y)$ in the image plane and it is assumed that the total derivative is zero, that is, all the changes in irradiance are due to motion. A fundamental difficulty remains as only the component of the flow parallel to ∇E (perpendicular to the edge), referred to as the 'vernier velocity' $\underline{v}$ or edge motion, is obtained. The lack of information about motion perpendicular to ∇E (parallel to the edge), referred to as the 'aperture problem', is simply eliminated in the solution given in the following section.

The image irradiance values $E(\underline{r},t)$ are always corrupted by sensor noise and can smoothed using a Gaussian filter $G(\underline{r},t)$ over both space and time (see Buxton and Buxton, 1983). To obtain reliable estimates of $\underline{v}$ where both $\partial E / \partial t$ and ∇E are large at the moving edge features, the ratio of estimates of the slope in space and time is taken at the zero crossings of the visual signal

$$S(\underline{r},t) = - \left[\nabla^2 + \frac{1}{u^2}\frac{\partial^2}{\partial t^2}\right] G(\underline{r},t) * E(\underline{r},t) \qquad (2.3)$$

Details of this calculation have been given elsewhere (e.g. Buxton and Buxton, 1984) and involve spatiotemporal convolution, determining the zerocrossing locations and estimating the vernier velocity $\underline{v}$ in a small neighbourhood in space and time. The calculation maps straightforwardly onto an SIMD array as similar calculations must be performed at every pixel in the image and the masking facilities on the DAP enable a simple uniform algorithm to be written that only calculates the vernier velocity at the edge features required. A further point to note here is that these low-level calculations are extremely fast on the DAP so, for instance, for the ideal 1:1 mapping of image pixels onto the processor array (currently 64*64), calculations to obtain the vernier velocity at moving edge features located to subpixel accuracy can be carried out in approximately 36ms/frame using a mask of radius 8 pixels in space and time, even though this involves an effective 2000 pixel convolution and a least squares fit to the data in order to obtain the derivatives required in the motion constraint equation.

3. Mathematical Background to the 8-point Algorithm
The problem, then, is to interpret the edge motion by simultaneously solving the aperture and structure from motion problems. A more complete mathematical treatment can be found in Buxton,Buxton,Murray and Williams (1984). Only an overview of the derivation is presented here.

A consideration of the motion of rigid bodies through the spatial coordinate system (2.2) yields a formula involving the position $\underline{r}$ which is known, the vernier velocity $\underline{v}$ which can be measured, and the parameters we wish to find, namely $\underline{V}, \underline{\Omega}, \underline{N}$.

$$v^2 = (\underline{v} \cdot \underline{V}) + (\underline{r} \cdot \underline{N}) + (\underline{v} \cdot \underline{r})(\hat{\underline{z}} \cdot \underline{V})(\underline{r} \cdot \underline{N})/l + \underline{v} \cdot (\underline{\Omega} \times \underline{r}) + (\underline{v} \cdot \underline{r})[\hat{\underline{z}} \cdot (\underline{\Omega} \times \underline{r})]/l \qquad (3.1)$$

where the solution to the aperture problem hinges on the observation that the dot product of the tangential and the normal flow components is zero. To now solve for $\underline{V}$, $\underline{N}$ and $\underline{\Omega}$ requires the solution of a set of non-linear simultaneous equations. The parameters appearing in (3.1) may be expressed uniformly using:

$$p_{ij} = V_{ij} - \varepsilon_{ijk}\Omega_k - \delta_{ij}(V_3 N_3)$$

with the matrix of coefficients:

$$C_{ij}(m) = [v_i x_j - (\underline{v} \cdot \underline{r}) \, \delta_{i3} x_j / x_3]_m$$

where δ_{ij} is the identity matrix and ε_{ijk} is the antisymmetric matrix, as usual. Thus an expression in a form suitable for solution using the methods of linear algebra is obtained:

$$v_m^2 = \sum_{ij \neq 9} C_{ij}(m) p_{ij} \qquad (3.2)$$

The p_{ij} are found using Gauss Jordan elimination and can then be rearranged so that all the rotational components cancel leaving products of $\underline{V}$ and $\underline{N}$ only. Finding these involves the solution of five simultaneous quadratic equations, but fortunately the solution can be reduced to first solving a cubic equation for $V_3 N_3$ (Longuet-Higgins, 1984). Longuet-Higgins also shows that the middle root of this cubic may be used to generate the physical solutions for the components of $\hat{V}$ and $\hat{N}$ (to within the ambiguities mentioned above), the value of the product VN, and hence by back substitution, the angular velocity Ω. The outer two roots of the cubic may be used, if required, to find the value of $\underline{V} \cdot \underline{N}$ directly.

4. DAP Implementation of the 8 Point Algorithm

The main computational steps in the implementation of the SM-8-point algorithm above are described in detail in Buxton, Buxton, Murray and Williams (1985) and are summarised in the table below which gives the time taken for each step. The 8 coefficients are calculated at every edge point in the image and stored vertically under the DAP processing element (PE). Thus, for a 64 x 64 image the storage would be a 64 x 64 x 8 structure; henceforth CBLOCK. PE's which do not contain a zero-crossing have their 8 coefficients set to zero. Mathematically, the next stage involves selecting n edge points (n>=8) to form an (n x 8) matrix of coefficients. This process involves a selective rearrangement of the data from (conceptually) three dimensions to a planar matrix form. Initially, this was precisely how the data rearrangement was performed, with n chosen to be 64 in order that the matrix would fit in the 8 left-most columns of a DAP plane.

However, a parallel, uniform method of obtaining $[C]^t \cdot [C]$; henceforth CTXC, has been found which fully exploits the data throughput possible on the SIMD architecture. The method hinges on the observation that CBLOCK can be unfolded into an 8 x 4096 [C] matrix along a continuous seam. Thus the resulting [C] matrix can be regarded as being formed from 64, (8 x 64) arrays connected end to end, when it becomes obvious that CTXC can be obtained directly using the DAP Fortran sequence:

```
DO I=1,8|
DO J=1,8|
CTXC(I,J)=SUM(C(,,I)*C(,,J))
```

Furthermore, using the observation that the matrix of least squares coefficients is symmetric, the computation can be made even faster. Similarly, $[C]^t \cdot (v^2)$ can be obtained in a uniform parallel fashion. The rest of the computation requires no special mappings for efficiency.

Machine	Time (ms)	Operation on 64x64 image
DAP	36	Calculate the vernier velocity
DAP	4	Calculate product coefficients
DAP	35	Matrix multiplications
DAP	8	Solve 8x8 linear system (real*8)
DAP	7	DAP-2980 storage mode conversions
HOST	-	Solve the cubic
HOST	-	Calculate the structure and motion parameters
DAP	3	2980-DAP storage mode conversions
DAP	4	Find correct interpretation
Total	97	Total DAP cpu time

The time for the least-squares matrix multiplication steps is predicted by an analysis of the individual steps involved and is computationally expensive (35ms). This is still very fast considering the number of operations involved, but it is this stage in particular which should be optimised, particularly if the flow field has to be iteratively processed as may be the case if motion segmentation is required. Pseudo-inverse methods for solving rectangular linear systems could avoid the computationally expensive and time consuming least squares steps which produce the square linear system and give numerically more accurate results. Unfortunately, solution by psuedo-inverse methods in the form of a DAP library subroutine are not yet available but may be in the near future. The timings above are, however, encouraging and are fast enough to indicate that further development and perhaps a slight hardware improvement would give real-time processing of image sequences.

5. Structure and Motion Determination

In this section sample results obtained from a test run on a synthetic image sequence and on a sequence obtained by moving a camera on an optical bench are presented to give an indication of the expected accuracy and limitations of this algorithm. For the synthetic data, the image irradiance $E(\underline{r},t)$ of a textured moving plane is calculated and then corrupted with image noise. The depth, orientation and motion parameters used to generate the sequence are known and can be compared with the estimates from the algorithm. It can be seen from Table 2a that two of the four interpretations are possible for this data. The two-fold ambiguity in the instantaneous flow field can be resolved by data from subsequent frames, as discussed in Section 7. In this example, the correct interpretation is accurate to approximately 2% given noise in the data of 1% but it must be remembered that this is a global reconstruction. In fact, the flow field is from a single square texture contour that covers approximately a tenth of the image.

Once the intermediate parameters p_{ij} are obtained, there are cases for which the algorithm is known to fail (Buxton, Buxton, Murray and Williams, 1985) which include the obvious cases of no translational velocity or the plane at infinite distance. Other failures or indeterminacies occur for simple patterns of the image edge contours at which the flow is measured, for example, a single straight line or conic section, when the set of equations for the p_{ij} will be rank deficient. These do not seem to be a problem in practice, as in general, many more than 8 points are used and the texture contours are irregular (e.g. Figures 1abcd). The reconstruction is not robust for small angles of view, however, and it has been shown that although the component N_3 of the surface normal can be estimated reliably, the other two components N_1 and N_2 rapidly become inaccurate. Work on the stability is still in progress but the SM-8-point algorithm seems to be at least as stable as the Hildreth-Ullman variational principle for reconstructing the full flow field (Murray and Buxton, 1984). A formulation using a standard p^2 regulariser is being explored and involves the a priori expectations that $\underline{V}$ and $\underline{\Omega}$ will be small. This fits in neatly with the use of the p^2 measure for segmentation described in the next section. We can then pose the problem as an optimisation using weak constraints (Blake and Zisserman, 1985) so that the p_{ij} are smoothed except at the discontinuities at motion boundaries.

Figure 1a: A Single Textured Image Frame; 1b: Convolution Surface;
1c: Zero Contour; and 1d: Flow Field for the Optical Bench Sequence

Table 1a: Four Interpretations frame 10 for the optical bench sequence

****8 POINT SOLUTION 1***		INVALID INTERPRETATION
UNIT BIG N VECTOR	0.0497146600	0.0492756800	-0.9975474000
UNIT TRANSLATIONAL	0.4451951000	-0.8954331000	-0.0014286430
UNIT ROTATIONAL	-0.0000000948	-0.0000066943	-0.0000346538
****8 POINT SOLUTION 2***		INVALID INTERPRETATION
UNIT BIG N VECTOR	0.4451951000	-0.8954331000	-0.0014286430
UNIT TRANSLATIONAL	0.0497146600	0.0492756800	-0.9975474000
UNIT ROTATIONAL	-0.0212252500	-0.0105569800	-0.0016136000
****8 POINT SOLUTION 3***		FEASIBLE INTERPRETATION
UNIT BIG N VECTOR	0.0497146600	-0.0492756800	0.9975474000
UNIT TRANSLATIONAL	-0.4451951000	0.8954331000	0.0014286430
UNIT ROTATIONAL	-0.0000000948	-0.0000066943	-0.0000346538
****8 POINT SOLUTION 4***		INVALID INTERPRETATION
UNIT BIG N VECTOR	-0.4451951000	-0.8954331000	0.0014286430
UNIT TRANSLATIONAL	-0.0497146600	-0.0492756800	0.9975474000
UNIT ROTATIONAL	-0.0212252500	-0.0105569800	-0.0016136000

Table 1b: Four Interpretations frame 20 for the optical bench sequence

****8 POINT SOLUTION 1***		INVALID INTERPRETATION
UNIT BIG N VECTOR	0.0498063300	0.0509993000	-0.9974564000
UNIT TRANSLATIONAL	0.2694849000	-0.9630039000	0.0012842520
UNIT ROTATIONAL	-0.0000077247	-0.0000011511	-0.0000485971
****8 POINT SOLUTION 2***		INVALID INTERPRETATION
UNIT BIG N VECTOR	-0.2694849000	0.9630039000	-0.0012842520
UNIT TRANSLATIONAL	-0.0498063300	-0.0509993000	0.9974564000
UNIT ROTATIONAL	-0.0280333400	-0.0078461800	-0.0018491210
****8 POINT SOLUTION 3***		FEASIBLE INTERPRETATION
UNIT BIG N VECTOR	-0.2694849000	-0.0509993000	0.9974564000
UNIT TRANSLATIONAL	-0.2694849000	0.9630039000	-0.0012842520
UNIT ROTATIONAL	-0.0000077247	-0.0000011511	-0.0000485971
****8 POINT SOLUTION 4***		INVALID INTERPRETATION
UNIT BIG N VECTOR	0.2694849000	-0.9630039000	0.0012842520
UNIT TRANSLATIONAL	0.0498063300	0.0509993000	-0.9974564000
UNIT ROTATIONAL	-0.0280333400	-0.0078461800	-0.0018491210

To get a more realistic idea of the performance of the algorithm, sets of results obtained from the optic bench sequence (see Figures 1abcd) are given in Tables 1a and 1b with centre frame 10 and 20 respectively. Only one interpretation is found to be feasible given the instantaneous flow field in both cases and varies smoothly for the intermediate frames. Also, most importantly, it corresponds well with the scene geometry and motion which was set up with the camera being translated almost vertically (V_2), no rotation, and textured surface facing the camera (N_3). Again, it must be remembered that this is a global interpretation and the flow field used in the reconstruction covered the entire image. The results are, however, quite encouraging as visual motion algorithms based on gradient methods are only accurate at low image velocities and thus the perspective effects on which the 3D reconstruction depends are also small and frequently unstable.

6. Local Least Squares Solution

The previous sections discussed the mapping of the global SM-8 algorithm onto the DAP. The 8 coefficients from the motion equations at n edge features were collapsed into one 8x8 matrix which forms the left hand side of a system of linear equations. In general, however, a local, rather than a global, estimate of parameters will be required in order that the flow field can be decomposed into meaningful components i.e. segmented on the basis of the translation and rotation of objects in the scene and the orientation of their surfaces.

On the DAP, this can be accomplished by requiring every DAP processing element containing an edge feature to compute and store a local 8x8 matrix of least-squares coefficients. The matrix multiplication steps are performed in the manner described for the global solution, but the sum steps are now local to a neighbourhood of prescribed size around the processor containing the edge feature. Fixed size neighbourhoods (3x3) were used here but more sophisticated schemes can be envisaged to collect data from local windows e.g. Gaussian weightings of the coefficients propagated along the edge contours. This, too, could be implemented on the DAP without difficulty, but the basic scheme outlined above serves for demonstration.

Local summations on array processors can be performed efficiently using global shift operations to enable every processor in the array to fetch a neighbour in a particular direction - either North, South, East or West given the connectivity of the DAP array. Furthermore, such sum steps can be factored by decomposing the steps to gather N-S - gather E-W phases (a fact which was used to speed up the image-time-sequence convolution) rather than explicitly fetching all neighbours within the neighbourhood.

The aim of motion segmentation is to assign image features (sets of flow vectors) to interpretation classes, each class being defined by a particular combination of the scene and motion parameters, $\underline{V}$, $\underline{N}$, and $\underline{\Omega}$. If it is known a priori that there is only one interpretation class, we can simply apply the global version of the SM-8 algorithm to recover the desired parameter set. However, if there are several interpretation classes to be recovered, as would be the case for scenes containing many planar facets and moving objects, it is not possible to recover the various parameter sets without first knowing the correct motion segmentation.

Naively, if we have F flow vectors and I known interpretation classes there are I^F possible assignments of interpretation classes to flow vectors. Buxton and Murray (1985) describe the use of a global stochastic optimization technique based on the simulated annealing approach of Kirkpatrick, Gelatt and Vecchi (1983) to tackle the the search problem. This approach has the advantage of being able to cope with interpenetrating flow fields but, unfortunately, is rather slow and, due to the global nature of the processing involved, is not easily amenable to parallel processing (but see discussion below).

The motion segmentation described here (see also Murray and Williams, 1985) hinges on the observation that locally computed motion parameters will change abruptly at a motion boundary. The section above indicated how the local version of SM-8 is implemented and that the system of linear equations can be solved for every point which is the centre of a neighbourhood containing 8 or more flow vectors. For those neighbourhoods containing flow fields arising from the motion of a single planar facet, the p_{ij} will be more or less constant, but where the neighbourhood encompasses a boundary, and flow vectors from an adjacent field are included, the p_{ij} change abruptly.

As an example, consider a non-sparse flow field where every pixel is assosciated with a flow vector. A 3x3 mask is run systematically across the image and equation 3.1 solved at every pixel (i,j) for the nine flow vectors at the neighbouring pixels. The coefficients are then combined by computing the sum of squares p^2 of the 8 p_{ij} at each pixel. Motion boundaries can be found most simply by thesholding the p^2 signal. Figure 2a shows the extent of 4 separate flow fields with various motion parameters.

Figure 2a: Flow Field Extents; 2b: Synthetic Flow Field;
2c: High Threshold; 2d: Low Threshold; and 2e: Final Segmented Image

The results obtained with this synthetic flow data (Figure 2b), where three different flow fields were superimposed on the background flow using randomly oriented texture edges, are shown in Figures 2cde. The segmentation is easily derived by simple thresholding and is fairly indifferent to the level chosen as the boundary points have far greater values than internal points. The results from setting a high threshold (Figure 2c) or a low threshold (Figure 2d) are given for this data. Cleaning up isolated points yields the segmented image (Figure 2e).

The final output of this processing could be used to define subsets of the image for processing by the global motion and surface parameter estimation algorithm described in the previous section. This would allow full 3D analysis of scenes composed of large opaque surfaces but problems would still arise with interpenetrating flow fields or complex scenes. The boundaries detected could also be used in a more sophisticated iterative processing scheme in which the cost function defining an optimal parameter estimation and segmentation given the data is minimised. The boundaries would define the initial set of boundaries across which smoothness constraints are not enforced.

The full cost function needs to include constraints that minimise the number of segments and differences in interpretation within the explicitly marked boundaries (c.f. the line processes in Geman and Geman (1984)) and can be derived by application of maximum likelihood theory (Buxton and Murray, 1985). The cost function may be nonconvex but the minimum could be found using a stochastic search (Kirkpatrick, Gelatt and Vecchi, 1983). Implementations of the Geman and Geman algorithm and other stochastic optimisation problems on the DAP are being tested and will form the basis for a new, more powerful parallel algorithm for scene based segmentation and local 3D interpretation of motion and surface parameters.

7. Continuity over Time

In the previous section the combined segmentation and 3D interpretation problem was discussed but expected continuity over time was not enforced. There are many reasons for including the temporal predictability in the interpretation. For example, consider a tracking task. Simple 2D tracking in the image plane can be obtained directly from the vernier velocities as these give the instantaneous direction and magnitude of the contour movement. Similarly, 3D tracking in the scene is directly obtained from the estimated 3D translational and rotational motion parameters. The tracking could be made much more efficient and effective, however, if fully integrated with a dynamic scene representation that is updated rather than computed from scratch from moment to moment. This is also true for the motion interpretation and can be exploited to allow non-rigid interpretations to build up over time (Ullman, 1984).

```
-----------------------------------------------------------  -----------------------------------------------------------
|Table 2a: Input parameters specifying the 3-D motion and    |Table 2b: Input parameters specifying the 3-D motion and
|the orientation and offset of the plane with respect to     |the orientation and offset of the plane with respect to
|the viewer,the expected solution and four interpretations   |the viewer,the expected solution and four interpretations
|at frame 10 for the synthetic image sequence.               |at frame 12 for the synthetic image sequence.
-----------------------------------------------------------  -----------------------------------------------------------
|*** OBJECT MOTION AND PLANE VECTORS ***                     |*** OBJECT MOTION AND PLANE VECTORS ***
|ROTATIONAL    : (  0.0000,   0.0000,   0.0000 )             |ROTATIONAL    : (  0.0000,   0.0000,   0.0000 )
|TRANSLATIONAL : (  0.0000,   1.0000,   0.0000 )             |TRANSLATIONAL : (  0.0000,   1.0000,   0.0000 )
|PLANE NORMAL  : (  0.0000,   0.0000,  -1.0000 )             |PLANE NORMAL  : (  0.0000,   0.0000,  -1.0000 )
|PLANE START   : (  0.0000,   0.0000, 109.0000 )             |PLANE START   : (  0.0000,   0.0000, 109.0000 )

|*** EXACT 8 POINT SOLUTION ***                              |*** EXACT 8 POINT SOLUTION ***
|UNIT BIG N VECTOR   0.0000000000     0.0000000000  1.0000000000   |UNIT BIG N VECTOR   0.0000000000     0.0000000000  1.0000000000
|UNIT TRANSLATIONAL  0.0000000000     1.0000000000  0.0000000000   |UNIT TRANSLATIONAL  0.0000000000     1.0000000000  0.0000000000
|UNIT ROTATIONAL     0.0000000000     0.0000000000  0.0000000000   |UNIT ROTATIONAL     0.0000000000     0.0000000000  0.0000000000

|***8 POINT SOLUTION 1***       INVALID INTERPRETATION       |***8 POINT SOLUTION 1***       INVALID INTERPRETATION
|UNIT BIG N VECTOR   0.0836534500     0.9940037000  -0.0704231900  |UNIT BIG N VECTOR   0.0300261200     0.0218278400  -0.9993110000
|UNIT TRANSLATIONAL  0.0442604700    -0.0178777200   0.9988603000  |UNIT TRANSLATIONAL  0.1012257000    -0.9914972000  -0.0817768600
|UNIT ROTATIONAL    -0.0088223360     0.0008686832   0.0003651688  |UNIT ROTATIONAL     0.0000867692    -0.0000824302   0.0001469452

|***8 POINT SOLUTION 2***       INVALID INTERPRETATION       |***8 POINT SOLUTION 2***       INVALID INTERPRETATION
|UNIT BIG N VECTOR  -0.0442604700     0.0178777200  -0.9988603000  |UNIT BIG N VECTOR   0.1012257000    -0.9914972000  -0.0817768600
|UNIT TRANSLATIONAL  0.0836534500    -0.9940037000   0.0704231900  |UNIT TRANSLATIONAL -0.0300261200     0.0218278400  -0.9993110000
|UNIT ROTATIONAL    -0.0000111593     0.0000985218  -0.0000390427  |UNIT ROTATIONAL    -0.0067634100    -0.0007635884  -0.0000737594

|***8 POINT SOLUTION 3***       FEASIBLE INTERPRETATION      |***8 POINT SOLUTION 3***       FEASIBLE INTERPRETATION
|UNIT BIG N VECTOR  -0.0836534500    -0.9940037000   0.0704231900  |UNIT BIG N VECTOR  -0.0300261200    -0.0218278400   0.9993110000
|UNIT TRANSLATIONAL  0.0442604700     0.0178777200  -0.9988603000  |UNIT TRANSLATIONAL -0.1012257000     0.9914972000   0.0817768600
|UNIT ROTATIONAL    -0.0088223360     0.0008686832   0.0003651688  |UNIT ROTATIONAL     0.0000867692    -0.0000824302   0.0001469452

|***8 POINT SOLUTION 4***       FEASIBLE INTERPRETATION      |***8 POINT SOLUTION 4***       INVALID INTERPRETATION
|UNIT BIG N VECTOR   0.0442604700    -0.0178777200   0.9988603000  |UNIT BIG N VECTOR  -0.1012257000     0.9914972000   0.0817768600
|UNIT TRANSLATIONAL  0.0836534500     0.9940037000  -0.0704231900  |UNIT TRANSLATIONAL -0.0300261200    -0.0218278400   0.9993110000
|UNIT ROTATIONAL    -0.0000111593     0.0000985218  -0.0000390427  |UNIT ROTATIONAL    -0.0067634100    -0.0007635884  -0.0000737594
-----------------------------------------------------------  -----------------------------------------------------------
```

Tables 2a and 2b give the interpretations available from later frames in the synthetic sequence described in Section 5. It can be seen that an interpretation that is feasible at one moment becomes invalid at a later time. In addition, it is sometimes the case that incorrect but feasible interpretations change more rapidly than the parameters in the correct solution. The elimination of the ambiguous interpretations could, therefore, be achieved by an a priori expectation of low acceleration in the translational and rotational motion. These extra constraints would both help to stabilise the solution, acting as a regulariser, and by posing the problem as an optimisation, bias the solution towards the correct interpretation. Using stochastic search techniques over time to obtain the optimal solution and using such a cost function, would allow this temporal predictability to be directly exploited in speeding up the parameter estimation as a good starting point would be available from moment to moment. This kind of processing has been shown to be effective in the optic flow segmentation scheme of Buxton and Murray (1985) where a Markov random field was used over both space and time to model the redundancy in the neighbouring positions. Later frames were segmented an order of magnitude faster than the earlier ones.

8. Conclusion
In conclusion, these fast parallel algorithms represent progress towards real-time processing of visual motion to obtain the 3D structure and motion of the scene at the level of Marr's 2 1/2 D sketch (Marr, 1982) and would be amenable to future VLSI implementations. It is possible to perform the motion segmentation on image sequences and then obtain the full set of parameters for the surface slant, tilt and relative depth and the translational and rotational motion for simple scenes consisting of a few opaque surfaces in rigid motion relative to the camera. Many problems remain for more complex scenes however, as the reconstructions are not robust for small angles of view. Fortunately, as mentioned in the previous sections, there have been some recent suggestions as to how our processing scheme can be stabilised by prior constraints when the data is poor, both for the instantaneous interpretations and over time, to obtain fully dynamic scene descriptions.

Acknowledgement
We would like to thank Bernard Buxton and Christopher Longuet-Higgins who contributed so much to the mathematical background for this work. In addition, we would like to acknowledge the financial support of GEC Research (NSW) and an Alvey/SERC award within the IKBS 3D Vision Project (HB).

References
Brady, J.M., 1983, "Parallelism in vision", Artificial Intelligence 21, pp271-283.

Blake, A. and Zisserman, A., 1985, "Using weak continuity constraints", CSR-186-85, Univ. of Edinburgh.

Buxton, B.F. and Buxton, H., 1983, "Monocular depth perception from optical flow by space-time signal processing", Proc. Roy. Soc. Lond. B 218 pp27-47.

Buxton, B.F. and Buxton, H., 1984, "The computation of optic flow from the motion of edge features in image sequences", Image and Vision Computing 2 pp59-70.

Buxton, B.F., Buxton, H., Murray, D.W. and Williams, N.S., 1984, "3D solutions to the aperture problem", Proc. ECAI 84, Pisa, pp631-640.

Buxton, B.F., Buxton, H., Murray, D.W. and Williams, N.S., 1985, "Machine perception of visual motion", GEC Journal of Research 3 pp1-17.

Buxton, B.F. and Murray D.W., 1985, "Optic flow segmentation as an ill-posed problem and maximum likelihood", (submitted to Image and Vision Computing).

Geman, S. and Geman, D., 1984, "Stochastic relaxation, Gibbs distributions and the Bayesian restoration of images", IEEE PAMI 6 pp721-741.

Gibson, J.J., 1966, The Senses Considered as Perceptual Systems, Houghton Mifflin, Boston.

Helmholtz, H., 1925, A Treatise on Physiological Optics, Optical Society of America.

Kirkpatrick, S., Gelatt, C.D. and Vecchi, M.P., 1983, "Optimisation by simulated annealing", Science 220 pp671-680.

Koenderink, J.J. and van Doorn, A.J., 1975, "Invariant properties of the motion parallax field due to the movement of rigid bodies relative to an observer", Opt. Acta 22 pp773-779.

Lee, D.W., 1980, "The optic flow field: The foundation of vision", Phil. Trans. Roy. Soc. B 290 pp169-174.

Longuet-Higgins, H.C., 1981, "A computer algorithm for reconstructing a scene from two projections", Nature 293 pp133-137.

Longuet-Higgins, H.C., 1984, "The visual ambiguity of a moving plane", Proc. Roy. Soc. Lond. B 223 pp165-169.

Longuet-Higgins, H.C. and Prazdny, K.F., 1980, "The interpretation of a moving retinal image", Proc. Roy. Soc. Lond. B 208 pp385-391.

Marr, D., 1982, Vision, Freeman, San Francisco.

Murray, D.W. and Buxton, B.F., 1984, "Reconstructing the optic flow field from edge motion: An examination of two different approaches", Proc. First Conf. on A.I. Applications, Denver, pp382-388.

Murray, D.W. and Williams, N.S., 1985, "Detecting the image boundaries between flow fields for several moving planar facets",(accepted for publication Pattern Recognition Letters).

Reeves, A.P., 1984, "Survey: Parallel computer architectures for image processing", Computer Vision, Graphics and Image Processing 25 pp66-72.

Ullman, S., 1979, The Interpretation of Visual Motion, MIT Press, Cambridge, MA.

Ullman, S., 1984, "Maximising Rigidity: The incremental recovery of 3D structure from rigid and non-rigid motion", Perception 13 pp255-274.

Waxman, A.M. and Wohn, K., 1984, "Contour evolution, neighbourhood deformation and global image flow", CAR-TR-58, Univ. of Maryland.

Advances in Artificial Intelligence - II
B. Du Boulay, D. Hogg and L. Steels (Editors)
© Elsevier Science Publishers B.V. (North-Holland), 1987

Combining Image and Spatial Reasoning
for Model Retrieval

Radu Horaud[1]
LIFIA
BP 68, 38402 Saint-Martin d'Heres
FRANCE

Abstract

In this paper we address the problem of recognizing a three-dimensional object from a single perspective image. The approach consists in interpreting the sensory data on the basis of 3D geometric models. Linear features and linear feature groups are first extracted from the image. Each such feature is next interpreted in terms of model features. The interpretation is divided into two stages: image reasoning and spatial reasoning. The first stage consists in labeling the image features in such a manner that the individual feature labels are consistent with the relationships between features. The second stage consists in backprojecting these features out in the 3D space and interpreting them on the basis of the metric properties of the objects expected in the scene. This last stage has been implemented as a tree-search. The method is valid over a wide range of perspective images. It has been implemented for recognizing and locating a class of industrial parts.

Keywords: object recognition, feature grouping, perspective transform, geometric constraints, cognitive modelling.

1. Introduction

In this paper we address the problem of recognizing a three-dimensional (3D) object from a single view. This problem is difficult because there is no one-to-one correspondence between the object models and the sensory data embedded in a grey-level image. On one hand, the physical world is essentially 3D and therefore any representation of this world must describe its 3D shapes and properties. On the other hand, an image is a highly ambiguous collection of data. Aside from the fact that information is lost by projection, the value of any pixel in the image is the result of multiple reflexions of a beam of light travelling through the scene. A variation in intensity between a pixel and its neighbours cannot be simply interpreted as a change in the geometry of the scene. This suggests that an object in the scene is not directly encoded in the image and hence a purely data-driven recognition technique is likely to fail.

In order to overcome these difficulties a *model-based* approach to image interpretation has been developed in the last decade by several researchers, [4], [2], [5], [6]. In a recent paper, [7] we described a method for interpreting images in terms of a 3D object, i.e., *spatial reasoning*. We have notably shown that six degrees of freedom (3 rotations and 3 translations) of an object may be retrieved from a single view on the premise that some assumptions are correctly made. If these assumptions state clearly which object has to be found in the data, a hypothesize-and-test strategy can be used for establishing a unique correspondence between this object and a set of image features. The key-stone of this method is a *backprojection* technique allowing a set of three image lines, whenever they are interpreted as three non co-planar object linear edges, to constrain the spatial orientation of the object to a finite set of solutions.

---

[1]The work reported herein was performed while the author was part time with the "Laboratoire d'Electronique et des Techniques de l'Informatique", Grenoble, France

Nevertheless, if instead of just one object, a *memory of shapes* is available, model retrieval becomes untractable because of the combinatorial explosion of the search space. In this paper we try to investigate to what extent *image reasoning*, i.e., feature extraction, feature grouping and feature labeling may help the recognition process -- the selection of the right assumptions to be made about the identity of the objects present in the scene. Hence, image reasoning can reduce the explosion of spatial reasoning. In other words, image reasoning should provide a first pointer into the memory of shapes.

In order to better understand this approach, consider the following example. The memory of possible shapes is composed of a parallelipiped and a tetrahedron. What tells you in the line-drawing of Figure 2-1 that you shouldn't see a cube? Let us detail the matching process involved here. A 3-line image junction such as (a,b,c) has an infinity of 3D interpretations. Since our possible world is restricted to just tetrahedrons and paralellipipeds, there are 12 possible interpretations. Moreover, since both lines a and b belong to an image triangle and since an image polygon may be interpreted as the planar face of an object, the image junction considered above should belong to a tetrahedron.

2. Approach

The approach envisaged in this paper can be paraphrased as follows. Image reasoning comprises feature extraction, feature grouping and feature labeling. Feature extraction consists in edge detection and line finding and it is a data-driven process. Feature grouping takes into account *descriptive* properties invariant under the perspective transform. On this premise lines are grouped into *junctions* (two, three or more image lines intersecting in a common image point) and into *polygons*. Feature labeling consists in interpreting image lines and image groups as object features. Next, image reasoning is performed. The image features are backprojected onto the 3D space using the geometric constraints available with the perspective transform. Spatial knowledge is used in order to infer *metric* properties such as orientation and depth. Finally, a viewer-independent description in terms of the scene objects is produced.

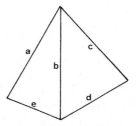

Figure 2-1: What tells you in this line-drawing that this is not a cube?

For this approach to be effective, explicit models for both the camera transform and for the physical world are required. We shall consider central (perspective) projection exclusively since it is the correct model both for the human eye and for TV cameras. A general framework for representing the physical world is beyond the scope of this paper. A simple scheme for describing 3D geometric structures and their topology will be used. It is a standard surface-edge-vertex description augmented with a network of pointers linking topologically connected features. Although this scheme is valid for a wide variety of objects built up of elementary volumes such as parallelipipeds, tetrahedrons, cylinders, cones, spheres, etc., we will limit our discussion to objects bounded by planar faces.

Previous approaches have concentrated on either image or spatial reasoning. In [4], [5] and [10] there are described techniques for predicting object appearances in the image and for performing the matching in the image plane. The authors have not addressed the problem of model retrieval when several objects are available. In [12], [1] and [3] backprojection is used in conjunction with global world properties such as *compactness* or *uniformity*. In [9], image reasoning is combined with backprojection. Orthography is used which is inherently more ambiguous than perspective. Again, the model retrieval aspect of recognition is not considered.

The results of each step of the recognition process will be shown throughout the paper on the image of Figure 2-2. This image has been gathered with a standard TV camera equiped with a 90mm lens. The image (8.8mm by 6.6mm) is digitized at a rate of 256 by 256 pixels. There are 64 grey-levels per pixel. The objects are approximately at 0.9 meters in front of the camera. With this setting the perspective effects are moderate. Figure 2-3 shows the final result of recognition: this is a display of a wireframe representation of the geometric model of the object to be recognized.

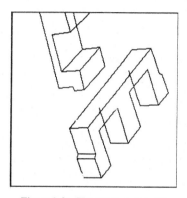

Figure 2-2: A view of two objects   **Figure 2-3:** The result of recognition

3. Image reasoning

Image reasoning is confined to the 2D array of sensory information. Within the context of our approach, image reasoning is aimed toward providing 2D figures which may be used as initial pointers to find those objects in the memory containing these figures. However, this reasoning is inhibited by the fact that metric properties are lost by projection. For example, a set of lines that are parallel in space project onto a set of image lines intersecting in a common point, called the vanishing point, [1].

Let us make the assumption that the scene is viewed from a general position such that the perceived figures are not accidents due to a particular viewpoint. The following descriptive properties are useful for our approach:

- a space line projects onto the image as a line;
- the projections of two colinear space lines are colinear in the image;
- the projections of two lines intersecting in space, intersect in the image and
- the projection of a space polygon is an image polygon.

Let us consider an object bounded by planar faces. Such an object contains vertices -- the intersection of three or more linear edges, and polygons -- the boundary of a planar face. When the object is projected onto the image, any of its vertices produces a limited set of figures: two-line junctions (*angles*) whenever one face of the vertex is visible, three-line junctions (if two or three faces are visible), four-line junctions and so forth. As we shall see in the next Section, junctions with at least three lines may provide a finite number of spatial orientations for the corresponding vertex. Therefore they are more useful than angles.

We implemented a relatively straightforward algorithm for finding image junctions. The lines are first considered pairwise in order to be grouped into angles: the intersection of the two lines is first computed. If this intersection falls within the image bounds, an angle is marked. Angles with common intersections are fused into a junction. Finally isolated lines that occur to pass through an angle are detected. Such a line may turn an angle into a 3-line junction or augment the number of lines of an already existing junction.

The completed list of image junctions is then used as an entry to a polygon finding algorithm. The junctions are mapped into a graph: each junction is mapped into a graph node and each line belonging to at least one junction is mapped into a graph arc. Two nodes are connected by an arc whenever their corresponding image junctions share a common line. Therefore, the problem of finding image polygons is equivalent to searching for closed paths in an undirected graph. This graph is planar, that is, it can be drawn on a sheet of paper in such a manner that its arcs never cross each other. The planarity is a direct consequence of the fact that lines never cross in the image. Hence, the amount of search is a linear function of the number of graph arcs.

In practice, polygon finding is a two-stage procedure. First, isolated junctions (which are not linked to other junctions) and open lines (which have a free end) are thrown out. Whenever a junction has been reduced to just one line, this junction and its line are thrown out. This stage is repeated iteratively until the graph cannot be reduced any more. Second, closed paths are detected in the reduced graph.

Figure 3-1 shows the image lines detected using standard edge detection and line finding techniques. Figure 3-2 shows the junctions detected in the image by the algorithm described above. Figure 3-3 shows the result of polygon detection. Notice the considerable reduction in the number of lines. Feature grouping has the intrinsic characteristic of eliminating irrelevant data since noisy lines are unlikely to form feature groups. However, such things as shadows and highlights still affect the data.

Figure 3-1: Lines extracted from the image   **Figure 3-2:** Image junctions

The last step of image reasoning is feature labeling. Image lines and image groups (junctions and polygons) are labeled in terms of possible object feature interpretations, i.e., physical labels. Each image feature is first labeled individually and second the number of labels of each feature is reduced on the basis of *compatibility* between features. This process is similar to the *constraint propagation* method for interpreting line-drawings developed by Waltz, [11]. Waltz used line labels such as **concave, convex** and **shadow**. He never dealt with realistic imagery. One can say in general that the *block's world* paradigm was aimed towards constructing percepts from images with no specific knowledge about objects in the scene. This approach fails whenever it deals with noisy data because it does not use higher-level geometric knowledge which undergoes the relevant data opposed to noise due to random processes.

The feature labeling algorithm that we implemented starts by assigning a set of possible interpretations to every feature in the image. Lines are labeled **linear edge**, junctions are labeled **vertex** and polygons are labeled **face**. For each line, there is a list of pointers to all the objects in the memory containing a linear edge. For each object in this list -- for each object assigned to this line, there is a list of pointers to all the linear edges in this object. To summarize, a line points to **all** the linear edges of the world.

Similarly, each image group is assigned all possible world interpretations. For each image group there is a list of pointers to all the objects containing a 3D structure matching this group. For each object in the list there is a list of pointers to all the object structures that match the image group. For example, a n-line junction points to all the vertices with at least n linear edges. A n-line image polygon points to all the n-edge faces in the world.

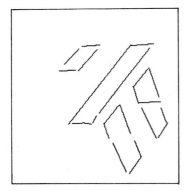 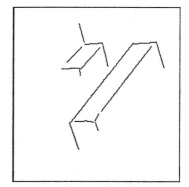

Figure 3-3: Polygon detection: 6 polygons   **Figure 3-4:** Two super-groups

The last step consists in reducing the number of possible assignments of each group and of each line within the groups by checking their mutual consistency. Whenever two groups share one or several common lines, those assignments that are not mutually consistent are thrown out. The result is a considerable reduction in the overall number of assignments. Next, the number of line assignments is reduced as well. The line assignments have to be consistent with the assignments of all the groups to which the line belongs.

Let us show how this work in practice. Consider again the task of interpreting the line-drawing of Figure 2-1 as either a tetrahedron or a parallelipiped. The image junction (a,b,c) is labeled vertex. Both the tetrahedron and the parallelipiped are assigned to this junction since they both contain 3-edge vertices. There are 4 pointers to the 4 vertices of the tetrahedron and 8 pointers to the 8 vertices of the parallelipiped. The image triangle (a,b,e) is labeled face. Only the 4 faces of the tetrahedron are assigned to this polygon. Let us now make the junction labeling consistent with the polygon labeling. Only the tetrahedron assignments are shared by the two image groups. Hence, the set of image lines (a,b,c,e) belongs necessarily to a tetrahedron. This reasoning could have probably been made without taking any junction into consideration. The reason for doing so is that junctions are more useful than polygons for determining the spatial metric properties of the sought object. Moreover, junctions are more likely to be detected than polygons. The latter are strongly affected by occlusions.

There are 59 junctions shown on Figure 3-2 but only 18 among them belong to polygons. The

super-groups shown on Figure 3-4 correspond to 3-line junctions connected to a polygon having the smallest number of labels, i.e., spatial interpretations.

4. Spatial reasoning

Spatial reasoning is aimed towards interpreting image features and groups of features in terms of *metric* properties of the three-space. Within the context of our approach, spatial reasoning comprises three stages: backprojection, image-to-object correspondence and matching.

The first stage consists in backprojecting image features and image groups of features out in the 3D space using the geometric constraints available with the perspective transform. The set of possible spatial configurations of the backprojected features is farther constrained using specific shape knowledge about the set of objects to be recognized. Under certain circumstances, the combination of these constraints provides a finite set of possible 3D orientations for the backprojected features. For example, if three image lines are interpreted as three non co-planar linear edges of an object, the three rotations and two translations of the object can be uniquely determined. Moreover, the *shrinking* inherent to perspective, the object size and the spatial orientation previously computed allow the third translation (depth) to be determined as well. The second stage computes an image-to-object correspondece on the basis of an image-group-to-object-group assignment. The third stage consists in the matching process -- find a unique correspondence between a set of image lines and a set of object features. This is performed by a hypothesize-and-test strategy implemented as a depth-first tree search. A search process is necessary because the initial image feature labeling is ambiguous. On the basis of backprojection, the search is entirely performed in three-space. Its combinatorial complexity is directly related to the degree of ambiguity of the labeling. Therefore, combining image and spatial reasoning is a crucial issue.

4.1. Backprojection of image lines
Backprojection of image lines has been extensively developed in [1] and [8]. It allows isolated lines, angles, junctions and polygons to be interpreted as 3D features. As we shall see below, junctions are the best suited image groups for backprojection.

Let us consider a viewer centered coordinate system with its center at the focal point. The image plane is parallel to the xy-plane at distance f (the focal length) from the origin along the z-axis (the viewing direction). A space point projects onto the image along a line passing through the focal point. Inversely, any image point defines a direction in space. Let us now associate unit vectors either with directions of lines or with normals to planes. Such a unit vector may be represented in cartesian coordinates by the triplet (x,y,z) or as a point on a unit sphere centered at the origin. This sphere is called the *gaussian sphere*. A point on this sphere has two angles as coordinates, the azimuth α and the elevation β. Azimuth is measured from the z-axis in the yz-plane and the elevation is measured from the yz-plane toward the x-axis. See Figure 4-1. The cartesian and spherical coordinates are related by:

$$x = \sin(\beta)$$
$$y = \sin(\alpha)\cos(\beta)$$
$$z = \cos(\alpha)\cos(\beta)$$

In practice only half of the sphere (the one oriented toward the viewer) is of importance. This hemisphere can be represented digitally as a 2D grid with the azimuth varying horizontally from $\pi/2$ to $3\pi/2$ and the elevation varying verticaly from $-\pi/2$ to $\pi/2$. The geometric constraints derived by backprojection will be represented as loci of points (curves) on this grid. Let us now associate an *interpretation plane* with an image line. This plane passes through the focal point and contains the image line. Any spatial interpretation of the image line belongs to this plane. Let us denote by L the unit vector associated with the direction of a line belonging to this plane and let P be the vector normal to the plane. The interpretation plane intersects the gaussian sphere along a great circle. The equation of this circle is

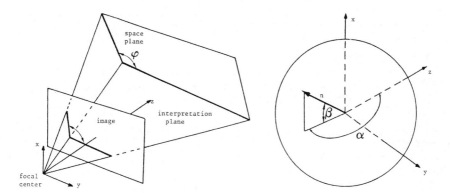

Figure 4-1: The geometry of the perspective transform

simply the dot-product of P and L:

$$P \cdot L = 0$$

Or, on the unit sphere:

$$P_x \sin(\beta) + P_y \sin(\alpha) \cos(\beta) + P_z \cos(\alpha) \cos(\beta) = 0$$

The great circle thus defined is the locus of possible orientations of the backprojection of an image line. Let us consider an image angle. We seek a locus for the possible orientations of a space plane containing the backprojection of this image angle. Let us denote by S the vector normal to this space plane. We also denote by l_1 and l_2 the lines forming the image angle, by P_1 and P_2 their corresponding interpretation plane normals and by L_1 and L_2 their corresponding backprojections. L_1 is the cross-product of S and P_1 and L_2 is the cross-product of S and P_2:

$$L_1 = S \times P_1$$
$$L_2 = S \times P_2$$

The cosine of the space angle formed by L_1 and L_2 is the dot-product of these vectors divided by the product of their magnitudes. If we denote by ϕ the space angle and if the value of this angle is known, we can derive a constraint on the spatial orientation of the space plane S:

$$(S \times P_1)(S \times P_2) = \| S \times P_1 \| \, \| S \times P_1 \| \cos(\phi)$$

Consider now a third line l_3 forming an image junction with the first two ones and let L_3 be its backprojection and P_3 be its interpretation plane normal. Two angles, θ and ψ define L_3 relatively with L_1 and L_2. Remember that L_1 and L_2 belong to the space plane S. θ is the angle made by L_1 and the projection of L_3 onto S. ψ is the angle made by L_3 and this projection. Hence, L_3 may be written as a combination of L_1, S, θ and ψ:

$$L_3 = \sin(\psi) \, S + \cos(\theta) \cos(\psi) \, L_1 + \sin(\theta) \cos(\psi) \, (S \times L_1)$$

Since L_3 belongs to the interpretation plane associated with l_3, we have:

$$P_3 \cdot L_3 = 0$$

By combining the last two equations we obtain an additional constraint on the orientation of S. Consider as an example the image junction of Figure 4-2. If this junction is interpreted as a vertex and if the values of ϕ, θ and ψ are respectively 110°, 60° and 45°, we obtain the curves shown on Figure 4-3. The intersection of these curves is the unique 3D orientation of the space plane S. The values of the space angles ϕ, θ and ψ have been arbitrarily selected. For an isolated junction such as the one of Figure 4-2 all the space angle values available in the memory of shapes must be considered. This leads to a huge search space. Image reasoning is the only way to reduce the explosion of this space.

4.2. Image-to-object correspondence

The image-to-object correspondence is a rigid transform that maps an object centered frame into the camera frame. With the homogeneous coordinate notation, it is a 4 by 4 matrix. When three image lines are put into correspondence with three non coplanar object edges, this transform is completely defined. Consider for example the three-edge vertex mentioned above. L_1, L_2 and L_3 are the axes of a vertex-centered frame. On the basis of backprojection, the direction of these lines may be determined in camera space. This is a direct consequence of the set of equations developed above. The position of the vertex in the camera frame -- the 3 translations, can be computed using the position of the junction in the image and the length of any of the three edges. Since we deal with a rigid object, the trasform from the object frame to the vertex frame is known. In conclusion, the image-to-object correspondence is completely defined under an image-junction-to-object-vertex assignment: it is an image-to-vertex transform followed by a vertex-to-object transform.

Notice that a similar result may be obtained for any group of image features which has, by backprojection, a finite set of spatial interpretations. In [1], image-polygon-to-space-polygon assignments are envisaged. Planar shapes such as polygons require strong perspective effects in order to provide a finite number of spatial solutions. This is one of the main reasons for which we deal with junctions.

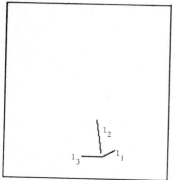

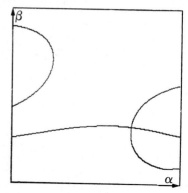

Figure 4-2: An image junction   **Figure 4-3:** Spatial constraints on the unit sphere
for the junction of Figure 4-2

4.3. The matching strategy

The matching consists in finding a unique correspondence between a set of image features and a set of object features. Such a correspondence means two things: first, all the objects in the memory which contain this set of object features are correct interpretations and second, six degrees of freedom are determined for each interpretation. We have implemented a hypothesize-and-test strategy which lies at the heart of many perception algorithms, i.e., [5]. It can be described in general terms as follows:

   1. **Hypothesize:** An image group is selected which has not been included yet in a match and which has the minimum number of model assignments. One of its assignments is selected and an image-to-object correspondence is computed on the basis of backprojection and of image-feature-to-object-feature assignment.

   2. **Predict:** For the object being hypothesized a list of visible features is computed. For each

feature which is predicted visible, its position and orientation in three-space are determined as well as its image location and appearance.

3. **Test**: For each previous prediction, look in the image lists of features for potential candidates. For each candidate that has not been included yet in another match, compute its possible backprojections and check whether it could be interpreted as the predicted object feature or not.

4. **Update**: If the previous test is successful, extend the current hypothesis to include the new image-feature-to-object-feature assignemnt and use the actual position of the image feature to refine the parameters of the image-to-object transform.

The algorithm repeats this loop until a satisfactory match is found, i.e, until a set if image features has a unique set of object feature assignments. Whenever the algorithm fails to find a predicted edge, it backtracks to the last choice point. Choice points arise when more than one image feature has the predicted properties or when an image group has more than one object assignment. Notice that the comparison between the hypothesized object feature and the potential image feature matches is performed in three-space. The object feature needs to be compatible with one of the many spatial configurations obtained by backprojecting the image feature. This is more reliable than matching them in the image plane: if the translational parameters are wrong the projection of the object feature onto the image plane is also wrong. Spatial matching depends only on the rotational parameters. The combinatorial complexity of the search described above depends directly on the number of choice points. Image reasoning is the only way to control this complexity.

Let us see how this strategy works when it is applied to the image of Figure 2-2. Figure 3-4 shows the best super-groups available in the image. The current implementation deals only with one object model. The group in the lower part of the image is composed of one polygon and three junctions. It matches six configurations in the model and hence six hypotheses may be generated. The hypothesis having the highest number of good verifications is the correct one. Figure 2-3 shows the final result of the recognition process.

5. Discussion

In this paper we have discussed and partially implemented a method for retrieving three-space properties from a single perspective image on the basis of image and spatial reasoning. We first select the groups of image features the best suited for further interpretation. Spatial reasoning takes these features as input, backprojects them onto the 3D space and interprets them in terms of object features.

If the memory of possible 3D shapes is very large, the combinatorial complexity of the search becomes a serious handicap. This is the reason for which we introduced image feature grouping and labeling. In the future we also plan to match 3D primitives as an intermediary step between backprojection and 3D object recognition. This may further constrain the amount of search.

The natural extension of this approach would be to allow objects with curved surfaces. This is difficult both from a qualitative and a quantitative point of view. First, 3D curved surfaces are seen in the image in terms of occluding contours that appear where the surface is turning away from the viewer. Surface nature must be inferred on the basis of the shape of these contours. Second, the mathematics of curve backprojection are not yet completely understood. Even in the case of an image ellipse being interpreted as a circle, the solution is unstable, [1], [3].

For these reasons, our short term goal is to fully understand and implement efficiently recognition of shapes bounded by planar faces. We plan to investigate as well to what extent global scene properties such as horizontality and verticality may be retrieved from a single view on the basis of the approach advocated in this paper.

Finally, this approach seems to be promising for cognitive modelling. If perception is viewed as a cognitive process, it involves two types of reasoning: geometric and semantic reasoning. However, semantic properties cannot be retrieved directly from the 2D image; they are inferred from lower level geometric properties. In conclusion, combining image and spatial reasoning may be the first step towards a more global understanding of perception.

References

1. Barnard, S. T. "Interpreting Perspective Images". *Artificial Intelligence 21* (August 1983), 435-462.

2. Bolles, R. C. and Cain R. A. "Recognizing and Locating Partially Visible Objects, the Local-Feature-Focus Method". *International Journal of Robotics Research 1*, 3 (1983), 57-82.

3. Brady, M. and Yuille, A. "An Extremum Principle for Shape from Contour". *IEEE Trans. on Pattern Analysis and Machine Intelligence PAMI-6*, 3 (May 1984), 288-301.

4. Brooks, R. A. "Symbolic Reasoning Among 3D Models and 2D Images". *Artificial Intelligence 17*, 1-3 (August 1981), 285-348.

5. Goad, C. Special Purpose Automatic Programming for 3D Model-Based Vision. Proc. Image Understanding Workshop, Arlington, Virginia, USA, June, 1983, pp. 94-104.

6. Horaud, R. and Bolles, R. C. 3DPO's Strategy for Matching 3D Objects in Range Data. Proc. IEEE International Conference on Robotics, Georgia, Atlanta, USA, March, 1984, pp. 78-85.

7. Horaud, R. Spatial Object Perception from an Image. Proc. 9-th International Joint Conference on Artificial Intelligence, Los Angeles, USA, August, 1985, pp. 1116-1119.

8. Horaud, R. Model-Based Interpretation of Single Perspective Images. Alvey Meeting on Computer Vision and Image Interpretation, University of Sussex, England, September, 1985.

9. Kanade, T. "Recovery of the 3D Shape of an Object from a Single View". *Artificial Intelligence 17*, 1-3 (August 1981), 409-460.

10. Lowe, D. Visual Recognition from Spatial Correspondence and Perceptual Organization. Proc. 9-th International Joint Conference on Artificial Intelligence, Los Angeles, USA, August, 1985, pp. 953-959.

11. Waltz, D. Generating Semantic Description from Drawings of Scenes with Shadows. In Winston, P., Ed., *The Psychology of Computer Vision*, McGraw-Hill, New-York, 1975, pp. 19-92.

12. Witkin, A. P. "Recovering Surface Shape and Orientation from Texture". *Artificial Intelligence 17*, 1-3 (August 1981), 17-45.

Advances in Artificial Intelligence - II
B. Du Boulay, D. Hogg and L. Steels (Editors)
Elsevier Science Publishers B.V. (North-Holland), 1987

PLANNING SENSOR-BASED MOTIONS FOR PART-MATING USING GEOMETRIC REASONING TECHNIQUES

C.LAUGIER & P.THEVENEAU
LIFIA Laboratory
BP68, 38402 Saint Martin d'Heres Cedex, France

April 3, 1986

Abstract

Automating robot programming within the context of mechanical assembly requires several well-known geometric and planning problems to be solved. In this paper we deal with the problem of automatically generating sensor-based sequences of movements (called fine-motions) for mating two parts in presence of uncertainty. We present a system that embodies a two-phase approach to construct a fine-motion program from a symbolic description of the task to perform. First, a geometric reasoning is applied for building a graph representing the different ways in which the assembled parts may be theoretically disassembled (without considering all the manipulation constraints). This reasoning is based on a symbolic analysis of the moving constraints applied by the contacts. Next, a sequence of guarded compliant motions is generated from a well-chosen reverse path in the disassembly graph. Various heuristics and expert knowledge are used during this phase.

Keywords : Automatic robot programming, geometric reasoning, fine-motions planning, compliant motion, manipulation knowledge.

1 INTRODUCTION

Programming a robot for a specific assembly task requires determination of robot actions to be executed, necessary sensing, and the way actions and sensing are to be embedded in an overall algorithm including conditional and loop statements. The main difficulty for performing such a programming task comes from the fact that the robot is a physical machine that operates in a real world. This means that both the environment and the actions executed by the robot cannot be predicted exactly at programming time, and that the resulting uncertainty may cause the program to fail.

One of the major problems to solve in this case consists of locating the points where uncertainty is too high according to the required precision (see [Brooks 82a] [Puget 85]), and reducing this uncertainty using sensory interaction. It is obvious that partmating operations constitute points where robots are more likely to fail, and where well-suited strategies aimed at processing uncertainty are to be applied. Many researchers have already attempted to solve the problem of automatically synthesizing what we call fine motions programs for part-mating [Taylor 76] [Lozano 76] [Lozano 81] [Brooks 82 b] [Dufay 83] [Dufay Latombe 83] [Lozano Mason Taylor 83] [Valade 85]. Basically, this problem consists in constructing sequences of sensor-based and guarded motions aimed at achieving a set of goal relations between two parts. These goal relations may be either explicitly given by the user, or automatically generated by the system.

All the work mentioned above has been done in the automatic robot programming context, in which the main problem consists in converting a task level description of an assembly task into a manipulator level program allowing the robot to carry out the task (see the projects TWAIN [Lozano Brooks 85] or SHARP [Laugier Troccaz 85] for more detail).

In this paper, we consider the problem of planning robot actions from symbolic descriptions of the task to perform when uncertainties have to be considered. More precisely, we focus on the problem of synthesizing fine-motion programs for mating two parts, despite the lack of precision of the robot and the uncertainty introduced by the physical nature or the real world. The presented method operates in two phases :

- In a first phase, the system constructs a symbolic graph representing the different ways in which the assembled parts may be theoretically disassembled (without considering all the manipulation constraints). This phase is based on geometric reasoning applied to object models.

- In a second phase, the system generates a sequence of guarded compliant motions for the part-mating operation. This sequence is obtained by choosing a good reverse path in the disassembly graph, and by computing all the motion parameters.

This new approach to the problem of fine motion synthesis is complementary to the one previously developed in our group by Dufay [Dufay 83], and is based on inductive learning. In fact it may be seen as a pre-processing phase for generating a first nominal plan (called the ground plan), to obtain a better understanding of the problem (and then to generate more intelligent corrective motions in case of failure at execution time).

2   ROBOT PROGRAMMING IN PRESENCE OF UNCERTAINTY

2.1   Effects of uncertainty

If there were no uncertainties, a robot program would merely consist of a sequence of goal-oriented motions. Because of uncertainty, individual robot actions never exactly achieve the expected results. This is not a problem as long as uncertainty is lower than the precision requirements of the task (this situation is often met in current industrial applications through a carefully engineered environment). In other cases, specially part-mating, it is of major importance and necessitates complex sensory interactions.

Errors and uncertainty may be processed in very different ways depending on their nature and on their potential effects on the robot control program [Puget 85]. Several sources of uncertainty may be identified: accuracy of robots, imprecision of sensor information, errors in robot control commands (language interpretor, numerical computation ...), position uncertainty of parts delivered by feeders, tolerances on mechanical parts. But, the resulting uncertainty cannot be exactly known at programming time. This means that the system (or the user in conventional programming) must reason about empirical knowledge like ranges of error values (bounds, magnitude), or statistical behaviour (systematic errors, random deviations ...). Some authors have developed mechanisms for representing and manipulating uncertainty [Brooks 82 b] [Puget 85]. This is important for checking the validity of robot programs, and for detecting where and how to correct these programs in case of failure. Other researchers have based uncertainty processing on learning techniques. Reasoning can then be made on the effects of uncertainty rather than on an explicit model of their behaviour [Dufay 83] [Dufay Latombe 83]. Such an approach is more realistic when executing tight-tolerance operations like mating two parts, but it requires a large amount of expert knowledge (see next section).

2.2   Fine motion synthesis

A fine motion program may be regarded as the implementation of a strategy to reduce uncertainty until the good relation between two parts is achieved. Such a program may typically include [Latombe 83]:

- Goal-oriented motions to achieve required relations,

- Corrective motions to improve position accuracy from unwanted relations,

- Information gathering motions to reduce position uncertainty,

- Conditional statements, which implicitly interpret sensory data in terms of spatial relations requiring different courses of actions,

- Loops to repeat goal-oriented motions that where previously unsuccessful,

- Variables representing uncertainty, and assignments to update them after either corrective or information gathering motions have been executed.

All the methods developed until now for automatically synthesizing fine-motion programs do not really solve the whole problem. The first approaches were based on the concept of procedure skeleton [Taylor 76] [Lozano 76]. The main difficulty lies in the identification of different classes of fine-motion strategies, and in the determination of the required parameters. Related work is mainly oriented towards the development of techniques for representing and propagating error bounds through relations among part features in a world-model. Later, Brooks [Brooks 82a] improved the method by introducing symbolic mechanisms for error analysis, but the basic drawbacks of the approach remained unchanged: many errors are difficult to estimate and error propagation techniques based on the worst case uncertainty hypothesis may result into unrealistic over-estimates due to error compensation phenomena; moreover, non-linear plans may introduce fix point computation problems which are not solved.

These drawbacks have motivated the investigation of a drastically different approach based on the fact that the use of learning techniques do not require a precise prior estimate of uncertainty [Dufay 83] [Dufay Latombe 83]. Basically, the method consist in assembling input partial local strategies described as expert rules into a complete manipulator level program by processing the execution traces of several attempts to carry out the task. Each execution trace is obtained by executing a first plan, called the ground plan, and by inserting on-line some corrective subplans in case of failure. This approach is very attractive and yields efficient and reliable part-mating programs. It is not directly applicable in the general case, because it necessitates a large amount of expert knowledge concerning assembly strategies, sensor behaviour, physical situations...

A more recent approach, based on geometric reasoning, has been proposed by [Lozano Mason Taylor 83], and further developed in [Mason 84] and [Erdmann 84]. It makes use of the configuration space method, for constructing a sequence of compliant motions allowing a point p representing the moving object, to reach a goal position located on the sub-assembly. This sequence of motions is determined in a reverse way (from the goal to the initial position), by computing at each step the range of starting configuration, allowing the mobile to reach the current goal configuration by executing a simple motion. Such a method is potentially more general than the previous one, but involves complex computation, and suspect the algorithmic complexity to go out of control in real situations.

As we will see further, our method is based on the same idea, but the geometric reasoning process manipulates more symbolic items and thus reduces the complexity of the search graph. It also makes use of expert knowledge both for reasoning and helping the system when generating the part-mating program.

3   OUTLINE OF THE SYSTEM

3.1   Principle of our approach

Our approach for solving the fine motion synthesis problem is based on two remarks: The first one is to say that compliant motions are very useful when motions to execute are very constrained by the task and when uncertainty needs to be considered; The second remark is that the sequence of assembly operations may generally be deduced from the sequence of disassembly. Then, the purpose of the method is to generate a sequence of guarded compliant motions for mating two parts, by reasoning on the geometrical model of these parts placed in the goal situation.

During the reasoning, the relative degrees of freedom of the two parts are analysed, and the possible sequences of disassembly operations are produced by successively relaxing each of the contacts existing between the features of the objects. This first phase leads to the construction of a graph representing the different ways in which the assembled parts may be theoretically disassembled. Then, the next step consists of choosing a good path in the previous graph by computing all the motion parameters. Various heuristics and expert knowledge are used during this phase.

3.2   Representing contacts and their associated moving constraints

As explained previously, we are interested in analysing contacts between two parts, and the possible relative motions generated by these contacts. This means that we have to manipulate three types of representation:

- a symbolic representation of the contacts between object features,

- an analytic model of the allowed degrees of freedom associated with the moving object,

- and a numerical characterisation of the moving parameters.

Geometrically speaking, very few types of contacts have to be considered: points, lines and surfaces. In reality, such contacts may be generated in very different ways depending both on the context and the objects features. Then, reasoning on contacts requires both geometric and symbolic information. As an example, the one-line determination of contact parameters in robotics applications leads to reason on objects features, and to make use of various contextual information like the manipulator position, the uncertainty interval, the moving direction and the exerted forces [Dufay Laugier 82].

In the context of planning sequences of compliant motions for part-mating, we are mainly interested in stable contacts (typically: contacts along surfaces) for guiding the motions, and in very instable contacts (typically: contacts between two parallel edges) which designates transition points to manage carefully. The first type of contact is named strong contact, and is created by two overlapping faces (planar or not). The face belonging to the fixed object is considered as the support of the contact and of the compliant motions. Then, punctual and linear contacts on this surface are viewed as temporary situations, occurring only during the realization of the goal relation. Other contacts are named adjacent contacts. They represent situations where the boundaries of two faces are possibly overlapping according to positions uncertainty within the system, contacts are represented by predicates as shown in figure 1. In order to make contacts manipulation more efficient, objects faces are initially decomposed into elementary elements like rectangular or triangular surfaces. This approach permits very simple computations to be used to determined contact parameters. It also permits a quick analyze of new situations and on-line modification of the disassembly graph in case of failure. Each contact reduces the set of degrees of freedom of the mobile object. According to our approach, the moving constraints are directly applied by the face supporting the contact. Then, it is easy to explicitly characterise all the possible translating directions of the moving feature on a unitary sphere (see figure 2): a planar face defines a valid domain represented by the half sphere located above the plane (relatively to the direction of the normal external vector), a couple of contacts determines a set of allowed motions represented by the intersection of the domains associated with each contact. Using this formalism, computation of the degrees of freedom may be executed in a two-dimensional space obtained by mapping the sphere on a plane (φ, θ), using the function:

$$\varphi = \arctan \frac{Nx \times \cos \theta + Ny \times \sin \theta}{-Nz} \qquad (1)$$

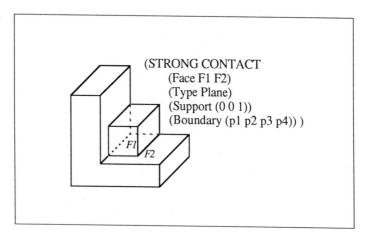

(STRONG CONTACT
(Face F1 F2)
(Type Plane)
(Support (0 0 1))
(Boundary (p1 p2 p3 p4)))

Figure 1: Representing Contacts

Where (Nx, Ny, Nz) represents the normal external vector of the face defining the contact (see [Theveneau 85] for more detail). An important property of this approach is that the allowed compliant motions may be easily extracted from the model as they are represented by the boundaries of the constructed domains (see figure 2). Each couple $(\varphi\ \theta)$ in the model defines an allowed moving direction, but it does not specify all the parameters of the motion. The compliance parameters may be easily determined from the geometry of the surface, and eventually the friction cone. A detailed study of this problem is presented in [Whitney 76]. The amplitude of the motion must be computed according to more global considerations, and must take into account collision problems. The principle of this computation is described in the next section. Within the system, a guarded compliant motion is defined by a statement of the type:

MOVE ALONG T WITH COMPLIANCE C UNTIL B

where T defines the nominal moving direction, C characterises the force conditions to satisfy during the execution, and B is a boolean expression representing the termination predicate. This predicate indicates that motion can be stopped either when the wanted relation is achieved, or when an unexpected event occurs (in practice: a collision or a failure when trying to obtain a particular contact). Such a predicate may be expressed either in terms of force conditions, or in terms of the covered path (distance or elapsed time). In the current implementation, the maximum amplitude of the movement is coded within the transformation T, and the force condition in B is a simple expression computed in relation with the characteristics of the commanded motion: for example, a force fz becoming higher than a predefined threshold value Fz will stop a movement executed along the -Z axis.

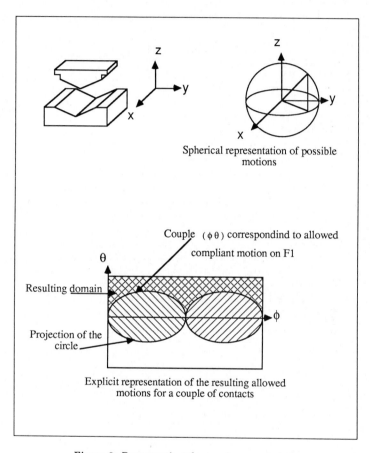

Spherical representation of possible motions

Couple ($\phi\theta$) correspondind to allowed compliant motion on F1

Resulting domain

Projection of the circle

Explicit representation of the resulting allowed motions for a couple of contacts

Figure 2: Representing the moving constraints

3.3   Constructing the disassembly graph

The basic idea when constructing the disassembly graph is to explicitly represent what we think to be the most relevant sequences of world states along with their associated transformations. As we will see further, this graph may be locally refined during the second phase under the control of dynamic advices.

Each node of the graph represents a key world state. It is characterised by a tuple of the type:

$$\boxed{\text{name, P , D, I, Q}}$$

where P represents the set of contacts, D characterises the degrees of freedom of the moving feature, I is a set of qualitative informations concerning the physical situation (for example: cylindrical or prismatic insertion, leaving an edge, leaving the subassembly ...), and Q denotes an heuristic assessment of both the quality of the situation (stability, robustness relatively to position uncertainty...) and the distance from the current state to the goal one. These data are computed from the world model. Contacts are modelled as explained previously, but only the moving constraints are explicitly represented in terms of inequalities. This approach permits unnecessary computation to be avoided, so that complex moving domains are determined only when some graph refinements coped us to do so.

Arcs characterise the transformations allowing to transfer between couples of compatible world states. Each transformation corresponds to a simple motion: a pure translation or a pure rotation. It defines the geometry of the nominal movement using a matrix expressed in homogeneous coordinates; It also designates the sliding surfaces, and eventually the faces that may stop the movement. An heuristic weight representing the quality of the needed compliant motion (roughness of the sliding surfaces, gravity action...) is associated with the arc.

The construction of the initial disassembly graph is realized using the following algorithm:

1. Compute the set of contacts in the assembly and create a node corresponding to the goal situation.

2. For each couple of strong contacts, apply the selected rule in the knowledge data base for choosing a small set of well suited moving directions. For example, four directions will be determined by a couple of contacts based on two non-parallel planar faces $F1, F2 : d1 = N1 \wedge N2, d2 = -d1$, $d3 = d1 \wedge N1$ and $d4 = d2 \wedge N2$, where $N1$ and $N2$ represent respectively the external normal vectors of $F1$ and $F2$ ($d1$ and $d2$ are the directions defined by $F1 \cap F2$, $d3$ and $d4$ are the orthogonal directions on $F1$ and $F2$). Similarly, a cylindrical contact combined with a planar contact determines three primary movements along the cylinder axis: a translation and two opposite rotations. For a single contact, the system generates a simple movement for relaxing this contact.

3. Check the validity of the moving directions selected in step 2, by considering the current set of constraints generated by the contacts. Determine the amplitude of the movement associated with each valid direction, in order to minimize the relaxed constraints and to avoid collisions. Usually, this is done

by computing the minimum distance (euclidian distance or angular distance) between the features of the two parts. The jaws of the gripper may be considered as components of the moving object for this computation.

4. Create an arc and a node in the graph for each movement computed at the previous step. The node corresponds to the new situation obtained after having moved the mobile part. It is characterised by the description of the new set of contacts. If this set contains strong contacts then go to step 2, else label the node as an entry point for the search phase. The algorithm stops when all pending strong contacts have been processed.

3.4 Generating the part-mating program

The first step when constructing the part-mating program consists in finding a good reverse path in the disassembly graph. As this graph may be dynamically expanded during the search phase, a classical A* algorithm which guarantee the optimality of the computed solution according to a particular cost function is not directly applicable. This is the reason why we have chosen to apply a method in which the search phase is guided both by a simple cost function, and a set of dynamic pieces of advices. Each node labelled as an entry point is seen as a potential starting point for the algorithm, and the node corresponding to the assembled situation is the goal one. Then, several possible solutions are examined and evaluated in parallel according to two criteria: the length of the path and the quality of the sequence of operations. This evaluation is done using an heuristic function combining weights attributed to the graph items (see section 3.3). The purpose of this function is to minimize the length term and to maximize the quality one. It also allows the system to always attempt to increase the constraints generated by the contacts, when constructing a solution.

Dynamic advices are recorded in the knowledge data base. They become applicable when some particular physical situations are detected in the current sub-graph. They may lead to modification of new situations, for example, when a transition between two states requires sliding on a rough or on a vertical face (the gravity may cause some disturbance). They may also correspond to the processing of unrealistic intermediate situations like adjacency contacts or very close world states (the needed movements are less than a predifined minimum value). For example, if a unique contact cannot be directly left because of the presence of an obstacle in the vicinity of the moving part, then it is advised to slide on the contact surface (and consequently to create new nodes and arcs in the graph). In the same way, an adjacency contact gives rise to the computation of a set of well-chosen intermediate strong-contacts along with their associated sub-graph. This approach reduces the algorithmic complexity, and permits new strategies to be integrated in the system. In particular, classical methods for solving some well-known mating operations like a cylindrical insertion may be directly coded by graph skeletons in the data base. This facility has not been implemented yet.

The last step consists in computing all the motion parameters of the selected solution. These parameters are easily determined from the numerical and the symbolic information recorded in the graph (see section 2.2): geometric transformations are explicitly represented on arcs, and force conditions are computed from the sets of contact and sliding surfaces. In the current implementation, the force associated with the termination predicate is opposed to the movement, and it is created by the goal contacts. The direction of the nominal force to apply during a compliant motion is obtained by adding the external normal vectors of the sliding surfaces, and its amplitude is a parameter given by the system. This force is assumed to lie within a tolerance domain characterized by a cone included in the friction cone, and by a small interval of values.

4   CONCLUSION

The system described in this paper is part of a larger project of our research group to automate robot programming [Laugier Troccaz 85]. It has been implemented in Franzlisp on a VAX-750 under the UNIX system. Several part mating tasks requiring only translating motions have been successfully processed in simulation using the LISP-3D system [Laugier 82]. The example shown in the appendix falles; 580 seconds CPU time, and built a graph of 50 nodes and 80 arcs. The generated program is composed of 4 guarded compliant motion statements expressed as lisp functions. A liaison between the system and the ITMI controller of a six axis SCEMI robot equipped with a force sensing wrist will soon be available; it will permit real-life experimentation.

Current work deals with the implementation of rotations, and the improvement of the role of expert knowledge within the reasoning. Later, we will study the interface with a learning module aimed at correcting unforeseen physical errors, and at generating efficient and reliable part-mating programs from the solutions initially proposed by the system. This module will be based on the method presented in [Dufay 83].

Acknowledgements

The work presented in this paper describes research done at the LIFIA laboratory. It was partly supported by the ADI (Agence de l'Informatique) and by the French National ARA project (Advanced Automation and Robotics).

References

[Brooks 82a]   R.A.Brooks 1982: "Solving the find-path problem by good representation of free space", 2nd American Association for Artificial Intelligence Conference, Carnegie-Mellon,
August 1982.

[Brooks 82 b]   R.A.Brooks 1982: "Symbolic error analysis and robot planning", International Journal of Robotics Research 1, 4, December 1982

[Dufay 83] B.Dufay 1983: "Apprentissage par induction en robotique - Application à la synthèse de programmes de montage" (in French), Thèse de 3ème Cycle, INPG, Grenoble, June 1983.

[Dufay Latombe 83] B.Dufay, J.C.Latombe 1983: "An approach to automatic robot programming based on inductive learning", 1st International Symposium on Robotics Research, Bretton Woods, August 1983.

[Dufay Laugier 82] B.Dufay, C.Laugier 1982: "Geometrical reasoning in automatic grasping and contact analysis", Proc of PROLAMAT'82, Leningrad, May 1982.

[Erdmann 84] M.A.Erdmann 1984: "On motion planning with uncertainty", MIT Artificial Intelligence Laboratory, Technical Report 810, 1984.

[Latombe 83] J.C.Latombe 1983: "Automatic synthesis of robot programs from CAD specifications", NATO Advanced Study Institute on Robotics and Artificial Intelligence, El Coccio, Italy, June 1983.

[Laugier 82] C.Laugier 1982: "LISP-3D: Logiciel pour la manipulation et la visualisation de scènes tridimensionnelles", Rapport de Recherche IMAG 328, Grenoble, Septembre 1982.

[Laugier Troccaz 85] C.Laugier, J.Troccaz 1985: "SHARP: A system for automatic robot programming of manipulation robots", Third Int. Symposium of Robotics Research, Gouvieux, France, Octobre 1985.

[Lozano 76] T.Lozano-Perez 1976: "The design of a mechanical assembly system", AI TR 397, Artificial Intelligence Laboratory, MIT, 1976

[Lozano 81] T.Lozano-Perez 1981: "Automatic planning of manipulator transfer movements", IEEE Transactions on Systems, Man and Cybernetics, SMC-11, 10, 1981.

[Lozano Brooks 85] T-Lozano-Perez, R.A.Brooks 1985: "An approach to automatic robot programming", AI Memo 842, Artificial Intelligence Laboratory, MIT, April 1985.

[Lozano Mason Taylor 83] T.Lozano-Perez, M.T.Mason, R.H.Taylor 1983: "Automatic synthesis of fine-motion strategies for robots", 1st International Symposium on Robotics Research, Bretton Woods, August 1983.

[Mason 84]   M.T.Mason 1984: "Automatic planning of fine motions:
                     Correctness and completeness, IEEE International Con-
                     ference on Robotics, Atlanta Ga, 1984.

[Puget 85]   P.Puget 1985: "Problèmes de prise en compte d'incer-
                     titude en robotique d'assemblage", Rapport de DEA,
                     (in French), LIFIA/IMAG, juin 1985.

[Taylor 76]   R.H.Taylor 1976: "Synthesis of manipulator control
                     programs from task-level specifications", AIM 228, Ar-
                     tificial Intelligence Laboratory, Stanford University, July
                     1976.

[Theveneau 85]   P.Theveneau 1985: "Une méthode de génération de
                     mouvements fins basée sur une analyse des contacts",
                     (in French), Rapport de DEA, LIFIA/IMAG, juin 1985.

[Valade 85]   J.M.Valade 1985: "Geometric reasoning and automatic
                     synthesis of assembly trajectory", Proc of ICAR'85,
                     Tokio, Japan, Septembre 1985.

[Whitney 76]   D.E.Whitney 1976: "Force feedback control of manipu-
                     lator fine motions",J.Dynamic Systems, Measurement,
                     Control, 91-97, June 1976.

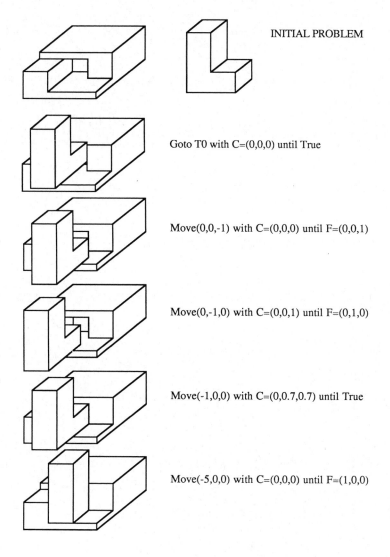

INITIAL PROBLEM

Goto T0 with C=(0,0,0) until True

Move(0,0,-1) with C=(0,0,0) until F=(0,0,1)

Move(0,-1,0) with C=(0,0,1) until F=(0,1,0)

Move(-1,0,0) with C=(0,0.7,0.7) until True

Move(-5,0,0) with C=(0,0,0) until F=(1,0,0)

Advances in Artificial Intelligence - II
B. Du Boulay, D. Hogg and L. Steels (Editors)
© Elsevier Science Publishers B.V. (North-Holland), 1987

ANALOGICAL AND PROPOSITIONAL KNOWLEDGE
IN INTELLIGENT PATH PLANNING

Lina Massone and Pietro Morasso

Department of Communication, Computer and Systems Science
University of Genoa — Via all'Opera Pia 11a
16145 Genoa —Italy — Tel. +39−10−310223/303651

Abstract

The cooperative roles of analogical and propositional knowledge are investigated as regards spatial reasoning, in general, and navigation/path−planning, in particular. Representations for the environment and the actor are proposed as tools for reasoning about space.

1. INTRODUCTION

This paper deals with the following generalized navigation problem: "Given an actor in a cluttered environment and a task to be carried out, find a sequence of actions that perform correctly that task". The task could simply be to *reach a target position* or might have more complex formulations like *move a certain object from one location to another location, pick up the red book in the bookshelf* and so on. In any case, the expected performance implies a safe trajectory to be covered, possibly concurrent with a set of *postural adjustments* to be performed by the actor along the trajectory in order to avoid undesired collisions with obstacles and/or other actors.

Although an actor may have a very complex geometric structure, it is acceptable, in the context of the navigation paradigm, to use a drastic simplification of the actor's shape in terms of its *extent*, i.e. the smallest vertical parallelepiped that contains the actor. Consequently, postural adjustments may be classified according to their effects on the actor's extent and on the environment. For example, the three following classes may be considered:

− Rotations of the extent around the vertical axis (e.g. when turning sideways in order to negotiate a narrow passage);

− Changes of orientation and/or dimensions of the extent (e.g. when bending down, crouching or passing over obstacles).

− Movements that affect the geometry of the environment, like pushing an object to open a path or moving it in order to accomplish a specific job.

Understanding and representing the strategies of an intelligent actor and their interactions with the environment is a everyday−life complex problem which requires different types of knowledge to co−exist and to be suitably processed.
1) Knowledge about the actor: its geometry, its motion capabilities, its subjectivity.
2) Knowledge about the environment: shape, space, specific features of objects.
3) Knowledge about the task: task decomposition into subtasks, subtask interaction, subtask concurrency.

The suggestion that is put forward in this paper is that modeling such multi−faceted behaviors can succeed only by viewing the problems from two different perspectives, which are neither dual nor mutually exclusive: an *analogical perspective* and a *propositional perspective* [Sloman 1971, Palmer 1975, Anderson 1976, Kossylin and Pomerantz 1977, Shepard 1978, Waltz and Bogges 1979, Funt 1980, Shepard and Cooper 1982, Ballard and Brown 1982, Pylyshin 1984]. The notion of mental or analogical model, in particular, was investigated by Johnson−Laird [1980]:

A mental model represents a state of affairs and accordingly its structure is not arbitrary like that of a propositional representation, but plays a direct analogical role. Its structure mirrors the relevant aspects of the corresponding state of affairs in the world.

On the contrary

A propositional representation is a description .... it is true or false with respect to a mental model of the world.

Analogical representations are coherent and continuous, and embody all the knowledge about the world in an implicit manner; information can be recovered, typically, by means of measurements and simulations. Propositional representations are explicit, scattered, discrete, abstract pieces of knowledge, with no geometric resemblance to the situation, naturally suited for posing direct questions and making logic inferences.

Sometimes the same entity can be modeled in both ways, sometimes one of the two representations does not make sense. In any case, we think that there are no hierarchical constraints among them; both representations are likely to play a role and one is not reducible to the other except in a trivial sense. Let us consider the following examples to make things more clear.

The road map

A road map of a town is an example of analogical representation which contains in an implicit manner all the information about topology, distances and so on. A table of distances between locations expresses a knowledge of propositional type which makes explicit a piece of information contained in the map. If the task is to find the way between two locations in the town, we would certainly prefer to have a look at the map rather than to read a book saying that street A is at the right of street B and crosses street C at midway and so on; but if the task is to know how far is location A from location B we would probably prefer to go through a table of distances rather than computing on the map the various subdistances while taking into account the scaling factor.

Fragility

The concept of fragility is very complex from an analogical point of view: it is a function of the molecular properties of the material, of the weight of the object, of the forces applied to it, of the acceleration of gravity, of the type of collision and of many other things. If we wish to warn people about the fragility of an object, we wouldn't certainly tell them about physics and dynamics; we would just write on the object "fragile", using an explicit, well understood propositional label.

Art Watching

Suppose you are in a museum looking at a painting by Raffaello, while reading a guide book to help you "see" what is important. The actual painting is a direct analogical record of what Raffaello did and how he did it. The book makes explicit – in an obviously propositional way – different aspects of the painting (the influence of such and such school, the special kind of illumination or color technique, and so on). Therefore, you are just combining an analogical representation (the painting) with a propositional one (the guide book) to understand Raffaello's art.

These examples show informally that real world problems require both types of knowledge to be present and to be used. This should be contrasted with the main stream of AI that focuses on logical methods, attempting to reduce everything else to it. In the case of spatial reasoning, a good example of this approach is the notion of *conceptual model* by Hagert [1985] who relies on levels of meta–knowledge in order to reproduce logically some features of mental models of spatial arrangements of objects.

In fact, the power of logical methods, the main tool to manipulate propositional knowledge, lies in a representation of the world in symbols that can be processed in well understood ways to produce inferences. However, most real world problems are not suited for representations in terms of precise logical formalisms: knowledge bases in real world problems are systematically inconsistent [Hewitt and De Jong 1983] from the logical point of view and violate the closed–world assumption that underlies most part of the AI research. For these reasons they have often been considered unstructured, ill–defined and thus difficult to capture from the computational point of view. On the other hand, geometric measurements and simulations of physical processes are computationally intensive activities which provide local information from which it is hard to make abstractions and to model global behaviors; they can carry only part of the representational burden imposed by concepts like space, shape, motion, action.

Consider, for example, the well known block–world paradigm, in which blocks have to be arranged according to a specified goal configuration. Viewing the problem only in analogical terms (for example representing blocks as sets of voxels with a spatial position) would make it difficult to say which block has to be moved next. On the other side, traditional STRIPS–like formulations [Fikes and Nilsson 1971] can take into account only that part of the problem which can be modeled by means of propositional statements: ON(A,B), CLEAR(B), etc.. Suppose now to plunge the problem into a real world of shapes, weights, equilibrium, space and time constraints, unaccounted events, concurrency and partial information. The only way to cope, at least partially, with this fascinating cocktail of reality would be, in our opinion, to integrate propositional statements with analogical models and to provide interfaces between them.

These statements are investigated, in the rest of the paper, in the framework of intelligent path planning, although we believe they reflect a general working philosophy to model interactions between intelligent actors and their environments, in which reasoning activities are strictly coupled with geometrical and physical constraints.

2. RELATED WORK

Finding a safe path among a set of obstacles is a well known problem in robotics. The standard approach − the configuration space approach − is based on the idea of computing those parts of free space which can be occupied by the moving object without colliding with obstacles. The problem is simplified by shrinking to a point the moving object while expanding the obstacles according to the size of the object. The main drawbacks of the approach are:

1) Limited domain (only polyhedric obstacles are considered).

2) Difficulty when dealing with changes of configuration and/or shape of the moving object.

Mathematical formulations for the configuration space have been provided by Lozano−Perez [1981, 1983] and Canny [1984], and the approach has been used with some variations by Moravec [1980] in two dimensions, Udupa [1977] and Lozano−Perez [1984]. In a different method proposed by Brooks [1983], free space is explicitly represented by means of planar specializations of generalized cylinders with straight spines which overlap at paths intersection. Khatib [1981] and Hogan [1981] followed an approach based on penalty functions to measure the distance between moving object and obstacle. Ahuja et al. [1980] proposed a method which detects overlap among the projections of the objects on a given set of planes and a method which represents obstacles by means of octrees. In all mentioned cases the amount of computations to be performed to plan a safe path increases exponentially with the complexity of obstacles, that is with the articulation of the environment. Moreover, since these approaches are mainly focused on global, off−line aspects of spatial modeling and planning, they cannot take into account local, unexpected events which may, at run time, interfer with the planned actions. Chattergy [1985] recently proposed some heuristics to help solving the navigation task in the case of unexplored environment, that is when a model of the world is not available. Massone and Morasso [1985a, 1985b] presented a heuristic approach aimed at distributing the navigation complexity into different components. Each component can be accepted to fail in several occasions without causing the overall performance to collapse. The components are:

a) A *3D Geometric Modeler*, which needs not to be restricted to polyhedric objects.

b) A *Planner*, which operates on a 2−D analogical representation of the environment (augmented with 3−D propositional attributes) and on a propositional representation of the actor.

c) An *Impact Avoidance Mechanism* which operates on local information acquired during the actual navigation monitoring the actor/environment interactions.

d) A *Navigation Expert* which computes the necessary representations according to the task and to the actor model, and updates it dynamically taking into account the actual performance.

In this paper the approach is further investigated by focusing on representations (of the environment, of the actor) to show how propositional and analogical knowledge can co−exist and can be used to reason about problems.

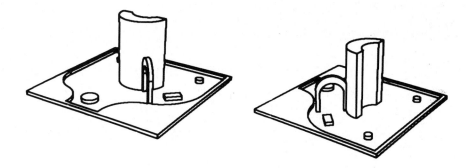

Figure 1. *Two views of a 3D street−like environment generated by means of PADL−2*

3. REPRESENTING THE ENVIRONMENT

The real world is a continuum of infinite complexity [Mandelbrot 1984]. Taking for granted that a representation can never fit it perfectly, the research problem which is still open is to avoid on one hand the combinatorial explosion of its complexity and on the other the triviality of a "toy world". This section shows that domain generality can be achieved by integrating analogical and propositional models and that their cooperation can reasonably constrain the computational load.

3.1 Modeling Free Space

Consider a synthetic three−dimensional environment (see figure 1) generated by means of any geometric modeler (specifically, we are using PADL−2 package [Brown 1982], but the whole approach is not constrained by this choice). For planning a path between two different locations, information about the topology of free space should be provided. Topological information can be captured, for example, by sectioning the environment according to a significant plane. It can be reasonably assumed that the environment has a floor on which the actor moves; hence, sectioning can be performed along a plane parallel to it at a meaningful height with respect to the actor. This section, observed downward in a direction normal to the floor, is a binary image containing free space and sections of obstacles (see figure 2−left). (From a practical point of view, these images can be obtained by means of PADL−2 computing the intersection between the CSG model of the environment and a thin parallelepiped.) In order to represent the structure of bidimensional free space we are using the *Skeletal Representation* (SR) of shapes described in [Gaglio et al. in press]. SR applies the medial axis transform [Blum 1973] to a low frequency representation of the boundary in order to avoid typical problems of sensitivity to noise and boundary details. Contours of objects are first extracted and then smoothed by means of a low pass filtering procedure which allows keeping the information about the main structure of obstacles stripping out noise and unsignificant details; the *skeleton of free space* is then computed together with the *thickness function* which says how far is the skeleton from obstacles boundaries (see figure 2−right). The result of these computations is a set of skeletal points and thickness values.

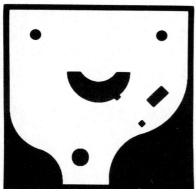 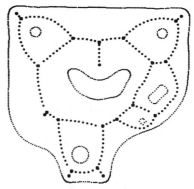

Figure 2. Left) Top view of a floor−section of the environment shown in figure 1. Right) Skeletal Representation of bidimensional free space.

This representation, however, is discrete, redundant and poorly structured. To reach a better configuration, SR is viewed as a graph with arcs (skeletal branches) and vertices; vertices can be either ending points (where the skeleton ends) or fork points (where the skeleton presents singularities). The topology of free space can then be coded in terms of connections among branches assigning symbolic names to branches and vertices. The behavior of a single branch (the shape of the branch and the associated thickness function) can be coded in terms of smooth parametric functions to provide a continuous analogical representation. In other terms, the initial representation

$$\begin{array}{llll}
& s_0 \; s_1 \; \cdots \; s_m & \text{(skeletal points)} \\
(1) & d_0 \; d_1 \; \cdots \; d_m & \text{(thickness values)} \\
& a_0 \; a_1 \; \cdots \; a_m & \text{(angles between skeleton and thickness segments)}
\end{array}$$

is transformed into

$$(2) \quad \begin{array}{l} s = S(u) \\ d = D(u) \end{array} \quad u = (0-1)$$

where $S(u)$ and $D(u)$ are two smooth functions of a running variable u normalized to a unit range and must satisfy the following boundary constraints:

$$(3) \quad S(0) = s_0 \quad D(0) = d_0 \quad D'(0) = \|S'(0)\| \cos(\text{alpha}_0)$$

$$(4) \quad S(1) = s_m \quad D(1) = d_m \quad D'(1) = \|S'(1)\| \cos(\text{alpha}_m)$$

Three classic identification problems have to be faced:
1. to choose the base functions;
2. to estimate the parameters;
3. to estimate the order.

With regard to the first problem, Bezier polynomials have been chosen [Rektoris 1969] because they are smooth and computationally convenient:

$$(5) \quad P_n(u) = \sum_{i=0}^{n} P_i \; \text{binom}(n \; i) \; u^i \; (1-u)^{n-i}$$

$n+1 \; --> $ polynomial order
$P_i \; --> $ polynomial guiding points

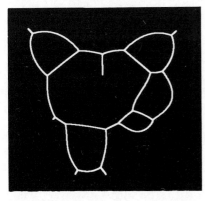

Figure 3. The synthetic skeleton of free space generated from the identified guiding points.

Although the identification problem is non linear, it is possible to separate it into a linear part, for which standard least square techniques can be used, and a non linear part, which can be dealt with by means of successive approximations. Figure 3 shows the synthesis of skeletal branches of figure 2—right obtained from the identified guiding points. SR can then be coded in terms of branches, vertices, skeleton's guiding points, thickness's guiding points. SR is a mixed logical/analogical representation: it is logical because it makes explicit the topology of free space and it is analogical because it preserves the metrics of free space and makes it possible to perform measurements on it.

However, the computations performed on a single section of the environment are not sufficient because they ignore the third dimension. To capture, at least partially, this information some features of the obstacles' layout over and under the considered section must be formalized. Specifically, given SR of a certain section, the intersection between a line normal to the section and the obstacles can be computed for each sample of the skeleton.

This computation (which can be performed again by means of PADL−2) provides two functions (a *positive height function* and a *negative height function*) which measure the distance between the skeleton and the obstacles over and under the section. These functions can be managed in terms of Bezier polynomials exactly like the thickness function in the plane. However, they do not need, for our purpose, to be totally stored: since the geometry of the actor is known (see next section), only "critical points" need to be singled out, i.e. points where the available height is lower than the height of the actor. This information can be coded by means of propositional statements which associate to each branch name a set of pairs (branch coordinate – critical value). By exploiting this knowledge the actor can take into account 3D environment features such as galleries, protuberances and so on.

3.1 Modeling Objects

If path planning is conceived simply in terms of avoiding collisions with obstacles, these representations of the environment would be sufficient, as shown by the authors in [Massone and Morasso 1985a], to find a safe path. In fact there are situations in which finding the path requires to modify the spatial location of certain objects, either because a safe path cannot be found otherwise (for example in a very crowded environment), or because such a path would follow a long, winding, unnatural way, or just because the task imposes it. Some specific features of the objects need then to be represented, at least in a propositional way.

Physical objects can be described at infinite levels of detail and from the most disparate viewpoints. Capturing their semantics by means of formal models is a crucial problem in robotics and AI [Hayes 1979, Hayes 1985, Adorni et al. to appear], which goes beyond the scope of this paper. Here we want just to show how some features of physical objects can be represented in a propositional model and how this model can be related to the analogical model of free space previously introduced.

A description of physical objects should include both objective and subjective (actor–dependent) features. Examples of objective features are geometry, material, etc..; actor–dependent features relate, for example, to the possibility of being lifted, pushed, passed over etc.., since these attributes involve the size and/or the strength of the actor. The former features can be coded by means of explicit statements, while the latter require rules involving statements about both objects and actor. At present we storing such information into a particular type of *frame* [Adorni et al. in press] where many possibilities are indicated for each feature (for example, a chair can be made of wood, plastic, metal, ..); such frames can be specialized for particular instances of objects. This is still a preliminary development that needs to be enriched by considering other issues – like, for example, functionality – and other more efficient representation schemes – like, for example, semantic networks. Appendix A shows an example of simple propositional model of a chair.

The link between objects modeling and free space modeling can be captured by observing that the structure of the skeletal representation of free space is such that (see figure 2–right) each branch has always one object on one side and one object on the other side. It is then possible to store, while computing the skeletal representation, the names of the objects (pointers to the propositional models) whose boundaries triggered a certain branch. In this way it is possible to know, for each spatial location of the actor, its position with respect to free space and which are the surrounding objects.

4. REPRESENTING THE ACTOR

For taking into account an actor which navigates in its environment, the actor needs to be modeled from both a geometric and a motor point of view. The actor's geometry can be coded (like the environment's geometry) at different levels of detail, according to the desired accuracy of the results. At the lowest level, the actor can be represented by means of its three–dimensional extent, i.e. the enclosing (vertical) parallelepiped or cylinder of minimum volume; such a model, even if rough and imprecise, is appropriate for sketching navigation plans on the basis of heuristics. Other more detailed models could be used for finer specifications of plans in critical sections [Massone et al. 1984].

Motor skills of the actor can be modeled, for example, by stating how movements affect the geometry of the actor when they are performed. Let us consider, for example, a human–like actor and let us assume that its standard position is the standing one; the actor can, for example, stretch arms up, sit down, lay on the floor, go on all fours and so on, each of these postures being characterized by a different 3D extent. The actor's model consists, at this stage of the project, of a standard extent and a set of rules which modify it, simulating motor skills. In Appendix B a simple example of propositional actor model is shown by means of a Prolog–like formalism.

It is worth noting that this model, being propositional, can neither take into account the actor's motion (velocity, acceleration ...) nor model an articulated body – a tree of kinematic chains with links and joints – which can move in an anthropomorphic way; both aspects, which are currently being investigated [Morasso and Tagliasco in press, Marino et. al. 1985], would require analogical models to be integrated with formalisms for expressing complex geometric structures and motor coordination patterns.

5. REASONING ABOUT REPRESENTATIONS

The computation of intersections with obstacles over and under the considered section of environment is time costly; it is then worth performing it only for those portions of space which appear to be promising. A strategy which could be followed is to plan a safe path in two dimensions (on the basis of SR and of the objects' features) and then verify its validity in three dimensions by computing critical points as shown in section 2 and by trying to overcome them by means of the motor skills of the actor. If this is possible, the required motions are stored for each critical point; otherwise some paths are labeled as "unsafe" and planning in 2D is started again on a better knowledge basis.

The representation of the environment which is being computed is composed of an analogical part (Skeletal Representation) which can be refined run−time by impact avoidance mechanisms and of a propositional, actor and task dependent part containing the following statements:

1) Critical Points <symbolic name of the branch, set of pairs (coordinate value − critical value)>

2) Actor's Motions <symbolic name of the branch, set of triples (motion name − initial coordinate − final coordinate), meaning that when the initial coordinate is reached by the actor the motion has to be executed and the posture maintained until the final coordinate is moved past>

3) Safety Attributes <symbolic name of the branch, attribute>.

Let us now describe how a safe path in two dimensions can be computed. (It is worth recalling that the goal is not just to avoid obstacles but to provide a strategy for acting also on the environment, if necessary.)

Being available the previously described representations of free space, actor and objects a reasonable strategy to reach a target location could be outlined as follows:

If the line joining the initial and final location is all contained in free space and there is enough space for the actor around that line, then follow that trajectory; otherwise search for alternative paths or try to change the obstacles' layout.

The first part of the condition can be easily verified on the binary image of the environment layout (another source of analogical knowledge which can be usefully exploited): it is true if the pixels of the connecting line are all black (or all white). The second part requires to relate the initial and final locations to the branches of the skeletal representation and to analyze the behavior of the thickness function. The term "enough space" must be quantified with respect to the actor's extent and position. Let us suppose that the actor is initially in a standard position with the larger of the dimensions of its 2D extent normal to the direction of motion (this corresponds to the position of a walking man). If the thickness is greater than this dimension everywhere along the trajectory, then the actor can proceed normally straight ahead. If the thickness is smaller somewhere (or it is too close to the actor's size leading to a high risk of collision), the actor can analyse the surrounding objects to see if slightly moving an object can make the path more comfortable. If this is not possible − for example because the surrounding objects are too heavy or because there is not enough free space around them − the actor has two choices: either turn, in such a way to "show" the smaller dimension of its extent (this would correspond to walk sideways) or to look for an alternative path. If, after turning, the thickness around the trajectory is still too small, an alternative path has certainly to be searched; otherwise the two alternatives must be evaluated in terms of length and burden of the alternative path versus the risk of collision while walking sideways and the fact that this posture is somewhat unnatural. If, on the contrary, the line joining initial and final location is not completely contained in the free space, an alternative trajectory has to be searched or objects need to be moved by applying the same strategy outlined above. Alternative paths can be searched by considering the topological links between skeletal branches, their length, the safety attributes, the extent of the actor versus the thickness function and by taking into account and evaluating the possibility of displacing objects.

These reasoning activities can be easily performed over the skeletal representation and the propositional models previously defined and have been coded in a set of rules (about 50 at this stage) whose preconditions can refer to any of the representations.

The result of this bidimensional exploration is tested in 3D − as explained at the beginning of this section − and provides a list of actions to be performed by the actor (either over its own geometry or over the objects) along a safe trajectory. The final trajectory is described in terms of symbolic names of skeletal branches and target points within the paths identified by those names. In fact, constraining the actor to move along the skeleton in many cases is a too conservative solution, since paths are covered "unnaturally", following all turns and concavities. Better trajectories can be computed by implementing over the Skeletal Representation some heuristic criteria like "shorten all turns", "keep right" and so on (see figure 4).

For example, to shorten turns target points can be chosen by fixing a minimum distance among them and by checking that the segments connecting each of them with the following one are completely

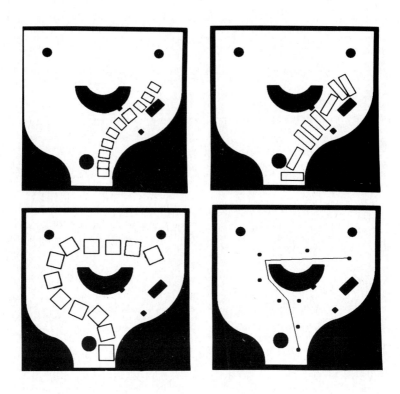

Figure 4. This picture shows four different navigation strategies obtained by fixing the initial and final location to be reached by the actor and by changing the actor's size. Top left) Extent's size (in pixels) 20x30x180; to pass under the arc the actor has to bend down; consequently the extent is altered by decreasing the height and increasing the width. Top right) Extent's size 60x20x100; the arc is now passed without bending down, but the actor has to walk twice sideways for a while. Bottom left) Extent'size 40x40x300; the actor is now very tall and bending down would not help it to pass under the arc; then it must follow a longer way to reach the target location since none of the obstacles can be displaced. Bottom right) The latter path can be covered more efficiently by applying the "shorten all turns" heuristics.

contained in the free space The resulting trajectories can be arbitrarily refined and smoothed by decreasing the minimum distance among target points and by performing more often the latter test.

Movements of the actor along the trajectory are described in mixed propositional/analogical terms, like, for example, "bend down near coordinate 0.7 of branch B3", "push object CHAIR towards coordinate 0.8 of branch B7 of an amount A".

Simulation results are available for most part of the heuristics described here (see figure 4).

6. CONCLUSIONS

This paper emphasizes the necessity of integrating different sources of knowledge for dealing with real world problems. Representations for the environment, the actor and the objects have been proposed, on which many types of reasoning can be performed. Promising simulations results have been obtained by implementing the strategies described in section 5. As a future development, it is worth extending the present set of rules in order to include also task contraints; hence a representation for tasks needs to be studied, which must differ from traditional planning formulations to take into account time constraints, overlaps and concurrency.

As a final observation, we would like to point out that the approach outlined in this paper provides also a framework for applying qualitative reasoning theories − like quantity space and qualitative proportionality − to spatial problems (to deal, for example, with terms like "enough space", "too close", "too small", "too heavy", "slightly moving" and so on), whereas the usual formulations [Bobrow Ed. 1984] constrain them to monodimensional processes.

The algorithms to compute the Skeletal Representation and to manipulate it have been written in C, while the reasoning is performed in C−Prolog. Interfaces have been provided between the two languages. The whole system runs on a MicroVax 2 under Ultrix Op. Sys.; graphic output of simulation processes has been obtained by means of a VDS 7001 system for image processing.

ACKNOWLEDGEMENTS

This work was partially supported by the ESPRIT project P 419 − Image and Movement Understanding.

APPENDIX A

Example of Propositional Model of a Chair

```
min__extent([40,60,80]).
max__extent([80,100,120]).
material(wood).
material(plastic).
material(metal).
min__weight(1).
max__weight(7).
can__be__lifted if adult(actor).
can__be__lifted if non__adult(actor) and weight < 2.
  ..
  ..
  ..
```

Adult, non__adult are attributes which
can, for example, be expressed in terms of actor's extent
(see section 3 and Appendix B).

APPENDIX B

Example of Propositional Model of an Actor

```
standard([180,50,30]).     /* dimensions of the 3−D extent (parallelepiped) */
actual([180,50,30]).
can__sit(man).
```

```
can_stretch_arms(man).
can_lay(man).
can_go_on_all_fours(man).
change(X) :- can_sit(X), standard(Y), mul(Y,[0.72,1,2.33],Z),asserta(actual(Z)).
change(X) :- can_lay(X), standard(Y), mul(Y,[0.16,3.66,1.66],Z), asserta(actual(Z)).
change(X) :- can_stretch_arms(X), standard(Y), mul(Y,[1.25,0.8,1],Z), asserta(actual(Z)).
```

/* mul(X,Y,Z) is a rule which multiplies each element of X by each element
of Y and appends the result to Z */

REFERENCES

ADORNI G, DI MANZO M, GIUNCHIGLIA F (in press) Reasoning about Scene Descriptions, Proc. of IEEE.

ANDERSON JR (1976) Language, Memory, and Thought.

AHUJA N, CHIEN RT, YEN R, BRIDWELL N (1980) Interference Detection and Collision Avoidance among Three- Dimensional Objects, Proc. AAAI, 44-48.

BALLARD DH, and BROWN CM (1982) Computer Vision. Prentice Hall:Englewood Cliffs,N.J.

BROOKS RA (1983) Solving the Find Path problem by Good Representation of Free Space, IEEE Trans on SMC, 13, 3, 190-197.

BLUM H (1973) Biological Shapes and Visual Science. J. Theoretical Biology 38:205-287.

BOBROW DG (1984) Qualitative Reasoning about Physical Systems: an Introduction. Artificial Intelligence 24:1-6.

BROWN CM (1982) PADL-2: A Technical Summary. IEEE J. Computer Graphics and Applications 2:69-84.

CANNY J (1984) On Detecting Collisions Between Polyhedra. In: Proceed. ECAI-84:533-542. Elsevier Science Publisher:Amsterdam.

CHATTERGY R (1985) Some Heuristics for the Navigation of a Robot, Int. J. of Robotics Research, 4, 1, 69-85.

FIKES RE, and NILSSON NJ (1971) STRIPS: A New Approach to the Application of Theorem Proving to Problem Solving. Artificial Intelligence 2:189-208.

FUNT B (1980) Problem Solving with Diagrammatic Representations, Art. Int. 13:3, pp 201-230.

GAGLIO S, GRATTAROLA A, MASSONE L, MORASSO P (in press) Structure and Texture in Shape Representation, The Journal of Intelligent Systems.

HAGERT G (1985) What's in a Mental Model? On Conceptual Reasoning with Spatial Descriptions, Proc. 9th IJCAI, pp 274-277, Los Angeles (CA).

HAYES PJ (1979) The Naive Physics Manifesto. In: Expert Systems and Microelectronic Age, D. Michie Ed., Edinburgh Univ. Press:Edinburgh.

HAYES PJ (1985) The Second Naive Physics Manifesto, In: Readings in Knowledge Representation, R.J. Brachman and H.J. Levesque Eds., pp. 467-486, M. Kaufmann Inc., Los Altos, Ca.

HEWITT C, and DE JONG P (1983) Open Systems. In: Perspectives on Conceptual Modeling (M.I. Brodie and J.L. Mylopoulos, Editors). Springer Verlag:Berlin.

HOGAN N (1981) Impedance Control of a Robotic Manipulator, Proc. Winter Annual Meeting of ASME, Washington D.C.

JOHNSON-LAIRD PN (1980) Mental Models in Cognitive Sciences. Cognitive Science 4:71-115.

KHATIB D (1981) Commande Dynamique dans l'Espace Operationelle des Robots Manipulateurs en Presence d'Obstacles. Docteur Ingenieur Thesis, Ecole National Superieur de l'Aeronautique e de l'Espace:Tolouse.

KOSSYLIN SM, POMERANTZ JR (1977) Imagery, Propositions and the Form of Internal Representations, Cognitive Psychology, 9, 52–76.

LOZANO PEREZ T (1981) Automatic Planning of Manipulator Transfer Movements, IEEE Trans. on SMC, 11, 681–698.

LOZANO PEREZ T (1983) Spatial Planning: a Configuration Space Approach, IEEE Trans on Comp., 32, 108–120.

LOZANO PEREZ T, MASON MT, TAYLOR RH (1984) Automatic Synthesis of Fine Motion Strategies for Robots, Int. J. of Robotics Research, 3, 1, 3–24.

MANDELBROT BB (1983) The Fractal Geometry of Nature. WH Freeman and Co:San Francisco.

MARINO G, MORASSO P, and ZACCARIA R (1985) Motor Knowledge Representation. Proceed. IJCAI–85 (Los Angeles, California, August 18–23):1110–1112.

MASSONE L, MORASSO P, and ZACCARIA R (1984) Shape from Occluding Contours. Proc. SPIE Conf. on Computer Vision for Robots, Cambridge (Ma), 521:114–120.

MASSONE L, MORASSO P (1985a) Navigation Among Three–Dimensional Shapes, Proc. Spie Conf. on Computer Vision for Robots, Cannes.

MASSONE L, MORASSO P(1985b) SMASH: an Approach to Soft Manoevering among Shapes, Proc. AICA Conf., Florence.

MORAVEC HP (1980) Obstacle Avoidance and Navigation in the Real World by a Seeing Robot Rover, Stanford Univ. Tech Rep., AIM 340.

MORASSO P, TAGLIASCO V Eds. (in press) Human Movement Understanding, North Holland.

PALMER SE (1975) Visual Perception and World Knowledge: Notes on a Model of Sensory–Cognitive Interactions, In "Exploration and Cognition", DA Norman and DE Rumelhart Eds., Freeman, San Francisco.

PYLYSHYN ZW (1984) Computation and Cognition. MIT Press: Cambridge.

REKTORIS K (Ed.) (1969) Survey of Applicable Mathematics. MIT Press:Cambridge Massachusetts.

SHEPARD RN (1978) The Mental Image, American Psychologist, 33, 125–137.

SHEPARD RN, COOPER LA (1982) Mental Images and Their Transformations. The MIT Press:Cambridge Massachusetts.

SLOMAN A (1971) Interactions between Philosophy and Artificial Intelligence: the Role of Intuition and Non Logical Reasoning in Intelligence, Art. Int. 2, 3/4, 209–225

UDUPA SM (1977) Collision Detection and Avoidance in Computer Controlled Manipulators. IJCAI–77 (Cambridge, Massachusetts).

WALTZ D, BOGGES L (1979) Visual Analog Representations for Natural Language Understanding, Proc. 6th IJCAI, 226–234.

Advances in Artificial Intelligence - II
B. Du Boulay, D. Hogg and L. Steels (Editors)
© Elsevier Science Publishers B.V. (North-Holland), 1987

PLAN GENERATION IN A TEMPORAL FRAME

Edward P K TSANG

Department of Computer Science
University of Essex
Colchester CO4 3SQ, UK

Abstract

This paper presents a new view of plan generation, which is based on and generalized from Allen's. It also describes how a complete planning process should look under this view. Finally, it gives a brief description of an implemented planner which is based on such ideas.

I   Introduction

The main purpose of this paper is (1) to present a new view of plan generation; and (2) to describe how a complete planning process should look under this view. A planner based on such ideas has been built. It will be described briefly in this paper.

II   Limitations with traditional planners

In traditional planners like NOAH [SAC 75] or NONLIN (as described in [TAT 76,77,84]), a problem is described by a set of propositions which hold true in the initial state and another set of propositions which we want to be true in the goal state. Planning is finding the means by which we can arrive at the goal state. A goal can be already true in the initial state and remain unchanged thereafter, or achieved by application of operators.

These planners assume that all actions and propositions are instantaneous. Hence the temporal relations (between two actions) that these planners can represent are limited to "before", "after" and "in parallel", (which in fact means no restriction). This limits the planners' ability to talk about goals like "finish cooking the meat and baking the potatoes at the same time" or actions like "make the soup during the period when the potatoes are being baked". Nor can they talk about durations of actions or propositions, like "put the pot on the fire for 15 minutes". Besides that, when it is found that actions A and B cannot take place "in parallel", these planners must commit themselves to either "A before B" or "A after B". Taking a wrong choice could rule out all possible plans. In this case, planners like NONLIN have to backtrack in order to find possible plans.

DEVISER [VER 82,83] tries to escape from the assumption that actions and propositions are instantaneous by introducing "packages". A "package" could be shared by one or more actions or propositions. It consists of a window which restricts the earliest and latest starting point of such actions or propositions, as well as their durations. A window has the form [E, L] where E is the earliest starting time and L is the latest starting time. Thus it can talk about something like "action A takes 5 seconds" or "event X starts at time T".

However, DEVISER uses networks like NONLIN's. So basically it can handle the same temporal relations as NONLIN. It can use windows to help it to say something like "events A and B start at the same time" only if:

(1)   events A and B share the same "window", which means that they must have the same duration; or

(2)   both A and B's windows are committed to [X, X], which forces both events to start at time X. But such a commitment might rule out possible plans.

For example, assume that DEVISER needs to state the fact that A and B must end at the same time in the following situation:

		window	duration
Event A	---------	[5,10]	5
Event B	--------------------	[0, 5]	10

DEVISER can do so by narrowing the windows of A and B to, say, [5,5] and [0,0] (or [6,6] and [1,1], [7,7] and [2,2], ..., etc.) respectively.

Besides, DEVISER has limitations in duration handling. Durations must have absolute values. For example it can say "to steam fish takes 15 minutes", but not "to steam fish takes 10 to 20 minutes".

III   Planning with a temporal world model

In [ALL 83a], Allen suggests a view of planning which uses a temporal world model. In such a model, each proposition has associated with it a time interval during which it holds. There are 13 possible primitive relations between pairs of intervals [note 1]. These relations are listed in Table 1 below.

Table 1. The set of all possible binary primitive relations

	Temporal Relation	Symbol	Graphical illustration (with interval B fixed)
			BBBBBBBB
1.	A *before* B	<	AAAA
2.	A *meets* B	m	AAAAAAAAA
3.	A *overlaps* B	o	AAAAAAAAAAAA
4.	A *finished-by* B	fi	AAAAAAAAAAAAAAAA
5.	A *contains* B	di	AAAAAAAAAAAAAAAAAAAAAAAA
6.	A *starts* B	s	AAAA
7.	A *equals* B	=	AAAAAAAA
8.	A *started-by* B	si	AAAAAAAAAAAAAAAA
9.	A *during* B	d	AAAA
10.	A *finishes* B	f	AAAAAA
11.	A *overlapped-by* B	oi	AAAAAAAAAAAAAA
12.	A *met-by* B	mi	AAAAAAAA
13.	A *after* B	>	AAAA

Intervals and their relations can be represented by a **relation network**, where the nodes are intervals and there exists an arc R_{xy} between any two nodes X and Y. Each arc represents the temporal relation between the two intervals which are joined by this arc. If a network is totally unconstrained, each arc can take any of the 13 primitive relations as its value. For every arc in any network there should be a nonempty set of possible values that it may take. For example the relation between X and Y could be [< m], which is a shorthand for "X is before Y or X meets Y".

All relation networks obey the **propositional constraints**. For a particular domain, a network obeys a set of **domain constraints**. They are both temporal constraints on the arcs of the networks. One propositional constraint is "if A holds at both T1 and T2, then T1 before T2 or T1 equals T2 or T1 after T2". An example of a domain constraint is "if on(a,b) holds at T1 and clear(b) holds at T2 then T1 [< m mi >] T2".

When this formalism is used for planning, the initial and goal states are represented by intervals I and G respectively. A problem is expressed as a set of **explained intervals** (S_1) each element of which "contains" I and a set of **unexplained intervals** ($S_{\neg}$) each element of which "contains" G. X "contains" Y here means Y [s = d f] X. We say that an interval is *explained* if it is, or can be identified as, (i) an interval which exists in the initial state; or (ii) an effect of an operator which is applied. Intervals in the goal state are said to have **causal gaps** from the initial state. This can be represented by figure 1 below.

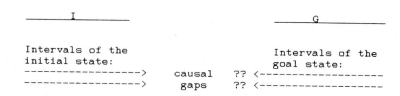

Figure 1   Problem specification under Allen's approach

Planning is the process of filling the causal gaps (which means explaining all the intervals) in this possible world.   All intervals in the initial state are themselves explained.   An interval can be explained by an interval which is already explained.   An operator can be used to explain some intervals, but might themselves introduce unexplained intervals (i.e. preconditions).   In trying to fill the causal gaps, some primitive relations between some pairs of intervals, for example "A equals B", could be found nonviable.   This would be a constraint on the arc R_{ab} (the relation between A and B).   If a solution exists, the planner should be able to produce a relation network in which there exists a nonempty set of possible values for every arc.

One of the major advantages of using a temporal world model for planning is that more complicated temporal relations (like the ones mentioned in section **II**) can be represented.   In addition, it provides a general approach to reasoning with temporal relations.   In the following sections, we shall generalize Allen's view to cover planning.   We shall also argue that his approach to plan generation is incomplete.

IV   Planning as a Partial World Description (PWD)

We shall define a **Partial World Description** as a set of intervals together with a set of **temporal** and **duration constraints** on them.   A temporal constraint is a constraint on an arc of the relation network, and a duration constraint is the constraint on the maximum and minimum duration of an interval.

Our view to planning is based on Allen's, except that there is no initial or goal states.   A problem specification is a partial world description, in which some of the intervals are explained and some are not.   The unexplained intervals are the goals which we want to bring into the world.   In such a problem specification, an unexplained interval need not be after an explained one.   Planning is seen as the process of explaining all the intervals in this world description.

An operator itself is also a partial description of a possible world.   Application of an operator means to superimpose the world described by this operator onto the world description of the problem.   During the plan generation process, many such partial world descriptions may be added.

An example of a problem specification in the blocks world is :

> We know that clear(a), on(a,b), clear(c) and on(b,e) are already true in the world, and clear(d) will become true sometime in the future. The goal is to achieve on(a,c) first, and then to achieve on(b,d) sometime later.

This specification can roughly be shown graphically below:

```
     Propositions            Intervals and their relations

     clear(a)          T1   ----->
     on(a,b)           T2   ----->
     clear(c)          T3   ----->
     on(a,c)           T4                 ?? <-------
     clear(d)          T5                       ------->
     on(b,d)           T6                              ?? <----
     on(b,e)           T7   ----->
```

Figure 2   A problem specification in terms of a
           Partial World Description (PWD)
           ---------> explain intervals
           ?? <------ unexplain intervals

At this stage, let us remind ourselves that this diagram cannot fully represent the world description because it can only show for each interval-pair one temporal relatoin that is allowed in the problem specification. For example the problem specification allows T4 [< m o ...] T5, but the diagram only shows the relation T4 [o] T5.

Assume that we have defined (in terms of a partial world description) an operator **move(X,Y,Z)**, meaning to move X from Y to Z, (where X, Y and Z are variables), as in figure 3.

```
     Propositions            Intervals and their relations

     move(X,Y,Z)       I1                 --------------
     clear(X)          I2   ?? <-------
     on(X,Y)           I3   ?? <-------
     clear(Z)          I4   ?? <-------
     on(X,Z)           I5                         -------->
     clear(Y)          I6                     ------------>
```

Figure 3   The operator move(X,Y,Z)

In order to explain T4 (in which on(a,c) holds) in the world shown in figure 2, we can apply the operator move(a,b,c). This will introduce 6 new intervals (I1 to I6) into our initial partial world description, augmenting our relations network and possibly imposing additional constraints on existing arcs. Now T4 can be explained by I5, which is defined to be *explained* in

the world description of the operator *move* (refer to figure 3).
The introduced unexplained intervals I2, I3 and I4 can be
explained by T1, T2 and T3 respectively. By merging the two
partial world descriptions, we obtain a partial world
description with more details.

In order to explain T6, we can apply the operator move(b,e,d),
introducing I1' to I6' similarly. The world description after
explanation of all the intervals can roughly be represented
graphically by figure 4 below.

<u>Propositions</u>   <u>   Intervals and their relations   </u>

```
clear(a)        T1, I2      ----
on(a,b)         T2, I3      ----
clear(c)        T3, I4      ----
move(a,b,c)         I1          --------
on(a,c)         T4, I5                    ----------------
clear(b)            I6, I2'         ----------
clear(d)        T5,    I4'       -------
move(b,e,d)            I1'                      ------
on(b,d)         T6,    I5'                          -----
on(b,e)         T7,    I3'    ----------------
clear(e)               I6'                          -------
```

<u>Figure 4   A world description with all its</u>
<u>   intervals explained</u>

V   Problem of Allen's approach to planning

(1)   Possible inconsistency of relation networks

In [ALL 83a], a plan is a set of intervals S_t such that
between any two intervals in S_t, there exists a nonempty
set of possible temporal relations. However, the
constraint propagation process does not guarantee that all
relation networks are consistent. [ALL 83b] gives an
example of an inconsistent network. Figure 5 gives two
more examples.

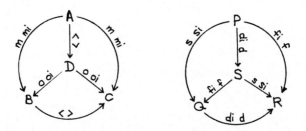

<u>Figure 5   Inconsistent relation networks   </u>
(A, B, C, D, P, Q, R & S are intervals)

In both examples, there exists no consistent labelling for the arcs (which are temporal relations). Finding a consistent labelling is a **Consistent Labelling Problem** (Constraint Satisfaction Problem). According to Nudel [NUD 83b], a Consistent Labelling Problem is defined as follow:

> We have a finite set Z of n variables. Each variable X_i in Z has a finite domain D_i from which X_i can take one of the M_i values. Constraints exist for subsets (of various sizes) of the variables in Z. The task is to find a solution-tuple (which is a n-tuple), which means the assignment of one value to each of the variables in Z such that all the constraints are satisfied.

Important publications about the consistent labelling problem are [MAC 75,77,85], [FRE 78,82], [HAR 79,80a,80b], and [NUD 83a,83b]. We shall call a solution-tuple of a relation network a **Definite Plan** to distinguish it from Allen's definition of "plans".

Inconsistency exists in some relation networks because the constraint propagation process in Allen's approach only guarantees 3-consistency [FRE 78]. The constraint propagation process would be extremely laborious if it were made to guarantee total consistency in the network [FRE78,82] [MAC 85]. Searching for solution-tuples could be nontrivial too [HAR 85].

(2) Allen's approach does not generate a readable plan

Under Allen's approach, a *plan* could be something like this:

> Intervals A, B, C and D are all explained; and we have
> R_{ab} = [fi si]
> R_{ac} = [fi di si]
> R_{ad} = [fi di]
> R_{bc} = [o oi]
> R_{bd} = [< m o di s oi]
> R_{cd} = [fi]
> where R_{ij} is the set of all possible relations between intervals i and j.

This relation network is consistent. But it is difficult for an agent to see how this plan should be executed. It would be easy to see how the plan in figure 6, which is one solution-tuple for the above network, could be executed.

```
Intervals                      temporal relations

    A          ------------------------------
    B          ---------------------
    C                      --------------------
    D                       -----------
```

Figure 6   A plan represented as a schedule

This is in fact the kind of schedules that we often see in offices or workshops.

(3)   The Duration Reasoner described in [ALL 83a] can only detect some inconsistencies. According to our understanding, it will not be able to detect the following inconsistency:

```
Intervals         temporal relations          durations

    T          ----------------------------      100
    A          ------------------                 70
    B                     ------------------       70
    C                      --------                60
```

**Figure 7   A network with inconsistent duration
                constraints**

The Duration Reasoner will not be able to detect inconsistency of this network because this network satisfies all its rules:

```
            A starts T, and    A - - (0.7 (0.7)) --> T
            B finishes T, and  B - - (0.7 (0.7)) --> T
            C during A, and    C - - (6/7 (6/7)) --> A
            C during B, and    C - - (6/7 (6/7)) --> B
```

where X - - (a(b)) --> Y is read as "the duration of X must be at least a but not more than b times the duration of Y".

The above example is inconsistent because the overlap between A and B is 0.4 of T but the duration of C is 0.6 of T. Therefore C cannot be *during* both A and B.

This example also shows that relation networks which can be labelled may not be consistent when duration constraints are considered. We believe that Linear Programming is the most general approach to detecting the consistency and finding the starting and ending time of intervals for a relation network [MAL 83]. The **AnalyzeLongestPath** procedure, according to [BEL 85a,85b], is a specialized linear programming approach for checking the consistency of such networks.

VI   A Complete planning process

We suggest that when the above temporal world model is used, a
complete planning process should consist of the following stages
and processes:

(1)   Accepting the problem
      This will give us a partial description of a possible world
      (PWD$_0$), which is basically a set of intervals together with
      a set of temporal and duration constraints on them.

(2)   Explaining all the intervals in the possible world
      The   result   of   this   process   will   be   a   partial   world
      description (PWD$_1$) in which all the intervals are explained
      and there exists a non-empty set of primitive relations for
      each pair of intervals.   It is at this stage that Allen's
      approach stops.

(3)   Labelling the temporal relations
      The result of this process is like PWD$_1$ except that the
      temporal relations between pairs of intervals are labelled
      by one primitive relation each.   As mentioned before, we
      shall call a network which has all its arcs so labelled a
      Definite Plan.

(4)   To determine the start and ending points of each interval
      This process should return the starting and ending time of
      each interval.   This is important because, as we have shown
      in section **V**, networks which can be labelled may not be
      consistent when duration constraints are considered.

VII   Implementation

Limited by space, the implemented system will only be described
briefly here.   A domain-independent planner based upon the above
ideas has been implemented.   Given a problem specification, it
generates a plan in the form of a chart, with the start and end
time of each interval labelled.   Perhaps it would be easier to
illustrate the system by an example:

      The Problem: Finish cooking a meal in 100 minutes.   The
      meal should have a soup and 3 courses, followed by a
      dessert.   The cooking of the soup and the 3 courses must
      be finished at the same time.   It takes 20 minutes to
      finish the meal, after which the dessert must be ready.
      John is free to cook the meal at the start and Mary can
      only join the cooking 20 minutes thereafter.   John must
      make a telephone call for at least 5 minutes sometime
      before the meal.

Traditional planners have difficulties in handling this problem
for at least the following two reasons:

(a)   There is no specific initial or goal state in this
      problem. Some goals (like finish cooking the 3 courses)
      has to be achieved before others (finishing cooking the
      dessert). The goal "make a telephone call" does not have
      to be achieved at a particular time during the 100 minutes
      as far as it takes place before the meal.

(b)   There are duration constraints like "at least 5 minutes".

This problem is input to the system with a **Partial World
Description (PWD) Language**, which specifies (among other things)
the existing intervals, the unexplained intervals, a set of
temporal constraints and a set of duration constraints on those
intervals.   Given this problem, the planner generates and
reports a plan in the following format:

<u>Actions or Propositions</u   <u>Intervals</u>

      make_apple_tart(mary)   ------------------
      apple_tart_ready   ----
      make_telephone_call(john)   ----
      steam_fish(john)   ----------------
      cook_rice(john)   -----------
      fry_vegetables(john)   --------
      make_soup(mary)   ----
      fish_ready & rice_ready &   ----
      vegetables_ready & soup_ready
      & to_finish_the_meal

<u>Figure 8   A plan for the example problem</u>

VII.1   The structure of the planner

The implemented system consists of a **Temporal Inference Engine
(TIE)**, a **Duration Handler (DH)** and a planner which uses TIE and
DH.   TIE takes as input a temporal constraint and propagates its
effects to other temporal relations.   This constraint
propagation process (which maintains 3-consistency) is based on
the one described in [ALL 83b].   DH propagates duration
constraints.   DH uses simple rules to detect inconsistency and
to propagate constraints.   Basically, inconsistency is detected
by the following rule:

      If T_1, T_2, ..., T_N are discrete subintervals of T, then
      the summation of minimum-durations of T_i must be less
      than or equal to the maximum-duration of T.

An example of a constraint propagation rule is:

> If T_1 is a subinterval of T_2, then an increase in the minimum-duration of T_1 could affect the minimum-duration of T_2

Since temporal and duration constraints can affect one another (e.g. if A is a subinterval of B, then the duration of A must not be greater than that of B), TIE and DH have to propagate their constraints to one another.

The planner is given a set of operators, each of which is defined as a world description. Each operator has certain effects, which are patterns saying when the operator can be applied. Side-effects are simply other explained intervals in this world description, and preconditions are unexplained intervals.

The planner consists of an **Interval-explanation Module**, a **Definite-plan-generator** and a **Plan-verification Module**. Each of these modules correlates to one planning step, which will be described in the next section.

VII.2 The planning process

The problem is input in the form of a partial world description (using the PWD Language) into the Interval-explanation Module. The process of explaining intervals is based on Allen's approach. The end product of this module is a relation network, which will be input to the Definite-plan-generator.

In searching for a definite plan, the Definite-plan-generator uses Nudel's **Fail First Principle**, assigning values to those relations which have the least number of choices first [NUD 83a]. Heuristics are used to improve the efficiency of the search and to search for a more efficient plan.

After a definite plan has been found, the Plan-verification Module will set up a graph from the labelled network. The nodes of this graph are the start and end points of the intervals, and the arcs are the minimum and maximum durations of intervals. For example, if the minimum and maximum durations of T are *Min* and *Max* respectively, then a directed path with length *Min* will go from Start(T) to end(T), and a path with length $-Max$ will go from end(T) to start(T). The AnalyzeLongestPath procedure [BEL 85b] is then used to detect the consistency of this graph as well as to compute the earliest start and ending time of each interval. After this computation, the plan can be displayed in the form of a schedule as shown in figure 8 above.

VII.3 More about the system

The planner does hierarchical planning, which means operators can be expanded into details. When the planner detects inconsistency in its relation network, it does chronological backtracking. One of its most important features is that it uses **Reference Intervals** to limit the computation needed for constraint propagation processes.

The idea is to organize all the intervals into a hierarchy. let us stipulate that two intervals are **referrable** to each other if they share the same reference interval, or one of them is the reference interval of the other. Only relations between referrable intervals will be stored explicitly by the system. A relation between two non-referrable intervals has to be looked up via paths through referrable intervals. If intervals X and Y are referrable to each other, then a constraint between X and Y is propagated only to those intervals which are referrable to both X and Y. Thus computation is limited. However, if X and Y are not referrable to one another, then we must decide how a constraint between them can be propagated properly.

Reference intervals have been used in Allen's system. Assume that we have a hierarchy like this:

        A is the reference interval of C;
        B is the reference interval of D;
        A and B are under the same reference interval:

and it is found that there exists a constraint between intervals C and D. Allen's system would create an extra reference link from C to B or from D to A so that any constraint between C and D can be propagated to relations among A, B, C and D (that makes the hierarchy a tangled tree). However, soon most of the intervals in the hierarchy will become referrable to each other as more and more constraints between non-referrable intervals arise. So reference intervals cannot serve their prupose of reducing the amount of computation needed for constraint propagation.

In our approach, if a constraint between C and D exists, the system will update only the relations R_{ca}, R_{ab} and R_{bd}. The risk of doing so is that the effect of such constraints may not be fully propagated, hence some infeasible relations might remain unrejected. But we argue that this is justifiable because, by using the constraint propagation algorithm described in [ALL 83b], we cannot guarantee that all unrejected relations are viable anyway. We do not spend extra effort to try to reject all possible rejectable relations just as we do not spend extra effort to guarantee total consistency of the network during the interval explanation process. Besides, these infeasible relations will be rejected by the Definite-plan-generator or the Plan-verification Module.

One of the problems in the implemented system is that when reference intervals are used, the effects of temporal constraints between intervals of different reference groups will not be fully reflected by the explicitly stored relations. This affects the system's ability to detect inconsistency before the AnalyzeLongestPath procedure is applied.

Detailed discussion of the use of reference intervals will be left for another occasion.

VIII   Summary and Discussion

In this paper, We have presented a new view to plan generation which is based on and generalized from Allen's. Basically we have adopted Allen's temporal frame and his approach to the explanation of interals. We have argued that Allen's approach to planning is incomplete, and presented a completed plan generation process. A planner which is based on this general view and complete plan generation process has been built.

It is worth mentioning that one can see the plan generation process described in section **VI** from another point of view. Steps 1 and 2 are the steps to identify the variables that are involved in our problem, as well as setting up certain constraints on these variables. Its product, a relatoin network, is a set of inequalities, possibly with disjunctions, which prevents us from using traditional linear programming techniques to solve them. Moreover, not all members of the cartesian product of these disjunctions are viable. Step 3 is the process of finding one set of (conjunctive) inequalities which satisfies the inference rules. Step 4 is to solve the linear inequalities, minimizing the duration of the plan based on the labelled relations.

[note 1]
At least intuitively, these 13 primitive relations exhaust all the possible temporal relations between any two intervals [BEN 83]. All those primitive relations can be derived from Meet [ALL 84]. The logic behind Allen's interval-based time structure will not be discussed in this paper.

Acknowledgement

I have to thank Chris Trayner, Sam steel and Jose Ambros for their valuable opinion on this paper. Also I would like to thank Jim Doran and Professor Turner for their supervision of this project.

References

[ALL 81]   ALLEN J F
            An Interval-based Representation of Temporal Knowledge
            IJCAI-81, p221-226

[ALL 83a]   ALLEN J F & KOOMENS
            Planning Using a Temporal World Model
            IJCAI-83, p741-747

[ALL 83b]   ALLEN J F
            Maintaining Knowledge about Temporal Intervals
            CACM Vol.26, No.11, November 1983, p832-843

[ALL 84]   ALLEN J F & HAYES P J
            A Common-sense Theory of Time
            Department of Computer Science and Philosophy
            University of Rochester, December 1984
            (A simplified version of this paper can be found in
            IJCAI-85, p528-531)

[BEL 85a]   BELL C E & TATE A
            Use and Justification of Algorithms for Managing
            Temporal Knowledge in O-Plan
            AIAI-TR-6, University of Edinburgh, 1985

[BEL 85b]   BELL C E & TATE A
            Using Temporal Constraints to Restrict Search in a
            Plan
            Proceedings, Alvey programme planning SIG workshop,
            Sunningdale, January 1985

[BEN 83]   VAN BENTHEM J F A K
            The Logic of Time
            D Riedal Publish Company, 1983

[FRE 78]   FREUDER E C
            Synthesizing Constraint Expressions
            CACM November 1978, Vol.21, No.11, p953-966

[FRE 82]   FREUDER E C
            A Sufficient Condition for Backtrack-free Search
            JACM Vol.29 No.1, January 1982, p24-32

[HAR 79]   HARALICK R M & SHAPIRA L G
            The Consistent Labelling Problem: Part I
            IEEE Trans PAMI-1:2, 1979, p173-184

[HAR 80a]   HARALICK R M & SHAPIRA L G
            The Consistent Labelling Problem: Part II
            IEEE Trans PAMI-2:3, 1980, p193-203

[HAR 80b]   HARALICK R M & ELLIOTT G L
            Increasing Tree Search Efficiency for   Constraint
            Satisfaction Problems
            AI 14(1980), p263-313

[MAC 75]   MACKWORTH A K
           Consistency in Networks of Relations
           Technical Report 75-3, July 1975

[MAC 77]   MACKWORTH A K
           Consistency in Networks of Relations
           AI 8(1), 1977, p99-118

[MAC 85]   MACKWORTH A K & FREUDER E C
           The Complexity of Some Polynomial Consistency
           Algorithms for Constraint Satisfaction Problems
           AI 25, 1985, p65-74

[MAL 83]   MALIK J & BINFORD T O
           Reasoning in Time and Space
           IJCAI-83, Vol.1, p343-345

[NUD 83a] NUDEL B A
           Consistent-labelling Problems and their algorithms:
           expected complexities and theory-based heuristics
           AI 21, July, 1983

[NUD 83b] NUDEL B A
           Solving the General Consistent labelling (or
           Constraint Satisfaction) Problem: Two algorithms and
           their expected complexities
           AAAI 83, August 1983, p292-296

[SAC 75]   SACERDOTI E D
           The Nonlinear Nature of Plans
           IJCAI-4, 1975, p206-214

[TAT 76]   TATE A
           Project Planning Using a Hierachical Nonlinear Planner
           D.A.I. Research Report No.25, Univ. of Edingurgh, 1976

[TAT 77]   TATE A
           Generating Project Network
           IJCAI-77, p888-893

[TAT 84]   TATE A
           Goal Structure -- Capturing the Intent of Plans
           Proceedings, European Conference of AI, 1984, p273-276

[VER 82]   VERE S A
           Planning in Time: Windows and Durations for Activities
           and Goals
           Technical Report D-572, Jet Propulsion Lab, July 1982

[VER 83]   VERE S A
           Planning in Time: Windows and Durations for Activities
           and Goals
           IEEE Trans PAMI-5, No.3, 1983, p246-267

Advances in Artificial Intelligence - II
B. Du Boulay, D. Hogg and L. Steels (Editors)
© Elsevier Science Publishers B.V. (North-Holland), 1987

Hierarchical Planning: Definition and Implementation

David E. Wilkins
Artificial Intelligence Center
SRI International
333 Ravenswood
Menlo Park, California 94025
U.S.A.

Abstract

There is considerable ambiguity involved in hierarchical planning. We present a definition of the latter, and examine several of the reasons for this confusion. An explication of hierarchical-planning implementations entails two distinct notions: *abstraction level* and *planning level*. A problem in currently implemented planners that is caused by mixing these two levels is presented and various remedies suggested. Three solutions that have been implemented in the current SIPE planning system are described.

Category: Problem Solving

Keywords: planning, hierarchical planning, granularity, abstraction, goal, operator

The research reported here is supported by Air Force Office of Scientific Research Contract F49620-79-C-0188.

1   Definition

It is generally recognized that planning in realistic domains requires planning at different
levels of abstraction [3]. This allows the planner to manipulate a simpler, but computationally tractable, theory of its world. The combinatorics of concatenating the most
detailed possible descriptions of actions would be overwhelming without the use of more
abstract concepts. This has resulted in numerous hierarchical-planning systems. However, hierarchical levels and hierarchical planning mean quite different things in different
planning systems, as is explained in the next section.

   In our view, the essence of hierarchical planning (and a necessary defining condition) is
the use of different levels of abstraction both in the planning process and in the description
of the domain. An *abstraction level* is distinguished by the granularity [3], or fineness
of detail, of the discriminations it makes in the world. From a somewhat more formal
standpoint, a more abstract description (in whatever formalism is being used) will have
a larger set of possible world states that satisfy it. When less abstract descriptions are
added, the size of this satisfying set diminishes as things in the world are discriminated
in increasingly finer detail. In complex worlds, these abstract descriptions can often be
idealizations. This means that a plan realizable at an abstract level may not be realizable
in a finer grain (i.e., the satisfying set might reduce to the null set). For example, one
might ignore friction in an abstraction of the domain, but find that the abstract plan
cannot be achieved at the lower abstraction level when the effects of friction are included
in the world description.

   To see how hierarchical planning can help avoid the combinatorial explosion involved
in reasoning about primitive actions, consider planning to build a house. At the highest
abstraction level might be such steps as site preparation and foundation laying. The
planner can plan the sequence of these steps without considering the detailed actions
of hammering a nail or opening a bag of cement. Each of these steps can be expanded
into more detailed actions, the most primitive of which might be nail-driving and wire-
cutting. Hierarchical abstraction levels provide the structure necessary for generating
complex plans at the primitive level.

2   The Many Guises of Hierarchical Planning

The planning literature has used the term "hierarchical planning" not only to describe
levels of abstraction, but also to describe systems containing various hierarchical structures or search spaces, metalevels, and what we will call *planning levels*. Examples of each
of these are given below. Planning levels are of particular importance because confusing
them with abstraction levels causes a problem in various implementations of hierarchical
planning that will be discussed in the remainder of this paper.

   Many planners produce hierarchical structures (e.g., subgoal structures) during the
planning process or explore hierarchically structured search spaces. Generally having

nothing to do with abstraction levels, they occur even in nonhierarchical (by our definition) planners that allow only one level of abstraction. STRIPS [1], while nonhierarchical, could be regarded as producing plans with a hierarchical structure, e.g., its triangle tables. The Hayes-Roths [2] use the term *hierarchical* to refer to a top-down search of the space of possible plans where more abstract plans are at the top of this search space. This involves a hierarchical search space that contains abstraction levels, but the levels in the hierarchy are not defined by these abstraction levels.

Hierarchical planning is also used to refer to metaplanning. Reasoning at a metalevel involves reasoning about the planning process itself. This is an entirely different domain, not merely an abstraction or idealization of the original domain. Stefik [7] states that ". . .layers of control (termed *planning spaces*) . . . are used to model hierarchical planning in MOLGEN". In this case, the three planning spaces are being used to implement metaplanning and, respectively, represent knowledge about strategy, plans and genetics; the first two are not abstractions of the genetics domain. (MOLGEN does provide for planning at different levels of abstraction through its constraints.)

The above uses of the term "hierarchical planning" describe processes or structures unrelated to the use of abstraction levels. Therefore, any confusion generated is terminological and is not an indication of possible conceptual problems within the planning system itself. Planning levels, on the other hand, have been confused with abstraction levels – which, as we shall see, can lead to problems within the planner, particularly if the planner incorporates the STRIPS assumption [9]. *Planning levels* are artifacts of particular planning systems and may vary considerably from planner to planner. They are not defined by a different level of abstraction in the descriptions being manipulated, but rather by some process in the planning system. Most planning systems have some central iterative loop that performs some computation on the plan during each iteration. This may involve applying schemas, axioms, or operators to each element of the existing plan to produce a more detailed plan. To the extent that such an iteration takes one well-defined plan and produces another well-defined plan, we will call it a planning level. Planning levels may correspond, in some systems, exactly to the hierarchical structures discussed earlier, but this is coincidence. They are defined by the planning process, not data structures, and may or may not correspond to hierarchical data structures within a particular system. In general, the term is admittedly vague, but in many AI planning systems of interest it has a very precise definition.

In particular, all planning systems in the NOAH tradition, including SIPE [10], NOAH [6], NONLIN [8], and ABSTRIPS [5], have distinct and well-defined planning levels. In these systems, a new planning level is created by expanding each node in the plan with one of the operators that describe actions. In the literature these levels are often referred to as hierarchical, which implicitly associates them with abstraction levels. In fact, they are independent of abstraction level; a new planning level may or may not result in a new abstraction level, depending upon which operators are applied. For example, in the blocks world described by Sacerdoti [6], there is only one abstraction level. CLEARTOP and ON are the only predicates and each new planning level simply further specifies a plan involving these predicates. Thus, all the hierarchical levels in the NOAH blocks world are actually planning levels, that result in adding further detail to the plan at the same abstraction level. Others have described such an omission of detail as an "abstraction", but we specifically require an abstraction level to involve different predicates with different grain-sizes.

Planning systems not in the NOAH tradition also have planning levels. Rosenschein's planning algorithm, using dynamic logic [4], attempts to satisfy a set of planning constraints. Running his "bigression algorithm" on each constraint in the set (which he claims is a straightforward extension of his system) would constitute a planning level. Agenda-based planning systems also have natural planning levels that are defined by the execution of one agenda item. These planning levels would be somewhat different from the others we have discussed, as they might not involve performing some operation on each element of a complete plan. Consequently, they are not likely to be confused with abstraction levels.

3   A Problem Encountered with Current Planners

There is a problem that can arise when planning and abstraction levels are interleaved in a planner making the STRIPS assumption, as they are in the aforementioned systems. (The STRIPS assumption states that things remain unchanged during an action unless specified otherwise.) This problem exists in many NOAH-tradition planners but has never been documented.

In such a planner, one element of the plan can attain a lower abstraction level than another element at the same planning level, depending upon which operators are applied. Thus, the plan at the current planning level could be **P1;Q1;G**, where **P1** is an action making the predicate P true, **Q1** an action making the more abstract predicate Q true, and **G** a goal that depends upon the truth of P for its achievement. With the STRIPS assumption, the planning system will find that P is true at **G**, since **Q1** does not mention changes involving any less abstract predicates (such as P). In fact, the truth of P may depend upon how **Q1** is expanded to the lower abstraction level, since it may or may not negate the truth of P. Thus, conditions may be evaluated improperly in these planners, resulting in incorrect operator applications.

For these planners to correctly test the truth of a condition at time N in the plan, they must ensure either that all relevant information at the proper abstraction level is available for the actions preceding N, or that subsequent expansions to lower abstraction levels will not change the truth value of the condition. However, many existing planners (e.g., NOAH and SIPE) do not provide this assurance. There are good reasons for this. Various solutions to the above problem are discussed later in this paper, but the most straightforward one is to impose a depth-first, left-to-right planning order that is sensitive to change in abstraction level. This means that, when a condition with predicates of abstraction level M is checked at time N in the plan, all possibly relevant information at abstraction level M or higher will be available for every plan element occurring prior to N.

However, this is not always desirable since many advantages can be gained by planning certain parts of the plan expedientially (or opportunistically) to lower abstraction levels. For example, in planning a trip from Palo Alto to New York City, it might be best to plan the details of the stay in New York first, as this could determine which airport would be best to fly into, which in turn could determine which Bay Area airport would be the best departure point. Thus, we do not want to restrict ourselves to depth-first, left-to-right planning, which would require choosing the Bay Area airport before the one in New York.

While the foregoing problem will be discussed in this paper in the NOAH-like terminology of "operators" and "goals", it applies equally well to any planner that must coordinate deductions over different abstraction levels. For example, Rosenschein's hierarchical planner based on dynamic logic [4] must address this issue in order to produce correct plans.

The definition of this problem will be made more concrete by looking at it in the context of an indoor robot domain, which will be used for expository purposes throughout the rest of this paper.

3.1   Abstraction Levels in an Indoor Robot Domain

We recently encoded a simple indoor robot world in the SIPE planning system that revealed the problem of coordinating abstraction levels. The robot domain consists of 5 rooms connected by a hallway in the Artificial Intelligence Center at SRI International, the robot itself, and various objects. The rooms were divided into 35 symbolic locations that included multiple paths between locations (which greatly increases the amount of work done by the planner). The initial world was described by 222 predicate instances, about half of which were deduced from SIPE's deductive operators. The description of possible actions in SIPE included 25 operators describing actions and 25 deductive operators. The operators use four levels of abstraction in the planning process. The planner produces primitive plans that provide actual commands for controlling the robot's motors.

The most abstract level of the planning process reasons about the tasks that can be performed, such as preparing a report or delivering an object. Our simple domain requires only one level for this, but more complex tasks might require several abstraction levels to describe them. The first level below the task level (referred to as the INROOM level since INROOM is the crucial predicate) is the planning of navigation from room to room. This plans a route that may require many planning levels for all the necessary operators to be applied, but it does not involve any reasoning about particular doors or locations. High-level predicates describing connections indicate that it is reasonable to move from one room to another, but without first considering any details as to how this might be done or whether it might even be possible in the current situation. When such a move is planned to a lower abstraction level, it may fail or many actions may have to

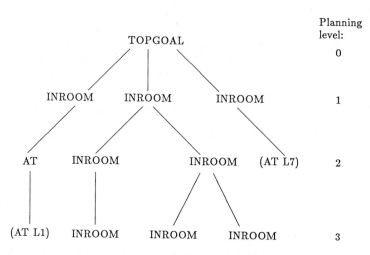

Figure 1: Hierarchical Plan in Robot Domain

be performed to clear a path.

Below the room level is the NEXT-TO level, which plans movements from one important object (that the robot is next to) to another. For example, to copy a paper, the robot will have to get next to the door of the copy center, then pass through the doorway, then get next to the desk of the operator, etc. This abstraction level plans high-level movements within a room but is still not concerned with actual locations. NEXTTO is the crucial predicate at this abstraction level.

The lowest level is the location level, where SIPE plans movements down to the level of the actual locational grid it has been given. This may involve planning to move obstacles so as to clear particular paths. AT is the crucial predicate at this abstraction level.

3.2   Coordinating Abstraction Levels

The problem of coordinating abstraction and planning levels arose during planning in the robot domain in the plan depicted in Figure 1. The initial goal produced three INROOM goals at the first planning level. Of these three subtrees, the first and last were transformed into the lowest abstraction level at planning level 2 (intervening NEXTTO goals have been disregarded for the sake of simplicity). The middle subtree, however, is still at the room abstraction level on planning level 3, as it required several operator applications to find a path through the rooms to accomplish its goal.

Now, when the planner applies an operator to the (AT L7) goal at planning level 2, any precondition that queries the AT predicate will find (AT L1) to be valid, since that is the last place at which AT is affected and the STRIPS assumption assumes all actions leave predicates unchanged unless they explicitly specify otherwise. But this is not correct, as AT may be affected after the middle subtree is expanded to the lowest abstraction level. If the operator depends critically on the value of the AT predicate, its application to (AT L7) may be incorrect. The resulting plan will have commands that move the robot from location L1 to location L7, whereas the robot is not likely to be at L1 when this part of the plan is executed (because of movements made in the middle subtree). Whether such an operator application will prevent the correct plan from being found depends on how a particular planner detects invalid plans and how the search space is organized.

4   Solutions

There are many alternative solutions to the problem discussed above. They range from calculating all possibly relevant information before it may be needed to ignoring the problem altogether and simply letting the user beware of the consequences. The former, and most straightforward, is to force the planner to plan in temporal order and to provide for calculation of all the predicates at one abstraction level that may be needed later. Many planners do this, though it is usually not made clear that they depend on several assumptions to avoid subtle problems such as this one. ABSTRIPS [5] is an example of planners that use this approach. It assigns abstraction-level numbers to the predicates and plans a lower level only when all necessary computations have been made. SIPE provides, as a user-selectable option, the ability to control hierarchical planning in this manner. This is useful for performance comparisons with the different techniques described below.

The problem with this approach is that the planner is limited in the order in which it can process goals. Quite often the order imposed will not be optimal (as in the Palo Alto-to-New York example). The flexibility to plan certain parts of the plan expedientially to lower abstraction levels is lost. Constraints generated during such lower-level planning can narrow down the search, thus resulting in potentially large gains in efficiency. For these reasons, planners like SIPE, NOAH, and NONLIN allow the mixing of planning and abstraction levels.

The approach used in these latter planners is susceptible to the level coordination problem and therefore requires the user to be alert. Incorrect checking of conditions similar to the one described can occur in these systems, depending on the task and the encoding of the operators. This can result in incorrect operator applications. The planning system may have mechanisms that later detect the plan is incorrect, as SIPE and perhaps NONLIN do. However, the proper solution may not be found if the operator applied incorrectly is the one actually needed for the correct solution, since it may not be retried. Its premature application should have been delayed one or more planning levels so that other parts of the plan could be planned to a lower abstraction level. The user is responsible for writing operators that will accomplish this delay. This process is facilitated by certain features of SIPE, as we shall see.

It is appealing to look for a technique between the inefficiency of computing everything in a certain order, and the expediential behavior of systems that perhaps miss valid solutions. This would involve reasoning about what properties will remain invariant during further planning of certain goals. For example, in Figure 1 the planner might calculate whether the possible expansions of the middle subtree will affect the value of the AT predicate. If not, planning can proceed expedientially. This is all the more appealing because reasoning about concurrency depends on determining invariant properties of a sequence of actions.

Despite the attraction of this approach, there are severe difficulties entailed in computing these invariances. It would be best if they could be computed automatically from the operators without requiring the user to supply additional knowledge. (The STRIPS assumption effectively makes this computation for predicates at one abstraction level, but the computation must be done for predicates at other abstraction levels.) In general, this is not computationally tractable. It is similar to the problem of regressing conditions through actions ([4],[9]), except that the regression must be done through every possible expansion of the actions for an indeterminate number of planning levels. Furthermore, simple schemes that simply check for predicate names that have possibly been changed will probably find very few invariances. For example, in the robot domain, every high-level goal will alter the values of AT predicates at the lowest level. More sophisticated schemes that check possible values for the arguments of the predicates, perhaps determining ranges of values they might acquire in all possible expansions, would themselves require solving a large search problem.

An alternative is to have the user provide information about what remains invariant over actions. While this may be useful for some domains, in general the same criticisms made above apply to this case. There will in general not be many things (at lower abstraction levels) that are invariant; moreover, it may even be difficult to indicate explicitly what they are, as the invariance may involve complex constraints on the allowable arguments to predicates. In addition, one of the chief advantages of abstraction levels is that specifying details is unnecessary at higher levels. Computing invariants would require information as to which lower levels are affected in what way by each higher-level goal, thus removing some of the advantage gained by not planning at the lowest level from the very beginning. The computational costs of this can quickly become overwhelming as we shall see in the next section.

4.1   Delaying Operator Applications in SIPE

For reasons given above, SIPE allows the user to assume the burden of encoding the domain in such a way that incorrect evaluation of conditions will not produce applications of operators that prevent solutions from being found. We have solved this problem within SIPE for the indoor robot domain in two different ways (in addition to the option of using the ABSTRIPS solution). One solution involves delaying the application of certain operators and the other solution involves the introduction of certain less abstract

```
OPERATOR: not-yet
ARGUMENTS: robot1,location2,area1,location1;
PURPOSE: (at robot1 location2);
PRECONDITION: (at robot1 location1),
     (inroom robot1 area1),
     (not (contains location1 area1));
PLOT: COPY
END PLOT END OPERATOR
```

Figure 2: Operator for Delaying Operator Application

predicates at earlier planning levels.

The first solution involves a novel use of operators, developed during implementation of the robot domain, that effectively delays the achievement of certain goals until the appropriate juncture, as long as the latter can be ascertained by conditions that are expressible as preconditions of a SIPE operator. This is best shown by returning to the robot domain example.

In the robot domain, only the planning of AT goals is affected when abstraction levels varied in the plan. Figure 1 depicts the type of situation in which the accomplishment of an AT goal must be delayed. This is done in SIPE by using the operator shown in Figure 2. It delays the solving of AT goals until the part of the plan preceding them has been brought to the same level of abstraction. This is done by checking whether the AT location of the robot is in the same room as its INROOM location. If the precondition of this operator matches, it means that the last AT predicate specified as an effect of an action came before the last INROOM predicate specified as an effect. Consequently, the latter action must still be planned to the lower level of abstraction. [1]

This operator is applied before any other to an AT goal. The plot of not-yet is simply the token *COPY* that copies the goal from the preceding planning level. It is necessary to use a special token rather than specify the AT goal in normal syntax. Normally SIPE inserts the precondition of an operator into the plan and maintains its truth. In this case the precondition will not be true in the final plan, so the COPY option inserts the appropriate goal without first inserting the precondition. With this feature and the above operator, SIPE can mix abstraction and planning levels freely in the robot domain without missing a solution on our test problems. However, there may be problems in the domain that cannot be solved without creating additional delaying operators.

---

[1] Of course, this operator could still be fooled if you planned a circular route that ended in an INROOM goal for the same room that contained the last preceding AT location. However, this would cause a problem only if the eventual location reached in the expansion of the INROOM goal were different from the one in the earlier AT goal. This situation never arises in our domain.

4.2   Introducing Low-Level Predicates in SIPE

Instead of using the not-yet operator, the second solution involves introducing lower-level predicates at higher abstraction levels in order to prevent the STRIPS assumption from causing a problem. In this case, we add a lower-level AT predicate (which includes an uninstantiated locational variable) to every higher-level NEXT-TO goal as a placeholder for the predicate that would be produced during some future expansion. When the NEXT-TO goal is expanded to the lower level, the location actually reached will eventually become the instantiation of the locational variable introduced. At the planning level of the NEXT-TO goal, any AT predicate in a condition being tested will match with the newly inserted AT predicate, preventing the planner's incorrect assumption that the NEXT-TO goal does not affect the truth-value of the condition.

This solution takes advantage of SIPE's ability to post constraints on variables. The newly introduced AT predicates effectively document the fact that the AT location may eventually change during any expansion of the NEXT-TO goal (even though the location is not yet known). Before and during such an expansion, the location variables can accumulate constraints on their possible values, so the planning process will not be hindered. The matching of conditions will always be correct because these AT predicates are present everywhere the AT location might change.

Incorporating this change into the SIPE operators written for the first solution was easy. Only three operators of the 25 posted NEXT-TO goals, so only those three had to be changed. The process of converting these three operators is illustrated by contrasting the original FETCH operator shown in Figure 3 with the FETCH operator including AT predicates shown in Figure 4. In the plot, each goal and process with a NEXT-TO predicate in its effects is given an additional effect that is an AT predicate involving a new locational variable. The latter is included in the arguments of the goal or process so as to permit appropriate matching with the variables in the operators that solve NEXT-TO goals. The locational variable is added to the arguments of the operator, whose precondition can also specify any predicate that constrains the variable. At a minimum, the variable can be constrained by its containing room; stronger constraints can sometimes be specified.

Once the three operators were converted in this manner, SIPE was able to solve all the problems in our test domain. This solution appears robust and should not prevent the planner from successfully dealing with any problems it might solve by means of an ABSTRIPS-like approach. Characteristics of the domain are again exploited in this solution. By having to plan about less abstract entities at a more abstract level, we are giving up some of the advantage gained by planning hierarchically. However, it is reasonable in this case because we need introduce only one lower level predicate early (albeit the most important one), and we need introduce it only a single abstraction level early. There is no difficulty in coordinating any other pair of abstraction levels in this domain. However, the introduction of more variables and constraints significantly increases the effort required. Using this technique to solve problems in the robot domain

```
OPERATOR: fetch
ARGUMENTS: robot1,object1,area1;
PURPOSE: (holding robot1 object1);
PRECONDITION: (inroom object1 area1);
PLOT:
    GOAL: (inroom robot1 area1);
        MAINSTEP: (holding robot1 object1);
    GOAL: (nextto robot1 object1);
    PROCESS
        ACTION: pickup;
        ARGUMENTS: robot1, object1;
        EFFECTS: (holding robot1 object1);
END PLOT END OPERATOR
```

Figure 3: Original FETCH Operator

```
OPERATOR: fetch
ARGUMENTS: robot1,object1,area1,location1;
PURPOSE: (holding robot1 object1);
PRECONDITION: (inroom object1 area1),
    (contains location1 area1);
PLOT:
    GOAL: (inroom robot1 area1);
        MAINSTEP: (holding robot1 object1);
    GOAL: (nextto robot1 object1);
        ARGUMENTS: robot1, object1, area1, location1;
        EFFECTS: (at robot1 location1);
    PROCESS
        ACTION: pickup;
        ARGUMENTS: robot1, object1;
        EFFECTS: (holding robot1 object1);
END PLOT END OPERATOR
```

Figure 4: FETCH Operator with AT Predicate

Problem:	NOTYET	introduce AT	ABSTRIPS
Original	29.5 (7)	54.2 (7)	32.1 (11)
Shorter path	24.8 (7)	46.7 (7)	25.1 (8)
longer path	43.7 (7)	57.4 (7)	35.7 (10)

Figure 5: Symbolics 3600 CPU time and planning levels for solutions

takes from one-third again to twice as long as using the not-yet operator (see next section).

4.3   Comparison of Solutions

The two techniques described above were tested on three different problems in the robot domain. The ABSTRIPS control regime was also used to solve these problems. (This involves using the same operators as were used while delaying operator application except that the NOTYET operator is eliminated.) The original robot problem involves a choice of different paths and entails seven planning levels for producing a primitive plan with 58 process/phantom nodes. The other two problems are similar, but one requires a shorter path to be found and the other requires a longer path. Figure 5 depicts the cpu time and number of planning levels required for each problem. It is to be expected that the ABSTRIPS control regime is as efficient as delaying operator application since these particular problems do not admit to simpler solution by planning later parts of the plan to a lower abstraction level. For problems and domains with this property, ABSTRIPS-like coordination of levels is preferred since it is both efficient and correct. (It does, of course, require more planning levels.)

The first solution (NOTYET) accomplishes the delayed application of operators when necessary, but permits expediential planning in other cases. This retains flexibility while remaining efficient by not regressing conditions through possible expansions of actions. As no lower-level predicates are introduced early, full advantage is taken of hierarchical planning. The disadvantages of this approach are that the user (though relieved of the necessity of specifying invariance properties for higher-level goals) must write appropriate delaying operators and, furthermore, must have anticipated all possible situations in which operators would need to be delayed. In complex worlds this means that novel problems might not be solvable. In addition, it may not always be possible to express the appropriate delaying conditions as a SIPE precondition. In an application in which efficiency is of paramount importance and failure to solve a particular problem can be tolerated, this may be a desirable approach.

The second solution (AT) is more robust and less likely to fail on novel problems. It was surprisingly easy to implement in SIPE. However, when low-level predicates are introduced at a higher abstraction level, it is significantly less efficient. The advantages of hierarchical planning can be readily seen, as the introduction of only one predicate (albeit the crucial one) at the next higher abstraction level nearly doubles the cost of computation.

5 Summary

Ambiguities in the planning literature involving hierarchical levels are explicated. The interleaving of planning levels and abstraction levels prevents some current planners from finding correct solutions. Various techniques designed to prevent this have certain drawbacks; three methods implemented in SIPE involve different tradeoffs between flexibility, efficiency, and robustness.

References

[1] Fikes, R. E. and Nilsson, N. J., "STRIPS: A New Approach to the Application of Theorem Proving to Problem Solving", *Artificial Intelligence 2*, 1971, pp. 189-208.

[2] Hayes-Roth, B. and Hayes-Roth, F., "A Cognitive Model of Planning", *Cognitive Science 3*, 1979, pp. 275–310.

[3] Hobbs, J.. "Granularity", *Proceedings IJCAI-85*, Los Angeles, California, 1985, pp. 432-435.

[4] Rosenschein, S., "Plan Synthesis: A Logical Perspective", *Proceedings IJCAI-81*, Vancouver, British Columbia, 1981, pp. 331-337.

[5] Sacerdoti, E., "Planning in a Hierarchy of Abstraction Spaces", *Artificial Intelligence 5 (2)*, 1974, pp. 115-135.

[6] Sacerdoti, E., *A Structure for Plans and Behavior*, Elsevier, North-Holland, New York, 1977.

[7] Stefik, M., "Planning and Metaplanning", in *Readings in Artificial Intelligence*, Nilsson and Webber, eds., Tioga Publishing, Palo Alto, California, 1981, pp. 272–286.

[8] Tate, A., "Generating Project Networks", *Proceedings IJCAI-77*, Cambridge, Massachusetts, 1977, pp. 888-893.

[9] Waldinger, R., "Achieving Several Goals Simultaneously", in *Readings in Artificial Intelligence*, Nilsson and Webber, eds., Tioga Publishing, Palo Alto, California, 1981, pp. 250–271.

[10] Wilkins, D., "Domain-independent Planning: Representation and Plan Generation", *Artificial Intelligence 22*, April 1984, pp. 269-301.

CONCLUDING

VISIONARY PAPER

by   Sir Clive Sinclair

Advances in Artificial Intelligence - II
B. Du Boulay, D. Hogg and L. Steels (Editors)
© Elsevier Science Publishers B.V. (North-Holland), 1987

THE WHY AND WHEN OF ARTIFICIAL INTELLIGENCE

Sir Clive SINCLAIR

Sinclair Research Limited, Milton Hall, Milton
Cambridge, CB4 4AE, England

To those embedded in the academic pursuit of Artificial
Intelligence the intellectual challenge suffices as
justification for the endeavour.   The rest must or
should seek more material ground for what promises to be
a long, risky and expensive argosy.   Just what is it we
hope to gain?   Any investment of resource should, in
some manner return a dividend.   Can we expect such from
the hundred, perhaps thousands of millions likely to be
spent on Artificial Intelligence in the decades ahead?
If we can, of what form is the dividend?

The increase in our wealth in centuries past has been
wrought by steadily reducing the human labour element in
the production of food and manufactured goods.   Now that
robots are proving cheaper than humans in ever more areas
of production we can forsee, in the not far distance, a
point where all the physical things of life, food,
housing, consumer durables, mechanical transport can be
made with the employment of only a small portion of the
population, say less than 10 per cent, leaving the rest
to provide services in teaching, medicine, entertainment
and the like.   There will then be little gain in our
individual wealth to be had from further productivity
growth in manufacturing industry.   Even a halving in the
labour needed would only raise our per capita wealth by
5%.

Significant further growth in wealth will only come then
through replacing human effort by machine effort in the
service industries.   Even if all our people were
employed in these industries we could not hope to meet
all appetite for medical aid, entertainment and education
as the capacity of the rich to absorb the services of the
poor demonstrates. But most of these employments require
more mental than physical agility so only through
Artificial Intelligence can we hope to lower their cost
and so continue our long history of growing standards of
life.

In many areas Artificial Intelligence will creep in at
first unrecognised.   The modern car contains several
silicon chips monitoring engine and vehicle performance.

Soon the elaborate wiring loom will be replaced by a pair
of wires or a glass fibre linking chips throughout the
car each controlling or monitoring a function.   As the
'intelligence' of the system increases, as it will, it
will subtley start to take control from the driver.

First it will warn him of danger, later, not content with
the lag imposed by his nervous system, it will act
directly.   The driver, lulled into false security by
small changes seemingly aiding his driving will one day
discover that really the car is doing the driving.   The
law will support the change on grounds of safety and our
right to drive ourselves will pass as surely as did our
right to carry swords and for much the same reason.

If machines can drive cars they can perform the generally
more trivial tests of flying planes and so they will.
It might then be that private planes become ubiquitous.
Given the power of vertical take off and total automation
they would far surpass the car in flexibility and speed.
Though our skies may be darker for the change we need no
longer feed our countryside into road making machines.

Doctors in the U.S.A. no longer make house calls.   They
never did other than for the relatively wealthy.   We
would like them o but no society can so arrange its
affairs to make this a universal enjoyment no matter how
large a proportion of our population is concentrated in
the service sector.   But this need can be met by the
electronic medic.   It will not be long before, on feeling
a pain, we go not to the surgery but to a box downstairs.
A friendly face appears, addresses us affectionately by
name and asks how we are.   Once told of the symptoms the
advice of this phantom mentor will be kindly told and
based on the best possible knowledge of the day together
with intimate and complete knowledge of the patient.

A more mobile version will be able to provide physical
help to the aged and infirm combined with solicitous
company, albeit inhuman.

These developments bode such benefit to man as to justify
almost any conceivable investment in Artificial
Intelligence   Similar help can flow to children not so
much, one hopes, from the cybernetic nanny which might
usurp a mothers love as from the robot tutor able to give
a child undivided attention.   This development may take
much longer than the medical changes as we have so much
to learn about education but the benifits will, again,
justify the most intense effort.

In entertainment too Artificial Intelligence will creep
upon us.   Indeed the creeping has begun.   The first
machines that attempt to understand us by parsing our

sentences exist in the unlikely form of games playing
programmes for home computers.   The sophistication of
the latest of these is astonishing and the pace quickens.
Now hugely more powerful computers are under development
for the home market featuring stunning improvements in
graphics resolution and speed.   As these are combined
with the ingenuity of our software houses we may expect
interactive games which begin to border on reality.   We
may enter a fully three dimensional world with scenes
created continuously in real time changing as we turn
them to fight monsters deriving from the 'imagination' of
the machine.   So seductive could these images become as
to rob us of our own reality.   A journey taken in the
computer will become more enticing than any real trip.

How real though are these dreams?   We can judge the
order of the problem by comparing the complexity of a
modern computer with that of a human brain and by looking
at our rate of progress.   In 1980 the simplest personal
computer contained about 10^5 components counting each
element on every chip.   Today's personal machines are at
least 10 times larger and the biggest computers in use
have, perhaps, 10^9 components and so are three orders
larger than the smallest.   The brain contains about 10^{14}
elements assuming there to be 10^{10} neurons each with
about 10^4 connections.   The brain is 10^5 times more
complex than the largest computer which is a daunting
number until one remembers how fast the size of computers
has been growing.

With an order of magnitude improvement every five years,
and we have been experiencing at least that, we are only
25 years away from a machine as complex as the brain and
one which would be enormously faster.

Within that time component geometries, now nudging the 1
micron level should have shrunk to say 0.1 micron or
below.   X-ray, electron beam or ion beam lithography will
have replaced the optical technology of today.

With components of the order of a tenth of a micron in
diameter a machine of brain like complexity will require
one square metre of substrate.   If this substrate is
divided into 100 layers, 1mm apart, the entire machine
need be only a 10 centimetre cube.   Not only will we
match the complexity of the brain but its size as well.

The material for the substrate is unlikely to surprise
us.   Only silicon seems a likely contender since no
other material is so developed.   There is simply not
time for a radical change.   Even if Gallium Arsenide
could be exploited fast enough, and that is not
impossible, it would seem to offer no advantage.   It is
quite possible that multi layer silicon, using laser or

electron beam recrystalisation of poly silicon layers
will be the method used to achieve very high packing
density.   Alternatively ribbon silicon technology may
have developed to the point where a continuous strip of
silicon can pass through the entire manufacturing cycle.

Though we may well have the power to make machines of
this complexity in the time described it is less sure
that we will, so soon, solve the architectural and
software problems.   The machine must clearly be hugely
parallel so the structure will be novel to say the least
and nothing like our current programming languages or
methods will suffice.   The problems are daunting but,
since we exist, soluble so the question is when not
whether.

Our android brain may cost more to develop than landing
man on the moon or the development of the atom bomb but
it is hugely more significant than either of these.
Once a working design is achieved, mass production will
surely lead to low unit cost.   The basic raw material,
170 grams of silicon, is not expensive, the energy input
not high and, given known redundancy techniques
production yields should be no problem.   Production time
should be extremely short compared with the competing
biological product.

Education will pose huge problems initially but here
again, once the trick is learned, the advantages are
great compared with humans.   Once we have an educated
android we can have as many clones as we like by doing a
massive file swap from the original to the copies.
There may be a core of programme common to all such
machines with specialist knowledge given to specific
models.   Individual machines would also learn by
experience of their particular environment.

The android population to come will have a peculiar
advantage over us humans.   We exchange data when we
talk, directly or on the phone, at a rate of only a few
hundred bits per second.   Even this low rate is of great
value to us.   Robots should be able to 'talk' at data
rates of megabits or even gigabits per second over large
distances.   They will not be intellectually our equals
but hugely our superiors.

When might all this happen?   I will make a guess knowing
that I cannot be proved wrong for many years to come by
which time my guess will be forgotton.   I imagine we
will achieve the first machine of human brain complexity,
huge in size and cost, by the year 2000.   By the year
2020 I think we will have solved the programming problems
and by 2040 I think these machines will be in such large

scale use that their intellectual gross product will exceed that of humans by a factor of 100.

And where will all this be achieved? It would be nice to imagine that a great international co-operative effort will handle the problem; nice but naive. Instead we may expect a growing competitive spirit among nations at first based on open and friendly competition but soon on great secrecy as the powers that guide us realise the monumental implications of the race.

Should one nation or group of nations attain a marked lead it will be serious for the stability of the world. Sadly the military possibilities of Artificial Intelligence will not be lost on our leaders. Nor on theirs for that matter. We can hope that if a lead does arise, as it most likely will, the guardians of that new wisdom and power are on the side of the angels.

We should not assume that the Artificial Intelligence problem can only be cracked by huge teams and vast resources. Almost certainly the pioneering work will be done by small groups probably in unexpected areas. Since the problems are essentially intellectual even amateurs will have a chance for glory. Once the fundamental problems have been solved it will take a large capital investment to achieve economic production but nothing too daunting compared with the rewards to be gleaned.

For the benefit to mankind of the coming age of robots is so great as to beggar exaggeration. It should mean the total ending of poverty and a level of individual wealth undreamed of by the Ceasers. Properly controlled, and that will be no simple matter, this technology that we discuss so gently here can take us at last to a truly golden age for all. Mishandled it could end the world but so could have so many things and they did not.

Given the success I anticipate the 21st Century will be the age of the coming of machine intelligence and the beginning of man's voyage into the galaxy.

AUTHOR INDEX